Dark Skies

Dark Skies

Space Expansionism, Planetary Geopolitics, and the Ends of Humanity

DANIEL DEUDNEY

OXFORD
UNIVERSITY PRESS

OXFORD
UNIVERSITY PRESS

Oxford University Press is a department of the University of Oxford. It furthers
the University's objective of excellence in research, scholarship, and education
by publishing worldwide. Oxford is a registered trade mark of Oxford University
Press in the UK and certain other countries.

Published in the United States of America by Oxford University Press
198 Madison Avenue, New York, NY 10016, United States of America.

© Oxford University Press 2020
First issued as an Oxford University Press paperback, 2022

CIP data is on file at the Library of Congress
ISBN 978–0–19–090334–3 (hardback)
ISBN 978–0–19–765649–5 (paperback)

1 3 5 7 9 8 6 4 2

Paperback printed by Marquis, Canada

To John Steven Welch, North Star

CONTENTS

PART FOUR ASSESSMENT

LIST OF TABLES AND FIGURES

ACKNOWLEDGMENTS

Stretching over many years, my thinking about space has been shaped by conversations with John Agnew, Bentley Allan, Peter Andreas, Jane Bennett, Wayne Biddle, Lester Brown, Barry Buzan, Luis Cabera, Arthur Clarke, Joseph Coates, Campbell Craig, Leonard David, Ron Deibert, Everett Dolman, Richard Falk, Peter Garretson, Nadivah Greenberg, Jairus Grove, John Logsdon, Tim Luke, Allyn McAuley, John McLucas, Beth Mendenhall, Zia Mian, Craig Murphy, Ethan Nadelmann, Michael Neufeld, John O'Looney, Scott Pace, Columba Peoples, Benoit Pelopidas, John Pike, Shane Pinkston, Robert Poole, Carol Rosin, Carl Sagan, Si Sheppard, Harlan Smith, Warren Tucker, Frank von Hippel, Ole Waever, Karl Walling, Wesley Warren, Alex Wendt, Jim Wirtz, and the students in my Politics of Outer Space course at Johns Hopkins University.

Valuable research assistance has been provided by Michael Byrne, Mason Cole, Kiernan Coleman, Zackery David, Kenny Eaton, Jacob Grunberger, Beckett Jackson, Ethan Landis, Ian Maddox, David Oh, Wang Jae Rhee, David Saveliev, Greg Sgammato, Yi Su, Sunil Vaswani and Grant Welby. Special thanks to Mason Cole for checking numbers and calculations.

Helpful comments on earlier versions of the manuscript were provided by Bentley Allan, Barry Buzan, Zackery David, Ron Deibert, Everett Dolman, Namrata Goswani, David Hendrickson, Joan Johnson-Freese, Daniel McCarthy, Beth Mendenhall, Clay Moltz, Sebastian Mazzaca, James Thompson, Phil Torres, and anonymous reviewers for Oxford University Press.

This project has also benefitted from comments on earlier versions of this argument presented at panels at the International Studies Association, Toronto (March 2019), Baltimore (February 2017), Atlanta (March 2016), Toronto (March 2014), San Francisco (April 2013), and New Orleans (February 2010); the Naval Postgraduate School, Monterey (May 2016); Department of Political Science, Johns Hopkins University (April 2015); School of Advanced International Studies, Johns Hopkins University (April 2014); Department of

International Relations, Graduate Institute, Geneva (December 2013); Danish Academy of Sciences and the University of Copenhagen (December 2013); Spruce Hill Atheneum, Philadelphia (July 2013); University of Copenhagen (June 2013); the Watson Institute, Brown University (March 2013); Program in Peace and Conflict Studies and the Institute for Space Policy Studies, George Washington University (May 2012); Jackson School of Public Policy, University of Washington (April 2011); Munk School, University of Toronto (February 2011); Peace and Conflict Studies Program, Colgate University (October 2010); Convention of the American Political Science Association, Washington, DC (September 2010); Department of Political Science, University of Frankfurt (July 2010); Eisenhower Center for Space Strategy, United States Air Force Academy (December 2009); Department of Political Science, Colorado College (October 2001); University of British Columbia, Institute of International Relations (July 1996); Program on Nuclear Policy Alternatives, Center for Energy and Environmental Studies, Princeton University (June 1985); United States Senate Foreign Relations Committee (May 1983); and the UNISPACE Conference, Vienna, (June 1982). Very early versions of the arguments of chapter seven appear in my MA thesis, supervised by John Logsdon at the Program in Science, Technology and Public Policy, George Washington University, were presented at workshops on space cooperation at the Space Science Institute, Moscow (September 1988), and appeared in the *World Policy Journal, Foreign Policy, Bulletin of the Atomic Scientists* and studies published by the WorldWatch Institute.

Special thanks to the editorial team at Oxford University Press and Newgen KnowledgeWorks, David McBride, Holly Mitchell, and Liz Davey, whose support and expert editing have been invaluable. Generous financial support for this project was provided by the Nadivah Philanthropic Fund in Memory of Barbara Feinstein. This project would not have been possible without the support, encouragement and tolerance from the members of my family, Ruth Deudney, Holly McGarragh, Heidi Pinkston, Robert Slater, and especially John Welch.

PROLOGUE

Machine Civilization and the Transformation of the Earth

> At long last, we begin to feel the effects of the finite, actual size of the
> earth in a critical way.
>
> —John von Neumann (1955)[1]

> On a steady diet of accelerating technology, strategic weapons have
> outgrown their traditional arena—the earth.
>
> —Robert Salkeld (1970)[2]

The Globalization of Machine Civilization

Humans are sprung from the Earth, have never lived anywhere but on Earth, and the features of this planet have shaped every aspect of human life. Over the past several centuries, and accelerating across the twentieth, the practical human relationship with the Earth has profoundly changed. Advances in natural science and technology, the globalization of a machine-based civilization, and the possibilities of planetary-scope technological catastrophes have combined to produce a radically novel and deeply unsettled human historical situation. In perhaps the most audacious and spectacular thrust of technological civilization, humankind took the first steps in the middle years of the twentieth century toward becoming an outer space–faring species by venturing out of the Earth's atmosphere and into the edges of the stupendous vastness of cosmic space.

Humans have always lived on a globe-shaped planet, but only recently have human activities become significantly global and planetary in their scope. The decisive root, widely recognized, of this far-reaching change is the superior human ability to make and employ tools with progressively increasing capabilities. Among the billion or so species of complex life that have existed on Earth, *Homo sapiens* is distinguished by a package of sociobiological attributes (most notably language and prospection) that have enabled humans to fabricate and instrumentally employ tools, which now exist in astounding numbers and varieties. Across the past several centuries, the pace of scientific discovery and technological development has greatly accelerated, producing a worldwide human civilization that makes and operates machines and systems of machines with increasing power, spatial scope, and complexity. Possibilities for technological advance are far from exhausted, and the commitment to technological progress is deeply entrenched.

The expansive trajectory of machine-based civilization that seems to lead to the stars has already transformed the physical features of the Earth by permitting vast increases in the number of humans, expanding the impacts of their activities, and altering habitats to make them more useful for human needs and wants.[3] Humankind has disrupted, exploited, and managed large parts of nature, constructed vast complexes of built and enclosed spaces, and deployed networks of machines spanning the planet. This exceptional human ability to make and use ever more capable tools has radically transformed the human estate, propelling initially tiny human populations, living a precarious animal existence at the edge of extinction, into a presence large enough to reshape major features of the Earth's ecology and geology.

Modern machine civilization has made the human world global and planetary by amplifying and accelerating human activities. This globalization has knit together many human "worlds," previously isolated and fragmented, into "one world." This globalization has been strategic/military, economic, cultural, and ecological.[4] The overall results of this multidimensional globalization, greatly intensifying across the second half of the twentieth century, are levels of planetary-scale interactions, interdependencies, stratifications, and vulnerabilities that were previously experienced by humans only on much smaller spatial scales. These transformations have produced the "abolition of distance," made a "global village" or even a "spaceship Earth," resulted in the "closing of the frontier" and the "acceleration of history," and placed in human hands "the fate of the Earth."

These widely employed characterizations of the human planetary situation produced by the globalization of machine civilization are all significantly geographical in character, and they convey the extent to which the practical geography of humankind has been revolutionized. What was once far has now become near, and what was once slow has become fast. Barriers have become passageways. The once difficult or impossible has become easy or routine. The scarce has become abundant, while what was once abundant has become scarce. Fantastic dreams have become mundane realities. As a result of these mutations in the practical geography of the human world, solutions have become problems, and what was once taken for granted and beyond human choice is now within the ambit of human decision-making.

These reconfigurations of practical geography have produced very uneven human effects. Some peoples, most notably in Europe and its settler colonies, inadvertently infected, killed, stole, traded, and innovated into positions of global ascendancy in wealth and power. But for peoples outside the privileged, predatory and productive core, the experience of European imperial globalization was often catastrophic, marked by conquests, enslavements, and genocides.[5] And as previously geographically separated populations were forcibly brought into contact, massive pandemics resulted, greatly altering the Earth's demography. The intensification and acceleration of technological advance with the Industrial Revolution initially increased Western advantages, leading to even more effective imperialism and larger empires, while at the same time amplifying the destruction of wars among industrial powers to catastrophic levels.

These rapid material transformations have been inspired by one of the most successful and pervasive modern ideologies: technological modernization. This project to transform the earthly human estate through technological advance, often dubbed "Promethean" in its aspiration, was articulated by Francis Bacon in the seventeenth century.[6] It became a broad movement during the European Enlightenment and began to bear practical fruit with the Industrial Revolution of "steam and electricity" in the long nineteenth century.[7] Over the past two centuries, these advances have made possible vastly enlarged populations living in much improved conditions.[8] These advances have been accompanied by the prospect of much more to come from the "endless frontier" of scientific-technological advance and the further "conquest of nature."[9] In its most expansive formulations, this Promethean technological program promises a total transformation of the human condition, a realizable utopia, likened by some to a return to a mythical Eden, a new "golden age" of human flourishing and abundance, even immortality.[10] Humanity seems to have found a road map to unlimited progress, and adherents of this worldview believe anyone standing in the way will be relegated to the "ash heap of history."

The Expanding Horizon of Catastrophic and Existential Threats

By the middle years of the twentieth century, this optimistic story of limitless progress through scientific and technological advance came to be rivaled and sometimes overshadowed by a much more pessimistic, even apocalyptic vision of the trajectory of the modern project. It began to seem increasingly possible that technology would come to master its creators and carry humanity toward unforeseen and possibly catastrophic outcomes. Premonitions of technological wizardry leading to disasters are extremely old, dating back at least to the myth of Icarus, who is said to have fatally fallen into the sea after flying too close to the sun on wings his father, Daedalus, constructed.[11] As the Industrial Revolution gathered steam, dark anticipations became increasingly widespread, in works such as Mary Shelley's *Frankenstein; or, the Modern Prometheus* and Karel Capek's *R.U.R.* Perhaps technology, not man, was "in the saddle," as Henry

Adams worried. And perhaps machines, becoming ever more capable and inter-connected, were the next step in the evolution of life, destined to dominate and eventually eliminate humanity, as Samuel Butler warned.[12] The contours of the future, H. G. Wells announced in his famous 1902 lecture, "The Discovery of the Future," were difficult to discern but would surely be unlike the past or the present, and definitely included disasters of new types and magnitudes.[13]

In the ghastly world wars, industrial genocides, and totalitarian tyrannies of the middle twentieth century, technological advances empowered barbarism on a new scale, destroying the credibility of the simple modernist faith that more potent tools are a straight path to human betterment.[14] Rather, technological advance has produced a cornucopia of double-edged swords, with amplified possibilities for both progress and disaster. A growing herd of horsemen of the anthropogenic apocalypse have ominously appeared on the human horizon of possibility: nuclear weapons, genetic engineering, total surveillance despotism, runaway artificial intelligence, and rampant environmental decay.[15]

All across the blood-soaked history of humanity, technological advances in killing tools have been sought and extensively deployed for purposes of war-making and coercion. But since the Industrial Revolution, military technological advances have come with increasing rapidity. With the development of nuclear weapons, something of an "absolute weapon" emerged. There have always been enough rocks, to say nothing of knives and guns, to kill every inhabitant of the planet many times over, but nuclear explosives are utterly novel in their concen-tration of vast quantities of destructive capacity. One nuclear weapon, an ob-ject roughly the size of a modern household refrigerator, can obliterate a large city and kill millions of people. At their peak, the arsenals of the United States and the Soviet Union, employing but a small percentage of the potentially avail-able nuclear material, contained several tons of TNT equivalent for every man, woman, and child on the planet. In "the most dangerous moment in human his-tory," the Cuban Missile Crisis of 1962, these superpower states came perilously close to a nuclear war that might well have obliterated industrial civilization, and perhaps so wrecked the planetary life-support system that human extinction would have resulted.[16]

The fabric of life itself has also come to be understood by scientists and manipulated by engineers. The discovery in the early 1950s of the DNA molecules encoding information at the heart of every living cell triggered explo-sively rapid advances in the science of genetics. These scientific advances opened the door for the development of techniques to manipulate the genetic codes of organisms, first the relatively small and simple codes of bacteria and plants, but then increasingly animals, including humans.[17] These new technologies, rap-idly advancing with lavish funding from both governments and corporations, have already made possible a variety of new medicines and therapies, with the prospect of much more to come. They also make possible the creation of ever more lethal diseases and plagues that might be deployed as bioweapons, by governments or even small groups of "terrorists."[18] And the day may be rapidly approaching when it will be possible to transmogrify the biological features of humans beings, opening the prospect of directed evolution of the human species into beings with superior intelligence and other abilities, a "transhuman" future. Alternatively, the uneven application of these techniques might produce the diversification of the genus *Homo* through the creation of other intelligent humanoid species, something not seen on Earth since the extinction of the Neanderthals some thirty thousand years ago.

A third technological hallmark since the middle of the past half-century has been the explosive expansion in human ability to manipulate, transmit, and gather information. The first electronic digital computers built in the early 1950s filled entire buildings and were composed of expensive and fragile vacuum tubes. But with the relentless progress in the miniaturization of electronic circuitry, it is now possible to shrink two million transistors, the basic processing unit of digital computers, to the size of the period at the end of this sentence, and some ten trillion transistors a second are being added to the worldwide inventory. As the costs of computation have fallen by a factor of about a billion since the first electronic computing machines, billions of highly capable computers have been deployed and linked together through the internet, producing vast disruptions across virtually every aspect of commerce and society. Increasingly harnessed by powerful corporations and governments, the technological capacities for total surveillance and monitoring now within reach cast a lengthening shadow over the prospects for individual human freedom.

Computer engineers also are racing to create increasingly capable forms of artificial intelligence, possibly leading to artificial superintelligence, a digital computer vastly more intelligent than any human. Such a machine could massively accelerate the rate of technological advance but may be difficult or impossible to keep under human direction, making such a device humanity's "final invention," one way or another.[19]

Accompanying these astounding technological leaps of the nuclear, biotechnological, information, and computer revolutions, human impacts on the Earth's biospheric life-support system have begun to reach critically dangerous levels. Humans have been altering and degrading parts of the Earth as a habitat since prehistory, but with the globalization of machine civilization these assaults have rapidly grown in magnitude, scope, and complexity.[20] In reconfiguring their environments to make them more commodious, humans have set in motion changes in natural planetary systems with far-reaching negative consequences. Most notably humans are loading the atmosphere with various greenhouse gases (produced by the widespread burning of fossil fuels and deforestation), making substantial climate change very likely, perhaps very rapidly, with far-reaching negative implications for the viability of existing human habitats.[21] Scientists speak of these massive human assaults on the biosphere as the "sixth great extinction event" in the history of life on Earth, placing humans alongside asteroidal collisions as general perils to the planet's myriad life forms.[22] Humans have become a force of such planetary magnitude as to mark a new epoch in the geological history of the Earth, which some geologists call the Anthropocene.[23]

These five developments indicate that the scope of consequence of human actions has increased to encompass civilizational catastrophes of planetary proportions, perhaps even the extinction of the human species. The emergence of a globalized Earth across several centuries of the modern era had been catastrophic for many peoples, while propelling others to new heights. But as further globalization has made the human habitat planetary and vulnerable, it is now possible that catastrophe will be universal, perhaps the secular end of history. Due to this cumulative technological precocity, the prospects, even the survival of the human species, as well as much of the other life on the planet, now permanently hinge on what humans do—or do not do—with their extraordinary new technological powers.

These five anthropogenic perils, in combination with recently appreciated natural disasters, most notably asteroidal collisions, compose a long and lengthening list of ominous possibilities. Every society has had its doomsday myths, but for the first time rigorous analyses of natural disasters, technological accidents, civilizational collapse, and existential risks are being widely conducted by scientists, security analysts, futurists, and philosophers. Whether from natural causes, military conflicts, technical errors, or "terrorist" employment, disasters of comprehensive scope are not only possible but perhaps eventually unavoidable. Any quantitative calculation of the contours of the perils ahead remains shrouded in uncertainty, but some sense of their magnitude is registered in the astrophysicist Martin Rees's recent estimate that civilization has only a 50 percent chance of surviving through the twenty-first century.[24] Even if not an assured road to perdition or extinction, technological development appears to be a series of mysterious doors, some of which should be opened, but others of which should remain permanently closed.

But can humanity develop the foresight capacities to accurately anticipate which novel technological capabilities open paths to actual progress and which lead to the slippery slopes of a civilizational and species abyss? And can humanity develop the self-restraint to reverse course on the basis of new information, and even relinquish opening the doors to seductive but particularly catastrophic technological possibilities? The record of foresight and restraint thus far is not encouraging. Human capacities to anticipate consequences of major novel initiatives remain primitive, and powerful actors have short-term incentives not to know the full consequences of their activities.[25] Efforts so far to restrain these new perils stemming from human ingenuity range from the partial but inadequate to the nearly nonexistent. Even when expert Cassandras warn of impending disasters, they are often ignored.[26] Furthermore, efforts to restrain technologies face fierce opposition from Promethean optimists and powerful entrenched special interests. Add the conceptual and practical difficulties inherent in designing and operating regimes of restraint with worldwide scope, and what is in principle quite possible becomes quite daunting in practice.

The Technological Closure of the Earth and the Outer Space Prospect

These reconfigurations of the planet's geography and the emergence of planetary perils are all rooted in the extraordinary growth in human abilities to understand and manipulate the natural world. But their effects and perilous potentials also directly stem from a simple and obvious—but often overlooked—fact of geography: these expansions are all occurring on the planet Earth, which has not been expanding in size. The vast increases in human capabilities to harness natural forces have all been taking place within the finite space of the terrestrial Earth, the now narrow and crowded confines of this planet. Thus, as the "limitless frontiers" of science have been successively stormed by human ingenuity, spatial frontiers have everywhere been closing on the Earth. Where once distances seemed vast, they are now "abolished"; where once resources and "sinks" to dump wastes seemed practically unlimited, they are now increasingly exhausted and saturated. Disasters, whether from wars, tyrannies, plagues, or ecological destruction, were previously ruinous for particular peoples and places but are now potentially universal in their scope. As a result, technological expansion on Earth has produced the *closure* of human historical experience on this planet.[27] More can be wrung from less, and manipulations can be increasingly conducted on ever smaller scales, but the planet is now rapidly approaching the point where the extensive spatial expansions that have marked human activities across history can no longer occur within the confines of this planet. Societies once possessed a relatively clear "inside" and "outside." But in the wake of the globalization of machine civilization within the finite space of the planet Earth, everyone is now inside a worldwide complex of intense interactions, interdependencies, and vulnerabilities. The only real outside exists beyond the Earth, in cosmic outer space.

Set in this context of historical closure produced by the globalization of machine civilization and the planetary vulnerabilities created by the supercapabilities emerging in the second half of the twentieth century, the opening of outer space—the topic of this book—has seemed to many people uniquely positive in its transformative potentials.[28] Human expansion into space, while arduous and not advancing very rapidly, is widely seen as having almost entirely positive potentials to solve, or escape from, Earth problems and troubles. But are these aspirations and hopes well placed? Are there convincing arguments that a "vertical expansion" off the planet into outer space can play a role, possibly a decisive one, in addressing the lengthening list of civilizational catastrophes and existential threats confronting humanity and the Earth? Or are humanity's steps to open "the ultimate frontier" of outer space intensifying the closure of the Earth and planetary vulnerabilities? And might human expansion into space be the most seductive but ultimately most disastrous of our species' Promethean enlargements?

PART ONE

THE EARTH, TECHNOLOGY, AND SPACE

1

The Promise of Space Revisited

Out of the oceans to the land. Out of Africa to the north. Out of Earth and into space.

—Robert Zubrin (1999)[1]

Our only hope for long-term survival is not to remain lurking on planet Earth, but to spread out into space. Once we establish independent colonies, our entire future should be safe.

—Stephen Hawking (2013)[2]

Space exploration is not just another government program. It may be the key to human survival and evolution and perhaps even more than that.

—Frank White (1987)[3]

From the Sky Age to Modern Astronomy

Long before humans realized they lived on a globe-shaped planet, they were keenly attentive to the sky and the awesome nightly spectacle of the cosmos. And long before humans could venture into space, what they thought about the sky played outsized roles in many aspects of their lives. Culturally, much of human history is appropriately called "the Sky Age" due to the enormous importance humans everywhere attached to patterns in the skies that majestically vaulted over their living spaces and seemed to govern much in them. Throughout their history humans have viewed the sky as "the heavens," the abode of mysterious but superior beings with great sway over human destinies. Peoples everywhere keenly followed the seasonal variations in the movements of the sun and moon, as well as the oddly shifting positions of the handful of points of light in the night sky that wandered in their position relative to other stars. They delineated their basic temporal units—the day, the month, the year—on familiar cosmic regularities. Unusual events, such as eclipses and comets, were widely viewed as portents of calamitous future events.[4] Stories and claims about the heavens and celestial phenomena are woven prominently into every human religion and culture. And systematic, mathematically precise, and observation-based astronomical investigation is among the most ancient of sciences. "The above" was not only more powerful but also generally viewed as better, and imagined ascents into the heavens were widely associated with spiritual and moral advance.

Humans also have long aspired to practically apply astronomical knowledge. Immense efforts have been made to divine the intents of superpowerful celestial beings, and then to propitiate their whims and follow their directives. Since the Neolithic era, peoples in many parts of the world have erected enormous mega-lithic structures aligned with celestial patterns.[5] Statecraft has also been closely linked with skycraft, as powerful political and religious leaders sought to gain cosmic legitimacy by ceremonially attaching themselves to heavenly forces and occurrences.[6] Astrology, an elaborately systematized method for predicting the life fates of individuals, has been widely practiced and influential as an "applied astronomy" (albeit one based on completely imaginary causal connections).[7] The study of celestial phenomena has also been intimately associated with the practical arts of navigation, particularly across oceans, and thus with explora-tion, trade, and war.[8]

Across most of history, the magnitude of the importance humans attached to what they saw in the skies was fully matched by the magnitude of their igno-rance about the real character of what they were seeing and about the actual lines of influence sky patterns exerted upon their affairs. How this ignorance came to be dispelled by the accumulation of accurate scientific knowledge is the story of modern astronomy. Early modern revolutions in knowledge about the heavens played a pivotal role in the emergence of science-based technological civilization. And for astronomy, as with so many domains of human life, the rise of this civi-lization has been revolutionary. Among the modern natural sciences, astronomy has no rival in terms of the magnitude or ultimate significance of its discoveries. Over the past several centuries, and accelerating across the twentieth, modern astronomy has produced a cascade of extraordinary discoveries that have utterly transformed human understanding of the universe and the place of the Earth in it. What sets modern astronomy apart from its predecessors is surely not the mental ability of its practitioners but rather the capabilities of its instruments. Starting with the small homemade telescope that Galileo first pointed into the sky and extending to contemporary telescopes that are the size of large buildings, the possibilities and pace of astronomical scientific advance have been tightly coupled with advances in instrumentation made possible by modern technology.

Storming Heaven

Long before humans had a clear understanding of the realms beyond the ter-restrial Earth, they had imagined flying into the heavens and traveling to other celestial bodies.[9] But in the early twentieth century, fantasy started to become practical possibility as engineers and scientists in Russia, America, and Europe developed the fundamental principles of rocketry, the basic enabling technology for all subsequent space activities. Inspired by these technological advances and science fictions about space travel, there was an explosion of ideas for doing things in space.

Space activities burst from the visionary into the actual suddenly—and ominously. In the early years of the twentieth century, fervent advocates of space exploration formed the first pro-space organizations and sought support from the public, corporations, and governments for the substantial economic resources needed to build the complex machines they hoped to propel into the heavens.[10] They found their largest sponsorship in the late 1920s from the German army, which was eager to evade the limits on heavy artillery imposed by the Treaty of Versailles, and then from Adolf Hitler, who poured resources into rocket development in the misplaced hope that this weapon would prove decisive in winning the Second World War.[11] In the 1950s the Cold War militaries of Soviet Russia and America pursued rocket development with even larger commitments in order to more rapidly deliver nuclear weapons at intercontinental distances. These rockets also made possible Earth-orbiting satellites, and then ventures to the Earth's moon and into the vast reaches of the solar system.

These beginnings of human activity in the unfathomably vast realms beyond the Earth's atmosphere have been particularly spectacular and visible, capturing the attention and imagination of large numbers of people, and space developments have at times played pivotal roles in human affairs. The Soviet launch of the first Earth-orbiting satellite in 1957, the American Apollo Project landings on the moon in 1969, and the explosive demise of two US space shuttles in 1986 and 2003 have been particularly dramatic and sensational. Also widely known are the fruits of space missions to expand human knowledge of the cosmos, such as landings of probes on other planets, and images of vastly distant celestial phenomena from orbiting space observatories such as the Hubble Space Telescope. For some observers, these initial steps beyond the Earth's atmosphere are so momentous and full of grand potential as to warrant referring to this period of human history as "the Space Age."

Since rockets first nosed their way out of the Earth's atmosphere three-quarters of a century ago, a wide array of very different activities has taken place in space. Aside from the fact that they are occurring in space, many have very little in common with each other. They have been undertaken by a diverse set of actors, most notably the militaries of rival nation-states, civilian government agencies, scientific researchers, private corporations, and international consortia. These actors pursue diverse goals, most notably national security, scientific knowledge, profit, and practical services. Although the goals of these varied space activities are clear enough, their actual consequences are harder to discern, despite—or perhaps because of—the claims of the many interested parties undertaking them.

The beginnings of human space activity have generated an extraordinary amount of commentary and reflection. The emergence of space travel as a practical possibility has triggered debate over very fundamental but difficult-to-answer questions about the place of humanity and the Earth in the cosmos. What should humans do in space? What will come from space activities? Is there a fundamental necessity to human space expansion? Debates about these questions have been particularly extensive in the wake of pivotal space developments such as the first satellite and the first lunar landings.[12] Answers to these questions, and judgments about the space enterprise, have come from many voices spanning an extremely wide spectrum. For some, human expansion into space is of vital importance and cosmic significance. President Richard Nixon proclaimed the Apollo landings "the greatest week in history since the beginning of the world, the creation."[13] Others condemned, often in sweeping ways, blasting space missions as meaningless frivolities, dangerous follies, or evidence of national and human civilizational priorities gone awry. The novelist Norman Mailer blasted NASA technicians as "barbaric" and "root-destroying people."[14] The sociologist Amitai Etzioni famously condemned the Apollo "moondoggle."[15] The technology critic Lewis Mumford called it "technological exhibitionism."[16] The Christian allegorist C. S. Lewis lamented space travel for allowing Fallen Man to spread damage across the universe.[17] Some populist conspiratorial thinkers doubt the Apollo moon landings actually occurred.[18] Also part of the space conversation are those who insist on the reality of UFOs and alien visitations, abductions, and interventions on the Earth or are devotees of UFO religions.[19]

Despite the extreme variety of views voiced about every aspect of space, the most developed and influential body of thought about human space activity has been produced by space advocates. They view significant expansion into space as an extremely positive, even necessary human undertaking. Vast numbers of people are aware of space, but most do not focus much on space. Most people who are heavily involved in space, or follow it closely, hold optimistic views about space expansion. And optimistic space advocates have been far more influential than their limited numbers might suggest. Advocates of space first conceived everything that has been done in space, have laid out elaborate visions for doing vastly more, and now believe they are on the cusp of another significant leap in the expansion into space.

This body of thought, which I refer to as "space expansionism," is the subject of this book. Space expansionism is a complex and captivating ideology. It extrapolates and amplifies the Promethean worldview of technological modernism into a project of literally cosmic scope. Space expansionism, as we shall see, contains many parts, crosscurrents, and disagreements. And many of its specific claims have been subject to criticism. However, among those who think most about space, strongly optimistic views of the desirability of human expansion into space overwhelmingly prevail. Those who think most about space do not commonly question whether space activities have been or will be positive in their consequences because their primary focus is making space activities more feasible.

This book advances a considerably darker view of the space enterprise. I argue that the consequences of what has actually happened in space are much less positive than space enthusiasts and many others believe. My case for this darker net assessment of actual space activities centers on the role of space activities in making nuclear war more likely. This darker view of space impacts is based in large part on a revisionist understanding of what has actually happened in space, which is, I believe, fundamentally more accurate than in virtually all descriptive accounts of the Space Age. Furthermore, I argue that many prospective space ventures are likely to be much darker in their consequences than advocates claim. Their pursuit and realization are likely to entail grave risks for security and freedom on Earth, and eventually for the survival of the human species. In sum, this book argues that the large-scale expansion of human activities into space, past and future, should join the lengthening list of catastrophic and existential threats to humanity, and that the ambitious core projects of space expansionism should be explicitly relinquished.

The basis for this revisionist view of the promise of space, past and future, is a set of arguments about geography, geohistory, and geopolitics. The arguments of space expansionists are filled with geographic assertions about the physical contours of the Earth and space, with analogies between space futures and terrestrial geohistory and with geopolitical propositions about the political consequences of technologies deployed in particular space geographies. Despite their manifest importance in space expansionist thinking, these arguments about geography, geohistory, and geopolitics have never been systematically assessed and evaluated. Optimistic thinking about space is marked, I argue, by important geography errors, misleading geohistorical analogies, and slanted and truncated geopolitics. Ambitious space expansion proposals also rest on dubious assumptions about human control of nature and technology and governance of superpotent new technologies. When these deficiencies are identified and corrected, space activities, actual and prospective, look very different, and space expansion loses much of its appeal.

This critical account is not, however, completely antispace. Instead it attempts to extend and vindicate a more modest, and more readily realizable, Earth-centered pro-space agenda focused on nuclear security and environmental protection. This agenda aims to protect the Earth rather than expand into space.

It opposes some space activities, most notably militarization and colonization, but supports others. And far from being a full rejection of the Space Age and what it has wrought or a return to approaches that predate the Space Age, the Earth-centered space program defended and extended here is better based on knowledge that has emerged during the Space Age. In contrast, the main ideas of space expansionism largely predate actual space activity and have not registered the profound new understandings of the Earth and its place in the cosmos that have emerged during this period.

The remaining four sections of this chapter survey space expansionist thought, profile the "boom and bust" patterns of space development, and offer reasons why the topic of space, and the arguments of space advocates, remain vitally important. Chapter 2 lays out the space-political questions addressed here, describes their explosive implications for major contemporary debates about the human prospect, outlines the geopolitical framework for assessing space arguments, summarizes the main conclusions, and provides a map of the chapters that follow.

Space Expansionism and Its Critics

What, then, is space expansionism? Who are the space expansionists, and what do they think about space?

Space expansionism is a subset of technological futurism, which creates "technological imaginaries" that are elaborate visions of future technological possibilities and their potential consequences. Technological futurism has been a prominent facet of Promethean modernism since its beginning. Space futurism, what some call "astrofuturism," is only a small part of technological futurism. While humans have long dreamed of machines with wondrous abilities to travel into the heavens, the growth in science and science-based technology over the past two centuries has stimulated a massive expansion in the volume, scope, credibility, and sophistication of space futurism.

The fullest sweep of technological futurism is found in science fiction, a body of literary writings in which imagined new scientific knowledge and technologies are employed to create worlds that are limited only by the human imagination. Space is not by any means the sole topic of SF or sci-fi (as its practitioners refer to it), but it looms large. Beginning with the archetypal works of Jules Verne and H. G. Wells in the late nineteenth and early twentieth centuries, many tens of thousands of SF stories about space have been published. Fictional space stories have also inspired actual scientific-technological advances, and some leading space scientists and engineers have written science fiction.[20] Across the twentieth century, imaginative renderings of space futures, UFOs, and aliens have permeated mass culture, making what the cultural historian Alexander C. T. Geppert calls "astroculture."[21]

But not all space futurism is science fiction. A substantial body of writings, often prominent and sometimes practically influential, makes very seriously intended, and often very bold, claims about actual space possibilities and their anticipated consequences. Space futurism emerged in the early years of the twentieth century, mainly in Russia, Europe, and America. This space futures literature has largely been produced by scientists, engineers, military planners, and a diverse assortment of independent space analysts and advocates. Some space futurists, most notably H. G. Wells, Konstantin Tsiolkovsky, Robert Goddard, Hermann Oberth, Wernher von Braun, Arthur C. Clarke, Buckminster Fuller, Carl Sagan, Stephen Hawking, Freeman Dyson, Elon Musk, and Jeff Bezos are space celebrities with global followings. Others, such as J. D. Bernal, David Lasser, Eugen Sänger, Krafft Ehricke, Dandridge Cole, Robert Salkeld, G. Harry Stine, Peter Glaser, Gerard O'Neill, John Lewis, Ben Bova, Frank White, James Oberg, Everett Dolman, Robert Zubrin, James Vedda, Peter Garretson, Ian Crawford, Michio Kaku, and Charles Cockell, are known mainly among space enthusiasts. Some of these figures were, or are, primarily visionaries, inspiring others to action, while some played influential roles in realizing space ventures. Some of the most prominent are what the historian W. Patrick McCray calls "visioneers," who operate at "the blurry border between scientific fact, technological possibility, and optimistic speculation,"[22] and combine hard engineering schemes with charismatic promotion. Their ideas and lives have been extensively discussed by legions of critics, commentators, journalists, biographers, and intellectual historians.[23] Their imagined projects have been rendered visible by talented space artists.[24] These astrofuturist visions provide the ideology for a small and sometimes very influential pro-space political movement. As with any other visionary ideology, the promotion of space is prone to distinctive forms of blindness and fanaticism. Ideas from space visionaries also have a vivid presence in popular astroculture and have been prominently voiced by many political leaders in making (or at least attempting to justify and promote) decisions about space activities.

Space futurists have many differences, some very important, and heated debates often occur among them. But nearly all space futurists are space expansionists. By this I mean that most space futurists are *advocates* of extensive human expansion into space. Most basically, space expansionists claim that a movement of humans into outer space is becoming *feasible*, and will become much more feasible in the future. More important, they argue that space expansion is *desirable* because it will benefit those who conduct it as well as humanity and the Earth in myriad ways.[25] Space expansionists believe that the enlargement of human activity into space will solve a variety of important earthly problems, thus positively transforming the trajectory of human development. Like other programs of technological modernism, space expansionism boldly claims to be able to better realize very basic human aspirations, most notably security from violence, a richer and more commodious human habitat, and various forms of freedom. Space expansionists often try to connect their proposed space activities with the specific interests of particular states and peoples, but they routinely characterize space expansion as beneficial to the human species and life itself.

Everything actually done in space was first imagined by space futurists. But what has actually been done is only a tiny part of what they have imagined and advocated (see Figure 1.1). These projects, realized and anticipated, are described and evaluated in detail ahead, but a brief glance at the overall vision can provide an initial sense of the scope of the expansionist agenda, as well as the high stakes of its claims. Already realized are visions for the development of rockets, the basic space technology, and their employment for a variety of purposes, most notably long-range bombardment, placing of satellites (some with humans on them) into orbits around the Earth, a few human visits to the moon, and many small robotic spacecraft launched across the solar system. The longer list of prospective projects starts with elaborate infrastructures in orbit around the Earth, and then proceeds to the colonization and industrialization of the Earth's moon, the asteroids, and Mars. Their proposed projects next extend to the distribution of humans and their machines throughout the outer solar system and, eventually, across the vast voids of interstellar space to a Lebensraum of galactic proportions. As these space expansions occur, many space advocates anticipate the physical modification of humans and celebrate biological and cyborg species diversifications as part of the spread of life in the universe.

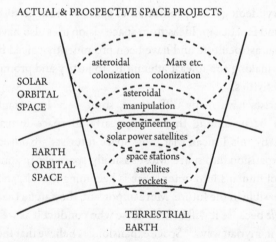

Figure 1.1 Actual and Prospective Space Projects

While their ultimate aim is to expand far beyond the Earth, space advocates have also proposed numerous projects for meeting needs and solving important terrestrial problems. Solving the Earth's problems with space technology not only benefits the Earth but also helps establish the foundations for ambitious expansions far beyond the Earth. Weather, communication, navigation, and monitoring satellites provide valuable services, some of which are infeasible or very costly to otherwise provide. Similarly, military organizations use space for a variety of purposes. The problems on Earth that space expansionists think can be solved from space are very diverse and have shifted across time. And advocates, as we shall see at length, fundamentally diverge about what the Earth's central problems are and what should be done about them.

Space expansionists also advance an array of vastly more ambitious projects that they believe can solve very large and important Earth problems. The problem of nuclear vulnerability looms especially large, with fundamental differences in how this might be solved. Space advocates also point to a large number of ways in which the Earth as a habitat for humanity is threatened, and they offer space projects as solutions to these problems. These contemporary habitability problems include ecological degradation and pollution, scarcity of resources and energy, overpopulation, and climate change. Space expansionists also look to space as a way to protect and realize various forms of freedom, but they have widely differing views of freedom that range from extreme libertarian to communist. Some hold that space expansion can alleviate tendencies toward world government and cultural enervation produced by global closure and planetary vulnerabilities, but others look to space expansion as a welcome catalyst for world unification and government. Space expansionists also point to a variety of cosmic catastrophes and other threats to the Earth and humanity, ranging from asteroidal collisions to the eventual dying of the sun, as arguments for major human space activities.

Advancing a solution from space presupposes the definition of a problem on Earth. In making their case for space solutions to major Earth problems, space expansionists grapple with some of the most important problems stemming from the globalization of machine civilization. Space expansionists typically emphasize that technological globalization has made humanity's terrestrial habitat increasingly vulnerable and marked by closed frontiers and many limits to growth. In contrast, space advocates view space as a vast new frontier where human expansion knows no ultimate limits, where painful choices can be solved or left behind, and where the expansive trajectory of humans across Earth history can be continued and enlarged. Thus competing claims about Earth problems are an integral part of the case for space, and their appeal rests as much on claims about the Earth as on claims about space. Viewing the many threats to humanity's terrestrial habitat as both inherent and severe, space expansionists are confident that their programs are not only beneficial but also necessary and eventually will be inevitable. Given this view of the human situation, space expansionists are often impatient with those who doubt the appeal, urgency, and inevitability of their ambitions.

The projects advanced by space expansionists, and the problems they seek to address, gain further intellectual power because they are embedded in a larger metanarrative about humanity, Earth, and cosmos, an epic story that connects past, present, and future. Space expansionism seamlessly combines Big History with Big Futurism. Space expansionism is more than the sum of its programmatic parts because it advances a comprehensive account, a narrative whole, in which its many projects are nested. The space expansionist narrative has extremely broad spatial and temporal scope, offering a macrohistorical, planetary-scale account of human development and its interaction with nature. Space expansionists tell this large story about the human past and present, and then extrapolate it into imagined space futures. In this story, the present sits at a decisive inflection point, culminating millennia of steadily rising interdependence and interaction on the Earth, but at the threshold of an ultimately limitless expansion across the "final frontier" of cosmic outer space (see Figure 1.2). In an era when Grand Narratives—particularly those associated with the Enlightenment—have become suspect among the humanistic intelligentsia, space expansionists cast themselves as the avant-garde of technological civilization and advance the most comprehensively progressive Grand Narrative of Enlightenment modernity.

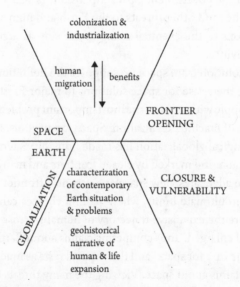

Figure 1.2 Space Expansionism

This narrative employs numerous geohistorical analogies suggesting that expansion into outer space continues patterns of spatial expansion across Earth history. In the largest temporal frame, the space enterprise is likened to the expansion of organic life on Earth, as well as many historical terrestrial expansions of humanity on Earth. Familiar Earth geographic features, notably oceans, islands, and frontiers, are analogized with the features of outer space. In this story, technological advancement, from the control of fire and the invention of clothing to large sailing ships and malaria prophylaxis turn formidable natural barriers into new frontiers, enabling humans to expand their habitats through further exploration, conquest, and colonization, a pattern that will continue as new technologies enable expansions into outer space. This expansion narrative gains further credibility by incorporating powerful high modernist Promethean ideas about the cosmos, nature and life, and scientific and technological progress. Although expansionists claim space ventures will benefit all humanity, they also anticipate special advantage for those who first undertake them, while peoples who fail to seize opportunities for space expansion will fall behind.

The broad narrative of space expansionism is in many ways a science-based and technology-dependent religion.[26] Space expansionism transmutes the Promethean modernism of globalizing scientific-technological civilization into a spiritual enterprise without earthly bonds and boundaries. Space expansionists transpose the divine significance humans once attached to natural cosmic phenomena onto the artifacts they aspire to fabricate in the heavens. Its strongest formulations offer a comprehensive understanding of humanity and life and set forth a challenging human vocation with cosmic significance. The human movement into space becomes a vital step toward the immortality of the human species and Earth-originated life, and eventually toward something approximating a species apotheosis in which the posthuman descendants of humanity acquire God-like powers. But unlike prescientific religions, full space expansionism takes its writ from the Book of Nature as revealed by experimental science rather than supernatural revelations. Unlike prescientific religions, the strong version of space expansionism sees human technology as the indispensable stairway to heaven, not as transgressive of divine order. Unlike prescientific revealed religions that are challenged by evolutionary biology, the full narrative of space expansionism advances itself as the culmination of the evolution of life on Earth and the cosmos. The long historical association of spatial elevation with moral and religious improvement gives this religiously infused space expansionist worldview an intuitive credibility. This narrative imparts to its believers a strong faith that their small and struggling steps inevitably contribute to something of vast cosmic import. It also justifies overlooking doubts and possible downsides inconsistent with its progressive trajectory of improvement through ascent, as well as the employment of whatever means are necessary to realize humanity's cosmic destiny.

In making the case for the cosmic expansion of humanity, space expansionism rests on strong claims about the ends of humanity, in both senses of this term. On the one hand, space expansionists hold that the movement of humanity into the cosmos is the distinctive end goal, or telos, of all of human history, indeed of life on Earth. Humanity has biologically ordained species objectives. The only questions are how soon and by which part of humanity this teleological human end will be realized. On the other hand, space expansionists advance their program as solutions to a growing list of frightful scenarios of the end or termination of humanity. Only by expanding into space, they insist, can humanity avoid a variety of catastrophic and existential threats, either from the blind forces of nature or from the very technologies that have propelled humankind to the cusp of cosmic expansion, but all linked to the vulnerabilities, fragilities, and finiteness of the Earth as the sole abode of humanity. If humanity stumbles, in some ghastly failure of nerve, in realizing its nature-given role as the guardian and carrier of life and does not move resolutely to expand its habitat beyond this planet, the outcome will inevitably be the elimination of the human species from the cosmos. If humanity fails to expand into space, it betrays its basic essence and will pay for this betrayal with extinction.

Space expansionism is a magnetically attractive and intoxicating ideology. It feeds off experiences of the technological and cosmic sublimes, of awesome roaring rockets and astounding gizmos, and of weirdly alien planets, incomprehensibly titanic cataclysms, and mesmerizing spacescapes. Everything about it is oversized: speeds, distances, magnitudes—and payoffs. To paraphrase counter- and digital-culture guru Stewart Brand, "space is the greatest thing (other than the internet) since LSD." With its many "out there" proposals, it is easy to lampoon, and it is often difficult to discern where the space movement's lunatic fringe begins and ends. Space-struck members of the international space movement, who fondly refer to themselves as "space cadets," become part of the elect, the self-chosen avant-garde of the species, indeed life, by preparing to embark on a heroic and elevating adventure of unprecedented scope. By hitching their wagons to the stars, as the quintessential American uplift guru (and astronomy enthusiast) Ralph Waldo Emerson advised, the lives of space cadets acquire cosmic purpose and value.[27] In the fractious contemporary political scene, big space visions attract from across the political spectrum, from astro-libertarian government-phobes, through military officers and pork-barreling politicians, to neo-Marxist supporters of Fully Automated Luxury Communism. Space camps, space SF theme parks, SF conventions, and space museums provide immersion experiences for the faithful and assist recruitment. With its intricate techno-jargon, captivating neologisms, and esoteric acronyms, spaceworld offers a comprehensively encompassing alternative reality.

The cosmic aspirations of the popular space movement are continuously nurtured by the space advocacy vanguard, composed of celebrity astronauts (Buzz Aldrin), superwealthy entrepreneurs (Elon Musk and Jeff Bezos), superstar scientists (Stephen Hawking), and a phalanx of charismatic proselytizers, busy bloggers, and sympathetic journalists. To gain support, costly, risky, and speculative engineering schemes are wrapped in the space expansionist macrohistorical, macrofuturist narrative. To mobilize on the basis of completely imaginary scenarios, pie-in-the-sky visions of unimaginably vast benefits are promised. But what are these pied pipers of the ultimate frontier really selling? Is it really going to have only benefits, with no downsides?

While space expansionist arguments are the most charismatic and developed body of thought about space and its promise, the space enterprise has also been widely criticized. These criticisms, explored at length ahead, come from every direction, sometimes with great force. Some philosophers, literary humanists, and cultural critics view space activities as another malignant manifestation of the modern machine-based civilization that is deranged and hurtling toward self-destruction.[28] More prosaically, many argue that space activities are too costly, and such objections have been extremely influential in shaping the actual pace of space expansion. Many criticisms are essentially internal to space expansionism, about how best to achieve expansionist goals. Most notably, many scientists criticize the high cost of manned exploration and advocate using increasingly cheaper robotic probes.[29] Other critics point to the inefficiencies of government space agencies and advocate greater reliance on the private sector. Perhaps most important, given the magnitude of military space activities and their potential consequences, advocates of arms control (including this author) have made extensive criticisms of space military activities and propose many arms control measures, as well as alternative uses of space technology to build a new global security system. And environmental thinkers criticize proposals to solve terrestrial habitability problems with space solutions and schemes to expand industrialization across the solar system.

While these critical arguments are often potent and compelling, and sometimes very influential, they are ad hoc, scattered, and unsystematically formulated and are less than the sum of their parts. These criticisms have not been taken very seriously by space advocates and have not diminished their optimism about the promise of space. As reactions to what space expansionists have done and proposed, these critical arguments are newer than advocacy arguments. As a result, they have yet to be assembled into anything approaching a general view of the space enterprise comparable to military and habitat space expansionism.

The Space Age Arrives

Compared to all previous history, there has been a recent explosion of space activity, but compared to what expansionists propose doing in space, virtually nothing has happened—yet. To begin thinking about the overall net consequences of space activities, past and present, it is useful to start with a brief outline of what has actually happened in space. Space activities are commonly seen as falling into five more or less distinct clusters (see Table 1.1), and have little in common. They have been undertaken by a diverse set of actors (militaries of rival nation-states, scientists, private corporations, and international consortia). These actors have set forth a diverse set of goals or purposes (national security, scientific knowledge, profit, and practical services) that they anticipate will be advanced by specific space activities.

First, exploration and science have been an enduring and astoundingly productive space activity. Probes and observatories, aimed at both the cosmos and the Earth, have yielded a greatly improved mapping of the features of the Earth, of the solar system, and of galactic and intergalactic space. This knowledge-gathering has yielded data with far-reaching implications for many of the most important questions that science has been asking since its beginning. And widely viewed images of the whole planet Earth from space, most notably the "pale blue marble" photographs, have become ubiquitous icons for globalizing humanity

Table 1.1 **Actual Space Activities**

	Description	*Objective*	*Patterns & Trends*
Science	Orbital satellite observatories and planetary probes	Increased knowledge of cosmos and earth	More looking out than at Earth; open science
"Manned"	Humans in orbit and six moon visits	Exploration, prestige, and biomedicine	Declining; tourism?
Military	Missiles, satellites, and antisatellite weapons	Increased national security	Highly erratic: build and partly dismantle
Utility	Satellites for communication and navigation	Economically valuable services	Steady growth and increasingly privatized
Regime	Treaties and practices to regulate space activities	Reduce conflict and permit orderly use	Partial strengthening and partial weakening

and inspirations for the worldwide environmental movement.[30] Space science is typically conducted openly, often through international cooperation.

Second, humans have actually traveled into outer space. For most people, probably the most memorable space events have been human orbital and lunar voyages. In a short burst between 1961 and 1969, crewed vehicles were first put into Earth orbit, and then briefly traveled to the moon. Several small space stations in Earth orbit have been inhabited for extended periods. The cumulative number of humans who have gone into space is minuscule, only about five hundred, and these astronauts (or cosmonauts or troikanauts) have mainly been military pilots and scientists and have undergone stringent fitness testing and training. Initially these manned space activities were driven by interstate rivalry and to divert rivalry from military to peaceful activities, but now they are largely an interstate cooperative effort. Despite aspirations and strenuous efforts to lower costs, humans have remained very expensive to transport to space, sustain there, and return to Earth, while robotic capabilities have grown successively cheaper, more capable, and more extensively used. And decades-long efforts to find militarily useful roles for humans in space have also proven largely fruitless. As a result, human expansion into space has largely stalled, and only three countries have gone to the expense of developing the ability to send humans into space. But many anticipate that growing numbers of people will soon go into space as paying space tourists.

Third, military activities have expanded into space. Militaries developed many basic space technologies and rely extensively on space capabilities. The single largest space activity (as measured by expenditures and the number of space launches) is military. Over the decades of the Cold War, rockets tipped with nuclear explosives became the paramount weapon in Soviet and American arsenals, and the proliferation of nuclear weapons capability to more states has largely paralleled the diffusion of large rocket technology. This integrated weaponization of space and nuclear technologies has cumulatively produced a planet-encompassing rocket-satellite infrastructure for transportation and information services for nuclear weapons, and increasingly also for conventional military forces. Rockets provide the transportation of nuclear explosive devices, while orbiting satellites provide information services (reconnaissance, surveillance, communication, navigation, and targeting). This astounding planetary architecture of networked machines is capable of wreaking unprecedented levels of destruction. Seeking security, states built this apparatus but also have pursued arms control to restrain and dismantle it. Given the magnitude of the harms from the extensive use of nuclear weapons, any evaluation of the overall net impact of actual space activities must hinge largely on whether they have made catastrophic outcomes more or less likely.

Fourth, several prosaic utilitarian activities have expanded into space. Most prominently, communication satellites designed to relay radio signals to and from distant points on the Earth have been extensively commercialized and are part of the explosion of information technologies over recent decades. Satellites also routinely provide remote sensing of parts of the Earth for the practical tasks of weather forecasting, disaster assessment, and agricultural, forestry, and fishery exploitation and conservation. Satellites also provide navigation services, most notably the Global Positioning System (GPS), which is routinely employed by hundreds of millions of widely dispersed users. The valuable information produced by these satellites is sometimes military and intelligence secrets, sometimes available for purchase, and sometimes freely disseminated. Over recent decades there has been a shift in the mix of organizations engaged in these activities, away from government and toward private for-profit firms. And the number of satellites in orbit is now rapidly growing, as large numbers of increasingly small satellites in low orbits are replacing the small numbers of large ones in high orbits.

Fifth, international law has expanded into space. A basic space constitution, provided by the Outer Space Treaty of 1967 enshrines "free passage" for space vehicles and the nonappropriation of celestial bodies.[31] Like other parts of world public order, the outer space regime privileges states, while embodying restraints agreed upon by states. Like other regimes, the public order of space is also contested, with some wanting its expansion and others its weakening.

The field of space history is largely placid, without major controversies. There is pretty much universal agreement about who did what when and why. But the presence of the items summarized here is curiously uneven in the larger stories told about the Space Age, suggesting a very different view of space activity and its consequences. First, almost all accounts of the Space Age hold that it began in 1957 with the launch of the Soviet Sputnik, the first artificial satellite, rather than in the 1940s, when the first human artifact, a German ballistic missile, actually passed beyond the Earth's atmosphere. Second, it is universally acknowledged that military organizations developed the first rockets capable of propelling objects beyond the Earth's atmosphere. But once orbital activities begin, the continuing development and deployment of increasingly capable ballistic missiles in steadily increasing numbers by the United States and the Soviet Union from the late 1950s through the early 1980s simply disappears as an event in the Space Age narrative.[32]

As a result of this odd disappearance, a very large use of space is ignored or treated as if it were occurring in some other realm. Once this move is made, the great controversies surrounding the security implications of ballistic missiles, and then the cooperative dismantling of large numbers of them in the later 1980s and 1990s, cease being parts of Space Age history. In short, ballistic missiles and arms control efforts to restrain them are "dark" space programs, in the sense that they are hidden in advocate accounts of space activity. Bringing these two enormous and consequential space programs back into thinking about space has, as we shall see, immense implications for a full assessment of the space enterprise.

From Boom to Bust

Despite the spectacular advances of the Space Age, the actual trajectory of human expansion into space has been disappointing for space advocates, and quite different than they anticipated. The overall pattern has been boom and bust, highly erratic in important and unanticipated ways, and marked by actual reversals. What was done, but then stopped or undone, now looms larger than what is being done.

Human expansion into space has been far slower than anticipated by almost all its advocates.[33] The Space Age began with an initial space boom of very rapid progress but over the past several decades has turned into something of a space bust. The initial boom lasted roughly a quarter of a century, from the launch of the first heavy rocket (the German V-2) in the early 1940s, through the Soviet launch of Sputnik in 1957, and to the first landing on the moon by Americans in 1969.[34] This rapid progress seemed to be a continuation of the extremely quick development of aeronautical technology, which had progressed within half a century from the first heavier-than-air flight in 1903 to routine transcontinental jet flight in the 1950s. The period of extremely fast space development encouraged space advocates to hope—or even assume—that this pace would continue. For example, the noted space thinker Dandridge Cole, writing in 1965, extrapolating from trends over the preceding decade, anticipated extensive colonies on the moons of planets in the outer solar system within fifty years, by 2015.[35] But after this first burst of major advances, the overall path of human space expansion has been much less rapid and successful than advocates had anticipated. As a result, there has emerged a progressively expanding expectations gap between the anticipations and hopes of space advocates and the actual pace of space development.

The list of disappointments, unrealized promises, and outright failures is now long. Many anticipated that the moon missions of 1969–72 would be followed by trips to Mars and the establishment of lunar bases. Leaders declared ambitious goals but did not commit the substantial resources needed to carry them out.[36] The Russian space effort, spectacularly successful in the 1950s and 1960s, has become a poor ghost of its former self since the collapse of the Soviet Union and the decline of Russia.[37] The space shuttle program, the largest American space project after Apollo, was initiated in the 1970s with high expectations of substantially lowering costs and thus catalyzing myriad activities in near Earth orbit.[38] But the shuttle, despite the expenditure of a quarter of a trillion dollars, was unable to reduce costs, was prone to catastrophic accidents, and was terminated long before planned.[39] Bullish expectations in the 1970s of profitable orbital microgravity industrial processing were unrealized. The proposals of American space militarization advocates for an orbital astrodome defense system to eliminate the vulnerabilities posed by nuclear weapons carried by ballistic missiles, under the rubric of the Strategic Defense Initiative (or "Star Wars," in popular parlance), loomed large in American military space policy in the 1980s.[40] But this effort, despite consuming over a hundred billion dollars and producing only incremental advances, was also greatly scaled back in the 1990s.

The International Space Station, built by the United States and Russia with the participation of other countries after the Cold War, is widely viewed as a very expensive white elephant and may be abandoned before the end of its useful life.[41] Communication satellites, heralded in the 1960s as producing a global village of instant information connectivity, now carry a small and shrinking share of the stupendously vast information flows associated with the internet and other contemporary telecommunications. There are now more derelict than operational satellites in orbit. High-velocity space debris is accumulating and increasingly menacing space activities. Orbital space is not yet Detroit, but it seems headed that way. The pattern of bust continues into the present, with the recent demise of the highly publicized companies Planetary Resources and Space Industries, backed by leading Silicon Valley and Hollywood figures, which had been planning to launch satellites to survey near Earth asteroids for valuable metals, and then to bring them back to Earth for processing and marketing.[42] Perhaps most telling, the cost of placing an object into Earth orbit (about ten thousand dollars per pound since the 1960s), widely viewed as the single most important indicator of the prospect for a substantial increase in space activities, has remained stubbornly high.[43] In contrast, during this same period the cost of artificial computation has fallen by many orders of magnitude, enabling the explosion of computer applications that have increasingly eclipsed the space enterprise as the most dynamic frontier of contemporary technological civilization.

As these disappointments and setbacks have accumulated, many commentators acknowledge that the Space Age has not yet lived up to the heady hopes associated with its early days. As anniversaries of various landmark space firsts have rolled by, commentaries have taken on pessimistic tones, heavy with nostalgia and melancholy.[44] The space historian Walter A. McDougall observed on the fiftieth anniversary of Sputnik "a mood of disappointment, frustration, impatience."[45] A telling indicator of these dashed hopes is the shifting status of the expression "the Space Age." While no one doubts this has been the first period in human history with space activities, hardly anyone now thinks such activities are the defining feature of this era.[46] Indeed space increasingly has the aura of something retro rather than future, like the Space Age tail fins on behemoth American automobiles of the 1960s.[47] The cutting edge of technological advance has shifted from extensive to intensive expansion, from outward expansion into the cosmos and into the infinitesimally small scales of microcircuitry, genes, and nanotechnology. And in a symbolic indicator of the fact that humanity is entering the Anthropocene far more decisively than the Space Age, many major American space facilities, located on coasts and islands, will soon be under water as sea level rises due to climate change.[48]

Despite half a century of disappointingly slow progress in the trajectory of space expansion, advocate thinking about space remains very optimistic. Space advocates have continued to develop and promote their visionary schemes. The lag in the economic and technological feasibility of ambitious space ventures has not undermined optimism about the positive impacts of accomplished space activities, or the longer-term space prospect. Pessimism has been confined to the question of whether much more can be done soon, leaving untouched a more important optimism about the desirability of space expansion, both actual and prospective. For advocates, the widely held presumption has remained not *whether*, but *when*.

Despite this general space bust, space activities continue to slowly advance. Important and sometimes spectacular advances continue to be made, most notably by robotic exploration and orbiting astronomical observatories. The number of countries and corporations conducting space missions has steadily increased, and a third country, China, has developed the capabilities to place humans into space.[49] But looking across the five decades since Apollo, it is hard to avoid the conclusion that optimistic expectations about the pace of space expansion have been dashed, and the overall space enterprise, far from breaking out and accelerating, has slogged along a bumpy and very slowly rising plateau.

Given the slow pace and modest progress of space development over recent decades, why should space expansionism still be taken seriously and critically evaluated? The simple answer is that actual space activities have had profound underappreciated contemporary impacts and have persisting potential to become immensely important again—possibly very quickly. More generally, the presumption that the human future is in space perpetually hovers influentially—and possibly misleadingly—over serious consideration of planetary problems and solutions. And an assessment of the overall space enterprise and its animating visions and rationales is now particularly timely—even urgent—given several recent developments over the past few years indicating that space may be at the cusp of another major boom.

An Emerging Space Boom?

Many space advocates now widely believe and loudly proclaim that a second golden age of space has dawned and major new strides are imminent. Such claims and expectations have been voiced many times before, only to be unrealized. But this time might be different for two major reasons: renewed great power military rivalry and very deep-pocketed private-sector activity and support. A new space boom with immense potential practical consequences—but with little critical assessment or significant opposition—appears to be now beginning.

First in importance, and in ability to ignite a major burst of space deployments, is the return, after several decades of relative calm and significant cooperation, of political conflicts among the great powers: the United States, Russia, and China. The nuclear arms control regime slowly pieced together across and at the end of the Cold War is rapidly collapsing, and efforts to limit space weapons remain stymied. Military spending for nuclear and space, as well as advanced conventional weaponry, is rapidly rising. Efforts to test and deploy antisatellite and antimissile systems of many kinds are accelerating. New hyperglide long-range missiles are emerging, as are hyperaccurate ICBMs equipped with conventional explosives for prompt global strike but low collateral damage, destruction of enemy ICBMs, high-value infrastructures, and terrorists. New military space information systems are being planned and deployed. Many countries are developing rockets, and some (most notably Iran and North Korea) have nuclear ambitions. And with the internet reaching everywhere, cyber warfare has also emerged.

Dramatic changes have also recently taken place in American military and space policy, with potentially far-reaching consequences, given the enormity of US military expenditure and its historic role in leading international cooperation and regime building. US president Donald Trump has called for the establishment of a space force to be coequal with the other military services. He and military officials in his administration have also proclaimed the goal of achieving "space dominance," a major departure from previous American military policies. And space activist Scott Pace, speaking as executive secretary of the newly revived executive National Space Council, has declared that the United States no longer considers space an international "commons," sharply departing from previous US policy and challenging a central feature of the Outer Space Treaty, which the United States did much to establish in the 1960s.[50] The technologies may be new, but the rationales voiced for these initiatives are old and familiar and widely persuasive: necessitated by geopolitical realities and guided by geopolitical theory, further space weaponization will increase national security. Looking at these trends, and recalling the pivotal role played by World War II and the Cold War in stimulating major steps into space, military space expansionists have very good reasons to expect that they and their projects are entering boom times yet again.

Second, recent developments in the civil and private space sector are propelling space into rapid forward motion and public prominence. The rhetorical commitment of leading governments to ambitious space expansion, always strong across the Space Age, crossed an important threshold, from embrace of exploration to support for colonization, with President Barack Obama's declaration in his 2015 State of the Union address that humans should be going "out in the solar system, not just to visit, but to stay."[51] Both China and the United States are taking steps toward lunar landings and resource exploration, and perhaps bases, sparking what the space analyst Leonard David calls a "moon rush."[52] NASA is developing an enormous new rocket, the Space Launch System, comparable in size to the Saturn V rocket used in the Apollo program.[53] And, abandoning the Obama-era focus on Mars missions, the Trump administration has announced a major new effort, Artemis, to return humans to the moon.

A new space boom is also beginning because of the emergence of space entrepreneurs with deep pockets and ambitious visions. A handful of very rich e-capitalists who are also strong space expansionists have initiated several highly visible and ambitious space ventures.[54] Elon Musk (cofounder of PayPal) has founded Space X to build reusable rockets to launch payloads at much lower costs. Amazon founder and CEO Jeff Bezos has established his own space company, Blue Origin, which is building a fleet of successively larger rockets, to carry supplies, then tourists and ultimately settlers into space.[55] Richard Branson, the British airline magnate, has established Virgin Galactic to build space vehicles to carry passengers to the edge of outer space for a few minutes, for a ticket costing about a quarter of a million dollars.

Space advocates widely hail Musk, Bezos, and others as visionary organizational pioneers of a fundamentally novel "new space" approach to storming the heavens, embodying the fierce "Move fast and break things" ethos propelling the rapid rise of tech and internet companies. Although lavishly lauded by space enthusiasts for bringing the dynamism of the free market to replace supposedly sluggish and unimaginative government space agencies, these initiatives are being propelled more by space expansionist visionaries than profit-making opportunities. The key figures in "new space" are first and foremost space expansionists, and their business ventures and the wealth they have produced are of prime value, they say, for making large-scale space expansion possible. Bezos was an undergraduate student of the space colonization visionary Gerard O'Neill at Princeton University and president of its campus chapter of Students for the Exploration and Development of Space. He speaks of a future in which millions, then billions, and eventually trillions of people will live and work in space. For Bezos, the goal is free-floating space colonies. For Musk, near-term colonization of Mars is the paramount—and quite achievable—goal. And the rationales they offer for these ventures are straight from space expansionist thought: expanding human habitat, solving Earth problems, and avoiding extinction by getting our eggs out of one basket. In Bezos, the world's wealthiest person, with a fortune of some $150 billion, the space cause may not have found its Messiah, but it may have found its Croesus.

The celebrity prominence and booster rhetoric of these superwealthy individuals has kindled optimism among advocates that a new era of rapid space progress has arrived. Space advocates herald these initiatives as a decisive break from previous government-led space efforts and have high expectations of dramatically lower costs and large new markets.[56] As these efforts have unfolded, space advocates increasingly speak the language of American libertarianism, with its conviction that government is primarily a problem and progress is assured only when market forces are fully unleashed. But whether these ventures are a critical step to renewed expansion into space, modest rearrangements in corporate-government roles, or vanity projects of space enthusiasts with too much money remains to be seen.[57]

Beyond rising military rivalry and these "new space" private initiatives are several additional plausible scenarios for another boom in space activity.[58] Most important, if new technologies and new organizational approaches are able to produce major reductions in launch costs, a cascade of new activities is likely.

Earth problems related to energy, resources, and environment may also stimulate a turn to space solutions. As climate change grows in severity, geoengineers may find support for their schemes to deploy space-based systems to regulate the quantity of solar radiation striking the planet, as might proposals to collect and beam energy to the Earth to reduce reliance on carbon-based fuels. Such projects are being investigated by several Asian space agencies and were promoted by the former president of India.[59] Or a highly visible or destructive asteroid strike (or even a scientifically credible prediction of one) could trigger major additional space activity.[60] Unlike many other problems, asteroid strikes do not depend on terrestrial trends or developments and are a matter of when, not whether, due to the vast population of space objects that cross the Earth's orbit. Numerous studies have urged deflection efforts, and advocacy groups, such as the B612 Foundation, relentlessly seek public awareness with measures such as Asteroid Day (June 30).[61]

And a new burst of space activity may result from the energetic promotion of space expansionists. An international network of advocates continues relentlessly pushing for more space activities. Organizations such as the Planetary Society, the Mars Society, the National Space Foundation, and the British Interplanetary Society, as well as various trade and professional organizations, showcase new ideas and sustain the hopes of the faithful. Captivating films, books, articles, and websites extolling the promise of space expansion reach wide audiences. Because space advocates are well-positioned in government space agencies, research institutions, and universities, have the prestige and authority accorded scientists and engineers, and are often skilled in media arts, it is certain that space possibilities will remain in policy debates. And their plans may be pursued because of support from the large number of people who are inspired and excited, captivated and fascinated by space.

Given how important their consequences might be (if the advocates are to be believed), it is remarkable—and disturbing—how little critical scrutiny these projects and their rationales have received. Are further big steps on the ladder of space weaponization really going to improve national security and global security? Are traditional realist versions of geopolitics really a sound guide for steering statecraft with planetary and species consequences? Given the new space boom gathering momentum, the absence of significant critical scrutiny, and the very high stakes in getting space choices right, a full and even-handed evaluation of the space enterprise and its visions, past, present, and future, is both needed and increasingly urgent.

Questions, Debates, and Frameworks

Space is really easy to overhype.

—Jeff Bezos (2016)[1]

All too often, rather than rationally offering a solution to a problem—over-population, developing sustainable energy—space advocates have decided that what they really want to do is to explore space and settle space. The arguments for doing so are often something of an afterthought, prepared as a justification for the goal of getting off this planet.

—Roger D. Launius (2003)[2]

There have been almost no critical analyses of space programs or projects by social scientists. . . . [The aim] of good social science research should be to "problematize" the entire space venture.

—James A. Dator (2012)[3]

Space-Political Questions

Books and studies on space continually pour forth, for both specialists and general audiences, and so it is appropriate to clearly specify the distinctive approaches and aims of this one. Most simply, this book differs from other treatments of space because it attempts to provide a full assessment of the claims of its advocates (and their scattered critics) about the overall consequences of both accomplished and anticipated space projects. And in contrast to virtually all treatments of the subject, this book aims to show that the expansion of human activities into space has had, and promises to have, severely negative consequences and should in large measure be reversed, regulated, or relinquished.

The core questions this book attempts to answer are simple: Is space expansion, as its advocates insist, a positive development for humanity and the Earth? Is space expansion desirable because it has produced and will produce the positive consequences anticipated by visionary space advocates? Or are actual and prospective space expansion more mixed in their consequences, perhaps even largely negative? These very broad questions unfold into a cluster of interrelated, more specific questions: Have space activities altered global closure and helped reduce planetary vulnerability? Or have they intensified global closure and increased planetary vulnerability? Can the large-scale development of Earth orbital space make important, even decisive, contributions to solving Earth problems? Or are such schemes unlikely to contribute to solving these problems, while entailing substantial unanticipated risks? And is the expansion of humanity into a multiworld species likely to beneficially transform the overall human situation? Or is such an expansion more plausibly viewed as the source of great, perhaps ultimately fatal, perils for humanity? How this flock of questions about space are answered clearly has profound implications for both the space prospect and the contemporary debates about the human situation on Earth.

Unfortunately, answering these questions with any degree of certainty is very difficult in some cases, and probably impossible in others. Space is filled with a great many "known unknowns," things we know we do not know, as well as "unknown unknowns," things we do not even know we do not know anything about. Despite these many hurdles, an assessment still has great potential value, if only because space expansionists continue to provide strong answers to these questions, often with a great deal of certainty. If the topic of space is so full of unknowns, how can space expansionists be so confidently certain that space expansion is desirable? Thus even if a full assessment of the space expansionist claims faces great uncertainties, it can still be very valuable simply by showing that the strong claims offered by space expansionists rest on erroneous, contradictory, implausible, or speculative grounds.

Surprisingly, no general assessment of the overall net impact of all actual space activities exists.[4] Also surprisingly, there exists nothing approaching a full critical assessment of whether the larger space projects envisioned by advocates are really as desirable in their consequences as is widely thought. Indeed for many space ventures, past and prospective, simply asking questions about negative impacts alongside positive ones is itself a novelty. The existing literature on space, while enormous and filled with many outstanding works, is largely written by advocates and sympathizers of the overall enterprise. And while existing treatments of space are numerous, they are also very fragmented. They typically examine some space activities, while largely ignoring others. Some examine what has actually happened in space, while others focus on prospective space activities. The treatment of military space activities has tended to be isolated and fragmented. Some focus solely or primarily on military activities, while many others downplay, segregate, or even ignore the military dimensions of space, both actual and prospective. Furthermore, while it is universally acknowledged that military activities have played a very large role in actual space expansion, prospective military activities and scenarios for large-scale violence largely disappear in nearly all visionary schemes for the industrial development and colonization of space near the Earth, as well as for space expansion across the solar system. If, however, the prospect of military activities occurring in the course of ambitious prospective space activities is not assumed away, the potential consequences, and thus the desirability, of these grand schemes may look very different.

Many arguments of space expansionists are space-political arguments, about the broad political consequences of space. They employ claims related to some of the most basic and contested questions in political science, political geography, and international relations but have never been systematically assessed as propositions in these social sciences. Instead of analyzing the political impacts of space expansion, the few political scientists who examine space topics have concentrated their efforts in offering explanations of how political factors, such as interstate rivalry, helped bring about space activities. In short, existing political science analyses of space largely explore the *causes* of what has happened in space, not the *consequences*.[5]

A complete assessment requires a thorough examination of the visions of space expansionists, as well as of the first fruits of the full range of actual activities in space. For an assessment to be complete it is necessary to include all the actual impacts of space activities, however undesirable and however unexpected by space advocates. Making an assessment that is even-handed requires a serious examination of the arguments of the critics, as well as the advocates, of space expansion. An even-handed assessment of space activities and prospects also requires stepping back from the pervasive optimistic assumptions about space that have loomed so large in the thinking of so many. If we stop thinking about actual space activities as frustratingly small steps in a much larger space expansion and see them as part of human expansion into nonterrestrial parts of this planet, we begin to see lessons and implications of the space enterprise that are sharply at odds with space expansionist thinking and expectations.

A new examination of space activities and thinking is also needed because so much of the space expansionist vision was formulated before the Space Age or during its early phases. Because so little of it has happened, it is easy to overlook the fact that the main visions of space expansion largely emerged in the first years of the twentieth century, decades *before* actual space activities. While space expansionism has been elaborated and altered in secondary ways, it is largely unchanged in its basic vision and has been slow to incorporate important knowledge about the Earth and nature, and lessons gained from the events— and nonevents—of the Space Age. This means space expansionist thinking may be based on discredited assumptions and superseded knowledge. A new assessment that is full and even-handed may also provide the basis for space programs very different from those now advanced by space expansionists, ones superior in realizing some of the basic goals and aims that animate space expansionism.

Sorting Space Arguments and Debates

The first step in making a full and even-handed assessment of the arguments of space expansionists and their critics is to establish a clear, comprehensive, and less biased understanding of what space expansionists and their critics say, the projects they propose, and the arguments for and against their feasibility and desirability. In short, before evaluating the strengths and weaknesses of their proposals, it is necessary to let them speak for themselves as accurately, fully, and fairly as possible. Unfortunately, simply grasping fully and clearly what they say is a formidable task because the proposals and arguments of space expansionists and their critics are scattered across a large literature of uneven quality produced over more than a century. Further difficulty arises because their arguments are extremely diverse and sometimes directly in conflict with each other. Space advocates support very different expansions into space, and they have differing and conflicting views about the consequences and desirability of different projects. The picture is further complicated by the existence of critics of space expansionist projects, whose concerns point toward much more modest space activities.

The full presentation of their claims is the work of several chapters ahead, but an initial sorting is appropriate here. While an overall classification scheme for space projects and rationales is vital for any overall assessment, there is not now any widely employed way to talk about the different parts of space expansionism. A sound classification system helps in establishing a coherent and accurate understanding of the character, components, and relationships of space arguments. In making their powerful and sweeping claims, space advocates employ a bewildering variety of overlapping, incomplete, and sometimes misleading—even propagandistic—terms and labels that are formulated in a variety of different theoretical conceptual idioms. Many appear aimed to inspire, or even obscure and mislead, rather than accurately describe. Taking the simple, seemingly mundane step of establishing coherent and consistent nomenclatures, taxonomies, and typologies sets the stage for an assessment of claims about space that is complete and even-handed. It is also directly valuable because it reveals gaps and inconsistencies with potentially serious implications for the appeal of space activities. It is these misleading characterizations and categorizations by space advocates and others that produce the unknown knowns that mark almost all treatments of some of the most consequential space activities.

The intoxicating macro-scale vision of human expansion into the cosmos summarized earlier is embraced by almost all ardent space advocates, but it incompletely represents the full range of space thinking and activity. It neglects military space expansionism, as well as a third, more inchoate and underappreciated vision and agenda for space centered around planetary security. For purposes of clarity, I will throughout refer to these three programs or paradigms as *habitat space expansionism, military space expansionism,* and *planetary security space expansionism*[6] (see Figure 2.1). The assessment here of the consequences of space, past and future, takes the form of a comparative assessment of the claims of the advocates of these three competing space visions and agendas.

In simple terms, habitat expansionists propose orbital energy, resource, and habitat infrastructures to solve Earth habitability problems, to be followed by the colonization and development of asteroids and other planets, for the survival and enlargement of humanity and life. In contrast, military expansionists propose the development of ever more capable space weapon systems in order to achieve national security. The planetary security approach proposes an agenda of arms control, space cooperation, and science and information-centric space activities in order to meet basic human survival interests and to strengthen international institutions and common global identities.

By including this third program, this way of grouping space projects and arguments departs from most contemporary thinking. Only by seriously considering the arguments of the critics of military and habitat space expansionism, and the positive alternatives for space activities they propose, can an assessment be full and even-handed. While criticisms of military and habitat space expansionist claims are numerous, diverse, often telling, and influential, they also are scattered and rarely taken seriously by space advocates. When gathered together they comprise an alternative way of thinking about space and space activities

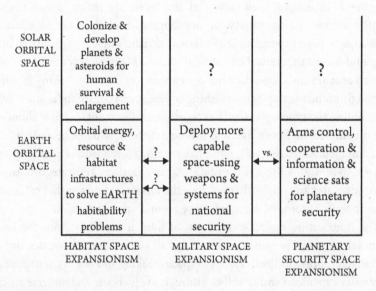

SOLAR ORBITAL SPACE	Colonize & develop planets & asteroids for human survival & enlargement		?		?
EARTH ORBITAL SPACE	Orbital energy, resource & habitat infrastructures to solve EARTH habitability problems	? ↔ ? ↔	Deploy more capable space-using weapons & systems for national security	vs. ↔	Arms control, cooperation & information & science sats for planetary security
	HABITAT SPACE EXPANSIONISM		MILITARY SPACE EXPANSIONISM		PLANETARY SECURITY SPACE EXPANSIONISM

Figure 2.1 Three Space Expansions

centered around planetary security. Such approaches are readily dismissed by advocates as against space expansion generally, when in fact they oppose some and support other space activities. No analysis leaving out arms control and environmental criticisms can possibly be even-handed or complete. Taken together more of these programs of the planetary security approach have been implemented and have been more successful in achieving their goals than is currently appreciated. Once brought fully into the assessment conversation, the possibility is open to see them as more consistent with developments and findings from the Space Age, making them—not military and habitat expansionism— the appropriate frame for space thought and activity for the foreseeable future.

Most obviously, these three programs are similar in extending into space types of activities long prevalent on Earth. And they are similar because the justifications and rationales deployed by their advocates speak to great contemporary debates about technology, humanity, and the Earth. But these three programs also differ profoundly, and each is incomplete in significant ways. Habitat expansionism has by far the largest vision spatially and temporally, stretching deep into the cosmos and across centuries and millennia. But almost none of it has been realized. In contrast, military and planetary security expansionism are focused almost exclusively on Earth orbital space, but significant parts of their agendas have been realized. And they are similar in that neither has significantly developed visions, projects, and expectations for the larger domains of solar orbital space.

Even more important than these differences are sharp disagreements. Military and planetary security expansionism are diametric opposites, and much of the jagged path of actual space development has been shaped by their competing agendas. Thus is posed the central question of what I will refer to as the *first great debate on space*: Which of their approaches is actually best suited to realize security objectives? Are the widely articulated and shared goals of realizing security from violence better served by the programs of military or planetary security space expansionism? Answering this question is the first main task of this work. After laying out the lines of difference and dispute (in chapters 5 and 7) and after laying out a geopolitical framework and a set of general geopolitical propositions (in chapter 8), I offer (in chapter 9) a comparative evaluation of these two expansionisms.

Beyond this first great debate about violence capabilities and security in near space around the Earth is what *should* be a second great debate on the desirability of the larger, almost completely unrealized habitat expansion program. With almost nothing accomplished to assess, and with the widespread and largely unchallenged belief that large-scale human expansion into the solar system is very desirable (however currently infeasible) holding sway, doubts about the actual desirability of realizing the habitat expansionist program are now almost completely nonexistent. Given this, the second task of this work is to *open* a debate about the actual desirability of large-scale habitat space expansionism, a debate I will refer to (hopefully not too prematurely) as the *second great debate on space.*

My strategy for opening this second great space debate here is to use geopolitical propositions to generate a set of anticipations about the character and consequences of large-scale human space expansion (in chapter 10). The anticipations generated in this manner are largely very negative, close to a mirror image of the optimistic scenarios of habitat expansionists. They provide strong reasons to think that large-scale space expansion across solar space will have catastrophic consequences for humanity and the Earth. While surprising, and likely to be very unwelcome to space enthusiasts, these dark scenarios are much more realistic and probable than the optimistic ones now so dominant. They are also better based, I argue, on a realistic assessment of how large-scale space expansion will likely interact with other potential catastrophic threats, both natural and technological, facing humanity. The clear implication of these findings is that humans should largely avoid pursuing the colonization and development of bodies in space. While these arguments may not turn out to be persuasive, in part or in whole, to the space faithful, and may not alter the actual trajectory of humanity into space, it is reasonable to anticipate that arguments of the dark sort advanced here, and thus the second great debate on space, will almost inevitably be increasingly salient when, or if, large-scale space expansion becomes a real possibility.

Aside from the obvious fact that space activities and visions are intimately linked to the great human fascination with the sky and the cosmos, mythic and real, evident across all human history, space expansionism is compelling to so many—and so important—because it purports to be the continuation of large-scale trajectories operating across human history and because it is so thoroughly entangled with major developments and debates about the human situation that have emerged since the middle years of the twentieth century. Only by situating space expansionist claims in the context of these larger historical patterns and very recent developments and debates does their character and importance become fully intelligible.

The first human steps into space are part of a cluster of technological and other developments that have recently explosively burst into human history. These developments are viewed by many space advocates, and many others as well, as milestone inflection points in patterns of human history that are basically driven by new scientific knowledge and technological innovations. And the visionary grand claims of space advocates about the larger import of space expansion are parts of several far-reaching debates about these recent developments and their implications for humanity and the Earth. Because space expansionists speak first and most basically to these recent developments and debates, grasping what they are claiming and the stakes in their claims requires a synoptic overview of these developments and debates, laid out in the next nine sections of this chapter.

From Global to Planetary Earth

Historical milestones and eras are defined by what one views as important, and for space expansionists and many late moderns, the most decisive novelties and defining features of human history are largely technological. Eras, from the stone ages through the agricultural and industrial revolutions, take a distinct character because of the technologies humans employed in conducting their basic activities. Major changes in technologically enabled and defined macrohistorical human trajectories also bring major changes in the spatial and geographic scope of human worlds. With major new technologies, what is possible changes, with far-reaching implications for core human activities. And with them also comes new choices and new debates about what is likely to happen and what should be done. For this way of thinking, the main pattern in the larger scale human trajectory has been rising empowerments and growing capacities to do more at a distance, and this process, occurring on a spatially finite planet, has produced successive globalizations (see Figure 2.2).

Overall accounts of this sort, while differing about many secondary and tertiary questions, register several junctures and eras. A major inflection point was in early modernity, producing what might be termed *Global Earth* radically

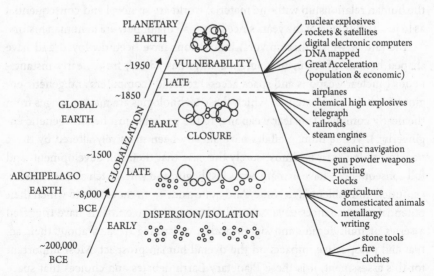

Figure 2.2 Planetary, Global, and Archipelago Earths

different in important ways from the much longer earlier period, which lacks a widely used label but which I will refer to as *Archipelago Earth*. And there is widespread agreement that Archipelago Earth can be divided into two rough periods, before and after the agricultural revolution and all that came with it. Similarly, Global Earth is also broadly recognized as having an early and late period, before and after the Industrial Revolution and its effects.

For thinking about space and the central contemporary debates that space expansionists address, it is essential to recognize an epochal juncture in technological development that occurred in the middle years of the twentieth century, marking the beginning of what can be appropriately referred to as *Planetary Earth*, or the planetary era of human Earth history. It is appropriate to think a fundamental juncture occurred during the rough decade stretching from the middle of the 1940s to the middle of the 1950s because this is when four extremely potent new technologies burst forth into the human world and when humanity's course to cross planetary sustainability boundaries was set. The first nuclear weapons (1945 and 1952), the first long-range rockets and satellites (1942 and 1957), and the first electronic digital computers (1953) all arrived during these years, as did the first mapping of the DNA molecule (1953). These years also witnessed the beginning of the "great acceleration" in human population and economic growth, which has been so consequential for the human impacts on the planet's biosphere and habitability. And it is these years which some geologists designate as the beginning of the Anthropocene as a distinct epoch in planetary geological history. Because of these developments, humanity is in a fundamentally new place and has a new future, or futures, with new possibilities just beginning to be glimpsed and understood. Taken together, these five fundamental inflections in the human relationship with the material world are so novel and consequential as to justify thinking of the years since them as a major new era in human history.

The rate at which these pivotal innovations have been deployed and have shaped human affairs in fundamental ways has varied, from nearly instantaneous (nuclear weapons and space access) to rapid (computers and genetic engineering). And the extent to which these technologies are mature ranges from the nearly complete (nuclear weapons) to the probably just begun (genetic engineering). While human affairs have already been massively altered by these new technologies, it is almost surely the case that their full development, and full consequences, have in many ways just begun and will stretch across decades, centuries, and millennia to come. And quite aside from the extent to which their potential consequences have been felt, these five developments have triggered a series of multidecade and significantly overlapping debates about their actual and prospective impacts on the overall human prospect. Most important for this assessment, it is these Planetary Earth debates and choices that space expansionists claim will be decisively shaped by large-scale space activities.

Space and the Great Debates on Planetary Earth

The massive and startling changes in the human situation on Earth produced by the globalizing spread of advanced machine civilization as it morphs into Planetary Earth have triggered a series of great debates about the human prospect and the practical implications of the new human planetary condition. These debates sprawl across the twentieth century and beyond and have grown greatly in scope, sophistication, and relevance. They address the most basic issues of humanity's future and include vying architectonic images and metaphors aspiring to simply capture the most important new realities. The core disputes in these debates are about whether the features of Planetary Earth and advanced technological modernity require fundamental changes in long-established practices and political arrangements in order to realize basic human species interests, particularly security from violence and habitat viability. For the great debates on Planetary Earth, the prospect of protecting, fixing, or leaving Earth through space activities is a potentially decisive wild card, with the potential to scramble lines of dispute, shape their conclusions, and even render their questions moot.

Claims about the Earth, past, present, and future, are also everywhere in space arguments, as noted earlier, and they play surprisingly crucial roles. And claims about space, knowledge derived from space activities, and images from space are a surprisingly extensive part of contemporary debates about the Earth and its problems. Yet the role of these Earth claims in space arguments, and of these space claims in Earth arguments, are both underappreciated and underexplored. While space expansionists make many claims about the Earth, they seldom make much effort to justify or demonstrate them or to consider alternative claims about the Earth potentially subversive of their views. While space advocates widely employ analogies from past Earths, they rarely explore whether such analogies may incompletely represent past experiences, or whether there are other analogies less favorable to their advocacy. And their frequent evocation of various contemporary Earth problems to establish the need for space solutions is rarely accompanied by serious consideration of the multiple political, economic, or social dimensions of these problems, whether the reasons for these problems might also afflict space solutions to them, whether space solutions to these problems are unique solutions to them, or whether these solutions will be plausibly available in relevant time frames. At the same time, the numerous and important claims about space that appear in arguments in contemporary debates about the Earth are rarely justified and explored.

Debates about the Earth and space are inextricably entangled. What happens—or does not happen—in space has direct and profound implications for seven great contemporary debates: about human vulnerability to catastrophic and existential threats; about the persistence or alteration of international anarchy and prospects for world government; about planetary closure, sustainability, and frontiers; about surveillance and information control; about freedom, markets and inequality; about superhumans and computers with advanced intelligence; and about the relationship between technology and politics. A brief glance at the terms and stakes of these seven great debates will provide a clearer picture of just how important space choices are to the future of humanity and the Earth.

Between Utopia and Oblivion

The first great debate, and the one with the largest scope, in which space choices and outcomes play potentially explosive roles concerns the overall prospects for human survival and flourishing. For most of human history, the prospects for major improvements—or comprehensive declines—were severely limited due to human dispersion and the incapacities of human technologies. But with the coming of potent science-based technology and globalization, the spectrum of plausible possibilities for humanity has enormously broadened (see Figure 2.3), forming what the economist and futurist Kenneth Boulding dubbed a "fan" of possibilities, spanning from some approximation of utopia to outright extinction.[7] For the first time humanity seems precariously perched, as Buckminster Fuller put it, "between utopia and oblivion."[8] Which choices humanity makes

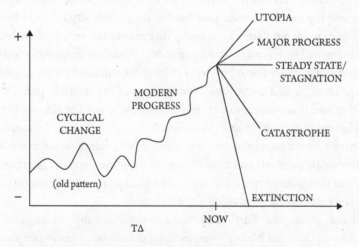

Figure 2.3 Steering between Utopia and Oblivion

about space, and which space outcomes are realizable—and realized—could decisively shape whether humanity progressively climbs or fatally stumbles.

In anticipating realizable utopian outcomes, habitat space expansionists join other Prometheans who believe that technological progress can and will fulfill the promise of Baconian modernity to realize paradise, not only on Earth but also on a cosmic scale. If the rate of technological progress over the past several centuries continues for at least several more centuries, humanity will possess powers to remake itself, the planet, and the near cosmos in ways that can now barely be imagined.[9] And if technological progress is accelerating, as Ray Kurzweil and other "singularitarians" maintain, a radical transfiguration of humanity and its worlds could come even more rapidly.[10] With visions of transhumanist reconfiguration of human bodies with genetic engineering, humanity itself can be radically improved. If these scenarios of perpetual progress on the ultimate frontier of science are realized, humanity will have advanced, in a geological instant, from precocious beast to near god. But are these scenarios achievable? Obviously one set of questions concerns technological feasibility. But perhaps more problematic for the high improvement scenarios is this question: Do the radical technological progress paths depend on improvements in humanity's capacities to steer and govern itself and its artifacts that are beyond practical reach? It is doubts about the limits of human abilities that transmute many promising technological advances into ominous perils to the species.

In the other direction, among the downward paths, questions about space loom even larger. As the five horsemen of the anthropogenic apocalypse and other perils, natural and human-made, have come into view, the expectation that space can play a uniquely and decisively positive role in either fixing Earth problems or escaping from them has become an unquestioned article of faith, endlessly repeated by space advocates as well as most analysts of catastrophic and existential threats. If "all humanity's eggs are in the one vulnerable and fraying basket" of the Earth, as widely proclaimed, then spreading human settlements into the cosmos seems a straightforward path to human survival. And if asteroids colliding with the Earth are a threat to civilization and the species, then a space program to detect and divert them becomes vitally necessary. The overwhelmingly dominant view is that space activities have an *entirely* positive role to play in addressing perils to human survival. In contrast to many technologies that promise both perils and benefits and that must, somehow, be partly restrained, the question is not whether space efforts are desirable but rather how soon they can be made feasible. Despite the breadth and sophistication of their visionary thinking, neither space expansionists nor analysts of catastrophes give much consideration to possible ways in which space activities might exacerbate or trigger existing threats or create new ones.[11] In futurist thinking about technogenic threats, large-scale space expansion enjoys a special status, a *space exceptionalism*, which in turn is supported by and supports a *space exemptionalism*, a free pass from a serious consideration of its possible downsides.

Is this strongly optimistic view of space and macrodisasters well founded? In opening this question and weighing space ventures as *sources* of such threats as well as solutions to and escapes from them, this analysis raises the possibility that many significant space activities should be restrained or relinquished on the same grounds that many now believe them to be an unalloyed good, and that human survival may actually hinge on the ability of governance to avoid rather than undertake major space expansions. It is certain that the Earth will become uninhabitable over the very long term of hundreds of millions and billions of years into the future, and that humanity can survive only by leaving the Earth and migrating elsewhere in the cosmos. But these threats are so temporally distant that they can have absolutely no relevance to current human choices and activities. Many of the threats imminent within the next centuries are significantly of human origin, and space expansionists rarely consider the possibility that the patterns of human activity producing these threats might be carried into space along with the spread of humans. Nor do they consider whether regimes to restrain threatening technologies, if established on Earth, can persist if human polities spread across the solar system.

Nowhere does how we resolve questions about space choices and outcomes more decisively shape human survival prospects than with nuclear weapons. The anthropogenic threat of nuclear war is widely rated by analysts of catastrophic and existential threats as a paramount contemporary danger, but most space expansionists view their enterprise as either unrelated to this problem or a partial solution to it. The clash between military space expansionists and advocates of the planetary security approach over nuclear weapons, arms control, and various types of space weapons speaks directly to this salient macrothreat. If we conclude, with the military space expansionists, that orbital weapon infrastructures to shoot down ballistic missiles are feasible and desirable, then the path to nuclear security is more—not less—weaponization. Or, if we conclude that the use of ballistic missiles is part of the space story and that these weapons have raised the probability of nuclear war, then we must view the overall space enterprise negatively.

The asteroid peril seems a simple and straightforward case for space activity, but it is actually quite vexed. These small celestial bodies, which swarm in vast numbers throughout the solar system and occasionally destructively collide with the Earth, can, with reasonable time and effort, very probably be detected and diverted. Because it is a matter of when, not whether a collision will occur again, asteroids are the wild card in the space futures deck. Asteroids are also central to any large-scale development of space near the Earth because they are the most readily accessible source of raw materials for building infrastructures in space. But once capabilities to move asteroids are brought into existence, how can we be confident that *intentional* bombardment, which some have proposed, will not open up an entirely new vector of catastrophic and existential threat? And what does the threat of intentional asteroidal bombardment imply about the actual consequences of extensive solar colonization, if it is accompanied by war between different settled worlds? Curiously, space advocates have almost totally ignored the proposition of the astronomers Carl Sagan and Steve Ostro that the development of capabilities to deflect asteroids will *increase* the probability of an asteroid striking the Earth due to their potential employment as intentional weapons of destruction, a line of thinking that has profound implications for the desirability of the cosmic diaspora that space expansionists, including Sagan, so ardently support.[12]

Anarchy, War, and World Government

Space choices and consequences also directly speak to the great contemporary debate about world orders and security from violence. Can time-hallowed "realist" security practices still provide security, given the violence capacities of modern technologies? And should or will international anarchy be significantly modified, with the Earth politically unified with a world government of some sort? Starkly different valuations of international anarchy and anticipations of world government play remarkably central roles in space expansionist thinking. What one thinks about space choices significantly hinges on whether one views world government as a natural and needed step to meet pressing world problems or a menace to freedom and diversity. And there are strong reasons to think what happens or does not happen in space will decisively influence whether world government arises.

All across human history, world political order has been anarchic, in the sense that an overarching government has been absent. But the prospect and appeal of exiting or significantly modifying anarchy by adopting different security practices and creating world government or strong international institutions have shifted radically across historical time, from impossible to possible to perhaps necessary and inevitable. For most of human historical experience, in Archipelago Earth, stretching from the Old Stone Age to about 1500 CE, human polities existed in significant isolation from each other, and world unification was technologically impossible. The dominant operating manual of security practices was everywhere the same: use violence to destroy, dominate, deter, or defend. Although beyond practical reach, many religious and ethical thinkers yearned for a pacific universal human community and political association. With the coming of globalization and then the Industrial Revolution, it became increasingly possible to interact at global distances, making a Global Earth, and raising the prospect that the world might be politically unified, either peacefully or violently. Since the middle years of the twentieth century, with the emergence of Planetary Earth marked by nuclear weapons, rockets, and satellites, very rapid long-range communication and transport, large-scale economic integration, and planetary-scope environmental degradation, the prospects for or at least necessity of world unification has greatly increased. These developments have stimulated efforts to abandon the security (and habitat) operating manuals from Archipelago Earth and instead govern the entire planet as an enlarged and modernized domestic realm with mutual restraints.[13]

Views of the relationship between the realities of Planetary Earth and the prospects and appeals of abandoning violence-based world orders and establishing some form of world government vary enormously. On one side, various strong globalists and world federalists, following in the steps of H. G. Wells and others, view some form of world government as vital for preventing catastrophic wars and global ecological collapse.[14] For these thinkers, the need to establish world government is the inevitable consequence of the rise of intense interaction and interdependence, particularly of violence, on a worldwide scale. All the reasons in the past why nation-states were needed now point to the need for world government.[15] Advocates also differ on whether a world government should be configured as a classic state, enlarged in size, or as a more circumscribed union or confederation. On the other side, a vastly larger group views world government as a menace to freedom and often sees even modest steps toward international cooperation and institution-building as dangerous moves onto a slippery slope toward world totalitarian government. While the need for postanarchic worldwide governance appears great and growing, the world, far from unifying, is politically fragmenting. Creating even modest international cooperative institutions has become extremely difficult, and no significant force in world politics supports creating world government.

Against this largely hostile contemporary landscape of thinking, space expansionist thought is filled with several paths, of varying plausibility, to several varieties of world government. Because orbital space completely envelops the terrestrial Earth, is adjacent to the territory of all states, and is above all states, whether and how it is governed potentially affects all states in profound ways. Do space activities make political consolidation of the planet more or less necessary and more or less likely? Numerous very different positions vie with one another. Some habitat space expansionists claim world government is here or near and inevitable and necessary given Earth's high levels of interdependence, but also is a menace to freedom. They embrace space colonization throughout the solar system as freedom insurance and a frontier where governments have limited reach. But other habitat space expansionists see world government as vital to provide the sustained effort needed to settle space and to avoid exporting conflict beyond the Earth. Alternatively some military expansionists believe the planet can be militarily dominated by a state controlling and garrisoning orbital space, an astro version of arguments pioneered by global geopolitical theorists who believed that global political consolidation, an "empire of the Earth," was feasible, given the capabilities of industrial technics and the planet's geographical contours.

In sharp contrast, planetary security space expansionists anticipate that views of the Earth from space and telecommunications systems with global reach will generate a new sense of shared planetary identity to displace national loyalties and underpin strong new international institutions. They also hold that arms control and large-scale space cooperation can moderate interstate rivalries, pushing world order toward a modified anarchy, but not a hierarchical world state. And the large-scale orbital energy, resource, and habitat infrastructures advocated by habitat expansionists are likely to have significant implications for world order in ways subversive of the persistence of anarchy. Looking even further ahead, if solar space colonization is successful, and if rivalrous relations emerge between worlds, could Island Earth in the Solar Archipelago be secured without a fairly hierarchical political consolidation? One way or another, understanding which space-political scenarios are most plausible, and the paths to their activation or avoidance, illuminates and helps resolve the great contemporary debate about anarchy, violence-based world orders, and world governments.

Sustainable Closure versus Frontier Expansion

The third great contemporary debate in which space choices and consequences could be decisive is over planetary closure, limits, and new frontiers (see Figure 2.4). As human numbers and economic activities have burgeoned, particularly since the "great acceleration" after World War II, human impacts on the planet's biospheric life support systems have also skyrocketed. As these impacts have grown, a worldwide environmental movement has arisen, and a wide-ranging reconsideration of the human-nature relationship has occurred, made even more urgent by climate change. In a variety of different formulations, the central concept is restraint and living within limits.[16] A steady state and sustainability must be reached. The "cowboy economy" must be replaced with the "spaceman economy." "Planetary boundaries" must be respected.[17]

On the other side of this debate are optimistic arguments about the ability of technological innovation to allow growth to continue without excessive environmental damage, exposed by various "cornucopians" and "ecomodernists."[18] In this vein, habitat space expansionists advance space projects

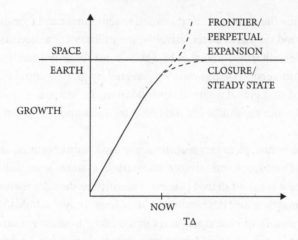

Figure 2.4 Frontier Expansion versus Sustainable Closure

as a way to transcend—permanently—terrestrial limits to growth by opening the final or ultimate frontier of outer space.[19] An entire ladder of steps is conjured to eliminate the closed Earth and make terrestrial sustainability irrelevant. Terrestrial resource and energy needs can be met from space. Artificial habitats can be created for vast populations, eventually allowing trillions of people to live in abundance beyond the Earth. The project of manipulating nature on successively larger scales to elevate the human estate has not reached its limits; it has just begun.

The clash between these competing schools of thought about earthly limits also plays out over different Earth-ship analogues and "earthcraft" visions.[20] Is the planet's character and potentials like a spaceship, a ship, a lifeboat, a raft, or a debris mat? And what arts of steerage, maintenance, and improvement are needed and obtainable?

Paradoxically, whether large-scale human expansion into space can move civilization beyond the material restraints posed by the finitude and fragility of the Earth depends on whether human abilities to manipulate and manage organisms and ecosystems can be radically improved. To make space expansion work, to establish societies capable of sustaining themselves in the harshly inhospitable and sterile wildernesses of space, it will be necessary to create and sustain completely contained ecosystems, which has thus far barely been attempted, let alone robustly demonstrated. But is it really plausible to think that humanity can ex nihilo create and sustain flourishing habitats on Mars, as it demonstrates its incapacity to cease wrecking the immensely diverse and vastly ancient ecosystems on Earth? Or does space colonization offer a chance to start again and to apply the lessons from terrestrial mistakes on a tabula rasa?

Information Explosions

New techniques and technologies of communication and information have played pivotal roles in the evolution of the human species and in the development of human societies.[21] The deployment of the electric telegraph in the middle years of the nineteenth century marked, and was widely observed as marking, an epochal shift in the human condition by making nearly instantaneous communication possible at global distances. With this technology, along with the railroad, declarations of the "abolition of distance" became widespread. As subsequent wireless telegraphy (the radio) and then television were rapidly developed and widely deployed, extensive ranges of the electromagnetic spectrum became available for human exploitation, yet another physical frontier of the planet opened by technology. As these technologies and their many important consequences emerged, futurists and global thinkers began to speak of the emergence of what Wells termed the "world brain," of the planet, what Vladimir Vernadsky and Teilhard de Chardin called a "noosphere" of consciousness, what Marshall McLuhan dubbed an "electronic global village" and what Benjamin Bratton has called a techno-geopolitical "stack."[22]

The invention of electronic digital computers in the middle years of the twentieth century, followed by rapid cascades of further innovations and deployments of computational technologies, is one of the defining features of Planetary Earth. As computers have become successively smaller and cheaper and linked together as the internet, the information environment of every human and virtually every human activity has been affected, often dramatically.[23] Space activities have been intimately interconnected with these recent revolutions in information technology, as an early stimulus to miniaturized computers, and by opening up the outer space around the Earth for the networks of communication satellites and synoptic observation platforms of many varieties and with many practical uses. It is also very plausible that progress in fabricating the underlying hardware of digital circuitry on even smaller scales may continue for some time, making for ever cheaper, more capable, and more widely dispersed information systems and a dense internet of things linking machines of all kinds together.

These extremely rapid and far-reaching developments are as conceptually bewildering as they are practically consequential. They have also triggered a debate about the oldest of political questions: Who will control and who will benefit? Beating back calls for a New International Information Order advanced by poorer countries seeking national sovereignty over information flows and content, the leading countries in the recent waves of information innovation, through a combination of intent and incapacity, have produced a largely laissez-faire information regime, which has quickly become dominated and often monopolized by a small number of private corporations, which have quickly ascended to the peaks of corporate size and value. At the same time, vast numbers of digital user communities have sprung up, creating powerful new forms of activism on behalf of a wide span of causes, from malign to beneficial. Efforts to establish various forms of consumer and citizen sovereignty over information and expanded privacy protections are also under way. All of these tendencies and struggles are sure to intensify as information systems become increasingly powerful and pervasive. Like previous struggles over territories, physical resources, and domains like the ocean and atmosphere, a worldwide struggle for control of the internet and its extensions is under way, an epic struggle which the media political theorist Ronald Deibert calls the "world brain war."[24] Because space systems, both for transmitting and for gathering information, are parts of the planet-enveloping cybernetic infrastructure, these general debates and struggles over the control of information will inevitably shape the ownership, governance, and control of space systems. And to the extent space systems become held by more actors or subject to regulations and regimes, they, in turn, will influence the outcome of the global brain war.

Freedom, Democracy, and Capitalism

The fifth great debate of Planetary Earth is about a set of perennial questions about human freedom, economic organization, and intergroup justice. Divisions on these questions extend into space thinking, and space advocates make competing claims about the relationship between their projects and these topics.

All across history, people have been quarreling, sometimes violently, about the desirability, preconditions, and prospects for political systems in which individuals and groups have a wide spectrum of freedoms and in which government is accountable to the great mass of people. The great rise in liberal democratic regimes over the past several centuries, and the extremely widespread—and perhaps deeply rooted—aspirations of people everywhere for government consistent with the realization of a full panoply of human rights has led many political thinkers to view human progress and the spread of liberal democracy as intimately connected and ultimately inevitable.

But political systems of hierarchical rule have been historically more common than republics, and in many ways free polities are difficult to establish and fragile. And with the coming of the industrial machine and then the dawn of the potent new technologies of the Planetary Earth era, the "friends of freedom" have been haunted by the prospect of modernized and ever more capacious and comprehensive hierarchical regimes. Many wonder whether steps needed to push world politics out of anarchy, to ensure biospheric sustainability, and to regulate potent new technologies are compatible with liberal democracy. As technologies become more complex and the role of expertise more vital, might technocracy, not democracy, be increasingly vital?

Because the great wars and struggles of the twentieth century that gave birth to space technology were conflicts about whether liberal democratic polities would survive, the historical relationship between space and questions of freedom has been intimate. Particularly for Cold War Americans, space ventures were touted as vital manifestations of the potency and innovativeness of the "free world." Arguments about freedom play prominent roles in space expansionist thought, particularly among American and British space advocates. On the one hand, many see freedom as in jeopardy on Earth and look to space colonies as a form of freedom insurance. Many see the space frontier as the natural incubator of many basic forms of freedom that flourished, they believe, on the terrestrial frontiers now closed due to rising interdependence and increased densities. On the other hand, advocates of collectivist and anti-individualist ideologies see the close confines of space colonies as locales for the realization of their preferred political forms. And many wonder, as we shall see at length in chapter 6, whether the ship-like governance requirements of space colonies makes liberty and political democracy dangerous and unlikely.

The heaviest atom in the modern liberal democratic molecule is private property and market capitalism. Much of the success of liberal democracy is linked to capitalism's ability to generate more military capability and more wealth, making possible widespread prosperity. But a recurrent pattern in capitalist economies is uneven distribution and socioeconomic stratification, which undermines democracy. Capitalist economic systems have never been confined to one country and have generated their own world system, which over the past five centuries has expanded to a global reach and penetrated deeply into every aspect of human life. The human metabolism with nature, of production and consumption, is largely organized along capitalist lines and profoundly shapes the prospects for environmental sustainability. While tamer versions of capitalism operate within liberal democracies, the operation of capitalist forms across societies was an integral part of the great modern European imperial and colonial expansion and its enslavements, mass murders, displacements, and thefts.

Space expansionists have widely varying postures on questions of political economy and capitalism, essentially mirroring competing terrestrial views. Most early space activities were conducted by governments. The outer space treaty regime, not even mentioning corporations, embodied the interest of what was then called the Third World in preventing the richest and most powerful from again appropriating frontier domains. Early versions of expansionist imaginaries make virtually no mention of corporations and capitalism. Early Marxist and collectivist space thinkers envisioned space colonies in which freedom from individuality could be accomplished. In contrast, many recent American space actors and advocates have enthusiastically embraced privatization. For American libertarian space advocates, space expansion offers an escape from government regulation and taxation, and unleashed capitalism offers the fastest way to make space happen in a big way. Whatever the virtues of market exchange within a well-defined system of property, capitalism – and the state-system – have been historically atrocious in making a fair "original distribution" when a *res nullius* (a thing of no one) is converted into property or sovereign territory. Will the further opening of space intensify the steep and growing stratification of wealth? Or can space regimes be built to ensure that the prospective riches from space will be distributed to benefit wide masses of humanity?

Superhumans and Silicon Successions

Of all the new technological possibilities and the debates they have spawned involving space, none are more conceptually challenging than prospects for employing genetic engineering to improve humanity, the program of transhumanism, and for the use of computer technology to create cybernetic intelligences superior to humanity. While other new technologies alter major aspects of how humans live in profound ways, genetic and cybernetic technologies promise to do something much more fundamental and intimate: to change—or supplant—the essential features of human being. In offering to alter the irreducible biological human of bodies and brains, these technologies create choices and pose questions radically more far-reaching than any ever confronting this species and for which humans are extremely ill-prepared to make and answer. Although very different in their technical character, these two technologies are similar in their complexity, potential significance, and rapid advancement, and are both based on sciences of the small. Both are also thoroughly intertwined with space expansionism. While there remain great uncertainties and controversies about their full possibilities, these technologies loom very large in contemporary anticipations of the future, in part because they have been prime topics of science fiction imaginaries for centuries.

Should humanity keep itself largely the same, incrementally augment itself, or pursue radical transfigurations to become superhumans? Should humanity view superintelligent machines as mortal perils or welcome them as the next steps, or leaps, in the evolution of life on Earth and the cosmos, as a "silicon succession"? Should humanity view such radical reconfigurations of bodies and brains as welcome, and hopefully inevitable, augmentations enabling more intelligent responses to the cascade of other daunting choices it—or someone—must properly make to avoid great perils and calamities? Further compounding the difficulty of these debates are questions about who—governments, corporations, or even individuals—should make such momentous choices and decisions. Lacking anything but the most rudimentary arrangements for world-wide decision-making, how likely is it that any species-wide decisions will actually be made in the relevant time frames? If humanity is somehow able to make these choices and decisions, who will guarantee their implementation?

The posture of many if not most space expansionists on these deeply perplexing and immensely significant questions is shockingly certain. Habitat space expansionists, as we shall see at length in chapter 6, view radical alterations in human bodies and brains and various silicon successions as integral, desirable, and eventually inevitable parts of large-scale space expansion. Whether one views this as a reason to embrace or eschew space expansion, there should be little doubt that if large-scale movement of humanity into space is possible and pursued, and if these humanity-morphing and -replacing technologies are feasible, then the debate over transhumanism and cybernetic succession will be decisively resolved for the affirmative. If, or when, the technologies enabling transhumanism, a silicon succession, and significant space expansion mature to the stage of implementation, it also seems very likely that their advocates and opponents will vie and clash in ways reminiscent of the most extreme religious and ideological conflicts across human history, making for wars not just over the Earth but over the cosmic destinies of Earth-originated life.

Technopolitical Alternatives

As technology has come to play increasingly influential roles in ever more domains of human life, questions and debates about its relationship to politics, the Earth, and humanity have become increasingly significant and contentious. Technology is the root reason why humanity faces the broadened spectrum of choices from utopia to oblivion, why the operating manual from Archipelago Earth appears so out of date, why biospheric limits are being violated, why comprehensive and repressive information regimes loom, why individual liberty and democratic government may be obsolete, and why posthumans and silicon successions might surpass current humanity. In many ways, the differences dividing space thinkers are simply extensions of broader disputes over appropriate levels of confidence in technology and its governance. Views of technology fall along a five-segment spectrum, stretching from Promethean Technophiles to Luddite Technophobes, with Techno-Optimists, Cautious Soterians, and Friends of the Earth in between (see Table 2.1). They differ in six major ways: on the overall human prospect, the role of technology, the character of humanity, relations to nature and the Earth, assumptions about society and politics, and

Table 2.1 **Technopolitical Alternatives**

	Promethean Technophiles	Techno-Optimists	Cautious Soterians	Friends of the Earth	Luddite Technophobes
Overall Prospect	Utopia, singularity, and apotheosis	Perpetual progress probable	Doomed without prudent steering	Dystopia possible; probably doomed	Dystopia likely; surely doomed
Technology	Path to unlimited progress	Decisive positive factor	Outcomes depend on foresight and steering	Generally skeptical	Source of trouble; massively repress
Humanity	Transhumanist radical change	Enhance and advance via technology	Some learning potential	Extensive restraint needed	Subsume or terminate for Earth benefit
Nature and the Earth	Completely reconfigure	Master and exploit	Use within limits	Respect and care	Worship as source of all value
Society and Politics	replace politics with technocracy	Technical fixes for social problems	Advance and change possible but difficult	Value tradition and restraints	Debased by technology imperatives
Knowledge	Complete confidence in science and engineering	High confidence in science and engineering	Information for steering possible but difficult	Nature and impacts partially opaque	Skeptical of science; confidence in intuition

assumptions about knowledge acquisition and reliability. Although labels for these different schools of thought are not fully settled, this continuum of clashing worldviews has increasingly come to supplement the older left-right political spectrum.[25] In making their claims about the feasibility and desirability of different space scenarios, different schools of space thinking rely on different views of technology. If some of these general technology positions are judged implausible or unappealing, the space scenarios they support must also be doubted.

Most bullish are the hypermoderns, the Prometheans, for whom utopia is within reach and some approximation of apotheosis is eventually likely.[26] For Prometheans, technology is white magic, leading to radical progress, and its development should be accelerated. Science is the only news, and failure of nerve is the greatest sin. Present humanity is transitional, to be succeeded by a TransHuman or SuperHuman species surpassing humanity's many limitations. Nature and the Earth are merely raw material to be completely reconfigured.[27] Society and politics are flimsy obstacles, to be flung aside and preferably replaced with a comprehensive technocratic enlightened despotism, as Bacon suggested. And they have complete confidence in the knowledge produced by science and technology.

The Techno-Optimists hold considerably more moderate versions of the same basic pro-technology worldview. They see perpetual progress as probable. They are highly optimistic that technological advances will be overwhelmingly positive and that negative effects can be readily identified and corrected, usually with more technology.[28] Environmental problems can be fixed with "ecological modernization" to produce a "good anthropocene."[29] Nature and the Earth should be mastered and exploited, and humanity should be gradually enhanced with bio- and cyber-technology. They believe most social and political problems can be solved with technical fixes and that technological misfires can be solved with different and better technologies. Many still embrace technocracy, but others, particularly American techno-optimists, embrace radical libertarian and total free market arrangements. They have high, but not total, confidence in scientific and technological knowledge.

At the other end of the spectrum are the Luddite Technophobes, for whom the overall prospect is surely doom and technology is black magic, the source of existential miseries and environmental catastrophes.[30] Luddites worship nature, whole and holy, as the source of all value. Embracing posthumanism, they want to subsume or terminate humanity to protect the Earth and its teeming nonhuman inhabitants.[31] They embrace small-scale social and political arrangements, oppose further technological development and economic growth, and see techno-administration as a source of alienation and oppression. They are deeply suspicious of science and its claims of authoritative knowledge, but completely confident in their intuitions.

The Friends of the Earth hold considerably more moderate versions of an Earth-centered worldview. They advocate "de-growth" for environmental sustainability.[32] They see only probable eventual doom for humanity and impose high burdens of proof on the introduction of any new technology in the form of stringent "precautionary principles." Nature should be treated with respect and care, and extensive restraints on humans are needed. They favor checks and balances, stakeholder vetoes, and public accountability in social and political arrangements and are conservative of traditions. Their presumptive caution is anchored in the conviction that both nature and human affairs remain significantly opaque to humans.

Sitting in the middle of the spectrum are the Cautious Soterians (named after Soteria, the Greek goddess of safety, preservation, and deliverance from harm).[33] Soterians believe humanity is probably doomed without capable steering. Whether technologies benefit or harm depends on foresight and steerage capacity. They believe that nature and the Earth should be used, but within limits. But the control of nature is difficult.[34] While acknowledging the difficult-to-change crooked timber of humanity, Soterians believe that steady, but potentially reversible, progress can be achieved with better education, knowledge, and institutions. While greatly valuing natural science, they are pragmatists, looking to practical experience as a vital source of knowledge. Like the Friends of the Earth, they favor deceleration to make better decisions. For both, the greatest sin is hubris. The vital information needed for successful steering is difficult but possible to obtain. Soterians identify various syndromes of human-technology interaction making steerage difficult, justifying regulatory restraints and even selective relinquishments. Technology, while a human product, is partly uncontrollable and opaque. While Center of the radical Enlightenment and Luddites trace back to the Romantic and counterrevolutionary Anti-Enlightenment, Soterians continue the pragmatic moderate middle Enlightenment.[35]

Using these distinctions, almost all conventionally understood space expansionism, of the habitat and military varieties, are Promethean and Techno-optimist. In contrast, the underrecognized planetary security school is largely Soterian, with some Friends of the Earth ideas. Being almost completely opposed to technological advance, Luddites are completely opposed to space technology and expansion. Thus the sides of the great debate over space alternatives are in significant measure extensions of different technopolitical worldviews. When we decide on technopolitical fundamentals, we are largely deciding on the plausibility of different space futures. To the extent assessments can be made about the plausibility and desirability of different space expansionist paths, different technopolitical worldviews are also vindicated or undermined.

A Framework for Assessment

A serious and systematic assessment of the arguments of space expansionists and their critics may be missing. And the stakes in such an assessment may be far-reaching. But is such an assessment really possible? And how should such an assessment be conducted?

Grasping the essential vision of space expansionism is fairly straightforward, but understanding all its parts and critically evaluating their claims is much more difficult. Evaluation is difficult because space expansionist writings fit within no existing discipline of knowledge, make claims relevant to all existing disciplines, and draw on virtually all existing branches of knowledge. Space expansionist claims stretch across physics, astronomy, and engineering to biology, geography, politics, and religion. These writings commonly combine an exuberant mix of genres and styles. They are part philosophical treatise, popular science, policy analysis, and manifesto. They purport to be accurate and scientifically progressive due to their reliance on scientifically acquired knowledge of nature and technological possibilities, but are about much else as well. They are stronger on bold and visionary ideas than systematic formulation, cumulative development, or critical assessment.

Despite their variety and complexity, these arguments all take a common form as practical arguments, thus providing the basis for this assessment. In saying that space expansionist arguments are *practical*, I mean that space expansionists assert that particular actors *should* do particular projects and that doing these projects will produce identifiable *consequences*. The arguments of the critics of space expansion against these projects are similarly practical in character.[36] Recognizing that the arguments of space expansionists and their critics take this practical character is the key to seeing how the varied parts in their arguments fit together (see Figure 2.5). The practical core, the main axis of arguments about space expansion is made up of a specified actor, a specified set of projects, and a set of goals or consequences that advocates believe will result from the realization of these projects. Practical space arguments thus assert that if particular actors undertake specific space programs, then important values or goals will be realized and overall world order shaped in ways that support and reflect the realization of these goals. The reasons space expansionists believe their proposed space projects will produce the consequences they anticipate rest squarely on a varied set of claims and assumptions. To get a clearer initial sense of what assessing space arguments with this practical framework entails, it is useful to

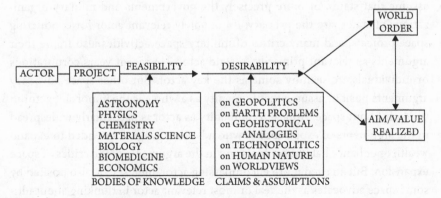

Figure 2.5 Framework for Assessing Practical Arguments

unpack its main features and note how this approach differs from other commonly used ways to think critically about space activities.

What space expansionists advocate doing in space, the actual space projects themselves, are the most straightforward part of their arguments. The typical space expansionist text devotes the lion's share of its efforts to simply describing the specifics of the projects they propose be undertaken. These project descriptions, whether of a rocket, an infrastructure in orbit, or a colony on some celestial body, are understandably so central in space expansionist treatments because what they propose is almost always unfamiliar and often initially quite fantastic. These project descriptions are commonly heavy with accounts of the space environments where the projects would be conducted and with engineering specifications for the actual technological apparatuses they propose to build and deploy. These descriptions are often accompanied with artist's conceptions that give their audience a vivid sense of what they propose to do and where they propose to do it.

These accounts seek to establish, first and foremost, the *actual* or *eventual* technological feasibility of such ventures. In making their feasibility arguments, advocates draw upon many bodies of scientific and technological knowledge, most notably astronomy, physics, chemistry, materials science, biology, biomedicine, psychology and economics. They also make many technological forecasts of what technologies are likely to emerge to make significant space expansion feasible. Whether these projects are, or will soon be, feasible, is now inherently unknowable with much certainty, but reasonable estimates and extrapolations, examined in chapter 4 at some length, are possible.

The question of *who* space expansionists envision doing their space projects also plays an important role in their arguments but one that is easy to overlook. There are some simple variations in the specified actor that have far-reaching importance for the desirability of their proposed projects. Some space expansionists, particularly those advocating military projects, posit or assume that states, or more precisely the governments and military organizations of states, are the primary, if not solely relevant actor for conducting space projects, and many critics of military space activities also frame their arguments as relevant primarily to state actors. In recent years corporations or individuals are seen by some as the key actor. But other space advocacy arguments posit or assume that humanity as a whole is the important actor in thinking about space. Appeal to humanity as actor is particularly widespread in the arguments of expansionists who advocate projects intended to expand wealth or enhance habitation goals and in the arguments of the critics of space expansion. But an even more encompassing actor, life itself, is also posited by some space advocates as the real or most relevant actor in thinking about ultimate space possibilities.

Along with the "what" and the "who," practical space arguments are distinctive in asserting a goal or aim, a result they anticipate will flow from the realization of their proposed projects. It is this assertion of ends or consequences that makes space expansionist arguments practical in character. Thus the arguments of space advocates speak extensively about the goals or aims of space activities and about the consequences that such activities will have, particularly with regard to overall political patterns. The ultimate desirability and appeal of the projects of space expansionists depends squarely on the question of whether the projects they advocate will actually realize the goals and produce the political patterns they anticipate. The range of aims and goals to which space arguments appeal is broad, but almost all fall into one of four clusters: knowledge, security from violence, wealth and habitat services, and freedom. Terms like "security" "survival," and "national security" all relate to security from violence. Space expansion is also advanced as the path to realize great advances in wealth and mundane material human well-being. And for others, the space enterprise promises to preserve or recover various forms of cultural plurality and political freedom, as well as the general vitality of human life.

In making their case that the pursuit of projects will produce the consequences they anticipate for the actors they designate, space expansionists deploy an extremely diverse set of supporting claims and assumptions. These are the most important part of space expansionist arguments because they are what connect—or fail to connect—space projects with the consequences of the projects. On their accuracy and plausibility rests the desirability of the projects that the expansionists advocate. If these supporting claims and assumptions are inaccurate, inconsistent, or implausible, the desirability of space expansion is seriously undermined. These supporting claims and assumptions are very diverse, but six are most prominent and are the focus of this assessment: (1) geopolitics, (2) Earth problems, (3) geohistorical analogies, (4) technopolitics, (5) human nature and its malleability, and (6) worldviews on science, nature, and life. These claims and assumptions are very different in character from the engineering schemes of their projects, and they are very different from each other. They draw on numerous bodies of knowledge and insight from the social and natural sciences and beyond: natural and human history, political science, political geography, economics, sociology, and anthropology, as well as philosophy and even sometimes theology. These supporting claims and assumptions are also very difficult, if not impossible, to evaluate fully with high certainty, and different standards of evidence and logic are appropriate for each type of claim or assumption. But because these supporting claims and assumptions are so central to the case for the desirability of space expansion, focusing on them is vital to achieving a full and realistic assessment. After completing an extended profile of the arguments of space expansionism and its critics, we will return to this framework (in chapter 8) and lay out specific propositions which can then be employed to test whether the claims of space expansionists are plausible.

It should be emphasized that the practical arguments made by space expansionists and their critics about the impacts or consequences of space activities are significantly different in character from the *explanatory* arguments commonly made by social scientists and many historians about the causes of the actual space activities. Practical arguments assert that specific outcomes will result from carrying out space projects, while explanatory arguments offer reasons why space activities have, or have not, taken place. Because almost all the social scientists and historians who have written about space have focused on explaining the causes of what has happened (or not happened) in space, comparatively little attention has been given to assessing the impacts and consequences of space activities or the plausibility of the impacts anticipated by space advocates.

This critical "impact assessment" approach also differs from "critical theory" efforts focused on the origins of space expansionist ideas. The founders of space expansionism were all white, all men, and all from Western imperialist countries, and many of them held views on many subjects deeply offensive to contemporary enlightened values. For some cultural critics, simply identifying these narrow origins and unsavory associations is sufficient to discredit their ideas. While sociological, gender, cultural, and psychological explanations for why these individuals thought what they thought about space activities and their consequences are interesting and insightful in many ways, they provide no insight into whether or not their expectations are accurate. Whatever their possibly problematic origins, space expansionists advance propositions about the consequences of their proposed space activities, which this inquiry aims to assess for plausibility and accuracy.

Assessments of this sort, while vital to decide whether these projects are in fact beneficial to pursue and to guide the decisions we are inevitably making (one way or another), are inherently limited in important ways. Looking at the questions in the two debates on space and in the seven great debates on Planetary Earth, at the vast number of factors in play, many ambiguous and significantly morphing, and at the inherent novelties of the features of nature revealed by science and of the technologies they make possible, the project of acquiring anything approaching adequate practical knowledge is probably inevitably doomed to remain significantly out of human reach. With so many novelties, the past and lessons drawn from it are inherently limited in their insight about what to expect. This fact should be extremely sobering for the decision-making that must inevitably take place.

Geography, Geohistory, and Geopolitics

Fully adequate answers to these questions may be nearly impossible, and gaining minimally adequate knowledge is very difficult. But among the many possible inadequate ways in which these questions might be addressed, there are some good reasons to think that a materialist-centered approach, focusing on geography interacting with technology and geopolitics, might be insightful. Materialist approaches, focusing on the actual contours of things and their interaction with human bodies, draws our attention to where the rubber meets the road, where human ideas and social arrangements encounter the realities whose features will heavily condition the success or failure of basic human practical projects of achieving security from violence and adequate habitat services. As for geography, the vision of its value laid out by Halford Mackinder, one of the founders of late modern academic geography, remains especially pertinent today: a broadly framed geography is best suited as a place for synthesizing the implications for practical choices of the torrents of new natural, technical, and social scientific knowledge.[37] An expansive and synthetic version of geopolitics is probably the best path for producing a framework and propositions melding social scientific theories of politics concerned with large-scale political structures and organized violence, with variable material contextual factors.

These approaches are also particularly suited to assessing space expansionist arguments because they rely so extensively on geographical, geohistorical, and geopolitical claims in advancing the case for their projects. Most simply, all arguments about space and space activities contain a central geographic element simply because they are about particular geographic places, such as Earth orbital space or solar space. Treatments of space topics routinely devote considerable attention to describing the character and features of the geography, or astrography, of outer space, and routinely do so not as a matter of controversy but rather as the simple presentation of facts. But space writings, particularly by advocates, contain assumptions and claims about the geography of outer space and its relation to other human places that are marked by surprisingly simple but far-reaching errors and mischaracterizations. While space scientists are continuously improving maps of space geography by acquiring better measurements and data, geographical errors of a more general type involved in classifying and placing are less routinely criticized and improved. Activities become misplaced when they are classified on the basis of function rather than location and when distance is conflated with effective distance. Such formulations assume a taken-for-granted status and lead to significant errors in thinking about the consequences of human space activities. When this happens, facts become *unknown knowns* whereby something that is known becomes effectively unknown because of misplacement or spatial misclassification. Once these unknown knowns become properly known by accurate practical geography, the entire landscape of human space activities looks radically different from the accounts of almost all space advocates and space observers, and the grounds for an accurate geopolitical assessment are established.

The use of geohistorical analogies in thinking about space is also extremely widespread and has been extensively discussed and evaluated. But these treatments, while offering many insights, stop short of a thorough examination of the central geohistorical analogies that space expansionists make about oceans, islands, and frontiers. None sets forth alternative analogies that are less flattering for the space enterprise but better in capturing the real similarities between space and historical terrestrial places and experiences.

Most important is the central place of geopolitical assessment. The term "geopolitics," like all the "big words" with long histories and wide usage, has a variety of overlapping but distinct meanings. Most commonly, geopolitics today is used in a relatively narrow sense to refer to "great power politics," a vital and even central dimension of space activities. But in a broader and older meaning, geopolitics refers to arguments about how differing material contexts composed of geographies and the technologies that interact with them shape, condition, and determine the need for and viability of different political arrangements, particularly those concerned with violence and its restraint. This broader sense of geopolitics, analyzed in chapter 8, is used to generate general propositions about the impacts of space activities, both in space near the Earth and in the larger realms beyond, thus enabling an assessment of claims of space expansionists and their critics. By thinking in a disciplined way about central geopolitical constructs such as anarchy and hierarchy, violence interaction capacities, and the distribution of power, it becomes possible to make a reasonably plausible assessment of space expansionist expectations. Because geopolitical claims are widespread in space expansionist writings, particularly by military advocates, and often play central roles in them, a geopolitical assessment is largely internal rather than externally imposed. The problem with geopolitical arguments in space expansionism is not their absence but their inconsistent, truncated, and slanted formulations.

The Argument and Its Implications

The overall conclusions that emerge from this assessment are very different in two main ways from the views of space expansionists. First, space activities have been, and promise to be, considerably less benign and more harmful than space expansionists think. The net impacts of actual space accomplishments and activities, heavily centered on military applications, as well as the prospective consequences of its longer term colonization-centered program, are not plausibly viewed as inevitably benign and beneficial to humanity and the Earth. Furthermore, not doing some things in space, and doing some things in space only in particular political arrangements, are more important than whether things are done in space. Indeed the net impact of actual space activities has only avoided being grossly negative because of the parts of the space vision *not pursued* (and even partially outlawed) despite fervent promotion by advocates of space expansion. And the ledger of actual impacts remains heavily weighted by undesirable military parts of the space expansionist vision that have been implemented but should be undone. Where space expansionists argue that space activities will decisively shape the human future, the main weight of the argument advanced here is the opposite, a brief for what might be termed 'the Terra Hypothesis': the human future for at least many centuries will be determined primarily by what humanity does – or does not do – on Earth.

Second, the view of space that emerges from this assessment is very Earth-centric. But this Earth-centric view of space is not completely antispace, antitechnology, or indifferent to the knowledge from the Space Age. Rather this Earth-centric view of space is grounded in the most important Space Age discoveries about space and about the Earth. This view of space is also marked by what space advocates derisively call "Earth chauvinism." But this Earth chauvinism is grounded in an understanding of space superior to space expansionism because it better employs new knowledge derived about both Earth and space developed during the Space Age and looks ahead with fewer illusions.

In summing up, the overall perils and promises of the human situation—and the basic arc of the argument in this book—are captured in very old stories about the Greek astronomer Thales about the prospects for people with widened celestial awareness. Thales, who lived over 2,500 years ago, is reputed to be the first scientist-philosopher of ancient Greece and the founder of scientific astronomy. It is said that Thales was so captivated with observing the skies that he lost his footing and fell into a ditch, evoking the laughter of a Thracian servant girl, the female voice of the Earth.[38] Thales is also said to have applied his new and superior knowledge of the heavens to make accurate forecasts of the rains. This enabled him to make a windfall profit after he shrewdly cornered the market for olive presses, which he anticipated would be in high demand for processing a bumper olive crop produced by atypically heavy rains.[39]

Our Space Age planetary human situation, with its problems and possibilities, is essentially Thales's situation, but with enlargements of the parts—and the stakes. Our ditches and our presses, our built infrastructures and our arrays of appliances are vastly swollen in size, number, and complexity. Their size is so enlarged as to be much of our world, making up much of the ground on which we walk. And their number and complexity are so increased that the choices we confront and (whether we know it or not) are continuously making defy enumeration. More ominously, the ditches into which we might stumble portend unexpected falls with fearsomely catastrophic dimensions. These ditches are also disturbingly numerous, not always obvious in either their location or appearance, and sometimes have slippery approaches.

Like Thales, space-gazing humanity risks disorientation and dangerous missteps. Like Thales, space-struck humans are at risk of becoming enraptured by celestial possibility and disoriented by sheer wonder at cosmic magnitude. The rapid expansion of human activities on Earth, the stupendous expansion in the size of the known cosmos, the intoxicating dreams of space expansionists, and the wondrous first steps of humans into outer space, all combine to produce the possibility of a profound and widespread practical disorientation about space and place and about where humans actually are. In forgetting where it actually stands in its Earthly home, spatially disoriented humanity risks losing its footing and could suffer a calamitously dangerous fall. But like Thales after he was reminded of where he was actually standing, walking, and living, humanity, equipped by science with a newly accurate cosmic mapping of its actual position and possibilities, could also apply its practical knowledge to the more fruitful cultivation of its earthly home.

Our Thalesian disorientation and possible loss of footing manifest in our collective misperceptions of our actual place and the real counters of our very particular place, the Earth. Overcoming Space Age disorientation and forgetting most basically requires getting our geography right. Overcoming Space Age disorientation starts with the simplest of moves: looking down at the features of where we are actually standing and walking in order to get the basic facts straight about the ground on which we stand and the path on which we walk. Getting such an improved orientation about this ground and path will also help reveal the locations and contours of the pitfalls we want to avoid stumbling into, while hopefully also pointing to possible paths for avoiding calamitous falls.

Map of the Chapters

The argument proceeds in four parts across ten chapters. Part one, "The Earth, Technology, and Space" in this and the previous chapter, surveyed the events of the Space Age and identified the scope and stakes in debates about the Earth and space. Part two, "Geographical and Technological Horizons," in two chapters, provides a background survey of geographic and technological realities relevant to space expansion. Part three, "Space Expansionism," in three chapters, provides a detailed picture of what advocates of the three programs propose and the consequences they anticipate. Part four, "Assessment," in three chapters, lays out geopolitical propositions and then applies these propositions to Earth space and solar space.

Chapter 3, "New Heavens, New Earth," overviews the main features of the realms beyond the Earth where space expansion might occur. Short surveys are provided of the ways the space environment is extremely inhospitable for humans, the features of the Earth's magnetic fields and radiation belts, the role of gravity in ordering all bodies in space, Earth orbits with especially useful traits, and the features of the Earth's moon. The scope widens to solar orbital space, particularly Mars, and then the even larger realms of the outer solar system and beyond. Particular attention is devoted to the asteroids, their features and the history and prospects of their collisions with the Earth. The chapter concludes with a brief summary of the evolution of thinking about the existence of life beyond the Earth and the revolution in thinking about the extraordinary uniqueness of the Earth that has emerged, quite unexpectedly, over the course of the Space Age.

Chapter 4, "Technological Imaginaries, Feasibilities, Syndromes, and Catastrophes," examines the intimate relationship between science fiction and space expansionism, the feasibility of the technologies necessary for large-scale space expansion, and syndromes limiting technological foresight and governance. Ten civilizational and existential threats are assessed, and the prospects for significant restraints on dangerous technologies are considered.

The three chapters of part three lay out in detail the actual proposals and claims made by space expansionists and their critics and examine their logic and consistency, thus laying the basis for their comparative assessment in the chapters of part four.

Chapter 5, "Absolute Weapons, Lightning Wars, and Ultimate Positions," provides an in-depth examination of the main projects proposed for extensive military activity in space. The full set of these projects, sequenced as a five-step ladder, starts with ballistic missiles and ends with proposals for controlling the planet by completely dominating Earth orbital space. Military space expansionists differ on whether the national security they seek is to be realized through deterrence or domination. They are thus sharply divided about whether their projects will perpetuate the anarchic state system or replace it with planetary hegemony or de facto world government.

Chapter 6, "Limitless Frontiers, Spaceship Earths, and Higher Humanities," provides an in-depth examination of the main projects that have been proposed by habitat expansionists, focusing on anticipated consequences and underlying assumptions as well as variations and inconsistencies. These programs, also a ladder of steps, start with proposals to refashion the geophysical features of the planet, fill its orbital space with infrastructures, and then colonize numerous other worlds in solar space. Also examined are the great diversity of space expansionist claims about their projects and world government and whether space colonization will bring the communist elimination of individuality or the preservation and expansion of individual freedom. Finally, the chapter establishes the shift from humanity to life as the agent in space expansionism, and the various ways in which the evolution of human life beyond the Earth is envisioned and uncritically embraced.

Chapter 7, "Superpower Restraints, Planetary Security, and Earth Identity," provides a comparable description and analysis of the scattered critics of space expansionism, mainly from arms controllers and environmentalists, and synthesizes these positions into an alternative, planetary-security view of space and the Earth. Of prime focus are the arms control criticisms of military expansion programs, the intimate connections between nuclear and space weapons, and the underrecognized space features of nuclear arms control. Dilemmas of asteroidal defection are explored. This chapter also assembles and extends scattered alternatives to conventional space expansionism centered on the extension of the outer space regime, the role of large-scale international cooperation, and expanded Earth monitoring, which together constitute an alternative, more modest and Earth-centered Whole Earth Security ladder of steps.

With the mapping of the geographical and technological horizons of space provided in part two, and with the claims of space expansionists and their critics specified in part three, the ground is laid for the full assessment of actual and prospective space impacts in part four.

Chapter 8, "Geography, Geopolitics, and Geohistory," considers the nature of the geography errors and how analogies guide and mislead. The chapter describes the nature and the strengths and weaknesses of geopolitical theory, with particular attention to the ways in which material contexts composed of geography and technology do, and do not, determine human choices. The chapter then focuses on material contexts and advances propositions connecting variations in them with different political outcomes. A brief summary of how these propositions illuminate the larger patterns of Earth historical development across three broad historical periods demonstrates the analytic leverage of geopolitical theory.

Chapter 9, "Earth Space, Planetary Geopolitics, and World Governments," applies the propositions of the geopolitical model to actual and proposed space activities in Earth orbital space. Several important geographical errors underpinning prevalent space thinking are identified and corrected, and leading geohistorical analogies are assessed and found to be significantly misleading. Accurate characterizations of Earth's space are plugged into the geopolitical model, and propositions are generated. The prospects for decreasing planetary closure and vulnerability and achieving planetary hegemony are considered, as are megastructural habitat proposals and anticipations of the emergence of planetary identity.

Moving into even more speculative terrain, chapter 10, "Solar Space, Island Earth, and the Ends of Humanity," explores the consequences of human expansion into the vastness of solar orbital space. Reasons why solar space expansion may not be feasible and may not be pursued are summarized. Then the propositions of geopolitics are employed to generate expectations about successful solar space settlement, providing multiple ways in which colonized solar space will be primed for conflict. Solar colonization as a source of multiple catastrophic and existential threats and the larger implications of this argument are explored.

Finally, a brief conclusion, "Space for Earth," summarizes the indictment against military and habitat expansionist programs and outlines an eight-part Earth-oriented space program to advance planetary security and habitability. This space program for Oasis Earth emphasizes further arms control, the avoidance of large infrastructures and colonization, cooperative asteroid deflection, a strengthened space regime, and greatly increased Earth and astronomical science.

PART TWO

GEOGRAPHIC AND TECHNOLOGICAL HORIZONS

New Heavens, New Earth

Magnificent desolation.
—First words spoken by the second man to step foot on the moon,
—Edwin "Buzz" Aldrin (1969)

The personal safety of civilized man extends outward from the police powers in his home town to a full and vigilant patrol of outer space.
—Allan O. Kelly and Frank Dachille (1953)[1]

What was significant about the lunar voyage was not that men set foot on the Moon, but that they set eye on the Earth.
—Norman Cousins (1975)[2]

Modern Astronomy and the Expansion of Space

Humans have been making maps of the heavens for as long as they have been making maps, but over the past several centuries knowledge of the realms beyond the terrestrial habitats of humanity has explosively advanced.All recent thought about human expansion into space rests upon these astronomical discoveries and are unintelligible without them. The notion that humans might travel to other worlds presupposes that astronomers have shown the existence and mapped the features of such places. While systematic astronomical investigation is among the most ancient and universal of sciences, progress in mapping the cosmos has been particularly rapid over the past several centuries, as a succession of advances in instrumentation has enabled astronomers to see vastly further into the heavens, bringing a cascade of extraordinary discoveries, far surpassing all other modern sciences in magnitude and ultimate significance.

The new cosmic map has one overwhelmingly salient feature: its staggering size.[3] Modern astronomy has discovered the astounding immensity of cosmic space, the vast number of objects in it, and the stupendous distances between them. As understanding of the enormity of the universe has grown, the Earth has been transformed from the center of the universe into an infinitesimally small speck. This great epic of scientific discovery, a crown jewel of modern technological civilization, has been exhaustively chronicled by historians, and the features of the new cosmos have been brought to large audiences by many gifted science writers and presented in many sumptuous and dazzling "atlases of the universe."[4] A brief overview here of the main features of the new cosmic map summarizes the features of the radically alien places that space advocates propose for human expansion, as well as several important Space Age discoveries about space and the Earth quite at odds with the assumptions of the founders of space expansionism.

Knowledge of the cosmos has been sought from the earliest times by astronomers in all parts of the world, but over the past several centuries, as a leading part of the globalization of modern science and technology, astronomy has become the most international of sciences, with practitioners, professional and amateur, all over the world. Where once there were distinct astronomies in different parts of the world, there is now only one astronomy with different parts. The history of astronomy can be divided, as the science historian Willy Ley suggests, into three ages, based on differences in astronomical tools.[5] The first age of astronomy pursued observations with the naked eye and was accompanied by the emergence of exact observations and the development of mathematical tools, most notably geometry and algebra. The second age employed telescopes, while the third age, only a half-century old, uses space probes and observatories. In each of these ages, exploration of the Earth and of space have been intimately linked, and the third age of astronomy is intertwined with what the historian Stephen Payne refers to as the third age of Earth exploration.[6]

The second age of astronomy emerged in one time and place—early modern Europe—and its advances are the foundation of all subsequent astronomy everywhere. Early modern European astronomers advanced their revolutionary new theories as superior alternatives to a very specific body of astronomy developed in Greek antiquity; these theories were then adopted as cosmological truth by the Roman Catholic Church, the dominant cultural institution in Latin Christendom. This mapping of the cosmos, synthesized by the Greek philosopher Aristotle and the Hellenistic Greek astronomer and geographer Ptolemy, put an unmoving Earth in the center of a quite small universe; had the sun, the moon, and the five moving stars revolving around the Earth; and understood the fixed stars to be points of light in an all-enveloping crystalline sphere of unchanging heavenly perfection.[7]

The cluster of astronomical advances known as the Copernican Revolution overthrew the Ptolemaic system by establishing that the Earth was a minor planet orbiting the sun. The Polish astronomer Nicolas Copernicus initiated the revolution with a simple version of the heliocentric model, and the German astronomer Johannes Kepler refined the model by showing that orbiting bodies moved in ellipses rather than perfect circles. The Italian astronomer Galileo Galilei made spectacular discoveries confirming this model with the first use of the telescope, and the English mathematician Isaac Newton set forth three simple "laws of motion" which explained the patterns his predecessors had identified. Newton's theory of gravity also offered a simple and compelling solution to the puzzle of why, if the Earth is moving, people did not experience it as moving and did not fly off such a moving body.[8]

This "new world system," as Galileo termed it, was understood to be vastly larger than previously thought. And the sun, although to the naked eye virtually identical in size to the moon, was found to be enormously larger and at a distance that seemed unimaginably great. This new cosmic view also held that the planets were not moving points of light but rotating orbs like the Earth, and that the seemingly innumerable fixed stars visible to humans at night were sunlike bodies at fantastically great distances. Because these distant suns might also plausibly have planets, the universe was likely to have a staggeringly large "plurality of worlds."

This early modern expansion in the size of universe has in turn been utterly dwarfed over the past century by the discovery of deep space, populated by over two *trillion* "island universes," or "galaxies," each containing several hundred billions stars.[9] Over the past several decades, astronomers have developed instruments and techniques capable of identifying planets orbiting other stars and now believe that most stars have numerous planets circling them. Thus over several centuries the size of the universe known to scientific astronomy has gone from being only small multiples of the size of the Earth to being millions of trillions of miles in extent, and the number of "other worlds" has gone from a handful to billions of trillions (see Figure 3.1). The magnitude of the cosmos

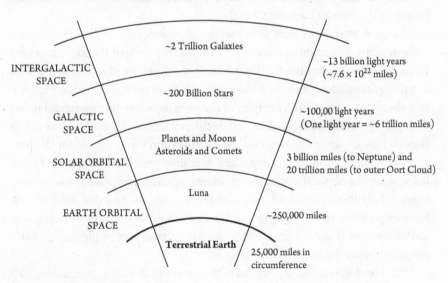

Figure 3.1 The New Cosmic Map

now mapped by astronomy can be formulated in simple numerical expressions, but is so large as to elude meaningful human comprehension. But one measure of its size is that if the entire universe were shrunk to the size of the Earth, then the Earth, proportionately shrunk, would be several orders of magnitude smaller than the size of one atom, some several trillion of which constitute the ink in the period at the end of this sentence.

Over the modern era the political context for astronomical investigations has also dramatically changed. Astronomy and cosmology were once intimately linked to politics but have become largely apolitical. When the heavens were understood to be the abodes of great powers, astronomy often received lavish support, but astronomical innovations deemed subversive were harshly suppressed. Perched atop the great pyramids in Babylonia and Mesoamerica, astronomer-priests were important cogs in the wheels of political power. In ancient Athens the natural philosopher Anaxagoras, who taught that the sun was fire and the moon a rock, was driven into exile, and the great philosopher Socrates was executed, in part for teaching similar theories. During the medieval period astronomers in the Islamic world gained extensive support because they could provide more exact orientations for those seeking to heed the prophet's call to pray in the direction of Mecca. Wide acceptance of the Copernican model was slow, despite compelling empirical evidence and elegant theoretical explanation, because established religious leaders, backed by the coercive power of states, sought to suppress what they saw as deeply subversive and threatening. Galileo's writings were banned and publicly burned, and he was forced to recant his views and then held for much of his later life under house arrest.[10] His less circumspect follower, Giordano Bruno, was tortured and burned at the stake for heresy by the Roman Catholic Church.

The new astronomy was also the paradigmatic case of the far-reaching early modern revolution in scientific method that provided the foundation for Enlightenment civilization.[11] By explaining the heavens, the new method of acquiring knowledge gained immense legitimacy and prestige. Of course science had always been significantly empirical and even occasionally experimental, but with the rigorously formulated new inductive experimental method laid out in Bacon's *New Organon* and elsewhere, the foundation was provided for the progressive accumulation of enormous and ever-growing bodies of reliable knowledge about the physical world. This modern scientific enterprise is now lavishly funded, fully institutionalized, and worldwide in scope. And this flood of new knowledge about nature has provided the basis for the cascades of technological innovation that have profoundly shaped every aspect of life and recently propelled humanity into Planetary Earth.

With Newton's mechanical model of the heavens ascendant, mechanistic naturalism was also widely assumed to be an appropriate model for understanding the human world and all aspects of nature and the Earth.[12] As mechanization took command, the new method and its view of nature also came to be applied in the establishment and expansion of the sciences of the Earth—geology, meteorology, oceanography, and ecology—which have slowly but surely generated enormous bodies of new geographic knowledge about this planet and the emergence and dynamics of its current features. This new modern worldview also meshed perfectly with the Baconian project of refashioning material reality to elevate the human estate, thus linking the immense prestige of the new cosmology with the powerful practical advances of science-based technology.[13] Nature was both potentially fully knowable by humans and reliably subject to their instrumental control and exploitation. The new cosmology, while greatly diminishing the magnitude and status of humanity, also seemed to offer a clear and practical path to vast advances in human knowledge, well-being, and power. Humanity might not amount to much cosmically, but it was now equipped to begin humanizing the Earth and inaugurating a new, human-centric age of terrestrial natural history—and perhaps much more.

Surprisingly, with the triumph of this cosmology and method for acquiring knowledge, the capacity of astronomical innovations to unsettle politics—and religion—has greatly declined. Many religions, which once seemed to have staked important parts of their doctrines to claims about the heavens, have persisted and proceeded without any discernable hindrance after the scientific demolition of these claims. And new theologies, such as deism, pantheism, and cosmism, seemingly attuned to the newly revealed cosmic realities, have failed to gain mass followings. While the terrestrial progeny of the new modern astronomy have massively altered major aspects of virtually every human activity, often with politically explosive results, new discoveries in cosmic astronomy, which continue to be rapidly made, have shown almost no ability to unsettle or influence politics, or even religion. While claims and arguments about the cultural and philosophical implications of advances in astronomy and scientific cosmology continue, cosmological astronomy is now in many ways the paradigmatic pure science, a search for knowledge largely untainted by practical applications and competing terrestrial interests and ideologies. Some, as we shall see ahead, continue to claim that new understandings of cosmological realities, and of the Earth's actual cosmic context, *should* greatly change how humans conduct their affairs, but such calls to action on the basis of heavenly realities and imperatives have generated only faint ripples of effect. Cosmological claims have evolved from being central to bodies of thought with fundamental links to how societies arrange and conduct themselves to now being close to completely detached from almost all the practical concerns of humans and their polities.

There is now one global community of astronomers, operating with common standards of acquiring, interpreting, and publishing evidence. International cooperation is extensive. Even acute ideological cleavages, such as the Cold War East-West divide, had no discernable distorting impact on astronomical inquiry and knowledge. While astronomy depends on society for resources, and rivalry among astronomers is often intense, the discrepancy between the magnitude and ultimate significance of what astronomers discover and the insignificance of their current impact on practical politics has become gaping. This ironic and often overlooked Space Age development is yet another surprise of the era, an outcome quite unexpected given the intimate linkages and great influences of thoughts and perceptions about the heavens prevalent across almost all of human history.

Geographic mappings of humanity's terrestrial habitats have always been inti-mately associated with astronomical knowledge and investigations, and the great early modern scientific revolutions were as much geographical as astronomical. The most important feature of the new geography of the Earth was the discovery that humans inhabit a sphere-shaped global body, an insight with immense prac-tical as well as astronomical implications. This primary insight was hypothesized and then empirically vindicated by the first circumnavigations of the Earth by European mariners before the Copernican Revolution had been launched. The discovery that the Earth was global in shape greatly enhanced the credibility of the new astronomy's characterization of the heavens as populated by spinning orbs rather than by points of light or disks.

With central features of the heavens and Earth now seamlessly integrated into one mechanistic model, geographers represented the Earth as a globe girded by a precise geometric grid of longitude and latitude, a spatial framework within which all distinct and particular places might be situated, subject to detailed mapping and examination by science, and eventually brought into conformity and exploited. The new geography had major implications for the conduct of military and economic activities, helping to empower European imperial and colonial projects with global reach. Better knowledge of position was a potent asset and enabled and augmented the power of other assets. The new Earth ge-ography also meshed well with Baconian aspirations to reconfigure the physical worlds of Earth to serve human projects of power and prosperity, an enterprise aggressively spearheaded by the modern states and capitalist market actors of Europe and its offshoots, much to the general misery of most of humanity.

The New Map of Space and Earth

As scientific astronomy has surveyed the awesome magnitude of cosmic deep space, it has also produced a much more detailed understanding of the realms of outer space nearest to Earth and discovered many fundamental ways in which cosmic events, past and future, shape the Earth and its habitability for humans. As these new mappings have been made, revolutionary advances and major reconceptualizations have also occurred in the Earth sciences, overthrowing major aspects of the terrestrial geography and related bodies of Earth knowledge dominant across the modern era. Some of these discoveries, made across the Space Age and partially made possible by space activities, are very different from geographic understandings informing the foundational formulations of space expansionism.

In assessing the arguments of space expansionists, competing geographies and geography errors for both Earth and space play central roles, making it vital to get the geography right. Doing this is both easy and difficult. On the one hand, there are very large areas of consensus among astronomical and Earth scientists about a large number of topics, derived from vast empirical databases generated by numerous new instruments of observation and information processing. Compared to what even the most informed humans knew about the planet and its place in the cosmos a mere century ago, contemporary science has produced cascades of major discoveries, providing a radically different understanding of planetary Earth and cosmic geography. On the other hand, many debates and uncertainties persist. There are many known unknowns and sure to be many unknown unknowns, and astounding, often quite unexpected, discoveries continue to occur. The inescapable reality is that whether significant space expansion is feasible—and desirable—partly hinges on discoveries not yet made. Of particular importance here are relatively subtle but hugely consequential geography errors, understood as mistakes in how phenomena and activities are geographically placed and categorized, and flawed assessments of the direct implications of geophysical realities for practical activities.

In this chapter's survey of the new mappings of space and Earth generated by recent scientific investigations and discoveries, there are four main, essentially uncontested realities with immense implications for humanity, Earth, and the space enterprise. Some of these realities are integral to space expansionist thinking; the implications of others are disputed; and some have yet to be acknowledged and engaged.

First, the spaces and places beyond the Earth are unimaginably vast and radically different from terrestrial realms. This basic fact sits at the center of late modern understandings of cosmic nature, undisputed and widely grasped. Second, features of the Earth, its continued habitability, and the possibility and fate of humans on Earth have been, and will inevitably continue to be, fundamentally shaped by myriad cosmic influences, some operating across vast time scales, but others occurring in an instant. Inherent in these realities is the possibility of *cosmocide*, the extinction of humanity by the operation of cosmic forces. This bleak reality is widely grasped, and compelling representations of scenarios of cosmocide (with varying degrees of more specific accuracy) permeate contemporary consciousness worldwide.

Third is the reality of what can be most simply referred to as *Oasis Earth*. Expanding for at least many trillions of miles in all directions from Earth is a completely desolate and harshly inhospitable wilderness, within which the Earth is a tiny oasis fabulously teeming with life. The heavens, modern astronomy has discovered, are a staggeringly vast array of hells. And the Earth, in comparative terms, turns out to be a splendid Garden of Eden. Often overshadowed by speculations and searches for pockets of microbes in a few cosmically near places, and for intelligent life at even greater distances, as well as by imaginaries of the expansion of Earth life into space, the discovery of the reality of Oasis Earth is occasionally discussed by environmental thinkers but rarely emphasized by astronomers and space advocates.[14] It is often overlooked that this discovery of the sterility of Earth's cosmic neighborhood was quite unexpected and sharply contrary to the widely held assumptions of astronomers and many others across the modern era. The realities of cosmocide and Oasis Earth have profound implications for the space expansionist enterprise which have yet to be registered adequately in the debates among the branches of space expansionism.

The fourth fundamental reality mapped by science is a revolutionary new view of the character of the Earth and the role of life in fundamentally shaping it. The newly apprehended reality is that the geophysical features of the Earth have been profoundly shaped by the presence and evolution of life, and that all major features of the planet interact and coevolve in complex, chaotic, and emergent patterns that defy human ability to predict and control. This newly understood Earth, emerging during the Space Age, has not been significantly registered in space expansionist thinking but has major implications for both the feasibility and the desirability of large-scale space expansion in important ways.

Beyond exploring the implications of these four important established geographic realities, this analysis focuses on a set of geography errors permeating contemporary space thinking, particularly among advocates, with major implications for the Earth and the space enterprise. Two of these geography errors, about the spatial contours of the planet Earth and the differences between Earth space and solar space, are discussed in this chapter. Three others, about the definition of "space weapons," about the practical size of Earth space, and about whether space is now a frontier, are explored in subsequent chapters, as is a general consideration of the types and origins of geography errors.

This survey of the new mappings of space and Earth examines the space environment, the geophysical features of the space near Earth, the inner planets, particularly Mars, and, at some length, the asteroids and their interactions with the Earth. It then proceeds quickly through the outer solar system, before looping back to view trends in thinking about life beyond the Earth, and then the features of the recently rediscovered Earth.

The Space Environment

Space contains innumerable bodies, each of which has a distinct geography. But these diverse worlds move through a vast void, which has a distinct physical geography radically unlike the various bodies populating it. The voids of outer space also radically differ from the familiar environments of the terrestrial Earth and are harshly inhospitable to human and other life forms. The environment of space has four main features, each of which can be best grasped by comparison with aspects of the terrestrial environment that all humans continuously experience but usually take for granted.[15]

First, outer space is marked by extremes of temperature, ranging from deep freezing in the shade to broiling in sunlight. Temperature variations are much more extreme in space than on Earth. The coldest known atmospheric temperature on Earth, about 90 degrees below zero Celsius, was recorded atop the miles-thick ice sheet in central Antarctica during winter's total darkness. The temperature of objects in deep space that are not exposed to much starlight hover around 250 degrees below zero Celsius, not far above "absolute zero," the coldest temperature that is physically possible. Exposed to extreme low temperatures, any object containing water—including all life forms—freezes instantly. The highest atmospheric temperature ever recorded on Earth is 56 degrees Celsius, in the summer in the desert of Death Valley in California. Temperatures of objects in space rise with proximity to the sun. Objects in space in the vicinity of Earth exposed to sunlight have temperatures of approximately 300 degrees Celsius, some three times the boiling temperature of water.

Second, outer space is washed by intense fluxes of radiation and rapidly moving particles that are harmful to life. Those from the sun are known as "solar winds." Fluctuating solar emissions produce "solar weather." Other radiations, known as "cosmic rays," come from all directions from deep space and are believed to be iron and nickel nuclei moving at extreme speeds from ancient cataclysmic explosions of giant stars at vast distances in interstellar and intergalactic space. Fortunately for the living organisms on this planet, these radiations are mostly deflected by the Earth's magnetic field and mostly blocked by its atmosphere. These radiations and particles harm living organisms by breaking the chemical bonds of the complex molecules composing life, wrecking the functioning of cells and causing genetic damage leading to cancers and birth defects. To colonize space heavy shielding against radiation will be necessary.

Third, the vast realms of outer space are close to being a perfect vacuum. In contrast to this cosmic emptiness, the Earth's atmosphere, the film of air around the planet that can seem so insubstantial, is vastly more dense with gaseous matter. The Earth's atmosphere at sea level contains several billion times more matter than is found in the vacuum of space. And the atmospheres of several planets, most notably Venus and the gas-shrouded giants of the outer solar system, have densities many times that of the Earth's atmosphere. This basic dif- ference between outer space and the Earth's atmosphere profoundly shapes the kinds of activities that can be conducted in both places. Most obviously, space lacks breathable air, the mixture of gases, mainly nitrogen and oxygen, that living organisms require, and a human exposed to the void of space would quickly suf- focate. Furthermore there is no atmospheric pressure in space, while the Earth's atmosphere exerts about 14 pounds of pressure per square inch. Terrestrial organisms are configured to operate with such pressures, and a human body exposed to the vacuum of space would rapidly balloon and then rupture.

Fourth is weightlessness. All bodies in space, while they inherently have mass, are weightless. Some people view short periods of weightlessness as an exciting experience, but longer durations are another matter. Humans exposed to pro- longed weightlessness suffer a variety of debilitating health effects, which are still poorly understood. When weightless muscles lose mass, bones lose calcium and become brittle, red blood cell levels decline, and eyes become deformed. These effects can be partly averted by massive amounts of strenuous exercise, and astronauts on long duration missions spend much of their time exercising. It is also possible to create artificial gravity by spinning a space vehicle, producing a centrifugal effect, in which case the interiors of a vehicle's outer walls become its floors.

Overall, space is a severely hostile environment for Earth life and poses im- mense constraints on all space activities involving humans. It is also notable— but rarely noted—that the extreme inhospitality of space to humans and other Terran life forms was largely unanticipated by the founding visionaries of space expansionism. The great advances in understanding the biomedical dimensions of extraterrestrial human life achieved across the Space Age are but one of sev- eral important areas of scientific advance undercutting the feasibility of ambi- tious space expansionism.

Orbits, Velocity, and Gravity Wells

Viewed in cosmic perspective, the Earth is quite a modest place in many ways. The terrestrial parts of this planet, composed of its metallic and rocky litho- sphere, its oceans, or hydrosphere, and the thin film of gasses of its atmosphere, is about eight thousand miles in diameter, with a circumference of about twenty-five thousand miles. Its oceans cover about three-quarters of its surface, with an average depth of about three miles, and its atmosphere is about a hundred miles deep, as thick on the planet as the fuzz on a peach. The atmosphere does not abruptly end, but instead gets successively thinner with altitude, and some 95 percent of its mass is in its lowest five miles. Above sixty-two miles (one hundred kilometers), the Kármán line, there is not enough atmosphere to support winged flight, but only above one hundred miles is the atmosphere thin enough to permit the velocities that objects must maintain to prevent falling back to the Earth.

While the vast and harsh realm beyond the Earth's atmosphere is largely empty, it is not featureless. Space is gravity's kingdom, and the spatial contours of gravitational attraction decisively shape celestial patterns. The possibilities for human space activities in the areas immediately beyond the Earth's atmosphere are largely dictated by the gravitational attraction of the Earth. The laws of gravity also govern the patterned movements of the innumerable other celestial bodies of widely varying size and character that populate cosmic outer space. These laws of gravity, which Newton formulated in a set of simple equations, provide the scientific foundation upon which rest all technologies of space travel. All objects in the universe gravitationally attract one another, and the larger the mass of a body, the greater its gravitational pull. But the force of this attraction falls off rapidly with distance, in a nonlinear pattern, with the strongest gravitational attraction in close proximity to bodies.

Objects within the grip of a planet's gravitational attraction can stay in its proximity without being drawn into a collision with it only if they are traveling at a velocity sufficient to counteract the planet's attractive force.[16] This orbital velocity varies according to the mass of the planet. For the Earth, orbital velocity is about 17,000 miles an hour, or about five miles a second. Any object within the close grip of the planet's gravitational pull not going at least this speed will quickly fall back into the atmosphere and then either burn up or collide with the ground at high speed. To leave the Earth's gravitational grip, an even higher speed, an escape velocity of 25,000 miles an hour, is necessary. To put these numbers in perspective, a commercial jet airliner at cruising altitude has a velocity of about 500 miles an hour, making the Earth's orbital velocity thirty-four times as fast. To accelerate an object to this velocity requires enormous quantities of energy, which explains why the vast majority of the mass of a typical rocket at its launch is fuel, leaving only a small share for its payload which reaches orbit.

Because gravitational attraction falls off rapidly with distance, most of the energy required to leave a body must be expended nearby. Space scientists visualize this as a *gravity well* (see Figure 3.2). This analogy conveys the important fact that one must climb out of a deep hole to leave a planetary body, and that

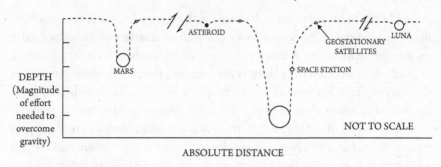

Figure 3.2 Gravity Wells

the depth of this well is much greater for larger bodies than smaller ones. For the Earth, the lip or rim of the gravity well is about thirty thousand miles up, a distance somewhat larger than the circumference of the planet. Once this altitude has been reached, an object has traveled about a tenth of the distance to the moon but has done about nine tenths of the work pushing against gravity necessary to get there. Thus the Earth System, composed of the Earth and its moon, has two gravity wells of very different depths, with a large, slightly sloped plain filling most of its expanse. This pattern is reproduced throughout the solar system and the universe, at larger scales. A practical upshot of this space geography is that it takes vastly more effort to go to the moon from the Earth than Luna the other way around.

The presence or absence of an atmosphere has profound implications for the speed with which objects can travel. The vacuum of space permits the liberation of speed, allowing velocities that are impossible to reach or sustain in the Earth's atmosphere. Conversely, an atmosphere imposes severe limits on the velocities at which objects pass through it, and the denser the atmosphere the more severe the limitation. Objects traveling through atmospheres are subject to air resistance and friction, slowing and heating them. As objects push their way through atmospheric gases, they lose velocity, and sustaining their velocity requires additional propulsive energy, whether from a propeller, jet engine, or rocket engine, setting limits on how long velocities can be maintained. Furthermore the kinetic energy lost as their velocity is reduced from friction takes the form of heat energy, which for objects traveling very fast can become extreme. But the absence of atmospheric gases in outer space means there is no air resistance and no air friction, allowing objects to travel at vastly greater speeds without heating up and slowing down. And without atmospheric friction to slow them, objects in space retain their velocities indefinitely, until they either collide with something or are subject to some other force. These facts explain not just why it is possible to achieve extreme velocities in space and not in the atmosphere but also why it is so arduous to return from space and land on the surface of the planet. An object leaving orbit and reentering the atmosphere has a great deal of kinetic energy it must shed, which friction with the atmosphere accomplishes. Atmospheric reentry produces very high temperatures, typically over a thousand degrees Celsius, more than enough to melt many metals.

In sum, the gravitational attraction of the Earth makes high velocities *necessary*, while the vacuum of space makes them *possible*. On Earth, all objects are stationary unless force is applied. But in space all objects are, and remain, in very rapid motion unless force is applied. Taken together, these distinctive features of the space environment—lethal radiation, hard vacuum, weightlessness, and fantastic speeds—are radically unlike the familiar terrestrial Earth, making analogies between these two realms fundamentally misleading.

The great speed that objects in space routinely travel also means that when they collide with another object they do so with frighteningly high levels of destructive force. Speed kills, and extreme speed kills extremely. On Earth, "Move fast and break things" may be a motto of brash techno-entrepreneurs, but in space it is a geographic description. Objects colliding at orbital velocities suddenly release as heat all the kinetic energy contained in their velocity. Because energy released is equal to mass times the *square* of velocity, very small objects traveling at enormous speeds can release devastating quantities of energy when they collide with something. With all this heat concentrated in such a small place, metals are quickly vaporized, the vapor expanding outward with explosive force. This means that any collision can be catastrophically damaging. Tremendously large destructive potentials are latent in all space objects simply because of their very high velocities. Thus destroying something in space does not require explosives but simple collisions.

Once an object has obtained the necessary speed to achieve orbital velocity, the geometry of orbits can take extraordinarily many shapes. Which orbital path an object will take is a function of the angle at which its acceleration is directed. Some orbits hug the top of the atmosphere, while others can be at very high altitudes, out to and beyond the moon. Very low orbits are ideal for closely viewing the Earth, while higher ones permit more synoptic vantage points. Orbits can also be polar in their configuration, meaning that they cross over the north and south poles, in which case the planet essentially rotates beneath them, allowing them to pass over its entirety every day. Another orbit, known as geosynchronous or geostationary Earth orbit (shortened to "GEO"), has unique and useful features. When an object is placed in orbit at an altitude of about 22,000 miles and angled so it is above the Earth's equator, its speed and the speed of the Earth's rotation on its axis are synchronized, and it thus remains stationary relative to all points on Earth. Satellites placed in this orbital band can readily serve as radio signal relay stations because dispersed receiving antennas can remain fixed in their positions.

Another notable geographic feature of Earth space is its zones of radiation, the Van Allan radiation belts, named for the American geophysicist who discovered them in 1958. For a planet its size, the Earth has an exceptionally large metal core and magnetic field, which deflects most of the charged particles flowing from the sun, thus protecting the gases in the upper layers of the atmosphere from being slowly stripped away. Without this protective shield, the atmosphere would be much thinner and radically different in composition. This strong magnetic field also traps large quantities of solar particles in the distinctively configured belts identified by Van Allan and concentrates them to levels inimical to human health, thus setting important limits to human activities in large areas of Earth orbital space.

Outer Earth Space, Luna, and the Lagrange Points

In an orbit about a quarter of a million miles above the surface of the Earth is the planet's sole natural moon, widely referred to as Luna.[17] This body has a surface area roughly the size of North America and has virtually no atmosphere or magnetic field. As a result, its surface is bombarded with the full force of the radiations and particles flowing through space. Luna has a mass eighty times less than the Earth, so a human on the moon weighs about a fifth of her weight on the surface of Terra. This low gravity makes it possible to throw objects at much greater distances than on Earth, as was demonstrated when the Apollo 14 astronaut Alan Shepard hit a golf ball that traveled "miles and miles," establishing a world record, of some sort. Escape velocity from the moon is less than a quarter of the Earth's, and without an impeding atmosphere, it is possible to accelerate objects to great speeds directly from the surface. This means that coming and going on Luna is substantially easier than on Earth. Its days and nights, alternating baking heat with deep cold, are fourteen Earth-days long. Luna is also completely devoid of life, and its surface is covered with innumerable craters produced by collisions of objects from space across the billions of years since its formation. The pocked face of the moon thus provides a good register of the bombardment the Earth has also endured, the signs of which have almost completely been wiped away by atmospheric weathering and plate tectonics, processes completely absent on Luna. Luna also has special places, most notably its two poles, where sunlight, blocked by surrounding mountains, has not shone for billions of years, allowing the persistence of water crystals, which might be harvested for habitats and rocket fuel.

Another notable feature of Luna is that it is in orbital lock, meaning that the periods of its rotation on its axis and its rotation around the Earth are synchronized. Orbital lock is common for smaller bodies in orbits around much larger ones and explains why Luna always presents only one side to the Earth. Luna thus appears to observers on the Earth not as the rotating sphere that it is but rather as a disc, unchanging except for the waxing and waning of sunlight and darkness on its surface. The hidden hemisphere of Luna, long known (misleadingly) as "the dark side of the moon," was first glimpsed by humans in 1959 when the Soviet Union sent a probe into lunar orbit and photographed this previously unseen realm. Luna also affects the Earth, most notably in producing the tidal movement of the Earth's oceans. Despite its inhospitable conditions, Luna will inevitably play a central role in any large-scale human movement into space simply due to its proximity.

Outer Earth orbital space (EOS) has one further geographic feature of note, the Lagrange points, named after the eighteenth-century mathematician who hypothesized their existence. Two of them, designated L4 and L5, and sometimes referred to as Trojan points, have unique features that make them particularly valuable (see Figure 3.3). Satellites in any orbit are subject to a variety of

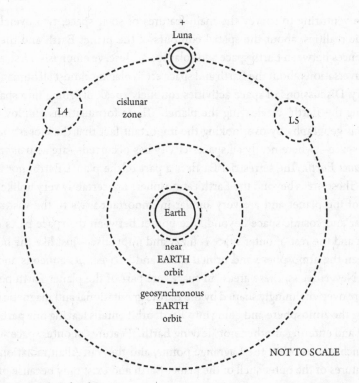

Figure 3.3 Earth Orbital Space

weak forces that cause them to gradually change paths over time. Objects closer to the terrestrial Earth are gradually slowed by friction with the extremely attenuated gases that trail off from the atmosphere, and their orbital lifetimes are measured in years. Objects further out have lifetimes measured in centuries and millennia, but their orbits are also gradually altered by weak gravitational forces from distant bodies, particularly the moon. In order to stay in their preferred orbital paths, additional energy can be expended for "station keeping," but doing this for large bodies or over long time periods is difficult. But at L4 and L5, located on the same orbital path as the moon, the gravitational pulls of the Earth and the moon combine to create effectively permanent orbits. As such, these two Lagrange points, also known as libration points, are the preferred locations for constructing massive orbital infrastructures proposed by space expansionists. Another such point of stable gravitational equilibrium, L1, sits nearly a million miles from the Earth and is always situated between the Earth and the sun, making it the preferred location for hypothetical infrastructures to regulate the amount of solar radiation falling on the Earth.

From the Earth's Astrosphere to the Solar System

Before venturing to survey the main features of solar space, two overall geographic realities, about the spatial contours of the planet Earth and the great differences between Earth space and solar space, deserve emphasis. First, almost all conversations about the Earth and space err in placing almost all human space activity. Discussions of space activities routinely speak of "going into space" as "leaving the Earth" or "leaving the planet." These formulations employ an erroneous geography by overlooking the important fact that the closest parts of outer space—where nearly all space activity has occurred—are actually *part of the planet Earth*. The terrestrial Earth is a part of the planet Earth, not its entirety. These areas beyond the Earth's atmosphere are certainly very unlike other parts of the planet and are very similar in important ways to the vast realms of solar and cosmic space beyond. The border between the space parts of the planet and the rest of outer space is fuzzy and imprecise—just like the borders between the atmosphere and orbital space and between its aqueous and land parts. Nevertheless, these areas "in space" are part of the planet Earth because they are overwhelmingly shaped by the Earth's gravitational and magnetic fields. Exiting the atmosphere and going into Earth orbit entails leaving one part of the planet and entering another, not "leaving Earth." Features of outer space such as geosynchronous orbit, the Lagrange points, and the Van Allan radiation belts are features of the outer shell of the planet Earth and exist only because of their relationship with other parts of the planet.

This space part of the planet, Earth orbital space (EOS), is appropriately referred to as the planet's *astrosphere,* its outer shell, sitting atop its atmosphere, hydrosphere, and lithosphere. The astrosphere of the Earth is this planet's "outer space." The astrosphere is the nearly empty attic of the planet rather than a place outside or beyond the Earth. With their eyes focused on how different the planet's astrosphere is from terrestrial Earth, space commentators commonly overlook the basic ways in which Earth's space is an integral feature of the planet. And with their imagination fixed on the vastness of the cosmos, and eager to leave home, space expansionists overlook the fact that very few human space activities have actually left the planet Earth. One complication with this corrected planetary geography concerns the moon. Luna, while bound in orbit by the gravity from the mass of the Earth's terrestrial body, is also a substantial body with distinct features and is best thought of as being part of the "Earth system," a formulation already in use by some geographers and astronomers.

Second, the planet Earth, even with its outer space, is vastly dwarfed by the size of solar space, the cosmic domain in which the sun's gravity holds sway. This fact has been definitely established and no one disputes it, but its profound implications for thinking geopolitically about human activities in these two realms is not always clearly registered. With comets included, the retinue of objects in the sun's gravitational sway stretches many trillions of miles into space, many tens of thousands of times further than the Earth's distance from the sun. And the volume of solar space is hundreds of millions of times greater than the volume of the Earth's astrosphere. If the sun were a beach ball, the Earth, proportionally sized, would be a pea, some fifty feet away. And comets, at most dust motes proportionally, would be hundreds of miles away. While the Earth's astrosphere and the vast reaches of solar orbital space have important similarities, particularly in contrast to the terrestrial Earth, their stupendous difference in size clearly justifies delineating them as two very distinct places. These realities mean that speaking of outer space as a domain that starts at the upper edge of the Earth's atmosphere and stretches across the solar system and the galaxy to the unimaginably distant edges of the cosmos is fundamentally misleading in conflating radically different spaces and places.

The staggering magnitude of the size difference between the full planet Earth and solar space means that the geopolitics of distance, interaction, and interdependence for these two places is guaranteed to be significantly different. What may be compelling restraints and opportunities for political practices and arrangements in Earth space are likely to be radically different, even opposite, in solar space. One geopolitical model applied to these two vastly different spaces can be expected to produce a set of planetary geopolitical propositions about tendencies and viabilities that are radically different from its propositions about solar space. Therefore, any thinking about space possibilities and outcomes that does not begin with this fundamental geographic difference is likely to severely mislead by reading the features of the larger realm into those of the smaller. Thus a geopolitics of outer space promises to significantly confuse, in sharp contrast to the insights provided by a dual geopolitics of Earth space and solar space.

The Empire of the Sun

The solar system is so large and diverse that mappings of solar space developed by astronomers commonly distinguish three relatively distinct zones, each successively much larger in size. The inner and outer parts of EOS are but a tiny part of the inner solar system space, or inner solar orbital space (SOS). The inner solar system (with distances of hundreds of millions of miles) encompasses four rocky planets (Mercury, Venus, Earth, and Mars) as well as smaller asteroidal bodies, many hundreds of thousands of which have been detected (see Figure 3.4). Most asteroids, and the largest ones, are in a belt beyond Mars, but some have orbital paths that cross the paths of the inner planets. Outer SOS, with distances of billions of miles, encompasses four giant planets (Jupiter, Saturn, Uranus, and Neptune) and their numerous moons. Jupiter, the first (and largest) of the outer planets, is nearly 500 million miles from the sun, five times the distance of the Earth, but Neptune, the furthest of the outer planets, is almost three billion miles from the sun. Beyond this vast realm are the even larger reaches of what astronomers refer to as the third zone, with distances of trillions of miles and containing enormous numbers of icy dwarf planets and the even more distant cloud of comets, which may number in the trillions.

This entire sprawling collection of bodies in motion is a system with an overall order produced by the gravitational influence of its largest central body, the sun, which contains more than 99 percent of the mass of the entire system. The sun

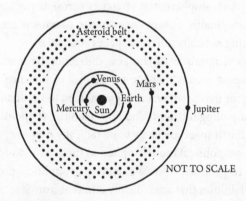

Figure 3.4 Inner Solar Orbital Space

is vastly larger in size than any other body in the solar system, with a diameter about 110 times that of the Earth. The sun is also radically different in character and composition, being vastly hot and emitting prodigious quantities of energy, without which all the other bodies in the system would be very cold.

Until the middle years of the twentieth century, one of the greatest mysteries of science was how it was possible for the sun to produce so much energy for so long. Because no substance on Earth known to science could produce such energies for very long, it was puzzling how the Earth could be as old as the geological record indicated. In one of the great breakthroughs of modern science, this puzzle was solved by advances in nuclear physics and astrophysics, and by the 1950s a remarkably full picture of the basic processes operating in the sun and other stars, and their life cycles, was in hand. These discoveries also had an immensely important practical application, because they provided the scientific foundations for the development of the most potent of nuclear weapons, the hydrogen bomb, which imitates, at a tiny scale, the process powering the sun and the stars.

About three-quarters of the mass of the sun is hydrogen, the simplest and lightest and by far most abundant element in the universe. Due to its immense mass, the central regions of the sun are extremely compressed, with a density some 150 times that of water. Under these immense pressures hydrogen atoms are pressed together with such force that some of them fuse together to form helium, a process that yields prodigious quantities of energy. Thermonuclear fusion heats the core of the sun to temperatures of some 15 million degrees Celsius, and it is the energetic output of these reactions that lights the skies. From the surface of the sun, comparatively cool at temperatures of around 5,600 degrees Celsius, pours forth a continuous flux of energetic particles and radiations, not just in the visible parts of the electromagnetic spectrum but also in infrared and ultraviolet wavelengths. The sun has been burning for about five billion years, but eventually its thermonuclear core will start to run out of hydrogen fuel. In about five billion years it will begin a lengthy death sequence in which it will first gradually increase in luminosity and balloon massively in size. As this happens the inner planets, including the Earth, will be turned into glowing cinders of rock and perhaps swallowed into its fiery furnace. Then, in a spectacular final act, the sun will undergo violent convulsions and eject about half its mass, obliterating the Earth and all its other planets. Of the answer to the ancient question of whether our world will end in fire or ice, there is no longer any doubt.[18]

Of more immediate concern are far more frequent and smaller scale variations in the sun's energy output. The sun has an atmosphere composed of very hot gases that are churning and circulating as it rotates on its axis, thus generating solar weather. At times, for reasons not well understood, the sun ejects large bursts of energy and matter, known as solar flares, and when these strike the

Earth, the electromagnetic behavior of the planet is dramatically altered. In 1859, just as the electric telegraph came into wide use, the largest solar eruption on record caused the entire system to collapse. An eruption of this magnitude today would destroy crucial components of the global electrical and telecommunications systems, plunging the world into a crisis that could require years for recovery and that could cost, according to a study by the insurance company Lloyds of London, some 2.6 trillion dollars.[19] There is also evidence that the sun's output waxes and wanes in multicentury cycles and that lower output periods may be implicated in triggering terrestrial ice ages, long periods when large parts of the planet are covered with thick sheets of ice.

Inner Solar Space and Mars

Beyond its lunar satellite, the Earth's closest celestial neighbors are the other inner planets of Mercury, Venus, and Mars, whose sizes are roughly comparable to Earth's. But "close" is a relative term, and the distances to these neighboring worlds, constantly shifting as they move in their orbits, are hundreds of times further away than Luna. These bodies are visible as points of light in the night sky of the Earth. Unlike the vast plenitude of visible stars, they move about in complex but recurrent patterns, and so the Greeks called them "planets" (literally, "wanderers"). Charting their movements was the central focus of early astronomy. With the coming of increasingly powerful telescopes, and then robotic space probes, planetary scientists have learned a great deal about these bodies.

Mercury is the closet to the sun, a mere 36 million miles at its closest. It has no atmosphere and is composed largely of iron. It is the smallest planet and has high surface temperatures. Next is Venus, a near twin of the Earth in size but radically different in character. Early telescopic observations of Venus revealed a thick, pale greenish atmosphere, giving rise to hopes that it might be like humid tropical regions on Earth. But closer observations, as well as probes landed on its surface, have revealed a hellish world: surface temperatures even hotter than Mercury's, crushing atmospheric pressure, an atmosphere of carbon dioxide laced with sulfuric acid, and continuous hurricane-force winds. Its atmosphere is so thick that little sunlight reaches its surface. But scientists believe that Venus was quite different earlier in its history, with ocean-size bodies of liquid water, which gradually evaporated as carbon dioxide accumulated in the atmosphere and trapped progressively more of the solar radiation striking the planet, producing a runaway greenhouse effect that culminated in the present oven-like conditions.

Mars, the next planet out from the Earth, is far closer to the current conditions of terrestrial Earth than any place known to science. Named after the Roman god of war because of its reddish tint, Mars has excited far more attention than any other planet. Telescopic observations in the late nineteenth and early twentieth centuries suggested to several leading astronomers, most prominently Percival Lowell of Harvard, a planet-spanning network of canals. Such claims inspired a large body of speculative literature about Mars being inhabited by intelligent beings who were attempting to combat the desiccation of their planet with an immense system of public works.[20] These ideas were thoroughly dashed in the 1960s, when closer images from probes and telescopes revealed much harsher realities.

While Mars has an atmosphere, it is very thin, about one percent as dense as the Earth's, composed almost entirely of carbon dioxide and devoid of oxygen. Mars is also quite cold, with an average surface temperature of sixty-three degrees below zero Celsius, but summer at the equator can reach twenty degrees Celsius. Because its atmosphere is so thin, much higher quantities of life-threatening solar ultraviolet radiation reach its surface. Humans on Mars would require elaborate spacesuits and would probably live mainly underground to escape radiation. Its dusty soil is rich in chlorine compounds toxic to humans. Despite its thin atmosphere, the planet has giant dust storms, and its polar ice caps are a mixture of carbon dioxide and water. But Mars too may once have had large bodies of liquid water, and its surface is marked with intriguing ravines and gullies, suggesting that liquids occasionally flow on its surface. Primitive forms of life may once have emerged on Mars, and it is possible that they, like many types of bacteria on the Earth, still live beneath its surface within the crust of the planet.[21]

Asteroids, Near Earth Objects, and Cosmic Collisions

Perhaps the most interesting class of bodies in the inner solar system are asteroids, or planetoids, the largest of which are now called "minor planets." These bodies exist in vast numbers and, most important, sometimes collide with other celestial bodies, including the Earth. Asteroids also figure prominently in space expansionist schemes, both to solve terrestrial problems and to expand into habitats beyond the Earth.

The first asteroid identified by astronomers, Ceres, was discovered in 1801; nearly nine hundred thousand of them have thus far been cataloged.[22] The vast majority of asteroids are located in the belt between Mars and Jupiter. These main belt bodies are thought to be the remnants of primordial material that did not coalesce into a planet due to the powerful gravitational pull of Jupiter. Asteroids vary greatly in size, and their populations vary inversely with their size.

The largest, Ceres, now classified as a dwarf planet, has a surface area nearly the size of India and contains a quarter of the mass of the main belt. Asteroids also vary greatly in their composition: some are stony, some are nearly pure metal, and others are composed of primitive organic compounds. Psyche, believed to be the core of a failed proto-planet, appears to be made almost entirely of metal, mainly iron and nickel.[23] Because of their small mass, even the largest asteroids lack atmospheres. Smaller asteroids are not even spherically shaped and take on lumpy potato-like forms. Some are rubble piles packed with dust and sand rather than solid bodies. Because they are so small they have negligible gravitational fields and escape velocities; with a good leap a person could achieve escape velocity. This also means that they have negligible gravity wells, making them easy to access and exit. Their low mass also means that altering their orbital paths should be relatively easy.

The most important population of asteroids for both the Earth and space expansionist visions are what astronomers refer to as Near Earth Objects (NEOs). The first of these, named Eros, was discovered in 1898; since then over 20,000 of them have been discovered. Unlike the large population of large asteroids in the belt beyond Mars, NEOs have orbital paths that cross the orbital paths of the inner planets, including the Earth (see Figure 3.5). They are commonly classed as either Apollo, Amor or Aten type objects, depending on which planetary orbits their paths intersect.

Over the past several decades scientists have come to understand that asteroids sometime collide with the Earth and that past asteroidal collisions have played a major role in shaping the Earth and its life.[24] Although astronomers, geologists, and paleontologists were slow to investigate and accept the realities

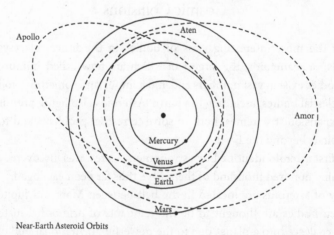

Near-Earth Asteroid Orbits

Figure 3.5 Near-Earth Asteroid Orbits

of cosmic collisions, the extensive body of now accepted scientific knowledge about collisions illuminates vital aspects of the Earth's history and future.

The evidence for collisions and their consequences is both extensive and startling. Results from preliminary exploration of the Earth's moon in the 1960s and 1970s decisively demonstrated that extensive cratering on the surface of the moon, long visible to astronomers, was the result of celestial bombardment, not vulcanism, as many thought. In the 1960s the geologist Eugene Shoemaker conclusively demonstrated that the highly visible half-mile-wide Barringer crater in Arizona was created by the impact of an object from space about 50,000 years ago.[25] In 1980 the case for cosmic collisions was greatly strengthened with the publication of an article by the physicist Luis Alvarez and others hypothesizing that the geologically abrupt mass extinction of the dinosaurs approximately 66 million years ago was the result of a collision with a celestial body some ten miles in diameter. Crucial evidence for this mass extinction hypothesis was the anomalously high levels of the metallic element iridium in the rock layers from this period. This indicated extraterrestrial origins because asteroids have much higher levels of this element than are present in the Earth's crust.[26] A few years later the impact crater from this epic collision was located, buried under hundreds of feet of sediments, on the Gulf Coast of the Yucatan Peninsula. The doomsday object that created this cataclysm has come be known as Chicxulub, after the Mayan fishing village that now sits above the center of the crater.[27]

Geologists estimate that this collision released energy equal to some 100 million megatons (MT) of TNT. The heat from this explosion set much of the planet's biomass on fire and injected enormous quantities of dust and soot into the atmosphere, which blocked sunlight for years, causing global temperatures to plummet, creating what some call an "asteroid winter." Scientists estimate that these disruptions killed some 90 percent of the organisms on the planet and drove to extinction some 60 percent of its species of complex life, including the giant reptiles that had dominated the planet's ecosystems for hundreds of millions of years. Artists's renderings of giant cosmic collisions vividly convey their Earth-smashing potential (Figure 3.6.a). Close examination of the Earth's surface from airplanes and satellites has mapped a large number of craters, known as "astroblemes," that were sites of ancient collisions, but many more remain deeply buried, in deep ocean waters, or have been completely erased by the subduction of parts of the Earth's crust at the seams of tectonic plates. How many other great extinction events in Earth history were caused by such collisions, or geophysically caused warming periods, remains in question.[28]

New evidence has also emerged that a collision between two asteroidal bodies some 466 million years ago produced a large cloud of dust, which spread across

(a)

(b)

Bolide Events 1994–2013
(Small Asteroids that Disintegrated in Earth's Atmosphere)

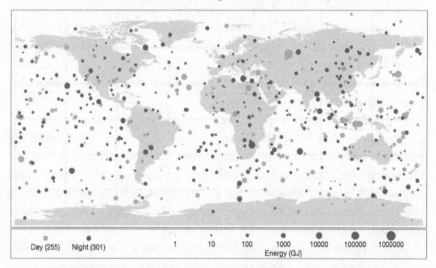

Figure 3.6 Depiction of Giant Asteroid Collision and Mapping of Bolide Events.
Source: (a) Wikimedia Commons/NASA; (b) NASA Planetary Science

the inner solar system and reduced solar insolation on the Earth, triggering a cooling period lasting some two million years.[29] Vastly larger numbers of much smaller objects routinely strike the Earth's atmosphere and violently disintegrate, in what are known as bolide events (Figure 3.6.b).

The largest cosmic collision in recent historical time occurred on June 30, 1908, when an object from space struck the remote Tunguska region in Siberia.[30] Local reports described a sudden giant explosion and fire in the sky and violent winds, and the sound of the explosion was heard thousands of miles away. The explosion flattened and scorched trees over an area of two thousand square kilometers, an area roughly as large as New York City and Washington, DC, combined. Scientists now believe that the Tunguska event was caused by a stony asteroid exploding in the atmosphere, which created a giant fireball but not a large crater. There is still uncertainty about the size of the object; early estimates suggested 100 to 300 meters in diameter, and more recently 45 meters has been proposed. The energy released by the collision is thought to be equivalent to the detonation of twenty to thirty million tons (MT) of TNT equivalent, the size of a large thermonuclear weapon explosion. If this object had arrived six hours later it would have struck over much more populated areas of Western Europe, and if it had been ten or twelve hours later it would have struck over the northern Atlantic Ocean, where it would have produced a tsunami twenty to thirty feet in height.[31]

Contingent Events, Risk Patterns, and Scientific Priorities

The Tunguska event suggests some fascinating "what if" historical counterfactuals. If this object had been traveling on an only slightly different path and struck an inhabited area of European Russia, Europe, or North America, instead of remote Siberia, it seems likely that the entire trajectory of twentieth-century history would have been radically different.[32] Space expansionist thought, taking form during this period, might have been focused less on leaving the Earth and more on protecting it. More consequentially, the leading nation-states, then squabbling over inconsequential precincts in the Balkans that would soon embroil them in the devastations of World War I, might well have banded together to demand scientific explanations and technological solutions for what would have surely been viewed as a perilous natural threat. Had they done so, heavy rockets, and possibly nuclear explosives as well, might have been developed earlier and in very different political contexts than the world conflicts of the 1940s that spawned them. Alternatively, had this collision occurred in an inhabited part of the world in premodern times, it might well have catalyzed the formation of a new religion.[33] If it had occurred fifty years later than it did, in 1958, at exactly the same spot, it might have triggered a nuclear war between the United States and the Soviet Union. These hypotheticals underscore the potentially major consequences from radically contingent variations in the timing of collisions and the ways in which the future trajectory of human development on Earth remains hostage to the indifferent orbital paths of distant and largely unknown—but not unknowable—space objects.

Based on the evidence accumulated by geologists and astronomers over the past several decades, a scientifically robust profile of the asteroidal collision hazard has been generated (see Figure 3.7). The scientific study of asteroids has definitively placed them on the list of major natural hazards to humanity's habitat. Fortunately, there is an inverse relationship between the probability of collision and the damage from collision simply because larger objects are less numerous than smaller ones. It is estimated that there are approximately two thousand NEOs of sufficient size to wreak planetary catastrophe. Astronomers estimate that there exist approximately 300,000 NEOs the size of the Tunguska rock, and that the natural rate of collision for such objects is somewhere between once every 100 to 500 years.[34] In the wake of the Cold War and the declassification of data from US satellites monitoring the planet for nuclear explosions, scientists gained more evidence on the frequency of collisions of objects exploding in the atmosphere high above remote areas, finding one explosion with the force of 15,000 tons of TNT and about ten in the 1,000-ton range annually.[35] It is also estimated that the probability of an average inhabitant of the Earth dying from asteroidal collision is higher than the probability of dying from a nuclear power plant accident or the crash of a commercial airliner. The fact that such objects have and will destructively interact with the Earth's biosphere clearly establishes that the environment relevant for thinking about environmental protection on Earth now extends across the solar system.[36]

Despite their immense practical importance for the human prospect on Earth, asteroids have been a low priority for both scientists and space programs. Geologists were slow to recognize that many terrestrial craters were produced by collisions with objects from space, preferring the explanation that they resulted from vulcanism, a purely geological explanation that did not

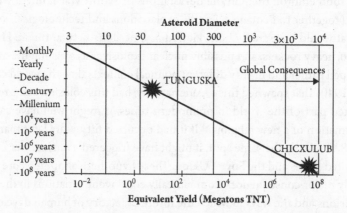

Figure 3.7 Asteroidal Risk Patterns . This image is based on a figure from Clark R. Chapman et al., "Impacts on the Earth by Asteroids and Comets: Assessing the Hazard," *Nature,* January 6, 1994.

entail attributing events in their domain of study to phenomena in the domain of another scientific field. Also, widely publicized claims of the Russian
émigré scientist Immanuel Velikovsky that the Earth was subject to cosmic
bombardment were discredited because he also advanced many elaborate
and thoroughly preposterous claims that gained wide public attention. This
created a sort of "pseudoscience by association" effect, discouraging geologists
and astronomers from seriously investigating the links between craters and extraterrestrial collisions.[37]

The priorities of astronomy and space science are largely set by scientists,
and comparatively little attention and resources have been directed to asteroids.
Instead efforts have been focused on the planets and the sun, and the larger
structures of the cosmos. Several small probes have been sent to asteroids in recent years and have produced important knowledge, but these missions have
been paltry in their numbers and costs compared to probes sent to Mars and the
other planets. Several major observatories have been placed in orbit, most famously the Hubble Space Telescope, as well as ones to survey the cosmos in infrared, ultraviolet, and x-ray bands of the electromagnetic spectrum obstructed
by the Earth's atmosphere. These artificial eyes on the cosmos commonly cost the
better part of a billion dollars apiece to build, place in orbit, and operate. But no
such observatory has been built for asteroid detection, even though one would
be relatively simple to design and cheap to build and launch.[38] As of this writing,
the single most expensive and technologically ambitious observatory, the Webb
Space Telescope, designed to detect faint radiation from the Big Bang (the event
thought to have brought the observable universe into existence roughly thirteen
billion years ago), is being readied for launch, despite cost overruns approaching
ten billion dollars, thus squeezing many Earth-oriented monitoring projects.
Should a major collision take place here on Earth, the peoples and governments
who have funded space astronomy while largely delegating priority-setting to
scientists will justifiably wonder how the quest to answer the big questions
about very far away and long ago events, such as the Big Bang, was allowed to
displace investigation of the much smaller bangs that, being here and now, will
have greater impact than anything else coming from the entire space enterprise.

The reasons for these priorities are not difficult to discern. Finding and mapping asteroids, while of potentially epochal *practical* value, does not promise to
answer any of the central *scientific* questions about the universe that animate
the modern scientific project. The scientific asteroid missions that have been
conducted mainly seek to answer questions about their features and formation, as a window to the early solar system. While the practical consequences
of the knowledge cosmological astronomy seeks may be minimal, the practical
consequences of not having the knowledge astronomers are not seeking could
be enormous.

Despite the historical general indifference of astronomy and space science to the problem of asteroidal collisions, growing awareness of this threat has slowly but surely begun to produce action. Prodded by the US Congress and a network of planetary defense, asteroid activists, and NEOphiles, the skies have been surveyed for objects large enough to produce civilization-ending levels of destruction. About 1,000 of the estimated 1,200 such objects have been discovered.[39] But there is almost no capability to detect objects of the size of the Tunguska rock. Some three-quarters of statistically hypothized NEOs at least 140 meters or larger have not been found (see Figure 3.8).

As for the development of technologies to actually defend against threatening asteroids, efforts to conceptualize deflection techniques have been extensive (as we shall see ahead) but have far outstripped even rudimentary implementation. The Deep Impact mission propelled a metal object into a comet at high velocity and studied the resulting ejecta for data about their primordial material. An ambitious NASA project, ARM (Asteroid Redirect Mission), to pluck a boulder from an asteroid, bring it back to the Earth system, and insert it in lunar orbit, was canceled in 2017. Another mission slated for launch in 2021,

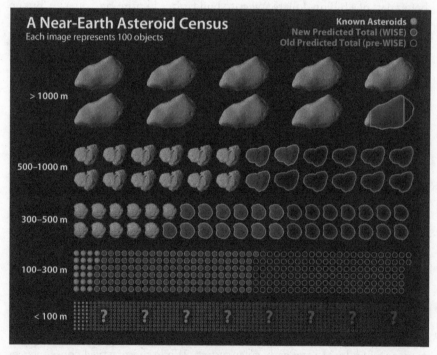

Figure 3.8 Estimated and Discovered Near Earth Asteroids . This figure makes use of data products from the Wide-Field Infrared Survey Explorer, which is a joint project of the University of California, Los Angeles, and the Jet Propulsion Laboratory/California Institute of Technology, funded by the National Aeronautics and Space Administration.

DART (Double Asteroid Redirect Test), will fire a high-velocity impactor into the tiny moon of the asteroid Didymos and measure how its orbit is altered, the first test with direct relevance to the practical deflection problem.[40] This pattern of almost complete inaction is also striking given the high priority attached to such efforts by public opinion and many space advocates. The bottom line is that humanity is now almost completely unprepared to take action if an imminent threat is discovered.

The overall implications of asteroids for humanity, the Earth, and the space enterprise are enormous and, as we shall see at length, fiercely contested. But these disputes are nested within a consensus about several basic realities revealed by science. As the reality of asteroidal collisions past and future has been firmly established by science, the interconnections between cosmic events and major features of the Earth and its life, and the possibility of cosmocide, have also been firmly established. Consciousness of this basic fact about the geography of humanity is now very widespread, in part due to compelling popular SF and cinematic representations. The fact that solar space is populated with vast numbers of celestial bodies with titanic potential collision energies means that the space environment is itself violent in fundamental ways. The fact that the Earth and its environments are inherently linked in very important ways to vast numbers of moving objects located at great distances from the Earth also confounds neat delineations of fully distinct places, borders, and zones. All parts of the solar system, whatever their many other differences, are similar in being potentially hit by asteroidal objects. This clearly means, as the geologists Allan Kelly and Frank Dachille argued in 1953, that humanity's safety inevitably hinges on asteroidal patterns and events stretching across the solar system. It is now indisputable that what humans do—or do not do—with asteroids will decisively shape, sooner or later, the future of the planet and the species.

Outer Solar Space, the Third Zone, and Beyond

The outer zone of solar orbital space is vastly larger than the inner zone (see Figure 3.9), as are its planets. Beyond Mars and the asteroid belt orbit the four largest planets, Jupiter, Saturn, Uranus, and Neptune. Astronomers refer to them as "gas giants" because they lack solid rocky surfaces and are composed of swirling masses of gases that become gradually denser in their interiors. Jupiter, the king of the planets, has a mass 318 times larger than Earth's. Its dense turbulent atmosphere has continuous hurricane-force winds, which generate Jovian-size bolts of lightning, of billions of volts. As Galileo famously discovered, this behemoth also has a retinue of orbiting moons, numbering about 80, making for an analogue small-scale solar system of its own. Having an extremely powerful

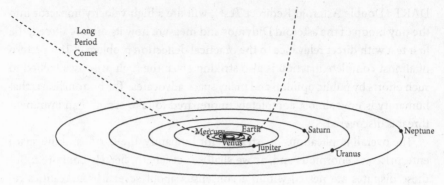

Figure 3.9 Outer Solar Orbital Space

magnetic field, Jupiter is girdled by belts of radiation vastly stronger and more lethal than those found in the Earth's Van Allan belt, and its astrosphere extends for tens of millions of miles. Some of the moons of the gas giants are substantial; the largest is Ganymede, which is larger than Mercury. The larger moons of the outer planets are very diverse in character and often have very active geologies and atmospheres. Particularly intriguing are the Jovian moon Europa, composed largely of water, and Saturn's Titan and Enceladus, which might harbor microbial life. The second largest planet, Saturn, famous for its distinctive rings, has a very weak magnetic field, making its moons more potentially habitable by humans than Jupiter's.

Beyond outer SOS and its gas giants is the third zone of space, governed by the sun's gravity, about which much less is known. The third zone is populated by a large belt of small icy worlds, known as the Kuiper Belt, and an even larger sphere of comets known as the Oort Cloud. And just as EOS is dwarfed by inner SOS, which is in turn dwarfed by outer SOS, the third zone is again vastly larger.[41]

Preliminary exploration of the third zone has been marked by interesting controversies about classification and nomenclature. After Neptune was discovered by telescopes in 1846, many astronomers believed there was still another planet to be found, and an extensive and widely publicized search for "Planet X" ensued. In 1930 a young American astronomer, Clyde Tombaugh, found evidence of a very distant body, subsequently named Pluto, that was widely viewed as the ninth and final planet. But from the outset Pluto was oddly different, vastly smaller than the four gas giants, and indeed considerably smaller than the Earth, and its orbit was wildly irregular, carrying it for long stretches inside the orbit of Neptune.

In recent decades astronomers have discovered other small bodies with oddly configured orbits. When one of them, named Eris, was discovered in 2005 and found to be larger than Pluto, a crisis of astronomical taxonomy ensued. If Pluto was a planet, then so too must be Eris, and if Eris was not deemed to be a planet, then neither could Pluto. Thus was born, after much debate, a new category, "dwarf planet," designed to include these objects and the now more than a thousand similar small icy bodies that have been located orbiting beyond Neptune.[42] Together they compose the Kuiper Belt, named after the Dutch astronomer who first hypothesized their existence. This controversy reminds us that astronomers and geographers are not simply accumulating observational knowledge (and generating explanations) but also making and revising classification schemes as they map spaces and places.[43]

The third zone is also populated by comets, bodies composed of frozen gases and dust, memorably dubbed "dirty snowballs," that remain most of their lives in the deep cold at enormous distances from the sun.[44] Unlike the planets, which are all on the same plane, comet orbits are found in three dimensions and thus form a vast spherical halo around the solar system, called the Oort Cloud for the Dutch astronomer who hypothesized its existence. Comets are thought to exist in staggeringly vast numbers, perhaps into the trillions. Some are hundreds of miles in diameter, and some have orbits whose furthest distance from the sun are several trillion miles away, an appreciable fraction of the distance to nearby stars.

Despite these great distances, comets are still within the gravitational sway of the sun, although their orbits may take thousands of years to complete. Some comets have orbits bringing them closer to the sun, where solar energy melts and vaporizes their outer layers. As this happens they develop the distinctive tails of luminous material that stretch millions of miles behind them. As their outer layers boil off into space, their mass declines and their orbits change, sometimes dramatically. When they come into the realm of the planets, some are drawn into collisions, particularly with massive Jupiter, while others plunge into the sun or are cast into interstellar space.

Across history the appearance of comets, with their tails sometimes arcing widely across the Earth's sky, was commonly interpreted as a dark omen of coming calamity. Even after their nature was better understood, many people feared comets would collide with the Earth or catastrophically contaminate the Earth with poisonous gases or spores.[45] Only an infinitesimally small share of their total estimated population has been detected, and comets previously unknown to astronomers regularly appear. If a comet hundreds of miles in diameter were to collide with the Earth, so much energy would be released that all the higher life forms would be driven to extinction. The approach of an unknown long-period comet on a collision course would afford relatively little warning time.[46]

Some indication of the destructiveness of such an event was provided in 1994, when a comet, Shoemaker-Levy 9, was ripped apart by Jupiter's gravity, and its pieces were drawn into a spectacular collision. The largest fragment released energies equivalent to 600 times all nuclear weapons on Earth and left a burn blemish in the Jovian atmosphere about the size of the Earth.[47] Long after comets have sped away or disintegrated, remnants of their sloppy passage persist as bands of dust and grit across the solar system. When the Earth passes, at predictable times, through these bands of fine debris, meteor showers made up of cascades of "shooting stars" appear in the night sky, as high-velocity sand-size grains vaporize in the atmosphere.

The solar system is in turn completely dwarfed by the size of the galaxy in which it sits. Galaxies, or "island universes," are giant assemblages of stars, and our galaxy, known as the Milky Way (for the hazy band of light arcing across the night sky, emanating from its densely packed central region), is quite typical in shape and size. A giant pinwheel with spiral arms wrapping around its dense core and rotating every 100,000 years, the Milky Way galaxy contains several hundred billion stars, most smaller but some vastly larger than the sun. And just as the planets in the solar system are held in gravitational thrall by the sun, so too bodies in the galaxy are governed by a central object, believed to be a black hole several billion times as massive as the sun, with a gravitational pull so strong that its escape velocity exceeds the speed of light.

Despite its plenitude of stars, the galaxy, like the solar system, is overwhelmingly empty, with vast gulfs between stars. The nearest star to our sun (actually a system of three stars) is some twenty-five trillion miles away. To measure such cosmic distances conveniently, astronomers employ the metric of the light-year, the distance that light, moving at about 670 million miles an hour (or 186,000 miles per second), travels in a year. To put these numbers in perspective, a satellite orbiting the Earth at about 17,000 miles an hour completes an orbit in ninety minutes. If light could be bent to travel in a circular path around the Earth, it would go around the planet about eight times in one second. Using this measure, the nearest star is a bit over four light-years away. Our galaxy is about 100,000 light-years in diameter and 10,000 light-years thick at the center, and our solar system is about 25,000 light-years from the galactic center. The nearest large galaxy is two and a half million light-years away, and the horizon of the observable universe is about thirteen billion light-years away.

Given the vast the distances of interstellar space, travel across these voids will be, even with the most advanced technologies feasible within the laws of physics, an extremely long duration enterprise, stretching across many human lifespans. Traveling at the speed of a satellite orbiting the Earth, a voyage to the nearest star would take thousands of years. The speed of light sets an absolute cosmic speed limit, and energies required to propel an object to even an appreciable fraction of this speed are extremely daunting, far beyond the capacities of current technology. Thus the sky is effectively unlimited but is so vastly unlimited that it severely limits human access.[48]

The larger galactic context of our solar system also poses potential hazards for the Earth and its life. Elevated levels of radiations from extremely violent celestial events such as the supernova explosion of a massive star or colliding black holes could sterilize the planet. Perturbations of the Oort Cloud or changes in the density of gas and dust in the interstellar medium could elevate the bombardment rate in the inner solar system. Fortunately, astrophysicists assign very low near-term probability to such events. But over the very long run these events, like the violent death of the sun, portend the end of the Earth as a viable habitat for humanity.[49]

Overall, the new mapping of cosmic realities across deep space and time has abundantly established that interactions between the cosmos and the Earth have played profound roles in shaping the features of the Earth and the evolution of its life forms. This mapping has also firmly established that the possibility and eventual inevitability of cosmocide is an escapable fact of nature for terrestrial humanity, a basic fact of life and death on the largest scale. As humans widely grasped in the Sky Age, our fate is indeed inevitably in the stars.

Life, Complex Life, and Intelligent Life

The new map of the cosmos contains many features unanticipated by scientists. But perhaps even more noteworthy is what science has *not found*: life and intelligent life. The question "Are we alone?" has animated inquiry and speculation throughout history and is one of the basic reasons for exploring space. But absence of evidence is not evidence of absence, and the universe is immeasurably larger than what has been explored, so the question remains fully open. But given the vast number of planets in this galaxy, and the staggeringly large number of galaxies populating the known universe, it is highly unlikely that life, complex life, and intelligent life exist *only* on the planet Earth.

Thinking about the existence of life and intelligent life in the universe has undergone a striking evolution across time (see Figure 3.10). A brief review of the evolution of thinking about life and nonhuman intelligent life forms in the cosmos establishes the unexpected novelty of the recent discovery of the lifeless universe proximate to Earth, and how widely thinking on this topic has varied and changed.

For much of history, humans thought the Earth and its places and objects were animated beings, possessing various levels of consciousness and intelligence. Many of these beings were thought to be vastly more powerful than humans. Even after the rise of monotheistic religions envisioning one all-powerful supernatural being, the Earth and skies were still understood to be populated with lesser intelligent beings, such as angels and demons.

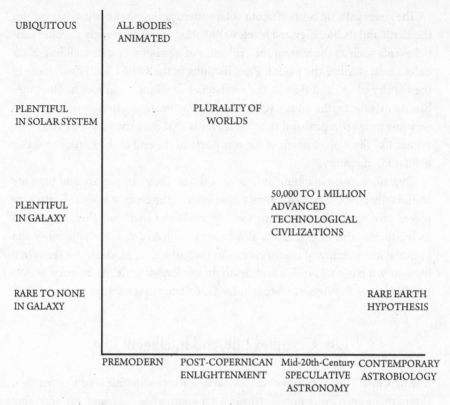

UBIQUITOUS	ALL BODIES ANIMATED		
PLENTIFUL IN SOLAR SYSTEM	PLURALITY OF WORLDS		
PLENTIFUL IN GALAXY		50,000 TO 1 MILLION ADVANCED TECHNOLOGICAL CIVILIZATIONS	
RARE TO NONE IN GALAXY			RARE EARTH HYPOTHESIS
	PREMODERN	POST-COPERNICAN ENLIGHTENMENT	Mid-20th-Century SPECULATIVE ASTRONOMY	CONTEMPORARY ASTROBIOLOGY

Figure 3.10 Shifting Views on the Frequency of Alien Intelligence

As the scientific and technological revolutions unfolded, a radically different cosmology took hold. The world became de-animated and disenchanted as the Earth and its myriad life forms came to be understood in terms of mechanism and matter, with humans occupying a special status. The discoveries of the Copernican Revolution discredited the animated heavens and supernatural intervention in terrestrial affairs. But as this cosmic de-animation proceeded, many scientists and philosophers came to think that life forms, including intelligent ones, were likely to exist on the innumerable "other worlds" discovered by astronomers.[50] Thus, as the moon and the planets ceased to be viewed as alive, they came to be viewed as places inhabited by life forms broadly comparable to life on Earth.

Much of this thinking about life in the universe was shaped by the Principle of Mediocrity, which holds that because the universe is so vast, anything present on Earth is likely to be very common cosmically. "What is true in one part will hold true over the entire Universe," the astronomer Christiaan Huygens asserted in 1698.[51] For several centuries a surprisingly large number of early modern European thinkers argued that extraterrestrial intelligent life forms existed, in great variety and in relative proximity to the Earth.[52] Such ideas were prominently discussed in the works of leading scientists, philosophers, theologians, and poets. Despite the absence of any supporting evidence, many offered detailed accounts of such beings.[53] Bernard de Fontenelle's *Conversations on Plurality of Worlds* (1686) brought this new cosmic view to wide audiences. The prominent French Enlightenment figure Voltaire employed the prospect of innumerable intelligent aliens to hammer Christianity, ridiculing the possibility that divine incarnation and resurrection would be repeated countless times for salvation to be universally available to believers. Such polemical, anticlerical arguments also appear prominently in the works of the republican revolutionary Thomas Paine, particularly in his widely read *The Age of Reason* (1794). At the same time, many theologians argued that the plurality of worlds doctrine supported religion because the abundance of life in the cosmos demonstrated the plenitude of divine creation and rebuked human pride.[54]

A particularly interesting version of Enlightenment thinking about extraterrestrial intelligent life appears in the writings of the great German philosopher Immanuel Kant, who wrote extensively about astronomy and geography in addition to his major works on metaphysics, ethics, and aesthetics. References to intelligent aliens play important roles in his cosmopolitan ethical system.[55] Kant speculated that many of the orbs in the solar system were populated by intelligent life forms with very different bodily designs suitable for their different worlds. But he thought that intelligent aliens would be fundamentally similar to humans because they possessed reason and autonomy, the marks of human superiority among terrestrial life forms. Although Kant did not seem to entertain the possibility of human interaction with extraterrestrial aliens, his cosmopolitan ethical system was just that, a system of rights and duties applicable to all reason-bearing beings, wherever they might live in the cosmos.

Across the nineteenth and twentieth centuries, a large number of scientists continued to think, entirely without direct evidence, that intelligent life was widespread beyond the Earth. As the severity of conditions on the planets in the solar system came into view, the focus of such expectations narrowed to Mars, where Lowell and others thought they had identified evidence of intelligent life. When it became clear later in the twentieth century that Mars was almost certainly barren of intelligent life, there was still a widespread assumption among many scientists that intelligent life was common in the galaxy and beyond. For example, as late as the 1960s the eminent astronomers Carl Sagan and I. S. Shklovskii estimated that this galaxy alone was home to between fifty thousand and one million advanced technological civilizations.[56] With this line of thought prevalent, it made sense to try to detect radio signals from neighboring civilizations, a project known as the Search for Extraterrestrial Intelligence

(SETI),[57] and to think seriously about scenarios and consequences of contact with alien intelligences.[58]

Over the past several decades the study of life in the universe, now known as astrobiology, has become much more extensive, systemic and scientifically respectable. Contemporary astrobiologists strongly disagree about many basic questions. But a strong astrobiological understanding about life in the cosmos has emerged to challenge the Principle of Mediocrity. This view, known as the "Rare Earth Hypothesis," is quite optimistic about the frequency of very simple life in the universe, but is very pessimistic about the prospects for complex and intelligent life.[59] This view is based on a clearer understanding of the factors shaping the emergence and development of life on Earth. Earth life falls into three broad classes: single cellular, metazoic, and intelligent.[60] Microbial life on Earth appears to have emerged not long after the planet had cooled from the extreme temperatures marking its formation, some 4.5 billion years ago. It now exists in an extraordinary diversity of environments, many of them previously thought to be inhospitable to living organisms. Particularly revealing is the discovery of extremophiles, microbial organisms that flourish in extreme environments, such as around ocean-floor thermal vents where temperatures range into the hundreds of degrees Celsius and the water is extremely acidic. Many scientists now expect simple life forms to exist wherever there are large quantities of liquid water for extended periods, while some maintain that even the emergence of primitive life requires so many fantastically unlikely steps that it too is likely to be very rare.

But the cosmic prospects for metazoic and intelligent life appear much dimmer. Metazoic life has complex, functionally differentiated parts, wherein cells of very different types, each specialized and performing distinct tasks, are integrated into one organism. Unlike its simpler predecessors, metazoic life did not emerge on Earth until about half a billion years ago, in a geologically sudden burst known as the Cambrian Explosion. The Rare Earth Hypothesis holds that the emergence of metazoic life is likely to be very rare because dependent on the simultaneous presence of a large list of factors not likely to be present on many worlds, at most a handful in this galaxy.

The cosmic prospects for intelligent life comparable to humans appear even dimmer. Since their emergence, approximately a billion distinct species of metazoic life have existed, well over 98 percent of which are now extinct. Of this vast number of life forms evolving over half a billion years, only one species, or one cluster of species in the genus *Homo*, have the attributes of intelligence.[61] In sum, the Rare Earth Hypothesis suggests that pockets of bacteria may be found widely where liquid water exists but that anything more complicated is likely to be extraordinarily rare, thus reversing the Principle of Mediocrity dominant since the Copernican Revolution. It is notable that this great downward estimate for advanced life in deep space stems not just from better astronomical observations but also from better understanding of the arduous, lengthy, contingent, and vulnerable emergence of advanced life on Earth across deep time.

Whatever the prospects for finding various grades of life in the vast reaches of the cosmos, modern astronomy has clearly established the reality of Oasis Earth. Life is staggeringly abundant on Earth, and the Earth is surrounded by at least many trillions of miles of harshly desolate and severely inhospitable spaces and places. Joined with the reality of the perennial possibility and eventual inevitability of cosmocide for terrestrial humanity, the implications of these new understandings of life in the cosmos are profound, suggesting to many that the extreme specialness of the Earth warrants placing an extremely high priority on protecting it, while implying to space expansionists an ethical imperative to spread advanced life in the universe.

The New Earth and the New Science

In some important ways what has been learned during the Space Age about the Earth is more revolutionary than what has been learned about the solar system. Space Age solar geography is Copernican, with much more detail, but investigations of Earth and its life have just passed through a Copernican-like revolutionary moment.[62] Significantly aided by orbital observation platforms and comparisons with Venus and Mars,[63] the scientific study of this planet now has a new central object, the Earth System, which subsumes the planet's rocks, waters, airs, and life forms into one complexly interactive whole whose parts are continuously changing. The Earth and its life forms are now understood to be coevolving, and the features of Earth are as much the product of biological as of geophysical and chemical processes. Life is integral to the geophysical composition and evolution of the Earth, which is sometimes referred to as an organism of organisms, a superorganism, alive not just in its parts but as a whole.[64] Life is not *on* Earth, it is *of* Earth.

Paralleling the great modern discovery of Deep Space, with vast spatial magnitude, has been the discovery of Deep Time, with vast temporal magnitude. Nature has a history, and its processes have unfolded across staggeringly great periods of time. And the Earth, in addition to being cosmically dwarfed, has been revealed to be enormously old, tens of thousands of times older than humanity. Investigations by geologists and paleontologists of the deep history of the Earth and its life have revealed a wide spectrum of past and possible alt-Earths, many radically inhospitable to humans and their activities. The new deep planetary history has also abundantly established the enormously powerful role of highly contingent, extremely rare, and catastrophic events in shaping the overall character of the Earth and the developmental paths of its life. Far from being designed for humanity and its well-being, as the vanity of *sapiens* supposed, humanity emerged late, the product of an incredibly long and vastly improbable series of natural events, and will almost inevitably eventually be catastrophically diminished or eliminated by one or more of a lengthening list of natural cataclysms. The Earth may be a Garden of Eden, a splendid Oasis, in cosmically relative terms, but its emergence has been shaped by a succession of freak events, and its violent demise is cosmically guaranteed.

The old adage "The more you know, the more you know you don't know" holds true for the study of the Earth and its life forms. The number of known unknowns is steadily rising. Estimates of the total number of distinct life forms on Earth now vary by orders of magnitude, and less than 1 percent of bacteria, by far the dominant life form on the planet, have been cultured and identified.[65] Organisms are now understood as biomes, with the human body containing some ten times more bacterial than human cells.[66] As astrobiologists struggle to identify faint hints of life on vastly distant celestial bodies, vast numbers of undiscovered Terran life forms are being extinguished by human encroachments. Perversely science has generated far more accurate and complete maps of several celestial bodies, most notably Luna and Mars, than of the Earth, vast parts of which under the oceans have been incompletely mapped.

The revolutionary new discoveries about the Earth and life have helped catalyze a new view of nature deeply subversive of the Newtonian mechanical universe that made Baconian engineering progress so plausible. The new scientific cosmology emphasizes the roles of complexity, chaos, and emergence, assigning to complex systems a potential for emergent creativity absent in earlier matter-and-energy cosmological models.[67] The Earth System and its myriad ecosystems are now understood to be powerfully shaped by nonlinear processes, unpredictable tipping points, and chaotic dynamics.[68] It is no longer intelligible as a homoeostatic system potentially modeled mechanically, or even cybernetically.

An implication of the new Earth system science understanding of the planet as one complex interactive system is that maps with geometric grids and state borders and territories, widely deployed in recent centuries, become more notable for what they hide and misleadingly represent than for their accurate representation of primary planetary geographic realities. Spatially the planet as understood by the new Earth science is an organism-like aggregation and assemblage of flows and entangled networks, utterly lacking in geometric lines and bordered, containerized spaces. Instead different parts fade into each other without sharp borders and powerfully interact with each other. Nonlinear geomorphic representations and mappings are now more accurate and abundantly generated and deployed, with multiple representations, each of which captures important realities, but no one of which enjoys the hegemonic or architectonic status previously held by the grid and bordered globes and maps propagated by early modern geographers and their successors.

Even more important, this new understanding of nature opens a significant gap between the human ability to impact nature and the ability to fully understand and control it. Like the other great scientific advances across the past several centuries, this new understanding of the planet is another towering monument to the continued supremacy of the Baconian project of progressively improving knowledge acquisition by empirical investigation. But its implications for the Baconian project of technological advance to elevate the human estate are profound and largely subversive. In undermining aspirations to fully know, predict, and master, this new view of nature calls into question the epistemological foundations of Promethean and Techno-Optimist ambitions to comprehensively contain and engineer nature and the Earth, as well as space expansionist dreams of seeding the cosmos with Earth-like habitats. The newly appreciated isolation, fragility, and vulnerability of humanity's terrestrial habitat provides a powerful rationale for significant human expansion into space, but the new understanding of nature diminishes its feasibility. The new opaque and untamable Earth and the new nonmechanistic cosmology produced by better "setting eye on Earth" mean that some of the most important scientific advances of the Space Age have seriously eroded the conceptual foundations of the practical prospects for the most ambitious dreams of space advocates.

Technological Imaginaries, Feasibilities, Syndromes, and Catastrophes

> At first we inevitably have an idea, a fantasy, a fairy tale, and then comes scientific calculation; finally execution crowns the thought.
> —Konstantin Tsiolkovsky (1911)[1]

> The world-altering powers that technology has delivered into our hands now require a degree of consideration and foresight that has never before been asked of us.
> —Carl Sagan (1994)[2]

> Relinquishment at the right level needs to be part of our ethical response to the dangers of twenty-first century technologies.
> —Ray Kurzweil (2003)[3]

Homo Faber Looks Ahead

That humans are outstanding in nature due to technology (and speech) had been recognized long before the arrival of advanced science-based technology. If Plato's account of the origins of humanity is to be believed, the gods assigned to the Titan Epimetheus (literally, "afterthought") the task of distributing survival-enhancing attributes such as speed, flight, and sharp fangs to the myriad creatures of the Earth.[4] Not being very good at anticipation, Epimetheus finished his work with no potent trait left for humanity. Sent to inspect his work, his brother Prometheus ("forethought"), fearing humanity would not survive, stole for them technical skills, speech, and fire from the gods, for which he was famously punished. Thus was born *Homo faber*, man the tool-maker, a mortal race but one equipped with some powers appropriately reserved for the gods.[5] Human use of technologies, starting with fire for cooking, has been so lengthy, intimate, and influential as to significantly shape the evolution of human bodily features.[6] From these ambivalent beginnings, humanity vacillates between its backward-looking Epimethean blindnesses and its forward-looking Promethean capabilities, a struggle whose stakes have grown as humanity lights ever more potent fires.

Among the speech-enabled traits allowing *Homo faber* to elevate itself so spectacularly above other life forms on the planet are robust cognitive capacities of imagination (seeing possibilities that do not exist) and prospection (seeing ahead). From the earliest cave paintings and oral tales, humans have exhibited a precocious ability to envision imaginary worlds and to mingle the real with the unreal in thought and action. Informal short-range anticipations and forecasts are part of all human activity.[7] Whether conducted by oracles or computers, prophecy, fortune telling, and forecasting are among the most valued human skills, imparting great benefits for even modest capabilities. Imaginaries are integral, not antagonistic, to scientific and technological progress and civilization, but not all technological imaginaries are created equal.[8] Some are dangerous illusions, while others are vital illuminations. As technologies become ever more potent, the ability to foresee their consequences and steer their uses away from catastrophic outcomes becomes increasingly essential for human survival and flourishing. Humanity's future increasingly depends on disciplined and systematic assessments of imaginary worlds, of the many possible realities, some dangerous, some desirable, which might come to exist. Without increasingly competent futurism, humanity may not have a future.

Nowhere does the interplay between imagination and foresight loom larger than in space, where imaginary visions and technological forecasts and assessments play foundational roles. While science-based technology is the indispensable means for the realization of the space expansionist cosmic quest of human enlargement, the path to the stars is not straightforward. The path of visionary space expansionism winds through the imaginative heights of science fiction and onto the hard road of technological forecasting and development, where it confronts possibilities for disastrous misfires while skirting the edge of an abyss of catastrophic and existential risks. This chapter explores the relationships between space expansionism and science fiction, the technological feasibility of ambitious space expansion, the ways technological choices can go awry, the overall horizon of catastrophic and existential threats, and the prospects for safely and soundly steering technologies.

Flights of the Imagination

Space expansionism is in many ways the offspring of science fiction, which is a modernized version of the universal human activity of imaginative storytelling. Throughout history, many different cultures have produced stories abounding

with beings, forces, and places not found in the real world of human-lived experience. And visions of cosmic travels have been part of the human social imaginary long before modern science and technology. While such stories occupy a
central place in many cultures and religions, they make no attempt to explain scientifically the nature and sources of these extraordinary beings and their powers,
leaving these topics shrouded in mystery, all the better for conjuring wonder,
awe, and fear. Their origins are commonly cast as miraculous, coming in the
form of dream or divine revelation, in circumstances not subject to general or
repeatable access. These tales are often filled with vivid visions of titanic forces
wreaking catastrophic fates on humans and their world, with no assurance of
happy endings.

From the standpoint of modern Enlightenment civilization, these stories
are "supernatural" because they presume the suspension of the laws of nature.
Whatever their literary, historical, moral, or theological value, they are deemed
essentially fantasies, lacking any necessary relationship with what is real or actually possible. With the emergence of the modern scientific approach to acquiring
knowledge and its skepticism toward all claims not produced with its methods,
supernatural narratives, while hardly disappearing, have come under relentless
assault as products of unenlightened superstitious minds. The early modern
avant-garde of Promethean modernism spent as much effort debunking the miraculous claims of the old religiously based cosmologies as they did accumulating
knowledge with the new empirical experimental methods. Despite the vast
accomplishments of scientific-based technology, the battle between religion and
science continues unabated, withstanding many attempts to force a surrender,
negotiate a truce, or establish a division of labor.

With the growth of scientific-technological modernity, flights of the imagination, far from disappearing, have taken on luxuriant new forms in speculative imaginings of further scientific and technological change. Indeed one of
the foundational works of the new civilization, Bacon's *New Atlantis,* was not a
treatise but an elaborate utopian political science fiction. By the middle years of
the nineteenth century, as technological advances were unmistakably altering
human life in wondrous ways, increasingly elaborate speculations about the trajectory of science and technology came to be produced, as "scientific romances"
and then "science fiction" but more accurately "scientific-technological fiction."
Science fiction has enormous general cultural influence and has been crucial in
the unfolding of the Space Age. In science fiction the civilization of the machine
finds its fullest and most compelling voice.

According to all accounts, the foundational figures in modern science fiction
are Jules Verne (1828–1905) and H. G. Wells (1859–1946). They were neither
the first nor only practitioners of this genre, but they were extremely prolific,
boldly original, and widely read. First came Verne, starting with *Five Weeks in*

a Balloon (1862) and *From the Earth to the Moon* (1866) and producing some forty-seven books in his Extraordinary Voyages series.[9] Even more prolific and far-reaching in his imaginary flights was Wells, who authored more than a hundred books and was a whirlwind of activity on radio and the public speaking circuit. Millions of copies of their books were sold, and many have been made into movies. Many of their basic story lines have remained foundational to subsequent science fiction.

Both ranged widely in their spatial scope, with journeys into the skies, the ocean depths, the interior of the Earth, and then outer space. Space is thus not by any means the sole topic of their writing, but their space stories, particularly Verne's moon book and *Off on a Comet* (1877) and Wells's *War of the Worlds* (1897), were widely influential in helping to make the previously impossible seem possible. Both closely followed emerging developments in science and technology, allowing them to quickly weave cutting-edge advances into their stories. A third widely influential figure, Olaf Stapledon (1886–1950), pushed the temporal and spatial frontier of the scientific-technological imaginary to the galaxy and the evolution of humanity across billions of years in his two "histories of the future," *The First and Last Man* (1930) and *Star Maker* (1934).[10]

Verne and Wells had a thoroughly Promethean modernist view of the human prospect, often articulated in long didactic speeches by the leading characters of their stories as well as in nonfiction books and essays. Both were also keenly aware that the new powers produced by the rush of science-based technological innovation held great peril as well as great promise, particularly by making war catastrophically destructive and world tyranny possible, making them as much scientific-technological dystopians as utopians.[11] Both dealt extensively with the spatial closure of the Earth produced by the globalization of industrial civilization and its implications for world government and empire, and both saw the human movement into outer space as a logical continuation of scientific-technological development and as a response to spatial closure.[12] Verne's wildly popular *Around the World in Eighty Days* (1873) dramatically portrays the great acceleration of movement brought about by industrial technologies. Wells's *A World Set Free* (1914) anticipated the destructive potential of the new nuclear physics to make an "atomic bomb." His *The Shape of Things to Come* (1933) portrays the devastation of civilization in a great world war and the subsequent pacification of the planet by a technocratic world government, which then launches expansion into space. And in Stapledon's epochal imaginary sweep, civilizations of humans and posthumans wax and wane across geological time scales, until eventually, as the sun dies, they migrate to the stars.

From these beginnings science fiction has grown in technical sophistication, audience size, and literary ambitions. In the early years of the twentieth century specialized SF magazines emerged, mainly attracting young male readers and with minimal literary aspirations.[13] But in the middle years of the twentieth century, often called the golden age of science fiction, a dazzling constellation of luminaries, led by Isaac Asimov, Arthur C. Clarke, and Robert Heinlein, produced a cascade of extraordinary of writings. Science fiction has expanded with the emergence of major female writers, such as Ursula Le Guin.[14] SF now has its own awards, professional associations, and conferences and is widely analyzed as an important cultural phenomenon.[15] Taken in combination, these writings constitute a scientific-technological imaginary of awesome and intoxicating dimensions, decisively shaping the horizons of modern civilization's future.

Science Fiction and Space Expansionism

With its pervasive message that the future lies in space, science fiction endows its space expansionist offspring with a presumptive plausibility, legitimacy, and inevitability. While intimate, their relationship is not untroubled, having three strong links and three important differences. Overall, space expansionism is a child of SF, but the entirety of SF provides a wildly unrealistic vision of space futures.

First, scientific and technological advances have often been influenced by science fiction.[16] Scientific advances depend not just on painstaking empirical research but also on imaginative intellectual leaps. Perhaps most consequentially, the Hungarian physicist Leo Szilard credited Wells's *A World Set Free* with inspiring his conceptualization of the chain reaction, a crucial step in developing nuclear reactors and explosives.[16] Of course the influence of imaginative ideas on science is not confined to science fiction. Perhaps most notably, Konstantin Tsiolkovsky's pioneering work was influenced by Russian technomystical theories of cosmism, which held that science would eventually resurrect the dead, making space colonies necessary to house everyone.[17]

Science fiction depends on scientific and technological knowledge, and it changes as they advance.[18] Without science, there is no science fiction. Space fiction, stories about travels to celestial bodies, especially Luna, long predate space science fiction.[19] The ancient Greek satirist Lucian described voyages to the moon, as did Johannes Kepler in his *Somnium* (The Dream; 1634). Both are only SF precursors because they offer no plausible account for how such extraordinary ventures might actually be realized. Sometimes scientific advances effectively terminate whole lines of science fiction stories, such as journeys to vast subterranean caverns hypothesized and then rejected by scientists.

Fictional portrayals of Mars and Venus have been heavily influenced by the progress of astronomical knowledge. Stimulated by hypothesized Martian canals, SF writers produced an outpouring of stories about intelligent Martians, extending from Wells's turn-of-the-century tale of Martian invasion, through Edgar Rice Burroughs's eleven volumes about the adventures of John Carter on Mars, to Ray Bradbury's *Martian Chronicles*.[20] But when the barren realities of the Red Planet were established in the 1960s, writers shifted to tales of the human colonization of Mars, such as Kim Stanley Robinson's epic *Mars Trilogy*, which chronicles centuries of struggle to transform Mars into a wet verdant world and achieve independence from Earth. When Venus was found to have a heavy atmosphere, SF writers conjured dense jungles, wide oceans, and wondrous animals. But when the hellish realities of Venus were discovered, visions of Venusian swamps disappeared. Most recently tales of heroic diversions of asteroids have flourished as science has recognized this threat.

Science fiction has profoundly influenced Space Age developments and expansionist thought. Pretty much everything space expansionists propose was first imagined in science fiction, and the pioneers of the Space Age attest that they got the space bug from science fiction they read in their youth. The rocket scientists Tsiolkovsky, Oberth, and Goddard attributed their fascination with space travel to science fiction, particularly the works of Verne and Wells, as did von Braun, many cosmonauts and astronauts, and e-commerce New Space moguls. Some leading space scientists and engineers are also contributors to science fiction. Clarke, who conceived of using geosynchronous satellites as radio relay stations, was also a leading SF writer. Sagan, drawn to astronomy by reading science fiction, was a planetary scientist, science popularizer, space advocate, and science fiction writer.

Despite these intimate mutual influences, science fiction and space expansionism differ in three important ways. First, the bounds of their imaginaries are different. Both envision radically new technological capabilities, but space futurism and expansionism limit themselves to technological possibilities consistent with scientific possibility. In contrast, many science fiction works are quite indifferent, sometimes brazenly, to scientific possibility. SF routinely employs fictional science rather than imaginative projections of future science-based technology. In response, some distinguish "hard science fiction," limited to non-fictional scientific foundations, from "soft science fiction" and "fantasy," where magical events transpire.[21] But this distinction depends on understandings of the laws of nature, understandings which have shifted and may shift again in the future.

While drawing sharp lines in all areas is difficult, defenders of hard science fiction insist on two key exclusions: faster-than-light travel and time travel.[22] Traveling interstellar distances quickly, and into the past and future, has obvious appeal for writers by vastly increasing their canvas for action. Among the canonical works depending on faster-than-light travel are Asimov's *Foundation*

series, *Star Trek,* and *Star Wars.* Time travel is also widely employed, in works
from Wells's *Time Machine* (1895) to James Cameron's *Terminator* films. The
fact that such works cloak their scientific fantasy with scientific-sounding
terms like "warp drive" gives them a patina of credibility, but they are actually only stylistically distinct from the medieval magic of Harry Potter and
Tolkien's *Hobbit.* These distinctions are, however, importantly beside the point
because SF aims to entertain and stimulate the imagination rather than provide remedial science education. But it is a sobering commentary on the trajectory of Enlightenment modernity that vast numbers of people today have
mental universes populated with essentially magical beings not fundamentally
different from the angels and demons filling the collective imaginations of pre-
Enlightened cultures. Aliens now occupy the heavenly spaces once occupied
by gods and angels.

A second important difference between space science fiction and space futurism is their intent. The primary purpose of SF is to tell entertaining and
edifying stories and provide social commentary. The stories are almost about
always a small set of humans who grapple with crises, doubts, and fears while
involved in some adventurous or perilous journey. Many SF stories are thinly
disguised commentaries on contemporary society transposed into distant places
and times. As such, they are heroic adventure stories, descendants of Homer's
Odyssey and Swift's *Gulliver's Travels,* with lots of esoteric machines and exotic
locales. Given these aims, violations of scientific and technological plausibility
are a routine result of taking literary license, distinguishing all fiction from history and science.

The third important difference, seldom noted but pointing toward the main
argument here, is the relative balance of positive and negative futures. Science
fiction abounds in future worlds and situations where things have gone seriously
awry.[23] Aliens invade, asteroids menace, and robots revolt. Science fiction does
not provide many utopian technological futures, probably because they are poor
settings for the drama and heroics that enliven stories. While utopian science
fiction was widely prevalent before World War I, it has since been almost completely eclipsed by dystopian stories.[24]

In contrast, space advocates rarely discuss dark futures and downside
possibilities. Moving and mining asteroids are advocated, but rarely explored are
the possibilities that such orbital diversions might cause, whether unintentionally or purposefully, bombardments of the Earth. Space colonies are portrayed
as utopias of diversity, accountability, and abundance, with little thought given
to the possibilities for tyranny and grim living. Space expansionists rarely consider the consequences of their plans if people exhibit the predatory and bestial
behaviors abundantly manifest across Terran history.

Technological Futurism and Forecasting

Space expansionism is clearly a type of technological futurism and rests squarely on technological forecasts about possible future technologies and technology assessments about their potential consequences. Technological futurism is broad-gauge thinking about the overall trajectory of technology; technological forecasting analyzes the developmental paths of particular technologies; technological assessment attempts to anticipate the multiple consequences of their deployment. Because these ways of thinking are at the heart of space expansionism, it will be useful to explore briefly their character and limitations.

Efforts to peer ahead to discern the shape of things to come, always valued, have become increasingly vital as technological change accelerates. Wells's *Anticipations* (1901), a landmark effort at technological prognostication, helped stimulate systematic futurism and futurology.[25] By the middle years of the twentieth century futurology was flourishing, with numerous institutes, journals, and conferences aimed at mass audiences as well as corporate and government patrons.[26] Leading futurists, most notably Herman Kahn, Buckminster Fuller, and Marshall McLuhan, were prominent public intellectuals who had something to say about virtually every topic.[27] Clarke, known as the "prophet of outer space," played this role for space.

Futurist prophets produce a dazzling stream of arresting images, oracular pronouncements, and dire warnings. Like their space expansionist cousins, they offer sweeping macrohistorical narratives in which technological change and rising interdependence define the future. Particularly fertile was the imagination of Fuller, in works such as *Operating Manual for Spaceship Earth* (1969).[28] But, as their critics observed, their skills as publicists far outstripped the epistemological basis for their anticipations. In many ways ambitious general futurism is a popular pseudo-science, the astrology of scientific-technological society. More charitably and modestly, futurism can be seen as efforts to consider alternative scenarios or perhaps to generate new myths and master narratives for planetary humanity.[29] And because the unanticipated cannot be averted, human survival increasingly hinges on progressively improving disciplined and systematic futurist evaluations of technological imaginaries and anticipations.

Technological forecasting is a more circumscribed and tractable enterprise. Claims about the trajectory of possible developments are integral to technological modernity. Accurate forecasts of technological trends assume immense practical importance as the scope of technological choices expands, and such analyses are now routinely conducted by a wide range of organizations. Many technological forecasts have been made, and some have been startlingly accurate. Among the more famous recent successful prognostications is the forecast, known as "Moore's Law," made by the electrical engineer Gordon Moore in 1965, that the number of transistors crammed into a microcircuit would double every eighteen months, a trend that has held for five decades.[30] But for every astounding success there are many more glaringly inaccurate forecasts, many made by leading experts.[31]

The simplest technological forecast is to extrapolate current trends into the future, which is what Moore did. This is also what space expansionists in the 1960s did in forecasting colonies on the moons of the outer planets within fifty years. The problem with straightforward extrapolation is that nothing expands indefinitely, and the nearly universal pattern of change is marked by slow initial takeoff, rapid growth, and then leveling off, represented graphically as the S curve. The big puzzle is ascertaining how long and how far the middle growth stage can continue, which varies greatly from one technology to another.

Civil aviation is a prominent example of an unanticipated stall in the pace of technological development. Between the first powered flight in 1903 and about 1970, with the introduction of the wide-bodied, intercontinental jet, the Boeing 747, the curve of technological development in aeronautics was extremely steep. It was widely anticipated that rapid advances would continue, but instead growth has largely leveled off, with only marginal improvements (in fuel efficiency, avionics, and lighter materials). The anticipated next major step, the supersonic transport (SST), would go faster than the speed of sound, halving transcontinental flight times. But its widespread use floundered on the loud sonic boom from flying at such speeds along its flight path.[32]

The Impossible, the Possible, and the Feasible

Space advocates believe the expansion of humanity into the cosmos is profoundly desirable and expect it will become much more feasible. How plausible is this expectation? In answering this question we must first consider general patterns and then the prospects for technologies necessary for space expansion. Between what is currently possible and what is excluded by physical law (such as time and faster-than-light travel), there is a vast domain of nonexistent but potentially possible technologies, and it is on these possibilities that expansionists pin their hopes (see Figure 4.1).[33]

But the fact that a venture does not violate fundamental laws of nature does not ensure its economic feasibility. And there are two very different standards of economic feasibility: whether those undertaking a project can afford it, and whether a venture can generate economic benefits exceeding its costs. Almost all space activities—military, civilian manned, and science—have been pursued without any expectation of generating direct economic benefits exceeding their

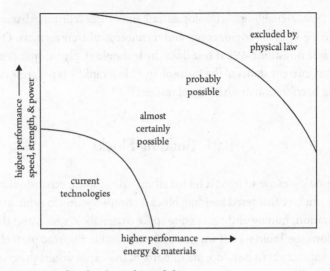

Figure 4.1 Horizons of Technological Possibility

costs because they are deemed to provide the valuable noneconomic benefits of national security, prestige, and scientific knowledge. Only communication, remote sensing, and launch services directly generate revenue. The feasibility of military technologies requires overcoming another major, and often changing, hurtle—the ability to operate successfully in the face of countermeasures produced by adversaries.

Thus arises the great puzzle of economic feasibility perpetually plaguing advocates of large-scale space expansion: what space activity can generate enough net revenue to justify large expenditures? A further hurdle is the time frame for revenue calculations. Even more daunting, a viable space settlement, argues the space advocate Scott Pace, must largely "live off the land" and generate some commercially valuable product. Until both conditions are met, the human presence in space will be confined to outposts like Antarctic science bases or off-shore oil rigs.[34] In wartime, societies accomplish Herculean resource mobilizations, but space has yet to be such a high priority. Very large space projects with long time horizons and many uncertainties will almost surely require major government support, despite the libertarian mania recently gripping space enthusiasts.[35] Thus China, with its powerful central government and tradition of mega-engineering, may be best suited to push ahead, as memorably envisioned in Liu Cixin's novel *The Three-Body Problem*. Faced with these constraints, space advocates propagandize on behalf of the priceless value of space activities and seek technological advances to lower costs.

The feasibility prospects for ambitious space expansion hinge upon the long list of technologies that are possible in principle but not yet demonstrated in practice. Space-enabling technologies fall into three clusters: basic building blocks, living systems engineering, and technological transformers. Of each we ask the same questions: What role does the technology play in space expansion? What is the current status of the technology? How rapidly is progress occurring? And what barriers constrain its development?

Basic Building Blocks

Four technologies are so important for all ambitious space expansionist schemes that they can be considered building blocks: cheaper access to orbit, asteroid orbital alteration, mining and processing space materials in space, and thermonuclear fusion (see Table 4.1). If any one of these possible-in-principle technologies remains impractical to develop, major parts of the expansionist program will be technologically infeasible.

Table 4.1 **Basic Building Block Technologies**

	Space Role	Current Effort	Rate of Progress	Main Barriers
Low-Cost Access to Orbit	Makes everything else more possible	Enormous	Incremental	Need much better materials or new approach
Mining, Processing, and Construction	Essential for large-scale EOS and SOS space development	Negligible (purely conceptual; no testing)	Rapid conceptual	Probably only absence of investment
Asteroidal Orbit Alteration (AOA)	Essential for planetary defense and resource extraction	Negligible (purely conceptual; no testing)	Rapid conceptual	Probably only absence of investment
Controlled Fusion	Provides large quantities of energy for deep space activities	Enormous	Incremental	Possibly intractable design trade-offs

Propulsion technology to get to space, and around in space, is the most basic technology for space expansion. The use of rockets to propel objects is now routine, but costs remain high, around ten thousand dollars per pound. Lowering costs by several orders of magnitude is widely seen as vital to more ambitious space activities.[36] Current rockets are essentially lineal descendants of the first rockets, because used only once, and propelled by burning liquid chemicals, with the combination of cryogenically cooled liquid hydrogen and oxygen being the most efficient. As many note, commercial aviation would also be prohibitively expensive if airplanes were not reused repeatedly. But this comparison, while capturing a basic difference between contemporary aeronautics and astronautics, fails to acknowledge that space launchers must accelerate to velocities some thirty-four times faster than airliners and withstand extreme reentry temperatures.

Much effort has gone to developing reusable spaceships, but the results have been disappointing. The most ambitious effort, the American space shuttle program, flew 133 successful flights between 1981 and 2011, but design flaws caused the destruction of two of the five orbiters. It was projected to reduce orbital access costs by an order of magnitude but was never able to achieve any cost reductions because of the extensive maintenance required to ready the shuttles for flight. Recent efforts by Space X and other corporations to develop reusable rockets have rekindled hopes for significant cost reductions, but it remains uncertain how many flights, with what levels of reliability, and with what refurbishment costs these new systems can provide. Achieving multiple-orders-of-magnitude cost reductions probably depends upon developing substantially lighter and stronger materials.[37]

A truly wild-card transport possibility, the "space elevator," could, if feasible, probably greatly lower costs, thus enabling many large-scale space activities.[38] The space elevator is simple in its basic outline, a cable stretching roughly sixty-two thousand miles between the Earth's surface and a large orbiting counterweight. Once built, substantial payloads could be hoisted up the cable, like elevators in skyscrapers, at costs of pennies per pound. A fundamental barrier to construction is that the cable must be nearly two-hundred times as strong as steel. Amazingly, researchers have discovered forms of carbon possessing such extraordinary strengths, but it remains unknown whether strands of this material can be expanded to lengths of thousands of miles. A space elevator would also have to be configured to withstand lightning strikes and severe storms and would catastrophically fail if the cable broke anywhere along its enormous length. However, should such wonders be possible, they might be constructed throughout the solar system.

For propelling objects through space on any significant scale, chemical rockets are inadequate, but a wide array of technological alternatives promise vastly greater efficiencies: ion drives, solar sails, lasers, and even nuclear explosives. For long-duration robotic space probes, nuclear energy is already widely used, and preliminary tests of other novel propulsion technologies have been conducted. Fusion reactors and propulsion are also extremely attractive in principle. Development of these alternatives is likely to remain rudimentary until demand for their services expands considerably, but it is reasonable to anticipate that one or several of these dark horse candidates for solar system transportation at reasonable costs will eventually be available.

The second building-block technology, altering asteroid orbits, is vital for preventing collisions with Earth and acquiring materials for building large-scale infrastructures. This has been often studied but never attempted, reflecting low priorities, not intrinsic difficulty. There is wide agreement that altering asteroid orbits faces no really fundamental technological feasibility problems. The first study, by a group of MIT engineering students in 1968, analyzed the use of hydrogen bombs launched by multiple Saturn V Apollo Program rockets to alter the orbital path of Icarus, a twenty-two-mile-long NEO.[39] The energy required for deflection varies with their mass and the point in their orbits when energy is applied, with the easiest at the apogee, the point when they are furthest from the object they are orbiting.

Deflection technology has received steadily more attention from researchers as the history of asteroidal collisions has come to light. The assumption that nuclear explosions are most suitable has waned with the realization that their brute force could fragment a body. Researchers have proposed a variety of nonnuclear techniques, all of which work slowly, increasing the importance of extended warning times.[40] One idea, the "gravity tractor," envisions positioning a spacecraft near the asteroid and then burning its engines slowly over an extended period of time, which would slowly pull both the asteroid and the spacecraft in a desired direction. Many asteroids are wildly spinning and tumbling and would need to be stabilized before gradual deflection techniques could be used. While many techniques appear viable in principle, actually attempting them could encounter unexpected problems and require lengthy trials and errors.

Third, technologies to process materials from the moon and asteroids into structures are vital for space expansion. Initial explorations have revealed a wide array of metals and resources, albeit in very different forms and concentrations than in the terrestrial lithosphere.[41] Unlike ores found on Earth, the metals in metallic asteroids are not combined in various oxide and salt compounds, making their conversion into useful objects significantly easier. The organic materials in carbonaceous asteroids, and the water, carbon dioxide, methane, and ammonia in comets, could provide the raw materials necessary to support life.[42]

While copious quantities of raw materials are available, no space material has yet been processed in space. Terrestrial industrial processes for mining and fabricating materials are mature technologies, providing the basis for processing in space. But differences in the raw materials themselves and the need to operate in a vacuum and in nearly weightless conditions are likely to limit the direct transfer of established terrestrial material processes. Learning to do in space what is routinely done on Earth will require investment in very basic material-processing technologies, requiring unknown amounts of effort, time, and money to accomplish. But because there are no winds or rain in the vacuum of space, structures might be made of much lighter and thinner materials, such as gossamer-thin reflective films that would quickly disintegrate in a turbulent atmosphere. And because objects are weightless they can be vastly larger than on Earth, perhaps many miles in size. But how such materials will weather harsh radiation and periodic solar storms and how long they will last are now unknowable but pivotal to their economic prospects.

A fourth building-block technology vital for ambitious space expansion is thermonuclear fusion as a source of energy. Because the energy of the stars and hydrogen bombs comes from fusion, there is absolutely no doubt as to its possibility in principle. Minuscule portions of the sun's outpouring of energy are routinely harvested in space by photovoltaic cells, which convert sunlight directly into electricity and are composed of the abundant element silicon. But the sun's luminous energies wane greatly in the outer solar system, and any large-scale space activity there will probably depend on some form of nuclear energy. Robotic probes sent to these distant and frigid realms are currently powered by the decay of plutonium, an artificial element created by nuclear alchemy from uranium. But this technology cannot be plausibly scaled up because the supply of uranium is relatively limited. This leaves fusion as the indispensable energy technology for large-scale deep-space ventures and interstellar voyages. Fusion is also highly attractive for generating energy on Earth, as it could produce vast quantities of energy from isotopes of hydrogen found in the water of the oceans.

The attractions of fusion have been recognized since the 1950s, and large amounts of money have been spent to develop fusion as a viable source of energy. A succession of extremely expensive experimental machines, typically costing several billion dollars apiece, have been built in several industrial countries, and their capabilities have steadily increased. But the pace of progress has remained frustratingly slow; fusion has come to be known as the energy technology that is always thirty years in the future. Re-creating the conditions present at the center of the sun and in hydrogen bombs for an extended period of time and then drawing energy from fusion reactions requires dauntingly difficult engineering. At temperatures of millions of degrees, hydrogen takes the form of plasma, which vaporizes anything it touches and is difficult to contain. Furthermore, fusion reactions emit immense quantities of subatomic particles, which make metal containment vessels very radioactive and brittle. Even assuming these difficult hurtles can be surmounted, it is likely to be many decades before this technology is ready for employment, and building such behemoth engines in space will pose further challenges.

New Earths?

The space environment, being extremely inhospitable to complex forms of life, poses formidable obstacles to human space activity and settlement. Microgravity is inimical to human health. Whether normal human procreation, egg fertilization, and fetal and child development are possible in reduced gravity environments, as found on Mars and Luna, remains completely unknown. Beyond the biomedical and reproductive hurdles are ecological ones. Three technologies for manipulating the environments of living organisms are vital for space expansion (see Table 4.2): artificial ecosystems to sustain human life in spaceships and colonies; geo-engineering space technologies to manipulate the geophysical features of the Earth itself; and, even more speculatively, terraforming, altering other planets to support human life. Building artificial ecosystems in contained spaces, manipulating the Earth's geophysics and biosphere, and reconfiguring other planets into Earth-like places differ greatly in their scale but are fundamentally similar in envisioning the manipulation and control of ecological and geophysical systems.

Are artificial contained ecosystems in a spaceship or colony feasible? Human life is currently maintained in spaceships by purely mechanical means. Air and water come from tanks and are recycled with industrial chemical processes. Food is brought from Earth and wastes are dumped into space. Breathable air, potable water, and edible food on Earth are produced by an extraordinarily complex and extended web of organisms several billion years old. Successful space colonization depends on the creation of artificial biospheres, miniature partial Earths. Despite the obvious importance of such ecological technologies, almost all biospace research is human biomedical studies of weightlessness and radiation effects.

There has been only one serious attempt to create a second ecosystem on this planet, the Biosphere 2 project in Arizona. Contained in a three-acre enclosed glass structure with six biomes (rainforest, ocean with coral reef, savannah grasslands, mangrove wetland, fog desert, and intensive agriculture), Biosphere 2 cost about 150 million dollars, contributed by a farsighted philanthropist. Its operation depended on an underground system of pumps, turbines, and ventilators, powered by electricity from the grid. During the two extended experiments, oxygen levels fell to dangerous levels, food supplies ran low, many species of plants and animals died, and the insect population exploded. The group operating the

Table 4.2 **Living Systems Macro-Engineering**

	Space Role	Current Effort	Rate of Progress	Main Barriers
Fully Enclosed Ecosystems	Essential for space colonization	Negligible	Negligible	Low investment; possibly inherently unpredictable
Geo-Engineering	Essential for space-based manipulation of solar insolation and planetary albedo to regulate global climate	Modest but growing (mainly for non-space applications)	Incremental (conceptual)	Low investment; environmental and political opposition; limited test possibilities; possibly inherently unpredictable
Terraforming	Essential for alteration of other planets for habitability of Earth-originated life forms	Negligible (purely conceptual)	Incremental (conceptual)	Low investment; limited test possibilities; possibly inherently unpredictable

facility developed cult-like tendencies, and the "biospherians" fell into conflict among themselves.[43] The facility was transferred to Columbia University and then the University of Arizona, but then closed for financial reasons. Biosphere 2 is now an educational and tourist site.

First tries are rarely successful; much more research—curiously not a priority for space expansionists—will be needed to determine the prospects for completely contained ecosystems. A combination of hydroponic gardening for growing food crops and the production of synthetic meats by bioengineered microorganisms may enable spaceships and colonies to achieve food independence without a diverse and complex ecosystem. But the prospects for even greatly simplified ecosystems are clouded by the difficulties of controlling unwanted bacterial and fungal microorganisms.[44] These life forms make up the bulk of the Earth's biomass, evolve rapidly, and are extremely difficult to control, as evidenced by the inability of scientists to completely sterilize space probes to achieve "planetary protection."[45]

Second is "geo-engineering," the recent term for schemes to manipulate the geophysical parameters of the Earth. Space expansionists have long proposed the construction of large orbital infrastructures to alter terrestrial environments, such as lengthening the growing season in northern climates, providing light at night, and preventing ice ages. But with the rapid emergence of anthropogenic climate change, geo-engineers are proposing measures to manipulate the geophysics of the planet to reduce or compensate for the buildup of atmospheric greenhouse gases. One class of geo-engineering schemes, Solar Radiation Management (SRM), attempts to alter the albedo, or reflectivity, of the Earth; one way this might be done is by placing particles or shades in orbit around the planet to deflect sunlight. Building "sunshades" of sufficient size to affect the planet's overall solar radiation budget would be an immense undertaking but in principle is quite feasible.[46] The fundamental puzzle for such infrastructural projects is whether they would alter the atmospheric and ocean circulation systems in predictable and desirable ways.

Finally, and even more speculatively, is terraforming, the alteration of other planets to make them more Earthlike and hospitable for human colonization.[47] If feasible, terraforming a planet would require vast quantities of energy and centuries or millennia to accomplish. Even assuming that engineering capabilities emerge for such planet-scale geophysical manipulations, their ability to produce biospheres is doubtful due to the unpredictability of organisms and ecosystems and their resistance to control.

Space colonization will be dependent on extremely high-competence ecological management, far beyond what is now possible. For existential risk reduction, such management would have to persist perpetually. Underlying all these speculative ecological technologies is the assumption that living systems can be manipulated and engineered in ways comparable to nonliving materials. While early ecological science expected to discover regularities analogous to those found in nonliving matter, the recent realization that ecosystems exhibit chaotic patterns and great complexity means ecological science cannot provide sound foundations for engineered manipulations, thus severely limiting the feasibility of projects dependent on the control of systems of living organisms.

Three Technological Transformers

A final trio of capabilities are not uniquely space technologies but have the potential to radically improve the feasibility of many ambitious space projects as well as to drastically alter terrestrial conditions: genetic engineering, nanotechnology, and robotics and artificial intelligence (see Table 4.3) These technologies have in common that they are based on the manipulation of matter at very small scales; they are often grouped together as "GNR technologies." Like space technology, they have a wide range of military as well as civil applications, and each potentially poses catastrophic and existential threats. As the advance of space technology has stalled since its spurt in the mid-twentieth century, GNR technologies have surged to the vanguard of technological progress and have come to occupy the central place once held by space expansion in Promethean technological imaginaries, while at the same promising to enable an off-planet trajectory.

These technologies are vastly complicated, but examining their main contours is vital for thinking seriously about the feasibility and consequences of ambitious space expansion. They are evolving very rapidly, and space expansionists routinely tout them as increasing the feasibility of large-scale space activities. Like space, these three technologies have been subject to many works of science fiction, abounding in extremely dystopian scenarios, and are being promoted aggressively by enthusiasts for their broadly transformative potentials.

But there is a fundamental difference between space and these three technologies that speaks directly to my critique of space expansionism. As noted earlier, a growing body of thought aims to restrain the development of

Table 4.3 **Radical Technology Transformers**

	Space Role	Current Effort	Rate of Progress	Main Barriers
Artificial Intelligence(AI) and Robotics	Enable mining, processing, construction, and design	Enormous (mainly for Terrestrial applications)	Very rapid	Software design
Genetic Engineering	Enable new life forms for extraterrestrial environments and human species change	Enormous (for Terrestrial applications)	Very rapid	Ethical, political, and environmental
Nanotechnology/ Molecular Manufacturing	Provide vastly stronger and lighter materials	Enormous (for Terrestrial applications)	Very rapid	Some environmental restraints

bioengineering, nanotechnology, and artificial intelligence in order to avoid their catastrophic potentials, but space thinkers have resolutely avoided considering catastrophic risks or restraining space technologies. But if these three technologies, with their broad range of very negative outcomes, are also components of the space expansionist program, then it is implausible to think that space expansion can be exempt from their possible downsides.

First is genetic engineering. While the ability of science to predict and control systems of organisms has proven elusive, the ability to manipulate the macromolecular codes governing cells has rapidly improved. Vast corporate and governmental resources are currently being devoted to genetic engineering in anticipation of valuable medical, agricultural, energy, and bioweapon applications. The genetic codes of small organisms are now routinely altered to produce drugs; gene therapies for diseases are emerging; and wholesale manipulations of human genes may soon be possible.[48] Because humans are so unsuited to extraterrestrial environments, biotechnology might be used for rapid and directed species change, making this technology a powerful enabler of ambitious space expansion.

Visions of improving humanity by eugenics are as old as Plato's *Republic*, and biotechnology has been a recurrent topic of science fiction, with scenarios from the utopian to the catastrophic.[49] Like space expansion, far-reaching genetic reconfigurations of humans to create a transhuman future is supported, often zealously, by an international advocacy movement. Transhumanists claim emerging technologies will eliminate disease, scarcity, and even death, and expect radically improved humanity will conduct large-scale space expansion.[50] These technologies raise far-reaching ethical and religious questions, and opposition from bioconservatives has already emerged. Whatever their consequences, it seems likely that capabilities to reconfigure the biology of the human species are becoming feasible, even if they do not produce the sweepingly positive effects their advocates anticipate.

A second transformative technology, nanotechnology, is also rapidly advancing and deeply implicated in the technological feasibility of space expansion. *Nano*, the Greek word for "very small," appears in the metric system as the label for a billionth of a meter. In a broad sense both biotechnology and production of microelectronic devices are nanotechnologies because they involve the precise manipulation of matter at extremely small scales. With techniques of molecular manufacturing, also known as atomically precise manufacturing, the atoms in materials are precisely aligned, giving them extraordinary properties. Advocates anticipate nanomachines, which might also endlessly replicate themselves. As with space expansion and biotechnology, nanotechnology has its strong boosters, who claim it will utterly transform and improve the trajectory of humanity.[51] Nanomachines might seek out pathogens and cancer cells and repair damaged cells, making possible the eradication of disease and vast longevity. Nanomachines dispersed in nature might perform many tasks, from concentrating metals to eliminating pollutants. Nanotechnology might help produce the high-performance materials needed to lower the costs of access to space and perhaps make space elevators feasible.[52] Nanoreplicators might be dispersed on celestial bodies to extract resources and help make terraforming feasible.

The third rapidly advancing set of technologies with transformative potentials for space are computers. The first electronic reprogrammable digital computer, with a processing capability of seventy-six kilobytes (about what an icon on a contemporary personal computer uses), went online in 1953.[53] It was composed of thousands of fragile vacuum tubes, filled an entire building, and cost millions of dollars.[54]

It was funded by the U.S. government, primarily to make calculations for designing hydrogen bombs, and even its brilliant main inventor, the mathematician John von Neumann, initially had difficulty conceiving other uses for it.[55] As the ability to shrink transistors has steadily improved, along the path of Moore's Law, powerful computational devices permeate ever more activities. Early integrated circuits were developed for military and space purposes and then found ever broadening civilian markets. This new, cheap, and durable computational machinery has had revolutionary implications for the conduct of space activities. Cybernetics also has been a recurrent theme of science fiction, which is replete with very dystopian scenarios.

Artificial intelligence (AI) is widely viewed as the ultimate objective of advancing computer technology. In a broad sense AI is already here, as computers routinely surpass the abilities of humans to do many specialized tasks, particularly numerical calculations. But these machine intelligences are currently quite narrow in the tasks they perform, and none yet approaches the overall capacities of the human brain in performing important tasks, most notably pattern recognition, control of complex movement, and situational judgment. This long-sought but stubbornly elusive form of intelligence is known as artificial general intelligence. Researchers are, however, making steady steps in this direction. Powerful computers are now widely used in virtually every aspect of space activities, and computing capability is rapidly improving and could become vastly more capable if quantum effects can be effectively harnessed. An IBM computer named Watson defeated the world champion player of the television quiz show *Jeopardy!* with the knowledge it had acquired from "reading" some four million books.[56] In 2018 a computer named Alphazero was given the rules of the ancient and complex strategy game Go; after playing itself millions of times, it defeated the world champion human Go player, and also invented completely novel strategies.[57]

The ultimate computer would have artificial superintelligence (ASI), vastly surpassing the mental capabilities of humans, with an IQ ranging into the thousands. Such a machine could have effectively unlimited memory capacity, process the data from billions of sensors, and copy and reprogram itself. Like existing computers, it would think about a million times faster than human brains and could be enlarged to the size of a small planet before reaching limits set by its internal communication speeds. Most experts expect ASI to emerge within this century. In the words of the computer scientist Irving Goode, an ASI would be humanity's "final invention" because it would be able to quickly solve all scientific and engineering problems capable of being solved. ASI might help solve many other potentially catastrophic threats, making it an all-purpose deus ex machina. Vast AI research efforts are under way, largely in secret, by military and intelligence agencies and corporations.[58] Advocates believe advanced AI could enable the full technological utopia of complete abundance and immortality anticipated by Bacon; some foresee uploading human brain patterns into machines, making for indefinite life spans. Such machines, advocates proclaim, would mark a major step in the evolution of life, from frail carbon-based forms into vastly more robust and capable silicon-based ones. Such entities, according to both cyber prophets and space advocates, would rapidly expand into space and fully colonize the universe.

Overall, further advances in these three transformative technologies appear very likely and are very likely to make space expansion considerably more feasible. It seems reasonable to expect that over the course of this century options for conducting space projects will expand considerably, presenting humanity for the first time with real choices about whether and how to expand beyond this planet.

However, technological advance may not unambiguously favor space expansion. Technological progress poses a *feasibility-necessity paradox*: as new technologies make space expansion more feasible, they may also make it less necessary. Most space-enabling technologies are moving rapidly forward to meet terrestrial needs, not to enable space expansion. To the extent space expansion is necessary to solve terrestrial problems, and to the extent technological innovations provide new terrestrial solutions, advances may undercut the need for space expansion as rapidly as they improve its feasibility.[59] For example, nanotechnological advances dramatically lowering the cost of accessing Earth orbit may also undercut the need to obtain resources from asteroids. Robotics could enable cheap fabrication of orbital infrastructures but could also reduce the need for space megastructures by facilitating terrestrial wealth generation.

Technological Assessment, Misfires, and Syndromes

Successful forecasting illuminates which technologies will be possible. But far more important for practical choices is the ability to foresee the consequences of technologies. The many claims of space expansionists about the prospective consequences of space projects are technology assessments, even if rarely so called. Thinking about the consequences of technologies has become much more developed since the middle years of the twentieth century.[60] The negative externalities of industrial society are so pervasive and significant, according to the sociologist Ulrich Beck, as to define late modernity as "the risk society."[61] Extensive study of what can go wrong with technologies has improved understanding of how technological misfires occur and syndromes of technological choice and governance. Taken as a whole, these insights powerfully subvert the assumptions of Promethean Technophiles and Technological Optimists, while supporting Soterian approaches. In identifying misfires and syndromes, technology critics justify decelerated decision-making and regulatory restraints and identify technologies best completely avoided. What fundamentally separates these approaches from the Prometheans and Optimists are not judgments about which technologies are possible, but rather doubts about the capacity of humans to successfully govern some technologies in ways that limit their downsides.

During the middle years of the twentieth century, "technology assessment" (TA) emerged as the label for techniques for analyzing the consequences of new technologies, as well as for a Soterian approach to technological choice, occupying a middle ground between the hard-core full-speed-ahead Prometheans and neo-Luddite technology critics and radical environmentalists.[62] Soterian technology assessors eschew talk of Technology-in-General as misleading because the real horizon of choice always involves myriad specific technologies. TA is ameliorative, seeking better informed social choices among technological alternatives by identifying unintended second-order consequences stemming from their deployments. TA takes heavy criticism from both strong supporters and radical opponents of technological modernism. The Prometheans fear too much scrutiny becomes "technology harassment," as Kahn famously put it. TA would retard useful technologies by empowering stakeholders threatened by change, but could not foresee or mobilize beneficiaries. Radical technology critics insist impact assessments are inherently incapable of foreseeing many negative effects of new technologies, particularly on complex ecosystems, thus encouraging unwarranted complacency.

Over the half-century since its emergence, TA has been greatly underutilized. Many major technological choices are made in secret by corporations and militaries without adequate analysis of full consequences. Institutionalizing assessment has proven difficult, as evidenced by the fate of the US Congress's Office of Technology Assessment, which operated between 1974 and 1995, when the Republican Party took control of Congress and their leader, Newt Gingrich (a strong space expansionist), engineered its abolition.[63] A parallel effort, requiring Environmental Impact Statements (EIS) analyzing the effects of major projects, has proven more lasting. This assessment requirement scored some very important successes, perhaps most notably the EIS processes for the SST and space shuttle, which led atmospheric scientists to investigate the effects of chlorine-based chemicals on the stratosphere and to discover that the widely used industrial chemicals chlorofluorocarbons (CFCs) depleted the stratospheric ozone layer, which shields terrestrial life from ultraviolet solar radiation. This discovery triggered a remarkably rapid international agreement to phase out CFCs, a milestone in environmental policy.[64]

Analysts of technology have identified at least four general ways in which the governance of technology can go seriously awry. The first root of technological misfires is epistemological. With the growing spatial and temporal scope of the consequences of powerful new technologies, impact assessment becomes simultaneously more necessary and more difficult. Seeing the future, always difficult, becomes much more so when technologies are novel. Furthermore the consequences of novel powerful technologies are difficult to accurately anticipate because they are so complex.[65] For example, to anticipate the consequences of the introduction of a new chemical in an ecosystem, a vast number of organisms, each very complex, and their even more complicated interactions must be understood, a dauntingly difficult task.[66] The list of failed anticipations of the effects of new technologies is long. Most recently the widely touted expectations that the internet would realize libertarian political visions has been dashed by the rise of predatory cyber-monopolies and authoritarian state surveillance. As a practical matter, actual deployment of technologies is often necessary to discern effects, which can sometimes be severely negative and difficult to reverse.[67]

A second way in which disastrous technological misfires can occur is rooted in the material character of complex artifacts and their interface with human users and operators. The sociologist Charles Perrow has demonstrated that technical systems are inherently prone to accidents when their components must be "tightly coupled" to one another and when their interactions are complex; nuclear power plants, nuclear weapons systems, and space missions are prominent examples.[68] Tight coupling is intensified when operations are fast, and reduced when slowed. Disasters also arise from human operator errors, which are impossible to completely eliminate, even with intensive training and monitoring systems.

A third set of problems concern Faustian bargains, in which societies assume long-term and difficult-to-carry burdens when they deploy larger-scale technologies with significant downsides. The physicist Alvin Weinberg famously suggested that committing to nuclear energy involved such a bargain: vast amounts of electricity could be produced, but preventing the disastrous effects of accidents and diversion of materials to make nuclear weapons requires that society be governed with great stability far into the future by a "guardian priesthood."[69] Societies should avoid deploying technologies with attached Faustian bargains because they will be unable to sustain their assumed obligations, thus dooming themselves to catastrophic outcomes.

Finally, there is the technocratic prospect. At least since Plato's proposal in the *Republic* to replace politics, with all its maladies, follies, and corruptions, with the rule of disinterested and virtuous experts, technocracy has been offered as a comprehensive solution to the problems of government.[70] With the coming of machine civilization and the great increase in the stakes of making correct choices about the deployment of technology, the appeal of technocracy has grown and been avidly promoted by leading Promethean modernists such as H. G. Wells.[71]

Despite the steadily rising need for technically informed decision-making, one looks in vain for historical cases in which technical experts actually govern. Experts are "on tap, not on top." Despite its apparent necessity, technocracy has remained essentially unobtainable due to the unwillingness of people to subject themselves to rule by experts with specialized knowledge. It is equally unrealistic to think that experts, being human, could govern without themselves falling prey to the interest-based and conflict-ridden politics motivating recourse to technocracy. Projects that presuppose technocracy for success are likely to be frustrated by the persistent chasm between the antipolitical aspirations of technocrats and the deep-seated political nature of human associations. Given this, any proposal that requires technocratic government to be successfully realized should be recognized as largely unrealizable, as requiring people to act in ways that it is deeply unrealistic to expect them to act. Proponents of technocracy claim that these problems can be solved with the great modernist nostrums of more information and better education. But pedagogy is at most an art and certainly not a science, and the crooked timber of humanity remains deeply resistant to straightening, particularly when exposed to the corrupting influences of great power.

Technocracy should be viewed not simply as extremely difficult to achieve but as deeply undesirable to pursue and approximate. Were such Promethean political ambitions somehow to be realized, the result is likely to be an oppressive political outcome. Although some regimes for brief periods have approximated total rule in the service of some modernist great leap forward, they stand as monuments to disastrous initiatives and large-scale oppression—and are widely and rightly viewed by the friends of freedom as monstrous abominations.[72] Once the give-and-take of pluralistic politics is replaced by the administration of things, large numbers of people almost inevitably get treated as things and disposed of accordingly.

The prospects for anticipating the full scope of a technology's consequences are dim, and complex technical systems have deep-seated proclivities to fail. It is unlikely that societies will be able to sustain the types of rule needed to employ many technologies with dangerous downsides. Eventually things inevitably will go wrong. These syndromes are especially disturbing due to the growing number of ways in which misgovernance of technology—or simple cosmic bad luck—might devastate civilization or obliterate humanity.

Catastrophic and Existential Threats

As the prodigies spawned by the Baconian project of torturing nature to reveal her secrets for the progressive elevation of the human estate have grown in their powers, modernity is increasingly haunted by the prospect that things might go horribly wrong. Humans, being fragile and vulnerable creatures and routinely subject to gruesome death from myriad sources, both natural and anthropogenic, have never had any difficulty in conjuring macro-scale scenarios of mass death. With the coming of scientific-technological civilization and the application of its products to wage more violent wars, expand the scope of imperialism, intensify exploitation, and even industrialize genocide, new large-scale calamities stemming from further technological empowerments have been easy to imagine. And with the enlarged understanding of the cataclysms unleashed by natural forces operating across deep time, the ways in which the human world might end through the blind and indifferent forces of nature have also lengthened the list of doomsday scenarios. In something of a landmark statement, Wells, in his 1902 essay on the future, spoke of numerous threats that could "utterly destroy and end the entire human race and story."[73]

The idea that terrestrial calamities necessitate celestial colonization, a basic tenet among both space advocates and big-disaster theorists, was fully articulated by Dandridge Cole and Donald Cox in 1962:

> There are many other ways [than nuclear war] in which all human life could be destroyed. Some are so-called "natural catastrophes" and others might be the result of man tinkering with the delicate "balance of nature." Among the life-destroying natural catastrophes we will only mention the possible collision of the Earth with a large

planetoid or comet, decrease or change in the quality of the sun's energy output, increase in the sun's output (including explosion of the sun), violent change in the weather, rearrangement of the Earth's crust, serious upsets in the Earth's ecology, rise of a mutant virus of unprecedented virulence, etc. Possible man-made catastrophes include many of the above list with the difference that they might be brought about through our own meddling rather than by natural processes. In addition, we must consider the possibility that some insecticide, medicine, detergent, food processing chemical, etc., will come into widespread use before it is discovered to have long delayed lethal effects. Of course, the probability of a world-wide catastrophe resulting from any one particular kind of natural or man-made event seems so low as to be of no real consequence. However, if we multiply this vanishingly small probability of catastrophe occurring, in, say, the next ten years by the number of possible occurrences, and extend the time period into the indefinite future, then the picture changes drastically. The vanishingly low probability rises to something very close to certainty. In other words, a major race-destroying catastrophe is bound to occur—if we wait long enough![74]

Anxious anticipations have triggered systematic assessment of the threat horizon, as well as measures to steer, or even stop, the accelerating juggernaut of scientific and technological advance. Thinking systematically about downside scenarios is a vital step in assuring they are not realized. As the computer engineer Bill Joy observed in his famous 2000 article in *Wired* magazine, the magnitude of growing technology dangers makes necessary the relinquishment of entire technologies and lines of scientific inquiry, particularly bio, nano, and cyber capabilities, which pose particular dangers because they self-replicate.[75] Despite the broad sweep of such assessments, visions of human expansion into space have largely escaped critical evaluation, as noted earlier. Both technological futurists and catastrophe analysts view space expansion as overwhelmingly attractive for its anticipated abilities to solve, ameliorate, or escape many looming perils. Space colonization is "probably the most promising way of preventing an existential threat, all things considered," according to the riskologist Phil Torres.[76] To take another step toward demonstrating why such optimistic views are unwarranted, it is useful to review some of the basic facts about catastrophes (events massively damaging civilization globally and killing a large fraction of humanity) and existential threats (events causing the complete extinction of humanity). Once this list of dark possibilities is brought into view, we can assess whether space expansion will escape or solve, or amplify and activate, many significant perils.

With the development of nuclear explosives, distant and abstract anticipations of technologically enabled annihilation suddenly seemed imminent. Debates over the nuclear question, intimately intertwined with the first major uses of space technology, have catalyzed the largest and most sophisticated consideration of the sources, consequences, and remedies of comprehensive human self-destruction. While human extinction from a general nuclear war had been routinely envisioned from the beginning, it was only in the 1970s that scientifically plausible scenarios for the complete extinction of humanity emerged.[77] It was on the basis of these studies that the New Yorker writer Jonathan Schell delineated in his 1982 book The Fate of the Earth the qualitatively distinct *existential* threat that technologically enabled human annihilation posed to all possible human futures, as well as the logic of assigning paramount practical priority to minimizing such threats.[78] This point, further developed by the philosopher Nick Bostrom and others, is a central insight in a new field called "existential risk studies" or "riskology," which systematically examines the larger perils to humanity.[79] These ominous analyses have gained wide, sometimes sensationalized public visibility, making secular apocalyptic thinking culturally pervasive. It is the shadow of this dark "end of history," not the universalization of liberal democracy, which has dominated the zeitgeist of the early twenty-first century.

Analysts of catastrophic and existential threats typically generate lists of perils, their entries heavily but rarely completely overlapping, and then discuss probabilities, triggers, and remedies.[80] A select composite list here contains ten entries, grouped in three clusters. This brief summation of knowledge and informed speculation focuses on the main threats and the key issues involved in thinking about adding space expansion to this list: the relative roles of natural forces and human agency, their dual-use, civil-military application, the breadth of their availability to human actors, and the problem of restraint through regulation and relinquishment.

Geophysical, Biological, and Ecological Threats

The Earth's geophysical and biological systems, and human interactions with them, generate a wide range of potential catastrophic and existential threats, usefully grouped into three types, each with distinct and complex characteristics: geophysical systems, disease, and environmental degradation (see Table 4.4).

Geophysical forces, both terrestrial and cosmic, imperil humanity.[81] Cosmocide, the destruction of humanity by cosmic events, is joined by what can be termed *terracide*, the destruction of humanity by natural terrestrial events. Supervolcanic eruptions are among the most severe global terrestrial geophysical threats. There are some 1,500 active volcanoes on Earth, and their eruptions

Table 4.4 **Geophysical, Biological, and Ecological Threats**

	Examples	*Human Causal Roles*	*Prospects for Catastrophe*	*Prospects for Extinction*	*Prospects to Avert*	*Barriers to Avoidance*
Geophysical and Astrophysical	Supervolcano, asteroid collision, and death of sun	None	Inevitable, but probably temporally distant	Inevitable, but probably temporally distant	None to total	Natural, technological, and political
Disease	Bubonic plague, influenza, and HIV/AIDS	None to indirect	Medium but growing	Possible but unlikely	Medium	Natural, technological, and political
Ecological Damage	Large and rapid climate change	Total	Very likely (climate change)	Possible but unlikely	Very high	Ignorance, interests, collective action problems, and cost

routinely produce catastrophic local and regional effects, and even severe global ones, when they propel large volumes of material into the upper atmosphere, as occurred in Indonesian eruptions in 1815 and 1883.[82] More ominously, the geological record demonstrates that some eruptions are massively larger than anything experienced in historical times. Supervolcanic eruptions can last for centuries, pouring vast quantities of dust and ash into the atmosphere, plunging the planet into a "volcanic winter," and causing mass extinctions.[83] Fortunately such mega-eruptions occur infrequently; unfortunately they are beyond human ability to prevent or ameliorate.[84] The word "disaster" itself, from the Greek for "evil star," attests to a long association between calamity and the heavens. Among the cosmic natural threats, collisions of asteroids and comets can in principle be averted. But others, such as fluctuations in the sun's output and its eventual explosive death, are likely to remain forever beyond human control.[85]

Of all the natural biological perils to human life, the most historically lethal is disease. As historians of the topic uniformly observe, diseases have killed vastly more humans than all wars. At various junctures massive epidemic and pandemic outbreaks of disease, such as the black plague in late medieval times and the Spanish flu in the wake of World War I, have killed large percentages of the populations they afflicted. Throughout history efforts to ameliorate or cure diseases have been widely sought and greatly valued but rarely very effective. With the coming of modern science, however, great advances in the medical arts have been achieved and, in terms of sheer human misery averted, are the most beneficial fruit of Enlightenment civilization.

Medical researchers once spoke optimistically about the complete eradication of disease, but a much more sobering prospect has recently emerged. Because the microbial organisms causing disease mutate extremely rapidly and share genes among themselves, they present a moving target for drugs and vaccines. Strains of disease completely resistant to all existing antibiotics are emerging, at the same time that the discovery of new antibiotics is slowing. Furthermore a succession of diseases previously unknown to medical science, such has HIV, SARS, Ebola, and Zika, have emerged and spread rapidly and widely in human populations through globalized transportation networks. And it is just a matter of time until a highly virulent strain of influenza evolves and kills tens or hundreds of millions of people. While it seems unlikely a naturally emerging disease will kill all humans, it is fairly likely that a catastrophic pandemic will occur.[86]

A third type of threat stems from human abuse of the Earth's natural environment. Starting with mastery of fire and fabrication of tools for hunting and then agriculture, premodern humans have left their harmful mark on the Earth's ecosystems. With the Industrial Revolution and the recent great spurt in human population, the magnitude of impacts on the biosphere have greatly increased. Vast quantities of novel industrial chemicals have polluted the biosphere, with effects largely unknown, and perhaps unknowable. While significant efforts have been mounted to combat these problems, and significant progress has been made in some important cases, the overall net human impact is not sustainable. Climate change caused by human activities is and will bring successively larger major disruptions, from changed weather patterns, rising sea level, ocean acidification, and mass species extinction. 'Hothouse Earth' poses both catastrophic and existential threats.[87] This unfolding and prospective anthropogenic mega-disaster potentially rivals naturally occurring major warming episodes across deep Earth history, which many scientists now believe caused several of the five great extinction events over the last half billion years. Major environmental disruptions may also trigger more general social collapse and conflict, further amplifying their impact.[88] Making any overall assessment of the full consequences of environmental problems is a vastly complex undertaking, but a sobering forecast by the eminent British scientist James Lovelock is that if humanity continues on its current path, the human population on the planet will number only in the hundreds of millions by the end of this century.[89]

Four Technogenic Threats

Currently unfolding environmental threats are essentially expanded versions of problems that humans have been producing on smaller scales across history. But four threats—from nuclear, genetic, nano, and computer technologies—are novel and are all technogenic, dependent on advances in the application of science-based technology (see Table 4.5).

The nuclear threat has been and remains the paramount actual technogenic threat to human civilization and survival. Nuclear technologies pose a significant dual-use problem because the same fissile materials and engineering skills needed to make explosive devices are also employed in civilian nuclear reactors used to generate electrical energy.[90] Fortunately the availability of these capabilities has been limited. But proliferation, the spread of nuclear weapons to additional states, and leakage, their diffusion to nonstate actors, are widely recognized as significant problems.[91] A distinguishing feature of the nuclear threat is its dependence on highly distinctive fissile material, making the complete containment and near elimination of this threat practically feasible, however politically difficult to accomplish.[92]

The nuclear threat highlights another signal feature of major technogenic threats: the likelihood of disaster heavily depends on the institutional context in which these capabilities are deployed. The nuclear threat also points to the absolutely central role of political-technological imaginaries in increasing survival

Table 4.5 **Technogenic Threats**

	Catastrophic and Existential Outcome	Current Threat Status	Dual Use?	Availability	Current Role of Military
Nuclear	War and biospheric collapse	Imminent and slowly growing	Medium to high	Low but growing	Very high
Biological	"Designer plagues"	Latent and growing	Very high	Potentially very high	Medium
Nanotech	War and runaway self-replicators	Hypothetical and growing	Very high	Potentially very high	Medium and growing
AI and Robotics	Hostile or indifferent ASI	Hypothetical and growing	Very high	Potentially very high	Medium and growing

prospects. There has never been a large-scale nuclear war, and experts offer widely differing explanations for this non-event. But surely a vital underlying factor has been the human ability to imagine, vividly and graphically, the disastrous character of such a war. Despite the fact that no one has ever experienced a major nuclear war, everyone knows that it might cause the end of the world. But the fact that you cannot avoid what you cannot imagine sets a sobering standard for the human prospect in the face of the many deep uncertainties inherent in projects of technology assessment and risk analysis for radically novel superpotent technologies.

The promising new technique of genetic engineering also poses a catastrophic threat. The use of biological weapons in war has a long history, and as microbiology advanced in the twentieth century, potent bioweapons were produced in large quantities. Fortunately modern bioweapons have never been extensively used in conflicts, and arms control measures greatly reduced stockpiles. But rapid advances in genetic engineering and synthetic biology (synbio) are creating possibilities for "designer plagues," and these technologies are rapidly becoming cheaper and more widely available.[93] Bioweapons appear well-suited to acquisition and employment by small nonstate groups for terrorist attacks.[94] Radical environmentalists seeking to save the planet by drastically reducing the human population, or apocalyptic religious movements, might find potent synthetic pathogens particularly useful for their purposes.[95]

Visions of disasters and horrors from technological manipulation of the biological fabric of humanity have an ancient lineage, dating at least to Daedalus, the master scientist of Greek mythology who is said to have fabricated fantastic monsters, both biological and mechanical.[96] Wells, in *The Island of Doctor Moreau,* provides an iconic anticipation of potent biological manipulation. Stimulated by Darwinism and advances in scientific genetics, eugenic agendas were extensively developed and partially implemented in the early twentieth century, just as space expansionism was emerging. Mingled with various spurious but reputedly scientific theories about race, eugenics was an integral component of the "master race" thinking and practice of the Third Reich, particularly its ghastly experiments on humans and its genocidal mass murder of "inferior races."[97] Of course the neo-eugenics movement of recent decades, now calling itself transhumanism, eschews *any* connection to its barbarous predecessor. Some transhumanists claim significant improvements in humanity are vital for solving catastrophic threats and enabling humans to maintain control over ever more capable machine intelligences.[98]

For critics, the grim record of early eugenic programs is but a hint of the potential horrors ahead. That the calamities of racist and Nazi eugenics emerged when the scientific foundations for human manipulation were so primitive suggests that powerful technologies based on solid scientific knowledge may spawn even more extreme outcomes. Bioconservative opponents of genetic alteration and transhumanism anticipate these technologies might create four major catastrophic outcomes: (1) *weaponization* producing arms races and superwarriors able to dominate others, (2) *diversification* leading to conflict and oppression, (3) *stratification* generating domination, and (4) *collectivization* producing extremely totalitarian societies in which individuals are drone extensions of a collective "hive mind."[99] Dark Enlightenment thinkers already espouse use of genetic technologies to create a neo-aristocracy of the elect, enhanced to rule over the inferior masses. Exploring these possibilities might require morally problematic experiments, giving advantage to the least scrupulous.[100] Control may be difficult, as DIY biohackers are already widely experimenting on themselves. And disputes over whether and how to pursue these technologies might lead to extreme conflicts or transgenic wars between humanists and superhumanists.[101] To avert these perils, some bioconservatives advocate research bans and international prohibition treaties.[102]

Nanotechnology also poses catastrophic and perhaps existential risks. One of the few studies of military nanotechnology concludes that an "all out nanotech war is probably equivalent" to a nuclear war in its short-term effects.[103] Further concern arises because nanotechnology manufacturing capability, like biotechnology, is rapidly decreasing in cost, permitting nonstate groups to make weapons. More speculatively, self-replicating autonomous nanobots released into the environment, either intentionally or unintentionally, might convert much of the planet into what the nanotech evangelist Eric Drexler memorably referred to as "grey goo."[104] Faced with these potential downsides, there are growing calls both for the careful regulation and restraint of nanotechnology as well as for its selective relinquishment.

ASI too may pose a macrothreat. While "AI could be the powerful solution to other existential risks," its downside potentials are probably as great.[105] Stories about artifacts achieving autonomy and turning on their makers have blossomed into an entire province of the imaginative empire of science fiction.[106] What would an ASI want? A widely held view among researchers is that, like all previous life forms, such an entity would minimally seek self-preservation and resource acquisition (to enhance prospects for self-preservation and realize all other goals).[107] An ASI with such goals would likely view humans as threatening and would seek to eradicate them.[108] In the view of the computer scientist Eliezer Yudkowsky, ASI is "probably the single most dangerous risk we face." A further disturbing feature of this threat is that an ASI might emerge very suddenly, in an "intelligence explosion."[109]

As the prospect of threatening ASI has appeared on the horizon, experts have begun to think about how such a machine might be kept under human direction. Can an algorithmic GO³D. (globally omniscient, omnipotent, and omnipresent device) be reliably augmented to GO⁴D. (globally omniscient, omnipotent, omnipresent, and *omnibenevolent* device)? In the most extensive treatment of the topic, Nick Bostrom considers a range of possible strategies but doubts their adequacy. Because such machines will be able to reprogram themselves, keeping them obedient to human goals may be impossible. With human annihilation as the default outcome, it may be necessary to relinquish the creation of such powerful and difficult-to-control machines.[110] But halting advanced AI will be very difficult because so much research is conducted in secret, incentives to make advances are very high, and dangerous code is hard to distinguish from benign. Restraints would need to be worldwide and would face opposition from the growing cadres of computer enthusiasts who embrace silicon-based life as the next step in evolution.[111]

Political and Wild Card Threats

To complete our brief tour of the megacalamities potentially afflicting humanity, three very different threats—totalitarian government, alien invasion, and unknown unknowns—deserve examination (see Table 4.6).

Table 4.6 **Totalitarianism, Alien Invasion, and "Monsters"**

	Definition	Catastrophic and Existential Outcome	Prospects for Occurrence	Role of Technology
Totalitarian Government	Unrestrained monopoly of coercive power in one body	Crushing of individual freedom and group identities	Low but growing	New information technology enables
Aliens	Arrival of intelligent life with advanced technology	Superior technology with xenocidal intent	Unknown but probably very low	Increases human cosmic visibility and probability of contact
"Monsters"	Unknown natural feature or process	Triggering unforeseen astrophysical or ecological collapse	Roughly proportionate to spatial scope and scientific and technological advance	Nearly total

A historically familiar catastrophic but probably not existential threat is world totalitarian government, a peril looming large in space expansionist thinking. Governments that are strongly hierarchical, concentrating capacity and authority in the hands of a small elite headed by an absolute ruler, have been viewed by most of Western political thinking since ancient Greece as an ultimate political evil. Prior to the advent of modern technologies of communication, transportation, and destruction, the creation of a globally encompassing "universal monarchy" was impossible, and even the most putatively despotic regimes faced extreme difficulties in imposing their authority at a distance. But with the coming of the industrial machine, the specter of "a Genghis Khan with a telegraph, the steamship, the railroad" appeared on the horizon of possibility, increasing the feasibility of achieving worldwide rule.[112] By the middle of the twentieth century, this dark trajectory seemed well on its way to realization in the monstrous totalitarian tyrannies of Hitler, Stalin, and Mao, who murdered tens of millions.[113] Looking ahead, Stapledon warned in 1948 of a "world-wide totalitarian ant-state, based on atomic power and the reduction of all human beings to robots."[114]

In George Orwell's dystopian *1984* the enabling technologies are surveillance and communication, and recent advances in information technologies are being rapidly employed by authoritarian regimes to tighten their grip on power, despite the libertarian ethos pervading the American infotech sector.[115] A major restraint on recent totalitarians was that they had to compete with more technologically dynamic liberal democratic regimes. But if a highly hierarchical regime emerges on a world scale, the new information technologies might provide the basis for a long-duration totalitarian order, a dark one-world "end of history," with no escape or effective resistance.[116]

Totalitarianism has significant synergies with other global threats and possible solutions to them. Environmental collapse, or steps necessary to avert it, might produce the iron rule of a global Leviathan. An ASI yoked to human objectives could rule as an omniscient and omnipotent enlightened despot, ushering in administered utopia. But with a different guiding algorithm, it could turn ruthlessly omnicidal. Genetic engineering might solve the perennial problem of violence, as Aldous Huxley imagined in *Brave New World,* by refashioning humans into pacific, obedient, and efficient workers, but at the cost of transforming humanity into a fully socialized species, similar in organization to the social insects, and perhaps eventually with a silicon queen bee fully commanding the planet. Efforts to restrain microtechnologies posing macrothreats might require the erection of globally comprehensive control regimes that would either be or easily become a highly hierarchical world government.[117]

A ninth macrothreat is alien invasion from space, producing the conquest, or outright annihilation, of humankind. A staple of science fiction, this peril appears unevenly in recent threat assessments but is obviously distinctively space-related. Assessments of its seriousness are tightly linked to estimates of the frequency of intelligent life in the cosmos, which remain speculative and vary enormously. Any species capable of traversing the stupendous distances of interstellar space will be vastly superior technologically, and so humanity's fate would rest almost entirely upon alien intentions.[118] If aliens behave as humans have behaved toward one another and other life forms, human survival is unlikely— unless technologically advanced alien civilizations have somehow achieved moral enlightenment.

Last, but unfortunately probably not least, are major unknown unknowns, or "monsters" understood as "something-we-know-not-what," and "currently unimagined risks posed by future, not-yet-conceived of technologies."[119] It is tempting to discount double unknowns as the product of overly active imaginations, but they may be the most deadly threat because they might strike without the slightest warning. There may be major aspects of the universe that the human mind is cognitively incapable of comprehending but that human actions are capable of interacting with. And the acceleration of technological advance may be rapidly increasing the number of ways in which humans may unwittingly trigger disaster or annihilation.

Analysts of catastrophic and existential threats emphasize that the cumulative danger to humanity is growing. By bringing into existence potent new supertechnologies, modern humanity may be, contra Marx, "posing problems which it *cannot* solve." The ability of humans to avoid negative outcomes ranges from nonexistent to complete. Human abilities to avert cosmocidal and terracidal outcomes vary but overall are fairly low. For anthropogenic threats, the prospects for calamity are heavily shaped by human behavior, and thus by cultural, social, economic, and political arrangements. As with nuclear war, the prospects for genetically engineered diseases, runaway nanotechnology, and malevolent artificial intelligence heavily depend on the institutional settings in which these technologies are employed. For many macrothreats, the prospects for calamity still stem from human choices and are only as inevitable as the inevitability of particular long-established patterns of human behavior. Overall the combination of recalcitrantly Epimethean humanity and ever more potent Promethean technologies bodes ill for human prospects.

Reversal, Regulation, and Relinquishment

Many of the major threats shadowing the human future are novel in important ways, but the essential features of what humans must do to survive are in their essence extensions of arrangements of restraint that make civilization possible. Every new empowerment, from the slingshot to the hydrogen bomb, has required new measures of restraint tailored to its contours.[120] In general terms, restraints fall into three broad categories: *reversal* (undoing something that has been done), *regulation* (continuing to do something in circumscribed ways), and *relinquishment* (completely forgoing a technology or activity). The logic of these measures is straightforward, but achieving them requires surmounting difficult obstacles. Restraint of novel advanced technologies faces inherent epistemological limits in assessing their effects. Restraints also depend upon surveillance capabilities to monitor compliance and some mechanism to sanction violators. Clearly seeing ahead is difficult, but effectively steering may be even more difficult.

Each of these types of restraint has somewhat different attractions and difficulties. Reversal is appropriate when unanticipated major negative effects of a newly deployed technology are discovered. But some actions, such as the dispersal of radionuclides and toxics in the environment, are effectively irreversible, although further emissions can be prevented. Once a technology is widely used, it generates beneficiaries with interests in its continuing use, but reversal efforts can benefit from the extensive knowledge that wide deployment produces. Second, restraint through regulation is appropriate for the many technologies with significant positive and negative consequences. But regulatory restraint is often difficult to achieve and sustain. Negative and positive activities are sometimes difficult to distinguish. Actors tend to push the limits of the permissible, making regulatory regimes perpetual attrition struggles. Third, relinquishment is appropriate when the negative consequences of employing a technology are very severe. Completely foreclosing a particular technology or scientific investigation faces the ideological obstacle of pervasive techno-optimism and Promethean modernism.[121] Relinquishment also faces an epistemological problem because the consequences of novel technologies are difficult to discern before development.

Looking at the full matrix of factors shaping the prospects for restraint through reversals, regulation, and relinquishment, three generalizations emerge. First, institutional settings marked by high levels of secrecy, competition, and weaponization make restraint very difficult. Because so much research on emerging superpower technologies is occurring in secret laboratories between competing states and corporations, much of it for weaponry, the prospects are disquietingly low for identifying their negative effects before they occur and for effectively restraining them. Second, technologies with both civil and military applications are particularly difficult to restrain.[122] Third, restraining technological capabilities with low barriers to acquisition, and thus wide availability to large numbers of actors, faces daunting problems due to the large numbers of potential actors whose activities must be regulated and monitored. Institutional reconfigurations could significantly lower the probability of macrodisasters, but the rate of appropriate institutional change is much slower than the advance of technology, making for potentially lethal lags.

Looking ahead, humans are very likely to continue empowering themselves with new technologies, creating an ever widening "cone of possibility" (see Figure 4.2). Perhaps the most important reality of this steadily widening cornucopia of ever sharper double-edged swords is that the scope of what humans will be able to do, but not benefit from doing, will grow faster and become much larger than what we will benefit from doing. This is most obvious for biotech, nano, and AI, where the possibilities for monstrosities and menaces will vastly exceed the number of applications consistent with human survival and flourishing. Given this narrow set of desirable applications situated in an ever-widening set of negative possibilities, human survival and advancement requires staying within a path of preservation and enhancement, the borders of which are architectures of restraint. Only by assuredly and permanently closing off many options will

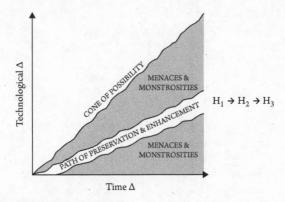

Figure 4.2 The Path of Preservation in the Cone of Possibility

technological advance yield human progress rather than catastrophes. Achieving Bacon's goal of "effecting all things possible" will probably doom humanity. On this multisided obstacle course, just because we get one—or several—choices right does not mean that we will get the next one right.

Given this, the crucial question emerges: Will major initiatives—such as space expansion—negatively impact the integrity and sustainability of the barriers of restraint? Any venture that weakens or destroys the architecture of reversals, regulations, and relinquishments holding back monstrosities and menaces becomes an indirect but assured path of unacceptable risk. Because the same powerful technologies enabling space expansion also pose so many existential threats, *whether* and *how* humans expand into space assumes a central role in any consideration of humanity's survival prospects.

PART THREE

SPACE EXPANSIONISM

5

Absolute Weapons, Lightning Wars, and Ultimate Positions

[Rockets] will give to future warfare the horror unknown in previous conflicts and will make possible destruction of nations, in a cool, dispassionate and scientific fashion.

—David Lasser (1931)[1]

This is the first day of the space age. We have invaded space with our rocket and for the first time have used space as a bridge between two points on Earth.

—General Walter Dornberger (1942)[2]

Control of space means control of the world. . . . That is something more important than any ultimate weapon. That is the ultimate position—the position of total control over Earth that lies somewhere out in space.

—Senator Lyndon B. Johnson (1958)[3]

Weapons, War, and Space

An adage of the Romans, *Homo lupus homini*, "Man is the wolf of man," sums up the grim fact that humans have been killing each other, often in great slaughters, since before the beginning of recorded history. Whether defending themselves from attack or dominating and despoiling others, all primary human groups have placed an extremely high premium on the effective mastery of violence. The harsh historical reality is that the fates of nations, states, and empires in every part of the world have been decided with dreary regularity by the clash of arms. With the emergence of modern science-based technology, the pace of innovation in killing tools has quickened, first with gunpowder weapons and global-range sailing vessels and then, as the Industrial Revolution bore its lethal fruit, with chemical high explosives, steel guns, and steam-powered ships and railroads.[4] As with so much else, this relentless "progress" in killing technologies accelerated rapidly across the twentieth century, as military-technological revolutions occurred with dizzying speed and far-reaching effects. During the world wars unprecedented levels of violence were unleashed, and states began the systematic pursuit of military research and development. Out of these cauldrons of violence innovation have poured killing machines with ever greater lethality, range, and speed, first chemical and biological weapons, then submarines and long-range bomber aircraft, and finally nuclear weapons and ballistic missiles.

The development of nuclear explosives during World War II seemed to mark an unmistakably revolutionary watershed in the capacities of humans to wreak violence in warfare. Quickly dubbed "the absolute weapon," nuclear weapons are so destructive that they required a whole new yardstick for measuring their capacities, first the kiloton (thousands of tons of TNT equivalent), and then in the 1950s, with the development of the hydrogen bomb, the megaton (millions of tons of TNT equivalent). It is the deployment of these weapons in prodigious numbers in the later decades of the twentieth century that has placed for the first time in the hands of the leaders of states the ability to catastrophically damage civilization, and perhaps render humans extinct.

The production and deployment of these weapons also has been one of the largest enterprises of the twentieth century, producing a planet-spanning military infrastructure without historical precedent.[5] Over the past seven decades, nearly 130 thousand nuclear weapons were fabricated, and there is enough of the fissile material necessary to make many more.[6] These weapons played central roles in interstate politics during the Cold War, and efforts to restrain them have generated a historically unprecedented level of international arms control. Due to the immense consequences of their use, these great engines have triggered a wide-ranging debate about their implications for the security and survival of nations and humanity. This debate remains fundamentally contested and unresolved. But because the use of space and space technology has been so thoroughly intertwined with preparations for waging nuclear war, any evaluation of the impact of space activities is inextricably dependent on judgments about the implications of nuclear weapons.

Although most space expansionists see the nuclear revolution as unrelated to the ascent of humans into space, military technological imperatives and interstate rivalries have played central roles in opening and exploiting space, and most military space activities have been intimately linked to preparations to wage nuclear war. Military organizations, with the US Air Force in the lead, remain the most extensive users of space. Despite wide recognition of these historical facts, the full extent of the involvement of space in the apparatus for nuclear annihilation remains dramatically underappreciated by space expansionists.

Because the combination of renewed interstate rivalry and new technology is stimulating significant and potentially very dangerous design, testing, and deployment of new space and nuclear weapons systems, an examination of the record and rationales of military space expansionism is particularly timely, even urgent. And because the military employment of space and space technology speaks so centrally to the core proposition of this book about negative space impacts, a close look at military space is necessary here. As a first step in this assessment, this chapter describes the main proposals made by military space expansionists and their rationales, with particular attention to their geographical, geohistorical, and geopolitical claims, and briefly summarizes the main roles military space systems have played in the interstate rivalries of the Space Age. Beyond these descriptive tasks, this chapter aims to correct two prevalent geography errors: about the character of space weapons and about whether space weapons designed to intercept ballistic missiles are defensive. Chapter 7 similarly examines the arguments of the arms control critics of military space expansion, thus setting in place the main claims of the two radically opposing views of military space expansion. With these two positions specified, we are prepared for the deployment of geopolitical theory in chapter 8 and to adjudicate between them in chapter 9.

Military space expansionists, while often disagreeing about secondary questions, all quite explicitly aim to enhance the national security of their states, although some also claim their initiatives will improve international security as well. But this pervasive *intent* does not, in itself, demonstrate that improved national security has in fact been the *consequence* of these deployments, and it is precisely here that arms control critics level their objections. Military space expansionists also have consequential differences about whether security requires deterrence, defense, or domination, with some explicitly aiming for planetary control. This means they also strongly disagree about whether their projects will preserve the anarchic state system or replace it with planetary hegemony or world government. Military space expansionists also differ on whether military rivalry is deeply rooted in human nature and geopolitics or is a more contingent and changeable feature of world politics.

The Von Braun Program and Beyond

In simplest terms military space expansionists advocate the deployment of space capabilities that are either weapons directly capable of destruction or are configured to enhance the destructive capabilities of other weapons. Space military activities have been anticipated and accompanied by strong, elaborately developed, and relentlessly promoted arguments, and the movement of war into space has been explored extensively in science fiction and technological futurism.[7] Advocates of military space expansion are not as widely known as leading visionaries of general space expansion. But if influence is measured by results, advocates of military space capabilities have been the most influential space expansionists. Much of this advocacy, and probably its most influential formulations, have occurred in the dark of national security state secrecy. But advocates of military space expansion, particularly in the United States, have produced many openly published works outlining the technological possibilities for military space and offering arguments, often quite urgent and sometimes alarmist, for their implementation.

Thinking about military space possibilities has been a part of the much larger and older enterprise of military futurism, which, like so much else, has exploded in volume and sophistication with the advent and acceleration of scientific technological modernity. Military futurism, particularly its space wing, has generated its own distinctive utopianism of ultimate capabilities, either decisive and unmatchable weapons or commanding and unassailable geographic positions and infrastructures. These quests for decisive advances are fueled and haunted by the long historical record of catastrophic strategic blunders by states and epic disasters by militaries.[8]

Like its civil siblings, military futurism has had both great successes and failures in its anticipations. As the ability of novel military technologies to exercise decisive influence on war outcomes has been unmistakably demonstrated, and as the pace of innovations with military applications has increased, military organizations across the world have become extremely future-oriented and routinely conduct extensive and sophisticated technological forecasting and assessment, research and development, and field testing. Conducted by large and well-funded organizations, military futurism and technological arms racing are now integral parts of modern statecraft and international politics. Quite contrary to their historical reputation as backward-looking and sluggish, the military organizations of leading states have over the past century been relentless innovators and technology early adapters. As the reach and speeds of modern machines have become global and planetary in scope, Earth's vast extraterritorial spaces and media have been transformed into battle spaces, extensively explored and scientifically studied. As the scope of wars became total, no rock has been left unturned for potential weaponization. In order to effectively conduct technological arms races, leading states have become scientific states, massively invested in scientific research and technological innovation, and have reaped numerous civilian spinoffs, such as civil nuclear power and digital electronic computers—and basic civil space technologies. The United States has been a particularly fierce innovator as it has sought qualitative superiority to off-set the quantitative and geographic advantages of its adversaries.[9]

Alongside all the many now-realized significant civilian Baconian elevations of the human estate, the military Baconians have achieved equally enormous and astounding successes in conceiving and deploying violence technologies able to massively, and suddenly, wreck everything humans have built—and much else as well. Because of these astounding advances in killing tools, errors of perception and judgment by states and militaries are now possible sources of civilizational catastrophe and species annihilation. War has been a scourge of humanity from time out of mind, but the possibility of wars total in planetary scope and destruction is the unique gift of scientific-technological modernity.

Despite its volume and sophistication, the violence futurism of militaries and states has systemic slants and blind sides. Being conducted by the core organs of suspicious and rivalrous states obsessively focused on relative power and capability, most military futurism about new technologies is framed by two practical questions: What advantage might be gained by our early or sole possession of an innovation? And What disadvantages will result if rivals and potential adversaries gain early or sole possession? With leads always deemed beneficial, and lags potentially calamitous, military technological innovation is completely appealing to states. The question of what general disadvantages might result from widespread innovation and deployment tends to be crowded out, a problem for someone else's department.

All across history, the politics of violence and interstate conflict has been intimately connected with geography and its implications. As global space started to close with the spread of industrial machines in the late nineteenth century, a large literature, soon using the new term "geopolitics," urgently examined the implications of the new technologies and their geographies for insight into the trajectory of the world political order and the fates of empires and states, as well as for guidance in steering through the torrents of change and peril that were widely anticipated. This explosion of geopolitical writing, the dominant international theory of the era, typically incorporated harshly realist understandings of world politics, often recast with metaphors and analogies drawn from Darwinian evolutionary biology, naturalizing nations and states (and "races") as biological entities or even organisms locked in perpetual life-and-death struggles for Lebensraum (living space). These theories are part of a broad nineteenth-century turn to historical materialisms, which spanned the political spectrum and treated both domestic and international domains. Although (as we shall briefly see in the following two chapters) other political theories and ideologies, both domestic and international, also developed geopolitical and materialist arguments and sought to ground or legitimate themselves as most suitably Darwinian, realist geopolitics was so extensive as to become more or less synonymous with geopolitics. Not surprisingly, explicitly realist geopolitics is most extensively developed by military space expansionists, who have also sought to extend the frameworks and categories developed by Friedrich Ratzel, Alfred Thayer Mahan, Halford Mackinder, Karl Haushofer, and other classical geopolitical thinkers in order to grasp the emerging possibilities of outer space for military activities and state interests.

The technological systems promoted by military space expansionists are bewilderingly complex and arcane in their details, but their essential features are relatively straightforward. The first steps of military space expansion, in space near the Earth, compose what I will refer to as the "von Braun program." What has been proposed by space expansionists far exceeds what has been done, but military space expansionists have been able to realize a much greater share of their visions than other space advocates.

Before turning to these projects, it is appropriate to justify using the name of the German American rocket engineer and charismatic space promoter Wernher von Braun to label the *military* path of space expansionism. In recent space discussions, "the von Braun paradigm" sometimes refers to a *nonmilitary* space program that von Braun also did much to conceive, popularize, and realize.[10] It is centered on human exploration and colonization through a series of specific steps (space shuttle, space station, moon landing and colony, culminating in a Mars landing and colony). This attribution also seems fitting because he played a leading role in building the gargantuan rockets used by the United States to send humans to the moon in the Apollo Project during the 1960s. But associating von Braun's name with the overall project of near-space militarization is even more appropriate because he also played a key role, first in Germany and then in the United States, in developing early rockets for long-range bombardment and was among the first to advocate establishing planet-wide military domination from space platforms equipped with nuclear weapons capable of striking anywhere on Earth on very short notice.[11]

Using von Braun's name to refer to civil rather than military space development has a propagandistic effect, whether intended or not, of evading some important and ghastly historical facts about the origins of the Space Age in Nazi Germany. The V-2s that were the first rockets powerful enough to lift objects out of the Earth's atmosphere were fabricated by a brutalized captive labor force composed of Russian prisoners of war and other groups targeted for extermination by Hitler's genocidal regime. In "planet Dora," one survivor's term for these labor camps, thousands died from subhuman conditions or summary execution by Hitler's SS squads.[12] As the historian Michael Neufeld notes, the V-2 is unique in the history of war because more people perished making them than were killed by their use.[13] Furthermore, after being snatched from Germany and relocated in the United States, V-2 technology and the von Braun team played important roles in the development of the long-range rockets to lob nuclear weapons at distant targets. And he prominently called for nuclear-armed space stations to dominate the planet. In sum, employing von Braun's name as the label for the space militarization program is not only substantively justified by what he did and advocated; it also serves as a reminder of the fact that while von Braun and his team may have "aimed for the stars, they hit London."[14] Employing his name may help remind us that, while space expansionists in the nuclear age "aim for the stars, they might obliterate the Earth," and that, whatever the intent of their deployers, widespread use of these weapons will be genocidal, or even omnicidal. Using von Braun's name in this way also highlights the "where the rockets come down is not my department" mentality so prevalent among space enthusiasts.[15] It will also help the future remember that the first objects to pass beyond the Earth's atmosphere were built by humans designated as Untermenschen (subhumans) for the benefit of a self-styled Übermenschen (master race). And von Braun stands as the outstanding exemplar of the seductions—and dangers—of the persisting habitat space expansionists' gambit of hitching their ambitions to ongoing military rivalries.

The space expansionist military program has five more or less distinct projects, which can be seen as steps in a ladder (see Table 5.1). It begins with the employment of space for long-range bombardment and culminates in elaborate orbital infrastructures designed to shoot down ballistic missiles and militarily dominate the planet. In between are satellites for military support services (reconnaissance, communication, navigation, early warning, mapping, and targeting), followed by orbital war fighting by attacking and defending satellites and potentially establishing operational space control. Some have been deployed (ballistic missiles and support satellites), while others have long been readily possible but not substantially deployed (antisatellite weapons and space control). Its final

Table 5.1 **Von Braun Military Space Expansionism**

	Plan	Extent Pursued
Planetary Hegemony	Orbital Earth-net infrastructure to negate ballistic missiles	Negligible
Space Control	Ability to achieve sole military use of orbital space	Negligible
Orbital Space Fighting	Orbital offensive and defensive weapons capabilities	Limited tests and deployments
Force Multiplying	Augment many military capabilities by surveillance and communication	Extensive
Bombardment	Missiles to deliver nuclear explosives at intercontinental distances	Very extensive since 1950s

Note: Read from the bottom up.

and most ambitious step (space-based ballistic missile defense and Earth dominance) remains technologically daunting and far from deployment.

Rockets and Ballistic Missiles

Long before their underlying scientific principles had been discovered, primitive
short-range rockets were used for military purposes.[16] Employing their early discovery of gunpowder, Chinese military craftsman built "fire arrows" and "flying
fire lances." In the nineteenth century British Congreve rockets with a range of
two thousand yards were deployed on naval vessels for coastal bombardment.
Unlike cannon, rockets do not recoil, making them particularly well-suited to
deployment on ships, but they lack the destructive power of heavy cannon due
to their small size and limited accuracy. Numerous families of vastly more potent
and accurate short-range missiles are now deployed by contemporary navies for
attacking ships and littoral targets.

The basic principle behind rocketry is found in Newton's Second Law, "For
every action, there is an equal and opposite reaction," but it was only early in
the twentieth century that rocket science was developed. Three individuals,
Konstantin Tsiolkovsky in Russia, Robert Goddard in the United States, and
Hermann Oberth in Germany, independently developed the basic principles of
rocketry. One of their key insights was that the velocity a rocket could achieve
was a function of the velocity and mass of burning fuels passing out of the
back of the rocket, and the best prospects for achieving orbital velocities were
liquid fuels, ideally a combination of liquid oxygen and hydrogen. Inspired by
space science fiction and fervently believing in human space expansion, each
encountered great difficulties in finding support for their projects. With support
from the US government and private foundations, Goddard built the first small
rockets that reached high atmospheric altitudes. But it was only with the support
of the German army in the 1930s that a rocket powerful enough to pass outside
the atmosphere was developed.[17]

This rocket, the A-4, dubbed "Vengeance Weapon 2," or V-2, by Hitler's
Propaganda Ministry, stood forty-seven feet high, weighed fourteen tons fully
fueled, and had a range of two hundred miles. Each cost as much to build as
several heavy bombers, and the program exceeded the cost of the American
Manhattan Project, which yielded the atomic bomb. Nearly six thousand V-2s
were built, with production continuing late into the war in mountain caverns.[18]
Although marking a decisive milestone in opening space, the V-2 was of limited
military value, far less than its cost, because it could not be guided accurately.
However, because its descent velocity exceeded the speed of sound, it struck
with no warning, making it a particularly effective terror weapon.

During the death throes of the Third Reich in early 1945, the advancing Allied armies sought to capture Germany's military technological resources. Most of the V-2 assets were grabbed by the Americans, who transported several hundred rail cars of material and most of the personnel to the United States, where they formed the nucleus of American rocket development. Relocated in New Mexico, near where Goddard had launched his rockets in the 1920s and the test site of the first nuclear explosion, teams of German and American engineers launched numerous reconditioned and modified V-2 rockets, achieving altitudes of several hundred miles, well beyond the atmosphere.[19]

With the realization in the 1950s that hydrogen bombs could be miniaturized to sizes small enough to be feasibly propelled at intercontinental distances, the floodgates of support opened for developing large rockets. Both the Soviet Union and the United States, having been drawn into World War II in 1941 by devastating surprise attacks, feared that hydrogen bombs hurled by long-range rockets would provide decisive military advantages, and so both poured resources into the development of several families of powerful rockets.[20] These crash projects soon yielded an awesomely capable force of missiles, some with ranges in the several thousand miles (intermediate range ballistic missiles, IRBMs) and others with ranges of over ten thousand miles (intercontinental ballistic missiles, ICBMs). Initially each rocket carried one nuclear weapon, or warhead, but during the 1960s it became possible for one missile to carry many warheads, each of which could be independently aimed at a different target (multiple independent reentry vehicles, MIRVs). Many thousands of these weapons were deployed between the late 1950s and the early 1980s; it was their unprecedented combination of destructiveness, speed, and range that made them the paramount military capability of the Soviet-American Cold War.

These rockets also made possible the first steps in civil space exploration. The instrument that James Van Allan used to discover the radiation belts around the Earth was lofted by a Redstone rocket, a descendent of the V-2. The rocket that the Soviet Union used to launch the first Earth-orbiting satellite, as well as Yuri Gagarin's first human flight into orbit, was the R-7, a powerful ICBM. The first American in space, Alan Shepard, was lifted into his suborbital flight by a Redstone IRBM. John Glenn, the first American to orbit the Earth, was launched by an Atlas ICBM, and the American Gemini missions used Titan ICBMs. Only with the construction of the behemoth Saturn rockets for the Apollo Program and then the space shuttle were large rockets built explicitly for civilian purposes. For many decades the three classes of heavy rockets routinely used for launching most American satellites, both military and civilian, were the Deltas, Atlases, and Titans, each first built to deliver nuclear weapons.

As with nuclear technology, there has been a steady diffusion of rocket capability to many countries. Despite the occasional use of rockets to launch a civilian satellite, the main purpose of many space programs is military. The close connection between nuclear weaponry and space launch capability, begun by the United States and the Soviet Union, is reflected in the fact that the members of the nuclear and space clubs closely overlap. Of spacefaring states, only Japan has forgone nuclear development. The most recent entrants to the nuclear club—India, Israel, Pakistan, and North Korea—have all developed rockets powerful enough to orbit satellites, and to lob nuclear weapons at their enemies.

As with nuclear technology, the spread of rocket capability has been marked by a schizophrenic, and not fully successful, attempt on the part of the superpowers to share or sell civilian technology while simultaneously preventing the diffusion of military missiles. In the late 1980s the major industrialized nations established a missile technology control regime to stem the spread of this technology. But several states with missile technology to sell are not part of the regime; several states party to the agreement are circumventing it; and considerable technology was transferred before the agreement.[21]

Another important milestone in the development of rockets for delivering nuclear weapons was the return to solid rocket fuels. Early small rockets had gunpowder propulsion, but this material did not produce enough energy for larger and longer range rockets, leading the pioneers of rocketry to liquid fuels, the most efficient of which used hydrogen and oxygen liquified at extremely low temperatures. These fuels, as well as other, less efficient liquid chemicals, had a major military drawback: they could not be safely deployed in the limited confines of submarines. With the development of highly energetic solid rocket fuels in the 1950s, it became possible to deploy nuclear-tipped missiles on submarines, and during the 1960s both superpowers fielded specially configured submarines as mobile underwater missile batteries. Roughly comparable forces were also fielded by Britain, France, and to a lesser extent China. Unlike previous submarines, which attacked surface vessels or other submarines with torpedoes from proximate locations, missile-launching submarines, known as "boomers" in US Navy slang, lurk in remote areas of the ocean with the sole purpose of firing a devastating barrage of nuclear weapons at intercontinental distances.

Both sides developed these fearsome weapons to improve their national security, but they had quite different implications for their relative positions. Prior to the deployment of their ballistic missile force, Soviet Union's ability to strike with nuclear weapons at the United States was considerably less than the US ability to strike them. Although the United States fielded a reliable nuclear rocket force before the Soviet Union did, the long-range missile was initially of much greater strategic value to the Soviets because it offset US advantages in long-range air power, overseas bases, and antibomber interceptors.[22]

The ballistic missile profoundly altered the operational security situation of states by greatly increasing the *speed* of attacks. In preindustrial times the deployment of military force at distance was arduous and slow, and the fastest weapons transport, the oceanic sailing ship, had an average speed of about 15 miles an hour. With the coming of industrialism, speed of movement, particularly over land, was quickened considerably by railroads, with sustained velocities of around 50 miles an hour. With military aeronautics speeds leaped up rapidly, and by the 1950s bombers were deployed with intercontinental range and speeds of around 600 miles per hour and with travel times between the interior of North America to the interior of Eurasia of ten to twelve hours, making warfare vastly more rapid than ever before (see Table 5.2). But ballistic missiles moved considerably faster, with velocities in the range of 10,000 miles per hour, roughly twenty times faster than bombers, and with intercontinental flight times of about thirty minutes, a speed that is effectively instantaneous in the world of politics.[23]

Arguments about the dangers posed by the high speeds of ballistic missiles are, as we shall see, at the heart of the case for nuclear arms control, but there are two undisputed consequences of missile military acceleration. First, the time in which a global nuclear war can be fought with ballistic missiles is extremely short, making possible wars of unprecedented spatial scope and destructiveness within mere hours. This greatly narrows the time available for nuclear decision-making. Speed also encourages states to keep their nuclear forces at extremely high levels of alert. Prior to World War II it was possible, at least for geographically favored insular states such as the United States, to build up their military forces after hostilities had commenced. But with the coming of the long-range bomber, "there will be no time," as the title of an influential 1946 book by William Borden ominously announced. Any forces relevant to the outcome of a great power war would need to be in place prior to the outbreak of hostilities, thus requiring unprecedented levels of permanent military mobilization.[24] With ballistic missiles, there would be even less time, and the outcomes of wars would come to hinge on the ability to nearly instantaneously use forces perpetually

Table 5.2 **Military Acceleration**

When	What	Speed
Before 1830	Sailing ship	15 mph
After 1830	Railroad	50 mph
1920	Propeller aircraft	350 mph
1955	Jet aircraft	600 mph
1957	Intercontinental ballistic missile	10,000 mph

poised for immediate use. Second, the speed of ballistic missiles makes the defensive task of shooting them down extremely difficult. The prospects for such antiballistic missiles (ABMs) hinge on achieving even faster speeds, as well as the ability to hit small objects moving extremely rapidly at great distances.

Ballistic Missiles as Space Weapons

While their historical development, military capabilities, and political consequences are widely recognized, ballistic missiles are almost completely absent in discussions of the impacts of space activities. Ballistic missiles are widely characterized as strategic weapons, not as space weapons. At least since the 1960s the term "space weapon" has been nearly universally used to describe weapons that are either *based in orbital space* or *operate against objects in orbital space*. Thus space weapons strike from Earth to space, from space to space, and from space to Earth, but not from Earth to Earth through space.[25] With this definition, space weapons, with the exception of a few tests, are a prospective possibility. But there are very strong reasons why ballistic missiles are inherently space weapons. To see why this is so, consider the geographic features of ballistic missile trajectories and the primary role the features of space play in making possible their distinctive features as weapons (see Figure 5.1).

In the course of their half-hour flight from launch to impact, ballistic missiles spend most of their time hurtling through the vacuum of space. Even more important, their passage through the vacuum of space is intrinsic to the distinctive military task they perform. The frictionless space medium enables ballistic missiles to sustain their extraordinary velocities of several miles per second. If

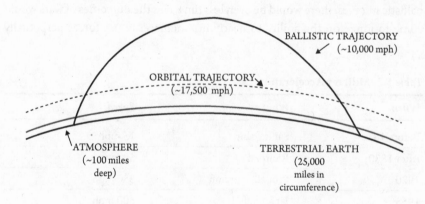

Figure 5.1 Ballistic Missile Trajectories

ballistic missiles could not use this empty space path, it would be impossible for them to travel at such high speeds without burning up and without carrying impractically large quantities of fuel. Speed distinguishes ballistic missiles from other types of weapons and is their most militarily attractive feature. Ballistic missiles are thus inherently space weapons because their basic features and functions as weapons intrinsically, not incidentally, depend on the unique features of space. If ballistic missiles are inherently space weapons, then any general analysis of space activities that does not include them is flawed by a simple but extremely consequential error of geographic misplacement.

This more accurate understanding of ballistic missiles also means that the widely employed distinction between the "militarization" of space and the "weaponization" of space is essentially misleading. Space is widely recognized as militarized due to the presence of numerous military-support satellite systems, but not yet weaponized due to the general absence of weapons in orbit or for attacking satellites. Once ballistic missiles are properly recognized as space weapons, it is obvious that *space has long been weaponized* and that much of the militarization of space provides support services for these space weapons. It is also notable that the term "strategic weapon" is a category of significance, not location, and the only systems commonly referred to as "strategic space weapons" are those designed to intercept ballistic missiles.

Once we recognize that ballistic missiles are the quintessential space weapon, the scope of space programs is dramatically enlarged. It is widely recognized that the total expenditures for military space activities exceed those for civilian activities, but with ballistic missiles included as part—indeed the most important part—of military space activities, the proportion of total space activities devoted to military activities becomes considerably larger. There are multiple ways in which the magnitude of the ballistic missile space weapon on the overall ledger sheet of space activities might be measured. Perhaps the simplest is the share of ballistic missiles in the total inventories of launch vehicles that have been produced. Looking at the American record, more ICBMs have been produced than NASA rockets. If the many US Air Force satellite launches to support nuclear missions are added, the gap grows considerably larger. Similar disproportionate numbers mark the Soviet and Russian space programs. If supporting basing systems and radars are added, the economic preponderance of the nuclear space enterprise grows further. And if efforts to shoot down long-range nuclear missiles are added, the gap grows still further.

Furthermore, recognizing ballistic missiles as space weapons means that what is commonly referred to as "nuclear arms control" is primarily (but not entirely) "space weapons arms control." Most actual nuclear arms control has aimed at restraining the numbers and capabilities of nuclear delivery vehicles, the most important of which have been ballistic missiles, rather than nuclear weapons themselves. Finally, and most important, recognizing ballistic missiles as space weapons has major implications for the overall net impacts of human space activities simply because these weapons have played such a pivotal role in the prospects for general nuclear war.

Information Force Multipliers I:
Satellite Surveillance

The realization that an object, if propelled rapidly enough, could be placed in an orbital path around the Earth where it would stay indefinitely had been an implication of Newton's Laws of Motion, and schemes to create such "artificial moons" had been common in early space expansionist thinking. But with the deployment of the V-2 and anticipation of even more powerful rockets, military analysts began to think seriously about possible military satellites. In one of the most prescient works of military space futurism, a 1946 RAND Corporation report, "Preliminary Design of an Experimental World-Circling Spaceship," outlined the many uses of military and civilian satellites.[26]

The first artificial moon, the Sputnik launched by the Soviet Union in October 1957, was a simple aluminum-sheathed sphere weighing 187 pounds, and it did nothing more than broadcast radio signals for a few weeks until its battery died. While this satellite had no military value, its existence ominously demonstrated that the Soviets possessed a rocket powerful enough to propel nuclear weapons over intercontinental distances, thus making the United States vulnerable to devastating, unstoppable, and sudden attack.

Unexpectedly Sputnik was a great propaganda coup for the Soviet Union, generating near hysterical panic in the United States, and seemed to demonstrate that the communist regime was a contender for world technological leadership.[27] Although both the Soviets and the Americans had announced plans to launch a satellite as part of the International Geophysical Year of 1957–58, political leaders had not anticipated the tremendous psychological impact of the first satellite on world public opinion.[28] With the American public and Congress clamoring for a suitable response, the Eisenhower administration initiated a far-reaching reconstruction of the relationship between the government and science and technology, including the establishment of NASA.[29]

Since the late 1950s several thousand satellites have been placed into orbit to perform intelligence and military tasks. These satellites are not themselves weapons but are force multipliers; like a scope on a rifle, they increase the potency of actual weapons. Such information force multipliers serve many roles, five of which—surveillance and reconnaissance, mapping, targeting and early warning, navigation, and communication—warrant examination because of their vital roles in the nuclear force structures of the superpowers (see Table 5.3). In their overall effect these space-based information systems have been yet another technological double-edged sword. On one side, they have greatly increased the ability of states to conduct nuclear military operations, while on the other side, they are vital tools for verifying arms control agreements.

The first military use of satellites was for reconnaissance and surveillance. Because satellites travel around the planet above the atmosphere, cameras and other sensing devices placed on them can gather information about activities on the ground and in the atmosphere. In the terms of military geography, orbital space is like a hill overlooking a battlefield, a high ground ideal for observation. The extensive use of these satellites has produced a far-reaching *transparency revolution* in the military relations between rival states, greatly increasing the difficulty of keeping many military activities secret.[30] Where the ballistic missile left states vulnerable to nuclear attack, surveillance satellites left them naked to inspection. But they have also greatly contributed to the *accuracy revolution*, which has increased the ability of missiles to hit targets precisely.

As with ballistic missiles, the first observation satellites initially had very uneven effects on the rival superpowers. The Soviet Union's tight internal controls over people and information within its vast territory impeded American intelligence agencies from monitoring Soviet military capabilities. Throughout the 1950s the United States sought to negotiate an "open skies" agreement to allow surveillance aircraft flights to be conducted over both countries, but the Soviets repeatedly rebuffed such proposals. In lieu of an agreement, the United States conducted clandestine aerial surveillance with a high-altitude airplane, the

Table 5.3 **Military Force-Multiplier Satellites**

	Main Function	*Additional Consequences*
Communication	Command links to distant bases, ships, and aircraft	Increase ability to make coordinated attacks and counterattacks
Navigation	Increase accuracy of weapons	Increase first-strike advantage
Mapping	Increase accuracy of weapons	Increase first-strike advantage
Early Warning	Provide more time for military response to attacks	Reduce pressure for launch-on-warning
Surveillance	Improve information about adversary's military forces	Arms control verification

U-2. But as Soviet surface-to-air missiles steadily improved, the United States, knowing the days of this venture were numbered, launched a crash program to develop satellites for surveillance. When a U-2 was shot down and its pilot captured by the Soviets in the spring of 1960, a full-blown Soviet-American crisis ensued.[31]

Many of the first American satellites were military spy satellites, although this purpose was carefully hidden from public view.[32] Over the course of the 1960s and beyond, the capabilities of satellite intelligence systems dramatically improved. Initially packets of film were dropped into the upper atmosphere with parachutes, which were then snagged, if all went well, by specially designed aircraft. Later satellites became completely digital and now radio-transmit copious streams of high-resolution imagery. Later generations of American KH (for "keyhole") satellites, each the size of a bus, cost about a billion dollars and can resolve objects the size of people and vehicles from their very low-Earth orbits.[33] Overcoming their initial strong opposition to such spying, the Soviets built roughly comparable systems, and over the past several decades many additional countries and corporations have deployed increasingly capable observation satellites.[34] In recent years declining costs of digital imagery and transmission have made possible smaller and more numerous satellites costing less to build, launch, and operate and which can be quickly replaced if they malfunction or are attacked. The observation satellites launched by corporations are now in some cases ahead of governments in technology and capabilities.[35]

Observation satellites have played important roles in the international politics of the Space Age. The information from the earliest surveillance satellites dispelled American fears, widely voiced during the presidential campaign of 1960, of a "missile gap" favoring the Soviet Union. Satellites revealed that the bold claims of Soviet premier Nikita Khrushchev that the Soviet Union was making ICBMs "like sausage" were a brazen bluff. Several years later President Lyndon Johnson claimed that the space program had saved ten times as much as it cost by reducing arms expenditures. As the missile gap was shown to be in America's favor, the Kennedy administration averted vast further procurement of missiles, while the Soviet Union turned to desperate measures to restore their position by placing nuclear IRBMs in Cuba in 1962, which triggered the hair-raising crisis bringing the world to the brink of nuclear war.

During the 1960s and early 1970s satellite reconnaissance and surveillance were widely viewed as helping to stabilize the superpower military competition, encouraging both unilateral restraints and bilateral treaties. By providing both sides with a high degree of confidence that they knew the numbers and locations of the other side's strategic forces, observation satellites also played a key role in the first halting steps to control the nuclear arms race during the late 1960s. Even after the acceptance of extensive on-site inspection in the Intermediate-Range

Nuclear Forces Treaty of 1987 and the Strategic Arms Reduction Treaties, satellites still provide wide-area surveillance necessary to detect locations for on-site inspections.[36] To monitor compliance with the Limited Test Ban Treaty of 1963 and the Nuclear Non-Proliferation Treaty, the United States placed observation satellites in high, large-vista orbits to scan continuously the remote regions of the globe for nuclear detonations.[37]

But the transparency revolution had another, more dangerous consequence that raised fears of nuclear attack. Once satellites provided detailed information about the number and extent of rival military forces, it became increasingly feasible to attack such forces in a disarming first strike. One potential response to this vulnerability is to adopt a "launch on warning" strategy, wherein missiles would be launched during the short period between their detection and their devastating impact. But this posture is exceedingly dangerous because it requires launching large numbers of nuclear weapons on the basis of electronic signals. Also, it would be difficult to keep the civilian political leaders in the loop in such short periods, forcing the delegation of launch decisions to military watch officers.

The solution to this ominous puzzle of how to avoid being the victim of a catastrophic nuclear first strike while avoiding the deployment of retaliatory forces on hair-trigger alert was to deploy forces capable of surviving an attack, which would then be available to launch a retaliatory second strike. According to the logic of deterrence theory developed during this period, the existence of such a secured retaliatory capability would ensure that any attacker would be subject to a devastating counter blow, and thus it would be suicidal to initiate an attack in the first place. But for this to be feasible in practice, a substantial share of a country's long-range nuclear strike force had to either be configured to somehow survive a barrage of nuclear explosions or be located where it could not be confidently targeted in the first place. Since the late 1950s, as the contours of this fateful problem came to be understood, many alternatives have been investigated, including placing missiles in deep underground missile bases (with the unfortunate acronym DUMB) and in very high Earth or lunar orbits or on the moon, where sheer distance would provide a time buffer.[38]

Two expedients have been judged most appealing, and Soviet and American long-range nuclear forces were reconfigured according to these ideas. First, missiles were placed in elaborate steel-reinforced concrete underground silos topped with heavy blast doors. These deployments were deemed invulnerable from first-strike destruction because ballistic missiles, though very fast, were not initially very accurate and so could not reliably knock out hardened missile bases. The second expedient was to base ballistic missiles on submarines. This strategy exploited a key and often overlooked exception to the transparency revolution, the simple geophysical fact that electromagnetic radiation does not propagate in water at distance, making the oceans a vast sanctuary from the full glare of transparency and making it possible to hide objects the size of submarines from detection and thus quick destruction. Thus, to the extent a second-strike capability was possible, it depended on the inaccuracy of ballistic missiles and a stubborn oceanic opacity residue.

Information Force Multipliers II: Mapping, Navigation, and Communications

A second cluster of military support satellites, for navigation and mapping, has also become an integral part of the planet-spanning nuclear force structures. For most of history, the stars have been used to navigate, particularly across open ocean. Maps of terrain and topography have been vital tools of war-making, and advances in geography and cartography have been intimately intertwined with military activities. During its naval and maritime ascendancy, Britain systematically mapped the planet's oceans, and the science of oceanography was born in these investigations. With long-range aircraft, submarines, and then missiles and satellites, the scope of military activities became truly planetary, creating the need for better maps and understandings of these far-flung terrains and exotic operating environments. Increased resources were poured into previously underfunded sciences of oceanography and atmospheric sciences as well as geology and studies of planetary space beyond the atmosphere. These investigations also generated many important advances in knowledge about the Earth, with applications and implications far beyond military uses.[39]

Since their first deployment in the 1960s, weather satellites have been an icon of the Space Age, providing meteorologists with detailed real-time images of weather patterns otherwise difficult to observe, particularly over the oceans. Storms have played a surprisingly large role in shaping the outcomes of battles across history, and the operation of many weapons systems, particularly aircraft and ships, remains heavily dependent on favorable weather conditions.[40] Although weather prediction beyond a few days remains stubbornly inexact, satellites greatly improve warnings of severe storms such as hurricanes.

Another well-known satellite force multiplier, for navigation, is the Global Positioning System (GPS) provided by the Navstar constellation of some two dozen satellites, each of which emits a continuous stream of signals that provide extremely precise three-dimensional locations virtually anywhere. Although civilian GPS uses have grown explosively in recent decades, this system was built by the US military to provide accurate and reliable navigational information for military forces, and access to the most accurate versions of its information was initially confined to military users. Unwilling to remain dependent on a US military system, Russia, China, European countries, and others have built increasingly capable navigational satellite constellations.

Less well-known satellite observation systems for mapping the lithosphere have also been significant force multipliers. The Earth is not perfectly spherical in shape, and its gravitational attraction varies enough to alter the trajectories of objects traveling long distances, such as missiles. Using geodetic satellites, these gravitational anomalies have been precisely mapped, and this knowledge is used to adjust missile flight paths, making them more accurate.

Communication satellites have also boosted the potency of military forces. As with mapmaking and weather, communication technologies have played powerful roles in shaping military outcomes throughout history. For most of history, communication was no faster than transportation, and vast efforts were expended, particularly by empires with large territories, to maintain communication at great distances. The electric telegraph forever severed the dependence of communication upon transportation, and message transmission speeds leaped to nearly light speed. With radios, communications no longer depended on a sprawling infrastructure of vulnerable wires. But because the transmission of radio waves at global distances was limited by the curvature of the Earth, it was only with the radio-relay satellites lofted in the early 1960s that truly planetary-scope communications became possible. The volume of information flowing through communication satellites has become astoundingly large as electrical engineers have learned to squeeze ever more information into electromagnetic waves.

Military communication satellites have had far-reaching impacts on military operations. With nuclear delivery systems dispersed throughout the planet's air, water, and land, communication satellites enable central coordination and direction and the command and control of protracted nuclear wars. As satellite communications became progressively more capable and cheaper, conventional military forces were networked with space links. Ground receiving stations for satellite transmissions shrank from the behemoth dish antennae of the early Space Age to the size of large dinner plates, making them portable and cheap. During the Persian Gulf War of 1991 to expel Iraqi armies from Kuwait, American forces made such extensive use of satellite information that this conflict was referred to as the "first space war," even though it employed no weapon in space and nothing in space was destroyed.[41] And in the ongoing American global war on terrorism, satellite links make it possible for "virtual pilots" in Nevada to remotely steer aerial drones and fire missiles at targets on the other side of the planet.

Overall, information satellite force multipliers have greatly amplified the military potency of ballistic missiles by increasing their accuracy.[42] In nuclear war, as

in the game of horseshoes, near misses count, as the destructive radius of a large
nuclear explosion is so great that approximate hits on "soft targets"—military
jargon for cities and industrial complexes—are extremely devastating. But for
hardened targets, such as ICBM silos and underground command bunkers, near
misses are not lethal, and the inaccuracy of early long-range missiles made it
plausible that such protective expedients would guarantee a survivable second-
strike capability. However, by the later 1970s mapping and related information
gathered from satellites made it possible to calibrate the flight trajectories of
intercontinental-range ballistic missiles to hit targets the size of a football field,
assuredly destroying even the most hardened targets.

This improvement in the precision of long-range missile targeting created
what strategic analysts called a "window of vulnerability" and a decline in the
confidence of any fixed target as part of a secure second-strike force. Navigational
advances have helped improve the accuracy of sea-based ballistic missiles to the
point where it rivals that of land-based missiles, thus turning these weapons into
potential first-strike weapons.[43] The full consequences of this amplification in
the potency of a nuclear strike force was not, however, fully experienced due
to the unexpected end of the Cold War during the 1980s and the subsequent
drawdown in Soviet and American long-range missiles. Advances in targeting
continue, and some war planners claim long-range ballistic missiles are now
so accurate that they can be equipped with powerful nonnuclear conventional
explosives and used for "prompt global strike" against hardened targets with
high confidence and negligible collateral damage.[44] Further advances in capability and vulnerability are resulting from extensive efforts to integrate increasingly capable AI into numerous military systems and to conduct espionage and
warfare through the internet.

Similar amplifications of the potency of conventional bombs dropped from
airplanes have resulted from satellite information services. Early prophets of
war-winning airpower anticipated highly accurate bombardment of military
targets, but this turned out to be dauntingly difficult in practice, and as a result
strategic bombing during World War II devolved into indiscriminate bombing of
cities. Over the past several decades, however, cheap precision aerial bombardment has finally arrived, largely due to the navigation services provided by the
GPS. For example, in the 2001–2 American invasion of Afghanistan, the US Air
Force transformed cheap and inaccurate "dumb bombs" into cheap and accurate
"smart bombs" by equipping them with strap-on flaps controlled by a GPS tran-
sponder, allowing them to be dropped from very high altitudes and strike targets
the size of a truck.[45] These technological upgrades are rapidly diffusing into the
militaries of many countries, heralding the very wide availability of precision
aerial bombardment, as recently demonstrated by Russia's space-assisted precision bombardment in Syria.

Antisatellites, War Fighting, and Space Control

With the next steps up the von Braun ladder to war fighting and space command, satellites become weapons and targets of weapons. The first antisatellite (ASAT) weapon tests were conducted in the early 1960s; since then several different approaches have been tried. Despite the steadily increasing importance of military satellites, deployment of ASATs has been limited. But many military space expansionists advocate deploying ASATs to fight wars in space. Some aim for space control, a situation in which one state is so militarily dominant as to effectively monopolize space for its purposes.[46]

Because satellites travel in predictable orbits, move at extremely high speeds, and are physically fragile, they are quite vulnerable to destruction. Satellites can be destroyed by nuclear explosions, by attack from so-called killer satellites that maneuver into proximity for attack (or mutual destruction), by missiles launched from the Earth to intercept them, and by directed energy weapons. Each of these techniques has been tested, and each has distinct advantages and disadvantages (see Figure 5.2).

Starting in the early 1960s, the United States explored weaponizing the van Allen radiation belts by filling them with charged particles.[47] In tests over the Central Pacific, nuclear weapons were detonated beyond the atmosphere, readily disabling the target satellite but also unintentionally destroying several operational satellites and knocking out the electric power grid in Hawaii.[48] Were nuclear weapons exploded today in near-Earth orbital space, large numbers of both civil and military satellites would be disabled. Tests of this ASAT were halted

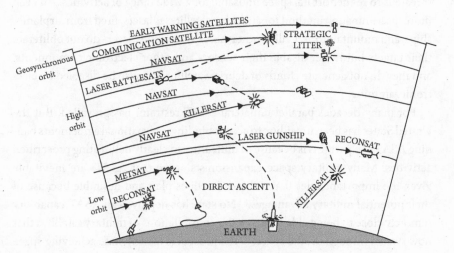

Figure 5.2 Destroying Satellites. Source: U.S. Department of Defense with author's modifications.

after the Limited Test Ban Treaty of 1963, which banned nuclear detonations in space (as well as in the atmosphere and oceans). But because nuclear weapons can be lofted into orbital space by ballistic missiles, all nuclear states possess a latent indiscriminate ASAT capable of eliminating large numbers of satellites.

Several more discriminating ASATs weapons also have been tested. The Soviet Union tested a co-orbital ASAT in which a killer satellite maneuvered into close proximity with its target and blew itself up with conventional explosives, showering its target with disabling shrapnel, making a "suicide satellite." In 1985 the United States tested a direct-ascent ASAT. In this technique a torpedo-size missile was launched from a fighter aircraft high in the atmosphere. The payload of the missile, a breadbox-size homing vehicle, collided with a satellite, obliterating it. This ASAT depended on its ability to rapidly process the information necessary to steer itself precisely into the path of its target. Compared to its predecessors, this ASAT was cheaper, more rapidly usable, and could be widely based. In 2007 China joined the ASAT club by destroying a satellite in a five-hundred-mile-high orbit with a direct collision by an intermediate range ballistic missile.[49] In 2008 the United States shot down a low-orbit satellite by striking it with a missile launched from a naval vessel. India joined the ranks of ASAT testers in early 2019.

These techniques, while robustly able to destroy satellites, have a major drawback: the generation of substantial quantities of debris. This wreckage, often destined to remain in orbit for long periods, poses a threat to other satellites because of its high velocities. The small number of ASAT tests thus far conducted have contributed significantly to the overall inventory of space debris, and any significant ASAT testing program, let alone their large-scale employment in war, threatens to render orbital space unusable for a wide range of activities. An even more discriminating method for attacking satellites is lasers, fired from airplanes, ships, and mountaintops. Unlike other ASAT techniques, lasers do not obliterate their targets but rather disable their sensors and other electronic components, and they do not generate clouds of debris. Satellites can also be disabled by electronic jamming.

For many decades parallel unilateral ASAT restraint has prevailed. But the United States has been unwilling to accept binding international agreements banning ASATs. In part this is because of difficulties in clearly delineating proscribed activities. Many military space expansionists argue that ASATs are inevitable given the important roles that military satellites play, and desirable because of their potential military advantages.[50] No state has deployed an ASAT capability remotely close to being able to attack the constellations of military satellites that now swarm through orbital space.[51] The prospects for any state achieving space control are clouded by the many potential countermeasures to ASATs, such as satellite proliferation, hardening, and maneuverability. The ASAT horizon is also complicated by the important overlaps between the technologies of destroying satellites and of intercepting ballistic missiles. Even a limited capability to shoot down ballistic missiles would have substantial ASAT capability, and an extensive ASAT system would have some ability to shoot down missiles. On the other hand, an effective ASAT test ban would also eliminate crucial avenues of technology development for shooting down missiles.[52]

Ballistic Missile Interception I: From ABM, BMD, and SDI to GMD and THAAD

Across the history of warfare, every innovation has triggered a quest, successful in widely varying degrees, to find yet another weapon to counter or defend against it. Thus the sword and spear evoked shields and body armor, and aircraft stimulated the development of anti-aircraft guns and missiles. As soon as ballistic missiles appeared on the horizon of possibility, military thinkers started searching for ways to shoot them down.[53] These technologies, first called ABM (antiballistic missile) and then BMD (ballistic missile defense), have been slowly improving, but formidable obstacles stand in the way of anything approaching a full defense against ballistic missiles. The main reason shooting down ballistic missiles is so difficult stems directly from their most attractive attribute: their extreme speed. Shooting down an intercontinental ballistic missile is often likened to hitting a bullet with a bullet, but this comparison considerably understates the difficulty, as an ICBM travels several times faster than a typical bullet. Not surprisingly, most progress in developing ABM technology has been made in intercepting slower moving, shorter range missiles.

Within the visionary horizons of military space expansionists, countering ballistic missiles has an especially lofty status. Greatly reducing, or eliminating, the dire vulnerabilities produced by nuclear weapons and their missile delivery systems would demonstrate unmistakably that military space systems can solve the most important security problem. This step up the von Braun ladder of military space projects is also appealing to many habitat space expansionists because it would require vast deployments of hardware in orbit, catalyzing further space development. At the same time, efforts to curtail such systems have been central to the arms control project. To begin to get a handle on this momentous topic, it is useful first to survey the political history of this technology, and then examine how ballistic missiles might be intercepted.

The history of antiballistic missile programs is long, winding, and filled with controversies. The technologies involved are extraordinarily complex and evolving. But the main outlines of both are subject to intelligible summary. Ballistic missiles are so militarily important that enormous efforts, now accelerating, have been made to develop a viable ABM system, and these efforts have often been at the center of superpower political relations. During the 1960s both the United States and the Soviet Union conducted extensive research and testing of ABM systems and began to deploy them, but these efforts were cut short by the ABM Treaty of 1972, which severely curtailed further testing and deployments.[54] Another factor was that the deployment of MIRVed ICBMs had greatly complicated the prospects for achieving a full defense.

In 1983 the antiballistic missile project was suddenly and unexpectedly renewed and thrust back into the center of American-Soviet relations when President Ronald Reagan announced his strategic defense initiative (SDI), aiming to "render nuclear weapons impotent and obsolete."[55] This effort, which quickly became known (to the chagrin of its backers), as the Star Wars program, triggered a high-stakes debate about its feasibility and desirability. Convinced emerging space technologies made his vision realizable, Reagan launched a major research effort, which yielded only modest advances.

Reagan's initiative evoked an extraordinary outpouring of military space expansionist thinking touting orbital space weapons as a solution to the threat of nuclear annihilation. Studies from retired army general Daniel Graham's High Frontier project, prominent SF writers Jerry Pournelle, Jerry Niven, and Ben Bova, and Lyndon LaRouche's Fusion Energy Foundation claimed the vulnerabilities produced by nuclear weapons could be greatly reduced or eliminated by a massive rapid deployment of space-based interceptors.[56] They viewed the Soviet Union as an intractable threat and arms control as largely futile. But, like Reagan himself, they sometimes mentioned sharing this technology with the Soviets so they too could escape from the menace of nuclear destruction. Some argued for mining asteroids for shielding of orbital battle stations, thus catalyzing a "space industrial revolution." A recurring geographic theme is orbital space as the planet's high ground, offering special potential for dominating the whole planet for the country bold enough to seize it. Some likened these systems to a protective continental "astrodome."

While no weapons were deployed, some claim that the technological "shadow of the future" cast by Reagan's SDI program played a key role in ending the Cold War on terms favorable to the United States.[57] But others maintain that the Soviets were willing to enter into large-scale symmetrical reductions in offensive nuclear forces only after they became convinced that SDI was a "paper tiger."[58] After the Cold War, the Americans scaled back this research and its ambitious goals, shifting efforts to the still very difficult task of shooting down a few or slower, shorter range missiles.[59]

Another burst of US BMD activity began around the turn of the century when the George W. Bush administration decided that nascent nuclear and missile programs in the "rogue states" of North Korea and Iran could not be deterred and therefore required American interception capabilities. In order to escape its stringent test bans, the Bush administration withdrew from the ABM Treaty in 2002, a move vigorously condemned by the Russians as an assault on a key piece of the arms control architecture at the center of the settlement of the Cold War.[60] By 2004 the United States had rushed into deployment a rudimentary Ground-based Midcourse Defense (GMD) system composed of largely untested and unreliable interceptors based in Alaska, and a behemoth but fragile sea-based X-band radar system.[61] A theater missile defense system (THAAD, for Theater High-Altitude Area Missile Defense) has been more extensively deployed on Aegis navel vessels, and a new version of its interceptor may be capable of intercepting ICBMs. In 2017 the Trump administration initiated a major increase in both these programs, as well as a renewed push to develop space-based interceptors.[62] Viewing these systems as threats to their capacity to deter the United States with a credible threat of retaliation, Russia and China are embarking on expanded deployments of ICBMs and are exploring other exotic nuclear delivery technologies, pushing the world toward a rekindled strategic nuclear arms race. China's and Russia's recent moves to expand space counterforce activities, combined with Trump's recent effort to create a Space Force and expand US military space activities, are likely to further accelerate space weapon deployment.

Ballistic Missile Interception II: Profile and Earth Control

To understand why ballistic missile interception is so difficult, and why the most potentially effective approach is both the most difficult and least plausibly defensive, it is necessary to review the basic geographical and technological facts of ICBM interception. Between its launch and target impact, a ballistic missile passes through three distinct phases, each of which offers distinct opportunities and constraints for interception. These phases—the boost, midcourse, and terminal—correspond to the parts of the flight that are in the atmosphere over the launch site, in the free-fall trajectory through space, and in atmospheric reentry over the target (see Figure 5.3). A technology effective in one phase of a missile's trajectory will seldom work in another, and thus a full-scale defensive system would require three interrelated but quite distinct layers, each with different strengths and vulnerabilities.[63] A central feature of any system is its kill mechanism, three of which are most important: nuclear explosions, collision, and energy beams. Each has distinct attractions and limitations, and none is suitable for all three phases of interception. They vary greatly in their technological maturity, from being established for nuclear weapons, improving but still limited

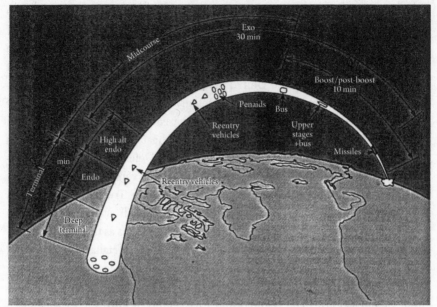

Each of the phases presents specific opportunities to the corresponding defensive layer. The phases are boost, post-boost, midcourse and terminal.

Figure 5.3 Ballistic Missile Interception. Source: U.S. Department of Defense.

for collision, and nascent for energy beams. An additional compounding complexity arises because all these approaches require elaborate systems of sensors, communication links, and command-and-control arrangements, which also vary greatly in their capabilities, vulnerability, and technological maturity. To grasp the main features of these systems, it is most useful to start at the end, the terminal phase, and work back to the beginning, the boost phase, roughly following the actual pattern of historical development.

The terminal phase of a ballistic missile flight trajectory, occurring as the warheads reenter the atmosphere over their target, involves the least use of outer space. Operating within the airspace of the target country, such systems are unmistakably defensive in character. Unfortunately for a defender, this phase of a missile's flight lasts only two to three minutes, requiring any potential defensive interceptor to accelerate extremely rapidly. The ABM systems that the United States and the Soviet Union tested and started deploying in the 1960s were designed to intercept warheads during the terminal and late midcourse, just before they reentered the atmosphere; they employed nuclear explosions as a kill mechanism (see Figure 5.4). Aside from the fact that this defense entailed nuclear detonations in the atmosphere above their targets, such explosions, although quite effective in destroying in-coming warheads, had the unfortunate effect of blinding and disabling the large radars that the system used for target

Figure 5.4 Soviet Moscow Terminal Defense System

acquisition and directing interceptors, making the system both impossible to realistically test and essentially self-defeating.[64] Furthermore, because only a limited area could be protected by a terminal system, extensive deployments of radars and nuclear-tipped missiles near populated urban industrial areas were necessary. Another weakness was that an attacker could overwhelm a terminal defense system by proliferating the number of attacking warheads. Doubts about technical feasibility and public safety, combined with fears of a costly missile-antimissile race, led the superpowers to agree to stringent restraints on both testing and deployment in the ABM Treaty of 1972.

The midcourse phase of an ICBM's flight poses different difficult tasks for an interception system. Midcourse is the long quiet part of a warhead's trajectory, after the large rocket has fallen away, leaving only a small object, or swarm of objects, hurtling through the vacuum beyond the atmosphere. The half-hour transit time for missiles traveling between the interiors of Eurasia and North America affords a more leisurely response time, at least compared to the first and third phases. But detecting the warheads in midcourse is much more difficult, as they are small, emit no radiation, and move rapidly. And if the missile was MIRVed, there are many warheads. Countermeasures include cheap and numerous decoys and maneuverability. Some have also proposed sending clouds of gravel into orbit to disable missiles and satellites, turning litter into a strategic weapon. To intercept fast-moving swarms of nuclear weapons requires a vast orbital array of sensors and communication links, as well as an armada of satellites filled with interceptor missiles. In addition to being vastly expensive, such an orbital infrastructure would itself be vulnerable to various types of attack.

During the first, boost phase of a missile's flight trajectory its engines are burning. A boost-phase rocket is easy to detect and target because burning rocket engines emit an enormous and impossible-to-cloak infrared signature which can be reliably detected at great distances. A missile in its boost phase, while rapidly gaining speed, is still moving much more slowly than it is when it has obtained its full velocity. A boost-phase missile is also relatively large, as it contains large quantities of fuel, fuel tanks, and rocket engines. Missiles in this first phase are especially inviting targets if they contain many independently targeted warheads. However, boost phase lasts only about two minutes and takes place in the atmosphere, where energy beams are attenuated, making them less effective than in the void of space.

While rockets in their boost phase offer the most promising targets, intercepting them poses the greatest difficulties due to *where* this must occur and *where* potential interceptors must be located. To strike at a rocket ascending its boost phase, an interceptor must be located more or less directly above it, in a low orbit.[65] The destruction of the ascending rocket must occur within the airspace of the country launching it. Further great difficulties arise because satellites carrying interceptor missiles or energy-beam weapons must be continuously on station, requiring a continuous row of satellites so that one would come into range as another passed out of range. Providing such continuous coverage over the territory of a large continental state, as well as the ocean expanses from which missiles can be launched from submarines, would require an immense planet-enveloping network of satellite battle stations and their support systems, what can be termed an *Earth Net* (see Figure 5.5). The overall cost of such a system, difficult to estimate with any precision, should realistically be viewed as comparable to an entire branch of the military rather than a single major weapon system. Finally, striking in the several minutes available for attacking boost-phase rockets would require an automated command system.[66]

The deployment of such an extraordinarily complex and expensive system by one state acting without opposition would be a monumental project, but if a rival state attempted to build a comparable system or take a cheaper path and deploy antisatellite weapons capable of attacking its battle stations, the difficulties

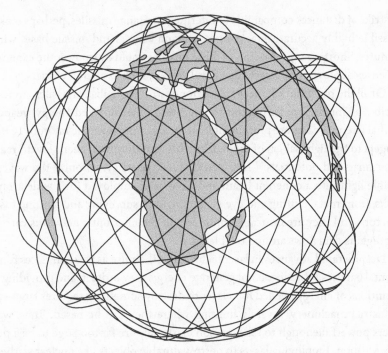

Figure 5.5 Earth Net Orbital Ballistic Missile Interception Architecture

in achieving a boost-phase interception would become vastly more daunting. And with vast numbers of weapons platforms swarming around the planet, many configured for autonomous automatic operation, accidents might trigger general conflagration.

Advocates claim technological advances in computers and sensors make large-scale interceptions increasingly possible. As the power of computers has increased, the enormously complex tasks of sensing missiles, aiming interceptors, assessing damage, and coordinating defenders very quickly have become more feasible. In one vision of the possibilities, dubbed "brilliant pebbles," numerous very small and cheap interceptors with small powerful computers would operate in autonomous swarms, thus eliminating the need for complex and vulnerable centralized coordination.[67]

The overall prospects for intercepting missiles of all ranges is further clouded by emerging hypersonic missile technologies.[68] Two distinct versions of this technology are in development. Boost-glide hypersonic vehicles, shaped like wedges, are lofted into a ballistic trajectory by a long-range missile, but then glide and maneuver as they reenter the atmosphere, thus greatly compounding the difficulty of tracking and intercepting them. In contrast, powered-flight cruise missiles operate continuously in the atmosphere and employ advanced scramjets to fly at some five to twenty times the speed of sound for enough time to strike at distances comparable to intermediate-range missiles, perhaps making possible highly accurate attacks on command centers and missile bases within minutes. Shorter range versions of these missiles could overpower the expensive defenses deployed to protect large naval vessels, such as aircraft carriers.

Of all the potential kill mechanisms for destroying ballistic missiles, none has excited as much popular interest as lasers and other directed energy weapons. Lethal energy beams are prominent in science fiction, from the ray guns of Buck Rogers to the light sabers of the Jedi knights, but they have been slow to realize their imagined potentials.[69] Invented in 1960, lasers synchronize the waves of visible light into a coherent beam and have been employed for a wide array of tasks, from metal cutting and eye surgery to land surveying and igniting fusion reactors, and they are critical components in the fiber optic networks carrying prodigious data flows around the planet.

Despite rapid advances in laser technology, their use as weapons faces fundamental barriers.[70] Lasers do not generate energy, they order it, and providing the quantities of energy needed for a laser to destroy something requires large-scale industrial machinery, severely limiting where they can be based. Thus, while lasers powerful enough to kill a person exist, they are far too large to be a portable weapon. Employing lasers to destroy durable objects like nuclear warheads at distances of thousands of miles requires yet further increases in their size, making them unsuitable candidates for large-scale deployment, particularly in the harsh environment of space. But beam weapons do have one unmistakable advantage over all other weapons ever devised: their extreme speed, transiting thousands of miles in a small fraction of a second, some 500,000 times faster than ballistic missiles. Should powerful military lasers ever be developed, they would fully complete the historical trajectory of violence acceleration.

Deep-Space Nuclear Basing, Planetoid Bombs, and Planetary Dominance

The technological imaginary of military space expansionists is not exhausted by ambitious schemes for intercepting ballistic missiles but extends much further into space. Ideas for the deep-space basing of nuclear weapons were developed in the 1960s by Dandridge Cole and Donald Cox and by the aerospace engineer and space visionary Robert Salkeld. Cole and Cox also envisioned maneuvering asteroids to serve as an ultimate deterrent capability, a "planetoid bomb." These plans were advanced as solutions to the general problem of nuclear war, and more specifically to the vulnerabilities of nuclear weapons based on the Earth, and each rested on elaborate claims about the geography of the Earth and space. Never attempted, these schemes are shockingly extreme, even among the Strangelovian apocalyptic military imaginaries of the 1950s and 1960s (see Table 5.4).

According to Cole and Cox, the underlying rationale for placing powerful weapons far into space is geographic: the size of the destructive effects of nuclear weapons has outgrown the size of the Earth. They point out that nuclear weapons have a destructive radius some three thousand times that of chemical high explosives, a perilous development because the Earth cannot be proportionally enlarged. But space is vastly larger, and if humans expand into a three-million-mile sphere of space, there would be a "return to the relative security of the pre-atomic age" and "even the hydrogen bomb will lose much of its terror."[71] Salkeld similarly observes that "on a steady diet of accelerating technology, strategic armaments have outgrown their traditional arena, the earth."[72] But in the "broadening perspective of lunar and planetary scales" he argues that "even the largest nuclear bursts begin to dwindle to insignificance," amounting to "no more than pebble splashes in an ocean."[73] These arguments seem initially compelling but ultimately fail because the populated targets of H-bombs on Earth are not proportionally expanding, leaving them just as vulnerable even if weapons become much more spatially dispersed.

A more specific reason for placing weapons of mass destruction into deep space is that terrestrial basing modes are inexorably becoming vulnerable as technology advances. It is inevitable, Salkeld argues that "no earthbound weapon system will be adequately secure from detection, surveillance and massive on-target attack," and as a result the "dependability of deterrent systems is melting away."[74] Basing nuclear weapons in near orbits would not remedy this problem because they could be de-orbited in a matter of a few minutes, making them potent first-strike weapons. But basing nuclear weapons in high Earth orbits provides "unprecedented degrees of survivability" because they are "insulated

Table 5.4 **Military Astro-Archimedeans**

Advocate	Proposal	Problem Addressed
Salkeld	Deep-space basing of nuclear weapons for deterrence	Vulnerability of second-strike nuclear forces
Cole and Cox	Asteroid planetoid bombs for deterrence	Vulnerability of second-strike nuclear forces
Stein, Vaucher, and Dolman	Complete military control of Earth space by Earth Net	Interstate rivalry and war

by astronomically large distances" and can "hide in vast, still unexplored regions" of space.[75] Salkeld details the spatial advantages of deep-space basing: the volume of space contained within a sphere out to a distance of 600,000 miles (over twice the distance to the moon) is some 7.5 billion times greater than the space contained within near-orbit space (which he defines as extending out 600 miles to the inner edges of the van Allan radiation belts).[76] In these "vast stretches" military space vessels are "very difficult to locate and less continuously tracked," enabling them to "cruise undetected and battle ready for weeks and months."[77] Another advantage of this scheme is that it would be impossible to employ such weapons for a sudden surprise attack because it would take days for them to strike at targets on Earth, making them a unique combination of survivable and unsuitable as a weapon of surprise. In recovering effective distance, time for human decision-making is also recovered.

An even more audacious scheme for maintaining an ultimate deterrent is Cole and Cox's proposed "planetoid bomb." Their book, *Islands in Space: The Challenge of the Planetoids*, advocates altering the orbits of asteroids for military and other purposes. They claim that a "captured planetoid" of between one and five miles in diameter would have the "impact energy equivalent to several million megatons," would create a crater twenty to fifty miles in diameter, and "would destroy whole countries through Earth shock effects."[78] But they hasten to add that such devastation would "not be anything near as bad" as a general nuclear war because there would be "no nuclear fallout carried by the winds to all parts of the Earth."[79] They also assert that such a system could be acquired at a cost comparable to existing strategic weapons systems and "could be a by-product of a vigorous manned interplanetary program."[80] A captured planetoid would be "the ideal deterrent system" because it could not be de-orbited in less than several hours and thus "would not be feared by a potential enemy as a surprise attack weapon."[81] Furthermore "an onrushing planetoid" could not be intercepted or deflected "even if detected several days before impact," and such an attack might be carried out "without much danger of retaliation" because it would be difficult to distinguish from a "natural catastrophe."[82] However, both high-orbit basing and use of planetoid bombs could be surprise attack weapons if only one side had them or their existence had been kept completely secret. Terrestrial states would be compelled to maintain extreme vigilance of their neighbor's space activities and remain perpetually prepared to embark on programs of their own. Curiously neither Salkeld nor Cole and Cox took the next obvious logical step to consider what such weapons might mean in the context of lunar or solar space colonization. Although this scheme suggests criminal insanity, it fits comfortably alongside other—fortunately abortive and outlawed—Cold War investigations of geophysical weaponization, of harnessing hurricanes, tornados, earthquakes, volcanoes, and tsunamis for military purposes.[83]

Another group of military space visionaries are the astro-Archimedeans, who claim space contains special places with the potential to dominate Earth space and the Earth. The astropolitical vision of planetary dominance is the practical realization of Archimedes's bold claim that "if offered a place of his choosing, he could move the Earth."[84] Extrapolating from ideas of late nineteenth- and early twentieth-century geopolitical theorists such as Ratzel, Mahan, Mackinder, and others, the school of space geopolitics or astropolitics includes Cole and Cox, G. Harry Stine, Marc Vaucher, and Everett Dolman. They identify space analogs to the sea lanes, chokepoints, high grounds, and other terrestrial geopolitical constructs. Von Braun's early proposal for a nuclear-armed space station emphasized the advantages of seizing the planet's high ground to dominate the Earth, a vision of global political transformation that subsequent astro-Archimedeans have further developed.

Cole launched this strain of space military thinking in 1960, advancing the Panama Theory, according to which "there are strategic areas in space which may someday be as important to space transportation as the Panama Canal is to ocean transportation." He also asserts that "in colonizing space, man (and/or other intelligent beings) will compete for the most desirable areas."[85] The main ideas of astro-Archimedeanism were clearly formulated by the space engineer G. Harry Stine in 1979. Pointing to the centrality of the gravity well in shaping military advantage in Earth space, he claims that "control of the Moon means control of the Earth" and that "control of the L4 and L5 Libration points in lunar orbit means control of the Earth-Moon system." He also observes that lunar "mass drivers" (a catapult-like device to accelerate mass off the moon) will be a "critical system" in "the overall industrialization of the earth-Moon system" but will "have a military utility" because they could be readily "converted into an earth bombardment system."[86] In a similar vein, Vaucher argued in 1981 that "control of geosynchronous orbit means control of all near earth space," and that "control of the Trojan points means control of the entire earth-moon system."[87]

The fullest version of Archimedean astropolitics is provided by Dolman, a professor at the US Air Force's School of Advanced Air and Space Studies, in his 2002 book *Astropolitik: Classical Geopolitics in the Space Age.* "The resource potential of space," he observes, "like Mackinder's heartland, is so vast that should any state gain effective control of it, that state could dictate the political, military, and economic fates of all terrestrial governments."[88] He advances what he terms the "neoclassical astropolitical dictum": "Who controls Low-Earth Orbit controls Near-Earth Space. Who controls Near-Earth Space dominates Terra. Who dominates Terra determines the destiny of humankind."[89] To take advantage of this opportunity, the United States should "seize military control of low-Earth orbit." He optimistically asserts that "from that high ground vantage, near the top of the Earth's gravity well," the United States "could prevent any other state from deploying assets," thus becoming the "shepherd (or watchdog) of all who would venture there" and

establishing a "benign hegemony."[90] He claims this plan has "tremendous political advantage and virtually no political liability." If American dominance were
"perceived as fair, non-arbitrary and efficient," then "other states would quickly
realize that they had no need to develop space military forces."[91] To ensure that
rapid development of space resources takes place, he calls for scrapping the Outer
Space Treaty and relying on private space development. It is notable that Dolman
specifically proposes the United States quickly deploy ballistic missile interception systems in an Earth Net configuration, further confirming that such systems
are intrinsically offensive. While this military imaginary is technologically improbable, it is starkly utopian politically: It is no more plausible that other states would
passively accept an American "Dolman grab" for planetary hegemony than that
Americans would accept comparable Chinese or Russian moves.

Beyond this small but lucid literature on the visionary outer horizons of von
Braunian space expansionism is the vast province of science fiction imaginaries
of future weapons and destruction, where a great many scenarios of staggering
violence are found. Just as on Earth, everything is imagined as weaponized and
vastly amplified in power and spatial reach. Interplanetary war is chronic (*The
Expanse* and *Halo*); planets are obliterated (*Star Wars*); fleets of warships with
powerful beam weapons swarm solar and interstellar space (*Star Trek*). Total
and genocidal wars between different intelligent species rage for eons (*Starship
Troopers* and *The Forever War*). Planet-size rogue battleships programmed to
exterminate life everywhere run amok (*Berserker*). Artificial intelligences stage
bloody revolts against their masters (*Battlestar Galactica*). Bioengineered living
weapons are unleashed on unsuspecting sentient species (*Aliens*), while time itself becomes weaponized in the boundless matrix of temporal warfare (*Doctor
Who*). Interstellar and galactic-scope empires rise and fall and collide (*Dune,
Foundation, Hyperion, Halo, Warhammer, Mass Effect*). Like military futurism
on Earth, many of these imagined weapons and scenarios may prove impossible
or impractical. But if, as on Earth, some do become feasible, the prospects for
ever more lethal von Braunian scenarios and their accompanying politics and
consequences appear cosmically large.

The Von Braun Programs and World Orders

The projects of the von Braun ladder program involve very advanced
technologies, but the rationales justifying their desirability are very old and very
familiar, not essentially different from those offered for technologically primitive
violence capabilities across human history. In claiming space weapons are desirable because they advance state security, advocates of the von Braun program
draw straightforwardly on the ideas of realpolitik and geopolitics derived from

the operating manual from Archipelago Earth to explain how and why space weapons will achieve this goal. Nation-states are seen as vying for security and power in an anarchic interstate system; relations between states are inherently rivalrous; and the prospect of war is ever present. They employ an age-old repertoire of practices: destroy, dominate, deter, balance against, or defend against their adversaries. Given this, states are assumed—and advised—to act on the assumption that their rivals will exploit the military advantages of emerging space technology. Restraints are at best fleeting, and any attempt to institutionalize them are illusory, even dangerous, and inevitably destined to fail.[92]

Despite shared basic views about international politics, military space expansionists differ in profoundly important ways about which strategies are necessary, about the relationship between military space activities and the nuclear revolution, and about the world order their proposed measures would produce (see Table 5.5). The vast destructiveness of nuclear weapons is a central fact for all advocates of space military expansion, but they fundamentally differ about their implications and whether space military capabilities can diminish their influence.

Aside from those who advocate world government, thinking about the nuclear revolution by self-styled "realists" has been dominated by two schools of thought.[93] The most intellectually dominant approach, what can be called "deterrence statism," sees nuclear war as fundamentally irrational and emphasizes maintaining a robust deterrence by means of a secure second-strike capability.[94] The most practically dominant school, "war strategism," sees nuclear war as potentially winnable, and deterrence as requiring a full range of capabilities to wage and prevail in a nuclear war.[95] For both these schools, space is an essentially ancillary topic, but they differ on which space capabilities are desirable. For adherents of the deterrence school, the development of space war-fighting capabilities is potentially destabilizing, while the war strategists view space as simply another arena for capabilities to deter, defend, or prevail. The world order produced by deterrence remains anarchical but is frozen in place, immune to the great historical change agent of major war. Conversely the world order produced by war strategist practices is much more militarized and much more likely to be subject to change—or termination—by large-scale violence.

Full BMD advocates and astro-Archimedeans advance agendas with far more revolutionary implications for world order. For advocates of space-based strategic defense and planetary dominance, the acute vulnerabilities created by nuclear weapons can be eliminated by the deployment of a vast new complex of space weaponry. Defending against nuclear weapons in an astrodome configuration would diminish the offense-dominant world of nuclear deterrence and war fighting. And states, or at least the most powerful ones, could once again actually secure their territorial realms, thus returning world order to some semblance of its prenuclear character. But the deployment of space infrastructures

Table 5.5 **Von Braun Strategies, the Nuclear Revolution, and World Orders**

	Relation to Nuclear Revolution	*Role of Space Systems*	*World Order Outcome*
Dominance	Reverse and escape	Pivotal	De facto world government and end of interstate anarchy
Deterrence	Revolutionary	Ancillary	State-system frozen from major war and change from war
War-Fighting	Not revolutionary	Ancillary	State-system and war persist; nuclear war more likely
Defense	Escape	Pivotal	Security foundation of state-system recovered

to comprehensively intercept ballistic missiles in an Earth Net configuration would not be defensive in character. It would be tantamount to creating planetary dominance, a situation in which one state has the capacity to both defend itself against all states and to devastate all other states. If the astro-Archimedeans are correct in viewing control of Earth space as a potentially decisive military high ground affording effective control of the entire planet, then the anarchic state-system would be replaced with a de facto world government, marking the most revolutionary change in world order in history. The tension between the von Braunians's optimism about technological change and pessimism about the prospects for political changes producing mutual restraint ultimately gives military space expansionism a tragic cast quite at odds with the optimism of most space advocates.

Despite their profound differences, advocates of the von Braun programs are united in their conviction that war and preparation for war will be an integral part of any expansion of human activity into space. And they largely view efforts to avoid rivalry and violence in space as utopian and dangerous if seriously pursued. Viewing humanity's nature as essentially fixed, they expect rivalry and violence to occur over anything of value, particularly over the living spaces, habitats, and resources that provide the material foundations for all societies. If true, these views have profound implications for the largest and most central of space expansionist visions, to expand human habitat and transcend human corporeal limitations.

Limitless Frontiers, Spaceship Earths, and Higher Humanities

> This is no way to run a spaceship.
> —Kenneth Boulding (1966)[1],

> There is no recognizable limit to growth.
> —Krafft Ehricke (1974)[2]

> This then is the goal: To make available for life every place where life is possible. To make inhabitable all worlds as yet uninhabited, and all life purposeful.
> —Hermann Oberth (1957)[3]

Lebensraum Unlimited

As the features of the new cosmology of Copernicus and his successors came to be known across Europe, the philosopher Blaise Pascal famously mused, "The eternal silence of these infinite spaces strikes me with terror," and wondered whether the aspirations of humankind, long bolstered by the illusion that the Earth occupied a central position in the cosmos, could be sustained.[4] In a similar vein, the philosopher Hannah Arendt, reflecting on the first artificial satellite, suggested that modern astronautics was producing a "dwarfing of man" that would diminish human self-confidence.[5] The essence of habitat space expansionism is the exact opposite of these reactions, eloquently voiced by the playwright George Bernard Shaw: "Of life only there is no end; and though of its million starry mansions many are empty and many still unbuilt, and though its vast domain is as yet unbearably desert, my seed shall one day fill it and master its matter to its uttermost confines," and "press on to the goal of redemption from the flesh, to the vortex freed from matter, to the whirlpool in pure intelligence."[6] Where Pascal and Arendt see the cosmic glass as being infinitesimally filled, space expansionists see unlimited potential for humans to fill it.

Harnessing space technology to perfect the instrumentalities of violence may be the largest space activity, but most space expansionists have their sights set on a vastly larger—and seemingly more benign—trajectory of expansion. They aim to fill space with useful infrastructures and habitats and then to spread colonies to other celestial bodies, initially in this solar system but ultimately into interstellar space. This epic vocation of technologically refashioning the Earth and then elevating humanity into a fully multiworld species is the real heart of space expansionism, however much it might be waylaid by the petty rivalries and violent proclivities of Earthbound states. It proceeds from the deep belief that humanity has been given a "cosmic mandate to inseminate the universe with the human."[7] It is this vision of improvement and expansion and elevation that space expansionists view as unquestionably beneficial and ultimately vitally necessary, even inevitable, despite the many obstacles to its realization.

Like all other biological organisms on Earth, human life depends on a suitable habitat and cannot exist without the myriad geophysical and biological services that the diverse environments of the Earth have provided, however unevenly and in many places grudgingly, for every minute of human existence on this planet. All organisms attempt, with widely varying degrees of success, to alter their habitats to improve their prospects for survival and to expand the spatial range of their activities. And all organisms, at varying rates and with varying degrees of success, evolve in ways that alter their ability to live in different habitats, which are themselves changing in a variety of ways, at variable speeds, and for many reasons. Among the innumerable species that have emerged on Earth, humans have been exceptionally and spectacularly successful in both remaking and expanding their habitats, due in large measure to their precocious ability to employ tools.

The heart of the habitat space expansionist vision is essentially an extrapolation of this biological trajectory of enhancing and expanding living space, or Lebensraum (to use the term favored by space expansionists, borrowed from nineteenth-century German biologists, geographers, and geopoliticians). In these visions, everything associated with life, from the Earth as a habitat to the biological fabric of humanity, can, should, and will come to be fundamentally transformed by a succession of ever enlarging expansions of technological civilization into the ultimate frontier of cosmic space. These space expansionist visions, in meshing biological imperatives with technological enablements and then projecting them onto a cosmic expansionary path, bring the modern Promethean project to its epic culmination.

Habitat space expansionism, like military space expansionism, extends long lines of thinking and practice about terrestrial habitats and their consequences. Thinking about variations in human habitats and their political implications has long been a primary concern of geographers, even more central than the geographies of war and violence. Habitat theory also has a well-developed geopolitics in analyses of the political consequences of both natural and built habitat spaces and places. And visions of ideal habitats, natural and built, are a common part of utopian imaginaries. Systemic thinking about the spatial patterns of arable lands, climate, and resources and their implications for politics appears in the work of Greek geographers and political theorists and remains a primary focus of contemporary geographers, who are increasingly focused on climate change and its relations to habitability.

Where one lives powerfully shapes how well one lives. The flourishing of peoples is everywhere understood to be dependent on salubrious and abundant habitats, and many miseries of famine, poverty, drought, earthquakes, and severe storms stem from habitat deficiencies. Gardens of Eden attract because they are appealing habitats, while hells inspire fear because they are unappealing ones. Visionary hopes of remaking the Earth for larger and better human habitats animate the Baconian project of Promethean modernity. And fears that human activities, amplified by enlarged human numbers and powerful new technologies, are ruining Terra's habitats haunt the many critics of technological modernity. Given how comprehensively important habitats are to human beings, it is only natural that habitat space expansionism would occupy such a central role in the imaginaries of space advocates.

The grand scenario of habitat space expansion is the work of many visionaries, stretching back to the beginning of the twentieth century, and has grown greatly in sophistication in recent decades. But its basic outlines were drawn at the very beginning by the great Russian inventor and visionary Konstantin Tsiolkovsky, and thus this entire enterprise is appropriately referred to as the Tsiolkovsky program.[8] In addition to his pioneering work on rocketry, Tsiolkovsky envisioned the full industrialization of the Earth, space stations, asteroidal colonization, enclosed ecosystems, terraforming, the transmutation of humans into higher, more spiritual beings, and the eventual expansion of most of humankind into space, as well as the ultimate migration into interstellar space. And he warned of "disasters that can destroy the whole of mankind or a large part of it."[9]

Like the von Braun programs, the Tsiolkovsky programs are a ladder of relatively distinct steps. But connecting them all is a comprehensive narrative not just of space projects but of humanity, its place on the Earth and space, and its role in cosmic evolution. This narrative has many features in common with a religion, and the religious-mystical dimension of human ascent to the heavens was particularly pronounced in Tsiolkovsky's thought. While habitat space expansionists disagree about some things, they are largely united in holding some version of this overall cosmic-historical narrative, reading all human history, indeed all the history of life on Earth, as preparatory steps toward expansion off the Earth and throughout the cosmos.

The American astronautical engineer and space activist Robert Zubrin provides a particularly full statement of this larger cosmic evolutionary narrative in his book *Entering Space: Creating a Spacefaring Civilization* (1999). Building on the work of the Russian theorist Nikolai Kardashev, Zubrin deploys a three-tier scheme for classifying civilizations, with Type I mastering its planet, Type II harnessing the resources and energies of its solar system, and Type III commanding its galaxy. Zubrin claims humanity is now graduating from Type I and taking the first baby steps toward Type II civilization. He reads history as the successive mastery of environments through technological innovation. Humans, biologically ill-adapted to living outside the warm climates of the tropics "became *Homo technologicus*" when they first left Africa and developed technologies enabling them to "conquer all the environments of the world."[10] The spaceship is as epochal a step in evolution as the development of the egg.[11]

Arguments for going into space rest on the identification of some problem on Earth, and the most commonly identified recurring and important problem for virtually every expansionist is the vulnerability of the Earth to asteroidal bombardment. As Zubrin puts it, the asteroids "offer nothing but mass death for the pre-sentient biosphere or Earthbound Type I humanity, [but] hold the promise of vast riches for a Type II spacefaring civilization."[12] Beyond this problem, space expansionists diverge, sometimes sharply, on which terrestrial problem for space expansion to solve. In Zubrin's version, "the earth's challenges have largely been met, and the planet is currently in the process of effective unification," but a "Pax Mundana" of cultural homogenization and stagnation imperils human progress and freedom.[13] In Arthur C. Clarke's colorful formulation, humanity will stagnate if forced to "endlessly circle in its planetary goldfish bowl."[14] But more typical is the opposite view, that Earth problems are of such magnitude that rescue from space, or escape to space, is a species survival imperative.[15]

Another dominant theme is frontiers, which have closed on the Earth but opened in space. In Zubrin's telling, civilizations need challenges to innovate and flourish. Across much of history, war offered a powerful competitive spur to development, but modern war has become so destructive as to be "unthinkable," and "military stresses have thus largely been eliminated as a major driver of the world system."[16] But "frontier shock" has also been profoundly stimulative of innovation and growth. Western civilization surged to global dominance because it opened the ocean frontier in the early modern era, while China turned inward and fell behind. Frontier-challenging civilizations are also more free, as freedom flourishes on frontiers, producing a "culture of innovation, anti-traditionalism, optimism, individualism, and freedom."[17]

This spatially expansive trajectory is characteristic not just of humanity but of all life: "Out of the oceans to the land. Out of Africa to the north. Out of Earth and into space."[18] The expansion of technology-empowered humanity assumes cosmic significance: "Humans, with their intelligence and technology, are the unique means that the biosphere has evolved to blossom across interplanetary and interstellar space."[19] Humans thus become the "stewards and carriers of terrestrial life."[20] Technology-endowed humanity becomes the reproductive organ of Terran life. Expansion into space becomes "the most profound vindication of the divine nature of the human spirit—domination over nature, exercised in its highest form to bring dead worlds to life."[21] Failure to pursue space expansion *"constitutes a failure to live up to our human nature and a betrayal of our responsibility as members of the community of life itself."*[22]

The Varieties of Habitat Space Expansionism

The technological imaginaries spun by space expansionists for the progressive enlargement of the human habitat are dazzling in variety and ambition. Here any analytic scheme to categorize runs the risk of becoming a proverbial Procrustean bed, painfully stretching one part while chopping off another. Nevertheless a loose typology of these projects that brings the overall habitat expansionist vision into an intelligible whole with more or less distinct parts is an essential first step toward a general assessment of their consequences and desirability. To this end, this chapter examines the main projects proposed by habitat space expansionists, with a focus on their underlying assumptions, variations and inconsistencies, and anticipated consequences as well as their geographical, geohistorical, and geopolitical aspects.

As with military expansionism, habitat expansionism can be sequenced as a series of steps, a ladder of life into the sky, each step named after a leading visionary who articulated a prominent version of it (see Table 6.1).[23] First is the "Fuller Earth program," named after Buckminster Fuller, which seeks to convert ever more of the planet into a built infrastructure and to geo-engineer the climate. In close conversation with environmental thinking about planetary limits and technology, the Fuller program aims to turn the planet into ever closer approximations of a built spaceship, producing a "geodesic-hydroponic" Earth. Second, is the Ehricke-Glaser-Lewis program, which envisions the construction of infrastructures in Earth orbit to harvest energy and resources from space for terrestrial use and to build space infrastructures. These projects would produce an artificial Glaser Ring of fabricated structures around the planet. Third is the Bernal-O'Neill program for even larger orbital megatechnics for the large-scale industrialization and urbanization of Earth orbital space, with vast canister cities in high Earth orbit. This program produces a Bernal-O'Neill Belt around the planet, with the population of humans living off-world growing into full-fledged human societies.

Table 6.1 **Tsiolkovsky Habitat Space Expansionism**

	What and Where	*Rationale/Goal*
Goddard	Migration across interstellar space to galactic expanses	Ensure survival of humanity from cosmic events
Dyson	Colonize Kuiper Belt and Oort Cloud with diverse intelligent and other life	Help life expand in universe and preserve plurality with species radiation
Cole	Colonize interiors of asteroids in solar space and species radiation	Ensure species survival and provide freedom insurance
Mars-Zubrin	Colonize and then terraform Mars	Ensure species survival if Earth humanity destroyed and frontier cultural stimulus
Bernal-O'Neill	Colonization in artificial habitats in high Earth orbit and beyond	Expand habitat and preserve social and cultural plurality
Ehricke-Glaser-Lewis	Energy and materials from sun, moon, and asteroids for Earth	Provide energy and resources for more wealth and less environmental impact
Fuller Earth	Mega- and geo-engineering of terrestrial and orbital Earth	More wealth and stable habitat for more humans

Note: Read from the bottom up.

The first three habitat expansion programs all take place within the Earth system, but the next four expand into the vastly enlarged domain of solar orbital space. Fourth is the Zubrin Mars program, which envisions the establishment of self-sustaining colonies on Mars and the eventual greening of the Red Planet with techniques of terraforming. Fifth, the Cole program, after Dandridge Cole, envisions the colonization of distant asteroids, thus achieving a great diaspora and a human habitat composed of "many worlds." Sixth, the Dyson program seeks the colonization and industrialization of the distant and frigid moons of the outer planets and the comets of the Oort Cloud. As habitat expands far beyond the Earth with the Cole and Dyson Diasporas, it is assumed that distinctly different biological branches of humanity will emerge, thus filling the distant reaches of the solar system with multiple forms of alien intelligences. Seventh and finally is the Goddard program to realize the "ultimate migration," the movement into interstellar space and the colonization of the galaxy.

This list of seven roughly distinct major habitat expansion programs is unlikely to be exhaustive and will surely be amended if these projects get under way. Also, these projects, while here sequenced on the basis of their distance from the Earth, may well be pursued in a different sequence, with asteroidal exploitation and Martian colonization occurring before the Glaser Ring or the Bernal-O'Neill Belt are constructed.

Despite their diversity, habitat space expansion projects are unified by two general postures toward the Earth. First, space expansionists envision transforming the Earth into a spaceship. The trajectory of habitat expansion starts with projects to convert the Earth from a purely natural spaceship (in the sense of a body moving through space) into a built and designed spaceship, analogous to the vessels humans have designed for plying the seas and air of Earth, but on a vastly greater scale. Making the Earth into a spaceship, requiring the construction of vast orbital infrastructures with resources drawn from solar space, lays the technological foundations for the expansion of humanity into a multiworld species. Second, space colonization requires creation of Earth-like conditions supporting life within the metal shells of artificial worlds, a plenitude of canned Earths. As humanity ascends an ever progressing curve of power over nature by harnessing ever more natural powers, the terraforming of other worlds, starting with Mars, enables planetary-scale approximate reproductions of the Earth. Ultimately these technological Earth offshoots prepare for propelling multigenerational arks across the abysses of interstellar space. Thus habitat expansionism starts with technics-in-ecosystems and progresses to ecosystems-in-technics, a move made possible by ecosystems-as-technics, the conversion of ecosystems into predicable, controllable, and reproducible engineered systems.[24]

The diverse programs of the habitat space expansionists, being animated by some problem or vulnerability of the Earth, propose space projects as remedies. They propose solutions to the terrestrial problems of insufficient Lebensraum for the expansion of human populations, of environmental deterioration, of shortages of energy and material resources, and of vulnerabilities to the Earth from cosmic catastrophes. Threats to civilization and human survival from nuclear war, plagues amplified by biotechnology, and other ghastly technological misfires are repeatedly evoked as providing an imperative for a significant human movement into space. The same technological accelerations and enablements that produce these new terrestrial perils also make space activities possible, providing either new solutions or new escapes. As space expansionists often say, "All humanity's eggs are in one basket," the natal Earth. As a result of this simple *geographic* fact, many threats, both natural and human-made, pose an existential threat as long as humanity is confined to one planet. The difference, space expansionists often proclaim, between humans and dinosaurs is that humans have a space program.

Terrestrial Habitat Expansion and Infrastructures

While expanding over the terrestrial Earth, humans have altered the planet in many ways, but among the most consequential and enduring has been by constructing physical infrastructures of "built space."[25] These infrastructures, particularly cities, but also dams, canals, and roads, are what some geographers refer to as "geotechnics" to distinguish them from more mobile and ephemeral artifacts.[26] Geotechnics have been a foundational part of human historical expansion and have their own extensive technological futurism and utopianism, most recently under the rubric of "macro-engineering."[27] It is this mundane and basic human vocation of constructing infrastructures that habitat space expansionists propose to complete and extend beyond the terrestrial Earth.

Beavers build dams, birds weave nests, and insects construct hives, but humans have been particularly adept in the variety, durability, and size of their habitat infrastructures. Around ten thousand years ago, as humans began to adopt sedentary abodes, buildings and then cities emerged. For several millennia irrigation systems, cities, roads, military fortifications, and cosmically aligned ceremonial megastructures, such as the great pyramids of Egypt, were the leading edge of human infrastructure activity. The early Chinese were particularly precocious in building large infrastructures, with the Great Wall, the Great Canal, and agricultural terraces. At the other end of Eurasia, "the nether lands" were ingeniously converted from swamps into arable land with dikes and wind-powered water pumps.

With the coming of the Industrial Revolution, the pace and scale of built-space construction greatly increased. The invention of steam-powered digging machinery enabled massive infrastructures such as the Suez and Panama canals, numerous large dams to divert rivers, and ever longer and sturdier bridges and tunnels, radically reconfiguring landscapes all over the planet. Cities, only rarely having a million inhabitants, exploded in size and in the sophistication of their infrastructures. With ever longer and more capacious roads, aqueducts, railroads, wires and cables, and pipelines, densely built urban-industrial nodes were linked to far-flung webs enmeshing large parts of the planet. Through these networks flow the torrents of material, energy, and information that give the human world its distinctive, and naturally disruptive, metabolism.

Despite their great importance in providing the literal foundations for civilization, infrastructure politics has rarely attracted much attention from political thinkers. An exception, the "hydraulic despotism" thesis suggested by Karl Marx and developed by Karl Wittfogel and others, hypothesized that early societies heavily reliant on large and capital-intensive hydraulic systems for irrigation were prone to economic stagnation and political centralization.[28] The basic logic of this argument is that the building and maintenance of large infrastructures to sustain food production required centralized despotic bureaucracies. In a similar vein, analysts of urban studies and architecture have developed many arguments about how the contours of built space embody different power projects and agendas, and in turn shape social and economic outcomes.[29]

Infrastructures also have ecologies. From their beginnings, human habitats have depended upon steadily improving techniques for managing the interior ecologies of enclosed spaces. The ecological history of cities is thus Janus-faced: on their outside face, in the spaces beyond their borders, cities have imposed mounting ecological burdens with their voracious resource consumption and generation of wastes, but on their inside face, they are completely dependent on technical infrastructures to tap, purify, and distribute water supplies, to collect, transport, and dispose of wastes, and to abate various forms of air and noise pollution.[30] The history of urbanization is thus in significant measure the history of successful environmental management, of designing and operating the ecologies of partly enclosed and partly built spaces, practices often overlooked by environmentalisms aiming for the protection of pristine nature.

Although typically overshadowed by anticipations about their flashier cousins—flying, killing, and thinking machines—habitat infrastructure also has a long history of technological futurism and utopianism, which habitat space expansionism continues. The basic premise of these visions is that properly designed built spaces can embody social and political goals and contribute to their realization. Across the past several centuries utopian urban planners have created—fortunately mainly on paper—boldly novel plans for cities and buildings which they believe will embody, and help realize and maintain, revolutionary improvements in society and politics and mass well-being.[31] Such anticipations and efforts are also found among the many contemporary space thinkers working to design appropriate habitats in space.

With the coming of the industrial machine, infrastructure futurists increasingly imagined comprehensive conquests of nature, often intermingled with frightening genocidal schemes for "demographic engineering."[32] William Delisle Hay, in his widely read *Three Hundred Years Hence* (1881), envisions a world population of 130 billion, living on a planet fully reconfigured for supporting humans, with leveled mountaintops, floating and submarine cities, geothermal heating of the polar regions, and the systematic extermination of all wild and domesticated animals.[33] He also envisions "the Great Extermination," the liquidation of the "colored races," in order that only "the fittest and the best may eventually survive," making his vision both a culmination of the Baconian Enlightenment project for the complete dominion of humans over nature and an anticipation of the ghastly industrialized genocides of the twentieth century enabled by the technological domination of some humans over others. Even

Wells, in a revealing passage of high modernist enthusiasm, wrote favorably of a country that "sterilizes, exports, or poisons its people of the abyss."[34]

An even more audacious and frightening vision of a Fuller Earth planetary infrastructural reconfiguration is provided by Tsiolkovsky himself in his 1928 essay, "The Future of Earth and Mankind." He proposes expanding human Lebensraum by eradicating "the hostile forces of vegetation and animals," covering the oceans with vast rafts, and enclosing the atmosphere with a "thin transparent roof," measures that would allow the human population to expand to 400 billion.[35] With humans bred to use less oxygen, the planet could support even larger populations. Extension of human habitats across the solar system would eventually allow populations of 10^{21} and "achieve perfection and banish all possibility of evil and suffering in the solar system."[36] Updating and extending this line of thinking to its logically absurd conclusion, the philosophers Milan Cirkovic and Nick Bostrom, in what they call their "astronomical waste argument," calculate that in the next billion years some 10^{32} humans could exist in this galaxy and beyond if humanity colonizes space as rapidly as possible, something they conclude is an absolute moral duty to pursue.[37] In leaving Terra, hypertrophic humanism morphs in what can be appropriately called cosmically malignant humanism.

Many less comprehensively ecocidal, genocidal, and utopian visions of large-scale habitat engineering have been proposed. A recurrent theme of Herculean engineering has been ever larger hydrological schemes, such as a dam across the Bering Sea, flooding the Sahara and the Congo basin, and diverting rivers flowing "uselessly" into the Arctic to irrigate vast tracts in Central Asia and North America.[38] Another family of macro-engineering schemes, particularly popular in Cold War America and the USSR, envisioned the widespread use of "peaceful nuclear explosions" as a powerful new "Earth-moving" technology. The American Operation Plowshares envisioned using nuclear explosives to dig new harbors, excavate an enlarged Panama Canal, and blast deep underground caravans to collect natural gas.[39] In the early twenty-first century, these mega-engineering schemes look like yesterday's tomorrows, futures that time has passed, as they have been halted by stakeholders adversely affected by their negative environmental consequences and by their dubious economic prospects. But these visions of reengineered landscapes have not so much disappeared as they have been elevated and projected into the vast realms of outer space.[40] Meanwhile, as these dazzling infrastructure visions flutter across the horizon of future possibility, the largest infrastructure *deconstruction* event in human history, the flooding of major coastal cities due to sea level rise from climate change, inexorably unfolds on Terra.

The Politics of Ships and Cities

The ultimate built space is the ship. The term "spaceship" is universally used to refer to vessels capable of traversing outer space, but in a more general sense of this term, humans have been building "space ships" since before recorded history, and these vehicles, growing successively more capable, have played vital roles in the spatial expansion of humans on Earth. Ships to ply the seas, then aerial and submarine realms, are in many ways the most advanced and complete of human-built, enclosed, and managed environments and have been the most complex of human artifacts for much of history. While cities are firmly planted in particular places on terra firma, ships are defined by their mobility, and they uniquely provide the means by which humans have progressively been able to traverse the fluid, gaseous, and vacuous parts of the planet. With large parts of the Earth accessible only with such complex machines, advances in ships have paced the globalization of human activities and shaped its very uneven results. With the development of ships to traverse the atmospheric heights and the submarine depths, the reach of humans started to become planetary and more fully three-dimensional. Ships for different media have radically different appearances, their shapes tightly determined by their functions and for passage through specific media.

All ships also must be configured to provide an enclosed livable habitat, however cramped and impoverished, for a temporary period. The progress of maritime, aeronautical, and submarine technologies has been dependent on advances in providing enclosed habitats for their human occupants. Long ocean voyages required techniques for storing food and water. Airplanes were able to fly into the less turbulent layers of the upper atmosphere only after pressurized cabins were developed; submarines require artificial atmospheres. With ships to traverse outer space, the construction of enclosed and built spaces approaches completeness.

The distinctive technological and geographic features of ships give rise to distinct political forms. The governance of ships is highly hierarchical and technocratic. Ships always have a captain, one individual invested with supreme decision-making authority, and crews, which have distinct functional technical tasks to perform and who must obey the commands of their superior officers. Ships sometimes carry passengers, who, from the standpoint of the governance and operation of the ship, are essentially animate cargo. The governance of ships is also technocratic, placing the highest premium on technical expertise, particularly navigation and propulsion. Ships are never governed as democracies, and the rights of all are massively circumscribed by the operational needs of the machine.

Dissent and disobedience on ships are acts of mutiny, quickly and severely punished. The captain of the ship is not a tyrant, but rather a technocratic despot.

The reason hierarchical technocratic regimes prevail on ships is extremely simple: the acute vulnerability of all ships to catastrophic destruction. Cities may eventually fall into various types of ruin and decay if not governed well, but ships at every instant of their passage may sink or crash. As a result, the rigidly authoritarian governance of ships enjoys very high legitimacy. Beginning with Plato's *Republic*, the metaphor of the polity as ship in perilous waters requiring skillful steerage has been used to discredit democracy and justify expert rule.[41] Not surprisingly, apologists for hierarchical rule of territorial polities often speak of "the ship of state" to legitimate claims of complete authority, and they justify this analogy by characterizing foreign policy as steering through a perpetually dangerous "sea of anarchy" requiring centralized and competent rule for the safety of all.[42] Nautical analogs are pervasive in political thought: the word "government" derives from the Latin for "helmsman," and political shipwrecks, storms, castaways, mutinies, and odysseys are common evocations.

Cities are also significantly artifactual, but very different lines of thinking prevail about the politics of cities. A long tradition, dating from antiquity and developed by early modern political thinkers such as Montesquieu and Rousseau, sees cities as being likely, or at least possible, sites for more democratic and republican rule.[43] The key argument is that the small size and close proximity of cities enable the bulk of the population to effectively organize to advance their interests, which is much more difficult for scattered rural populations. These arguments thus pose the question of whether space colonies will be more like ships or like cities or like some city-ship hybrid. Will the astropolis be a ship or a city?

The Fuller Earth Program and Spaceship Earth

These two intertwined historical trajectories—habitat expansion by means of infrastructures and ships as completely built spaces governed by technocratic elites—converge in the thinking of Buckminster Fuller about "spaceship Earth" and its "operating manual." The quintessential futurist guru of the 1960s, Fuller was a paradigmatic visioneer.[44] He cast himself as a general purpose designer and design philosopher with comprehensive planetary aspirations.[45] During the 1930s Fuller designed and built a variety of what he called "dymaxion" habitats and vehicles, the most successful being the geodesic dome, several hundred thousand of which have been built. These domes combine simple design, easy fabrication, and extreme strength and are architecturally iconic for late twentieth-century technological modernism. Fuller's fabricated enclosed megastructures are in turn dwarfed by the "archology" (a combination of architecture and ecology) of the visionary Italian architect Paolo Soleri, who envisions city-buildings a kilometer in size containing a "tamed facsimile of the regional climate" and in which people will become accustomed to "living inside instead of on top."[46]

Fuller's thinking on "spaceship Earth" was disseminated in numerous lectures and his 1969 manifesto booklet, *Operating Manual for Spaceship Earth*.[47] This concept gained wide currency as a metaphor for high levels of global interdependence, particularly among environmental thinkers. Fuller's starting point is the observation that the Earth itself is a "spaceship" and that "we are all astronauts."[48] The spaceship is "the first perfect environment," and Fuller aims to elevate the conduct of Terran affairs to this standard. This concept produces a pointed mandate: humans, whom Fuller calls "Earthians," should start behaving as if they are astronauts, or they will suffer catastrophic consequences. The alternatives are extreme: either utopia or oblivion.[49] Spaceship Earth is poorly run and did not come with an "operating manual." This Fuller proposes to create by mobilizing a global network of designers and "world planners" employing his synergistic and comprehensive design philosophy so the planet can be "comprehended and serviced in total."[50]

Continuing the strand of technological futurism that measures progress through larger infrastructures, Fuller proposes a variety of immense megastructures, such as the enclosure of lower Manhattan in a colossal geodesic dome, vast wind farms in remote areas, and a fully globally interconnected electricity transmission system with transoceanic links.[51] The ultimate completion of this vision produces the total fabrication of the surface of the planet, thus making a Hydroponic Earth and a Geodesic Earth, in which infrastructural built space is comprehensively enclosed. A complete technological reengineering of the planet violates nothing natural because the "universe is *nothing but* technology."[52]

Despite his visionary mega-engineering projects and his agenda to ultimately refashion the planet into a ship-like totally built space, Fuller's design philosophy is centered on the strategy of doing more with less. Throughout his work, his foil is Malthusianism, the view that there are not enough resources, particularly energy. The Earth may be a closed system (with the crucial exception of the influx of solar energy), but it does not follow, Fuller argues, that humanity is condemned to a Malthusian future of overpopulation, mass poverty, and social conflict. Ephemeralization, "the accomplishment of much greater performance with much less material," is the key to avoiding these outcomes.[53] Fuller points to the relentless miniaturization of electronic components as a signature example of ephemeralization. He sees this design approach in the operation of ships, and its fullest realization in the first space vehicles. Only by radical efficiency improvements can Earthians, vast in number and great in appetites but confined to their spherical space ship, escape catastrophic breakdown and make their habitats sustainable.

A crucial space component of the Fuller Earth program is orbiting infrastructures to regulate the planet's atmosphere. Just as aerial, submarine, and outer space ships are unthinkable without technological control of the gases within their hulls, so too a full spaceship Earth is unthinkable without the technological regulation of the planet's atmosphere. For early peoples, the apparent ability of celestial beings to control the weather by bringing storms, floods, and droughts was particularly awe-inspiring and practically consequential, a universally intelligibly measure of just how powerful such beings were relative to humans. Indeed, much of the obsession with astronomy in early civilizations (which were crucially dependent on reliable rain) stems from their conflation of the celestial with the meteorological, making their cosmic megalithic structures costly, but impotent, weather and climate prediction and control projects.

As anticipation of human technological ascents into the heavens began to emerge in the imaginative vanguard of the Space Age, schemes for weather and climate control became space futurist staples. Oberth in the 1920s foresaw large space mirrors to alter the weather and illuminate the night as well as to incinerate cities in wartime.[54] Clarke spoke casually about space being exploited not just to understand the weather but to control it. As the recurrent pattern of planetary cooling producing periodic ice ages over the past several million years came to be understood, space expansionists envisioned projects to increase the amount of solar radiation falling on the Earth by mirrors and lenses deployed in orbit.[55]

But over recent decades, as the opposite problem of global warming has risen in importance, some space expansionists have joined with geo-engineers in promoting solar radiation management (SRM) projects to reduce the amount of solar radiation falling on the Earth, and thus partly compensate for the greenhouse heating of the atmosphere.[56] Most SRM schemes involve injecting particulate matter into the upper atmosphere, but some space analysts propose orbiting apparatuses or debris belts to make massive planetary "sun screens" to block the amount of solar energy striking the Earth's atmosphere.[57] Although not taking the form of an actual geodesic dome, space-based SRM infrastructures would produce a Geodesic Earth, with a managed planetary atmosphere appropriate for the gaseous components of spaceship Earth.

Fuller's vision of spaceship Earth is accompanied by a quite explicit politics deriving directly from his projection of naval-maritime governance to a planetary scale. His conceptualization of the politics of spaceship Earth is straightforward technocracy, the rule of the master designers of his integrated system design science, thus making him the "captain of spaceship Earth."[58] In laying the groundwork for this vision, Fuller spins a quite fantastic history of the modern era in which nautical and navigational designers and innovators are the "power behind the throne" of the leading European imperial states, particularly Britain.[59] In contrast, he expresses contempt for both politicians and capitalists, seeing them as obstructive parasites in the path of progress.[60] Despite his very strong commitment to a democratic-utilitarian "greatest good for the greatest number," Fuller has little patience for Marxism or political revolution and essentially expects politics to wither away as a worldwide network of designers, architects, and engineers steps forward with innovative technological solutions to human problems.

Although Fuller emphasizes that everyone, particularly the young, should become problem-solving designers and engineers, he clearly envisions the replacement of politics by the administration of things, leaving the vast majority of humanity consigned to the roles of obedient crew members or passive passengers. Like prophets of earlier grand historical projects for comprehensive human improvement, Fuller speaks of "cosmic evolution" being "irrevocably intent" on realizing his new Earth ship.[61] With the Earth reconfigured into a vast and highly efficient machine sustaining the prosperity of everyone, or, as he puts it, "omni-integrated humanity omnisuccessful," Fuller's world ship relies upon the virtue and training of the technocrats to keep the vast powers of the Earth ship-machine directed for the general welfare.[62]

Energy and Minerals from Space

The progressive enlargement of human habitats has required growing inputs of minerals and fuels, provided by a planet-spanning extraction and processing infrastructure. As machine civilization has ripped and sucked ever greater quantities of material from the lithosphere, environmental impacts have grown, and the specter of depletion and shortage haunts its future. But as Earth is an infinitesimally tiny speck in a stupendously vast cosmos filled with effectively unlimited quantities of energy and materials, space expansionists propose to tap extraterrestrial resources for terrestrial needs.

Early space expansionist visions focused more on leaving than supplying Earth, but since the 1960s, space projects to collect energy and mine metals have been a major part of the agenda. These proposals are typically responses to an environmentalist "limits to growth" perspective, which energy shortages in the 1970s seemed to confirm. Krafft Ehricke, the German American engineer who helped develop and popularize these projects, speaks of "extraterrestrialization" and "a benign industrial revolution minimizing pollutive and biocidal side-effects."[63] Two clusters of such schemes, collecting solar energy and beaming it back to Earth and mining asteroids for metals, have been the most extensively developed. These projects are a central way in which space advocates argue that space expansion can help solve current terrestrial problems while laying the foundations for vastly enlarged solar space expansions. If there are limits to growth on the Earth, then moving into space and tapping its unlimited resources allows growth to proceed without limits.

Proposals to tap solar energy from space came onto the space scene in 1968 in the proposals of Peter Glaser, an engineer and management consultant. Glaser proposed a constellation of solar power satellites (SPS), or sunsats, placed in geosynchronous orbit.[64] Each satellite would be composed of large arrays of photovoltaic cells that would convert solar energy into electrical energy, which would be beamed as microwaves to giant receiving antennas on Earth. Collectors located in space could harvest energy continuously, and the sunlight falling on them would be a third stronger than on terrestrial collectors because unobstructed by the atmosphere. Glaser proposed a ring of sixty satellites, each the size of Manhattan, which would produce some 500 billion watts of electrical power, equal to roughly half of the generating capacity of the United States. The amounts of potentially available energy are prodigious: a "single kilometer-wide band of geosynchronous orbit experiences enough solar flux in one year (approximately 21 terawatt-years) to nearly equal the amount of energy contained within all known recoverable conventional energy reserves on Earth."[65]

As the energy crises of the 1970s unfolded, the SPS proposal for astro-electricity received considerable attention for about a decade, until energy prices declined. Three large studies of SPS proposals by organs of the US government concluded that sunsats were technologically feasible but not economically competitive, mainly due to the high costs of lifting materials for their construction into orbit.[66] Analysts also noted that Sunsats could provide energy for beam weapons or be modified into beam weapons, but would be highly vulnerable to attack.[67] In response to cost problems, advocates proposed using lunar and asteroidal materials, but calculating how much lunar and asteroidal bases, manufacturing facilities, and transportation systems would cost remains largely speculative.

With the recent growing concern over climate change, new versions of these proposals, now referred to as space solar power (SSP), have been advanced. Advocates claim new thin films and more efficient photovoltaic cells can greatly reduce fabrication costs. These projects may become economically competitive if the full environmental costs of terrestrial energy production are taken into account.[68] Interest in SSP is growing in large developing countries, such as India, where one former president tirelessly promoted such schemes.[69] Advocates also claim these infrastructures could provide energy for ambitious military space projects. Their construction in geosynchronous orbit would require a complete reshuffling of the communication satellites currently located there. Advocates liken this project to a combination of the Manhattan and Apollo programs. These behemoth infrastructures would transform the Earth's geotechnical landscape with a new feature, the Glaser Ring. Control and use of this mega-infrastructure would surely become a major issue in world politics, but its construction would expand the role of space in human affairs to an unprecedented level.

The idea that asteroids could provide prodigious quantities of minerals and be stepping stones in humanity's cosmic expansion dates back to Tsiolkovsky, but in recent decades detailed proposals to exploit asteroidal resources have been developed. Proponents emphasize that the planetary defense agenda of preventing catastrophic asteroidal collisions dovetails with a vision of turning threats into a resource base, of transforming a potential "rain of iron and ice" into "fertile stars" (see Figure 6.1). As with SPS, rising mineral prices in the 1970s stimulated interest in asteroid mining, which then declined along with prices, only to revive recently as rapid industrial development in China bolstered commodity prices.

A leading figure on this topic is John S. Lewis, an American planetary scientist who has written a stream of books touting asteroidal mining, whose titles make the pitch: *Resources from Space: Breaking the Bonds of Earth* (1978), *Mining the Sky: Untold Riches from the Asteroids, Comets and Planets* (1996), and *Asteroid Mining 101: Wealth for the New Space Economy* (2015). The case for asteroid mining is both economic and environmental. As use of metals grows, it becomes necessary to process ores of progressively lower value, which is more expensive,

Figure 6.1 Moving and Mining Asteroids. Source: Maciej Frolow/Getty Images

environmentally damaging, and energy consumptive. Preliminary inventories of valuable metals in space, most notably nickel, iron, platinum, and titanium, compiled by Ehricke, Lewis, and others, indicate staggeringly vast amounts.[70] Advocates speak of asteroidal mining as a trillion-dollar industry and anticipate a "third industrial revolution" in space.[71] Lewis claims that "resources from space change all the rules" by offering humanity a "boundless increasing-sum game" and making "affluence for all possible."[72] Looking further ahead, he projects that the entire mass of the main asteroid belt is sufficient to "provide for the material needs of a million times as many people as the Earth can hold."[73] Neo-Marxist advocates of Fully Automated Luxury Communism with abundance for all also look to asteroid mining for resources.[74]

The astral abundance analyses of Lewis and other sky-mining advocates focus on science, technology, and economics and rarely consider political or military possibilities, despite the earlier proposals of Cole and Cox to utilize asteroids as "planetoid bombs." It is unclear how the wealth from these mines in the sky will trickle down to elevate general living standards, particularly if mining is conducted by corporations owned by a handful of already extremely wealthy individuals. It is also unclear why the often violent conflicts over mineral resources on Earth would not also expand into space. Regardless of how the anticipated benefits are distributed and who controls these celestial grubstakes, mining asteroids would mark a watershed in the expansion of human activity into space, while laying foundations for much larger ventures.

The Bernal-O'Neill Program
for Urban-Industrial Orbita

Early imaginings of humans in space were almost entirely about traversing the cosmic voids to visit and explore other celestial bodies, mainly Luna and Mars. Anticipations of fabricated habitats in space begin to appear only in the nineteenth century, with Edward Everett Hale's *The Brick Moon*, in which a human residence is launched into Earth orbit.[75] Early in the twentieth century, Hermann Noordung envisioned a wheel-shaped space station that could be rotated so that centrifugal force could provide a sort of artificial gravity. This idea was popularized by von Braun and others in the 1950s, thus establishing the donut-shaped space station alongside the sleek phallic rocket as visual icons of space futurism. Starting in the early 1970s, the Soviet Union and the United States orbited a variety of small space stations in which crews lived for months.[76]

In the wake of the Cold War, this path of space development led to a joint American-Russian project, the International Space Station, which also includes

European, Japanese, and Canadian—but not Chinese—contributions. This structure, which has been continuously occupied by international crews since 2000, cost some 250 billion dollars to build and service and has about as much habitable space as a six-bedroom house.[77] It is humankind's most substantial and sustained presence in space. The primary research activity of the station is biomedical studies of the effects of long-duration weightlessness on human health. The station is completely dependent on food and oxygen supplies lofted from the ground, but its large solar photovoltaic arrays supply all its energy needs. Despite the fact that this complex crewed object is moving at over 17,000 miles an hour, it is referred to as a station rather than a ship, reflecting the fact that it is not really going anywhere but endlessly circles in its relatively fixed orbit.

These first long-duration habitats stand in relation to the larger expansionist vision of space colonization roughly as the cramped accommodations of the *Mayflower* stand to the entirety of contemporary urban-industrial America. Tsiolkovsky had anticipated vast numbers of humans living in artificial habitats, but an elaborate version of this idea was set forth by J. D. Bernal in his prophetic *The World, the Flesh and the Devil* (1929), and then developed much further by Gerard O'Neill in *The High Frontier* (1977) and other works. While the Fuller Earth, Ehricke-Glaser-Lewis, and von Braun programs all envision the construction of infrastructures in space, the Bernal-O'Neill program goes a major step further, to the humanization of space through large-scale human space settlement. This would add a much heavier infrastructural formation—a belt—to create a whole new domain of human habitation, whose population could eventually exceed terrestrial ones in size. Taken together, various satellite nets, the Glaser Ring, and the Bernal-O'Neill Belt would constitute Orbita, an eighth continent, a purely artifactual extension of human habitat large enough to change the planet's geography.

The idea of colonizing the outer reaches of Earth orbital space with city-size habitats is now primarily associated with the American aerospace engineer Gerard O'Neill.[78] In the work of O'Neill and his followers, stretching from the late 1960s through the early 1980s, such schemes reached a level of sophistication and public prominence vastly greater than any before or after. During this brief zenith of space colonization enthusiasm, numerous technical studies were conducted, press coverage was extensive, and a grass-roots organization, the L5 Society, promoted rapid colonization.[79] O'Neill says a barrier to recognizing the potential for such free-floating urban megastructures is the prevalence of what the SF maestro Isaac Asimov labeled "planetary chauvinism," the presumption that the surfaces of other natural celestial bodies are the most suitable places for colonization. Unlike the voids of space, the surfaces of planetary bodies are disadvantaged by low levels of gravity (which cannot be artificially increased), by gravity wells requiring great exertion to surmount, and by levels of gravity impeding construction of very large structures.

In O'Neill's vision of space colonization, materials mined from the surface of Luna could be cheaply flung into high Earth orbit by solar-powered electromagnetic rail guns. This material would then be processed into structural elements and assembled into habitats. The canister-shaped colonies would be rotated, at the rate of about three revolutions a minute, providing a gravity substitute for persons standing on their inner surfaces comparable to standing on Earth. Sealed from the vacuum of space, artificial atmospheres would be provided, and greenhouses enjoying continuous sunlight would produce food. One side of the canister would be a large latticework of windows, permitting the entrance of sunlight, reflecting off moving external mirrors to provide Earth-like cycles of day and night. By packing the walls of the canisters with lunar soil, the interiors would be shielded from radiation to levels comparable to Earth's. In O'Neill's Model One, some 500,000 tons of lunar material would be fabricated into a pair of counterrotating cylinders, each half a mile long and six hundred feet in diameter, providing a habitat for ten thousand people. In Island III, the canister would be twenty miles in length, four miles in diameter, have five hundred square miles of "land" area, and support a population of several million. Over time, large numbers of such city-ship worlds could be created throughout the solar system employing material form the asteroids and then the moons of the other planets, with populations exceeding the Earth's. O'Neill claimed that Model One could be built with existing technology for about 30 billion dollars and could be in place by the late 1980s. He emphasizes that the interiors of these colonies could be made to be very Earth-like, with forests, streams, and lakes, but with the inescapable oddity that people and objects on the other side of the cannister would be "above," giving such can-worlds wrapped rather than open horizons (see Figure 6.2).[80]

In making his case for these canned Earths, O'Neill argues that space colonization is necessary because of terrestrial resource shortages and environmental decay. He is relentlessly sensitive to emerging ecological sensibilities, suggesting space arks could be refuges for endangered species of Earth life. He anticipates that most industrial activities on the Earth eventually would be moved to space, leaving an "industry-free pastoral Earth" with large wilderness areas, which might attract tourism *from* space.[81]

O'Neill extensively discusses social, security, and political aspects of his envisioned worlds. He has a conservative view of human nature but a liberal view of the sources of violent conflict. Humans "change only on the time scale of millennia," and off-worlders will be "guided by the same desires, instincts, and fears that have dominated history."[82] He attributes most terrestrial wars to "battles over limited, non-extendable pieces of land," which "will be muted"

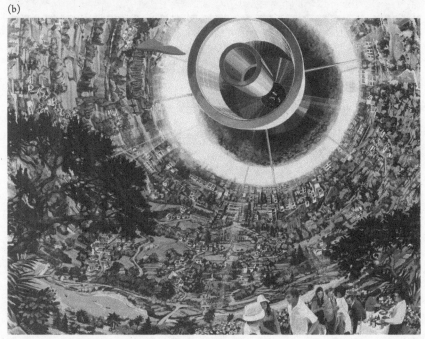

Figure 6.2 Space Colonies. A. Exterior view. Artwork by Rick Guidice. Source: NASA ID Number AC76-0965, https://settlement.arc.nasa.gov/70sArtHiRes/70sArt/Bernal_Exterior_AC76-0965_5688.jpg. B. Interior including human-powered flight. Artwork by Rick Guidice. Source: NASA ID Number AC76-0628, https://settlement.arc.nasa.gov/70sArtHiRes/70sArt/Bernal_Interior_AC76-0628_5716.jpg. C. Agricultural modules in cutaway view (multiple toroids). Artwork by Rick Guidice. Source: NASA ID Number AC78-0330-4, https://settlement.arc.nasa.gov/70sArtHiRes/70sArt/Bernal_Agriculture_AC78-0330-4_5726.jpg. D. Exterior view. Artwork by Don Davis. Source: NASA ID Number AC75-2621, https://settlement.arc.nasa.gov/70sArtHiRes/70sArt/Torus_Interior_AC75-2621_5718.jpg.

(c)

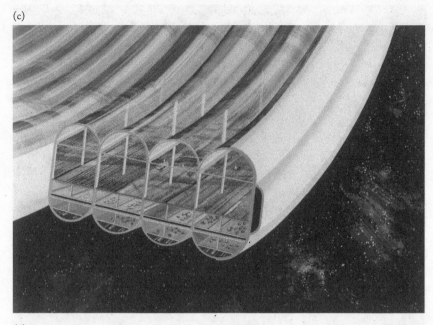

(d)

Figure 6.2 Continued

in space worlds that are "replicable so that no one need feel constrained by a fixed boundary" but will be "independent of each other for essential needs" and "movable."[83] More generally, he postulates that "moderation and empathy come with technical maturity."[84]

O'Neill also briefly considers the military situation of space colonies in relation to Earth, observing that they are "unpromising sites for weapons or military bases" and are sufficiently vulnerable that "no one in such a habitat can be tempted into believing that he can attack someone else without risk to himself."[85] Because these worlds would be "separated by at least one or two days of travel time" they can "never be used as effective sites for an attack on the home planet," and his overall expectation is that "the probability of wars between habitats" is "at least considerably smaller than of war between nations on Earth."[86] But as the Earth becomes dependent on energy from space, he acknowledges, terrestrial nations will insist on maintaining ownership and control, keeping them "tied to the earth governmentally," at least initially.[87]

On the internal governance of his space islands, O'Neill says the humanization of space is "quite contrary in spirit" to "classical utopian concepts," which center around "escape from outside interference, and tight discipline within the community."[88] He expects new worlds to "decrease rather than increase concentration of power and control" and produce extensive "diversity" and "experimentation."[89] Off-world migration will allow "special-interest groups to 'do their own thing' and build small worlds of their own," some "sharing a passion for a novel system of government" but others devoted to music or "nudism, water sports, or skiing."[90] The overall vision that O'Neill provides is not so much the urbanization of outer Earth orbital space as its suburbanization.[91] In this vision of astropluralism, the demands of building and operating such city-ships have no major influence on the social and political possibilities that can be pursued within them, a vision completely contrary to Fuller's spaceship Earth politics.

Writing half a century earlier, the British Marxist chemist J. D. Bernal provides a much less technically specific vision of an even more transformative space colonization in his book, *The World, the Flesh, and the Devil*.[92] Like others, Bernal postulates the necessity of migration from the Earth due to its finite size and limited resources. He postulates that there are three great enemies of "the rational soul": "the world" (resource limits and climate variability), "the flesh" (biological limitations of human bodies), and "the devil" (the limitations imposed by human emotions and intellectual incapacities). Space worlds, Bernal argues, can help overcome all three. First comes the replacement of human organs with artificial substitutes and then genetically reengineered human capabilities for a "much more complex sensory and motor organization," made necessary due to the increasing complexity of technology; he suggests that these posthumans will be shaped like crustaceans.[93] For overcoming the limitations of the human psyche, Bernal hints at various cybernetic enhancements but mainly expects new educational psychologies and socialist organization to produce perfect communal group minds "where memories are held in common." All this he characterizes as the "progress of dehumanization."[94] Where O'Neill foresees space colonies as laboratories for social experimentation, Bernal sees them as sites for much more radical change. Where O'Neill wants to make space habitats *like Earth* for humans who will stay the same, Bernal wants to employ technologies in space to fundamentally *change humans*.

Bernal envisions spherical artificial worlds, ten miles or so in diameter and made of very light "new molecular materials."[95] Initially they would be in hollowed asteroids, but then they would be fabricated with "the rings of Saturn or other planetary detritus."[96] Making these worlds viable will be very difficult, requiring the empowerment of scientists and intensive cooperation.[97] Scientists will be workers, and scientific workers will be the government. "Globe life" will be "extremely dull" without the "diversity of scene, of animals and plants and historical associations which exist in even the smallest and most isolated country on earth,"[98] but human interests will evolve to focus solely on scientific research. This new hive-like collectivized branch of humanity will leave "old Mankind" in "undisputed possession of the earth," which might be "transformed into a human zoo" and "so intelligently managed that its inhabitants are not aware that they are there merely for the purposes of observation and experiment."[99] Bernal says nothing about the potential military capacities of these higher humans and thinks of their interests toward "old Mankind" only in terms of scientific research. Thus Bernalian space colonies are the sites for the emergence of superspecies of collectivized intelligent life, a vision starkly different from O'Neill's astropluralist social diversification of humanity.

The question of how colonies dispersed across the solar system will interact with Earth receives very uneven treatment by colonization advocates. For O'Neill, the movement out is essentially an escape from scarcity and interaction toward independence. Bernal envisions a benign zookeeper overlordship; Cole and Cox say nothing about it. Frank White, another prominent space thinker, addresses this question in the course of his anticipation of a "solarian civilization" emerging in colonies across the solar system. Assuming that "psychology is shaped by physicality," the colonies of Solarius will "question their ties to Earth," and a "Declaration of Independence from Earth will probably come from one of the new space settlements within the next fifty years."[100] Space colonists will "stop identifying with the Earth itself" and "will jealously guard their incipient independence."[101] He also notes that rival terrestrial nation-states will abandon their military conflicts because of "more significant matters" emerging from "a potential split between Terra and Solarius over political control, economics, and philosophies of life."[102] How the Terrans might fare in such disputes is not considered, but White does characterize the new Solarian civilization as the next step in human evolution.

Colonizing and Greening the Red Planet

The planet Mars, the celestial body most resembling Earth in this solar system, has occupied a special place in thinking about the movement of humanity beyond the Earth. Although Luna is obviously much closer, its limited gravity, half-month days, and complete absence of an atmosphere make it unpromising for anything but scientific research and resource extraction.[103] Before astronomers revealed how desolate and inhospitable the Red Planet actually is, visions of Mars populated by intelligent life were elaborately developed and widely held. As human capabilities of space travel have started to emerge from the imaginary into the prospectively actual, a wide variety of plans have been developed to bring to Mars the intelligent life forms that nature had so disappointingly not provided. For von Braun and other space visionaries through the early and middle years of the twentieth century, the exploration and colonization of Mars was in many ways the ultimate objective of their efforts, something they thought could be realized during their lifetimes. In his 1953 book *The Mars Project*, von Braun envisioned a flotilla of a dozen space vessels making the journey to Mars and back, and he likened this voyage to that of Columbus and other explorers of the European global reconnaissance.[104]

In the wake of the successful voyages to the moon by the Apollo Project, many space advocates anticipated that a crewed mission to Mars would be the next step in the exploration of space. In the United States a succession of high-level studies, panels, and prominent figures have endorsed such Mars missions, but none has ever received the funding necessary to even begin to carry it out, in significant measure due to high costs, ranging into the hundreds of billions of dollars.[105] Instead robotic craft in steadily growing numbers and capabilities have been sent to orbit and land on Mars, and they have sent back a growing trove of data on its geophysical features. Despite the frustrating lag in sending humans to the Red Planet, a vibrant community of space expansionists associated with the Mars Society and other groups has developed and promoted a variety of new and imaginative schemes to go to Mars cheaply. The vision of establishing a viable human colony on Mars also animates many of the new entrepreneurs that have recently become such visible presences in the space enterprise. Apollo 11 astronaut Buzz Aldrin proposes a fleet of spaceships cycling out and back.[106] S. Fred Singer, the founding director of the U.S. weather satellite program, proposes to establish bases on Mars's tiny moons, Phobos and Deimos, and then proceed to the surface from there. Robert Zubrin, president of the Mars Society, proposes a "Mars Direct" scheme of sending automated rocket fuel production facilities ahead of the arrival of humans.[107] While earlier visions of Mars expeditions had emphasized the goal of exploring rather than immediately settling Mars, space expansionists now typically see the establishment of a permanent Mars colony as the most important immediate goal of their efforts.

Zubrin, who has done more than anyone else in recent years to conceptualize and promote Martian colonization, argues that exploring Mars and establishing scientific bases will require large initial government investment, but that "to be viable, a real Martian civilization must be either completely autarkic (very un-likely until the far future) or be able to produce some kind of export that allows it to pay for the imports it requires," and that "Mars will not be able to be self-sufficient until its population numbers in the millions."[108] He argues that Mars has great positional advantages in trade with the asteroid Main Belt because the "launch burden for sending a cargo to Ceres is about fifty times less for missions starting from Mars than those starting from Earth."[109] He envisions a robust "tri-angular trade," with Mars supplying food and low-value manufactured goods to the asteroids, Earth supplying high-value manufactured goods, and the asteroids providing metal to Earth.[110] Zubrin does not consider the possible military dimensions of this arrangement.

In addition to making the case for the feasibility of colonizing Mars, space expansionists devote considerable energies to explaining why it is desirable, even vitally necessary to expand the human habitat by settling Mars. Because Mars is distant from the Earth and its problems, advocates of Mars coloni-zation rarely claim their projects can contribute directly to solving problems on Earth. The key argument deployed by Mars colonization advocates is that various catastrophes may afflict humanity on Earth, and having a second plan-etary home would increase the prospects for the long-term survival of the human species. Mars advocates ritualistically repeat that "humanity has all its eggs in one basket" and must spatially diversify its habitat. Because Mars is at least 30 million miles away from the Earth, and radio communications, trav-eling at the speed of light, take at least twenty minutes to traverse the vast void between the planets, advocates of Mars colonization typically maintain that a Mars colony would inevitably become self-governing and politically independent.

Arguments about the culturally regenerative value of frontiers are also fre-quently deployed by Mars advocates. With rising pressures for conformity and regimentation on Earth due to human numbers and dense interactions, a Mars colony reopens a frontier where cultural innovation and political freedom can thrive. Zubrin claims that "an open frontier on Mars will allow for the preser-vation of cultural diversity," which is declining "within the single global society rapidly being created on Earth."[111] But for Soviet anticipations of Martian col-onization, the Red Planet has held a special attraction as a place for building the perfect communist society that has so long been thwarted by the "dead hand of history" on Earth.[112] A related argument frequently made for Mars col-onization is that humans can begin again, avoiding the mistakes afflicting hu-manity on Earth. Mars colonists, we are told, "will be determined not to repeat old madnesses, and they may be extremely intolerant of even the seeds of divi-sion, violence, and waste."[113] In short, new worlds make possible new and better societies.

Once humans have gained a foothold on Mars with a viable self-sustaining colony, they will, according to many space expansionists, want to make their world more habitable, more like the Earth, by beginning to terraform the planet. Zubrin confidently proclaims, "If Mars is colonized, then it will be terraformed."[114] Terraforming is planetary-scale macro-engineering to alter the geophysical features of other planets, starting with the supposed easy case of Mars. The idea of terraforming emerged in the middle years of the twentieth century, migrating, like so much else, from science fiction to space futurism, and has been steadily developed by the American engineer James Oberg and a small community of enthusiasts. Terraforming is essentially the application of geo-engineering techniques to other planets, and its advocates point to terrestrial macro-engineering projects and proposals as precedents and inspirations. Because Mars is cold, has a thin atmosphere, and lacks significant water, Martian terraforming would aim to make the planet warmer, thicken its atmosphere, and add water. In envisioning how this might be done, space expansionists think in grand scales and time frames across centuries, as memorably envisioned in Kim Stanley Robinson's *Blue Mars*. Manufacturing extremely potent greenhouse gases and releasing them into the Martian atmosphere might raise the atmospheric temperature enough to vaporize the large qualities of frozen carbon dioxide on the planet's poles, thus contributing to further warming. Others envision the use of thermonuclear weapons, giant space mirrors, and directed comet bombardment. To provide heat, solar energy would be collected or concentrated in space. To add water, comets could be brought from the outer solar system and directed to collide with Mars, recapitulating the planetary hydration that may have produced the infant Earth's oceans. While not holding out terraforming as anything but a long-term project, Oberg anticipates that eventually "dwindling wild areas on Earth may have to be replaced with wild areas on other planets."[115] Once terraformed, Mars would be a fully habitable by humans, capable of supporting large human populations.

Unlike the many habitat space expansionists who ignore the question of potential military applications of the technologies they promote, Oberg candidly acknowledges that the tools of terraforming "could be used for military purposes."[116] He admits that "the ability to rebuild planets can be applied to any planet, including earth, and can be used for any purpose, including destructive ones," and that "making sterile planets habitable . . . is just another side of the coin in making habitable planets (such as Earth) sterile."[117] Mirrors that might "control hurricanes, illuminate rescues, save crops, and ultimately warm distant planets were first conceived as weapons for burning enemy countries," as, of course, were thermonuclear explosives. Asteroids and comets can be directed toward as well as away from the Earth, and manipulations of rainfall patterns and the stratospheric ozone layer could bring "damaging ultraviolet radiation onto an enemy, country, continent, or planet."[118] Acknowledging that these possibilities are "chilling," Oberg ominously observes, "Human history demonstrates that people do what suits them and seek rationalizations afterwards."[119]

The Cole Diaspora, Asteroidal Colonization, and Freedom Futures

In the visions of habitat space expansionists for the movement of humanity into space, the smallest celestial bodies, the asteroids, loom large. Beyond the collision threat and resource prospect, asteroidal colonization is widely linked in space expansionist thinking to the preservation and expansion of diversity and freedom. As Zubrin puts it, asteroidal colonization will "make available thousands of potential new worlds, whose cultures and systems of law need never fuse," allowing a "bewildering myriad of societies" to "flower and bloom." Like a prism breaking down light, asteroidal colonization will yield a vivid rainbow of colorful cultural and political alternatives.[120]

An early well-developed vision of the colonization of the interiors of asteroids as human habitats was set forth by Cole and Cox in their 1962 book, *Islands in Space*. As with most space expansionist writings, their treatise is substantially devoted to describing the features of asteroids, how their orbits might be moved, and how their interiors might be hollowed out for human habitats.[121] But beyond this early technical analysis, their work is particularly interesting because, in addition to their previously discussed pioneering survey of planetary catastrophes, they examine the problems of freedom on Earth, world government, and colony freedom.

Freedom on the Earth is also in jeopardy, but space colonization offers the remedy. Modern technology has produced a "complex interdependent society"; this, along with the threat of nuclear war arising from states in international anarchy, creates the "need for a strengthened world organization . . . so great that it will inevitably evolve."[122] While necessary, a world government poses a "potential threat of the ultimate tyranny and the possible total elimination of individual freedom." Because of "advances in weaponry, drugs, psychology and communication, etc., a revolt against such a dictatorship would be impossible." Given this, space colonization should be viewed as a "freedom insurance policy."[123] They also see a "reproduction race" occurring on Earth, in which "the advanced nations" cannot "hold their present position" without "serious overcrowding and resultant increase in regimentation and government control."[124] Because "television and rapid transportation" have begun to produce "greater uniformity in language, culture, custom, and law," the "variety, flexibility, and personal choice offered by the old mix of diverse cultures" have been reduced.[125] In contrast, the colonization of space offers "new lands where there are no rules" and where colonists can "make the rules as they want them."[126]

Given the primacy of freedom in Cole and Cox's argument for space colonization, the question of whether space colonies will tend to be islands of freedom or micrototalitarian hives gains critical importance for their space vision. They first observe that a "planetoid colony" would not seem a promising place for freedom and diversity as it "would necessarily be highly organized, with cooperation, specialization, and interdependence of the inhabitants approaching that of the cells of the human body."[127] They also acknowledge that such a "closed-cycle society" would be "far more sensitive to aberrant behavior, asocial, and destructive behavior."[128] Furthermore, the "possibilities of physical resistance, or violent rebellion" in a "delicately balanced closed-system would be catastrophic."[129]

Despite these daunting obstacles, Cole and Cox are very confident that freedom will flourish. While some colony governments might attempt to establish a totalitarian regime, such a situation would "contain the seeds of its own destruction" because "men naturally resist compulsion" and "forced cooperation cannot be as productive as free cooperation," while "bottled up resentments will eventually explode into violent rebellion."[130] They conclude that the "new world society, like any society, would have to be democratic to be stable. And stability would be essential for the safety of the whole society."[131] As a result, they reassuringly conclude that space worlds will "probably have a government generally approximating those of the western democracies."[132] In sum, for Cole and Cox, the very high vulnerability of space worlds to violence ensures that they will be politically free rather than totalitarian. But it remains something of a mystery how the same forces jeopardizing freedom on Earth can be relied upon to preserve freedom in space colonies. And it is also notable that the authors give no consideration to how such asteroid worlds will interact militarily with the Earth, despite the prospect of the fearsome planetoid bomb.

The prospects for freedom in space colonies have recently received their most extensive discussion in the work of the British astrobiologist Charles S. Cockell in his book *Extra-Terrestrial Liberty: An Enquiry into the Nature and Causes of Tyrannical Government beyond the Earth* (2013), and in a series of conferences and edited volumes sponsored by the British Interplanetary Society.[133] Cockell's main theme is that "the extra-terrestrial environment's tendency to solidify and give succour to tyranny works at many different levels."; His great fear is "a population of contented extra-terrestrial slaves—a cryptic natural tyranny" in a "colony of automatons" with their "freedom reduced to a withered core."[134] Over the course of his wide-ranging discussion, Cockell identifies fourteen distinct ways in which space colonies will tend toward unfreedom, tyranny, and despotism in their politics, cultures, and economics. Unlike many space expansionists, Cockell does not consider alterations in humanity, holding that the human character "remains invariant."[135]

A dauntingly long list of factors predispose space colonies to unfreedom. First is the fact that such colonies, situated in the harshly inhospitable environments of space and other planets, will inevitably have central control over the necessities of life, most notably oxygen, water, and food, whose access has been largely taken for granted in all terrestrial human societies.[136] Second, space colonies will be spatially isolated, with a "natural Berlin Wall" preventing the flights to freedom that were available on Earth.[137] Third, there will be high barriers to the free flow of information between space colonies and societies elsewhere.[138] Fourth, free assembly, vital to permitting the mobilization and expression of popular grievances, will be difficult in the cramped and totally built spaces in extraterrestrial colonies.[139] Fifth, picking up on the point made by Cole and Cox, "unpredictable and criminal actions against the infrastructure represent a continuously present and potentially catastrophic" threat, thus justifying extreme constraints on individual activity and expression.[140] Sixth, space colonies will have "the need for a most intrusive and thorough-going surveillance regime" that will be easy to achieve and will extinguish privacy and erode individual autonomy.[141] Seventh, space colonies will be prone to cultures of intense conformity and will lack cultural diversity.[142] Eighth, the isolated and confined life of space colonies is likely to give rise to various forms of new religions with cultic tendencies inimical to individual freedom.[143] Ninth, turning to economics, collective efforts, not individual, will be necessary for converting raw resources into valuable goods, unlike on Earth, where sole proprietor and "homestead" ventures are both viable and widely viewed as a foundation for free societies.[144] Tenth, laissez-faire economic systems will be infeasible in space colonies, precluding a basic feature of free market economies on Earth.[145] Eleventh, space colonies are likely to require some type of welfare state to ensure that everyone has at least basic life-support services. Twelfth, the economies of space colonies are likely to be more autarkic than those on Earth, reducing the prospects for free trade, widely viewed as associated with free societies on Earth. Thirteenth, economic activity in space colonies is likely to require high levels of central planning.[146] Fourteenth and finally, population rates would need to be effectively regulated.

The future prospects for freedom in space, Cockell argues, are not just relevant to space but could also decisively shape the destiny of free societies on Earth. Space colonies could "exert a disproportionate effect on the Earth compared to their size and populations" because their position atop the gravity well would give them the ability to threaten the Earth with bombardment from space, hide weapons in the "unpoliceable vastness of the interplanetary void," and better exploit the vast resources of the solar system.[147] With stakes this high, and with such daunting obstacles to preserving freedom in space, one might expect Cockell to reach the cautious conclusion that space colonization should be avoided in the interest of human freedom. But this is most definitely *not* his conclusion. He compiles these arguments not to undercut the appeal of space colonization but to identify potential problems that he believes can be avoided through careful anticipatory planning and engineering design in creating both built spaces and institutions. Continuing on the path of terrestrial urban designers and architects, he proposes that the preservation of freedom should be an important factor in the design of space colonies as well as in the founding charters for governing space colonies.[148]

In the course of considering the prospects for freedom in space, two other members of the British Interplanetary Society group, the SF writer Stephen Baxter and the astronomer Ian Crawford, consider aspects of interplanetary warfare that might arise from attempts by space colonies to wage war to become independent from the Earth in ways analogous to how colonies on Earth, such as those in the Americas, became independent. After a careful quantitative assessment of violence potentials of asteroidal bombardment, they conclude that an interplanetary war "would be catastrophically lethal, even compared to our modern capability of all-out nuclear war," and would jeopardize "the survival of the human species itself."[149] Space colonial wars for independence "would likely wreck both civilizations if not exterminate the warring populations entirely."[150] More generally, they observe that the "ease of inflicting enormous damage through an attack from space" means that "it is doubtful that the planet and its cargo of life, including the human, could be adequately protected in the event of an interplanetary war."[151] But like Cockell's treatment of the many barriers to freedom in colonies, Crawford and Baxter do *not* draw the cautious conclusion that colonization is an undesirable goal. Instead they conclude that it is "essential that an interplanetary political framework is established that guarantees colonial liberty without recourse to conflict."[152]

Building on a suggestion by Olaf Stapledon in 1948 that the goal of human space expansion should be a "commonwealth of worlds,"[153] Crawford argues that "interplanetary anarchy is not desirable" and that an interplanetary federation is uniquely able to guarantee that colonies remain free rather than totalitarian and that interplanetary warfare does not occur. Drawing extensively from the history and theory of the founding of the United States of America in the late eighteenth century, Crawford argues that the federal form of the US constitution enabled continental expansion while preserving democracy and individual rights, and that the effective distances for communication and transportation in the solar system are roughly comparable to those at the time of the American founding.[154] Unlike most advocates of space colonization, Crawford sees continued political union between space colonies and the Earth, not space colonial independence, as vital to preserving freedom in space and avoiding interworld war. And he argues that a world federal government on the Earth is a vital prerequisite for space colonization because only such a political order could "effectively regulate the use of potentially dangerous space technologies" to ensure that "they cannot become military tools for one or more nation-states to threaten others."[155] World federal government will also permit the pooling of the vast resources, estimated at a hundred billion dollars a year for several decades, needed to accomplish human expansion across the solar system.[156] He hopefully expects that "a federal form of organization able to encompass both Earth *and* her colonies" will "co-evolve in a mutualistic manner." He insists that it is vital to "establish a framework for interplanetary federation *before* the colonies begin to see themselves as potentially independent entities" and that such a government be federal, rather than confederal, in order to avoid the weaknesses of entities such as the American Articles of Confederation, the League of Nations, and the United Nations.[157] Along those lines, the legal theorist Thomas Gangale suggests that colony government initially be a trusteeship, which could evolve into a federal union.[158] Crawford also claims that a world federal government does not present a threat to freedom but is increasingly needed to grapple with a growing list of distinctively global problems that independent nation-states, even cooperating together, are unable to effectively manage.

The Dyson Diaspora and Species Radiation

The next step in the ladder of habitat space expansionism is less developed and more distant spatially and temporally. These projects, aiming for the Dyson diaspora, envision further spatial extensions of the fabricated worlds imagined by Bernal, O'Neill, and Cole into the vast frigid reaches of the outer solar system and life forms unbound by containers. These projects constitute a distinct step in the habitat expansionist program because they are typically accompanied by strong anticipations that humanity will branch into different species, producing what biologists call "species radiation." In these scenarios, human biological evolution, propelled by the need to adapt to environments very unlike that of the Earth in which humans emerged, and accelerated by advances in genetic engineering, cybernetics, and robotics, will produce new forms of intelligent life. In short, the Dyson projects anticipate that there will be intelligent alien life in the solar system. But these intelligent alien life forms will not come from beyond the solar system, as so often imagined in science fiction; rather they will be the descendants of humans from Earth.

The notion that humans would evolve into another species as they moved into space has been advanced by many early space visionaries, notably Bernal and Cole. In the writings of the British American nuclear physicist Freeman Dyson, this vision of corporeal transformation is promoted and enlarged. Dyson, by no means solely a space visionary, has been a significant voice at the fringes of many science and technology issues for over six decades and has carved out a distinctive intellectual identity as a voice of heterodoxy.[159] He first burst onto the public stage in 1960 with an impassioned essay condemning a limited nuclear test ban treaty as a great affront to the progress and independence of science.[160] Its ban on nuclear explosions in space meant the end of Project Orion, an Atomic Energy Commission project on which he and other nuclear scientists were working to use multiple nuclear weapon detonations to rapidly propel space vehicles.[161] Although Dyson soon disavowed his criticism,[162] he later prominently supported strategic defense, doubted anthropogenic climate change, and promoted do-it-yourself genetic engineering. Dyson combines an expansive Promethean technological optimism with antipathy to social restraints, producing a technological libertarianism with cosmic scope.

During the centuries when the "plurality of worlds" doctrine held sway, it was routinely assumed that the creatures inhabiting other worlds would be suited to their distinct geophysical environments and would thus have very different physical forms from inhabitants of Earth. Habitat space expansionists posit that the diverse niches of other worlds, now known to be devoid of intelligent life, will come to be occupied by a diverse array of new species that will emerge from the diversification of the descendants of humans emigrating to other worlds. Anticipations of human species radiation and evolutionary advance in space come in four more or less distinct varieties.

The simplest but slowest path to human species radiation in space would be the old-fashioned way, through natural selection. Many advocates of space colonization observe that small and isolated populations of humans would over many generations come to be different simply through a process of genetic drift. Higher levels of solar and cosmic radiation could accelerate this process by causing more mutations, some of which might be adaptive. The rate of evolutionary adaptation can vary greatly due to the operation of metagenes that control which genes get expressed in the morphology of organisms. Over time, off-world humans will come to be different in their features and suited to aspects of their geophysical environments, particularly differences in gravity.

The second path to the transformation of humans in space is through cyborgization. The term "cyborg" (short for "cybernetic organism") has widely permeated popular culture through its many treatments by science fiction writers.[163] The term was coined in 1960 by two biomedical scientists working for NASA, Manfred Clynes and Nathan Kline. They concisely explain why merging machines and flesh into "artifact-organism systems" may be necessary for extensive human space activities: "Altering man's bodily functions to meet the requirements of extraterrestrial environments would be more logical than providing an Earth environment for him in space."[164]

Cole also points to cyborgization as having far-reaching implications for human space expansion. He anticipates "closed-cycle man," with complete mechanical organ replacements; "superman" genetically reengineered to frolic in the methane snows of Titan; and ultimately "saucer man," reduced to a computer-operating brain (see Figure 6.3).[165] His closed-cycle man, which could completely recycle its wastes, would need no external supplies except electrical power, which could be provided by plug-in cables. Such cyborgs "could move about at high speed through the atmosphere, underwater, in space, on other planets, through fire and radiation, and could withstand enormous acceleration."[166] While their physical appearances would be radically different and their abilities would far outstrip those of purely biological humans, Cole sees such supercreatures as supermen rather than as some altogether different species of being. Aggregated into large spaceships as "macrolife," these beings "will exceed in power and survival value any previous product of evolution known to us" and will be "undisputed masters of the known universe." They will be "practically indestructible and immortal" and perhaps be "the end product of the evolution of life."[167]

The third path to human species radiation widely discussed by space habitat expansionists is through the use of technologies of genetic engineering. White, for example, says that it is "quite possible" that such technologies will be "used to optimize adaptation to environments like a space habitat or Mars," and then casually notes that if such efforts succeed, "the state of the art will probably be pushed as far as it reasonably can go."[168] The anthropologists Ben Finney and Eric Jones observe that the human movement into space embarks "on an adaptative radiation of hominidae that will spread intelligent life as far as technology or limits placed by any competing life forms will allow."[169]

The most sweeping anticipation—and advocacy—of off-world human species radiation is provided by Dyson, explicitly building from both Bernal and Tsiolkovsky, in his 1979 essay, "The Greening of the Galaxy."[170] Dyson criticizes the space colonies envisioned by O'Neill as inhabited by people with "hygienic and protected lives, insulated from both the wildness of earth and the wildness of space."[171] Fearing space city-ships will devolve into space versions of Huxley's *Brave New World*, where human diversity is managed and freedom stunted, he declares the decline of diversity, both cultural and biological, to be the greatest threat facing humanity, both on the Earth and in space. As techniques of genetic manipulation become available to produce vastly greater human biological diversity, there would be a "splitting of mankind into a clade of noninterbreeding species."[172] However, this would produce intolerable strains on social institutions

(a)

(b)

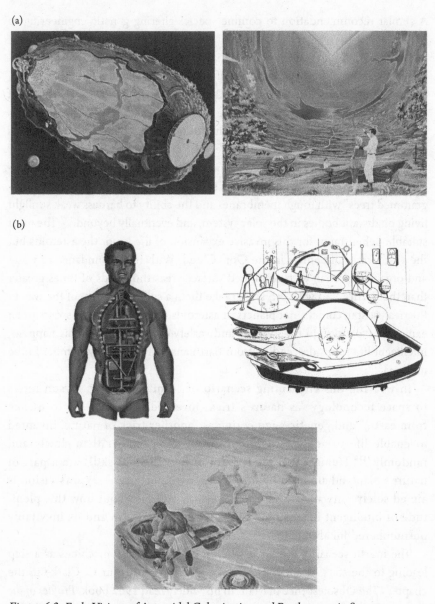

Figure 6.3 Early Visions of Asteroidal Colonization and Posthumans in Space.
Source: Dandridge M. Cole, *Beyond Tomorrow; The Next Fifty Years in Space* (Amherst, WI: Amherst Press, 1965).

because such diversification would be vastly greater than that created by the "diversity of human skin color."[173] He concludes that "as long as mankind remains confined to this planet, the ethic of human brotherhood must prevail over our desire for diversity."[174] An Earth-bound humanity is for Dyson inevitably doomed to both cultural and biological homogenization and stagnation.

A similar recommendation to confine species-altering genetic engineering to space also has been recently advanced by the astrophysicist Martin Rees.[175]

But by going into space, the potential of biotechnology to expand the biological diversity of human and other life forms can be unleashed on an essentially unlimited scale. Picking up on Tsiolkovsky's astounding anticipation of creatures living *on* asteroids and *in* the vacuum of space, Dyson hypothesizes that biotechnology will enable humanity to "adapt our plants and our animals and ourselves to live wild in the universe as we find it," rather than just in cans.[176] Noting that the expansion of life into new habitats occurs not by just one species but by a whole raft of interrelated species, Dyson envisions "suitably programmed trees" with tough membranes and the ability to harness weak sunlight living on distant bodies in the solar system, and eventually beyond.[177] The most suitable Lebensraum for this invasive expansion of life is not the asteroids but the vast swarm of comets in the Oort Cloud. With their abundance of water and organic material, with combined surface areas thousands of times greater than the Earth's, and with orbits that take them a substantial part of the way to the nearest star, comets, not planets or asteroids, provide the open space for an explosive expansion in the number and variety of life forms. As this happens, intelligent life forms descending from Earthians will potentially number in the millions.[178]

In weaving this enchanting scenario of cosmic greening, Dyson refers to space technology "as nature's trick, invented to enable life to escape from earth," and genetic engineering as "another trick of nature, invented to enable life to adapt rapidly and purposefully rather than slowly and randomly."[179] Humanity is the servant of life: "All our skills are a part of nature's plan and are used by her for her own purposes." Dyson's vision is aimed solely outward and upward; he says nothing about how this plenitude of intelligent beings might interact with the Earth and its inevitably outnumbered inhabitants.

The fourth scenario, the full evolution of humans into machines as a step leading to the stars, is anticipated and advocated by Arthur C. Clarke in the chapter "The Obsolescence of Man" in his widely read 1962 book, *Profiles of the Future*. Clarke views the human movement into space as part of an inevitable— and desirable—process of evolution in which humanity will be augmented and then replaced by machines. Tools made, and will eventually unmake, humanity. Initially there will be a cyborg "synthesis of man and machine," but eventually "the purely organic component" will be discarded as a hindrance. This replacement of *Homo sapiens* by *Machina sapiens* is the inevitable path of evolution and opens the path to extensive space expansion. "Creatures of flesh and blood" are too frail to cope with extraterrestrial environmental extremities, and "only creatures of metal and plastic can ever really conquer it."[180] Clarke declares that the notion that intelligent machines "must be malevolent entities hostile to man is so absurd that it is hardly worth wasting energy to refute it." He further claims that the "higher the degree of intelligence, the greater the degree of cooperation."[181] This evolutionary leap to machines and the stars resulting in the extinction of humanity is for Clarke neither bleak nor frightening, and he forthrightly acknowledges that "*extension* may be replaced by *extinction*." Just as no individual lives forever, so too it is unrealistic to expect that any species will live forever. Humanity's cosmic vocation is to serve, as Nietzsche prophesied, as a rope "between animal and super human."

A striking feature of recent anticipations of the emergence of artificial superintelligence is the widespread claim that such cybernetic beings will rapidly expand into space. For most such technological singularitarians, the passing of humanity is also viewed as a positive, indeed eventually inevitable advance in the evolution of intelligence in the universe, a benign transition from carbon-based to silicon-based life forms. But even in Bostrom's darker scenario of an ASI suddenly emerging and quickly eliminating humanity, rapid space expansion is anticipated. Such an entity acting to realize the goals of threat avoidance and resource acquisition would quickly seek "to colonize and re-engineer a large part of the accessible universe" in order to better survive in competition and conflict with comparable entities possibly emerging elsewhere in the universe.[182]

With these scenarios, Promethean ambitions to challenge the gods explicitly morph into ambitions to *become* gods in a cosmic apotheosis of matter into mind and an ascent to complete rule of the cosmic heavens. As Simon Young's "Transhumanist Manifesto" (2006) proclaims, "an immortalized species, *Homo cyberneticus*, will set out for the stars" and eventually "spread throughout the galaxy, a neural net diversifying at every turn." Eventually, "in an unimaginably distant future, the whole universe" will come alive and be "awakened to its own nature—a cosmic mind become conscious of itself as a living entity—omniscient, omnipotent, omnipresent."[183] Where Bacon could dream of technological advance returning humanity to the Garden of Eden, prophets at the convergence of cybernetic transhumanism and space expansionism dream of humanity, or at least its distant offshoots, ascending into god-like powers and expanse.

Aside from their extraordinary audacity, the anticipations and arguments of Dyson and other cosmically ambitious space expansionists for radical species radiation and a cybernetic silicon succession have two notable distinguishing features. First, the further they get spatially and in diversification, the less consideration is given to how these fantastic beings will interact with humanity. Second, the more extreme these visions become, the more they promote themselves as advancing the cause of life, or evolution, rather than humanity.

Galactic Horizons, Interstellar Travel, and the Ultimate Migration

Grand are the proposals of space expansionists for remaking the Earth, the solar system, and humanity itself. But far grander are their anticipations of human migration across the vast voids of interstellar space to the staggeringly vast number of other stars in this galaxy. Notions that humans would eventually migrate from this solar system date to the beginning of space expansionist thought and have been steadily developed since then.[184] Tsiolkovsky wrote of this eventuality, as did Goddard in his short paper "The Ultimate Migration" (1918). As Zubrin puts it, "ultimately the outer solar system will simply be a way station to the vaster universe beyond." To realize these possibilities, the space visionary Peter Garretson calls on humanity to formulate and pursue "a billion-year plan" to industrialize and settle the galaxy and beyond, producing a Type III civilization exploiting all the energy of the galaxy.[185] Given that the sun will eventually begin to die and render the Earth uninhabitable, the movement of humans across interstellar space is the ultimate step in the space expansionist ladder of ascent. Sooner or later humanity will leave the solar system or perish.

With distances between stars measured in light years, and assuming that faster-than-light travel is impossible, most speculation about interstellar voyages has clustered around two topics: how to propel objects to some appreciable fraction of the speed of light and how to keep human travelers alive for centuries. A wide body of scientifically informed speculation has considered the propulsion problem, and many possibilities have been explored. Goddard believed that harnessing what he termed "intra-atomic" energy is essential, and a great deal of attention has been focused on the prospects for highly efficient fusion engines, as well as other exotic possibilities at the edges of science. Alternatively others have proposed building stupendous infrastructures to collect and concentrate solar energy to propel the starship.

Assuming that speeds roughly a thousand times those produced by current propulsion technology can be obtained, travel times of multiple decades or a few centuries become possible, thus posing the question of habitat design for the human passengers. Voyages would extend beyond the lifetimes of individuals and necessitate an artificial habitat with a suitably sized population and sustainable ecosystem. Such "generation ships" would need to be very large city-ships, and how they would be internally organized and operated across multiple generations by humans who would have no direct experience of Earth has long fascinated SF writers. Others have envisioned "suspended animation" to keep the star travelers in some form of long-term hibernation, as "corpsicles," or sending human germ protoplasm for the generation of humans, which would then be raised by robots, or even uploading human brain patterns into durable computers. It is generally assumed that interstellar migration would occur only after solar colonization was well under way and would build on its advances.

Patterns and Puzzles

Among the technological imaginaries of Promethean machine civilization, the visions of the Tsiolkovskian habitat space expansionists have no rival in scope and audacity. In these programs the Baconian modern project of transformative technological improvement merges with a strand of Darwinian evolutionary life philosophy to produce programs that are the telos toward which all life, and all human activities, are—and should be—inexorably moving. When situated in a narrative of this scope, engineering projects become steps in the cosmic evolution of life, and each step, however arduous or apparently banal, acquires an ethical imperative of the highest caliber. From the perspective of this grand expansionary program, opposition is inevitably short-sighted and a betrayal of human destiny—and ultimately doomed to fail. With its ultimate objective of making the inanimate and insensate matter of the universe alive and conscious, Tsiolkovskian space expansionism elevates the trajectory of scientific Enlightenment civilization into a new cosmic religious vocation grounded in the revelations of the Book of Nature. It offers a secular technological path to the realization of the core aspiration of religions promising salvation—to deliver humanity from the vale of tears and mortality into a paradise of limitless abundance and eternal life. Although beginning as programs to save the ailing Earth from a variety of serious—and inevitably eventually fatal—maladies, Tsiolkovskian space expansionism rather quickly leaves the mere Earth behind. And although beginning as programs to address definitively the woes of long-struggling humanity, the Tsiolkovskian trajectory also inevitably abandons humanity for a new class of beings far more suited to cosmic expansion.

In moving to evaluate whether this astounding ladder of ascent leads to new heavens or new hells, there are three notable patterns and puzzles that emerge from this synoptic descriptive summary of habitat space expansionism, first about their general political assumptions, second about the prospects for freedom and war, and third about the fateful move from humanity to life as the agent and beneficiary of these efforts.

Habitat expansionists often make many claims, some of them sweeping, about the political aspects of space activities, but most have little or nothing to say about the political prerequisites or consequences of their visions or about their military potentials. Overall their postures toward political questions, particularly about war, are evasive, dubious, or utopian.[186] They implausibly combine visions of total control over things with total liberation of people, and vacillate between visions of totalitarian habitat closure and radical frontier freedom. Some attribute violent conflict to scarcities and the rivalries they generate. They point to the limitless resources in space, overlooking the reality that there will be richer lodes and better positions in space to fight over. They conjure astronomical abundance as a solution to the wide poverty on Earth but offer no explanation for how this wealth abundance will be distributed to alleviate poverty. Some explicitly anticipate that vertical spatial expansion will produce new stratifications between superior spacekind and inferior Terran humankind, but they do not explore how such a bifurcation is compatible with solving terrestrial problems from space or whether these technologically and spatially privileged Übermenschen might oppress or exterminate their inferiors. While most habitat expansionists ignore the military implications of their projects, the von Braunians assume violent rivalries and war will inexorably follow Lebensraum expansion, thus posing the question of what might happen if the vast apparatuses and titanic energies involved in habitat expansion are deployed in wars.

Among the political forms discussed by habitat expansionists, some version of technocracy is the default preference or assumption. The politics of expertise has been vitally important to the overall technological modernization project since its beginning, because the promise of machine civilization hinges on the competent design and operation of complex machines. Because humans in space are totally dependent on machines, highly competent rule of machines becomes absolutely necessary for human survival. But technocracy is extremely rare on Earth, and habitat expansionists provide no insight as to how it might plausibly emerge and persist in space. Thus is posed the question: If space expansion is not possible without technocracy, and if technocracy is not possible, is large-scale space expansion possible? Is space expansionism politically utopian?

A second set of patterns and puzzles emerge from the insightful debate about whether space colonies are prone to internal forms of hierarchical rule, independence, and war. Advocates of space colonization advance a quite diverse set of positions on this question (see Figure 6.4). For O'Neill, Zubrin, and Dyson, the situation of space colonies is highly permissive, allowing an extreme plurality of regime types and freedoms; they also either discount or do not consider the possibilities of interworld war. Another cluster of arguments, offered by Bernal and Cockell, sees severe situational constraints strongly favoring highly hierarchical and collectivist colony government, a tendency embraced by Bernal the communist and abhorred by Cockell the libertarian. Also anticipating strong tendencies toward internal hierarchy, Cole and Cox argue (implausibly) that the high mutual vulnerability of the inhabitants of space colonies will lead to liberal democracy, thus eliminating the problem. Taking the position that internal government will tend strongly toward hierarchy and that interworld war is inherent in independent colonies and would be catastrophic, Crawford and Baxter

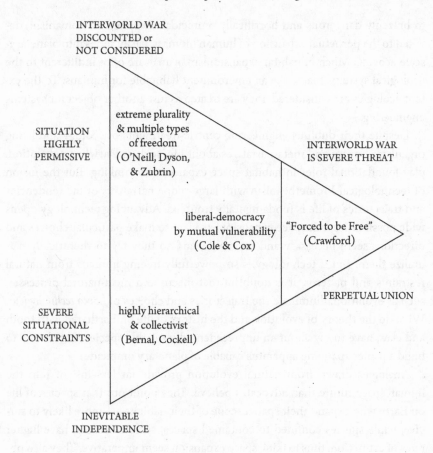

INTERWORLD WAR
DISCOUNTED or
NOT CONSIDERED

extreme plurality
& multiple types
of freedom
(O'Neill, Dyson,
& Zubrin)

SITUATION
HIGHLY
PERMISSIVE

INTERWORLD WAR
IS SEVERE THREAT

liberal-democracy
by mutual vulnerability
(Cole & Cox)

"Forced to be Free"
(Crawford)

PERPETUAL UNION

SEVERE
SITUATIONAL
CONSTRAINTS

highly hierarchical
& collectivist
(Bernal, Cockell)

INEVITABLE
INDEPENDENCE

Figure 6.4 Varieties of Space Colony Government

argue that a federal union joining the space colonies with the government of the Earth is needed to avert war and to guarantee the preservation of liberty in space colonies. The desirability of the central colonization project of habitat space expansionism rests on which of these views is correct. Far from escaping from oppressive and difficult social engineering, space colonization may well require its near perfection, sustained indefinitely. Paradoxically, only if "forced to be free" can space colonies avoid despotism.

The third important pattern with puzzling implications emerging from this tour of habitat expansionism is the shift from *humanity* to *life* as the decisive agent and beneficiary of the movement into space. The Tsiolkovskian problems with life begin with their stunningly implausible views on ecology. The Fuller Earth visions of fabricating Geodesic and Hydroponic Earth are utopian given the turbulent Earth and its unruly life. In their treatment of life, the Tsiolkovsky programs range from nominally sensitive, hopelessly archaic and merely ignorant to brazenly dangerous and horrifically omnicidal. Exponential humanism, devoted to the perpetual expansion of human biomass, easily slides into planetary-scale ecocide. Much of habitat expansionism is unaware of or indifferent to the ecological systems that make an environment habitable for humans. To the extent ecologies are considered, they are treated as just another object for systems engineering.

Despite their dubious engineering-centric treatments of ecology and living organisms, macro and meta-narratives about life, such as Darwinian evolution, play foundational roles in habitat space expansionist thinking. But the fusion of technological Prometheanism with large-scope narratives of the tendencies and trajectories of life is fundamentally troubled. Advancing technology opens wide possibilities, but space expansionists want to make particular choices and directions seem necessary and inevitable, and so they try to rhetorically naturalize them. But if technology is so powerfully freeing humans from natural restraints and patterns, it is doubtful that macro and meta-natural processes, such as evolution, illuminate the trajectories and choices of *homo technologicus*. What do the theory of evolution and the history of life on Earth, red with tooth and claw, have to say about an unprecedentedly capable species that *chooses* to build a planet-spanning apparatus capable of planetary omnicide?

Analogies drawn from natural evolution provide far less insight into the human space future than advocates believe. They point out that species of life on Earth who expand their spatial scope of their habitats are more likely to survive, while species confined to contained spaces, such as islands, have higher rates of extinction, thus making space expansion seem imperative. They also observe that species that expand spatially tend to fragment into multiple species, thus bolstering the appeal of human species radiation. But they rarely point out that diversifying species also lethally compete, with some driven to extinction, as humans might by their spacekind descendents. Unfortunately, the fact that all these patterns of life on Earth potentially map onto space choices and outcomes provides little or no guidance about which of them are appropriate models for successful space choice. Natural history and theory provide many arresting analogies, but very limited guidance for practical human choices.

Even larger problems afflict the upper rungs of the Tsiolkovsky ladder. In the first steps, interests of humanity and its natal abode are said to propel expansion. But once species radiation starts to occur, it is no longer humanity but life whose interests are advanced. In making the case for colonizing solar and then interstellar space, Dyson explicitly appeals to the interests of life itself, not humanity-in- general. This shift beyond humanity results from the expectation that humans will mutate—or be mutated—into multiple species of intelligent life. Once humans are just one of many intelligent spacefaring species, human survival ceases to be vital for the survival and success of cosmically expanding life.

This life to which the Dyson diaspora appeals is endowed with an all-encompassing purpose—to expand into new habitats and take new forms that enable the expansion into further new habitats. Life's paramount interest in expanding its living space is driven by the basic motor of evolutionary development of life on Earth since its emergence several billion years ago—to increase survival prospects. Life is thus too precious and vulnerable to be confined to the Earth, where it will inevitably, sooner or later, suffer complete extinction. Of the billion or so species of multicellular life that have emerged on Earth over the last half-billion years, humans have a particular status and importance, not as some "crown of creation" or apex of excellence and value but rather as the means by which life can escape the confines and vulnerabilities of its birth planet Earth. Humans are no longer just one precocious and highly successful Terran life form but are elevated into something vastly more important: the carriers of the seeds of Earth life to unimaginably immense new spaces and habitats. Humans and their space enterprise thus are transformed into instrumental tools and intermediary steps in an evolutionary trajectory of life expansion with galactic significance.

How these new forms of life might interact with mere humanity is, however, curiously not considered in the astro-Darwinian arguments supporting the Dyson diaspora and species radiation. This poses several questions and potential problems. What will be the prospects for Earth habitability and human survival if the intelligent alien descendants of humanity interact with humanity in the same fashion that humans have interacted with other human groups and with other living species? In part this question is evaded by characterizing the movement as ever *outward*, simply ignoring the possibility that new forms of intelligent life will expand in all directions, including back toward the Earth. And in part this question is evaded by the pervasive assumption among expansionists that vertical elevation will make *Homo spaciens* and its successors morally better as well as vastly more powerful and capable. The lion will not lie with the sheep, but vastly improved lions will acquire sheep-like beneficence.

The more central answer of space advocates to this momentous question, which is only rarely articulated directly, is that this expansion and radiation of intelligent life equipped with advanced—and ever advancing—technology will assuredly bring about the eventual extinction of *Homo sapiens*. For those who have appointed themselves the agents of life in general, the eventual extinction of humanity cannot be viewed with any real alarm because they anticipate humanity will be succeeded by creatures who are significantly better than humans. But for humans and the societies of humans on the Earth being exhorted to embark upon this path, this outcome is likely to be quite alarming. To the extent this inevitable terminal outcome is recognized, might it diminish enthusiasm for space expansion?

Perhaps even more troubling for the grand space expansionist ascent, humans are cast as playing a role that is uniquely contradictory among life forms. Space expansionists assign to humans tendencies that contradict their basic assumption that all life is survival-seeking. Habitat space expansionists are in effect saying that humanity will—and should—pursue a series of steps that will lead inevitably to its own demise. Space expansion may be an agenda of survival for life, but for humanity it is an expensive suicide cult. While the history of life provides many examples of both individuals and species pursuing paths that led to their own destruction, habitat space expansionists are saying that humanity will—and should—*intentionally* pursue arduous steps that are ultimately suicidal. Whether humans are this self-sacrificing, this incapable of pursuing their survival interests, or this gullible remains to be seen. But there is little doubt that space expansionism ultimately rests upon the assumption that humanity is uniquely stupidly suicidal, something that space expansionists are—perhaps not paradoxically—doing their best to demonstrate.

Superpower Restraints, Planetary Security, and Earth Identity

> Our earth is but a small star in the great universe. Yet of it we can make, if we choose, a planet unvexed by war.
>
> —Franklin Delano Roosevelt (1942)[1]

> When cosmic energies are turned loose on a small planet over-whelming destruction is the result.
>
> —Jonathan Schell (1982)[2]

> It's no use saying that all technologies can be used for good or ill. . . . when the "ill" achieves a sufficiently apocalyptic scale, we may have to set limits on which technologies may be developed.
>
> —Carl Sagan (1994)[3]

Critics and the Clarke-Sagan Program

The proposals of military and habitat space expansionists have been subject to significant criticisms. Many of these criticisms are linked to an underappreciated and underdeveloped alternative third general narrative about space activities and their relation to the Earth, as well as a set of alternative space programs, which is more modest and more Earth-centered. This neglected planetary se-curity approach offers what I will refer to as the Whole Earth Security program. These criticisms and this program view large-scale space expansionist projects in Earth space with considerable skepticism and propose much less ambitious space activities than those proposed by military and habitat expansionists. Because this approach proposes to significantly undo large parts of what has been done in space, particularly in the military realm, and because this agenda is comparatively modest, most space expansionists tend to view these critics and alternatives as essentially antispace and an astro-Luddite antitechnologism. But advocates of this way of thinking about space, including this author, argue that this underrealized approach best embodies the lessons of the Space Age and realizes the most practically possible use of space technology to accomplish the most important of humanity's goals: the protection of the Earth and its myriad inhabitants from self-destruction.

Like cosmic rays, criticisms of military and habitat space expansion come from many directions and often pack a potent punch. Arguably the most practically influential objections have come from budget directors, for whom space activities simply cost too much. But criticisms of the desirability of major parts of the space expansionist program have also been a recurrent feature of the conversation and debate about space, however much space advocates seek to ignore or belittle them. Many scientists have perennially criticized projects extending human activities into space as far too costly for the scientific knowledge they produce. But the most intellectually significant criticisms come from arms controllers, environmentalists, technology critics, and justice advocates. These criticisms are complicated in their specifics but quite simple in their essentials. Arms controllers argue that military space expansion reduces national and global security by increasing the probability of nuclear war. Environmental critics doubt the feasibility of engineering small, fully enclosed ecosystems and argue that the space infrastructures proposed by Fuller Earth expansionists are mismatched to actual Earth habitat needs and pose inherently unpredictable environmental risks. In a similar vein, technology critics doubt that objects and systems of objects designed and built and operated by humans are subject to predictable full human control. Justice advocates insist space ventures should not exacerbate steep inequalities of wealth and power between and within states.

Space is a minor side issue within the larger enterprises of arms control, environmentalism, technology criticism, and justice advocacy. Beyond their skepticism, these critics appear to have little in common with each other. Their criticisms commonly address only parts or aspects of space expansionism, rarely attack its general vision, and seldom advance an overall alternative to it. While these critical arguments are often quite compelling in their specifics, and sometimes have been quite influential on actual space policies, they are disconnected and incomplete and are ignored or caricatured by space advocates. These criticisms also have significant limitations, most notably in not addressing the desirability of the larger visions of human colonization across the solar system and beyond.

These criticisms do not, however, amount to a general rejection of space activity; rather they provide the foundations for the positive planetary security program for employing space and space technology for the construction of a global security system and the protection of the planet's habitability. The Whole Earth Security program is a series of steps making a ladder, like its larger and better-known rivals. The basic logic of this program is to restrain those capabilities that threaten the security and habitability of the Earth, while deploying combinations of institutions and hardware to reduce interstate conflict, support arms control, sustain planetary habitability, cultivate global consciousness, and advance scientific knowledge. No single individual makes all these arguments, but two well-known space figures, Arthur C. Clarke and Carl Sagan, voiced many of them, and it is thus appropriate to refer to the Whole Earth Security program as the Clarke-Sagan program.[4] Like the von Braun program, the Clarke-Sagan program has been partially implemented, but these measures have been underappreciated, particularly by most space expansionists. And like its rivals, this program extends a long line of earlier terrestrial ideas and activities.

Advocates of the Whole Earth Security approach to space argue that the most fundamental Earth problem stems from disjunctures between territorially based nation-states and the new violence technologies capable of wreaking planetary-scope destruction, as well as the environmental problems produced by inappropriate economic expansions occurring within the planet's biosphere.[5] The basic problem, in the words of the World Commission on Environment and Development, is that "the Earth is one but the world is not."[6] Planetary security requires comprehensive restraints on technological superpowers combined with the neutralization and selective employment of orbital space. The acid test for the Whole Earth Security program is not whether a space venture contributes to the movement of humanity into the cosmos but whether it contributes to solving primary terrestrial security and habitability problems. This program, while orders of magnitude smaller than what military and habitat space expansionists advocate, aims to make a potentially pivotal near-term contribution to protect the Earth, and thus provide a crucial contemporary service to the planet and humanity.

The Clarke-Sagan approach is knowledge- and information-centric. It envisions Earth space dominated by infosats—comsats to link, navsats to guide, and watchsats and science-sats to look and learn, both inward and outward. It champions astronomy, Earth system science, and astrobiology. It anticipates hopefully that the bountiful harvest of revolutionary knowledge and the thickening of informational interaction will not only be instrumentally useful but will also transform human collective identities, diminishing or displacing the nation-state. The Clarke-Sagan program extends Enlightenment and modern liberal republicanism into space. It embodies the liberal agenda of civilizational progress through knowledge enlargement and consciousness raising, and the republican agenda of power restraint in the interest of the many. For the astroliberal and astrorepublican project, planetary domestication and pacification become vital responses to the enlarged powers generated by Promethean modernity's commitment to scientific and technological progress.

Realizing the Whole Earth Security program would essentially terminate the von Braun ladder, both directly through arms control measures and indirectly—but more permanently—through changes in the world political relations that give rise to large-scale military competition. In incorporating the objections of environmental and technology critics, the Whole Earth Security program also rejects the feasibility and desirability of the heavier versions of the Fuller Earth program and its near-Earth extensions. But its relationship with the larger habitat program for solar space is quite unsettled. Many advocates of the Whole Earth Security programs—including Clarke and Sagan—combine a strong rejection of the von Braun military program with strong support for solar habitat expansion. Like the von Braun program, the outer reach of the Whole Earth Security program largely ends within the Earth system, the point where the habitat expansion program really begins its distinctive vocation. Thus is posed the crucial question, explored in subsequent chapters, of whether solar space habitat expansion is compatible with the Whole Earth Security approach.

As with the other expansionist agendas, asteroids play a crucial but unsettled role in the horizons of the Whole Earth Security program. Because this program is fundamentally a planetary security program, asteroidal diversion would seem to be a natural component and extension. In actuality, asteroidal diversion is subject to fundamental disagreements. One line of thinking, advanced by Sagan, holds that asteroidal diversion should be delayed until world politics has been significantly reformed. But others, including this author, argue that diversion should be pursued in ways that make it a valuable part of this program.

Arms controllers and advocates of a Whole Earth Security system advance their programs as crucially necessary for realizing the primary interests of a distinct actor: humanity as a whole. This places them in sharp opposition to the almost purely national-state interests served by the von Braun militarization program. This basic difference also points to a fundamental disadvantage under which the Clarke-Sagan program labors: the absence of any substantial organized voice of humanity. States are powerful organizations and nations are deeply entrenched identity formations, and nothing comparable exists for humanity as a whole. This gap between actual particular identities and organizations and vital but underrepresented general interests gives rise to claims about the emergence of a global or planetary common identity and the special role that the human advance into space can play in its formation. These anticipations of an emergent "Whole Earth identity," a Space Age "WE identity," are centered around the global telecommunications system partly based in orbit, as well as the iconic Whole Earth photographs taken of the planet from space, and are a space-one-worldism. Taken together, they are, according to this line of thinking deployed by Clarke and Sagan and others, producing a sense of shared planetary place and common fate, diluting or displacing the strong inherited parochial identity formations associated with nations, while also underpinning the political institutions needed to provide planetary security.

This way of thinking and the agendas it generates would at first glance seem to have nothing to do with "geopolitics," a term largely either avoided or vilified by thinkers about global peace, security, and habitability. But this apparent absence of geography and geopolitics is quite misleading, for the argumentation of globalist thinking contains a central core of claims about material realities, about the Earth and its transformations by technology. Although seldom noted by self-styled geopolitical thinkers over the past century, major ancient and early modern thinkers, most notably Aristotle and Montesquieu, advanced numerous arguments about the relationship between domestic political forms, including democracies and republics, and geographical and technological factors. And the great debates among the global geopoliticians and others a century ago actually included arguments advanced by Wells, Dewey, and many others about the obsolescence of realist political practices and arrangements and the increasing necessity of various types of federal republican world government. For those who like their arguments buttressed by analogs from Darwinian biology, there are works by Wells, Peter Kropotkin, and Lester Ward about the survival value of symbiotic cooperation and about superior fitness being about environmental congruity, not inter- or intragroup competition.[7]

Perhaps the simplest and most comprehensive version of such materialist thinking in globalist thought is found in the core argument of *The Public and Its Problems* (1928), the most important political book of the great American philosopher of pragmatism and democracy, John Dewey. Publics, he says, are groups produced by high levels of interaction and interdependence, which vary greatly across time in different geographies and with different technologies.[8] Given this, the central political problem becomes what forms of community (understood as a primary identity group) and of government (understood as authoritative political institutions) are necessary to serve the fundamental interests of the public? The central problem of late modernity, Dewey argues, is that deployed industrial technologies have created greatly enlarged publics, which in turn require significantly different and spatially enlarged forms of community and government. Whether members of publics come to realize the facts of their interdependence and can then successfully generate appropriate forms of community and government is not guaranteed and becomes the locus of political action and contestation.

Cast in the terms of Dewey's materially driven framework on the formation of publics and their problems, the core claims of much of subsequent globalist thinking, especially since the emergence of Planetary Earth, are simply stated: there is now a planetary and intergenerational public, and new substantive forms of worldwide government and community must be established if the fundamental interests of the new and vastly enlarged public are to be adequately served.[9] For globalists the paramount problem with self-styled "Realist" international theory and practice is its unrealism—its failure to grasp and act on the new and critically important material realities brought forth by scientific-technological modernity interacting with the finite and fragile planet Earth. For self-styled "Realists" threats come from enemies, and without enemies there are no threats. But for globalists there are "threats without enemies" (such as climate change), as well as threats from enemy-centered politics in a superpowered planetary material context.

This is the implicitly geopolitical framework of planetary security space expansionism, which directly challenges the geopolitics of the von Braunian military space expansionists. And it is this clash that is at the core of the first great debate on space. This debate between these globalists and these realists is not between an idealism and a materialism but rather is a clash of materialisms, both of which cannot be correct.

As in the preceding two chapters, my aim here is primarily to assemble, summarize and situate the arguments and proposals of these critics and advocates, with particular attention to the role of geography and geopolitics, and their assumptions about politics and political outcomes, particularly regarding world government and freedom. The chapter proceeds in four main steps: first a consideration of the arms control critics and actual arms control measures, then the environmental and technology critics, then the six steps of the Whole Earth Security program, and finally reflections on the areas of disagreement and agreement between these positions and those of the military and habitat space expansionists, thus setting the stage for their competitive assessment in the following chapters.

Nuclear Weapons and World Orders

International arms control, particularly for nuclear weapons but also for space, has been an increasingly salient feature of world politics since the middle of the twentieth century. In simple terms, space arms control seeks to reverse or block almost all the steps of the von Braun military space expansion program. Because military activities in space have been inextricably intertwined with nuclear weapons, space arms control has been deeply linked to nuclear arms control.

Efforts to restrain nuclear weapons sit at the center of a broad and powerful new way of thinking about the relationship among weapons, security, and political order that emerged during the twentieth century and come to significantly influence the global political system. Given the importance of security from violence in all times and places, the questions of *who* controls arms and *how* they are controlled have been elemental to all polities. At least since the agricultural revolution, the ability of governments to establish order, regulate violence, and control killing tools within particular territorial spaces has been at the center of their appeal as a way to organize human societies. But between polities, peace has been more difficult to establish and maintain, and for most peoples "arms control" has meant having a good control of their arms in order to effectively wage war, and "disarmament" something imposed by victors upon the vanquished. At the same time, across the blood-soaked annals of history, vast numbers of people have yearned for a more enduring end to the miseries of war and for the establishment of a durable and just peace, aspirations powerfully manifest in the ethical teachings of religions everywhere. But these widespread aspirations by the many have seldom produced much restraint on the ambitions of the powerful few. Despite wide popular hopes for deliverance from violence, elites routinely use violence to advance themselves, and even peace-seeking peoples have had to take up arms and prevail by force to defensively protect themselves from the predations of others.

With the great expansions in violence capabilities enabled by science-based technology, there has emerged a different way of thinking about the relationship between arms and security, which the Clarke-Sagan Whole Earth Security program embodies and extends. As the violence of wars grew, and with anticipations of greater devastations ahead, new ways of restraining arms and avoiding violent conflicts seemed increasingly vital for national security, and perhaps for the survival of civilization itself. The nineteenth century brought an explosion of serious thinking about how war and the tools of war might be restrained by peace movements, international leagues, and international law.[10]

Over the course of the twentieth century "arms control" came to refer to a relatively new agenda for interstate political relations and international order-building through mutual and symmetrical agreements. Spurred by the unexpectedly massive industrial slaughters of World War I, arms control treaties became a significant feature of international politics during the interwar years. But they were limited in scope and aspiration and ultimately were overwhelmed by the antagonisms igniting World War II. With the development of nuclear weapons and the specter of a war that would obliterate civilization and perhaps extinguish humanity, however, arms control assumed an unprecedentedly central role in international politics, and arms control thinking became much more developed. The years since the 1940s have been the Nuclear Age far more than the Space Age. At its heart the Clarke-Sagan program seeks to exploit the possibilities of space activities to help resolve the problems of the Nuclear Age.

Thinking about the implications of nuclear weapons for world political order during the early nuclear era was dominated by the ideas of nuclear-one-worldism.[11] In this view nuclear weapons, combined with rapid aerial and rocket delivery, rendered even the largest and most powerful of territorial states obsolete for providing security. This obsolescence thesis was commonly linked to the claim that an authoritative world government with an effective monopoly of violence capabilities, accompanied by the substantial disarmament of all states, was required to provide security.

This way of thinking was revolutionary in its practical implications but was actually quite conceptually conservative in its assumptions about the relationship between violence capability, political order, and security. It essentially envisioned taking the final step—at least for the Earth—of increasing the size of the security-providing units to match the spatial scope of the new violence capabilities, thus culminating a trend operating across history.[12] Although endorsed by a wide a range of political leaders and prominent intellectuals, and seemingly based on the application of the general lessons and logics of world political history, the world state solution soon reached something of a practical and conceptual dead-end.[13] Advocates were unable to provide a plausible path of transition to such a world sovereign, or convincing reasons why such an entity would not devolve into an oppressive world totalitarian state.

Subsequent thinking about the path to nuclear security has largely sought to steer a middle path between the Charybdis of catastrophic nuclear war arising from interstate anarchy and the Scylla of a totalitarian world state. A raft of internationalist and globalist projects and plans have sought not to replace territorial nation-states with an omnistate but rather to supplement and complement them with increasingly substantial arrangements of mutual restraint, thus moving world political order out of anarchy but not toward hierarchy. Within this broad middle path to a mixed world order sit all the nuclear and space projects and efforts considered here—arms control, the Outer Space Treaty, and the program for cooperative space activities—as well as international measures to sustain planetary habitability.

Nuclear Arms Control

Arms control as a distinctive way of dealing with superpower violence emerged during the late 1950s, just as the fateful mating of the nuclear weapon and the long-range rocket was yielding its monstrous offspring. As thinking about short-term and immediately politically feasible measures to avert nuclear war came to center on the notion of deterrence, concepts of arms control for both nuclear and space weapons were first framed. In the first major statements on the topic produced in the late 1950s and early 1960s, arms control was advanced as something distinctly different from general disarmament or the creation of a world government.[14] The key notion of arms control thinking was that the deployment of nuclear weapons for deterrent purposes was potentially unstable in ways that might result in an unintentional or accidental nuclear war. After the Cuban

Missile Crisis of 1962, arms control became an important part of the US-Soviet relationship. Many arms control treaties were negotiated and implemented and were central parts of the settlement of the Cold War in the late 1980s and early 1990s.[15] As these treaties grew in number and importance, the distinction between arms control and disarmament largely disappeared, and various deep arms control proposals became disarmament measures. A key construct in the arms controllers' relatively modest institutional program is the "regime." During the 1970s this term came to be widely used to describe institutional arrangements between states stopping short of the delegation of substantial authority to international organizations but still entailing regularized patterns of cooperative behavior. Arms control came to be widely characterized as efforts to build regimes. Such regimes supplement or complement rather than replace sovereign territorial states as the prime feature of world political order.

In the political struggles and theoretical debates over nuclear alternatives, arms controllers have been in a protracted struggle with very well-developed programs and arguments commonly cast as realist or based on geopolitics. In response to this arsenal of concepts that seem so well-established and hallowed by historical experience, arms control advocates and theorists generally make modest claims based on practical considerations, propose incremental steps and eschew comprehensive visionary agendas. Their arguments for the desirability of arms control derive directly from their claims about dangers associated with nuclear weaponization, not an overarching understanding of world political order and its relationship to the Earth and superpower technology. The arms control program also came to be seen, by both advocates and opponents, as embodying various normative and idealistic understandings of politics and political order. Arms control thinkers also emphasized the importance of processes and learning.[16]

A much more Earth-centered view of the implications of nuclear weapons for world political order was provided by Jonathan Schell in *The Fate of the Earth*. Drawing on scientific studies and reports about the planetary environmental effects of a large-scale nuclear war, he argues that a fundamentally new case against nuclear war had emerged: a nuclear war would not only kill vast numbers of people and smash the urban-industrial infrastructure of modern civilization; it would also potentially so damage and alter the atmosphere and biosphere that higher forms of life—including humans—could be rendered extinct. The large-scale nuclear wars that could have been conducted during the 1950s and 1960s would have produced completely unanticipated catastrophic effects on the Earth, dooming the victors and well as the vanquished. It is the fragility of the Earth's biosphere that sets limits on the levels of terrestrial violence compatible with human survival. Once this is recognized, the traditional calculus of risk informing nuclear strategy is rendered obsolete. With the fates of innumerable future generations of humans, as well as the panoply of complex life forms on the planet, at stake, security policy must resolutely aim toward the creation of a world political order in which biospheric destruction leading to nuclear extinction is made as practically unlikely as possible. If industrial killing tools made war too important to be left to generals, then nuclear weapons have made war too consequential to be left to states.

Arms Control and Space Weapons

The pursuit of arms control in space has been a prominent feature of the Space Age, and arms control measures are a significant part of the space political order. From the very beginning of the Soviet and American military space activities in the 1950s, arms controllers have sought restraints, both formal and informal. With the Limited Test Ban Treaty of 1963, the superpowers agreed not to test nuclear weapons in space, and both sides built sophisticated surveillance systems to detect violations. Then, in the Outer Space Treaty of 1967, the superpowers and almost all other states produced a rudimentary constitution for outer space and agreed not to station nuclear weapons in space or to put any weapon on any celestial body.

Arms controllers have mirrored the error of the military space expansionists in not recognizing ballistic missiles as space weapons. A series of major bilateral agreements, the first and second Strategic Arms Limitation Treaties (SALT I and II), the first and second Strategic Arms Reduction Treaties (START I and II), the Intermediate Nuclear Forces (INF) Treaty, and then New START and Strategic Offensive Reductions Treaty (SORT) are viewed by arms controllers as landmark measures restraining superpower nuclear arsenals. Yet it is often overlooked that these treaties do not typically directly limit nuclear weapons, only their "delivery vehicles," the most important of which are ballistic missiles. Thus what is conventionally understood to be *nuclear arms control* is mainly *ballistic missile space weapons arms control*. These treaties did not specifically focus on nuclear weapons because they are small and thus easily hidden, objects whose numbers could not plausibly be monitored except through a highly intrusive surveillance of the complete stockpiles of fissile materials and the behemoth industrial facilities producing them. Arms controllers focused on ballistic missiles for precisely the same reason that military planners saw them as so attractive: their extreme speed and the great difficulty in intercepting them, as well as the ease of counting their numbers. Once these great drawdowns in nuclear forces are recognized as focused on ballistic missile space weapons, these arms control measures emerge as one of the most extensive and consequential actual *space programs*. This giant space program, hiding in plain sight, has the sole purpose of restraining the doubly dark space program of ballistic missile space weaponization, also hiding in plain sight, sitting at the center of the planet-spanning military complexes generated by the great Soviet-American rivalry.

Despite the centrality of ballistic missile space weapons in so-called nuclear arms control, thinking about complete bans on ballistic missiles has had a remarkably underdeveloped role in arms control agendas. But some have proposed comprehensive restraints, or "zero ballistic missiles" (ZBM).[17] In one simple step, a ZBM regime would roll back the acceleration of violence, lower escalatory crisis pressures, reduce first-strike fears, and render ballistic missile defense moot. A further attraction of a ZBM regime is its ready verifiability because clandestine testing of ballistic missiles is extremely difficult. As hypersonic missiles have come onto the horizon of possibility, arms controllers have proposed test bans to prevent these destabilizing weapons from adding to incentives for preemption and rapid escalation.[18]

Another space weaponization measure, promoted by von Braun himself, is nuclear weapons in orbit, where they could be called down to strike their targets. Orbital basing for nuclear strike forces was militarily appealing for the same reason that ballistic missiles were: their extreme speed. While the intercontinental flight path of a ballistic missile would take roughly half an hour, a nuclear weapon could be de-orbited and strike its target in under ten minutes, making warning, let alone response, very difficult. These orbital bombardment systems were identified by early Space Age arms controllers as particularly dangerous precisely because of their extreme speeds, which made them militarily attractive. In an often overlooked arms control accomplishment, all states agreed in the Outer Space Treaty to forgo their testing and deployment.[19]

Beyond the enormously important but unacknowledged space program of nuclear arms control, the attention of arms controllers has focused on preventing or undoing steps in the von Braun ladder of space military expansion. Because arms control proposals for restraint are essentially reactive to the steps on this ladder, they amount to a series of blockages or reversals of its steps. Across the decades of political struggles over space weaponization, arms controllers have developed arguments in opposition that are quite straightforward in their essentials (see Table 7.1).

The swarms of force-multiplier satellite systems have been subject to virtually no arms control measures, or even proposals. The basic problem with arms control here is that these information-providing satellites are largely indistinguishable from many civilian systems, making it extremely difficult to design a regime prohibiting military uses while allowing civilian ones. In some cases, such as GPS navigation satellites, the military system is the civilian system. In other cases, such as mapping and geodetic satellites, the knowledge produced is valuable to myriad scientific disciplines and, once acquired, difficult to eliminate. As advances in information technology increase the potency of weapons, controlling weapons becomes increasingly important.

Table 7.1 **Arms Control Criticisms of Von Braun Programs**

Von Braun Program	*Arms Control Criticism*
Global hegemony	Rivalry impedes realization; war more likely
Space control	Crisis instability increased and debris created
Orbital space fighting	Crisis instability increased and debris created
Force multiplying	Crisis instability increased
Intercontinental bombardment	Acceleration decreases control; war more likely

But another type of information satellite, for surveillance, has come to occupy a special—and much celebrated—role in efforts to realize the arms control and disarmament agenda. With each arms control treaty, skeptics questioned whether the United States would be able to detect possible cheating by the Soviet Union, and the military and intelligence organs of the US government routinely provided assurances that their space-based monitoring capacities were up to the task of verifying Soviet compliance. The importance of these satellites for verification was so great that the SALT I treaty explicitly banned "interference with national technical means of verification," a euphemism for space systems.[20] Because these satellites played such important roles in verifying arms control treaties, they have been widely credited as a major space contribution toward preventing war and making possible reductions in advanced weaponry.[21] Because of their value in crisis monitoring, some have proposed to establish an international satellite monitoring agency to provide the UN Security Council with independent information.[22]

It is on the next step in the ladder of the von Braun program, for antisatellite weapons, where the conflict between arms controllers and space weaponeers has been most extensively waged. The basic argument of arms controllers is that ASATs are particularly dangerous because of their ability to strike at the networks of satellites that the superpowers rely upon for early warning, surveillance, and the command, control, and communication of their far-flung nuclear forces. In the absence of an agreement banning ASATs, their nondeployment has largely been the product of parallel unilateral restraints.[23] For the United States, heavily reliant on military satellite systems, the logic of this self-restraint is vividly captured by the space analyst John Pike's wry observation "People in glass houses do not organize rock throwing contests."[24] Precisely because the United States is so dependent on military satellites, it has more to potentially lose if antisatellite weapons become widely deployed. With the growing use of space information systems to support conventional military forces and the growing incentives to target such systems, nuclear and conventional systems are becoming "entangled," creating a new danger of escalation to nuclear war.[25] At the same time, the increasing deployment of large numbers of smaller satellites to replace a few large ones is greatly decreasing the prospects for successful ASAT attacks. For arms control critics, visions of space warfare as detached and casualty-free are as appealing as planning a shootout in a dynamite warehouse.

Another important objection of arms controllers is that testing and using ASATs creates space debris, which degrades the usability of orbital space for all other activities.[26] Because objects traveling at orbital velocities release such enormous quantities of energy when they collide with other objects, debris in space is a particularly lethal form of pollution, which has no analog in terrestrial experience.[27] Weapons testing is only one source of such debris, along with defunct satellites and discarded objects. Because this debris poses such a hazard to all space activities, the radars and telescopes of the US Space Surveillance Network currently track some 23,000 objects larger than a softball (10 centimeters) (see Figure 7.1), but its new "space fence" system aims to track some 200,000 objects. Not tracked are some 500,000 fragments between 1 and 10 centimeters and an

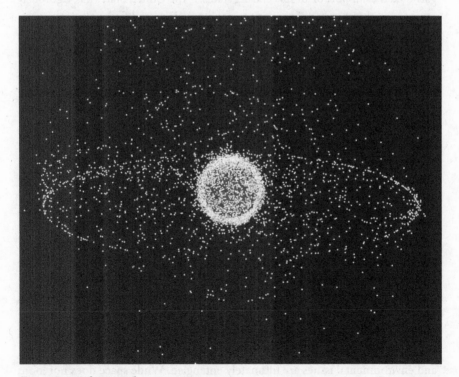

Figure 7.1 Orbiting Debris. Source: NASA.

estimated 100 million–plus pieces smaller than a centimeter. Larger objects such as multiton rocket bodies and satellites make up much of the 6,200 tons of debris.[28] And as objects strike other objects, a "Kessler Cascade" of multiplying debris results.[29] Early Soviet and American ASAT tests produced significant quantities of debris, but the first Chinese ASAT test, in 2007, produced by far the largest single contribution to the planet's debris cloud, thousands of trackable objects which are rapidly spreading into a large swath of Earth orbital space. Due to these side effects of ASAT testing, the space analyst Clay Moltz speaks of the "environmental security" of space being jeopardized.[30] And "the Archduke Francis Ferdinand of World War III may well be a critical reconnaissance satellite hit by a piece of space debris during a crisis."[31] As recognition of the debris problem has grown, space analysts have proposed a voluntary code of conduct specifying best practices to minimize the further creation of debris from routine space activities, with measures such as designing satellites to reenter the Earth's atmosphere after they expire and configuring rockets and vehicles so they shed less material while operating.[32]

Proposals for an international treaty banning ASAT weapons have been put forward since the 1960s, and more recently measures of restraint, under the rubrics of Preventing an Arms Race in Outer Space (PAROS) and Prevention of Placement of Weapons Treaty (PPWT), have been proposed but have not garnered the support of all spacefaring states.[33] The United States has vigorously opposed such measures. American negotiators claim codified restraints are infeasible because of difficulties in defining what specifically constitutes a weapon in space, pointing out that many routine techniques of orbital maneuver are indistinguishable from an ASAT capability. American defense planners also think the United States might gain significant advantages from the possession of a robust ASAT capability, and so they do not want this possibility to be foreclosed. Perhaps most important for American calculations, a ban on destroying objects in space would foreclose testing ballistic missile interception technologies.

Environmentalists, Technology Critics, and Justice Advocates

Beyond its intimate relationship with globalist nuclear arms control thinking, the Clarke-Sagan program partially draws ideas from environmentalists, technology critics, and justice advocates. Across the past century, environmentalism has ballooned into a major facet of human affairs, dwarfing by multiple orders of magnitude concern about space. Because claims about Earth habitats sit at the center of both the Tsiolkovsky and Clarke-Sagan programs, space expansionism and environmental issues are intimately entangled. While space does not loom very large as a concern among environmentalists, their views are extremely diverse, ranging from complete opposition to enthusiastic support.

On the critical side, *moral hazard* is the most general concern. If people believe space expansionist claims that viable habitats for human settlement can be found or created in space at reasonable spatial and temporal distances, they are less likely to make strenuous efforts to sustain the habitability of Earth. A key trope of environmental thinking is that there is only one Earth. If there is a reasonably available Planet B, then there is no need to worry too much about the degradation of Planet A. Earth would have a backup planet in case there is a crash. Some space advocates vigorously reject such thinking and insist, as the astrophysicist Martin Rees says, "it's a dangerous delusion to think that space offers an escape from Earth's problems."[34] But many others embrace such thinking, with proclamations like "Earth First! We will strip-mine the other planets later." Fatalistically treating habitat degradation and frontier expansion as the inevitable cyclical pattern of history, they contribute to a "disposable planet mentality."[35] In his *Late for the Sky* the cultural critic David Lavery indicts "the mentality of the Space Age" for producing a "lack of genuine alarm over the wholesale destruction of this planet through ecological catastrophe or nuclear Armageddon."[36] For these critics, space expansionism is far more a symptom of the maladies threatening the Earth than a remedy for them.

Environmentalists also generally object to large-scale space activities as having excessively high *opportunity costs*. Given the legions of the poor and sick, any expenditure can always be faulted on such grounds, but more directly environmentalists ask whether space expenditures justified as reducing catastrophic and existential risks by establishing self-sustaining colonies might better realize these goals by supporting short-term terrestrial catastrophic risk reduction measures, like limiting atmospheric carbon emissions. Other environmentalists doubt Earth-rescue-from-space schemes are viable in relevant time frames, question the viability of enclosed ecosystems in space, worry about the effects of numerous rocket launches on the atmosphere, and advocate protecting the pristine "wilderness" of celestial bodies.[37]

The positive side of the ledger is also full and diverse. Most generally, environmentalists have employed images of the Earth from space to powerfully convey their core message that the Earth is finite and vulnerable, and various "whole Earth" photographs have served as archetypal symbols for the environmentalist worldview and project. Environmentalists also speak of "spaceship Earth" but with very different emphasis than Fuller's Promethean technocratic vision. In her 1965 book *Spaceship Earth*, the British environmental economist Barbara Ward emphasized the vulnerability, intimacy, and community of humanity produced by closure and interdependence.[38] Further playing off the ship-planet comparison, the ecologist Garrett Hardin spoke of "Lifeboat Earth" to convey the draconian choices imposed by environmental restraints.[39] More tangibly, satellite-based scientific observations have made major contributions to improved understanding of the immensely complex planetary dynamics of the Earth and to the sustainable management of terrestrial fisheries, forests, watersheds, and crop lands. Some follow Fuller in arguing that the development of space technologies which "do more with less" make valuable contributions to more frugal terrestrial energy and resource systems.[40]

In the debates about space entangled with more general debates about technology, the Clarke-Sagan program draws straightforwardly on Soterian and Friends of the Earth thinking. From the latter it draws the normative centrality of protecting Earth, the Oasis Earth finding of space exploration, and epistemological limitations from the newest science. From Soterians, the Clarke-Sagan program draws caution stemming from anticipations of technological misfires and syndromes and the implausibility of enterprises dependent on technocracy. The Clarke-Sagan approach rejects the more general pessimism and technophobia of the Luddites and is cautiously optimistic that humanity can develop new identities and realistic interests, and then adjust their political institutions to reflect the realities of Planetary Earth.

Further criticisms come from justice advocates concerned about the impact of space enterprises on the terrestrial distribution of wealth and power between and within societies. These critics assume that extremes of inequality constitute a significant global problem and ask whether space ventures will exacerbate or ameliorate them. Justice advocates believe assuring the pie is justly distributed is as important as expanding it. For this perspective, the space activist Peter Diamandis's declaration that "the first trillionaire will be made in space" is a threat, not an inspiration.[41] Further doubts are raised because many libertarian space advocates aspire to an off-planet exit from governments and taxes, a standard SF scenario, memorably envisioned in the 2013 movie *Elysium*. A justice standard for assessing space ventures is the "golden rule" suggested by the astronomer William K. Hartman and others: "Space exploration must be carried out in a way as to reduce, not aggravate, tensions in human society."[42] Concerns about distribution are not intrinsically hostile to space activities, only those ventures that enrich or empower the few at the expense of the many. Also of concern are questions about which population groups are selected for space settlements and doubts about a tiny minority claiming to act in the name of Humanity.

The Whole Earth Security Program

These insights lead toward a positive alternative agenda for using space and space technology to construct a global security system. These measures encompass, complete, and build on the essentially negative or restraining agenda of arms control. Where arms control proposes to not do or undo, the full Clarke-Sagan agenda aims to do and do together. These alternatives are more scattered and inchoate than the programs of the arms controllers and are underappreciated by space advocates and security analysts. But taken together, these Clarke-Sagan aims constitute a ladder of steps comparable in their potential near-term political impact to the von Braun and Tsiolkovsky programs (see Table 7.2). Like

Table 7.2 **Clarke-Sagan Planetary Security/Whole Earth Security Program**

	Description	Extent Pursued/Status	Additional Proposals
Whole Earth (WE Identity) Formation	Satellite communication and Whole Earth imagery to change identity and consciousness	Very extensive	Universalize and ritualistically privilege
Infrastructure Collaboration	Joint science and exploration capabilities	Extensive: international space station (ISS)	Add China to ISS, moon science base, and asteroid deflection
Earth Habitability Science	Satellite monitoring of Earth system	Greatly underfunded compared to need	Massively expand
Astronomy and Exploration	Probes and observatories in space	Very extensive; pronounced trend toward robotics	Massively expand
Outer Space Treaty	Free passage and nonappropriation	Nonappropriation challenged by developers	Space traffic control regime and debris mitigation
Antisatellite (ASAT) Arms Control	Restraints on ASAT testing and deployment	Parallel unilateral restraints in decay	Test Ban Treaty
Arms Control Verification	Passive information systems to support arms control	Extensive, with growing private activity	Add capacities for international organizations?
Strategic Arms Control	Reduce numbers and capabilities of ballistic missiles	Extensive since 1960s but incomplete	Zero ballistic missiles (ZBM) and test ban

Note: Read from the bottom up.

its rivals, the Clarke-Sagan program has numerous parts, which have been ad-vanced and promoted by numerous analysts, including this author, across the Space Age. Some of these projects have been implemented, making them as much a part of the actual Space Age as their rival programs.

Like its rivals, the Whole Earth Security program rests on assumptions about the threats confronting humanity and the Earth and world political order. The core claim of the Clarke-Sagan Program is that space and space technology can be employed to construct a world political order that complements the territo-rial nation-states by addressing the security and habitability problems of nuclear war and environmental destruction created by the globalization of machine civi-lization. The basic insight is that there are some capabilities and some places that cannot be effectively mobilized and employed by any state without placing into jeopardy the security of all other states. Rather than consolidating authority over these assets into the hands of one global-scope actor tasked with employing them for the benefit of all, as advocates of a world state propose, the Whole Earth Security approach seeks to symmetrically demobilize these capabilities, neutralize these spatial domains, and then selectively employ them coopera-tively to secure all.

Having already examined the first three steps in the ladder of the Clarke-Sagan programs, concerned with arms control, we turn to the Outer Space Treaty, space cooperation as a security strategy, cooperative asteroidal diversion, and space connections and perspectives as catalysts for a planetary common identity and consciousness.

The Outer Space Treaty: Friends and Enemies

Efforts to restrain the deployment of weapons in space are part of a more ge-neral project of building an international legal regime for the orderly conduct of peaceful activities in outer space. These efforts bore major fruit early in the Space Age with the Outer Space Treaty and other ancillary agreements on liability and registration. Because of this treaty, space is not a legal vacuum, however inher-ently it is a physical vacuum. As with other space activities, this extension of international legal order into outer space was preceded by a burst of visionary an-ticipation and advocacy during the late 1950s and early 1960s. These legal space futurists and expansionists considered multiple alternative space and cosmic regimes.[43] Neither the Outer Space Treaty, nor this general project, have been popular among ambitious space expansionists, and over the past several decades the treaty has been increasingly eroding and under assault from both military and habitat space expansionists. For some, weakening or eliminating the Outer

Space Treaty is a step toward space expansion. But for the Whole Earth Security approach, the treaty is an important contribution to solving the Earth's problems and should be strengthened and extended.

The Space Treaty extends agendas and patterns of activity with long and recently accelerating histories. This longer term historical project by the leading members of international society seeks to erect international legal orders for the extraterritorial realms of the planet that do not readily lend themselves to territorial partition but which are increasingly sites for human activities due to advances in technology. Efforts to build extraterritorial legal orders stretch back to the early modern era and the emergence of the Law of the Sea, but have became much more expansive during the twentieth century. Emerging from the 1919 Paris and 1944 Chicago conferences was a legal regime for airplanes and airspaces. Although visionary "air age globalists" sought to create an aeronautical free-passage regime, the Law of the Air codifies the vertical extension of national sovereign territory, with free passage only over the oceans.[44] With the coming of wireless radio communication, a negotiated international regime for the allocation and use of the electromagnetic spectrum was established. Then in 1959 the major states with claims in the continent of Antarctica agreed to suspend their territorial claims, to prohibit all weapons, and to submit to a de facto regime of complete on-site inspection in the form of open visits to all scientific research stations.[45] During the 1960s and 1970s international conferences also produced a major revision and expansion of the Law of the Sea. Despite visions of extensively circumscribing state claims, this order also essentially codifies the primacy of state territorial sovereignty, which it extends with the semisovereign rights into the two-hundred-mile Exclusive Economic Zones, a measure that effectively nationalized most valuable ocean resources. Although each of these regimes is composed of a distinct body of laws and rules, the efforts to design and sustain them have mutually influenced one another, particularly through analogical extension of regimes for one realm to another.[46]

Within this effort the Outer Space Treaty is partly typical and partly unique. Aside from prohibiting nuclear weapons in orbit, the two main features of the treaty are provisions for the "free passage" of space vehicles and satellites and a prohibition of national sovereign appropriation of celestial bodies. In allowing free passage, this regime extends into space the arrangement that had long existed on the Earth's ocean surfaces. But in prohibiting the extension of national sovereignty to bodies in space, the Treaty broke important new ground, as no one had ever conceived of a Law of the Sea prohibiting state appropriation of islands and lands bordering seas. Instead of nation-states owning such bodies, the treaty stipulated that they were the "common province of mankind" (see Table 7.3).

The outer space regime was viewed by its creators as analogous to key features of the Antarctic regime.[47] But these provisions were the product of practical necessity, as well as the very time-specific aspects of the Soviet-US competition in space in the mid-1960s. While states certainly preferred to simply extend their sovereign rule of the atmosphere above their territory into the voids around the planet, such a move would have had the practical effect of precluding the orbiting of satellites, which must inevitably pass above many states as they circuit the Earth. The nonappropriation clause of the Outer Space Treaty was a reflection of the fact that neither the United States nor the Soviet Union could be certain who would get to the moon first and thus be able, according to international norms, to claim it. Rather than risk being second to the moon and losing any claim, both sides agreed to forgo the possible benefits of getting there first.[48] The Outer Space Treaty also followed the Antarctica model in prohibiting the placement of weapons on any celestial body and permitting on-site inspections of all bases.

A major feature of all these efforts to build international legal orders for the fluid realms of the planet has been a political struggle between the global haves

Table 7.3 **Outer Space Treaty: Supporters, Critics, and Proposals**

	Precedent and World Order Project	*Supporters' Plan*	*View of Critics*	*Critics' Plan*
Free Passage	Law of the Sea; allow wide access	Growing congestion requires space traffic control regime	Incompatible with hegemonic military employment	Centralized military control of passage
Nonappropriation of Celestial Bodies	Antarctica treaty; diminish conflict	Treat as common heritage and cooperative science	Impedes development	Evade, end, or modify to permit private appropriation
Common Province of Mankind	Law of the Sea; treatment of seabed; allow wide access	Scientific cooperation; widely distribute benefits	Impedes development	Avoid treating as common heritage

and have nots, between the few wealthy industrialized states and the many poor countries, many of them recently freed from imperial domination. During the lengthy negotiations over the Law of the Sea, the developing countries were determined that the next great boundary-drawing episode on the planet not leave them as dispossessed as those of previous centuries. The Global South was successful in achieving the creation of an International Seabed Authority, which would lease areas on the deep seabed for mining, as well as itself mine, with revenues distributed to disadvantaged countries. In part because of opposition to this measure, the United States, despite playing a leading role in negotiating the treaty, did not actually ratify it. A similar struggle played out over the 1979 proposed "Moon Treaty," which aimed to use the "common heritage of mankind" principle to govern the development of lunar resources.[49] Although the Moon Treaty is not supported by any spacefaring state, the prospect of such provisions animates opponents of the Outer Space Treaty and remains an unresolved issue for ambitious space development.

Although the Outer Space Treaty is highly permissive of state activities, and its loopholes are big enough to fly ballistic missiles and a constellation of military satellites through, many military and habitat expansionists see it as a serious hindrance to the achievement of their visions and actively seek to end or evade it. Dolman explicitly calls for the United States to withdraw from the Treaty.[50] Zubrin declares the treaty a "tragedy because it drained away the energy the remaining twenty years of the Cold War could have provided space exploration," which would have propelled humans to Mars before the end of the century.[51] Many habitat expansionists view the treaty's nonappropriation clause as an impediment to the commercial exploitation of asteroids and lunar settlements. In reserving celestial bodies as a "common province of mankind," the treaty raises the specter of wealth from development being shared with less fortunate members of the international community. Despite their frequent appeals to the needs of humanity, this prospect is utterly anathema to the pure free market, winner-take-all ideology of the new space entrepreneurs. Space expansionists who view the movement into space as an escape from the excessive government regulation choking innovative risk-takers on Earth see the treaty as the forward-leaning shadow of precisely what they aspire to leave behind. Opponents of the treaty scored a major victory in 2015 with the enactment of legislation in the United States authorizing private firms to appropriate asteroidal and lunar resources as property, a measure avidly sought by expansionists and the new space entrepreneurs.[52] Little Luxemburg, long the haven of wealthy tax evaders, has enacted similar legislation, perhaps initiating another regulatory race to the bottom. But, as is so often the case in other realms, the ideological libertarian antipathy to any regulation often collides with the practical business need for stable regulatory frameworks, particularly for congested places.

In contrast, arm controllers and others advocate a significant extension of the treaty by establishing a space traffic control regime.[53] The objective of such a regime would be prohibit space vehicles from coming too close to one another. Analogous control regimes to permit the safe and orderly passage of vehicles are well-established for terrestrial activities on roads, at sea, and in the air. It is notable that even though the skies over the ocean expanses of the planet are not possessed by any state, all states routinely conform to a global air traffic regime in these realms. Parts of a space traffic regime exist in the 1975 treaty requiring states to announce space launches, and the allocation of orbital slots in geo-synchronous orbit by the International Telecommunications Union. But once vehicles are in orbit, they are otherwise unregulated in their movements. The United States has resisted restraints on movement as a barrier to testing space weapons, while arms controllers support such a regime to inhibit further space weaponization.

Space Cooperation as Security Strategy

Since the beginning of the Space Age, the idea that the planet's enveloping space shell was particularly suited for international collaboration has been widely voiced. Unlike space arms control, which is really "co-non-operation" involving parallel restraints, space cooperation entails jointly conducted activities. The proposition that cooperative space exploration and colonization could significantly ameliorate world politics was advanced in the 1930s by David Lasser, one of the founders of the American Interplanetary Society, whose 1931 book, The Conquest of Space, first brought the prospect of space travel and the work of Robert Goddard to wide audiences.[54] Recognizing that rockets would make war vastly more rapid and destructive, Lasser looks to cooperative expansion into space as a solution. A "space-minded" generation would have "a sense of the community of mankind, sharing a common destiny on this little Earth."[55] Having "failed to find the basis for cooperation from the ground up," humanity should instead seek to do so "from space down." To "establish the idea of the common heritage and common destiny" of humans, space travel should be an "international venture directed by an Interplanetary Commission headquartered in the Swiss Alps."[56]

International cooperation has been a significant part of space activities, and any account omitting them would be significantly incomplete. Military space expansionists see little potential value in such efforts, and most habitat expansionists are indifferent whether states conduct space activities together or alone, as long as they do it. And many expansionists see interstate rivalry, even military competition, as valuable spurs toward their overriding aim of going into space. But other space thinkers (including this author) have advanced space co-operation as a security strategy and envision major cooperative space infrastructural projects not primarily as a means to do more in space but to achieve and sustain pacific political relations among spacefaring states.[57]

There are many rationales for conducting space activities cooperatively, not all related to security strategy. Among space activities, science has been the most extensively conducted internationally. Modern science is extraordinarily international, and scientific research is the most open major human activity, despite extensive military and commercial secrecy. Not surprisingly, space scientists have been among the most consistent and influential advocates of international space cooperation. Because space ventures are extremely expensive, conducting them cooperatively spreads the costs among more contributors. For small countries cooperative space ventures have been essential, and the now extensive space activities of the European Union are a large-scale working model of how numerous countries can achieve significant space advances by pooling their resources. But even when goals are well aligned, cooperation is often difficult in practice due to differing organizational cultures, budgetary systems, languages, and time zones.

Beyond these compelling economic reasons, space cooperation is a technique for building better political relations among states and thus sustaining arms control co-non-operation. Weapons are expensive, and if there are fewer weapons, more resources are available for civilian needs—with fewer guns, there can be more butter. The oft-quoted call from the Book of Isaiah, to "forge swords into plowshares," captures the strategy of making positive civil use of the capabilities necessary for war. In this vein, critics of high military spending, such as President Dwight Eisenhower, speak of preparations for war as robbing vital civilian needs. Another variant of such thinking, classically articulated a century ago by the American philosopher William James, is that foreign threats seem uniquely capable of generating great exertions, and so peace advocates must create a "moral equivalent of war" (with the unfortunate acronym MEOW).[58] Also along these lines is the strategy developed by the British political scientist David Mitrany during the 1940s for a "working peace system" built incrementally with "low politics" cooperation to achieve common, but mundane, "welfare" goals, which will over time produce "spillovers" of pacifying effects in the realm of "high politics" traditionally dominated by jealous sovereignties and military rivalries.[59]

The strategy of cooperation in space embodies these approaches, but then goes a step further by proposing to cooperate in places, and with technologies, having more, not less, military significance. This approach of cooperatively developing civilian applications of powerful technologies with great military potential can be seen in the early nuclear era, in the proposals for the cooperative international development of nuclear technology advanced by the Baruch Plan and Atoms for Peace plans of the Truman and Eisenhower administrations.

Because space and space technology are such vital domains of military competition, and because the manned space programs are such prestigious symbols of national technological prowess, cooperative activities could have a disproportionate influence on political relations. In short, "forging tanks into subways" has its appeal but is less strategically important than "forging missiles into spaceships." Furthermore, arms control is difficult to achieve in part because weapons-building organizations have a vested interest in continued production. But by diverting organizational, financial, and technological resources from weapons production to space cooperation, an influential constituency is created for sustaining pacific political relations. Once cooperative projects reach an organizational and financial critical mass, it becomes costly to disentangle their melded parts, thus providing a break if political relations deteriorate for other reasons.[60]

During the Cold War, both civil competition and cooperation in space played important and visible roles and were pursued primarily to shape interstate relations rather than to advance space expansionist goals. Even during the most tense periods of this rivalry, leaders of both countries often rhetorically endorsed cooperative ventures. It is often forgotten that the first satellites launched by both the Soviet Union and the United States were part of a major international scientific effort, the International Geophysical Year, which was devoted to studying the geophysical aspects of the Earth, particularly the polar regions and outer space. In the early 1970s, during the detente period, a much publicized rendezvous was conducted between Russian and American crewed vehicles in orbit.[61] During the tense early 1980s, several leading space figures, including Carl Sagan, proposed "to go to Mars with Moscow" as a means to help improve superpower relations.[62] Similar proposals were prominently promoted by Roald Sagdeev, the director of the Soviet Space Sciences Institute.[63]

After the unexpected transformation of superpower relations in the late 1980s, advocates of this strategy of joining the American and Russian manned space programs achieved their largest victory with the jointly designed and constructed International Space Station (ISS). This project, often disparaged by prominent space enthusiasts for not going anywhere and by many scientists for its high costs, has been the leading edge of the endeavor to expand the human presence into the cosmos for the past two decades. Modest in comparison to the ambitious visions of space expansionists, the ISS is the most expensive artifact ever built. Successfully executing this project required overcoming not just gravity but also the very different organizational cultures and technologies of two space agencies that had in significant measure been called into existence to compete with each other.[64] With the unanticipated retirement of its space shuttle fleet in 2012, the United States became completely dependent on

Russian launch vehicles to transport American astronauts to the station, a situation that will last at least until 2020. It is also notable that in the deterioration of Russian-American relations, the joint operation of the ISS has continued unchanged, thus setting at least a partial floor on the downward spiral of their relations, as advocates had anticipated.

Another underappreciated case of space activities as a strategy to improve superpower political relations is the largest single US civilian space project, the Apollo program. The American entry into a race to the moon, initiated during a period of tense rivalry and costing as much as the interstate highway system, Apollo was a gambit in the Cold War competition rather than reflecting an American commitment to space exploration. But recent research by John Logsdon, the leading American lunar space political analyst, reveals that the Kennedy administration viewed Apollo in part as a means to *divert* competition away from its dangerous military focus and toward civilian goals.[65] It is also notable that when the Kennedy administration came to office, the military was preparing to massively increase its manned space activities, but all these programs were terminated by the late 1960s.[66]

Combining these ventures, a strategic pathway emerges for employing space capability to alter the political relations of major spacefaring states (see Figure 7.2). Starting from a baseline of military competition, the first step is civilian competition such, as the Apollo project, followed by civilian cooperation, such as the International Space Station. Other frequently proposed large cooperative projects are Mars missions and lunar bases and removal of orbital debris. These projects prepare the way for the final step, security cooperation, which has yet to be attempted. What form might strategic cooperation take? The most plausible candidate for an international cooperative security venture of significant magnitude is the cooperative monitoring and diversion of asteroids.

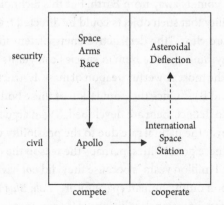

Figure 7.2 From Military Competition to Security Cooperation

Planetary Defense and Asteroidal
Deflection Dilemmas

While asteroids loom large in the horizons of habitat and some military expansionists, they receive little attention from arms controllers and most global security thinkers. As a planetary defense project, diverting asteroids seems a logical part of a Whole Earth Security program and international space infrastructure security cooperation, but opponents of military space expansion are sharply divided about asteroidal diversion. In part these disputes carry over from Cold War nuclear debates, with Edward Teller, Darth Vader for arms controllers, pushing nuclear solutions to the asteroid threat, and arms controllers raising alarms.

An important analysis of the dangers inherent in the deflection of asteroidal bodies is provided by Carl Sagan and Stephen Ostro.[67] Few figures of the Space Age have been as productive and prominent as Sagan, a planetary astronomer, science educator, and SF author.[68] Over the later decades of the twentieth century Sagan's work on planetary science, particularly Mars, his television series *Cosmos*, and his science fiction, most notably *Contact* (coauthored with Ann Druyan), made him an international celebrity and influential voice for science and space exploration. Unlike virtually all other space scientists and engineers of his era, Sagan also was active in advancing nuclear arms control, studying—and publicizing—the "nuclear winter" hypothesis and promoting cooperation in space to improve Soviet-American relations.[69] Although a strong supporter of the larger habitat expansionist vision, Sagan insists large-scale space activities should occur only *after* nuclear disarmament and planetary habitat stability have been achieved because of an ominous asteroid "deflection dilemma."[70]

The essence of the deflection dilemma is simple: species and civilizational survival inevitably will eventually require the development of the ability to deflect asteroids and comets away from Earth, but this technology also inherently creates the possibility that such objects could be directed *toward* the Earth. The existential stakes are clear: "the destructive energy latent in a large near-Earth asteroid dwarfs anything else the human species can get its hands on," making them potentially "the most powerful weapon of mass destruction ever devised"[71] (see Table 7.4.A and B).[72] Once the population of these bodies is fully mapped, and technologies to deflect them are developed, Sagan argues, the prospects for collision *increase* over the natural rate due to the possibility of intentional bombardment. Given these possibilities, perhaps the reason the dinosaurs lasted for nearly two hundred million years is because they did *not* have a space program.

In his major book on the human space future, *Pale Blue Dot*, Sagan lays out several scenarios for intentional collisions. His arguments are essentially the

Table 7.4.A **Nuclear Weapons: Volumes of Violence**

Nuclear Weapons	Volume of Violence
All Nuclear Weapons (1945–2020)	13,000 MT
Tsar Bomba (1961) (largest test) (USSR)	50 MT
B-41 (largest US weapon)	25 MT
Castle Bravo (1954) (US test)	15 MT (megatons)
Hiroshima (1945) (US on Japan)	13 KT (kilotons)

arguments of nuclear arms controllers. Madmen exist, and some "achieve the highest levels of political power in modern industrial nations."[73] Recalling the extreme destruction caused by Hitler and Stalin, Sagan posits the possibility that a "misanthropic psychopath" or a "megalomaniac lusting after 'greatness' or glory, a victim of ethnic violence bent on revenge, someone in the grip of severe testosterone poisoning, some religious fanatic hastening the Day of Judgment, or just some technicians incompetent or insufficiently vigilant" will bring about a catastrophic collision.[74] Earth-approaching asteroids amount to "30,000 swords of Damocles hanging over our heads," for which "there is no acceptable national solution."[75] And, like Cole and Salkeld (not mentioned), Sagan points to the possibilities of clandestine use of this technology.

Sagan's solution to the dilemma is to be found in the fact that "the timescales of the two dangers are different."[76] The natural threat is long term, while the human-made threat is potentially short term, and so delay in both mapping and deflection technology is prudent. Delay should occur until "the reliability of world political organizations" and the "confidence they inspire" have made

Table 7.4.B **Near-Earth Object Violence (Historical and Potential)**

Asteroids (Near Earth Objects)	Impact Energy (TNT Equivalent)
>1,000 meters (1,000 objects)	43 million MT (megatons)
500–1,000 meters (2,000 objects)	31 million MT
300–500 meters (3,000 objects)	8 million MT
100–300 meters (15,600 objects)	4 million MT
Chicxulub (11–81 km) (66 MYA)(Yucatan)	100 million MT
Tunguska (60–190 meters) (1908) (Russia)	15–30 MT
Chelabynsk (20 meters) (2013) (Russia)	300-500 KT (kilotons)
Annual event	10 KT

"significant strides," permitting them to be "trusted to deal with a problem of this seriousness."[77] But because deflection must eventually occur if humanity is to survive, the asteroid threat provides a "potent motivation to create effective transnational institutions and to unify the human species."[78] Sagan's argument for delay and extreme caution hinges on political claims about the limitations of the international system and of states in restraining the use of violence, and about the potential viability of world institutions. Danger of use arises because rivalrous states are likely to weaponize asteroids, as they have done with so many other militarily significant capabilities, and because hierarchical and secretive states are prone to reckless and aggressive behaviors.

Advocates of planetary defense, most notably James Oberg, reply that Sagan's scenarios are not plausible because altering an orbit to strike a specific target is more difficult than deflection.[79] A RAND study of asteroid weaponization concluded that "much cheaper, more responsive weapons of mass destruction are readily available," making planetoid bombs militarily unattractive.[80] And, like the "nuclear winter" blowback from nuclear war, the effects of a large asteroidal bombardment might also afflict the territory of an attacker.

An alternative approach to the collision threat, advanced by this author and others, proposes that an international consortium of spacefaring states undertake such efforts. In order to prevent cooperatively developed techniques and infrastructures being redeployed for unilateral ends, the planetary defense consortium would need to be combined with a firm agreement that no one state would conduct comparable activities without the participation of the others. This security regime for asteroids would have the added benefit of reinforcing the nonappropriation provisions of the Outer Space Treaty, while also laying the foundations for possibly jointly exploiting asteroidal resources in a manner that did not exclude the less advantaged members of humanity.

A key reason for thinking that this "do together, never alone" approach is superior to Sagan's strategy of delaying until the interstate system has significantly evolved is that a lengthy delay may not be feasible. While collisions with global catastrophic or existential consequences are sufficiently rare to reasonably risk delay, collisions with severe regional effects occur more frequently. The collision of a moderate-size body, particularly with a populated area, or even the mapping of an eventual collision, is reasonably likely—and is likely to trigger a technology-development response. Furthermore, nascent efforts to exploit asteroidal resources also entail the development of orbital alteration techniques, thus starting humanity, or at least some tiny fraction of it, on the path to access the immense energies contained in sky rocks. Furthermore, an international planetary defense consortium might help catalyze the international political transformation seen by Sagan as a prudent prerequisite for starting on this fateful path.

Sagan's strong argument for delay sits awkwardly alongside his strong advocacy of space colonization as necessary for ensuring the survival of humanity from various possible calamities. His bombardment scenarios are probably *misplaced*—more plausible after successful colonization than among Earthbound states. The picture he paints of a solar diaspora is surprisingly ominous. Human inhabitants of other worlds will develop a "very different set of perceptions, interests, prejudices, and predispositions" from those living on Earth. And humans living on other worlds will become different due to mechanical and genetic alterations.[81] He also off-handedly observes that "humans in space will hold the upper hand in any serious dispute with those on Earth."[82] But he does not consider the possible intentions that inhabitants of diverse other worlds might have toward terrestrial humanity, or how his earthly "madman scenarios" might be avoided in the vast reaches of the human space diaspora that he embraces so enthusiastically.

Global Village and Whole Earth Consciousness and Identity

The Clarke-Sagan program also offers powerful claims about how space-based communication systems and views of the Earth from space can contribute to the emergence of new forms of global and planetary consciousness and identity, supplanting those associated with the nation-state (see Table 7.5). How humans view themselves in relation to each other and to the Earth will be revolutionized, making for new Whole Earth (WE) identities.

Humans do not live by bread alone. They act on the basis of their identities and consciousness about themselves and their place in the world. All human groups, from the smallest family to the largest empire, persist in part because their members hold identities and ideas that make these groupings seem appropriate and legitimate, and a major part of statecraft has been soulcraft, the fashioning and reproduction of identities and ideas. With the coming of the machine civilization and its globalization, the human world has been made one materially, but forms of identity and awareness forged in preglobal times for groups of much smaller spatial scope have not only persisted but strengthened, as the new tools of modern communications and education have been harnessed for their reproduction. Against these lively psychic ghosts of earlier Earths, many internationalists, globalists, and cosmopolitans have sought over the past two centuries to forge new "one world" identities and consciousness better matched to the realities of intensifying material interdependence and interaction. To this end, they have conjured a wide array of programs and schemes, ranging from

Table 7.5 **Generating Common Planetary Identity and Consciousness**

	Description	Effect	World Order Outcome
Dwarfed Earth	Astronomy shows Earth as infinitesimally small	Realization of common fate and Earth's fragility	Decline in nationalism and war and rise of ecological awareness
Telcom Satellites	Global-range instantaneous television	Cultural and identity homogenization	Decline in nationalism and rise of common identity
Whole Earth Photographs	Synoptic views of Earth from space	Realization of common fate and Earth's fragility	Decline in nationalism and war and rise of ecological awareness
Overview Effect	Direct experience of Earth from space	Realization of common fate and Earth's fragility	Decline in nationalism and war and rise of ecological awareness

artificial languages to new cosmopolitan ethical systems.[83] These efforts have been motivated by the realization that the emergence of a worldwide common identity will make solving many global and planetary problems much easier and add greatly to the survival prospects of humanity. Alongside these efforts are what can be called a "space-one worldist" agenda to elevate and unify human consciousness and identity with satellite telecommunications and shared views of the Earth from space.

The idea that the unification of humankind is dependent on the ability of people to communicate with one another dates back at least to the biblical story of the Tower of Babel, in which the political divisions and spatial dispersal of humanity are attributed to differences in language. With the coming of telegraphic and other forms of very rapid communication produced by the Industrial Revolution, many anticipated that international peace and global unification would soon result. Anticipation of the emergence of new and strengthened forms of global identity and consciousness from the exploitation of space technologies, as well as from human ascents from the terrestrial sphere, finds some of its strongest formulations in the work of Arthur C. Clarke. Over the course of a career that stretched from the late 1940s into the first years of this century, Clarke produced a prodigious outpouring of space expansionist advocacy, technological futurism, and science fiction.[84] Perhaps most well-known is the movie *2001: A Space Odyssey*, written in collaboration with the director Stanley Kubrick, which stands as one of the iconic works of space SF.[85] Perhaps Clarke's most enduring claim to fame, however, is his 1946 proposal for the use of geosynchronous orbit as the site for communication satellites, or "global radio relay stations," as he put it, a vision that came to be extensively realized during his lifetime. Also in 1946, in what the historian Robert Poole calls "one of the founding manifestoes of the Space Age," entitled "The Challenge of the Spaceship," Clarke proclaims that "interplanetary travel is the only form of 'conquest and empire' now compatible with civilization," ranks rockets and atomic energy as inventions comparable to the control of fire and the invention of agriculture, and promotes space expansion to avoid civilizational stagnation.[86]

With the rapid deployment of communications satellites beginning in the 1960s, Clarke's technological vision came to be realized, and instantaneous communications with global reach became an integral part of the global revolution in information technology. The most enduring formulation for the new human reality created by instantaneous global communications is the "global village," provided by the Canadian media theorist Marshall McLuhan in 1966.[87] This concept has gained extremely wide currency to convey high levels of global interdependence. Known for his breathtaking oracular pronouncements, McLuhan proclaims, "We have extended our central nervous system itself in a global embrace, abolishing both time and space as far as our planet is concerned."[88] As they are linked together by the new globe-spanning media, people everywhere have a level of informational interaction comparable to what had previously been possible only in the much smaller spatial scale of a village. Clarke anticipated that television and satellite transmission would "remove all national barriers, and eventually create not merely the global village but the global family, sharing at least one language in common."[89] These new technologies, in creating the "TeleFamily of man," would make human consciousness as unified as the material world had become in the wake of the globalization of machine civilization.

Clarke's anticipations of the positive effects of space activities on human life extend much farther. Humans will not only shed their national affiliations; they will become generally improved because "with superhuman knowledge must go equally great compassion and tolerance."[90] The logic of this startling claim is that "morals and ethics must not lag behind science, otherwise the social system will breeds poisons which will cause its certain destruction." He speaks of waning "tribal divisions and squabbles" and declares it is "infinitely improbable" that "interplanetary warfare can ever arise."[91] He believes readers of science fiction "quickly realize the absurdity of mankind's present tribal divisions."[92] His claim that humans improve in their moral character through spatial ascents is a mild version of the cosmic narrative of humanity evolving to higher states of consciousness found in much of his science fiction, from his *Childhood's End* (1951; aliens rescue humanity from its petty conflicts by the transmutation of human consciousness, triggering migration into space) to *2001: A Space Odyssey* (a mysterious transcendent agent periodically intervenes to spur evolutionary leaps in humanity). These spatial elevations are presumably stepping stones to the eventual replacement of humans with highly intelligent machines he anticipates hopefully.

A second cluster of Whole Earth thinking claims new views of the cosmos and the Earth from space will catalyze the emergence of strong new planetary identities and consciousness.[93] Notions that astronomy and the study of the stars would elevate and unify human awareness are extremely old, appearing widely in the writings of ancient cosmopolitan thinkers. With modern astronomy showing the Earth dwarfed by the vastness of cosmic space, and eventually obliterated by the death of the sun, many hypothesized that a global revolution in consciousness was possible, as "the threat to human extinction eliminates differences of class, ethnicity and gender."[94] Others look to the new cosmology to provide a "transnationally shared, believable picture of the cosmos" with a "mythic-quality story of its origins," enabling humanity to see its problems in "an entirely new light" and "almost certainly solve them."[95] Related efforts to situate human development in a cosmic "Big History" (pioneered in Sagan's *Cosmos*), or even to consecrate science, also seek to construct a shared planetary WE identity strong enough to support global institutions and problem-solving.[96]

As anticipations of space travel became widespread, the idea that viewing the Earth from space would profoundly alter human consciousness in ways supportive of peace and unity was voiced by leading scientists, science popularizers, and futurists such as Wells, as well as by prominent literary figures such as Virginia Woolf.[97] In 1950 the astronomer and SF writer Fred Hoyle observed that "once a photograph of the Earth, taken from outside, is available," and the "sheer isolation of the Earth becomes plain to everyman," it "will have the effect of exposing the futility of nationalist strife."[98] With the first travels of humans to space and the first images of the Earth from space, strong expectations of a new planetary consciousness and identity became widespread. As the Apollo astronaut Russell Schweickart observed, "When you go around the Earth in an hour and a half, you begin to recognize that your identity is with the whole thing."[99] Images of the Earth from further distances, showing only a "pale blue dot," are also said to compellingly demonstrate humanity's comic insignificance and common destiny. The expectation and hope is that these new perspectives will produce what might be termed "planetary topophilia," a love of place for the whole planet, contributing to an Earth nationalism.[100]

The potential for space activities to trigger transformations in human identity and consciousness is developed at length by the American space thinker Frank White in *The Overview Effect: Space Exploration and Human Evolution* (1987). White starts with the observation that geographic position powerfully shapes human consciousness, as "mental processes and views of life cannot be separated from physical location."[101] After an extensive analysis of the reports by astronauts and cosmonauts of their experiences viewing the Earth from space, White posits the "Overview Effect": astronauts and space settlers have a "different philosophical point of view as a result of having a different physical perspective."[102] Noting that going into space is a "modern metaphor for the journey to higher awareness," he claims that the Overview Effect is "seeing and feeling the unity of Earth," and this "metaexperience" "heralds the creation of a planetary civilization and planetary consciousness."[103]

This transformative insight is not, however, confined solely to those who actually travel into space but is stimulated by viewing the "whole Earth picture" taken of the Earth from space. This "whole Earth symbol" is a "metaidea" based on the Overview Effect, has been widely disseminated through the satellite-centered global telecommunications system, and "makes the metaphor of a planetary nervous system into a reality."[104] This "disseminated Overview Effect is the foundation of terran awareness, providing the fundamental symbol of the new planetary civilization."[105] As this new planetary civilization emerges, humanity becomes a "more peaceful, self-aware, and ecologically careful species."[106] This new planetary order means the "demise" of the nation-state "as the dominant form on Earth" and the replacement of the international anarchic state of nature by a "terran constitution."[107] However, the "peaceful evolution" of this emergent planetary civilization is threatened by the "projection of military values into space," by nation-states that "seek to extend their dominance wherever possible, including outer space."[108] Solving this problem, as well as realizing an even more ambitious leap in human civilizational evolution, requires, White concludes, the colonization of space.

Whatever the vantage point—Earth from space, near and far, Earth special or typical, or cosmic space dwarfing Earth—the lesson these thinkers draw is the same: human unity based on shared planetary and cosmic reality. Whatever their merits, these Whole Earth identity and consciousness arguments should be thought of as "terrapolitan" rather than cosmopolitan because they aim to unify humanity through experiences of the Earth as a place rather than abstract ethical universals.[109]

The Great Debate on Earth Space

Bringing the projects and arguments of the Clarke-Sagan Whole Earth Security programs into view reveals why there are such fundamental disagreements among space advocates about what should be done—and not done—in the parts of space closest to the terrestrial Earth. Quite aside from the larger ambitions of habitat expansionists to make humanity a multiplanet species, space expansionists sharply disagree in four fundamental ways about the desirability and consequences of near-space activities.

First, and most consequentially, the von Braun and the Clarke-Sagan programs directly clash over the desirability of weaponizing space and space technology. Both programs are advanced as solutions to insecurity and vulnerability. But they propose essentially opposite strategies and differ on what they seek to secure—the nation-state or humanity and the planet. Because nation-states are well-established, and humanity and the Earth have almost no organized voice, the von Braun agenda would seem to have the upper hand, except for the inconvenient fact that no nation-state can be secure if humanity and the Earth are in jeopardy. At the heart of their differences lies a basic disagreement about what nuclear weapons mean for national and global security and world order. As such, the basic clash between these space programs is largely an extension of the great debate about nuclear weapons and world order. The von Braun programs are about how space should be employed in a nuclear world, assuming the continued primacy and viability of autonomous and rival states. And the Clarke-Sagan programs outline how space should be employed, assuming nuclear weapons pose a revolutionary challenge to the security-providing function of states that requires significant changes in the state-centric world political order. In short, where one stands on space depends on where one stands on the nuclear Earth. Despite their profound differences, both defend the desirability of their proposals with claims about geography, geohistory, and geopolitics, thus opening the possibility of resolving the main dispute between them by assessing these aspects of their arguments.

Second, there is a fundamental difference between the first steps of the Tsiolkovsky and the Clarke-Sagan programs. The Tsiolkovskians propose heavy infrastructures extending the Fuller Earth project into orbital space, while the Clarke-Sagan program envisions much lighter information-gathering satellite networks. While the habitat expansionists give little attention to military uses of space, and the Clarke-Sagan projects focus on reversing and relinquishing military space activities, they offer radically different accounts of the terrestrial problems requiring space solutions. For habitat expansionists, the basic problem is shortages of energy and materials, to be remedied by imports from space, and habitat limits and vulnerabilities, to be solved by artificial worlds. For the Clarke-Sagan approach, the basic planetary problem is the disjuncture between the cascade of material interdependence, interaction, and vulnerability created by the enlargements and accelerations of machine civilization and the inherited fragmented and conflicting patterns of authority and identity associated with the nation-state and the largely anarchical organization of world politics.

Third, asteroids play large roles in all three programs, but in very different ways. Avoiding natural collisions is a no-brainer for all three, but the salience of this threat and its relationship with other agendas vary enormously. Despite its focus on security and violence, diverting asteroids does not figure prominently in the von Braunian agenda, aside from hydrogen bomb enthusiast Edward Teller conjuring them to avoid nuclear disarmament. Only at the speculative edge do they appear, as sources of shielding for space battle stations or weaponized for bombardment. Unwilling to conceive of threats without enemies, the von Braunian security radar screen ignores naturally occurring asteroidal collisions. For Tsiolkovskians asteroids are pivotal, as resources for terrestrial and space development and sites for colonization. Skeptical of astro-mega-engineering and further weaponization, the Clark-Sagan program, notwithstanding Sagan's misplaced fears, has the most modest agenda, toward cooperative diversion efforts, with hopes for integrative institutional fallout. The diverse postures of the three programs toward asteroids reflects the protean and disruptive features of these cosmic crumbs, which will assuredly be prominent in any human space future.

Finally, these competing space approaches have clashing assumptions about humanity's relation to modern technological enlargements. While both embrace technological advance, the Clarke-Sagan projects are informed by the sobered Soterian realization that further technological empowerments will lead to enlarged disasters unless the quality of human decision-making improves. Such advances require the emergence of new global institutions and identities, which properly chosen space activities can help realize. In contrast, the Promethean Tsiolkovsky programs are politically underdeveloped but tend toward reliance on technocratic rule and amelioration through ascent.

While Clarke and Sagan see hard choices to be made about space near the Earth, their assumptions about politics in the larger solar and galactic expansion are straightforwardly ascentionist, indistinguishable from the core views of the Tsiolkovskians. Clarke finds interplanetary war unthinkable, while Sagan ignores the applicability of his fears over misuse of asteroidal diversion techniques by Earth-based states to the eventual space-based colonies he anticipates and advocates. Thus is posed the question: Are the types of doubts raised by Clarke and Sagan about the von Braun projects in near space applicable to the larger space diaspora of humanity to a multiworld species?

PART FOUR

ASSESSMENT

8

Geography, Geopolitics, and Geohistory

The "geographical setting" is only a stage; it is not the script, though it does suggest the plot and influences the cast of characters.
—Colin S. Gray (1996)[1]

Men make their own history, but not in the conditions of their own choosing.
—Karl Marx (1852)[2]

The longer you can look back, the farther you can look forward.
—Winston Churchill (1956)[3]

Answering Big Questions

What have been the effects of space activity? And what will be the impacts of the large future space projects proposed by space advocates? The overall claim of space expansionism is that human movement into outer space has had, and will have, desirable consequences of great magnitude. The core claim advanced here is that these positive views of the space enterprise rest on geography errors, misleading geohistorical analogies, and slanted and truncated geopolitics. With accurate geographic mappings, appropriate geohistorical analogies, and full geopolitical theory, it becomes clear that large-scale space activities pose underappreciated catastrophic and existential threats and that reversals, restraints, and relinquishments are desirable.

The benefits that space expansionists anticipate from human activities in space are many, but security from violence and the preservation and expansion of freedom are among the most consequential. Given the extreme destructiveness of nuclear war and the immense violence potential latent in fast-moving space objects, the question of whether space expansion is desirable roughly approximates into the question of whether space activities increase or decrease the likelihood of war. As we have seen, the question of whether military space activities have enlarged the probability of nuclear war sharply divides adherents of the von Braun programs from advocates of the Clarke-Sagan programs, and this momentous dispute extends into space the basic dispute about the nuclear revolution itself. As we have also seen, the question of whether large-scale violence is likely to accompany movement into solar space has not been given much consideration by those who view this expansion as the ultimate goal of the space enterprise, indeed of humanity itself. Similarly, given the immense threat to freedom from a highly hierarchical or totalitarian world government, the question of whether space activities advance or threaten freedom quickly simplifies into the question of whether space activities increase or decrease the prospects for such an oppressive world government. On this vital question, space expansionists hold an even wider range of views, both on the desirability of world government generally and on the relation of space activities to its realization or avoidance. How these questions are answered and how these disputes are resolved ultimately determine whether the space expansionist project is desirable to pursue or better reversed and relinquished.

Unfortunately the magnitude of the stakes in these questions and disputes is fully matched by the deficiencies of theories to authoritatively answer and resolve them. Despite the efforts of many thinkers and researchers over centuries, the project to build a reliable science of human behavior, and of society and politics, remains significantly incomplete. Particularly on large topics like war and peace and freedom and oppression, disputes and disagreements remain extensive. This fact should be—but rarely is—quite sobering to advocates of novel ventures of great magnitude and high stakes. Despite these severe limitations in the basis for answering the core political questions upon which the desirability of space expansion hinges, careful systematic evaluation of these issues is still potentially valuable. As we have seen, space expansionist argumentation heavily relies on geopolitical claims, in the sense that they attribute political influences and outcomes to geography and technology. Thinking systematically about such claims provides a basis for assessing the plausibility of their geopolitical arguments without making the assumption that the theories of geopolitics are themselves anything approaching a full and empirically vindicated model for explaining large-scale human political outcomes.

In this and the next two chapters, this assessment is undertaken in three main steps. In this chapter, types of geographic errors and misleading analogies are examined. Then the assumptions of a broadly geopolitical approach to politics are summarized and a set of general geopolitical propositions are advanced which are applicable to historical and contemporary Earth patterns as well as actual and prospective space expansions. These propositions are a synthesis of the insights developed by theorists of geopolitics and related bodies of international relations theory, political science, macrohistory, and historical sociology.

The ways these propositions illuminate the larger patterns across Earth history are briefly summarized, thus providing some at least loose historical vindication for their value. In the next chapter these propositions are employed to show that the claims of space arms controllers are superior to those of the von Braun programs and that large-scale development of Earth orbital space runs significant risk of leading to a hierarchical form of world government. In the final chapter the propositions illuminate the multiple ways in which solar space expansion is likely to lead to highly violent war, extreme levels of oppression, and the eventual extinction of humanity. Over the course of these three chapters leading analogies employed by space expansionists are also assessed and more appropriate ones are provided.

Geography and Geography Errors

Space is a geographic category, and characterizations of the geography of space play a prominent role in virtually every space expansionist argument. These deployments of geography by space expansionists contain errors with far-reaching implications and come in several varieties. Identifying and correcting these errors provides a more accurate view of the space enterprise and its consequences, while also providing a sounder basis for geopolitical theorizing about the political implications of space geography interacting with technology.

Accurate geography is universally valuable. Carrying out any activity significantly depends on accurate information about the places where it is conducted. All mobile organisms depend upon capacities to discern and remember spatial locational information, and superior abilities to do so provide important survival advantages. The ability of humans to make maps, exosomatic encodings of spatial information, has enabled locational information to be readily communicated, easily preserved, and cumulatively improved. The making and use of maps has been of special value to war-making, for knowing the features of the terrain and the location of mountains, rivers, straits, and shoals can spell the difference between success and disaster. As with writing, maps afford their possessors considerable power, and great efforts have been undertaken to make accurate maps and to sustain elite monopolies of them, often by treating them as secrets.[4]

Improved mappings of the Earth and sky have been intimately connected historically. Ptolemy provided the authoritative synthesis not just of ancient astronomy but also of ancient geography. The triumph of modern heliocentric astronomy and the emergence of modern geography organized around a globe-shaped Earth were intimately linked by the discoveries by explorers of new places, most notably the New World of the Americas, and the discovery by astronomers with telescopes of new orb-shaped worlds in the heavens.[5] Astronomical knowledge had extremely high practical value because it provided the navigational techniques making possible extended travel across the oceans, and voyages of geographic discovery often provided improved astronomical observations.[6] The new explorations of the Earth and the recent investigations of celestial bodies during the Space Age are thus different parts of one enterprise, and their advances are registered with improvements in the accuracy of the maps they produce.

As with every empirical inquiry, the making of maps and the production of geographic information about both the Earth and the cosmos are subject to several types of errors that distort spatial knowledge and the ends to which it is put.

Over the past several decades geographers have explored how maps and geographic investigations have been shaped and distorted by the normative goals and power projects of those who produce and use them. Under the rubric of "critical geography", geographers, in essays such as "Should the History of Geography Be X-Rated?," have demonstrated that many geographical investigations were motivated by predatory power objectives and geographic knowledge was often employed to assist imperialism and colonialism.[7] This corruption also entailed using maps for directly propagandistic purposes, an activity in which German fascist and imperial geographers excelled.[8] In the stronger versions of critical geography, all geographic knowledge is viewed as purely socially constructed and as essentially manifestations of the power projects of the actors. The valuable lesson of critical geography is that all representations of spatial phenomena should be skeptically interrogated for distortions and employments that serve parochial interests, particularly of the powerful.

The errors of interest here in expansionist thinking about space are of a different, indeed almost opposite character. Where critical geographers identify societal interests that distort the production and use of maps and geographic knowledge, this investigation focuses on a set of errors in geographic accuracy that distort practical realities in ways that hobble practical activities and assessments.[9] The most important geography error prevalent in space thinking is the conflation between *geophysical geography* and *practical geography*. The former is mappings of absolute spatial relations, particularly of distances, while the latter emerges from investigations of places and spaces as they relate to human activities enabled by technology. The most common example is the difference between *absolute distance* and *effective distance*, which depends on the speed of available transport technology interacting with absolute distance. Sometimes geomorphic symbols—the shape of geographic formations on maps—are misleadingly used as the basis for assessing practical geography.[10] Another simple error is *misplacement* or *displacement,* which occurs when an object is identified or classified on the basis of its function rather than its spatial locations. When simple geography errors of these kinds occur, places seem much larger than they actually are and objects disappear from where they are located.

Ascentionism and Disorientations

Another consequential geographic error commonly made by space expansionists—and indeed most thinking about space—is ascentionism. As we have seen, many space expansionists claim, or simply assume, that spatially ascending from the Earth will produce many improvements and that the conduct of human affairs, so frequently troubled on Earth, will get better in major ways as humans travel into the heavens. This pervasive linking of spatial elevation with moral and other forms of improvement undercuts the need to consider possibly undesirable downsides. It contributes to the presumption that space activities, almost alone among late modern high-technology ventures, are exceptional in being able to resolve or ameliorate rather than produce or exacerbate catastrophic and existential threats, thus making them exempt from serious critical scrutiny.

The vertical axiology of ascentionism appearing in space expansionist thought has intuitive appeal and credibility because it is woven extensively and deeply into human thought and language. Many familiar turns of phrase and expressions embodying ascentionism can be readily listed. The word "superior" is used to mean both higher and better. The wealthy are the "upper" class, while the poor are "lower" class. "Uplifting" experiences improve the spirit, while depressive mental states are "downs." "Elevated" conversation is better conversation. People with special talents and accomplishments are "stars." Positive outcomes are "upsides," while negative ones are "downsides." States growing in power are "rising," while weakening ones are "falling."

One possible explanation for the prevalence of this vertical axiology is its strong presence in many philosophies and religions. For Plato and Aristotle, the heavens were realms of unchanging spiritual perfection, while the Earth was the realm of change and corruption. It is strongly present in the Judeo-Christian georeligious constructs that are culturally pervasive in the places where space expansionism emerged and flourished: God in heaven is "above." The expulsion of Adam and Eve from the Garden of Eden is "the Fall." The savior and the souls of the saved "rise" into heaven, while the wicked "descend" into hell. While the cultural radiation of these vertical ethics may partly account for ascentionism, this explanation leads to a more basic question: Why is this vertical geo-axiology in religion, when it could have been completely reversed?

To grasp the primal basis for the intuitive appeal of ascentionism in cosmology and religion as well as space expansionism, it is useful to consider this tendency in the light of the basic insights of the body of philosophical thought known as phenomenology. Among the schools of modern philosophy, none excedes phenomenology in the impenetrable obtuseness of its main texts. This inaccessibility is, however, deeply ironic—even comic—because the basic insight of phenomenology is the simple idea that human perceptions of the world are always framed, influenced, and limited by the ways in which human sensory experience is embodied in corporeal living bodies that are always in particular places.[11] While obvious enough, this fact, according to phenomenologists, has been displaced in the quest by philosophers and scientists to understand the deeper and more abstract reality of things. Whether generated by deductive logic or empirical experimentation, the truths discovered by philosophy and science, whatever their actual validity, are often not experienced as valid by humans. In a passage speaking directly to our topic, the founder of phenomenology, Edmund Husserl, famously declared about the Copernican Revolution that "the Earth does not move."[12] By this he did not mean to challenge a central finding of modern astronomy but rather to say that humans do not experience the Earth moving, even if they know from the investigations of astronomers that it is hurtling and spinning through space at fantastic speeds. Even though we *know* from astronomy that the Earth is revolving around the sun, we still *experience* the sun moving across the sky of what feels like an unmoving Earth.

Thinking about ascentionism phenomenologically, the tendency to conflate spatial elevation with greater value and virtue becomes readily understandable. Because the human sensory apparatus is located on the top of the human organism, and the light of the sun, which illuminates the day, provides warmth, and stimulates growth, is located in the sky above, humans are naturally inclined to view spatial elevation as better.[13] As Buckminster Fuller puts it, with his typical extremity, "the vertical characterizes life and the horizontal characterizes death."[14]And much of human activity is spent overcoming the downward pull of gravity. In short, the basic geography of the human lifeworlds in places on the Earth, combined with biological features of human bodies that have evolved in these places, make spatial elevation seem intuitively linked to improvement. Thus the tendency to overvalue—and misperceive—the heavens is primordially rooted in the human corporeal body shaped by its earthly emergence. While the origins of this tendency and its strong and enduring intuitive appeal may be clear, it is equally clear that there is no basis whatsoever for thinking that human ascents into the heavens are going to produce or be accompanied by any improvement in the character and behavior of humans or their institutions.

A similar disjuncture between the experienced and the known is at the root of the disorientation afflicting Thales and the inhabitants of contemporary machine civilization. As Bacon observed in his classic analysis of the types of misperceptions afflicting humans, "people falsely claim that human sense is the measure of things, whereas in fact all perceptions of sense and mind are built to the scale of man and not the universe."[15] What is significantly vast, far, and alien relative to the scale of human bodies—such as outer space—is subject to perceptual Thalesian disorientations. As powerful observing instruments and enormously fast machines have conquered space, human capabilities to relate these newly revealed and created realities to lived experience lag painfully—and dangerously—behind. Perception of such objects and places are always abstract and largely dependent on the interpretative frames brought to them, particularly analogies making the unfamiliar seem familiar. Acting on the basis of such misleading constructs is sure to end poorly.

Geographic and Geohistorical Analogies

In making their case for the feasibility and desirability of space expansion, advocates deploy a wide array of analogies. In addition to "the big three" analogies of frontier, ocean, and islands ("space is a frontier to an ocean, in which there are islands") space expansionists analogize various technologies (the railroad and the spaceship[16]), various historical experiences (out of Africa and out of Earth), and diverse activities (mountaineering and space exploration). Geographic and geohistorical analogies are so prominent in space expansionism that they must be considered part of any general assessment. Analogies are pervasive in human thinking and often help stimulate important scientific insights.[17] Space expansionists deploy analogies between Earth and space geography and geohistory, the features of the Earth's geography and features of space, and Earth historical events with anticipated events in space. Analogs are pervasive and attractive because they help make what is unfamiliar and unexperienced into something that is familiar by association with something that has been experienced. As the frontier historian Patricia Limerick notes, an analogy "makes some alternatives seem logical and necessary, while making other alternatives nearly invisible."[18] Because space is so unfamiliar and so largely unexperienced by humans, analogies between the familiar on Earth and the unfamiliar in space help make otherworldly realms more comprehensible.

The use of analogies by space advocates and in thinking about space has been extensively analyzed. The historian Howard McCurdy shows how advocates such as von Braun skillfully tapped into popular American historical mythologies about the attractions of frontier expansion to gain support for their visions.[19] The political scientist M. J. Peterson shows how diplomats negotiating the Outer Space Treaty frequently discussed the ways in which the provisions of the Antarctica Treaty were suitable for space application.[20] And the historian of science Steven J. Dick shows how astrobiologists develop ideas about life in space with analogies to aspects of life on Earth.[21] However, these studies are not typically critical, but instead offer insight into how various analogies were deployed for persuasive purposes by advocates, how analogies influenced decision-making about space, and the positive ways in which analogies can illuminate the paths and benefits of space expansion. They focus extensively on frontier analogies, largely ignoring ocean and island analogs.

How can analogies be critically assessed? Analogies are not identities, and so dissimilar features are inevitably mixed with similar ones. Because analogies do not purport to be identities, it is difficult to say they are false, as one can say, for example, that the claim "There are oceans (of water) on Luna" is false. (Astronomers once thought this was the case, but observational evidence led them to abandon such views.) But analogies can be judged to be *misleading* when they emphasize similarities of lesser importance over important dissimilarities they obscure.[22] Misleading analogies that are employed in framing and guiding decisions can lead to disaster, as historical studies of analogies in political decision-making amply demonstrate.[23] When actions are undertaken under the influence of misleading analogies, unrealistic expectations are produced and dangers are underappreciated.

Being essentially parts of an advocacy brief, space expansionist analogies are designed to mislead. Their analogies mislead by making space seem familiar, space activities feasible, and space expansion desirable. Such analogies can be shown to be misdirecting by showing that they emphasize "like" aspects that are favorable to the space project over aspects that are "unlike" and unfavorable. Analogies from geohistory are misleading when they privilege successful and normatively appealing past events over failures and morally problematic ones. Space analogies can be judged misleading when they favor upside over downside consequences. And analogies that seem obviously appropriate, such as "Space is a realm of oceanic vastness," can mislead when applied to more specific parts of near space where they are inappropriate. The contribution of analogy evaluation to accurately understand space prospects is further increased by identifying other, less misleading and less appealing analogies that can alert thinking to the very steep potential downsides of large-scale space ventures.

What Is Geopolitics?

The term "geopolitics," like so many political and international keywords, comes with a bewilderingly large number of different meanings. Most commonly, "geopolitics" is now widely used as a vernacular term for international politics generally, particularly when great powers are involved in rivalry and conflict. In this common way of speaking of geopolitics, no particular importance is assigned to geography or material factors, and there can be said to be a geopolitics of virtually any international issue. A second meaning of geopolitics is associated with realist international relations theories and arguments about the roles that material factors, particularly geography, play in the power relations among rival states.

But this common use of the term can easily lead to a slanted and truncated appreciation of politics and material realities because it falsely assumes that analysis of the relationship between material factors and political arrangements and outcomes is confined solely to the international domain and solely to the political arrangements assumed or favored by realist international relations theory. It also tends to downplay the importance of various types of interdependence. In fact there is a long history of theorizing about the relationship between material realities and domestic politics, about the material in relation to nonstatist republican political forms and about interdependence. A more complete approach, of most value in analyzing the claims of the space expansionists, is best referred to, in simple terms, as full geopolitical theory. Full geopolitics refers to arguments about how differing material contexts composed of geographies and technologies shape and determine the viability and occurrence of different political arrangements, particularly those concerned with violence and political freedom. Only an approach of this character and scope can assess the claims about politics and world orders permeating space expansionist thought.

Before unpacking the assumptions and propositions of full geopolitical theory, it should be noted that this approach, while currently uncommon, has an extremely long history at the center of Western political science. Although the term "geopolitics" was coined only at the turn of the twentieth century, full geopolitical arguments are extremely old, tracing back to the beginnings of Western political thought. Arguments about the shaping effects of myriad geographical factors (particularly climate, topography, distance and proximity, and land-sea interactions) appear prominently in two of the three thinkers commonly regarded as the founders of political science, Aristotle and Montesquieu.[24] And claims about material factors sit at the heart of the arguments of influential theorists such as Hobbes, Rousseau, and Kant about the scope and features of the state of nature and the social contract that are held to be at the foundation of all governments. In many ways, political science, including the topics that are now thought of as international relations, began as a *naturalist* political science.

This broadly integrated way of thinking about the influences of nature on politics, or what can be called "natural-social science," fell into wide disfavor in the nineteenth century in favor of "social-social science," which explores the social causes of social events. In part, naturalist social science declined because of its apparently limited ability to explain historical change, changes across time in the same place, as well as the growing realization that technology was of increasing importance in shaping politics. In response to this problem, a variety of historical materialist theories continued and advanced the basic project of full geopolitics by incorporating technology, along with geography, as the material "base" that decisively conditions the viability and occurrence of different social, economic, and political formations.[25] Perhaps most notably, the large body of global geopolitical theory produced in the years around the beginning of the twentieth century attempted to understand how the new technologies produced by the Industrial Revolution, such as the railroad, steamship, and telegraph, interacting with the large-scale features of the Earth would shape the number and character of the units in the system, as well as whether the new material context was configured to make likely a world empire or the preservation of the plural state system.[26]

Despite the continuing and growing importance of technology and nature in world politics, efforts to theorize the material and its influences remain scattered. Although grappling with the Anthropocene is spurring a revival of materialist theorizing, the attention of theorists of world politics remains largely focused on social structures, ideas, and processes. Despite this emphasis, thinking about the influence of material realities on world politics has not so much disappeared as become fragmented, and virtually every approach to theorizing politics ascribes considerable importance to material factors, even if in a truncated, ad hoc, or implicit manner.[27] The result is that the landscape of contemporary theory does not have one materialist theory of the influence of geography and technology but rather a large number of theories that do this in a partial way. To employ this great wealth of insight in ways useful for assessing space expansionist arguments, it is therefore necessary to synthesize propositions, and before doing this, to state the underlying assumptions of such a full geopolitics or geopolitically inflected systems theory about determinism, the interaction of agents, and interests and structures, as well as to articulate a simple framework within which specific propositions can be formulated.

Assumptions, Determinations, and Frameworks

The objection commonly leveled against every theory asserting that political effects stem from material realities is determinism, the notion that variations in geography and technology can explain pretty much everything. Many versions of early natural-social science advanced what seem to be very strongly deterministic accounts of this relationship, and technological determinism is often seen as an error afflicting any theory that advances claims about the effects of technology upon human social and political arrangements. This problem would also appear to be particularly acute for the historical materialist response to the rise of social-social science, as it is one thing to say that geography stands outside the human world as an influence but quite another to say or imply this about technology, since technology is in very important ways itself the product of social and political choices.[28] Rejection of geography and technology as determining influences on the human world has been particularly vigorous in constructivist and postmodern theories, which have enjoyed great popularity over recent decades.

One way to resolve this problem is to distinguish between science, technology, and technics, each of which is very different, and quite mixed in the ways social construction and material determination occur (see Table 8.1).[29] Scientific research is clearly a social activity, and which research and explorations are undertaken is a matter of social choice.[30] But what is discovered by such investigations is most definitely not socially constructed or chosen, although it is perennially subject to differing interpretations strongly shaped by social and cultural factors. Thus the decision by the Spanish crown to fund the voyages of Columbus can be explained only by examining social and political influences. But what was "discovered," a "new world" of continents previously unknown to European geographers, rather than islands off the coast of Asia, was most definitely not socially constructed, even though Columbus himself never recognized the actual scope of what he had "found."

Technology in the strict sense of the term is engineering know-how, knowledge about the consequences of manipulating different natural materials to produce desired outcomes; technology in this sense is also a mix of the socially constructed and naturally determined. Which engineering research projects are pursued is straightforwardly within the domain of human social choice. But any feasible technology is ultimately dependent on natural phenomena that are most definitely not socially constructed.[31] If technological possibility were solely a function of social choice and construction, the menu of technologies available to humanity would be radically larger than it is. No matter how much effort is spent researching faster-than-light or time travel, the success of such investigations is ultimately determined by the features of nature that humans can potentially discover and cleverly manipulate but not create or eliminate.

Finally, there are technics, which are tangible apparatuses, devices, and artifacts that are produced by combining labor, engineering know-how, and natural resources. Technics are dependent on technology, but they are quite

Table 8.1 **Social Construction and Its Limits**

	Socially Constructed	*Not Socially Constructed*
Science	Extent and goals of scientific research	What is discovered
Technology	Extent and goals of engineering research	Natural phenomenon that engineering manipulates
Technics	Whether are built or operated	Full scope of consequences of their operation

different in character. Which technics are possible to construct is shaped by whether there are natural principles that can be exploited and manipulated, but within these often broad limitations the decision to construct technics is essentially social in character.[32] And simply because it is possible to construct something does not mean that it is socially necessary that it be constructed, although this is the strawman view that some take to be technological determinism. But the socially determined aspects of technics have very important limitations: once a technic has been fabricated, it is part of the material world shared by many actors, and the uses to which it can be put and the consequences of its operation are not confined to the intentions and purposes of those who construct it. For example, the Romans built an elaborate and expensive system of roads to serve their imperial purposes, but this infrastructure was also employed by Germanic tribes to rapidly invade the empire and sack Rome, a possibility inherent in the roads themselves, whatever the intent of their builders. Unlike scientific and engineering knowledge, which is difficult to eliminate, technics can be dismantled or destroyed through the same sorts of social choices that led to their construction.

Geopolitical theory assumes that human agency is practical and interested. But it occurs in circumstances, both material-contextual and social-structural, which are both enabling and restraining in roughly patterned and predictable ways. While social and political arrangements are socially constructed and can over time be changed, at any given time they powerfully shape and channel patterns of activity in ways as fully determinative of outcomes as material contexts. The goals or aims that animate human agency are diverse, but some, most notably security from violence and perhaps also freedom, are assumed to be primary interests, rooted in human nature and the corporeal vulnerability of human bodies. They claim primary status because the pursuit of other goals and interests is compromised without their at least minimal realization.

Many versions of both material-contextual and social-structural theorizing are often associated with rationalism, the idea that actors actually usually pursue their interests. But for geopolitics, actor rationality is viewed as an aspiration often difficult to achieve rather than as an assumption. In reality, the pursuit of fundamental security interests rooted in human nature is often confounded by the pursuit of secondary interests generated by social contexts and socially generated identities. And misperceptions and misinformation of many types can also lead activity away from paths consistent with fundamental interests. Especially in material contexts being rapidly revolutionized by technological change, the persistence of inherited established practices and identities, and the social structures they produce and depend upon, pose major obstacles to the realization of fundamental interests. Given these often powerful obstructions, geopolitics supports the project of practical political science by identifying which activities, practices, and social arrangements are actually consistent with fundamental interests in particular material contexts and which are not.

Given this way of thinking about practical human activity in constraining and enabling contexts, geopolitical theory seeks to answer two types of questions. First, which political arrangements are *necessary* to realize fundamental interests in which material contexts? Here geopolitical theory offers functionality arguments, specifying which political practices and orders serve basic interests in different material contexts. For example, in a particular material context, is peace or government irrelevant or necessary to realize security objectives? In illuminating what is necessary, geopolitics can provide actors critically valuable insight about what must be done to realize fundamental interests.

Second, geopolitical theory offers insight into how *possible* it is to achieve outcomes consistent with the realization of fundamental interests. Both material contexts and social structures can hinder and assist the realization of favorable outcomes, and the degree to which they do so provides insight into the likelihood that such outcomes will occur. Some contexts are so favorable to the realization of human ends that little or no actions are needed; others make the realization of desired human arrangements difficult or nearly impossible. Such assessments of context can provide vital insight into just how much of an uphill battle is required to achieve a desired outcome. Prudent choice avoids embarking on enterprises that will turn out poorly unless very difficult things are done. The roads to perdition are often paved with baselessly optimistic assumptions about capacities to accomplish and sustain strenuous or heroic arrangements.

Taken in combination, the degrees of necessity and possibility map a matrix of situations ranging from the tragic vital but nearly impossible to the trivial and easy, with the domain of practical politics in between. Thus if it is judged that space expansion will turn out disastrously if war and unfreedom prevail off-world, and if a reading of the lay of the land with the lenses of geopolitical theory indicates that putting in place institutional arrangements to prevent war and strong hierarchy is likely to be a strenuous to nearly impossible undertaking, then prudence dictates against expansion.

To move from these general assumptions toward actual propositions, a simple framework for posing the more specific claims and insights is useful (see Figure 8.1). Will the outcome tend toward security and freedom, or will it be insecurity and oppression? Answering this question requires an examination of material contexts and political orders. The shaping influence of the material context has both compositional and distributional aspects. Composition refers to the qualitatively different ends to which particular

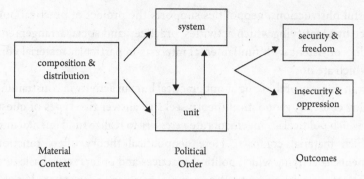

Figure 8.1 Material Contexts, Political Orders, and Outcomes

material assets and contexts can be put. For example, a hammer can be readily used to pound nails but not cut wood. Distributional analysis refers to how much of some asset is present in the hands of different actors. International political orders are commonly composed of units, of distinct polities, which in combination compose the system. With this framework it is now possible to turn to specific factors and propositions, five clusters of which are set forth in the next five sections.

Violence Interdependence, Anarchy, and Government

The first core cluster of propositions of geopolitics concerns the political effects of interdependence and interaction, particularly regarding violence capacities. Violence interdependence is the capacity of actors to inflict damage on each other, largely independently of the distribution of violence capabilities among them. The essential logic of this compositional factor can be grasped by considering the situation of people in a room. If the violence capability of individuals is initially only pencils and pens but then some obtain knives, the level of violence interdependence increases, even if some have more knives than others. If guns are introduced, the level of violence interdependence increases further, regardless of whether some have more guns than others. Violence interdependence varies along a simple spectrum from *absent*, through *weak* and *strong*, to *intense*. When violence interdependence is absent, actors in a particular space have no ability to harm one another. In situations where the level of violence interdependence is weak or strong, actors have the capacity to harm one another but not readily fatally. When the level of violence interdependence in a space is intense, actors can readily damage one another fatally.[33]

The level of violence interdependence in a particular space is a function primarily of the volume of velocity that can be brought to bear on inhabited territory, and secondarily on the speed with which this can be done. When the ratio of violence volume to territory becomes annihilative or *saturated*, the crucial ingredient of intense violence interdependence is present. But distance also matters, and calculations of distance and effective distance, sometimes referred to as a "loss-of-strength gradient," determine what is close and what is far. Calculations of effective distance, a ratio of speed of passage over terrain traversed, are elemental to geopolitical theory and important for determining the level of violence interdependence present. Thus, as transportation technology progresses, the effective distance between locations declines, even as their absolute distance remains unchanged. In sum, the interplay of violence volumes shaped by destruction technologies interacting with the size of inhabited territory, and the interplay of violence velocity shaped by transportation technologies interacting with geographic distance is what constitutes violence interdependence, the most important factor in full geopolitical theory.

The level of violence interdependence in a particular space is decisively important in determining whether anarchy (understood by international theorists as simply the absence of authoritative government, not as dangerous chaos) is tolerable for security, or whether government is necessary for security (see Table 8.2). In situations where violence interdependence is absent, government is both unnecessary and typically impossible. At the other end of the spectrum, when intense levels of violence interdependence are present in a space, anarchy is intolerable for security and government is necessary. In the middle range of the spectrum, where violence interdependence is weak or strong, government is possible but not necessary, and anarchy is compatible with security. In the middle range of the spectrum, anarchy may at times make life nasty and brutish but almost never short. But with intense violence interdependence, life in anarchy is potentially lethal, and an exit from anarchy is necessary for security. It

Table 8.2 **Violence Interdependence, Anarchy, and Government**

Absent	*Weak*	*Strong*	*Intense*
Actors cannot harm each other	Actors cannot seriously harm each other	Actors can seriously harm each other	Actors can readily destroy each other
Government impossible and unnecessary	Government unnecessary but potentially beneficial	Government unnecessary but potentially beneficial	Life in anarchy too insecure and government necessary

is in the middle range of the spectrum where ordinary international relations occurs and where various modest institutions such as alliances and public international law have been employed to moderate, but not fundamentally abridge, the anarchic features of international order. Another way to simply formulate the essential points here is to distinguish between a *first anarchy*, a situation without government that is marked by intense levels of violence interdependence, and a *second anarchy*, a situation lacking government in which violence interdependence is strong or weak. Despite the central importance of violence interdependence in geopolitical theory, many contemporary realists, including theorists of military space expansion, neglect this factor, which makes their arguments slanted and truncated.

The most important fact about violence interdependence across time is that the size of the space within which intense violence interdependence is present has been relentlessly increasing due to technological advances in communication, transportation, and destruction. Initially, intense violence interdependence was present only in the very small spaces of a tribe or a city-state, and a situation of anarchy within such a space was viewed as the most intolerable of security situations. With the coming of gunpowder weapons, the size of spaces with intense violence interdependence expanded to that of a nation-state, and then with the Industrial Revolution it leaped up again, to the size of a continent. Thus, with the coming of industrial capabilities, Europe went from being a second anarchy in which the major actors could damage but not readily kill one another, to a first anarchy in which war was total in its levels of violence. As this change occurred, the anarchic organization of European politics, moderated at the margins by various weak international institutions, was no longer compatible with security, and various forms of union, long viewed as unnecessary and utopian, were widely recognized as necessary to move the region out of perilous first anarchy.

With the development of nuclear weapons and ballistic missiles, the spatial scope of intense violence interdependence has grown to planetary scope, making worldwide interstate anarchy intolerable for security and making a government or binding restraints necessary. As we saw, this line of thinking led many in the early nuclear era to embrace the nuclear-one-worldist view that security on a planet with nuclear weapons required some minimum world government. The space within which weak and strong violence interdependence has been present has also expanded across time due to technological advances. For much of history since the agricultural revolution, quasi-continent-size regions, like Europe, South Asia, and East Asia, were second anarchies. In the early modern period, with the expansion of interaction across the oceans, second anarchy became global in scope, initially with weak violence interdependence and then, with the coming of steam and electricity in the Industrial Revolution, with strong violence interdependence. But after the nuclear revolution created first anarchy with its intense violence interdependence on a planetary scale, second anarchy has completely disappeared from Earth and might be recovered only through expansion into space.

The level of violence interdependence in a particular space depends on the technologies of communication, transportation, and destruction interacting with geography. In the example of the room with shifting levels of violence interdependence, changes in destructive capacities alone decisively shifted the levels present because all the actors were assumed to be in a small space where neither communication nor transportation was limited. But across most of human history, the shape, or topography, of land and sea played a major role in determining the levels of violence interdependence in particular spaces simply because technological capacities of transport and communication were so limited. Arguments about violence interdependence thus took the form of claims about the influence of topography. Topographies with broken terrain that impeded movement were thought to support the rise of plural political orders, while flat and open topographies, such as plains and large bodies of water, were prone to political consolidation.

According to this line of thinking, open topographies are spaces in which offensive military force has decisive advantages over defensive forces, while broken topographies provide natural defensive advantages. In more general terms, the insight here is that configurations of topography interacting with technologies shape the extent to which a space has *integral tendencies*. As technologies have improved and the spatial scope of interactions has expanded, new spaces with distinct integral tendencies have emerged. Within classical global geopolitics, Alfred Thayer Mahan argues that the flatness of oceanic space means it has highly integral tendencies, thus offering a partial explanation for the naval supremacy underlying the vast British Empire. Similarly, Mackinder argues that the flat interior regions of the Eurasian steppe have integral tendencies, which enabled the erection of the largest land empire by the Mongols.

A final important geographic variation related to interaction and interdependence is the difference between territory and extraterritorial media. People and polities are almost always land-based, and they are secure when the territorial space they occupy is protected from the application of violence. But beyond inhabited terra firma the planet also contains great extraterritorial realms of water, air, and orbital space, often called the "global commons." Human access to these realms is completely dependent on technology, and human activities in them are closely paced with what is technologically possible. An extraterritorial medium is in between landed spaces and can be either a barrier or a passageway. Before technology made activities possible in these spaces, they were formidable barriers to interaction, but with technological advances in ships, airplanes, and rockets, they become passageways to transit from one inhabited place to another. Although technological advances have made it possible to traverse these spaces, they remain uninhabited. Systems can vary greatly depending on whether they are entirely or largely territorial, a mix of territorial and extraterritorial media, or largely extraterritorial. Almost all historical international systems have been either the first or the second configuration; the only example of the third is the international system that came into existence in the wake of the Polynesians' colonization of the tiny scattered islands in Pacific.

System Scope, Closure, and Frontiers

Situations with intense violence interdependence are ruinous for security without government, but situations at the other end of the spectrum, when it is absent, are also quite consequential, because they determine the *scope* of the system. In our example of the room, interaction outside the room was assumed to be absent, and so the space and actors in the room are the system. But there may be other rooms containing other systems and actors. When a world order is marked by absent levels of interaction capacity and interdependence, separate systems coexist without interaction and some-times even knowledge of each other's existence, as when the Romans and Mayans both flourished unknown to one another. But the scope of systems changes when doors or passageways between them are opened. When systems are connected, the consequences can be extremely disruptive. As a door is opened between rooms, the scope of the system changes to encompass the space and the actors of both rooms. The opening of a passage between systems causes the interaction capacity in the spaces between the systems to go from absent to low, and as this happens one system emerges and the patterns of power and authority in both can be radically altered, particularly if the actors from one system have significantly more capacities than those in another.

When a door between rooms opens, there is a new frontier. Systems can either be spatially closed or open, and open systems are open because they have frontiers. A system is closed when all the space accessible to actors in it has been subject to exploration and colonization and brought under the rule of some government. Systems become closed when they are hemmed in by geophysical barriers that do not permit significant passage. In contrast, a system with a frontier abuts spaces that have not been explored, settled, or brought under rule but that are accessible to passage. Systems with frontiers become closed when expansion has filled the available accessible space, and closed systems become open when new frontiers are opened, typically by new technologies enabling passage through or over previously insurmountable barriers. Frontiers also vary in whether they are *nascent*, when high costs and inaccessibility severely limit the extent of human activities, or *full*, when access has become cheap and many activities are possible.

Opportunities for expansion into newly opened frontiers are typically uneven and benefit actors who are proximate to the new frontier and have developed the technologies to overcome barriers. Initially, as expansion occurs across frontiers, the core region of the system acquires an enlarged periphery. If the newly accessible spaces are large enough and suitable enough for development, the actors who exploit them gain relative advantage over actors who are either ill-positioned or ill-equipped to take advantage of the new possibilities opened at the frontier. But this advantage will often be short-lived, as colonies that grow large tend to become independent, particularly if they are located at a distance from the core and if they are located in places that are very different from the core. If the spaces accessible across the frontier are larger than the entire original core of the system, units in the periphery can form a new enlarged core and turn the old core into its periphery.

Frontiers are also places particularly prone to conflict and violence, often extreme. As the historian Frederick Jackson Turner observed, "at the frontier, the bonds of custom are broken, and unrestraint is triumphant."[34] Frontier spaces are often described as "power vacuums," which core powers tend to seek to fill as best and as fast as they can. The absence of established territorial borders and property claims is also a potential source of conflict. While the spaces and resources of frontiers often appear, from the perspective of the core, to be unlimited, there are always places that are particularly desirable and terrains with more abundant resources. The initially low densities of actors, low interaction capabilities, and absence of restraining institutions combine with locally great asymmetries of power to produce extremely violent conflicts. Frontier areas are also marked by a scarcity of labor relative to resources, which, combined with weak governmental authorities, make domination particularly attractive.

Distribution, Special Places, and Distinctiveness

The densities of interactions and the levels of violence interdependence are of primary importance in shaping the need for government and the scope of political systems, but they are followed closely in importance by how much power different actors have relative to each other. In our example of the room, whether one has knives while others have only pencils, and how many knives one has relative to other possessors of knives, have very significant impacts on the relative security of the actors and the types of government that might arise among them. The second cluster of propositions of full geopolitics concerns the sources and effects of the *distribution*, or balance, of power assets, on politics. The idea that the relative distribution of power capabilities significantly shapes political outcomes and arrangements is held in varying degrees by virtually all schools of thought about politics, despite their many other differences. Full geopolitical theory places its main emphasis on the distribution of material power assets, particularly capacities of violence. The basic proposition of geopolitics on the distribution of power is that situations in which power is heavily concentrated in the hands of one actor or group will tend to be hierarchical in character, and that situations in which power assets are widely distributed among multiple actors will tend toward political outcomes that are less hierarchical and more pluralistic. The basic notion is that when power is concentrated, this power will be used to establish political arrangements that subordinate the less powerful to the more powerful.

Just as topography plays an important role in shaping levels of interdependence, power distribution also has significant spatial and geographic aspects. In a mundane but often important manner, the geographic distribution of resources heavily shapes the relative power among actors. Power distribution geography also analyzes elevation or ascent and special places or master assets with potential influences beyond their size. That which is above is not only thought to be better; it is also often more powerful, as those positioned above, on the high ground, can both see and project power further and more effectively. Prior to the development of airplanes and then satellites, achievable elevation and ascent was relatively small, but on a micro scale considerable local advantages could be achieved by placing fortifications in elevated locations and with walls, which afforded not only defensive protection but also a relatively elevated fighting position.

Special places and assets also can have important distributional implications that are disproportionate to their absolute size. Straits between bodies of water and passes through mountains, often referred to as "choke points" by geopolitical writers, are often very small in size but afford those who possess them the power to influence who passes and who is excluded. In general terms, places that have the potential to significantly shape the overall system in which they are located can thus be thought of as *axial regions*. In a system with an axial region, the power positions of all the actors will tend to revolve around the control of this space, and access to it, unless it can be neutralized. As with topography and integral tendencies, shifting technologies and expansions into new terrains alters which spaces are axial in their potential influence.

A long line of geopolitical and strategic thinkers, extending, as we have seen, into the arguments of the astro-Archimedeans, has analyzed different places as axial regions. Following a syllogistic format first employed by Mackinder, they postulate that whoever controls X space (the ocean, the heartland, the atmosphere, or orbital space) controls the world. Actors having better access to the axial region have advantages in controlling it. If such a region exists and can be effectively controlled by one actor, then the system will tend toward hegemony or empire. Conversely, if the actors in a system are able to neutralize the axial region by effectively taking it out of the reach of any one actor to control, then the system shifts from anarchy to one ordered by mutual restraint. In effect this strategy postulates that if no one controls the axial space, then no one can control the world. Axial regions that also have integral tendencies present these choices in a particularly acute manner, as the integral tendencies facilitate one actor dominating the axial region, and thus the system. But axial regions, with or without integral tendencies, that are extraterritorial are more readily subject to neutralization than axial territories.

Master assets with system-wide influence potentials can also be technological and infrastructural. Throughout history, but particularly since the emergence and acceleration of modern machine civilization, revolutionary technological advances in capabilities of destruction have been avidly sought in the hopes of gaining a decisive distributional power advantage. "First possessor" advantages can often be great, but they rarely last very long, particularly in recent times, as states have made great efforts to stay abreast of scientific and technical advances with security implications, to spy on each other, and to quickly copy each other. Technological master assets are thus highly prone to diffuse to other actors in the system, unlike geographical axial regions, which are spatially fixed. Another possibility is that a built infrastructure could be a master asset with system-wide influence potentials. Fortifications and walls and systems of roads, railroads, telegraphs, and submarine cables have been among the prominent historically significant military infrastructures, but they, while often very important in the systems in which they have been deployed, probably fall short of being master assets. But on a political microscale a castle in a town is a master asset.[35]

Another variation in the material context of human action with significant political influence is civil-military *distinctiveness*, a measure of how different a particular militarily important violence capability is from routine activities prevalent in particular societies. Distinctiveness has varied greatly across time and space in terrestrial history and is likely to vary greatly in outer space. At one extreme, the military prowess of the Mongols, based on their superb riding and archery, was virtually indistinguishable from their main economic activities of hunting and herding, and so distinctiveness was low. At the other extreme, the technologies and materials of nuclear and space power, although not completely lacking civilian application, are highly distinctive from the mundane world of even advanced industrial societies. In between, the heavy industrial capacities for civilian and military activities, for example a truck and tank factory, are of medium distinctiveness because they are convertible to one another but not without considerable time and effort. Thus, because the United States had an extensive automotive industry in the 1940s, its lead time for building tank armies was far less than it would have been had it not, but a major effort was still needed to redirect this civilian productive capacity for military purposes.

The degree of civil-military distinctiveness has profound implications for the extent and speed with which societies can be mobilized for war, and for the character and feasibility of efforts to regulate and relinquish violence capabilities. When distinctiveness is low, societies can be prepared for war very rapidly, and restraining such capabilities is extremely difficult, as it requires wholesale changes in the routine aspects of civil life. Conversely, when distinctiveness is high, it takes considerable effort and lead time to prepare for war, but it is relatively easy to regulate or relinquish a violence capability. When the civil-military distinctiveness between different societies varies greatly, their relative power also varies considerably, with polities marked by low distinctiveness gaining a decided advantage over those with a high distinction between civil and military capacities.

Governments and International Systems

Governments exist when anarchy has been replaced with authoritative arrangements regulating the possession and use of force. Governments that are hierarchical in their patterns of authority and capability, based on concentrations of power, are not, however, the only type of government. Just as anarchies vary depending on the level of violence interdependence, so too governments vary significantly with different distributions of power and configurations of authority, as well as different levels of violence interdependence. Governments that are authoritative, in the sense that they regulate the occurrence of violence and have regularized systems of rules and laws, can be either hierarchical or republican in character. Republican governments are those in which the people as a whole hold ultimate power. In republican governments, violence capacities and authorities are configured through mutual restraints and various forms of checks and balances, not in top-down patterns. Until very recently such nonhierarchical republican governments have been relatively rare. In recent times republican governments have come to be referred to as liberal democratic constitutional governments.

Theorists of republican government hold that unlimited hierarchical governments are as much a threat to the security of the people under their sway as first anarchy is, thus making the overall achievement of security dependent on avoiding the full forms of both anarchy and hierarchy. Unlimited hierarchies take varied forms, both inside and among polities. When power is highly concentrated and unlimited within a polity, tyranny, despotism, and totalitarian rule occur; between polities such power asymmetries produce empires. Thus, in the simplest of terms, there are two extremely undesirable possible security outcomes: *crash*, associated with ungoverned situations of intense violence interdependence, and *crush*, associated with highly asymmetrical hierarchies. Space expansion, as we shall see, poses great risks of both these outcomes.

These multiple types of political order can be usefully combined into a simple typology, presented in a triangular configuration (see Figure 8.2).[36] The three pure types, located at the three apexes, are anarchic, hierarchic, and what I have elsewhere referred to as "negarchic," to capture the basic form of republican states and confederal and federal unions of such states. The pure types sit at the ends of three spectrums of mixed types. This typology encompasses both domestic and international political arrangements. Anarchy can exist either within a unit, as a state of nature and civil war, or between units, in the form of a state system; hierarchy can exist as a despotism within one polity or an empire encompassing multiple subordinated polities; and negarchic republican forms can be either internal republican governments or external unions of such polities. While authority and capacity are concentrated in hierarchies, they are distributed in both

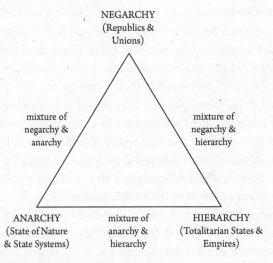

Figure 8.2 Typology of Political Orders

anarchical and negarchical forms but in quite different ways. In an anarchy there are no or minimal restraints on the employment of the distributed power, while the distributed powers in republican forms are muffled and channeled by institutional restraints. Another key reason the system theorizing of so many realists and von Braunians is truncated and slanted is because they operate with dyadic rather than triadic concepts of political order.

Thinking about this full set of possible political orders and their relationship to violence and security points to the fact that each is fundamentally constituted as a different system of arms control. Although the term "arms control" is commonly used to refer to mutually agreed reductions of armaments by independent states, in actuality hierarchical states, as well as republics, are orders in which the control of arms are centrally important but differently configured. Arms in hierarchical systems, whether states or empires, are the monopoly, or near monopoly, of the center. In contrast, the control of arms in republics is in the hands of multiple actors and then restrained and channeled. And arms control, like government, is absent in anarchies, and so violence capacities are neither centralized nor constrained by mutual institutions.

Patterns of political authority also vary on the basis of how extensively the actual authority reaches the social atom of the individual. *Penetration* can vary along a spectrum, from light to full. When penetration is light, the authority of government on the ground is not very extensive, and a great deal of de facto freedom exists. When penetration tends toward full, all aspects of life come under its sway. The degree of penetration that governments can realize is largely a function of the capabilities of communication, transportation, and surveillance at their command, as well as their organizational competence in deploying such assets. Until very recently, achieving anything approaching full penetration on any significant scale has been effectively impossible. This fact had a profound implication for the actual degree to which hierarchical government was oppressive and a threat to the security of its subjects. While hierarchical states and empires with unlimited authority concentrated in the hands of one actor have been extremely common, until very recently their actual capacities to do things at distance and to apply unlimited power to the nanosocial level of the individual have been quite constrained due to limitations in interaction capacities.[37] But with the coming of the industrial machine and its mobilization for hierarchical rule, much more fully penetrated hierarchical rule has emerged as a practical possibility, making possible the novel form of a large and comprehensive hierarchy, the ultimate state of unfreedom, the totalitarian state.

The difference between hierarchical top-down and republican bottom-up types of government captured in the triangular typology of political orders is of prime importance, but it is not the only way in which polities differ from one another. Political orders vary in myriad other ways that have consequences for the kinds of interactions they have. States have differing identities influenced by location, language, religion, ideology, economic systems, and the historical memories and ideas their peoples and leaders hold. Geography also helps account for why polities differ in so many ways. Polities that are located in places with similar ecological, topographical, and climatic attributes will tend to be similar, and vice versa.

Attempts by political scientists and historians to identify patterns of behavior linked to these myriad differences have not yielded much beyond the perhaps obvious proposition that states tend to be more suspicious and more conflictual and less cooperative when their unit-level attributes are significantly different, and vice versa. As differences between states become larger, they more readily see one another as threats and are more willing to employ greater extremes of violence in conflicts. When states differ from one another greatly, the prospects for avoiding war in second anarchy are lower, as are their prospects for avoiding total war and successfully exiting a first anarchy to create a common government or strong mutually restraining regimes.

International Systems, Modes of Protection, and World Governments

Much of the value of the triangular typology comes from its ability to encompass a diversity of mixed political orders. In moving along the axis from anarchy to hierarchy, government emerges based on concentrations of power, and in the middle range of this spectrum are hegemonic state systems, a hierarchy-anarchy combination in which many states are still independent but are ruled indirectly and lightly by a hegemon that has a concentration, but not a monopoly, of power in the system. As movement from anarchy to hierarchy takes place, patterns of authority based on asymmetrical binding occur, effectively transforming material power asymmetries into laws and rules that privilege the rulers over the ruled. Moving along the axis from anarchy to negarchy, government emerges but in very different ways and with very different results. Moving from the anarchy end of the spectrum, anarchy is moderated, but not replaced, by various interstate alliances, public international law, and regimes. Movement out of anarchy occurs as increasingly authoritative forms of mutual restraint emerge through cobinding. At the negarchy end of the anarchy-negarchy spectrum are unions of full mutual restraint. Movement can also occur along the hierarchy-negarchy spectrum, toward hierarchy as authority and capacity, both military and economic, become more concentrated, and in the other direction as power is devolved and more widely distributed in empires or hierarchical states.

These observations also help shed light on the different ways in which governments form, four of which are historically the most important. First, governments arise out of the need to regulate the interaction, particularly the violent interaction, of actors in spaces marked by intense violence interdependence, as well as myriad other frictions and externalities that afflict humans living in close interaction with one another. The fact that governments are needed in such circumstances does not in itself guarantee that they will necessarily emerge, as the repeated occurrence of civil wars and other varieties of intrastate disorder demonstrate. Second, governments arise because of threats posed by outsiders who seek to destroy or dominate. Polities situated in second anarchies, as almost all have been, need governments in order to amass and employ the capacities needed to protect from outsiders. Third, governments arise because of uneven distributions of power within a particular space. An extremely common pattern of state formation across history has been through conquest and domination, made possible by asymmetric distributions of power. Finally, most rarely, governments arise from the consent of the governed. It is notable that the second and third paths to the formation of government reinforce one another, as outside threats necessitate the concentration and mobilization of power, which can then be used not just to repel external threats but also to dominate internal rivals and adversaries. The relationship between the first and third paths out of anarchy to government is, however, potentially quite antagonistic. When levels of violence interdependence become intense but power is widely distributed, the path to government by domination and conquest is blocked, and it can arise only through mutual consent and restraint.

A further valuable concept of full geopolitical theory is the *mode of protection*, understood as a cluster of related security practices that over time give rise to and are supported by political structures of authority and related ideas and identities.[38] Hierarchical states are configurations of authority supported by the *real-state practices* of power mobilization, concentration, and acceleration, placing power in the hands of an autonomous actor for employment against threats, internal and external. The real-state mode of protection, the security operating manual of Archipelago Earth, is functional for security goals in material contexts in which it is difficult to mobilize, concentrate, and accelerate violence capabilities because its practices offer solutions to these problems. But real-state practices are dysfunctional for security in material contexts marked by violence abundance and high violence velocity. To the extent these practices persist in such contexts, their dysfunctionality is intensified. An alternative and historically rare republican-federal mode of protection seeks to demobilize, separate and divide, and decelerate in order to prevent employment. These practices were ill-suited to provide security in historical material contexts marked by violence scarcity and slowness but are viable in material contexts with violence abundance and high velocities. These practices and the mutually restraining arms control structures they generate have been increasingly appealing on Planetary Earth and would, if pursued sufficiently, move the international system out of anarchy toward systemic negarchy.

Much of the attention of international relations theorists, particularly realists, has been on anarchic systems, which have several powerful syndromes making war more likely.[39] First, lacking, by definition, overall government, the units in anarchies must largely rely upon their own devices to secure themselves. Second, typically having different interests and identities, governments in anarchic state systems are prone to conflict and war and spend considerable effort preparing for and engaging in conflict. Third, life in anarchic systems tends to make units hierarchical, and the typical unit of such systems, the state, is commonly defined as an institution marked by a central monopoly of violence, situated in the hands of an organization, the state apparatus, that mobilizes and then employs the resources of the polity to preserve its security and autonomy against outside threats. Fourth, states in international anarchies have high incentives to keep a close watch on other states and to emulate innovations that have significant implications for security. And fifth, states in international anarchies, placing a high premium on military capabilities relevant to preserving their security and autonomy, have high incentives to develop new technologies that might offer them a competitive advantage and are thus prone to push technological frontiers, usually with as much secrecy as possible. Of course the extent to which any state actually does all this varies greatly on the basis of perceptions of the magnitude of external threat, which are difficult to make accurately. And many states are unable, for a variety of domestic institutional reasons, to take the steps needed to preserve their security and autonomy, and as a result sometimes suffer loss of both their security and freedom and come to be dominated or absorbed by stronger outsiders.[40]

These features of anarchic state systems also help shed light on why republican forms of government have been relatively rare historically. To the extent that the mobilization, concentration, and employment of violence capacity is necessary for security in anarchic state systems, the arms control and authority patterns of republican states are ill-suited. Furthermore, until very recently, republics tended to be small in size, making their survival problematic. As a result, republics often depend upon various geographic features that afford them defensive advantages that compensate for their size.

Over the past century, as successively higher levels of interaction and interdependence have grown on a global scale, efforts to conceptualize—and achieve—some form of authoritative world government have been extensive. Although such postanarchic arrangements are commonly referred to as a "world state," the actual main thrust of most of these efforts, as we saw regarding nuclear arms control, has been toward a worldwide political order of sufficient weight to be beyond anarchy but not hierarchical. Over this same period the prospect of a hierarchical world state has also emerged as a real possibility, and a great deal of effort has gone into thinking about the role of special assets in enabling its erection, as well as the measures by which such an outcome can be thwarted.

As levels of violence and other forms of interaction over successively large spaces have grown, making anarchic state systems increasingly dangerous to the security of their members, efforts to move out of anarchy while avoiding hierarchy have grown in their appeal, providing a strong impetus to build various forms of international institutions. Efforts to conceptualize the features of increasingly negarchic systems have produced a bewildering variety of terminologies, but one of the most widely used is "regime." As regimes become more significant in the tasks they perform, the system becomes less anarchic and more negarchic. A measure of the significance of regimes for the system structure of world order can be fashioned by distinguishing between regimes that are *incidental, supplementary,* and *complementary.* Incidental regimes provide valuable services for the state units in the system, but not so valuable that any state depends upon them for their continued existence. Supplementary regimes provide even more valuable services, which smaller states depend upon for their basic viability as states. Finally, a complementary regime provides services of such magnitude that even the largest and most powerful states depend on it for their existence. The ability of a system with complementary regimes to exit anarchy without creating hierarchy makes them appealing, and the ease with which they can be created and sustained is improved if the assets and activities to be governed by the regime involve extraterritorial media and high levels of distinctiveness.

To sum up, the main claims of full geopolitics relevant to outer space can be summarized in twelve propositions (see Table 8.3).

Geohistory and the Three Earths

Because space expansionists base their expectations about space futures on claims about the Earth past and present, grasping and assessing the contours of the human future in space hinges in significant ways on views about the past and present Earth. And the plausibility of the propositions of full geopolitics applied to outer space expansion rests on their ability to explain the large patterns of Earth past and present. Human history is not, for either space expansionism or full geopolitics, one bloody thing after another, but instead exhibits patterns and trajectories which, if properly understood, offer important insights about the future.

Table 8.3 **Geopolitics: Main Propositions**

1. Violence interdependence (VI) is the capacity of actors in a space to inflict damage on one another. In situations of anarchy combined with VI (first anarchy), actors can readily kill one another, producing annihilative saturation of inhabited space, making exit from anarchy and establishment of government necessary for security.

2. Open topographies tending toward consolidation have integral tendencies, while fragmented topographies produce multiple-polity systems. Closed systems lack full frontiers, while open systems have full frontiers with cores and peripheries, which tend to be conflictual.

3. Concentrated balances of power tend toward hierarchical consolidation, while distributed balances tend toward anarchy and pluralism.

4. Special places or master assets capable of system-wide domination will tend toward hierarchical political consolidation unless neutralized, which is easier for extraterritorial media.

5. When civil-military distinctiveness is low, mobilization is easy, but mutual restraint is difficult. When distinctiveness is high, mobilization is difficult, but mutual restraints are easy.

6. Patterns of authority at unit and system levels can be anarchic, hierarchic, and negarchic. Arms control is absent in anarchies, asymmetrical in hierarchies, and mutual in negarchies.

7. The penetration of authority to the individual level becomes total when enabled by interaction, surveillance, and organizational capabilities.

8. Polities vary in numerous ways. Dissimilar polities tend toward conflict and find mutual restraint and cooperation difficult, and vice versa.

9. Governments form to overcome first anarchy, to defend against outside threats, as expressions of power concentration, from common identities, and by mutual consent.

10. Anarchic international systems are war prone, producing high incentives to weaponize new technologies and high barriers to institutionalized mutual restraint and cooperation.

11. The real-state mode of protection, a cluster of practices, mobilizes, concentrates, accelerates, and autonomizes violence capabilities. It is functional in violence-scarce and slow material contexts, and dysfunctional when violence is abundant and rapid. Conversely, the republican-federal mode of protection demobilizes, separates, slows, and checks power. It is dysfunctional when violence is limited and slow, but functional when violence is abundant and rapid.

12. Systems evolve from anarchy or negarchy to hierarchy as power concentrates. Systems evolve from anarchy to negarchy as international regimes evolve from incidental to supplementary to complementary in significance, or as extraterritorial axial regions or master assets are neutralized.

The overall space expansionist narrative of the trajectory of human history on Earth is, as we have seen, quite simple: technological advances enabled human spatial expansion. These new capabilities have made the overall human condition vastly better, while also creating major problems that can be solved only with further expansions, off the planet into space. The basic Earth problem for this spatially inflected technological Promethean project is shortage of space. Occurring within the finite space of the planet Earth, successive enlargements of the scope of human activities have produced a closed Earth beset by numerous problems. But these problems can be remedied by developing new technologies and continuing the overall pattern of human spatial expansion vertically off the planet into the limitless vastness of cosmic space. For space expansionists, the future and the past, while surely differing in important aspects, are essentially parts of one story, that of space expansion by technological advance. Expanding across the Earth has both enlarged and improved the human condition, and expanding into outer space will continue both enlargement and improvement in cosmic dimensions.

The propositions of full geopolitics are particularly well-suited to assessing such claims because the master geopolitical variable of interaction and interdependence is essentially about spatial patterns, and its other variables offer further insight into the shaping influence of material contexts. But full geopolitics, unlike Promethean space expansionism, does *not* offer a comprehensive philosophy of history. Full geopolitics is not committed to the view that there necessarily is a pattern of improvement in the trajectory of human spatial expansion and technological development. For geopolitical theory the question of whether more extensive space and more capable machines are desirable or disastrous depends on whether such enlargements are matched in their scope and powers by configurations of restraining institutions. As the German critical theorist Theodor Adorno put it, "No universal history leads from savagery to humanitarianism, but there is one leading from the slingshot to the megaton bomb."[41] With its concern for the employment of enlarged technologies for expanded violence, the propositions of full geopolitics offer insight into what must be done, what kinds of institutions of domestication and restraint are needed to ensure that consequences are desirable, and how easy or difficult such measures are to achieve. But it provides no guarantee that humans will rise to the occasion to produce and sustain the political restraints vital to avoid disasters.

Thus emerges a fundamental difference between the space expansionist view of the Earth-human relationship, past and future, and the basic logic of full geopolitical theory. Space expansionists argue that the expansion of humans across the Earth, empowered by ever more capable machines, has improved the human condition. And they anticipate that the movement into the vast realms of the solar system and then beyond will mark another stage in both the spatial and technological enlargement of humanity and the overall well-being of humanity. In sharp contrast, the propositions of full geopolitics illuminate the ways in which spatial and technological expansions have, or fail to have, desirable consequences depending on the contours of these enlargements and humanity's relationship to them. Progress for habitat space expansionists results mainly from spatial and technological enlargements. But for geopolitical theory, progress, in the sense of desirable outcomes, depends on whether human political arrangements are suitably configured in relation to the enlargements. Geopolitical theory identifies a variety of spatial and technological material contexts that are particularly prone to producing very undesirable outcomes. This means that it is perfectly possible, according to the propositions of geopolitical theory, for humanity to spatially and technologically enlarge in ways that produce extremely undesirable outcomes. The future, far from continuing to produce improvements, may produce regressions and catastrophic and existential threats. If the contours of the material contexts produced by future spatial and technological expansions resemble those of earlier periods marked by extensive conflict and oppression, then similar results should be anticipated for the future. Thus the movement out spatially could well amount to a replication of the patterns of the past, so that the further humanity goes into outer space, the further its situation will come to resemble in important ways its ever deeper past.

Vindicating any proposition by appeal to historical evidence is an inherently difficult undertaking. Evidence is often incomplete and ambiguous. For every example there are counterexamples. And the sheer diverse detail of the human historical experience ultimately confounds the ability of any single theory to explain everything. Despite these inherent limitations, overall patterns in macrohistory are discernable and provide a general test for the main propositions of full geopolitical theory. While nearly everything humans have ever done has occurred on the planet Earth, the relationship between humanity and the Earth has dramatically changed over time, and as this has happened the viability of different political arrangements has changed greatly in ways keyed to the categories of full geopolitical theory. Over the 200,000 years since *Homo sapiens* first appeared, the relationship of the human species to the material Earth has changed fundamentally in its levels of interdependence and interaction, making for the three quite distinct human Earths: *Archipelago Earth, Global Earth,* and *Planetary Earth* discussed earlier (chapter 2). Each of these three Earths marks a different stage in the globalization of the human relation to Earth, a process beginning with the first enlargement of the range and technological capacities of primitive humans in East Africa and culminating since the middle years of the twentieth century with the complete enclosure of the planet by human activities. A brief look at the main features of each Earth, and the ability of the propositions of full geopolitics to explain these features, provides an overall vindication of their usefulness, and thus some minimal confidence in the value of their insights into space expansion, actual and prospective.

Archipelago Earth and the Great Expansion

For almost all its history, humanity lived in a spatial and material situation radically unlike those which have emerged over the past half-millennium. Between the emergence of *Homo sapiens* and the beginnings of the explosive globalization of modern machine civilization over the past five centuries, humans lived in Archipelago Earth with a spatial pattern akin to scattered chains of isolated islands of differing sizes and physical features. Archipelago Earth is appropriately divided into two parts: before and after the agricultural revolution. The single most notable occurrence in early Archipelago Earth was the great expansion in the spatial range of humans, first throughout Eurasia and eventually to the Americas.[42] The first human technological capabilities, simple stone tools and weapons, mastery of fire, and clothes, provided the basis of this expansion. This migratory expansion, the greatest of the human species to date, occurred quite slowly and incrementally and left no written accounts. Perhaps the most notable feature of this great expansion was that it paralleled—and probably caused— the complete extinction of several other tool-making species of the genus *Homo* who had earlier emerged and spread out of Africa.[43] Although humans became widely dispersed, their population densities were very low; they lived precarious and short lives and were as much the hunted as hunters.

During the early phase of Archipelago Earth, often referred to as prehistoric times, humans everywhere lived similarly and primitively, in small peripatetic hunter-gatherer bands that had little social or political stratification or functional economic differentiation. Although the total human population numbered only in the tens of millions, it is estimated that some 600,000 of these simple polities existed in 1500 BCE.[44] Cultural and linguistic diversity was very high, and identities tended to be highly parochial. Given the primitive condition of communication and transportation technology, groups interacted at distance only slowly, weakly, and sporadically and along lines strongly shaped by the physical contours of Earth. The Archipelago Earth habitat was also marked by formidable natural barriers, nascent frontiers, and vast unoccupied wilderness spaces into which humans rarely ventured and never lived. The intergroup interaction that did occur, routinely with immediately neighboring groups and episodically at greater distances, was often very violent, with recurrent migration, war, conquest, and colonization, sometimes culminating in enslavement and genocide.[45] As a result of these patterns of habitation and interaction, the overall political system of Archipelago Earth was anarchical; cooperation and trust existed within groups but rarely between them. Although their lives were heavily circumscribed by natural scarcities and vulnerabilities, humans in this Earth were not subject to hierarchical political oppression simply because oppression required far more organizational capacities than any polity could muster.

With the development of agriculture beginning about ten thousand years ago, humanity began fundamentally different ways of life and patterns of interaction, a second phase of Archipelago Earth. With agriculture came sedentary built habitations and cities, as well as great increases in population, the domestication of numerous animals, metallurgy, pottery, textiles, and writing, developments marking the beginning of civilization. With denser populations employing an expanded suite of technologies, economic differentiation and social and political stratification emerged.[46] Writing enabled a great expansion in human capacity to preserve and transmit knowledge and the beginnings of observational science. Horses, roads, and ships expanded the range and volume of communication and transportation, enabling trade and war-making at extended distances. Weapons became more lethal, and strata of societies specializing in violence emerged. Proto-states with settled borders, central administrative organizations, and organized militaries also emerged. This basic set of developments arose, probably independently, in several regions of the planet—in Egypt, Mesopotamia, the Indus and Ganges river valleys in south Asia and China, and then later in Mesoamerica, places with adequate soils and water. But this new way of life did not become universal, allowing hunter-gatherer societies to persist in vast areas of the planet.

Cultural and linguistic differences continued to be extensive, and patterns of violent intergroup interaction continued on a larger and more destructive scale. In the regions of the Earth with developed agriculture and cities, highly destructive wars became common. Conquests frequently culminated in razed and looted cities and large-scale massacres and enslavements, as well as empires encompassing large populations and extensive territories. Despite the improved technologies of transportation, topography and the configurations of land and water continued to powerfully shape the capacities and extent of interactions of all types. During later Archipelago Earth, nomadic horse-based peoples living on the great steppes running across the center of Eurasia would periodically burst with great violence into surrounding sedentary lands for conquest and looting, but their small numbers were insufficient to sustain imperial rule over the more extensive populations they conquered.

Despite—or perhaps because of—the advances of material civilization, the vast majority of the population lived in a condition of acute unfreedom. The larger and more technologically advanced polities were highly hierarchical and despotic. Small groups of elites lived in luxury, while the masses were enslaved or subordinated into lives little better than those of farm animals. The essential political operating manual of later Archipelago Earth was the real-statist one of "destroy and dominate." Realist political practices prevailed in these times and places because they fit so well with the particular but recurring security circumstances and problems of this human habitat. But within polities, these harsh approaches were challenged and somewhat moderated by various religious and ethical cosmopolitan value-systems that sought to limit violence and domination and defend the interests of the downtrodden, and that emphasized the moral unity of mankind and the moral superiority of world political unity. Some of these cosmopolitanisms were rooted in philosophy, others in religions with universalist aspirations. But all advanced a program whose practical prospects were, for their times and places, essentially utopian because severely impeded by the basic contours of the actual human habitat and actual human capabilities.

Humans in Archipelago Earth were often as harsh in their interactions with their natural environment as they were toward members of other human groups. With the emergence of cities, habitat practices started to bifurcate into a mixture of external rapacious and violent expansion and exploitation and internal nurturing symbiosis. With hunting tools and the control of fire, humans began wreaking massive damage on ecosystems, and as *Homo sapiens* spatially expanded numerous species of animals were essentially hunted and eaten to extinction. With the domestication of animals and the beginnings of agriculture humans came increasingly to nurture the biological resources they lived off of and depended upon, and gradually they learned to enhance the fecundity of the grounds their bodies depended upon to live.

Global Earth: Expansion and Closure

The advent of the global in the human situation is widely recognized as having begun five centuries ago, as humans mastered the technological and organizational capability to travel long distances over the Earth's oceans. With the first circumnavigation of the Earth, the more general reconnaissance of the world ocean, and mapping of the main features of the terrestrial Earth, the multiple previous human worlds started to become interactive and interdependent and increasingly "one world." As this happened, the use of the term "global" to discuss something important in human affairs become increasingly widespread, and theorizing the implications of "global" starts to grow as an aspect of theorizing about the human world.[47] This great shift in the spatial contours of the human world was registered in the shift from flat maps to spherical globes to represent that largest scale of the place where humans lived and traveled. Global Earth is also appropriately divided into two periods, the first beginning around 1500 CE and the second beginning in the middle of the nineteenth century, as the fruits of the Industrial Revolution started to be widely influential.

Global Earth was marked by a second great expansion of one group of humans, originating in the European peninsula of the great Eurasian World Island, at the expense of peoples residing virtually everywhere else. Exploiting the new technologies of oceanic transport, the initial European expansion was limited to the ocean, its islands, and some of its littoral areas.[48] With the discovery of the New World of the Americas, European explorers eliminated the absence of interaction between Eurasia and peoples of these two continents. Quickly exploiting their technological superiority in weaponry, small numbers of Europeans conquered and toppled major American imperial states in Mesoamerica and the Andean highlands of South America, looted their accumulated wealth in precious metals, and reduced their populations to various forms of bondage for further exploitation. This rapid expansion and rapacious domination was greatly assisted by the outbreak of massive epidemics caused by diseases that the Europeans had unintentionally and unknowingly brought with them. These plagues are estimated to have killed some 90 percent of the population of the Americas within a century of Columbus's arrival and largely cleared North America of the indigenous populations, opening vast temperate areas to subsequent waves of European colonization.[49] The emigration of Europeans was most successful in temperate climate zones, where a suite of organisms from Europe proved to be as ecologically imperial as the humans who brought them, but not in the humid tropics, particularly much of Africa, where a "disease curtain" thwarted both European exploration and settlement.[50]

The early phases of Global Earth were marked not just by advances in ocean transport but also by new technologies of violence, most notably gunpowder weapons, which rapidly diffused into the hands of many states. Within the long-civilized regions around the great crescent of the World Island's Rimland, stretching from Europe through Southwest, South, and East Asia, the exploitation of these weapons triggered efforts to form enlarged regional universal states or gunpowder empires. Despite repeated efforts to consolidate the European region, universal monarchy in this area was thwarted, due in significant measure to the exceptionally fragmented topography of Europe, enabling a robust balance-of-power system to emerge. Thus early modern Europe remained an anarchic state system, while regions elsewhere in Eurasia of comparable size and population became or persisted as hierarchical empires. The ocean was a great extraterritorial medium, with integral tendencies due to its flatness, and came to be dominated by one state.[51]

The early phases of Global Earth were marked by new political innovations that made possible the enlargement and international viability of republican governments that were based on wider sharing of political power as well as an

ideological commitment to growing forms of individual freedom. And the inces-
sant wars transpiring within the European anarchic state system triggered novel
efforts to conceptualize and construct various modest international institutional
restraints on war. Thus polities in Europe moved away from hierarchy internally at the same time they were starting to moderate anarchy externally. These
expanding islands of relative freedom were, however, metropoles within a global
system of slave-based economic exploitation at the periphery. The presence
of these wars, empires, and enslavements indicates the continued hegemony
of the real-state security practices. But this operating manual was increasingly
challenged both domestically and internationally by advocates of an alternative
set of practices and institutions centered on mutual restraint and more extensively institutionalized freedom, manifest in the rise of republican revolutionary
movements, the expansion of the franchise, and the abolition of slavery.

The second phase of Global Earth is defined by the introduction of new
technologies of communication, transportation, and destruction produced by
the Industrial Revolution, which were the first major practical fruits of the new
science of the moderns and its technological application. By the middle years
of the nineteenth century the widespread deployment of the railroad, the telegraph, and the steamship began to alter the temporal and spatial frames of previous human existence and were widely hailed as abolishing distance. These
technologies enabled the Europeans and their settler colonies to rapidly expand
into the continental interiors, opening large areas of arable land and resources
to development. The invention of potent new weapons made of steel, for both
land and sea, gave decisive new advantage to the initially small group of states
with the industrial capacity to fabricate them, and enabled the Europeans to decisively overpower the other long-civilized regions of the World Island, at the
same time that tropical medicine helped open Africa to rapid exploration and
conquest.

As interaction capacity and violence interdependence on a global scale was
pushed from weak to strong, and as the distributional advantages of early industrialization were exploited, the spatial size of the shrinking number of remaining
states and empires grew even larger, with the multicontinental empire of the
British encompassing some quarter of the land area on the planet. By the turn
of the twentieth century, global closure was widely recognized. As Mackinder
famously observed, humanity was "for the first time presented with a closed
system" in which the "known does not fade any longer through the half known
into the unknown," "there is no longer elasticity of political expansion in land
beyond the Pale," and "every shock, every disaster or superfluity is now even felt
to the antipodes, and may indeed return from the antipodes."[52]

By the early years of the twentieth century, another set of consequences
started to flow from the new material possibilities and their employment. Within

the European state system, violence increased from strong to intense, making the persistence of interstate anarchy increasingly incompatible with security, as the great destructions of World War I and II demonstrated. In the face of these new material realities, efforts to achieve an exit from anarchy through imperial conquest were thwarted only by the concerted efforts of continent-size neighboring states from the previous periphery. And efforts to exit anarchy into some sort of regional confederal or federal union became increasingly seen as necessary for security. The exploitation of the new industrial technologies within states to build modernized hierarchical regimes produced the novel system of oppression that came to be known as totalitarian. At the same time, the scale-up of republican governments was enabled, producing another novelty: a federal national republic of continental scope. At the same time that these new enlarged hierarchical polities were coalescing, the diffusion of industrial weaponry and modern national forms of mobilization were distributing violence capabilities to the peripheral peoples in the European empires, leading to their rapid collapse in the middle years of the twentieth century.

Planetary Earth: Vulnerability and Closure

Although the terms "global" and "planetary" are often treated as synonyms, it is appropriate, as noted earlier, to refer to the overall human situation that has emerged since the middle years of the twentieth century as Planetary Earth to capture its starkly novel features.[53] As with the years around 1500 CE, the decade between the middle of the 1940s and the 1950s sharply delineates the outset of a new human-Earth period. The first development of nuclear explosives, long-range rockets, Earth-orbiting satellites, and electronic digital computers and the cracking of the DNA code of life, as well as the Great Acceleration in economic activity and fossil fuel consumption signaling the beginning of the Anthropocene, clearly inscribe a bright line of *before* and *after* this decade.

Although less than a century old, patterns of human activity in Planetary Earth are already marked by a set of distinctive features, starting with the first technogenic threat to human existence from nuclear weapons and a general increase in the vulnerability of civilization and humanity to a growing list of severe threats. Planetary Earth is also marked by intense levels of interdependence, particularly of violence, as well as high levels of network complexity, transborder flows, and material entanglement, high levels of political and economic stratification, and the acceleration of both movement and general change.[54] The spread of machine civilization and its commitment to scientific discovery and technological development have brought about a great diffusion in advanced capabilities of production and destruction, enabling increasing numbers of actors of ever smaller size to wield powers of increasing potency and spatial scope.[55]

The human world of Planetary Earth is also politically segmented and stratified, with a cluster of advanced industrial democracies, numerous authoritarian and autocratic regimes, as well as numerous failed and smashed states with quasi-anarchic endemic civil conflict. Planetary Earth is also acutely stratified economically, with a tiny handful of individuals possessing as much wealth as much of the rest of humanity combined. Despite the high levels of communication and information interaction, nothing approaching a common identity has emerged, and diversity and fragmentation have explosively increased. As interdependence and interaction as well as spillovers, neighborhood effects, and crowding have increased, there are more imperatives to create effective worldwide governance and government, at the same time that the vast increase in the number of capable actors and in the number of sovereign states makes effective collective action and institution-building increasingly difficult. The world is thus pulled in opposite directions simultaneously: toward unification by rising interaction and interdependence and the problems they create, and away from unification by the growing numbers of empowered actors with increasingly diverse identities.[56]

It is upon this Planetary Earth that the impacts of human expansions into outer space, actual and prospective, must be gauged. As we have seen, the seven great debates about Planetary Earth mark fundamental divides over the trajectory of humanity and the planet, and will be significantly determined by space choices and outcomes.

Earth Space, Planetary Geopolitics, and World Governments

Everything that rises must converge.
                                    —Teilhard de Chardin (1973)[1]

Since Sputnik and the satellites, the planet is enclosed in a manmade environment that ends *Nature* and turns the globe into a repertory theater to be programmed.
                                    —Marshall McLuhan (1970)[2]

The price of a reliable solar satellite power system, or any analogous enterprise, might be thoroughgoing world government.
                                    —Nigel Calder (1979)[3]

High Stakes in Earth Space

The full visionary project of space expansionists is immense, but big things begin small, and the first steps in their grand ascent are proposals to do significant things in Earth orbital space. By bringing into view the underappreciated Clarke-Sagan program, space expansionism is revealed to be deeply conflicted about the most significant actual and prospective human steps into Earth space. Having seen in detail what competing expansionist programs propose, the consequences they anticipate, and their sharp disputes about the desirability of employing Earth orbital space for military purposes, and having set forth the assumptions and propositions of a theoretical framework suitable for assessing their claims, we can now assess the major claims of space expansionists. The first step is an assessment of the accuracy of their geographic mappings and the appropriateness of their analogies. Then, most important, the propositions of full geopolitical theory are employed to adjudicate the great debate between the von Braun militarization programs and the Clarke-Sagan arms control and Whole Earth Security programs, finally providing an answer to the pivotal question: Has the net effect of actual space activities been negative or positive for human survival? These propositions also provide the basis to assess the world order consequences of the light, information-centric projects associated with the Clarke-Sagan programs, the von Braun programs for a planet-spanning military Earth Net and planetary domination, and the Fuller Earth habitat expansion programs for the construction of civil Orbita.

Earth Space Geography, the Astrosphere, and Planetary Closure

Analysis of space begins with geography, with accurate mappings of locations and spatial relations. The features of near-space geography routinely referenced by space expansionists have become uncontroversial, but these characterizations are flawed by several significant geographic errors. Beyond the previously discussed major errors of failing to recognize that the Earth's astrosphere, the planet's outer space, is part of the planet and of failing to treat ballistic missiles as space weapons, space expansionists make two simple but significantly consequential misreadings of near-space geography: about (1) size, distance, and effective distance; and (2) whether the edge of space is a full rather than nascent frontier. Correcting these errors provides a significantly revised understanding of Earth space as a domain for human activity (see Table 9.1).

First, space expansionists err in characterizing the size of the Earth's astrosphere. The space parts of the planet Earth are practically very small. Labeling anything associated with outer space small is strongly counterintuitive because cosmic outer space is so unfathomably large. In cubic miles, the voids of the Earth's astrosphere do considerably exceed the size of its atmosphere. A shell around the planet extending from 100 to 600 miles above the planet's surface has a volume of some 100 billion cubic miles, while the atmosphere has a volume of

Table 9.1 **Earth Space Geography and Closure**

Space Expansionist View	Corrected View	Implications
Going into space means leaving Earth	Orbital Earth space is part of planet Earth	Actual space activities intensify closure
Space is very large	Because of low effective distance, Earth space is practically small	Actual space activities intensify closure
Space is a frontier	Space is a nascent frontier, but now largely a formidable natural barrier	Actual space activities are not significantly diminishing closure

some 20 billion cubic miles, making near-Earth space five times larger.[4] Despite its large size, the astrosphere is smaller than the atmosphere in the ways that practically matter for human activity. Absolute distances are great, but *effective distance* is very small. In comparison with the Earth's atmosphere, both the size of Earth orbital space and the velocities of objects in it are vastly larger. But effective distance in EOS is small because velocities have increased proportionally more than distances. Orbital velocities are some ten to thirty times greater than atmospheric velocities. The most important practical implication of these facts is that the shortest path in time (but not in miles) between any two points at significant distance from each other on the surface of the Earth is *through* orbital space. This practical smallness also increases the likelihood that this realm will be particularly prone to crowding and various types of degradation. Thinking of space as vastly large makes it easy to imagine that there is plenty of room for both military and civil activities. But recognizing that the astrosphere is small underscores the fact that there is *not* room for both and that extensive further space weaponization will severely inhibit civil development. An accurate mapping of practical planetary geography is thus radically different from the views prevalent among space expansionists (see Figure 9.1).

Second, the omnipresent expansionist characterization of space as a frontier is more inaccurate than accurate. While certainly no longer just a *potential* frontier, space is still a *nascent* rather than a *full* frontier. The intrinsic natural features of space (vacuum, temperatures, radiations, and absence of air, pressure, weight, water, and food) make it a deeply inhospitable habitat for humans. More important, passage between the terrestrial Earth and the space part of the planet is very arduous and costly. Until costs of accessing space are dramatically reduced, calling space a frontier is more booster propaganda than an accurate geographic description. The technologies of access to space may improve in the future, but until they do very significantly, the sky literally is the limit for nearly all human

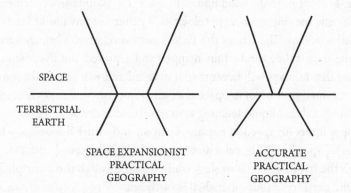

Figure 9.1 Corrected Practical Geography of Earth Space

activities. The existence of a formidable barrier-boundary between the terrestrial Earth and the astrosphere also means that all the growth of human numbers and interactions is occurring within an effectively closed space, inexorably increasing interdependence.

Thinking accurately about the geography of the planet strongly confounds the claim that expansion into space has reduced the closure produced by the expansion of machine civilization within the finite confines of the terrestrial Earth. Space activities are bringing parts of the Earth into much closer interaction rather than reducing their interaction through spatial expansion. Because effective distance in Earth's space is so low, and the fastest path between any two distant points on the surface of the Earth is through the space part of the planet, *activities in Earth space overwhelmingly reinforce closure and intensify interdependence*. Activities in the space part of the planet have altered the relationship of the other parts of the planet to each other as much as or more than altering the human relation to cosmic outer space. Until human activities significantly expand into the outer realms of Earth space and then into the solar system, further activities in the astrosphere will intensify, not reduce closure.

Recognizing these geographical features of the Earth and its space also undercuts the pervasive space expansionist analogy that space is an ocean. In initiating the American lunar-landing project, President Kennedy spoke of space as a "vast new ocean," and William Burrows's magisterial history of the Space Age is entitled *This New Ocean*. Building on this analogy, several analysts have drawn from naval history and strategy to guide space military activities.[5] Yet the analog between the geophysical features of outer space and terrestrial oceans is more misleading than illuminating. Like outer space, the Earth's oceans lack the solidity characteristic of the terrestrial spaces inhabited by humans. They are also vast in comparison with the realms humans inhabit, although cosmic space is so vast that comparison with any terrestrial feature is basically misleading. Furthermore the solid bodies in space, its "islands and continents," are continuously moving at extreme velocities, a pattern utterly unlike lands within the Earth's oceans. The size of the Earth's oceans relative to humans and their machines means they can be fully mapped and explored, but the cosmic ocean is so vast that humans will never map it in detail and will never visit more than an infinitesimal portion of it. Space is a radiation-washed lifeless vacuum, while the ocean is a dense liquid teeming with life. The density of water imposes very low upper limits on speed of passage, both on and under the ocean, while the vacuum of space permits velocities approaching light speed. Because transit through the hydrosphere is so slow while transit through the astrosphere is so rapid, the Earth's vacuous outer shell is vastly smaller in effective distances than its aqueous shell.

Given the oceans' extensive geohistory, the question is posed: Which historical period of human interaction with the oceans is analogous to which parts of space and which space activities? The favored expansionist ocean analog is the early modern period, when European navigational and nautical advances turned a formidable natural barrier into a frontier. But the actual geography of Earth space suggests comparison with more recent oceanic activities and different oceanic bodies. The historical trajectory of human interaction with the oceans has been marked by a great increase in the density of human activities, turning what was originally inaccessible into open and then increasingly closed space. As human activity in the oceans has grown, so too has crowding, degradation, and conflicts between different users and interests. As this has happened, ocean space has been increasingly enclosed politically and regulated. Due to the geographic features of the astrosphere overlooked by space expansionists, this place is also very prone to crowding, degradation, and conflicts. Indeed these patterns have *already* become significant, even though the currently very difficult and costly access to space indicates only the beginning of a frontier opening. Further evidence for the effects of the smallness of the Earth's astrosphere is the unanticipated threat to terrestrial astronomy from the recently launched Space X Starlink satellite constellations.[6]

On the basis of this corrected understanding of the planet's full geography, we should expect that a significant opening of the astrosphere as a full frontier will quickly produce an extreme density of interaction, interdependence, and degradation. Space today, when it is still a nascent frontier, is already more crowded and degraded than were historical terrestrial full frontiers. Earth space is more like contemporary Lake Erie or the Mediterranean Sea than the open ocean experienced in early modernity. If access to orbit becomes easy enough to open a full frontier, and space debris is not vigorously managed, the astrosphere will come to resemble the contemporary Aral Sea, which has been largely ruined by human activities. The most important actual use of space, as a corridor for bombardment, suggests the astrosphere is more like a narrow strait than an open body of water. And, as Salkeld suggested, the lower parts of orbital space are like shallow coastal sounds between beaches and reefs, which are analogous to the perilous radiation belts of the magnetosphere.[7]

The military geographies of the hydrosphere and astrosphere are also quite different. Some parts of the inhabited terrestrial Earth have ocean shorelines, making them vulnerable to naval assault, while vast interior hinterlands are inaccessible by maritime powers. From this basic difference stems the traditional geopolitical distinction between land powers and sea powers. In contrast, all terrestrial territories have shorelines to orbital space perfectly matched to their areal size, and all are equally vulnerable to assault. Thus an oceanic hegemony was inherently limited in its ability to dominate the entire international system, while an orbital hegemony would have no such limits. And the ocean, unlike the astrosphere, is not filled with derelict vessels and their detritus dangerously hurtling about at enormous velocities. Furthermore, there is nothing analogous in the oceans to the role strategic litter might play in military space conflicts.

In pointing to these ways in which near space beyond the atmosphere is part of the planet, small in its practical dimensions, and only a nascent frontier, as well as that ballistic missiles are inherently space weapons, I am pointing to the prevalence in space thinking of a particular type of very simple but very consequential geographic error. But the argument advanced here does not rest on newly discovered facts. Instead established facts such as the physical features of a ballistic missile trajectory or the ratio of speed increase to size increase in orbital space become effectively unknown due to misplacement and spatial misclassification. Once these unknown knowns are recovered by accurate placement and classification, the entire landscape of human activities across the Space Age looks radically different from the accounts of almost all advocates and observers.

These simple geography errors and disorientations arise because the features of the realms beyond the Earth's atmosphere readily lend themselves to misperception. Overall, space is very alien, radically different from the conditions of the terrestrial Earth humans inhabit. The main features of space— weightlessness, hard vacuum, high radiation, absence of air, and atmospheric pressure—are almost completely unlike any environment that humans experience on terrestrial Earth and can be only partly and temporarily approximated with specialized machines. Space and human space activities are also largely inscrutable to terrestrial viewers. While many different celestial bodies, some relatively close but others vastly distant, are visible from the surface of the planet, it is not immediately obvious what these objects are or where they are relative to the Earth. The modern understanding of realities beyond the terrestrial Earth is highly dependent on telescopic technologies and required several centuries to be widely accepted, in part because it was so radically unlike terrestrial realities. And, despite their proximity, the webs of artificial satellites surrounding the terrestrial Earth are largely invisible to terrestrial observers. Perceptions of space would be quite different if satellites produced contrails marking their passage, like jet aircraft do. If this were the case, terrestrial observers would see a dense webbing of lines in the sky and quickly perceive that these objects are not in some far distant realm but quite proximate. They would see not a portal to the cosmos but rather their terrestrial habitat densely wrapped and enveloped by flocks of super-fast-moving machines.

With these corrected understandings of the geography of the Earth and its space, it is possible to assess rival space programs with the propositions of full geopolitical theory. Because the large-scale detonation of nuclear weapons is the most salient contemporary catastrophic and existential threat facing humanity, the question of whether space activities contribute to its amplification or amelioration is the most important indicator of the overall impact of space activities. The Great Debate on Earth Space, pitting the von Braun against the Clarke-Sagan projects, each partially implemented, extends the central debate of the nuclear era, within which the central activities and main impacts of the Space Age are nested. Which approach is more likely to be successful in providing security according to the propositions of geopolitics?

Planetary Geopolitics I: Nuclear Violence and the State System

The most important primary propositions of geopolitics concern the relationship between different levels of violence interdependence and the security of actors in anarchy. In situations where violence interdependence is intense, the main actors can readily destroy one another, making the persistence of anarchy incompatible with security. The development of nuclear weapons and capabilities to deliver them reliably at global distances generate intense violence interdependence on a global scale, and an exit from anarchy, or substantial modification of it, is now required for security. The basic claims of nuclear-one-worldism about the obsolescence of territorial units of less than global scope as viable providers of security are strongly supported by the core propositions of full geopolitical theory. The basic material reality is that the volumes of violence afforded by nuclear technology are capable of saturating territorial units. The intense violence interdependence of even continent-size territorial units is further amplified by the vulnerability of the shared planetary biosphere to the catastrophic disruptions of ozone depletion and nuclear winter likely from an extensive nuclear war.

Geopolitical theory argues that this combination of anarchy with very high levels of violence potential created by nuclear weapons is inherently perilous and that an exit from or significant modification of the anarchic world political order is necessary for security. The move beyond anarchy required for security in material contexts marked by intense violence interdependence can take either of two paths: through mutual restraints leading toward negarchy or through concentrations of power leading to hierarchy (recall Figure 8.2). Although successfully moving from anarchy to hierarchy, from an interstate system to a world state or empire, diminishes or removes the set of insecurities related to system crash, it creates its own distinctive and potentially severe violence insecurity, in the form of imperial or totalitarian oppression or system crush. Once anarchy has been replaced by hierarchy, the ruling center has secured itself, but all other actors in the system are insecure. The final step of the von Braun ladder to global dominance by deploying an Earth Net capability would move the system out of anarchy and into hierarchy, producing a secure center but general insecurity, while risking devolution into totalitarian crush.

The core proposition of geopolitical theory on the relationship between violence interdependence, anarchy, and government finds, we saw, significant historical supporting evidence across the long era of Archipelago Earth as well as the shorter era of Global Earth. But in applying this proposition to the contemporary Planetary Earth, an additional important structural reality must be taken into account. In previous Earth epochs, exits from anarchy within particular territorial spaces marked by intense violence interdependence tended strongly toward hierarchical rather than negarchical forms because such polities were almost always situated in a more spatially extensive anarchical system where levels of violence interdependence were lower but where outside threats from other polities were an omnipresent reality. Successfully navigating the often perilous realms of international politics placed a high premium on doing the tasks that state hierarchies and realist practices were well configured to accomplish: mobilizing, concentrating, accelerating and employing violence capabilities against external adversaries.

Planetary Earth presents a fundamentally novel configuration of security threats because, barring substantial space colonization or threatening aliens, a world polity would be alone and thus not need to mobilize, concentrate, or employ violence capacity against outside threats. This means that the state hierarchical form and the tasks it is configured to accomplish are obsolete at a planetary scale, solutions to problems that no longer exist. In this situation, less historically prevalent negarchical approaches become an appealing way to exit from anarchy. This is another way of saying that the statist mode of protection has been rendered obsolete and that the republican-federal mode of protection now fits with the planetary material context in providing security. This points to the illogic of transposing the state form to a global or planetary scope with the creation of a world government equipped with an autonomous centralized monopoly of violence. And it points to the logic of demobilizing and decelerating power and placing checks and balances on state leaders. In embodying these practices and seeking to produce such patterns of authority, the nuclear arms control project is vindicated by full geopolitical theory as the approach best able to provide security in the novel material and structural circumstances of Planetary Earth. If this project were realized, a complementary regime would exist, and world order would have moved out of anarchy significantly toward negarchy.

Because the practices and structures now needed for security are effectively the opposite of those so successful, and so prevalent, across the entirety of human political history, the arms control project has acquired a misleading aura of being idealistic and purely normative. In actuality, the arms control project is motivated by the traditional normative goals of security from violence but is pursued with a more realistic understanding of the material conditions now existing on Earth. By the same token, however, the relative novelty of this approach, combined with the heavy weight of the dead hand of history, explain why such efforts are so politically difficult and why the political system is prone to lag in its adjustment and persist in contradiction with the planetary forces of destruction.

Stepping back and reflecting on the ambivalent trajectory of humanity's encounter with its first technogenic existential threat is sobering. Decades after the links between large-scale nuclear war and human extinction were compellingly illuminated, many thousands of high-yield nuclear weapons remain prepared for nearly instant use, and there seems little likelihood that this will change soon. What needs to be done is clear enough, but political capacities to do what is necessary are absent. Arms control is unraveling, and great power interstate rivalry is reemerging. And in a bizarre twist illustrative of the staying power of real state institutions, the newly resurgent Russian Orthodox Church has sanctified Russia's nuclear arsenal.[8] If humanity's encounters with synbio, nanotech, and ASI are as fumbling, survival prospects are dim.

Planetary Geopolitics II: Space Weapons and Acceleration

With this understanding of the core security imperatives created by nuclear explosives, we next employ the propositions of geopolitical theory to understand the implications of employing space and space technology for military purposes. Because violence interdependence is an aggregate of the volume of violence relative to territorial space and of the velocity of violence, any activity that increases the violence velocity increases the overall level of violence interdependence. Given this, the primary impact of the first part of the von Braun program that has been implemented—the deployment of ballistic missiles and the employment of orbital space as a corridor for the delivery of nuclear weapons—significantly increases the velocity of nuclear violence, and thus the intensity of violence interdependence on a planetary scale. Nuclear weapons produce saturated levels of violence volume, and the use of space and rockets to transport them produces nearly instantaneous violence velocity. This means that the implemented first step of the von Braun programs is judged to have amplified the intensity of violence interdependence and exacerbated the contradiction between the material forces of destruction and the world political system organized in territorial units. By accelerating nuclear violence, the von Braun accomplishment has increased the probability of civilizational catastrophe and human extinction. The main space program of ballistic missile space weapons, although transformed into an unknown known through geographic misplacement, is darkly negative in its impact on the fate of humanity and the Earth. If this situation persists, and if the propositions of full geopolitical theory are sound, then a systemic crash is sooner or later very likely.

What evidence supports the proposition that the employment of space and space technology to accelerate the transport of nuclear weapons has made nuclear war more likely? The fortunate fact that nuclear war has not occurred means that the empirical record can provide only a partial and imperfect test of the validity of propositions about the nuclear revolution. Why has nuclear war not occurred? Is it, as many leaders have attested, through luck? Is it *because* of particular policies, or *despite* them? Has this nonevent been produced by strategies of deterrence or strategies of war-fighting? Or is it because of the arms control restraints that have been implemented? Because all these measures have been partially pursued and all point toward nuclear war *not* occurring, it is impossible to cleanly resolve this momentous debate with appeals to the empirical historical record. In the absence of empirical resolution, we are left with good judgment and common sense—notoriously contested standards—and appeals to the fit between deductive theory and significant events of the nuclear era.

Despite these caveats, the case for thinking that the coupling of ballistic missiles with nuclear weapons increased the probability of nuclear war is robust. There is general agreement among statesmen, historians, and theorists that the great Soviet-American crisis of October 1962 was in significant measure both triggered and made more dangerous by the extreme speeds that the newly deployed nuclear ballistic missiles provided. The Cuban Missile Crisis was, in the often-quoted words of the historian Arthur Schlesinger Jr, "the most dangerous moment in human history."[9] Its peaceful outcome, according to the historian Martin Sherwin, was "the most important event in the twentieth century."[10] In its wake President Kennedy estimated that the prospect of the crisis sliding into general nuclear war was one in three to one in two, but had he known the full extent of Soviet forces deployed in Cuba, he would likely have deemed the odds of disaster even higher.[11]

As its name registers, ballistic missiles were central to the origins and dangers of this crisis. When the United States deployed Jupiter intermediate-range nuclear missiles, capable of striking Moscow within ten minutes, in the territories of its NATO allies (Turkey, Italy, and Britain), the Soviet Union responded by secretly placing comparable missiles in Cuba, along with a large inventory of other nuclear weapons and conventional forces to protect the island from an American invasion, which they believed had recently been attempted and would soon be again. Judging this an intolerable situation, the Kennedy administration demanded that the Soviets remove the missiles, deployed an armada of naval vessels to blockade Cuba, prepared forces to invade the island, and seriously considered bombing the missile sites. In the course of this mobilization, US military forces were put on the highest alert level of the Cold War, DEFCON-2, which meant that virtually every US nuclear weapon was poised for immediate launch.[12]

With the arsenals on a hair trigger and their far-flung forces beginning to violently interact in the air and at sea, the leaders of both superpowers feared that events—and their forces—were slipping out of control.[13] At the eleventh hour they negotiated a face-saving deal in which the Soviets would withdraw their nuclear forces, the United States would not invade Cuba, and the American Jupiters in Europe would be withdrawn.[14] Within this complex matrix of anxious political maneuvering and massive military mobilization, what stands out is the speed with which the missiles in Europe and Cuba could reach their targets, making them potent first-strike weapons, as well as the dangers of accidental escalation from the high levels of alert.

Further evidence for the nuclear space weapons transportation system making nuclear war more likely is found in the accuracy revolution of the 1970s. Made possible by military space information systems, highly accurate ICBMs increased the difficulty of deploying nuclear forces capable of surviving a first strike. As the accuracy of ballistic missiles was increased to the point where they could destroy any target that could be located, land-based missiles in hardened underground silos became vulnerable to preemptive first strike. This vulnerability created great incentives to keep ballistic missiles on alert status, prepared to be launched within minutes, and to adopt launch-on-warning strategies in which the missiles would be fired on the basis of electronic information that an attack was under way, creating the chronic possibility of nuclear war unintentionally triggered by accident or miscalculation. All these dangers have their root in the extreme speeds and accuracies of ballistic missiles, and as such must be seen as major ways in which the employment of space and space technology increases the probability of general nuclear war.

Geopolitical arguments about the perils of acceleration also strongly suggest that the next step on the von Braunian ladder to deploy antisatellite weapons will further increase the dangers produced by the first steps. Because military satellites provide essential communication and early warning services, developing robust capabilities to attack them adds to the ways in which accidental or inadvertent nuclear war might be triggered. Blinding an adversary equipped with large numbers of nuclear weapons prepared for rapid employment is a dangerous stratagem. The fact that the constellations of military satellites are traveling at extremely high velocities in an environment increasingly filled with space debris means that they might be suddenly disabled by a debris collision during a tense international crisis, sparking a general conflagration, a system crash.

Alternatively the Whole Earth Security program centered on mutually re-straining arms control moves the system out of raw anarchy and into a mixed anarchic-negarchic system. Geopolitical theory indicates that the practices of arms control through mutual restraint advanced by the Clarke-Sagan pro-gram are best suited to provide security in a material context marked by in-tense levels of violence interdependence. Reducing the number of ballistic missile space weapons has the effect of reducing the acceleration of violence, thus reducing the contradiction between the territorial state system and the forces of destruction. Because much of what is commonly characterized as "nuclear arms control" has actually restrained ballistic missile (space weapon) delivery systems, the great arms control treaties of the Cold War settlement are actually space programs. As such, this second great, dark, un-known known space program of space weapons arms control has had a sig-nificantly positive impact on reducing the probability of nuclear war and can justifiably be seen as *the single most important positive contribution* that any actual space program has had—and promises for the foreseeable future to have—on the greatest currently actual catastrophic and existential threat facing humanity.

Because the propositions of geopolitics about violence interdependence and anarchy are a set of functionality arguments, they indicate what must be done to be secure, but they provide no guarantee that the prescribed steps will be realized. Eventually, if the system does not move toward adjustment and a crash does not occur, then the propositions are falsified. Unfortunately there are several strong reasons why the adjustments necessary for security might not take place. State institutions and national identities are deeply en-trenched, and states have a variety of smaller and less consequential rivalries and conflicts that impede the pursuit of the measures needed for security in a material context marked by intense levels of violence interdependence. Also, nuclear weapons, being so far removed from ordinary human experience, are easily kept out of sight and out of mind, short-circuiting the clear perception of their stark implications. In short, there are robust reasons for concluding that the system will remain in fundamental contradiction and adequate adjustment will not take place.

But the historical record of the nuclear Cold War does provide important evidence of how extreme security vulnerabilities, when properly perceived, can trigger the far-reaching changes in interstate relations and world order that geo-political theory prescribes in the nuclear era. Although it is increasingly forgotten in both the United States and Russia, strong nuclear-one-world understandings played an unexpectedly catalytic role in the unexpected—and unexpectedly peaceful—end of the Cold War and the nuclear arms control treaties of its set-tlement. The historical record shows that Gorbachev's and Reagan's convergent views on nuclear vulnerability led them to alter Soviet-American political relations in order to reduce the probability of a nuclear war and massively reduce their nuclear arsenals.[15] These changes in political relations, and the arms control treaties they made possible, demonstrate that revolutionary statecraft, while not routine, does occur and can rapidly bring the international political system more into line with novel material realities.

Planetary Geopolitics III: Earth Net or Whole Earth Security?

The ambitions of the military space expansionists do not end with the deployment of ballistic missiles, satellite force multipliers, and antisatellite weapons, but extend to the construction by one state of an Earth Net system of satellite battle stations to intercept ballistic missiles and attack targets on the ground. And the Clarke-Sagan ambitions for a Whole Earth Security system do not end with nuclear and ballistic missile arms control but extend to the positive employment of space technologies to bring about and sustain changes in international relations and provide security and other benefits to the entire world. What do the propositions of full geopolitical theory indicate about the clash between these two diametrically opposed prospective space programs and their potential impacts on security and world order?

These programs differ massively in their cost and complexity. Both are centrally concerned with the threat to national and global security posed by nuclear weapons and their delivery through orbital space by ballistic missiles. The simplest and cheapest solution is clearly arms control, to ban ballistic missiles. In contrast, the von Braunians' proposal to build a vast Earth-encircling military infrastructure would be at least an order of magnitude more expensive and complex than anything yet attempted in space, with the primary objective of getting rid of ballistic missiles by shooting them down. As such, this scheme fails the Rube Goldberg test: an Earth Net is a fabulously elaborate and expensive gizmo to do something that can be done much more simply, directly, and cheaply. Similarly, Salkeld's proposals to solve the problem of basing mode vulnerability by dispersing nuclear weapons in high Earth orbit and beyond is a vastly expensive and complex scheme to solve a problem which the simple expedient of banning ballistic missiles can solve directly and cheaply. Both these competing programs would produce a significant change in world political order by pushing the system out of anarchy. Successfully building an Earth Net would push world order toward hierarchy, while the Clarke-Sagan program would move it toward a negarchical confederal system by establishing a complementary regime.

To start with the von Braunians, achieving an Earth Net–based planetary dominance paradoxically probably presupposes a world order in which the distribution of capacity is already decisively tilted toward hegemonic unipolarity. It is very unlikely that any state could create an orbital network of military satellites to prevent rival states from using orbital space as a corridor for bombardment in the face of determined opposition from rival states. Due to its size, an Earth Net project would be impossible to hide and would take an extended period to realize, providing rival states with plenty of warning and reaction time. Whatever its ultimate capabilities, the construction of such vast infrastructures is never going to be a quick coup, comparable to a military surprise attack or the secret development of a revolutionary weapon. Because so many states have access to orbital space, opportunities for response will be widely distributed. Because orbital space is an extraterritorial medium accessible from the territories of all states, no state has a significant positional advantage in attempting to dominate it (see Table 9.2).

Possibilities for effective blocking measures, both symmetrical and asymmetrical, are numerous. A blocking state could pursue a symmetrical strategy by deploying a parallel battle station infrastructure, in which case the current strategic stalemate would simply be transposed into orbit, at vast cost. Paradoxically, erecting dual networks would almost surely require a robust space traffic control regime. And the interaction of all this hardware whizzing around in Earth space is likely to create even more opportunities for accidents, and possibly first-strike advantages.

Asymmetrical responses, in which the blocking state deploys capabilities to negate but not duplicate, appear to be cheap and effective. Because objects in orbit, particularly large complex machines, are highly vulnerable to destruction and degradation from space debris, it would be possible to frustrate the construction of an Earth Net by intentionally creating debris, large quantities of which could be cheaply and readily dispersed. Because Earth space is so small in effective distance and has pronounced integral tendencies, its usability can be readily degraded. All these considerations support the conclusion that only a state largely or completely uncontested in its quest to dominate the planet from space would be able to do. While states have often failed to counteract the threatening measures of their adversaries, a balancing failure of this magnitude is difficult to imagine occurring in the contemporary world, which is marked by a wide distribution of economic and technological capabilities. The creation of an Earth Net thus presupposes the existence of what it aims to achieve, something approaching a planet-wide military dominance, a situation that no state, given the existence of

Table 9.2 **Planetary Geopolitics and Earth Net**

	Earth Space Features	Implications for Effort to Establish	Implications if Established
Distribution	Economic & technological capabilities widely distributed	Make very difficult to establish	Exploitation of space resources & energy likely to reinforce planetray domination
Proximity	Earth space is proximate to all points on Earth's surface	No state has significant positional advantage	Ability to readily threaten all assists planetary domination
Ascendancy	Earth space is ascendant over all points on Earth's surface	Provides incentives to attempt & resist	Enables planetary domination
Integrality	Earth space is highly integral	Makes asymmetrical response easier & symmetrical response more dangerous	Assists planetary domination
Extraterritoriality	Earth space is extraterritorial realm	No state has advantage	De facto annexation & governance of all space activities

large numbers of nuclear weapons in the hands of many states, now has or is likely to soon have.[16]

If, however, one state were able somehow to deploy an Earth Net capable of militarily dominating Earth space and everything beneath it, the anarchic state system would be replaced by some form of planetary world government. While the prospects of this outcome appear low due to the dim prospects for creating such an orbiting infrastructure in the face of blocking efforts by other states, the mere possibility of this outcome is something all great powers are likely to view with a combination of furtive aspiration and fearful anticipation. If such a planetary dominance from space were achieved, the ascendant state could sustain its rule by exploiting the panoptic potentials of satellite webs and by exploiting the energy and mineral resources of orbital and solar space, thus ending international history on Earth. Overall, the final step of the von Braun stairway to heaven is something of a lead zeppelin: extremely difficult to loft and prone to catastrophic crash or crush.

Beyond these distributional aspects of Earth Net scenarios, other positional geopolitical factors indicate that an Earth Net, if created, would have significant advantages in dominating the planet. First, features of the astrosphere and its relationship to the other parts of the planet strongly indicate that orbital space is an axial region. Because orbital space is so proximate to all terrestrial places on Earth, it affords ready access to every place. But even more important, orbital space is ascendant over all locations on the planet's surface, providing significant positional advantages to those actors capable of traversing and garrisoning it. Because of these features, an Earth Net would pose a severe threat to all states, and it would be difficult for other states to effectively challenge or overturn. Second, the astrosphere has strong integral tendencies because of the character of orbital paths. With the exception of geosynchronous orbit, the orbital paths of satellites pass over vast swaths of the planet's surface, and no state can deploy space vehicles over only its territory. Given this, extending territorial sovereign space vertically beyond the atmosphere into near Earth space would effectively foreclose the use of orbital space. Because of these integral tendencies, orbital space is difficult to effectively partition and will tend to come into the hands of one actor or one regime, or no one, if extensively degraded. Third, because Earth space is an extraterritorial medium touching on the territory of all states, and because it has such strong integral tendencies, a state militarily dominating it would be able to effectively annex it and thus control all space activities and reap their benefits, further bolstering its dominance.

What do the propositions of geopolitical theory indicate about the Clarke-Sagan Whole Earth Security program? In simple terms, all the geopolitical factors making the von Braunian projects difficult to realize and undesirable make the Clarke-Sagan easy to realize and desirable. The Clarke-Sagan program pushes world order out of anarchy to mutual restraining negarchy, while the von Braun program pushes toward world hierarchical government. But the key fact of interstate rivalry, which fuels the quest to realize the von Braun projects, impedes realizing the Whole Earth Security projects. Yet the widespread distribution of economic, technological, and military capabilities impeding the realization of planetary domination means that escaping the perils of anarchy through mutual restraint is appealing and feasible. Because the astrosphere is an axial region due to its proximity and ascendancy, the Clarke-Sagan project of strategic neutralization should be appealing to all states, except those aspiring to system-wide domination. The fact that Earth space has integral tendencies rendering it difficult to partition makes the provisions of the Outer Space Treaty guaranteeing free passage and prohibiting sovereign appropriation particularly suitable for the realization of the security and economic interests of all states, except those seeking general domination. The fact that orbital space is small in effective distance and easily degraded by space debris gives all spacefaring states a strong incentive to avoid weapons tests and to establish rules of the road to prevent its degradation. Because orbital space is an extraterritorial medium touching on the territory of all states but occupied by no one, it is particularly well-suited for strategic neutralization and for governance regimes facilitating its just and equitable employment.

Finally, there is the question of distinctiveness. With high distinctiveness between civil and military technologies, restraints are much easier to achieve. Because there are many different space technologies, calculations of their distinctiveness are potentially complex and indeterminate. The technologies employed in military information satellites and in civilian Earth monitoring are essentially identical, making any restraint of only military applications very difficult. The technologies employed in ballistic missiles are generally similar—but not identical—to those employed in civilian satellite launch vehicles. Solid fuels are widely used in military systems but not for civilian launches; the central military task of pinpoint terrestrial targeting has no civilian corollary. Ballistic missile tests are vital but impossible to hide. It should thus be possible to build an effective arms control regime for ballistic missiles without foreclosing civilian launch capabilities. Overall the propositions of geopolitical theory applied to Earth space geography and contemporary technological capabilities demonstrate that the Clarke-Sagan Whole Earth Security programs offer an effective path to security, avoiding both system crash and crush.

Light Webs, High Vistas, and the Planetary Panopticon

The use of satellites in Earth orbit to transmit and gather information and knowledge, championed by the Clarke-Sagan program, has been one of the hallmarks of the Space Age. Satellites providing information services are commonly divided into three distinct clusters: communication, remote sensing of the Earth (including weather satellites), and navigational services. As we saw earlier, military employment of the high vistas offered by Earth-orbiting satellites has been extensive and has been intimately connected both to preparations for nuclear war and to arms control verification. On the civil side, comsats, Earthsats, and navsats have been extensively deployed by growing numbers of governments and corporations, and together account for most commercially profitable space activities. Because these information satellite systems have been revenue generating, their payoffs, both direct and indirect, have been subject to several careful studies tabulating their benefits.[17] But such studies rarely consider the impacts of civil infosats on world order. Have the expectations of Clarke, White, and others of changes in global consciousness and identity been vindicated? Or are these systems enabling comprehensive surveillance, a planetary panopticon?

Anticipations by Clarke and others that the extensive deployment of comsats would produce much higher levels of communicative interaction at global distances have certainly been fully vindicated. Although comsats are only one component of a planet-spanning telecommunications infrastructure that also includes submarine and transcontinental fiber optic cables and microwave transmitters, the past several decades have witnessed an explosive growth in the volumes of information that are transmitted about the planet, as well as vast increases in the number of individuals using these systems. Virtually every facet of economy, society, and government is being significantly affected by the global information systems of the internet in ways that defy easy impact assessment.

But the main anticipation by Clarke and others, that this expanded information interconnectivity would produce the emergence of a new common global consciousness and identity, and corresponding dilution of traditional national affiliations, has most definitely *not* happened globally. In many ways, the emergence of an electronic global village has produced effects opposite those anticipated by Clarke, McLuhan, and others. The nearly limitless expansion in the number of broadcast channels and the capability of the internet to connect highly specialized groups has powerfully enabled ever smaller and more dispersed groups to coalesce into cyber communities. Nation-states have been as much subject to powerful centrifugal and disintegrative pressures as challenged by universal alternatives. And far from passively accepting their erosion, nation-states have increasingly sought to wall off, filter, direct, and manipulate information flows. Anticipations of connectivity have been abundantly realized, but anticipations of convergence have been fatally confounded.

Various "whole Earth" photographs have generated extensive excitement and commentary, with anticipations of catalyzing a humanity-wide WE identity to match the high and growing levels of material interdependence generated by the globalization of machine civilization. While these images have been extensively employed by the global environmental movement, the mental planetary re-placing they were anticipated to catalyze has *not* occurred with sufficient scale and intensity to subvert national identities or underpin robust global institutions.

While people may *know* they live on a highly interdependent and vulnerable planet, they do not directly *experience* this reality, and their lived worlds remain extremely localized and diverse. Just as people have a hard time perceiving the features of space, they have difficulty accurately perceiving the whole Earth. Furthermore, as many have noted, Whole Earth imagery makes humanity, and its artifacts and destructions, invisible.[18] Also, the debasing ubiquity of such reproduced imagery, their widespread use by advertisers to sell commodities, and the incapacity of environmentalists to situate and privilege Earth images in ceremonies and rituals rob the new planetary images of their full potential to shape identity and consciousness. But environmental sensibilities are likely to grow as climate change becomes more disruptive, and Whole Earth imagery might become symbolically primary if civilization comprehensively greens.

Claims by White and others for a powerful "overview effect" transforming global consciousness are also suspect. Only tiny numbers of individuals (well under six hundred) have been in space, and they have drawn diverse implications from their experience. It is notable that the Apollo astronaut Harrison Schmitt, the first scientist to visit the moon, returned to Earth and served in the US Senate, where he was active in advancing the interests of the fossil fuel industry. Where the astronaut Edgar Mitchell had a spiritual epiphany, and the astronaut Russell Schweickart experienced global interconnectivity, Schmitt saw a new resource base. In sum, the impact of even direct space experience of the overview effect seems to be significantly shaped by cognitive predispositions rather than directly simulative of a particular Earth-regarding narrative.[19]

On a more mundane level, satellite remote sensing has emerged as an important space application. Most notable are weather satellites, which have greatly increased the ability of meteorologists to track weather patterns, particularly severe storms such as hurricanes; this information has greatly reduced the human casualties and property damage from such events. Starting with the American Landsat satellites launched in the 1970s, numerous other such systems have been deployed by many countries and private corporations, and information from such systems is now routinely employed by a wide variety of resource managers to map patterns in forests and farmlands, water resources, pollution, and land degradation.[20] Such observation platforms have also been deployed for a wide range of Earth system science data collection (oceanography, Earth-sun interactions, geodesy, topographic mapping, ice-sea interactions, many features of the atmosphere, and ecosystems—forests, fish, desertification, and pollution). Taken together, these information-gathering platforms have been a major feature of the more general transparency revolution. Such synoptic mapping information, augmenting aerial sources and digitized in standardized formats of geographic information systems (GIS), has become widely available to multiple communities of users.

People have been using the stars to find their way about the terrestrial Earth since prehistoric times, but signals from artificial satellites have almost completely replaced earlier techniques of celestial navigation and printed maps. Navigation satellites did not loom large in early anticipations of space activities. The US GPS was developed for military purposes, to improve the accuracy of weapons delivery, but that application has been dwarfed by the largely unanticipated explosion in civilian uses. GPS has rapidly emerged as a central part of the global information infrastructure, providing navigational information for large numbers of ships, airplanes, trucks, and automobiles.[21] Mapping services of virtually every variety have come to depend on GPS locational information and have enabled billions of users to locate themselves with unprecedented accuracy and at negligible cost. GPS location and timing information has also become a backbone of the dispersed telecommunications and internet services brought about by the very rapid penetration of mobile devices, such as the iconic iPhone, that are now used by several billion people. And the widely anticipated next big thing in information technology, the "internet of things" (where computers embedded in machinery and appliances of every variety routinely exchange information), is also crucially dependent on satellite location and timing services.

These wondrous developments have been much discussed as bestowing a wide array of benefits and have rapidly changed wide swaths of human activity, from the delivery of pornography and demagogic tweets and the tracking of lost pets, through the conduct of terrorist attacks and counterterrorism drone strikes, to banking, retail shopping, and journalism. Information technology advocates promote these innovations in strongly libertarian terms, celebrating their ability to empower individuals, expand transparency, and diminish hierarchies. But the dark side of these new capabilities has also rapidly emerged. These new satellite-dependent information systems have enabled comprehensive corporate and state surveillance with profound implications for privacy and freedom.[22] Taken together, these new space-enabled information technologies make possible the penetration of hierarchical power down to the social atomic level of the individual, with planetary scope, making possible new forms of totalitarian rule far more complete than ever before possible.

The impacts of information satellites, while extremely varied, strongly support the proposition that activities in Earth space intensify planetary closure by increasing interaction and interdependence, not the opposite effects anticipated by the space expansionist notions of opening the frontier. The consequences of these information satellites are radically unlike what occurred when terrestrial frontiers were opened. When the Europeans explored the global ocean, many effects were felt in Europe, but among them were not increased interaction and interdependence *within* Europe. Sending ships into the Pacific Ocean did not reduce the difficulties of communicating between Berlin and Paris, did not improve maps of Europe, and did not make weapons delivery more rapid in Europe. If one thinks entering the space part of the planet is leaving Earth, these increasing interactions among terrestrial actors are unexpected. Ironically, orbital light webs supporting the planetary information infrastructure are made possible by exploiting the intensive frontier of microspace, not the extensive frontier expansions touted by space enthusiasts. Also, because important parts of the planet's information infrastructure are located in orbital space, potential space wars will be occurring not at some distant frontier but in what amounts to the utility room of our crowded planetary apartment building.

The Microfrontier and Intensive Growth

The rapid deployment of planetary information systems and the staggering advances in miniaturization suggest a new and unexpected answer to the puzzle of closure and growth animating Earth and space debates. It is instructive to consider an immensely significant, but rarely noted, divergence in trends in the scales of human observations and manipulations over the past several centuries (see Figure 9.2). Since the invention of the telescope, human capacities to observe the cosmos have increased massively; modern astronomy now maps a universe billions of light years in diameter. A similarly enormous advance in observations down in size has also occurred, as advances in microscopic technology allow single atoms to be observed. Modern science now observes phenomena across

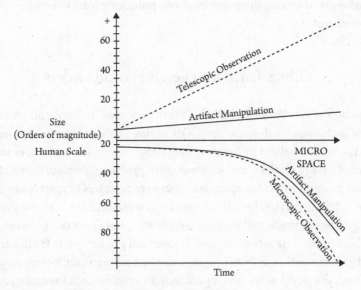

Figure 9.2 Macroscopic and Microscopic Observation and Manipulation

some forty-six orders of magnitude, from the observable universe to the diameter of an electron.[23]

These astounding parallel advances in macro and micro observational capability have been accompanied by a steadily widening divergence in the scale of human capacities to manipulate. The largest human artifacts have not increased much in orders of magnitude since early megastructures like the Great Wall of China. The largest contemporary artifacts, the communication and transportation networks girding the globe, are limited to the size of this planet. But small-scale manipulations now routinely produce artifacts such as microchips and complex synthetic molecules that are close to the scale of atoms.

To put this great divergence in artifact size in perspective, imagine what humanity would be doing if large-scale artifact construction had proceeded by as many orders of magnitude from the scale of human bodies as has small-scale construction. Such human artifacts would encompass multiple galaxies and many hundreds of billions of stellar systems. Compared to activities this large, even the most visionary space projects are vastly dwarfed. This divergence explains why the great frontier for human activities during the Space Age has been intensive and microscopic, not extensive and macroscopic. When the physicist Richard Feynman famously argued in 1959 that "there is plenty of room at the bottom," he was illuminating a path for expansion that has been far more realized than the manifestos of outer space expansionists.[24] Fuller's ephemeralization, not megatechnics, has prevailed. The technological future has turned out to be much smaller—and vastly more capacious—than most anticipated. The closing of extensive frontiers on the Earth has been followed not by stagnation but by explosive growth along the microfrontiers, producing intensive rather than extensive expansion.

Orbita, Earth Rescue, and World Orders

Alongside the von Braun and Clarke-Sagan programs, realized and unrealized, are the ambitious Earth space proposals of the Tsiolkovskians to alter and expand the human habitat by building mega-engineering infrastructures to solve terrestrial energy, material, and environmental problems. Because the realization of these projects will entail space activities several orders of magnitude greater than everything that has been done thus far, it is reasonable to assume that their macropolitical impacts will be quite significant. Thus arises the question: How will these macro-artifacts shape world order and the prospects for hierarchical world government? In approaching this momentous question, it is useful to consider both the world order presuppositions for erecting such immense projects, as well as their likely consequences once in place (Figure 9.3).

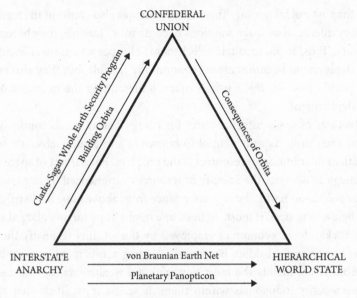

Figure 9.3 Impacts of Alternative Earth Space Programs on World Order

In moving from the modest accomplished uses of Earth space to the megaprojects of the Tsiolkovskians, the prospective terrain of activity expands considerably, out of the tight confines of the lower gravity well and into the vaster arena of high Earth orbits, including Luna, and the even larger spaces of the inner solar system with its Earth-crossing asteroids. As this enlarged realm comes into play, the "special places" geography of geosynchronous orbit, the Lagrange points, Luna, and the asteroid swarm become practically important.

Can Earth space infrastructures play decisive roles in solving Earth problems related to energy supply, mineral resources, and environmental deterioration? There are certainly stupendously large quantities of energy and material potentially to be harvested, but sheer quantity alone does not demonstrate that space solutions are superior to terrestrial ones. These Earth-rescue schemes suffer from a severe double standard—exaggerating the barriers to solving these problems on Earth while understating the difficulties of space infrastructural solutions. This is perhaps most pronounced with space-based geo-engineering for reducing solar insolation with shades or particle rings. Reducing terrestrial carbon emissions is likely to be much easier and cheaper than deploying immense infrastructures around the planet, a scheme that flunks the Rube Goldberg test. Deploying photovoltaic cells on rooftops is likely to remain easier and cheaper than fabricating and deploying them in orbit. Prodigious quantities of metals are to be found in the asteroid belt, but recycling and use of crustily abundant materials such as iron, aluminum, and silicon can meet terrestrial needs with less effort than asteroidal mining. These space schemes also confront the feasibility-necessity dilemma: as space solutions become more feasible, they become less necessary. Thus, as photovoltaic cells become cheaper and more efficient, their space deployment becomes more economically feasible, but they also become more readily used on the Earth's surface, undercutting the necessity of their space deployment.

Advocates of space infrastructures for energy and minerals routinely characterize their projects as beneficial to humanity and assume absolute scarcity rather than distribution of resources is the problem. For harvest of space metals and energy to alleviate the scarcity of resources experienced by large numbers of poor people on Earth, the new abundance from above must be distributed to those below who need it most. At best, one might hope for an enlarged version of the trickle-down economics employed by the wealthy to justify their special tax breaks and subsidies. Because the leading actors moving to exploit the high frontier are mainly the most powerful and wealthy states, and the strata of superwealthy individuals within them, it seems most likely that tapping space abundance will further exacerbate already severe international and class stratifications.

Advocates of Earth-rescue infrastructures propose technological solutions to problems with often intractable political dimensions, but actually deploying large space structures is likely to require the resolution of many political disputes. Given their magnitude and the geography of Earth space, significant civil orbital infrastructures are unlikely to be constructed without the cessation, or at least deep moderation, of interstate rivalries. Assuming resources for infrastructures will come from Luna, a governance regime for it will be necessary.[25] Conflicts may occur early over the water-bearing lunar poles. Although interstate competitive dynamics may propel the first stages of the erection of Orbita, anything approaching a full infrastructure will be built only if all spacefaring actors accept a fairly comprehensive regime allocating rights and property and restraining military activity. Military competition is likely to be quite incompatible with mega-infrastructures due to the extreme vulnerability of such facilities to destruction by high-velocity objects.[26] The ease with which destructive debris can be created gives any spacefaring actor a robust spoiler capability to bring down the house. Even if the costs of building megastructures decline to ranges where they are economically feasible, such apparatuses will still be immense capital investments and are unlikely to be built without strong assurances that they will be safe from catastrophic destruction. In thinking about historical analogies for the erection of Orbita, the construction of the Chunnel under the English Channel between France and England is a good model: unthinkable without robust interstate peace and cooperation. Building Orbita will require global political deals that will be difficult to achieve, but it would push world order out of anarchy, realizing the Clarke-Sagan aspiration to pacify world orders through space ventures. At least for Earth space, nothing much will rise without a fairly large degree of convergence, as suggested by the French cosmotheologian Teilhard de Chardin.

If Orbita is constructed, the planet's human habitat will be decisively altered. What were previously empty voids would be industrialized, the primordial matter of Luna and the asteroids processed and fabricated into structures more massive than any currently found on the terrestrial Earth. Once in place, the belts and rings of Orbita will constitute an eighth continent, but one whose geography will be radically unlike the landmasses of the terrestrial Earth. The erection of Orbita will further enclose the planet, its empty attic transformed into a complex of machines and infrastructures. Orbita also requires an ominous Faustian bargain because humanity must permanently maintain this orbital machine empire or suffer severe consequences. If terrestrial energy and material are provided by orbital infrastructures, new vulnerabilities will loom over the world economy, from terrorist attack, politically motivated sabotage, and accidents and breakdowns difficult to foresee, as memorably envisioned in Ben Bova's *Powersat*. If space systems provide a significant share of world energy needs, then another major part of the planet's technological infrastructure would be greatly accelerated, as energy would be produced and transported at effectively instantaneous speeds, like information.[27] And if such megastructures decay and cannot be adequately maintained, humanity could be saddled with a colossal orbital "rust belt."

While the creation of Orbita is likely to push the world political system out of anarchy, its existence is likely to pose a permanent threat of world hierarchical government.[28] In simple terms, *who controls Orbita controls the Earth*. Occupying the planetary high ground, Orbita has a positional ascendancy over the terrestrial Earth, inherently creating the possibility of its masters dominating the rest of the planet. Orbita might produce a planetary-scale analog to the hydraulic despotisms in early agricultural societies dependent on mega-infrastructures for irrigation. These civil space infrastructures will possess intrinsic military potentials of great power, making for low distinctiveness. Routinely slinging around large masses at high velocities means a powerful bombardment capability will always be close a hand. "Like the Cyclops of old," spacekind "will be able hurl rocks at the earthlings."[29] With sunsats collecting and transmitting immense energies, powerful beam weapons will also never be far removed. Once Orbita arises, the preservation of liberty on Earth will depend permanently on the ability of institutional arrangements to prevent its immense military potentials from being deployed against the terrestrial Earth.

These features of an Orbita infrastructure, and the threats they pose, also undermine the desirability of colonizing Earth space with large human settlements, as proposed by Bernal, O'Neill, and others. Creating and operating Orbita will be a very high-capital- and low-labor-intensive enterprise, with heavy reliance on robotics and a small, highly trained human workforce that would be rotated, like those on offshore oil rigs and submarines. Because most of Orbita will be above the Van Allan radiation belts, high radiation levels are also likely to inhibit early permanent human settlement. But once the transportation, mining, and fabrication capabilities needed to build Orbita are in place, the possibility of building Bernal-O'Neill canister habitats probably emerges. Once these settlements have significant populations, they become agents with the position and skills to potentially seize control of Orbita and cast the rest of terrestrial humanity into a position of permanent subservience. Should these colonial populations occupying the planet's high ground hold strong space expansionist views, and/ or come to develop a distinct identity as "above" the humans "left behind" on the terrestrial Earth, their incentives and inclinations for planetary mastery could be very high, as might their willingness to do what is necessary to achieve their Übermensch destinies.

Regardless of whether substantial human populations come to permanently inhabit canisters in Earth orbit, the creation of Orbita is very likely to make solar system colonization much more likely. Once asteroids are moved and mined, and once the technologies for the fabrication of large space structures have been extensively demonstrated, a human diaspora into solar space will be primed to proceed. This is, of course, an important part of the appeal of Orbita projects for the Tsiolkovskians seeking outward migration. But if a solar space diaspora entails significant dangers not acknowledged by their advocates, then the strong links between achieving Orbita and solar colonial expansion provide further reasons not to industrialize the Earth's astrosphere.

Whatever its impacts on world political order, the creation of Orbita will mark the beginning of a new epoch in Earth geological history, which can be referred to as the *Astrocene*. The Astrocene is the Earth geological epoch in which resources and energies produced or gathered by extraterrestrial human activities influence the Earth's geophysical and ecological systems. In the largest frame, all periods of Earth history have been fundamentally conditioned by astronomical events, such as variations of the output of the sun and asteroidal collisions. But the Astrocene epoch resulting from the erection of Orbita will differ from previous cosmic influences on the planet because of the essential enabling role of humans and their machines, which makes the Astrocene another, but very distinct, phase of the Anthropocene. As with the emergence of the Anthropocene, the Astrocene will occur in phases, first as resources and energies from space are detectable, then as they become influential in planetary balances, and finally as they come to dominate them.

Spaceship Earth, Technocracy, and the Industrial Heavens

As a final step in assessing the many prospective space expansionist megaprojects for Earth space, it is useful to evaluate the "spaceship Earth" construct of the Fuller Earth vision, and the logic of viewing and governing– and reconstructing—the planet as a comprehensive ship-like artifact.[30] Calling the Earth a spaceship is both descriptive and programmatic, attempting to justify a specific prospective agenda by linking it to a particular descriptive characterization. The ways in which the Earth is *not* like a spaceship point to fundamental limits of the mega-engineering agenda, while illuminating the ways in which such pursuits are largely politically utopian and, if realized, likely to be politically dystopian.

Viewing the Earth as a spaceship captures some essential features of the planetary situation, but is also significantly misleading. The Earth, like a ship, is situated in a vast and inhospitable realm and largely closed. And, like a spaceship, the Earth is marked by high levels of internal interdependence and interaction. But this analogy also misleads in more important ways. Ships are completely built artifacts, while the Earth, aside from a thin skein of human infrastructures and machine networks, was obviously not designed and built by humans, and the prospects for making the Earth fully artifactual are very low. As a candidate for the master metaphor of the human situation on Planetary Earth, the spaceship also erases the extensive violence, domination, and stratification marking globalization and its contemporary outcome. There is also a fundamental difference between celestial mechanics and navigational choice. The Earth, as it hurtles through space on its orbital path, is essentially going in circles and its path utterly beyond human choice and control. In contrast, ships can be steered to a great number of destinations, at the choosing of their human pilots. Astronomers can predict, with high levels of accuracy, the position of the Earth in space many millennia into the future, while the future location of a particular ship is utterly unpredictable because dependent on the choices of its human navigators. Characterizing the Earth as ship-like greatly amplifies in fundamentally misleading ways the prospect for steering.

While the technocratic hierarchic rule of ships has long served as a model for the creation of such regimes on land, there is a fundamental difference between all ships and full human societies and polities. Ships are almost always *total* in their hierarchic and technocratic rule but are always fundamentally *incomplete* as human polities and societies. No one lives their entire life on a ship, and everyone on a ship is from somewhere else. The human regimes of ships are always appendages to more complete human societies and polities situated on land. People may be conceived, be born, and die on ships, but their primary social and political associations are inevitably on terra firma. The destination of ships is typically set before boarding and decisions about destinations are never made democratically by the crew and passengers. Given these crucial differences, the ways in which ships are *not* like polities are more important than the ways they are similar.

Despite their important insights, neither the global village nor spaceship Earth can adequately serve to guide disoriented humanity. To be fully suitable, a master metaphor for Planetary Earth must incorporate its tumultuous and uneven process of formation, its accelerating pace of change, its fragmented authority structures, its potentials for novel catastrophes, and its severely limited steering capacities, along with a realistic range of its positive possibilities. Perhaps these several essential features of Planetary Earth and its past and future trajectories might be simply and vividly captured with metaphor of "the global debris mat," a sprawling and uneven assemblage emerging from many asymmetric historical collisions and now moving on a mist-shrouded, uncharted, and dimly lit river with a strengthening current and partially hidden rocks, but having limited raft-like possibilities for organization and steering.[31] While not very glamorous or heroic, competent and inclusive "raftcraft" is now probably our most realistic positive possibility.

Lost in Earth Space

The first steps of humans beyond the atmosphere are an extended story of disorientations and misplacements and have partially confounded the goals animating them and the anticipations preceding them. Seeking to improve their national security, states have exploited space to create a planet-spanning system to very rapidly deliver nuclear explosives, thus making nuclear war more likely and jeopardizing not only national security but also civilizational and species survival. Instead of opening a new frontier to reduce planetary closure, activities in the small and already crowded and degraded space part of the planet have intensified global closure, interdependence, and vulnerability. Instead of helping to forge a common planetary identity, new space-enabled communication links have exacerbated fragmentation. Inspiring new views of the Earth as a whole from space have failed to trigger a consciousness and identity revolution sufficient to diminish, let alone replace, nationalism and other parochial identities.

Overall, actual space activities have done more to increase planetary-scale interdependence and vulnerability than to planetize identity and consciousness or to catalyze new institutions. As a result the fundamental contradiction between planetary realities and parochial institutions and mindsets continues to grow. The fact that fundamental survival interests require new security practices and world institutions has not, thus far, been enough to bring them into existence.

Obsolete identity patterns robustly reproduce, despite their incompatibility with essential interests. Instead of thinking globally and acting locally, most people are increasingly *acting globally* while still *thinking locally*. The real world hurtles toward greater material interdependence and catastrophic vulnerability while identities and institutions resolutely face distant pasts.

The simple error of excluding ballistic missiles from the space story massively corrupts conventional and space expansionist assessments of the overall net impact of space activities. Space weapons have added to the intensity of this violence interdependence, and thus the obsolescence of the state mode of protection, by greatly increasing the velocity of violence, as well as making second-strike forces more precarious. Given the magnitude of the consequences of nuclear war, the net overall impact of actual space activities must be judged to be negative for increasing the probability of this major catastrophic and existential threat to civilization and humanity. Despite being an unknown known, arms control is the single most positive space program, and the single most important priority for a space program focused on catastrophic and existential threat reduction is the completion of the global nuclear and space weapons arms control project.

Properly putting ballistic missiles and the nuclear question on the ledger sheet of space activities produces another unexpected revision in thinking about space expansionism. It is widely observed—and patently obvious—that advocates of ambitious human space activities routinely exaggerate the consequences of those activities, both actual and prospective. But the opposite is actually true, at least for actual space activities. Space expansionists fundamentally believe that large-scale space activities *will* have species-transformative consequences, and they yearn to demonstrate these potentials by embarking on vast space projects. But in excluding ballistic missiles in their inventories of space activities, they are actually overlooking the space activity that has already had—and continues to have—the most significant implications for the survival of humanity. Space expansionists thus routinely *underestimate* the actual impacts of space, failing to recognize just how consequential their enterprise has been in shaping the prospects for civilizational and species survival.

Fortunately the next big things, the Earth Net of the von Braunians and Orbita of the Tsiolkovskians, face daunting hurdles and are unlikely to be realized any time soon, thus saving the planet from various calamities, including domination by a hierarchical world government. The features of Earth space, combined with the wide distribution of power, make the Clarke-Sagan program of strategic neutralization both particularly appealing and readily feasible. Building the Orbita of the Tsiolkovskians is advanced as a means to solve major Earth problems, but its appeal over terrestrial alternatives is doubtful. Exploiting the integral and ascendant planetary high ground would greatly intensify the closure of the Earth, produce a whole new set of vulnerabilities and dependencies and push the planet into a new geological era. Overall, the larger the space activity, the greater the potential for disastrous outcomes. While the high levels of planetary interdependence, interaction, and closure make the planet particularly well-suited for a movement out of anarchy and toward a modified anarchical or negarchical political order quite compatible with the preservation of liberty and the provision of security, the fact that this remains so elusive in practice should give serious pause to those who envision expanding even further into the solar system, onto terrain likely to be far less accommodating to the goals of security, freedom, and species survival.

Solar Space, Island Earth, and the Ends of Humanity

> If there are globes in the heavens similar to our earth, do we vie with them over who occupies the better portion of the universe?
> —Johannes Kepler (1610)[1]

> Short of a revolution in the heart of man and the nature of states, by what miracle could interplanetary space be preserved from military use?
> —Raymond Aron (1966)[2]

> When mankind moves out from earth into space, we carry our problems with us.
> —Freeman Dyson (1979)[3]

Here (Will) Be Dragons

Before humans ventured into space, they sent their best friends (dogs) and cousins (monkeys). One of America's trained astrochimps, named Ham, was lofted in 1961 into a suborbital flight, but the mission did not go as planned. Ham was subjected to greater than expected g-forces, and his capsule took on a great deal of water when it splashed down in the unexpectedly choppy Atlantic, far off course. When his little spaceship was finally hoisted onto the naval recovery vessel and opened, out came Ham, "a thoroughly infuriated space veteran" who "bared his fangs and bit anything, human or otherwise, he could reach."[4] Ham's transformation should stand as a cautionary fable for thinking about the consequences of large-scale space expansion: what goes out very friendly may eventually come back very unfriendly.

Whatever role space activities in the immediate vicinity of the Earth may play in the trajectory of humanity and the Earth, the ultimate vocation of space expansionism is the vastly grander evolution of humanity into a multiworld species through the large-scale colonization of other celestial bodies. The advocates of the Tsiolkovsky programs, as we have seen, view this expansive diaspora as playing an ultimately central role in the flourishing of life in the universe. While the feasibility of these projects remains uncertain, space expansionists, with quasi-religious fervor, view their desirability, even necessity and inevitability, as certain. And while this cosmic expansion may have important milestones, its ultimate potential is as limitless as the cosmos itself. The realization of even the first steps in these visionary programs might take many decades, if not centuries, to complete. But the ultimate confidence space expansionists have in the desirability of these audacious ventures gives value to every step, however modest, of this epic cosmic ascent.

The fabulous and captivating space expansionist account of this grand ascent is, however, marred by an important shift and a curious gap that provide openings for seeing this venture in a radically different light. When habitat expansionists unexpectedly shift the agent and beneficiary of this vast enterprise from *humanity* to *life*, they implicitly acknowledge that the human future in solar space will be eclipsed by something larger and different. But they provide only stray hints as to how and when humanity's exit from the cosmic story occurs. While expansionists certainly acknowledge (but rarely emphasize) that the path of human expansion across the heavens will have its share of disasters and setbacks, they rarely consider how their venture might produce a full dead-end for humanity. Most important, Tsiolkovsky habitat expansionists largely drop war and large-scale violence from their scenarios, paralleling how expansionists sidestep the role of actual space activities in amplifying the paramount planetary security problem of nuclear war. Even advocates of the Clarke-Sagan programs, sharply critical of Earth space militarization, generally ignore scenarios of violent conflict in solar space expansion. But if war does occur in solar space, then a plausible explanation for how humans exit the cosmic story emerges, and the desirability of the expansionist project disappears.

The theoretical lenses of full geopolitical theory, being ideally crafted to close this security-violence gap in solar expansionist thinking, illuminate how solar expansion could produce the termination of humanity. When the pervasive ascentionist assumptions of improvement through elevation are discarded, and the insights of geopolitics are employed to critically assess the likely consequences of this vast and seemingly so hopeful enterprise, a very unappealing picture of the humanization of the solar system emerges. In broad terms, geopolitical theory expects that human expansion across solar space will produce a Solar Archipelago with a radically novel combination of very inauspicious features. This expansion will probably produce a cascade of undesirable outcomes of sufficient severity to pose catastrophic and existential threats to humanity and the Earth.

The argument proceeds in three steps. First, a multistep scenario of successful expansion is summarized and its implausible assumptions are exposed. Second, the heart of the argument, in seven sections, the features of the Solar Archipelago, are analyzed with the propositions of geopolitical theory to generate specific expectations about the consequences of solar expansion, and related geophysical and geohistorical analogies are evaluated. Third, in two sections, how solar space colonization might alleviate, amplify, and activate catastrophic and existential threats and the broader cosmic implications of this new view of the human prospect in space are considered.

The (Improbable) Solar Expansion
Success Scenario

To start this assessment, it is useful to sketch a scenario of successful solar space colonization. This baseline scenario can then be subjected to two questions: How probable is its realization? and What do the propositions of geopolitics indicate about the likely consequences of successful solar space expansion?

Building a Type II civilization employing the full resources of the solar system is obviously a multistage process, four of which can be identified (see Table 10.1). This baseline scenario is not a prediction of what will happen, but rather is a summation of the state-of-the-art thinking of what space expansionists think could—and should—happen. This is a surprise-free scenario, and given the many uncertainties involved, the realization of this future would be surprising. It assumes that technological advance will proceed incrementally within the perimeters of currently understood and reasonably anticipated scientific knowledge. Cybernetics and robotics will be advancing, but not to an intelligence explosion producing an ASI; nanotechnology will be making more advanced materials possible, but not self-replicating nanobots; speeds of transportation will be rising, but faster-than-light and time travel will remain impossible; and astronomy and astrobiology will be advancing, but no extraterrestrial intelligent civilization will have been detected or arrived. Most important, the benchmarks of the scenario are geographical, technological, and demographic, and it is assumed that political impediments and conflicts will not occur.

Stage One is reached when small colonies have been established on Mars and asteroidal orbital alteration has been demonstrated. Despite visions of domed cities on Mars, underground habitats are likely to be more viable, but tunneling will be initially limited. Stage One expansion will not be sustainable without the continuing commitment of resources from the Earth. It is unlikely that species radiation to adapt to extraterrestrial environments will have even begun. Several important variants of Stage One concern whether the heavy or light variants of the EOS programs have been realized. If the construction of heavy Earth orbital infrastructure is under way or accomplished, asteroidal orbital alteration will be occurring for both planetary protection and resource extraction. If these steps

Table 10.1 **Four Stages of Solar Space Colonization**

	Features	*Variants*
Stage Four	Kuiper Belt and Oort Cloud colonization; extensive species radiation; population in billions	Extent of interstellar voyages and colonization; propulsion technologies at appreciable light-speed fraction
Stage Three	Martian urbanization; numerous colonies on asteroids and Saturn's moons; early species radiation	With or without terraforming; negligible or extensive trade
Stage Two	Large self-sustaining Martian colonies; small asteroidal colonies; small outpost colonies on the moons of Saturn; population in hundreds of thousands to low millions	With or without species radiation; with or without fusion
Stage One	Small Earth-dependent colonies on Mars; rudimentary asteroidal alteration; population in low thousands	Heavy or light Earth orbital infrastructures; Earth united or divided

are realized, the human population living off the Earth will number in the hundreds to a few thousands.

Stage Two is reached when large self-sustaining colonies exist on Mars, and smaller, not self-sustaining outpost colonies have been established on asteroids and the moons of Saturn. Tunneling on Mars will be extensive. Asteroidal orbit alteration will be extensively developed and routinely conducted, and efforts to turn asteroids into habitable worlds will be starting. Small outpost colonies will be on the moons of Saturn. The Kuiper Belt and the Oort Cloud will be extensively explored and mapped. Human expansion in the solar system will no longer be dependent on continuing efforts and resources from Earth. Stage Two will see the beginnings of species radiation, but spacekind will still be recognizable variations of humans. Off-world human populations will number from the hundreds of thousands to a few million.

Stage Three expansion in solar space will be realized when Mars has extensive population centers and self-sustaining colonies exist on numerous asteroids and the moons of the outer planets. Non-self-sustaining colonies will exist in the Kuiper Belt and the Oort Cloud. Efforts to terraform Mars will be beginning. Species radiation will be under way, and essentially nonhuman intelligent life forms will be emerging in the solar system. Serious consideration of interstellar travel will be beginning. The total population of intelligent life forms in the solar system will number into the hundreds of millions to low billions.

Stage Four of expansion into the solar system will be realized when large self-sustaining cities and city-ships exist through the entire solar system. Enabled by species radiation and robotics, intelligent life forms will be living on many bodies in the solar system. Terraforming infrastructure will be extensive. Initial ventures across interstellar space will be under way. The total population of intelligent beings in the solar system will range into the billions.

A crucial additional parameter of this scenario is temporal: How much time will be required to realize these steps? Optimistic expansion timetables presuppose large and sustained investments in space, which are unlikely.[5] But it seems plausible that these steps might be accomplished over several centuries. However, this schedule assumes that the Earth will be willing and able to provide significant initial support for colonization. The question of how rapidly self-sufficient colonies could be established has direct implications for their ability to serve as hedges to terrestrial catastrophic and existential threats.

Based on the earlier analysis of technological feasibility, the solar expansion success scenario is probably *possible*, with critical uncertainties about health and artificial biospheres. But this scenario is also very *improbable* for many strong reasons. Inaction, failure, or debilitating conflict are more likely than success. Colonization may not be attempted because it is too difficult and expensive, or because of growing Earth problems and troubles. Off-Earth living could be too unhealthy for humans, and reproduction and child growth in low-gravity environments may be infeasible, confining viable habitat to spinable artificial bodies. Potent pathogens might evolve in novel space environments. Artificial ecosystems could be too difficult to create and sustain. People may not want to live on Mars or an asteroid, for the same reasons they do not live in the middle of the Sahara or Antarctica. Or colonization might be attempted and quickly fail, like Norse Vineland in Newfoundland or Scot Darien in Panama. Or a colony might be only minimally successful and linger as a remote, climate-stunted backwater, like early modern Iceland. Space colonies might be like the many failed societies analyzed by the geographer Jared Diamond in *Collapse*.[6] The small population of a space settlement might succumb to disease or debilitating internecine conflict. Conflicts over the limited number of metal-bearing asteroids might start early.[7] The sponsoring Earth agent might abandon its colony due to shifting priorities, insufficient resources, or diverting conflicts. If interstate rivalry propels colonization it will happen more rapidly but will also be more likely to involve violence sooner. If rivalrous states establish colonies, conflict between them might beggar and hobble all. There may be a vast gap between a colony that can be kept operational with continual inputs from Earth and one that is capable of persisting without any Earth support. If, as Sagan proposed, large-scale settlement is delayed until after major terrestrial problems have been solved, the prospects for success rise, while the rationales weaken and the time frames lengthen. And as colonization becomes imminent, doubts of the sort voiced here may lead to organized opposition.

The success scenario, and much of space expansionist thinking, operates with the implicit assumption that space settlement will be propelled by numerous capable agents committed to advancing the long-term success of humanity. This is a dubious assumption, given that the Earth's growing problems have yet to stimulate the emergence of numerous powerful agents committed to advancing even the species' short-term success. And if powerful actors were motivated by long-term species interest, colonization would be much less necessary.

The success scenario also operates with what can be called the Benign Parent Model of Terra-Colony Relations. In this approach, Earth lavishes resources on its space colonial offspring and benignly supervises their development until they are able to direct and support themselves. Constitutions for space polities embodying the best of Terran political wisdom are established. This model, however, is almost entirely at variance with the historical experience of terrestrial colonization and the incentives of relevant self-interested actors. To the extent states or corporations invest in space colonies, they will want to maintain control and reap the benefits of their investments. To the extent they anticipate colonial independence, they will not invest; if they do, they will try to keep colonies small and dependent.

The success scenario also assumes that different space ventures build on each other when they might subvert and impede one another. The two central projects, Mars colonization and asteroidal resource extraction, might be quite antagonistic. Wealth generated from space resources will most probably be repatriated to Earth, not plowed into space habitat construction. Asteroidal exploitation is likely to be capital- and robot-intensive, with a minimal human labor force rotating through small off-world bases, as on off-shore oil rigs. If resources from asteroids are the bonanza some anticipate, the beneficiaries of this wealth will not want colonies to contest their access and possession and can be expected to actively oppose colonization. The more space mining benefits terrestrial actors, the greater their incentive to impede space settlements. And once the bombardment potential of asteroidal orbital alteration technology becomes obvious, the dangers of independent space colonies might be sufficiently obvious to thwart their realization.

A long list of powerful barriers stand between colonization visions and accomplishment. Given the many obstacles that render successful space colonization at scale very improbable, it is extremely imprudent for humanity to view space colonization as a hedge against catastrophe or extinction. With low probabilities of success and significant moral hazards and opportunity costs, space colonization should not be considered a viable response to severe Earth problems and troubles.

Solar space expansion may be improbable, but is it desirable? If we could do it, would we want to do it? What will be the consequences of successful human expansion across the solar system? Might success be even more disastrous than failure? Answers to these questions are, of course, necessarily significantly speculative because there are many known unknowns and are sure to be significant unknown unknowns. But space expansionists express great certainty that the consequences of humanity's becoming a robustly spacefaring multiworld species will be positive for humanity, Terra, and life itself. This confident optimism is greater than what can realistically be known about outcomes. Geopolitical analysis of human expansion into solar space, proceeding in seven steps, provides a much darker anticipation.

Solar Geopolitics I: Anarchy, Violence Interdependence, and Asteroid Analogs

The most important system features are the pattern of authority (or lack thereof) and the level of violence interdependence. The authority structure of the Solar Archipelago will almost certainly trend toward anarchy. Initially, in Stage One of expansion, the system structure will be an extension of Earth's. Colonies will be small dependent appendages of whatever state, consortium of states, or world government created them. But when space colonies become politically independent of Earth, the system will become anarchic. Whether this occurs in Stage One or in Stage Two, it seems almost inevitable that polities on other bodies in the solar system will become politically independent from whatever entity on the Earth established them. Most space expansionists assume this will happen and see colonial autonomy as a major benchmark for the progress of the overall expansion project. Whether this occurs peacefully or through violent rebellion, space colony independence will shift the system structure of solar space to anarchy, where it is likely to stay permanently. As colonies spawn colonies, further fission and fragmentation will continue to reproduce and extend anarchy. Distance and difference of circumstance also strongly point toward space colonial independence. Colonies will be tiny specks separated by a vast extraterritorial medium, making for extremely high topographical fragmentation.

The next basic system feature is the level of violence interdependence. To ascertain the level of violence interdependence in the Solar Archipelago requires an assessment of the volumes of space, and the volumes and velocities of violence likely to be present. As humans expand into solar space, the volumes of space within which they will be interacting will increase enormously. The volume of space contained within just the inner solar system is billions of times greater than the size of Earth, and the outer solar system, even more vastly larger. Colonies in the Solar Archipelago will be minuscule specks in an enormous empty void. As expansion moves to the outer solar system and then into the Kuiper Belt and Oort Cloud, absolute distances will further expand greatly.

The velocities with which violence can be transported will also increase, but not proportionally to increases in the volumes of space. The distances between bodies in the inner solar system are so great that effective distances between them will be high, with travel times initially measured in months. Over time, advances in propulsion technology are likely to increase speeds, but such advances are likely to remain dwarfed by the vast volumes of space. While velocities of travel will creep up, it will not be possible to accelerate substantial mass to speeds enabling passage about the solar system in the very short time periods that currently prevail on Earth. But giant lasers and energy beams employed as weapons might be able to deliver destructive levels of energy across the distances of the inner solar system in times comparable to ballistic missiles across terrestrial distances. But the distances in the outer solar system and beyond will ultimately prevent even this form of delivering destructive energy at speeds that would be classified as instantaneous. With regard to effective distance, a Solar Archipelago analogous to Archipelago Earth will emerge.

The volumes of violence available will also enlarge enormously with human expansion into solar space. The development of asteroidal orbital alteration technologies is likely to occur very early and will provide volumes of violence capability dwarfing the destructive power of existing terrestrial nuclear arsenals. Later the tools of terraforming, such as giant mirrors and energy beams, will provide other vast new capabilities for wreaking cosmically large-scale violence. Species radiation may open new possibilities for biological warfare. As long as all the adversaries in a conflict are human, the employment of comprehensively lethal bioweapons inevitably risks suicidal blowback, but this limiting factor disappears if adversaries have biologically diverged.

Because volumes of space will be so enlarged and effective distances so expanded, it is tempting to think that even the increased volumes of violence in solar space will be diluted, lowering the overall levels of violence interdependence to less than intense levels. But such calculations overlook the key fact that the volumes of violence *relative to the size of inhabited territories* will still produce extreme saturation. The size of inhabited territory will very probably remain tiny relative to both the volumes of space and the volumes of violence capability. While a hydrogen bomb explosion in solar space might be like a pebble splashing in the ocean, this weapon—let alone a planetoid bomb—will fully saturate space colonies with annihilative violence. Furthermore space habitats, as well as terraforming sun shields and space elevators, are likely to be extremely fragile, like easily smashed eggs. Thus the ratio of violence volume to the volume or size of inhabited territory will remain fully violence-saturated, just as it is now on the terrestrial Earth. Increases in effective distance will not obviate the extreme violence vulnerability of space colonies. Until velocities catch up with the enlarged distances, solar space will be like the Polynesian diaspora—with hydrogen bombs. Overall the level of violence interdependence in solar space will remain intense, making the moderation of, or exit from, anarchy necessary for security. The Solar Archipelago will thus combine the large effective distances found in Archipelago Earth with the high levels of violence interdependence characteristic of Planetary Earth—a particularly dangerous combination.

But might defensive or deterrent strategies be feasible? Defense against planetoid bombardment will be possible because what can be directed can also be deflected. But, as with nuclear weapons, defense will need to approach perfection because the violence volumes will be so enormous relative to inhabited territory. Overall, solar space is likely to be extremely offense dominant because of the enormous volumes of destructive capability combined with high absolute velocities. But might this widely shared vulnerability produce mutual deterrence, offering a semblance of security through deadlock, as with nuclear weapons? Might Solar Archipelago security come from MAD-MAD—Mass Asteroid Destruction–Mutual Assured Destruction? Deterrence might also be appealing because relative speeds would be reduced, thus lowering the dangers stemming from temporally tightly coupled technical systems, as now present on Earth. But deterrence might be difficult to sustain because discrimination (the ability to distinguish between natural and intentional events) and attribution (the ability to discern the identity of the attacker) could be very difficult to establish reliably. But solar space may be so offense dominant that fully annihilative first strikes may be possible.

Because asteroids as planetoid bombs play such a central role in shaping the levels of violence interdependence of solar space, it is instructive to critically examine the widely deployed analogy that asteroids are islands in space. This comparison accurately captures the geophysical facts that asteroids, like islands in terrestrial oceans, are relatively small bodies composed of solid matter surrounded by a vastly larger medium that is fluid or empty and not as habitable. But the differences between oceanic Earth islands and asteroids are much more important. Geophysically, asteroids are more completely insular than oceanic islands, which are firmly attached to the seabed, unlike asteroids, which are attached to nothing. This means that Earth ocean islands do not move, whereas asteroids do, and at extreme velocities. The winds and currents of the Earth's atmosphere and ocean blow and lap against oceanic islands, leaving them in place, while the invisible reins of gravity keep asteroids in perpetual motion. Thus, when the Spanish discovered the small island of Bermuda in the middle of the Atlantic Ocean, they did not have to wonder whether this body might be off the coast of East Asia in a few weeks or months. And they did not have to consider the possibility that it might at some point, quite of its own accord, crash into Spain with devastating consequences. Nor did they have to consider the possibility that its natural path might be intentionally altered by some rival power to collide with Spain. Thinking of asteroids as islands makes them seem safely and permanently fixed, distant, and unmovable, when in fact they are not fixed, are sometimes very close, and are readily movable. In making something so essentially novel into something that is misleadingly similar, the prevalent analogy of asteroids as islands hides precisely what is most important about them.

There is really nothing centrally analogous between terrestrial experiences and the realities of asteroids in solar space. Because of asteroids, the solar space geophysical environment is vastly rich in extreme and easily harnessed violence potentials in ways utterly unlike any terrestrial place. On Terra, humans fight with weapons over islands, but in space asteroidal islands are themselves potentially titanic weapons. But a somewhat illuminating analogy for asteroids is that they are like diseases, recurrent natural perils that can be reduced by medical intervention. But, like scientific and technological knowledge of diseases applied to fabricate bioweapons, asteroid orbits can be altered, producing devastating weapons.

Solar Geopolitics II: Unit-Level Variation

Systems are made of parts, and international systems containing units that are significantly different in their character are more prone to conflict and war and less inclined to mutual restraint and cooperation. Colonies scattered across the vast reaches of the solar system are likely to be very different in character from those on Earth and from each other. If species radiation and cyborgization occur in the course of the expansion of intelligent life from the Earth across the solar system, three different types of variation must be considered: a system composed of units that are exclusively human, a system in which biological species radiation has taken place, and a system with extensive cyborgization.

There are strong reasons why unit-level features of human colonies in space will be very different from terrestrial patterns. Insofar as identities emerge from an experience of place, space colonies will have radically different identities deriving from the vast differences between every place in space and any place on Earth. The entire physical texture of life in space colonies will be enormously different from any society on Earth. More than any society on Earth, space colonies will be completely machine-dependent and completely enclosed, mainly underground. Many space colonies will be in places with different levels of gravity than those experienced on Earth, and this will affect the fabric of social and cultural interaction in ways that will make space colony life very alien to Terrans. If the human tendency for some to have revelations and found new religions survives Earth escape, then great religious differences might also emerge.

If—or when—colonies in solar space develop populations biologically divergent from terrestrial *Homo sapiens,* an even more radical difference will separate off-worlds from Earth. The expansionist expectations of species radiation inevitably occurring through the slow processes of natural selection and of rapidly developing techniques to manipulate genetic codes being employed to greatly accelerate species radiation are quite plausible. Because extraterrestrial environments are so different in so many fundamental ways, starting with variations in gravity, it will be very attractive to alter human biology in major ways. Reengineered posthuman intelligent life forms would be able to effectively colonize much more of space and could come to be "at home" in a range of environments that will forever be harshly alien and unappealing to humans.

How far this branching of intelligent life forms might proceed is suggested by the extraordinary range in the shapes and capabilities of animal life on Earth. It seems reasonable to think that a fully developed technology of genetic engineering would be able to combine brains with the size and capabilities of *Homo sapiens* with wildly different body designs. Engineered intelligent life forms with more insectoid body types, with exoskeletons containing metal for radiation shielding and multiple legs for low-gravity environments, might be particularly suitable, as Bernal suggested. Engineered intelligent life forms configured for extraterrestrial environments might also emulate Terran social insects in being functionally differentiated for performing different tasks and having a centralized queen-bee-like coordinator. Although all of these organisms will be descendants of humanity, humans will surely perceive them as menacing monstrosities.

If solar space colonies come to have populations with biologically integrated cybernetic capabilities, a further radical difference will be present. Space expansionists are on firm ground in thinking that cyborgization will occur in space because humans are so ill-suited to environments beyond the Earth. Cybernetic augmentation could give humans greatly improved capacities that would enable the much more extensive colonization of solar space. Cyborgization combined with biological species alteration could also find wide appeal, further greatly expanding the variety of intelligent life forms that might come to populate the extended reaches of the solar system. Once cyborgization is in play, many additional levels and types of intelligences might be possible, as human-machine combinations exploit the extremely high memory and processing capabilities of digital computers.

If variations of these magnitudes do emerge, the Solar Archipelago will have much greater variation in its populations than anything experienced by humans on Earth. If the expectation of geopolitical theory linking higher unit variation with higher likelihood of conflict holds true, then the prospects for conflict are extremely high. If the Solar Archipelago comes to be populated by a diverse array of intelligent life forms, many radically different in physical shape from humans, and perhaps with mental and other capabilities exceeding those of humans, interplanetary relations will be interspecies relations, and wars will be xenocidal. Among life forms on Earth, interspecies relations vary along a wide spectrum, from extreme competition to symbiotic cooperation. To find an even partial historical experience similar to a Solar Archipelago populated with multiple different intelligent life forms it is necessary to go back to the very beginnings of Archipelago Earth, to the long era in which *Homo sapiens* spread out of Africa and encountered, and probably drove to extinction, its close but somewhat less capable relatives, *Homo erectus* and *Homo neanderthalus*.[8]

Several potentially mitigating and compensating factors deserve consideration. Life forms adapted to live in the radically different environments of the solar system might be uninterested in expanding into each other's habitats. An intelligent ant civilization swarming in the asteroid belt would not be viable on Earth, in the same way that humans are so ill-suited to extraterrestrial environments. Thus multiple distinct intelligent life forms specialized to live in extremely different environments might find a way to coexist, even trade with one another. But this outcome seems improbable because all these species, whatever their corporeal-based niching in different environments, would have high levels of intelligence and advanced technology and would thus probably see one another as inherently existentially threatening. Even if they did not want to live in each other's preferred habitats, their mastery of advanced technology would enable them to exploit resources from inhospitable places. Like Terran states in international anarchy, different intelligent species in solar space would reasonably fear that their rivals might make some great power-enhancing technological innovation. Another mitigating possibility is that the diverse intelligent life forms of the Solar Archipelago would become more capable of cooperation and trust, making possible at least mutual recognition and coexistence, or even the "commonwealth of species" envisioned by Stapledon.[9] While it is impossible to rule out this possibility, it entails evolutionary advances not seen among terrestrial life forms.

Solar Geopolitics III: Distribution and Distinctiveness

The patterns of power distribution and asset distinctiveness in the Solar Archipelago will also powerfully shape prospects for war and peace. Asymmetric power distributions tend to create hierarchical outcomes; shifting distributions make conflicts more likely; and uneven patterns of civil-military distinctiveness add to power asymmetries. The sheer volume and diverse bodies of solar space make it hard to discern axial regions, aside from the celestial bodies themselves, or ascendant positions, aside from the pervasive influence of the sun's gravity well favoring the asteroid belt over Mars and Mars over Terra, thus making solar geopolitics significantly unlike Earth planetary geopolitics.[10]

What will be the balance, or distribution, of power in a Solar Archipelago? There is no single answer to this question because the relative powers of the Earth and space colonies are likely to change very significantly over time. Initially space colonies will inevitably be small and weak and greatly outweighed by the large population and wealth of the Earth. But even when space colonies are small, they will have important positional advantages that will help at least partially compensate for their relative weakness in gross power indicators. Because the Terran gravity well is so much steeper than Martian or asteroidal wells, space colonies have an advantage. The large distances separating space colonies from the Earth also will greatly attenuate the relative power advantages of Earth. The large size of the Earth's human population, much of it poor, may negatively affect its power potential. And the Earth may be subject to further major wars, economic contractions, and the burdens of climate change that could dramatically reduce Terran capacities to mobilize and project power across the Solar Archipelago.

If space colonies expand as anticipated, the relative power between the solar diaspora and the Earth will inexorably shift in favor of the off-worlds. The growth potentials of the Earth are severely limited due to its finite size, its large existing population, and ecological vulnerabilities. Despite the visions of Hay, Tsiolkovsky, and Fuller, a geodesic and hydroponic Earth with large multiples of its current population is probably precluded by the geophysically active and ecologically complex crust of the Earth. But once the basic technologies of space colonization have been mastered, the scope for off-world growth is effectively unlimited. New technologies, difficult to exploit on Terra due to ecological constraints or the opposition of existing stakeholders, might find more rapid employment in space. Species radiation or cyborgization in off-worlds could also add significantly to their growth potential.

There are, however, potentially mitigating factors at least partially moderating this dire outcome for Earth. Assessments of the aggregate power potentials of Terra versus colonial off-worlds are directly meaningful only if these assets are in the hands of one political actor. To the extent political divisions are present on the Earth or within the solar diaspora, the potential viability of smaller and less powerful actors is considerably improved. If Terra remains divided into a multiplicity of states, its ability to counterbalance the capacities of the off-worlds will be greatly diminished. The prospects for the political unification of diverse polyglobal worlds are considerably lower than on Earth. If off-worlds become as diverse as space expansionists anticipate, their political consolidation will be extremely difficult, and they are likely to have very antagonistic and conflictual relations. Division among off-worlds opens the possibility for the balance-of-power politics familiar across Earth history, in which shifting alliances prevent the emergence of one power capable of dominating the entire system.[11] But even this mitigating factor will eventually reach its limits. If the expansion of space colonies continues, the day will inevitably come when Terra is reduced to a marginal player, at the mercy of its gargantuan, and probably monstrous, off-spring.

Civil-military distinctiveness will also shape the solar diaspora. Many of the technologies necessary for the expansion of humanity across solar space will have little relevance for creating violence capacity, but the overall distinctiveness of technologies pervasive in a Solar Archipelago must nevertheless be rated very low because one essential civil technology—asteroidal orbit alteration—has extremely high military potential. Such techniques are likely to be routinely employed for acquiring resources and fabricating infrastructures. Given the extremely high destructive potential of colliding bodies, this basic civil technology will constitute a violence capacity of enormous dimensions perpetually ready at hand for military use. The important civil technology of catapult mass drivers will also be readily employed for bombardment, as memorably envisioned in Robert Heinlein's *The Moon Is a Harsh Mistress*. If terraforming becomes extensive, very large mirrors and high-capacity energy beams will enable enormous devastations as well as expanded habitats. While the distinctiveness of technologies prevalent in solar space is likely to be quite low, those on Terra are likely to be very high, although this gap is diminished if heavy infrastructures are built in Earth orbital space.

In sum, if colonization assumes the expansive trajectory anticipated by space advocates, then it is inevitable that the Earth eventually will be overmatched in power potential. The more expansion into space proceeds, the further Terra is dwarfed in relative power. This shift can only be a question of when, not whether. As this happens, the fate of the Earth will inevitably rest in the hands—or claws—of diverse intelligent life forms not living on the Earth.

Solar Geopolitics IV: Frontiers

Systems vary from open to closed. With the movement of humans into the solar system, a frontier is opened and the system shifts from closed to open. And unlike previous terrestrial expansions, which eventually reached limits and closure, space expansion will produce a permanent frontier and perpetually open system. Like terrestrial frontiers, the space frontier will be primed for conflict. The writ of institutional restraints from the core will be attenuated by distance. Ownership rights will be weakly established, and the benefits of seizing assets and excluding others will be high. Core powers can be drawn into conflicts and wars over frontier access and control. The opening of frontiers also often leads to highly asymmetrical and horrifically violent encounters between previously separated peoples. The permanence of the space frontier ensures that the number of actors in the system and the distribution of powers among them will be in perpetual flux. The existence of a permanent frontier also guarantees that the Earth will eventually be overmatched in power. And as the frontier extends deeper into space, the system will come to have a concentric pattern of interaction capacity, with a dense core and successively less interactive peripheries. Eventually the pattern of Archipelago Earth, of peoples previously unknown to each other coming into violent conflict, will return. Overall, historical analogies of Terran frontier opening indicate more reasons why solar space will be very violent.

Space expansionists frequently compare future space frontiers with historical Earth frontiers.[12] Across Earth history, many groups of humans have moved across many frontiers, but the four most commonly deployed as geohistorical analogs to solar space expansion are the original human movement out of Africa, the spread of Polynesians across the Pacific Ocean,[13] the early modern explosion of Europe across the global oceans, and the westward expansion of the United States across North America.[14] Overall their similarities diminish desirability, while their differences diminish feasibility.

One fundamental similarity between these four expansions and solar space expansion is their dependence on technological advances, a point routinely made by advocates. From clothes and the control of fire to industrial transport, violence, and medicine, new technologies made possible human migration into new environments. Another fundamental similarity, rarely noted by expansionists, is that historical expansions were often violent and generated severe conflicts and produced greater differences among human societies. Even without indigenous peoples to conquer and despoil in space, historical similarities suggest solar space expansion will be quite violent. In the European global expansion, imperial states waged numerous wars among themselves over frontier possessions, borders, and resources. Successful settler colonies waged

wars to become independent, particularly in the Americas. Then independent
settler colonies fought to expand at each other's expense, as the United States
did with Mexico. If the analog of human global expansion is a reliable guide,
solar expansion will be chronically violent and thus less desirable than advocates
believe.

But in another way, all four of these terrestrial expansions are unlike space expansion because their prospects and pacing were mainly shaped by interaction
with indigenous human groups and with the many other organisms inhabiting
terrestrial environments. The human expansion on Earth is a social and ecosystem story in ways completely unlike the prospective expansion of humans
into the sterile wastes of space. All successful human terrestrial expansions were
successful because they moved into ecosystems with rich resources for human
exploitation and frequently other human groups who could be despoiled and
exploited. Human expansion on Earth was unsuccessful in the environments on
the Earth that most resemble those of space, such as the great deserts and polar
ice caps; it was successful in places that are radically unlike space environments.
But human expansion on Earth was also significantly shaped by disease patterns,
as diseases that had evolved in one part of the planet were inadvertently
introduced into others. If potent pathogens evolve in new space environments,
disease might also play a powerful but largely unpredictable role in shaping the
course of human space expansion.

The earliest human expansion, out of Africa, gave rise to the dispersed
habitations of Archipelago Earth and the great diversification in group identities.
When *Homo sapiens* expanded out of Africa into Eurasia, they encountered
other species of tool-using hominins who were less capable. But everywhere
sapiens arrived, their marginally less capable close relatives vanished, displaced
and destroyed. Only when humans first came much later to the Americas did
they expand into spaces without proto-human competitors. Thus early human
expansion was marked by competition with other intelligent tool-using species,
a pattern that is assuredly not going to happen in solar space expansion. It is also
notable that at the same time other species within the genus *Homo* were being
pushed to extinction, *sapiens* was beginning to biologically radiate, most notably
with regard to skin pigmentation, variations that emerged rapidly in response to
reductions in the intensity of solar insolation in northern climate zones.[15]

The extremities of violence and oppression stimulated by these cosmetic
differences should serve as a warning of the horrors likely to result from substantial species radiation in solar space. In thinking about the interactions between
different intelligent species in solar space, the multitude of horrifically violent,
often genocidal encounters between peoples with different cultures and different levels of technology across Terran history is probably a reliable guide. It
was, after all, the near annihilation of the native Tasmanians by British colonists

in the early nineteenth century that inspired Wells's classic story of a Martian invasion aiming to exterminate humanity in *War of the Worlds*.[16] And the fact that the discourse of genocide so routinely characterizes victim populations as inhuman is also a loud warning of what will be likely when humans interact with nonhuman intelligent life in solar space.

These differences have significant implications for the desirability and feasibility of space expansion. Expansion into space will be colonialism without imperialism and without guilt. Terrestrial expansions involved mass extinctions, but there will be no ecological destruction in the lifeless wildernesses of solar space. The global European expansion was possible because there were peoples to subjugate and exploit, but there will be no indigenous populations in solar space. And no conquest, domination, or displacement will be needed in order to begin space colonization. But feasibility will be diminished. The diverse ecosystems yielding a wide range of goods unavailable in other climatic zones provided the crucial economic foundation for the great expansion of the global trading system that motivated and sustained imperial and colonial expansion; these will be absent in solar expansion. The pace and prospects for solar expansion will be a function of the capabilities and incentives of humans interacting with the extraterrestrial physical environment and each other, and not in any way shaped by the relative power of the newcomers against the original inhabitants.

Overall the frontier geohistorical analogy is both alarmingly illuminating and partially misleading. Space and terrestrial expansion are similar in being dependent on technological advance. And they are likely to be similar in having violent conflict among expanding rivals. If solar space comes to be inhabited by additional intelligent species, the record of violent encounters and genocides across Earth history suggests even more extreme levels of violence. On the other hand, space is harshly desolate, utterly lifeless, and uninhabited, while historical terrestrial expansions were into commodious environments, filled with rich ecosystems of readily usable organisms and often inhabited by peoples who could be plundered and exploited. Life was everywhere humans went on Earth, but will be nowhere they go in space. As a result, solar expansion will be much harder to accomplish and will occur in radically different ways. Human expansions on Terra have been part of the shifting story of life on Earth, while solar expansion will involve the introduction of life into lifeless wastelands.

Solar Geopolitics V: Freedom in Space Worlds

Within the Solar Archipelago, marked by extreme regime-type diversity, raw anarchy, intense levels of violence interdependence, shifting power distributions, low civil-military distinctiveness, and permanently shifting frontiers, what are the prospects for freedom within units and institutionalized mutual restraints among them? Will the astropolis be free? What does geopolitics expect about freedom in space colonies? Humans disagree, sometimes violently, about whether freedom means the protection of individual autonomy or the integration of individuals into collectives. Reflecting the ideological differences fueling the great Cold War, many American and Western space expansionists anticipate that space colonies will be, or can be made to be, liberal democracies. Conversely, many Russian and Soviet space thinkers anticipate that colonies in space will be the sites for the complete subordination of the individual to the collective. For many contemporary American libertarian space activists and entrepreneurs, realizing and expanding individual freedom is a central reason why space colonization should be pursued. For advocates of space colonization as freedom insurance against the rising tides of conformity and bureaucratic domination on Earth, the appeal of space expansion must hinge on whether space colonies are likely to be free or can be made and kept free. For a large segment of contemporary space expansionists the answer to the freedom question should be strongly determinative of whether space expansion is actually desirable or something to be avoided.

Space thinkers disagree fundamentally on the freedom question, as we have seen. Tsiolkovsky and Bernal anticipate that the imperatives and opportunities of space colonial life will produce the complete submergence of individuality; being sympathetic to such political forms, they see this as part of the appeal of space expansion. In the earliest pro-liberty discussion, Cole and Cox provide a compelling list of reasons to think that the complete subordination of the individual would be necessary in space colonies, but then conclude that the ability of any dissenting individual to cause catastrophic damage would compel colonies to be governed much like contemporary liberal democracies. O'Neill and others see colonies as particularly suited to forms of democratic direct rule and diverse experimentation. The most sustained analysis of this question, provided by Cockell, Crawford, and other members of the British Interplanetary Society, provides a long list of ways in which the circumstances of space colonies will be prone to despotic and totalitarian forms of government but looks to careful anticipatory design and interworld federation as remedies.

The weight of argument on this question must be judged to be strongly against liberal democratic freedom outcomes and in favor of despotic and collective outcomes. The pro-liberty arguments appear more ideologically appealing than practically plausible. The threat to the whole posed by disaffected individuals is much more plausibly remedied with total surveillance and various forms of behavioral and cognitive therapy than with liberal democracy. And the system features of solar space are strongly mismatched to federal outcomes, as we shall shortly see.

This leaves the pro-freedom school dependent on what might be called the Good Seed Model of space colony development: start right and all will end right. This means designing both the physical infrastructures and the constitutions of new space colonies to ensure their compatibility with individual freedom. Considerable effort by space advocates has gone into writing founding charters for space colonies that embody advanced freedom and justice goals.[17] But these efforts presuppose the existence of a social science of freedom design, which is now at best rudimentary, as well as the political will to actually establish colonies based on these comprehensive designs. Ironically this approach entails an extreme degree of the social engineering that strong individual freedom advocates routinely decry and cite as a reason for escaping to the unregulated space frontier. Colonies started as mines owned by corporations or as military bases are unlikely to have an initial governance arrangement centered on preserving freedom. Even if colonies are somehow established with carefully crafted constitutions designed to protect individual liberty, they will inevitably be pulled and shaped as they expand by the very distinctive features of their environments.[18] How colonies begin is likely to shape their development, but not in ultimately decisive ways.

The arguments favoring despotic outcomes all rest, quite explicitly, on ships being the closest historical analog to the governance of totally built spaces. But as we saw, ships are fundamentally unlike polities because they are always incomplete as polities. And, as we also saw, a long line of thinking views cities as more likely to have free government than extended territorial polities. A historical analogy more favorable to freedom outcomes is the early modern city-state of Venice, which is as close to a city-ship as can be historically found. Being built on vast numbers of stilts driven into tidal flats and dependent on the regulation of water in its surrounding lagoon, Venice was a completely built habitat. For many centuries it enjoyed very stable internal government provided by its oligarchical republican constitution that afforded citizens extensive liberties.[19] Because its streets were waterways, a disaffected populace could not gather; discontent was also moderated by a generous welfare state, administered through church charities. Its citizens had a strong sense of group identity against outsiders. But it also had despotic aspects, most notably a secret committee with the authority to covertly murder any individual deemed subversive.

The arguments against freedom in space colonies are many and strong, but they may really be arguments against the feasibility of space colonies rather than their undesirability. If colonies are routinely despotically ruled, who would want to migrate into them? Perhaps people would become accustomed to extremes of unfreedom, as large numbers have across history on Earth. But this seems less likely for people with the advanced education, training, and skill sets necessary to make a colony viable. Free space colonial government probably should be viewed as a utopian aspiration, too difficult to realize in practice.

All the pro-freedom arguments about space colony government assume the only inhabitants of off-worlds are humans. If space environments do favor hierarchical rule, and if the direction of species radiation can be controlled, then it seems likely that gene technologies will help amplify the collectivist and totalitarian features of space regimes. Forms of hierarchical rule long sought, but only briefly achieved, among unruly human terrestrial populations might be realized in solar worlds. And if directed species radiation produces forms of intelligent life that employ radically nonhuman morphologies and intraspecies functional differentiation, the possibilities for comprehensive forms of centralized rule become extreme.

In sum, the association of space expansion with the preservation and expansion of individual freedom is probably extremely dubious. Space expansion, far from being a form of freedom insurance, is more likely to produce the perfection of despotism and the complete subordination of the individual to the collective. Those who value individual liberty should be strong skeptics and opponents of space expansion, not enthusiastic supporters.

Solar Geopolitics VI: Regimes, Unions, and Federations

What does geopolitics indicate about the prospects for establishing and maintaining mutual restraints and unions among the far-flung polities of a Solar Archipelago? This question is doubly important. First, if the diverse worlds in solar space do possess capacities to wreak catastrophic violence upon one another, persisting in political anarchy will be inconsistent with the provision of security, and establishing authoritative regulation of their violence capacities will be vitally necessary to achieve security. Second, if colonies can be kept free only through federation with Earth, particularly demanding mutual restraints will be needed. Unfortunately the prospects for achieving substantial mutual restraints are extremely unfavorable, for several reasons. If solar space polities do become very different from Earth's, and from each other, the barriers to establishing common institutions will be very high. If species radiation and cyborgization occur, these differences and barriers will grow to cavernous dimensions. And if civil-military distinctiveness of technologies in solar space is very low, there will be a further barrier to the establishment of mutual arms control. Being very distant and different from each other will make co-non-operation difficult, and cooperation extremely difficult. In sum, the presence of intense violence interdependence resulting from full saturation in combination with very low proximity and very high unit-level diversity will be nearly impossible to bridge with regimes. For the pursuit of security and peace, the geopolitical landscape of a polyglobal humanity in solar space looks like something approaching the worst of all possible worlds.

The prospects for solar federation seem much brighter when bolstered by historical analogy. As we saw, the British Interplanetary Society space liberty theorists draw a hopeful analogy between the establishment of a solar federation and the founding of the United States. Recognizing that interplanetary war could be catastrophically or existentially destructive, and that space colonies would have strong tendencies to become totalitarian microsocieties, they propose a solar federation to remedy these severe problems, and this vital expedient is made to seem plausible by the American founding example.

Unfortunately the establishment of the United States in the late eighteenth century is different in several major ways from what would be entailed in setting up a solar federation. Most important, the original thirteen former English colonies that banded together to form the American federal union were territorially contiguous with one another, enjoying a spatial proximity that would be radically different from the relationship between a Martian or asteroidal colony and the Earth. Also, the American states had a similar culture, religion, language, political tradition, and history and forged a nascent national community during the long and costly war during which they achieved their independence from the British Empire. Despite these many commonalities, the American union was difficult to achieve and was contested in a vastly destructive civil war less than a century after the founding. It is hard to imagine any Martian colony that would not have large differences in interests with the Earth. Commonly enacted laws would probably have little relevance to the vastly different circumstances of Mars, and any solar congress in which the Martian colonists had proportionate representation would be overwhelmingly dominated by Earth populations.

A better analogy for the prospects for a solar federation is to be found in the abortive efforts in the late nineteenth century to establish a British imperial federation. Although the British Empire encompassed about a quarter of the world's territory, its possessions, scattered all over the globe, linked by increasingly precarious maritime routes, and populated by an extreme variety of peoples, appeared very vulnerable to the growing power of America and Russia, based on vast continental territories. To remedy this problem, numerous schemes were developed for establishing closer ties with the parts of the empire that were colonies settled by emigrants from the British Isles, in Canada, Australia, and New Zealand, by establishing a federal national state, also inspired by the American federal union. Advocates pointed out that the abolition of distance brought about by the Industrial Revolution in steam and electricity meant that it would be possible to achieve a degree of political union that had not been possible in the late eighteenth century, when the American colonies achieved independence.[20]

Although such plans were widely advocated and discussed, no serious attempt was made to implement them. In any case, their prospects were very low, due to the still large effective distances (now measured in weeks rather than months), the divergent interests produced by their different locations, and the great asymmetry in population size between the small but densely populated British Isles and large but underpopulated spaces of Australia and Canada.[21] Like the far-flung English colonies, a Martian or asteroidal colony would be extremely difficult to federally unite with the Earth, and as it grew in size its aspirations and opportunities for achieving successful independence would also grow. To the extent that the desirability of space colonization hinges on avoiding planetary war and totalitarian microsocieties, and to the extent that the prospects for avoiding these severely undesirable outcomes hinge so heavily on the feasibility of solar federation, the suitable historical analog of the infeasible British imperial federation raises severe doubts about the desirability of the solar colonization project.

Solar Geopolitics VII: Island Earth in the Solar Archipelago

Finally, what does geopolitical theory anticipate about the impact of a Solar Archipelago on the Earth? As the Earth is transformed from the sole world of humanity into one of many, it becomes Island Earth in the Solar Archipelago. Overall, significant expansion into solar space will generate strong pressures toward a highly hierarchical terrestrial world government.

Initially, in Stages One and Two, the influence of solar space expansion on Earth's political order is likely to be uneven and highly dependent on who conducts it. If early solar colonial expansion is conducted by rival states, the anarchic features of terrestrial political order will be strengthened; however, if the first colonies are planted by a consortium of states, terrestrial anarchy will be modestly moderated.

The development of asteroid-moving techniques has considerably larger potential implications for terrestrial political order than the establishment of small space colonies. If these techniques are developed by rival military organizations to make planetoid bombs, the mutual threat level among the leading states on

Earth will take a quantum leap upward, producing a new technogenic cata-strophic threat rivaling nuclear war. Alternatively, if asteroidal orbital alteration techniques are developed by a consortium of leading states and conducted solely for purposes of planetary defense, interstate rivalry on Earth will be moderated at the same time that a general threat to the Earth will be mitigated. Another possibility is that such techniques will be initially developed by corporations seeking resources, in which case the effects on Earth would be primarily eco-nomic. Total economic output would rise, but wealth would probably further concentrate. But if these techniques are developed by corporations, it is hard to imagine that their violence potential would go unrecognized by states, opening up the possibility for a very rapid switch to either of the previous two institu-tional arrangements.

Once the third and fourth stages of solar expansion are reached, the influences of solar space upon the political order of the Earth will become ex-tremely powerful and are likely to be increasingly inimical to terrestrial secu-rity and freedom. Unfortunately, delaying colonization until after achieving the political unification or pacification of Earth, as Sagan recommended, is un-likely to retard the emergence of a violently rivalrous Solar Archipelago. If the Earth is not politically consolidated before solar expansion begins or gets very far, there will be growing pressures for consolidation as it progresses. As solar space comes to be extensively populated by polities that are very different from Terra's, as the balance of power shifts away from the Earth, and as the anarchic dynamics of the solar political system intensify, terrestrial political consolida-tion will be strongly encouraged. Protecting the planet from the threats posed by other worlds in solar space will almost surely require the political consolida-tion of the Earth. But Terra's ability to choose its own direction might still be severely circumscribed. For example, to sustain its competitive position, Earth might be compelled to genetically alter its population, or a subset of it, making it impossible to sustain the Bernal-Dyson-Rees exile of species-altering genetic engineering into space.

As humanity expands into solar space, world government on Earth ceases to be universal government and becomes one of many world governments, with very low prospects for a universal, multiworld government. Those who fear world government as a threat to freedom on Earth and look to space expansion as a freedom frontier fail to consider the effects of a Solar Archipelago on the trajectory of Terran political development. As world government advocates have long observed, a sure path to the political unification of the Earth would be the emergence of a threat from beyond, such as an invasion from Mars. The absence of such threats makes Earth unification difficult but permits unification on more confederal and nonhierarchical lines.

Unfortunately the world government that will emerge on Earth once it has been reduced to an island in the Solar Archipelago is likely to be highly hierarchical in character. The government of Island Earth will tend toward steep hierarchy due to the need to erect and maintain a significant space military infrastructure. If the construction of heavy civil infrastructure in Earth orbital space had not already created a master asset capable of dominating the planet, the measures necessary to protect the Earth from the other units in the Solar Archipelago surely will. The military capabilities deployed in space to protect the planet from threats beyond will also be readily available to dominate the Earth because they will be a high castle positioned on the planet's high ground. Should interworld wars and other conflicts occur, Terra is probably at a distinct military disadvantage. Securing the planet from outside threats will become successively more difficult and burdensome as the human, or posthuman, presence expands successively further, and the relative position of Earth in the system declines. Island Earth in the Solar Archipelago will thus tend toward a classic "garrison state" government in which the war-fighting arm of the polity is so large as to readily dominate the rest of the body politic, memorably envisioned in Heinlein's *Starship Troopers*. Eventually and inevitably, however, even such iron measures are doomed to defeat as Terra's share of total system capabilities shrinks to insignificance.

These observations suggest a rethinking of lessons drawn by space expansionists from China's abortive ventures in oceanic exploration in the early modern period.[22] Space advocates frequently note that China built a fleet of large seaworthy vessels, greatly exceeding the size of the ships used a century later by the Europeans in their global oceanic expansion. The Chinese fleets traversed the Indian Ocean and returned with a wealth of new information and goods. But then China abruptly abandoned this effort, allowing its ships to rot in port.[23] This decision, which Zubrin calls "the Great Ming Leap Backward," is commonly ascribed to China's large centralized government, which saw no benefit in transoceanic trade or colonization and which oppressively controlled the coastal regions of China that might have eagerly pursued such ventures. As a result of this decision, China fell behind the European latecomers and was eclipsed by them in power and wealth for several centuries. The lesson commonly drawn from this episode is that great benefits accrue to those who boldly explore rather than stay at home, and that large central governments are typically impediments to exploration and colonization.

But looking at China's larger and longer historical trajectory, a very different analogy is suggested. Because of the proximity of the populous regions of China to the great steppes stretching across its northern borders, China was continually threatened by invasion from nomadic horse-riding peoples. This posed an immense security problem that China was unable, despite strenuous efforts, to fully contain. Despite being vastly outnumbered, the steppe nomads repeatedly mastered the Chinese militarily with their superior mobility. The most substantial measure undertaken by the Chinese to deal with this chronic security problem was the construction of the vast network of walls and fortifications known as the Great Wall of China.[24] The heavy task of building and maintaining this vast military infrastructure helped make centralized government a vital and enduring feature of Chinese political development. This central experience of Chinese history suggests a revealing analogy for space futures: the Earth may find itself in a comparable position of military vulnerability to the less populous but highly mobile space diaspora, thus requiring a hierarchical central government on Earth to maintain a Great Wall of Earth against a "Genghis Khan with a planetoid bomb."

Overall, space expansion poses multiple threats to freedom. Large Earth orbital infrastructures are likely to produce a hierarchical world government. Offworlds are unlikely to be internally free. Island Earth in the Solar Archipelago will face strong pressures to consolidate in a highly hierarchical manner, putting terrestrial freedom further in jeopardy. The inescapable conclusion is that friends of freedom must look upon the space expansionist project as an ultimate threat and do everything they can to prevent its realization. Liberty might survive on Earth, but if large-scale space expansion takes place, it is almost certainly destined for extinction.

The Dark Skies of Solar Geopolitics

The propositions of geopolitics applied to solar orbital space strongly point toward outcomes deeply inimical to security from violence, freedom, and human survival, summarized in nine propositions (see Table 10.2). The greatest calamities will come from success, not failure. Human expansion into solar space will produce a Solar Archipelago, combining some of the most dangerous features of both Archipelago Earth and Planetary Earth. Vulnerabilities will be very high, but prospects for restraint will be very low. Several pervasive analogies hide these unappealing and perilous outcomes, but more appropriate geophysical and historical comparisons underscore them. Stripped of its ascentionist assumptions and with its slanted and truncated geopolitics corrected, space expansionism's positive anticipations collapse. Another way of putting this central conclusion is that the realization of the Tsiolkovsky programs will almost surely lead to the prevalence in solar space of appropriate extensions of the von Braun programs. In the simplest terms, major movement into the heavens promises a descent into the depths of hell.

Table 10.2 **Solar Space Geopolitics: Main Propositions**

---

1. Colonies large enough to provide catastrophic risk insurance are likely to be politically independent, producing an anarchic system structure, reinforced by fragmented topography, large distances, and great differences of circumstance.

2. Effective distance will be increased, but violence interdependence will be intense, with annihilative saturation of inhabited spaces due to the immense violence volume of planetoid bombs relative to minuscule inhabited areas.

3. Differences of circumstances will make units very different, further exacerbated by species radiation (undirected or directed).

4. Space settlement civil-military distinctiveness will be low because asteroidal orbital alteration will be a basic space civil technology. Distinctiveness will remain high on Earth.

5. The system will have full open frontiers prone to violence and producing perpetual shifts in power distribution.

6. The Solar Archipelago will be highly war-prone due to extreme unit-level differences, anarchic syndromes, conflictual frontiers, shifting power balances, and low civil-military distinctiveness. The real-state mode of protection will be prevalent.

7. Because of intense violence interdependence and high vulnerabilities, exiting anarchy and establishing mutually restraining government will be necessary for security but nearly impossible to achieve due to extreme unit-level differences, large distances, and difficulties in surveillance.

8. Numerous factors make likely totalistic hierarchical government in space settlements.

9. Island Earth in the Solar Archipelago will face strong pressures toward highly hierarchical political consolidation.

Catastrophic and Existential Risks from Solar Space Expansion

This dark scenario of solar space expansion produced by the application of geopolitical theory has profound implications for the argument that colonization of other bodies in the solar system is necessary to alleviate or escape the formidable catastrophic and existential risks facing Earth-bound humanity. Both riskologists and space expansionists strongly believe, with Hawking, that "once we establish independent colonies, our entire future will be safe."[25] If all humanity's eggs are in one fraying and vulnerable basket, then it stands to reason that spreading viable colonies of humans to other celestial bodies will help ensure the survival of the human species. While the role of existing space capabilities in amplifying the dangers of the great technogenic threat of nuclear war belies the astro-optimism of space advocates, what of their cherished larger vision of making humanity a multiworld species? While space advocates propose a variety of ways space expansion might *alleviate* or *escape* existing risks, they give almost no attention to whether expansion might *generate* new risks or help *re-activate* already regulated ones. The list of major threats facing humanity is dauntingly long, and the expansionist agenda for solar space has many parts, making assessment a complex undertaking. But there are six major ways in which the realization of the space expansionist agenda for solar orbital space is likely to generate or activate catastrophic and existential risks. Taken in combination these arguments provide a strong basis for putting ambitious space expansion on the list of megathreats potentially confronting humanity, and for making every effort to relinquish it. Large-scale space expansion must be viewed as something akin to a full-scale nuclear war and assiduously avoided. Unlike many of the other threats humanity faces, addressing those created by ambitious space expansion is now extremely simple: just say no.

The realization of the space expansionist program for solar orbital space enlarges the probability and scope of catastrophic and existential risks confronting humanity in six ways: *malefic geopolitics, natural threat amplification, restraint reversal, hierarchy enablement, alien generation,* and *monster multiplication* (see Table 10.3).

First, large-scale solar space expansion will produce a radically novel political and material landscape that is extremely inauspicious for security, freedom, and human survival, a perfect storm of unfavorable possibilities and tendencies. With a new word for a new phenomenon, borrowed from astrology for a conjunction of negatives, solar space patterns can be characterized as *geopolitically malefic.* Just as the space environment creates terrestrially inconceivable extremes of frigid and torrid temperatures on opposite sides of the same object, so too the prospective solar landscape combines geopolitical extremes in ways unknown to terrestrial experience. Most ominously, solar space geopolitics combines the extreme diversities and high effective distances experienced on Archipelago Earth with system-wide levels of intense violence interdependence found on Planetary Earth. Polities will be extremely different and spatiotemporally remote but will be capable of readily inflicting massive levels of destruction on one another. Add shifting distribution, wide accessibility, and low distinctiveness, and the contours of the violence-material landscape becomes even more prone to large-scale destruction. With system-wide common government and mutual restraints very difficult to create and sustain, solar space comes close to being maximally suboptimal for positive outcomes, a nightmarish worst of all possible worlds in geopolitical conjunction. Extensive mutual restraints will be vitally *necessary,* but they will be nearly *impossible* to realize. While humanity's

Table 10.3 **Catastrophic and Existential Threats from Solar Colonization**

	Definition	Catastrophic and Existential Threat
Geopolitically Malefic	Solar Archipelago combines worst of Archipelago Earth and Planetary Earth	Strong tendencies for interworld and interspecies war and weaponization
Natural Threat Amplification	Rate of naturally occurring threat increased by human employment	Increased risk of asteroidal bombardment
Restraint Reversal	Terrestrial regulations and relinquishments undone	Increased nuclear, genetic, nano, and ASI threats
Hierarchy Enablement	Securing Island Earth in Solar Archipelago requires planetary garrison state	Increased likelihood of despotic and totalitarian oppression
Alien Generation	Species radiation produces other advanced intelligent species with technology	Humans extinguished by superior and hostile posthumans
Monster Multiplication	Increased scope of geographic and technology interactions with adverse unknowable effects	Increased probability of unknowingly triggering large-scale disasters

eggs might be scattered among many baskets, egg-smashing with large rocks will be easy—and likely.

Facing this extensive list of major factors disposing the system toward large-scale violent conflict in solar space will require humanity's transmutation into Tsiolkovskian angels to avoid catastrophic and existentially threatening warfare. Perhaps the only saving grace of this key conclusion of geopolitical analysis is that the demons loosened by opening the Pandora's box of space colonization might start to wreak their damage early enough to throttle the colonial enterprise before it gets too fatally under way.

A second way in which colonizing solar space poses catastrophic and existential threats is through *natural threat amplification*. Because asteroids and comets collide with the Earth, and the total energy contained within the population of near-Earth objects vastly exceeds that contained in all nuclear arsenals, they pose the inevitable prospect of terrestrial calamities. The rate at which these objects strike the Earth is now solely a function of natural forces. Space expansionists advance human movement into space to avert this threat and promote their solution to this problem as a principal space contribution to reducing catastrophic and existential threats. But because the technologies to divert *away* from the Earth are essentially identical to those needed to direct objects *toward* the Earth, the rate at which these objects strike the Earth could *increase* if they become instruments of interstate rivalry and become weaponized as planetoid bombs. This prospect leads Sagan to recommend delaying the full mapping of asteroid orbits and development of diversion techniques until after some form of effective world government has been established on Earth. But with the spread of colonies across the solar system, the writ of any government on Earth will be severely limited. The same anarchical political configurations that Sagan views as incompatible with security from intentional asteroid bombardment on Earth will almost certainly be reproduced on a vastly larger, and more severe, scale in the Solar Archipelago. If, as seems extremely likely, systemic anarchy returns with the diaspora of humans across the solar system, then militarized rivalries are very likely to ensue, producing asteroidal weaponization. If this happens, a natural threat will have been amplified, enlarging the potential for the occurrence of a catastrophic event.

The third way in which ambitious space expansion could increase the catastrophic and existential risks confronting humanity is through *restraint reversal*. Barring civilizational collapse, the cornucopia of technological innovation will continue to pour forth its prodigies. If the monstrosities and menaces of the ever-widening technological cone of possibility can be thwarted only by staying within a narrow path of human preservation and enhancement, then space expansion must be assessed for its effects on the reversals, regulations, and relinquishments constituting the barriers of restraint. The record with nuclear weapons demonstrates that institutional architectures of restraint are not easy to erect and sustain on Earth. If space expansion makes the creation and preservation of restraints even more difficult, the probability of otherwise unrelated catastrophic and existential outcomes will rise, making it a potent catalyst for multisided disaster. Instead of mitigating the effects of multiple catastrophic and existential risks, large-scale space expansion promises to multiply them.

There are many reasons to anticipate that restraints established on Earth will be reversed if space colonization occurs. Restraints are unlikely to survive transplantation into diverse and demanding off-world environments. If humans are living on multiple worlds subject to different governments, regulation and relinquishment will be more difficult to establish, there will be more places for potential breakdowns, and verification of compliance will be vastly more difficult. If, as seems extremely likely, the many different worlds in the Solar Archipelago in systemic anarchy have violently hostile relations, establishing and sustaining restraints will become nearly impossible. Surveillance in the vast reaches of solar space will be vastly difficult. And if the human species radiates into multiple species, the barriers to regulation and relinquishment will become even more formidable.

A particularly dangerous case of restraint reversal may be technologies leading to artificial superintelligence, a particularly potent technogenic threat. Space activities are already heavily dependent on advanced computing and robotic technologies, and peoples living in space are likely to be far more cyber-dependent than those on Earth. Living in harshly inhospitable environments, spacekind will have strong incentives to push the development of cybernetic capabilities. If a robust regime for the restraint and relinquishment of ASI is not established, human extinction might occur before significant space colonization occurs. If an effective ASI-restraint regime is developed on Earth before extensive space colonization takes place, it seems unlikely that such restraints would survive the expansion of humanity across the solar system.

It might be objected that the breakout of an ASI in some remote world in solar space would not pose a general existential threat to humanity once all of humanity's eggs are no longer in one basket. If, however, we take seriously the standard scenarios of what an ASI would do once it emerges, the dispersion of humanity across multiple worlds would afford no protection whatsoever because an uncontrolled ASI, it is widely anticipated, will in short order expand not just on the planet of its origins but across the solar system, indeed the galaxy.[26] To the extent uncontrolled ASI is deemed something to avoid at all costs, large-scale space expansion must be viewed similarly.

Terrestrial arrangements to restrain nuclear, genetic, and nanotechnologies are also likely to be reversed as humanity expands to other worlds. The prospects of interworld and interspecies wars will provide high incentives for maintaining weaponized nuclear capabilities and for pursuing research into military genetic and nanotechnology applications. Any restraint regime for genetic technologies is unlikely to survive extensive human expansion into space, given the attractiveness of directed and accelerated species alteration in off-worlds. Solar space contains a vast number of islands for potential Doctors Moreau to work their alchemy, as memorably envisioned in Robinson's *2312*. If self-replicating nanomachines are possible and built on Earth, human existence will be threatened. But if a relinquishment regime is established on Earth, it is unlikely to survive in a solar diaspora. While interplanetary distances will afford a buffer from runaway replicators on other celestial bodies, this is unlikely to be permanently effective, thus delaying rather than foreclosing the gray-gooization of the Earth.

Fourth, solar expansion poses catastrophic and existential risks to humanity through *hierarchy enablement*. The emergence of totalitarian world government, nearly universally viewed as deeply undesirable, is reasonably judged a catastrophic threat to humanity. As we have seen, space expansion is likely to produce hierarchies in several significant ways. Many space advocates view large-scale space expansion as freedom insurance and anticipate that various forms of freedom and plurality deemed in jeopardy on Earth can be recovered and preserved in space. But anticipations of a freedom dividend from space expansion are largely illusory because large-scale space expansion into Earth orbital space is very likely to enable the erection of a highly hierarchical world government, either from one-state military dominance of the entire planet or from the control of a major infrastructure for resources or energy. The further large-scale expansion of human activity into solar space is likely to facilitate the emergence of a highly hierarchical world government on Island Earth that could then be prone to become totalitarian.

The fifth way in which ambitious space expansion poses catastrophic and existential risks is through *alien generation*. The human species radiation anticipated by expansionists will generate significantly different forms of intelligent life suited to other worlds. If these anticipations are realized, there will be multiple intelligent species, all descendants from terrestrial *Homo sapiens*, in this solar system and eventually across the galaxy. While space expansionists celebrate this as an expansion of life, they rarely dwell on its implications for the future of human life. If ascentionist assumptions about moral improvement resulting from vertical expansion are true, humanity and its descendant species will live in harmony. But if ascentionist assumptions are unfounded, then the generation of alien intelligent species in this solar system should be viewed as a catastrophic and existential threat to humanity. As the cyber visionary Hans Moravec observes, "biological species almost never survive encounters with superior competitors."[27] While habitat space expansionists embrace the Darwinian proposition that life inevitably expands, they do not seem to have thought through the implications of the corollary proposition that life forms often lethally compete.

The mechanisms for the annihilation of humans by advanced forms of extraterrestrial life, long a staple of dystopian SF, are easy enough to imagine. While it might be possible for humanity, mobilized and directed by a centralized world government devoted to planetary and species defense, to survive for a while, eventually the sheer number and variety of alien species with advanced technology is sure to prevail. Fictional accounts of alien threats to humanity are typically about life forms originating on other planets, and their eventual defeat commonly results from improbable expedients and heroics. The more realistic threat is probably from humanity's descendants, and this threat can simply be prevented from arising by relinquishing space colonization.

The sixth way in which ambitious space expansion is related to catastrophic and existential risk is through *monster multiplication*. The number of "monsters," threats that are unknown, has, we are told by riskologists, been steadily growing with the development of powerful new technologies. Some monsters are in principle knowable, but others may be unknowable to humans. Ambitious space expansion will clearly entail the development of powerful new technologies, and the actors developing these technologies will be spread in multiple worlds across the solar system. Therefore it stands to reason that the number of monsters posing potential terminal threats will inevitably increase as ambitious space expansionist projects are realized.

Taken together, these six ways in which the realization of the space expansionist program for solar space pose catastrophic and existential threats demolish the core proposition of space advocates that large-scale expansion is desirable. Space expansionists start with the persuasive proposition that technological capabilities for destruction are rapidly enlarging, while the Earth remains spatially finite. They then reason that expanding the spatial range of human activities through expansion into outer space will dilute dangers and bring the ratios between the powers of destruction and the spatial domain of human activity into safer proportions. But they fail to recognize or acknowledge that the potency of the destructive potentials inherent in space expansion also increases, and these capabilities can potentially be brought to bear on the finite and fragile Earth and its human populations, thus making the survival problem, at least for the Earth and humanity, much greater. If humans, or their alien progeny, occupying this vaster spatial realm behave in the same manner as they have on Earth, all that will have changed is that the magnitude of the threats will have been enlarged. For large-scale space expansion, there is no plausible human path of preservation bypassing its many very likely menaces and monstrosities. For humanity in space, there is only darkness at the end of the tunnel.

Astrocide—the extinction of humanity caused directly or indirectly by large-scale human space expansion—must join the list of threats to the survival of humanity that already includes cosmocide, terracide, and other technogenic threats. Like large-scale nuclear war, astrocide is a form of technologically enabled species suicide. But, just as graphic imaginaries and disciplined anticipations of nuclear Armageddon have probably played an indispensable role in averting, so far, nuclear species suicide, so too systematic and disciplined anticipations of the likely consequences of large-scale human space expansion might help avoid astrocide.

Irreversibility Thresholds and Departure Dilemmas

It seems very likely that the expansion of intelligent life across the solar system will generate a wide array of existential threats to humanity. But before concluding that these threats justify the relinquishment of space expansion, these negative possibilities must be weighed against the risk reductions that space expansion might provide. Aside from very long-term astrophysical threats such as the dying of the sun, the primary existential benefit of space expansion stems from the existence of a colony on another body in this solar system that could preserve humanity if all human life on Earth is eliminated. Might it be possible to expand into space far enough to reap the benefits of existential risk reduction and then stop expanding before the negative possibilities become activated? Once started, can space expansion be halted? Freeman Dyson observed, "The one thing that our descendants will not be able to do is to stop the expansion of life once it is well started."[28] But where is the line of no return? Somewhere between a small, lonely and precarious colony on Mars and a solar system teeming with very different, very powerful, and probably very hostile forms of intelligent life, there is a line beyond which space expansion becomes rapidly irreversible.

There are good reasons to think that the line of no return is located very early in space expansion and that it might be very difficult to avoid sliding across it. It seems likely that the line sits between a Martian colony large enough to survive on its own and one large enough to become politically independent of the Earth. But a colony on Mars large enough to sustain the existence of humanity is very likely to be capable, or close to capable, of becoming independent from the Earth, at which point the further direction and rate of expansion would slip out of terrestrial human control.

A colony on Mars with a small population dependent on Earth provides no existential threat protection but could be reversed simply by halting support. Stage One expansion produces neither existential benefits nor risks. It is too small and dependent to matter. To provide existential protection, a Mars colony would need enough population and economic viability to continue if the human population on the Earth is completely eliminated. How substantial a colony would need to be in order to be self-sustaining is very uncertain. A colony may appear to be viable but turn out to not be sustainable due to unforeseen developments. Being small and located in an inhospitable environment, it would be particularly vulnerable to setbacks that on Earth would be merely inconveniences or localized disasters. And for a colony to continue the existence of humanity, it would have to be completely isolated from whatever caused the complete extinction of humanity on Earth. Given the great discrepancy between the resources and populations of the Earth and the colony, a minimally viable Martian colony could be reversed, but this would obviously entail an effort that Earth might have little inclination to make.

How large would a space colony need to be to achieve independence? This estimate is also difficult to make because it is dependent upon the relative military capabilities of both the colony and the Earth and on the willingness of both Martians and Earthians to fully employ their capabilities. Distance would favor the colony, while its small size would favor Terra. A crucial factor would be whether asteroid bombardment capabilities were in play. It also seems likely that any colony capable of achieving its independence from the Earth would be, or would soon be, a potential catastrophic threat to the Earth. The large size of the Earth's population would favor the Earth, but much of this advantage would be offset by the Earth's being at the bottom of a much deeper gravity well. Because of its closer proximity to the main asteroid belt and its almost complete reliance on space technology, a Martian colony would probably achieve military superiority over Terra long before its population reached even a sizable fraction of the Earth's. If the benefits of existential threat reduction from a Martian colony are not realized until it is large enough to be self-sufficient, and the existential threats of a Martian colony become effectively irreversible approximately as soon as it becomes independent, space colonization is clearly an undesirable strategy for existential risk reduction.

These observations suggest humanity faces a terrible and tragic *departure dilemma*: if we do not leave, we are surely doomed, but if we leave, we are also surely doomed. Yet this dilemma may be more apparent than real because the time frames of the threats are radically different. In the very long term, humanity must leave the Earth to survive, but this is so far in the future as to be irrelevant for current decision-making. For the foreseeable future—at least the next several centuries—our best strategy is to stay home; bring our planet into better order; survival-steer through the nuclear, climate, cyber, bio, and nano revolutions; and leave distant generations a firm base to grapple with problems and possibilities we can only dimly imagine.

Rethinking the Fermi Paradox, the Great Silence, and the Great Filter

These considerations also have significant implications for the claim that space expansion will almost inevitably occur as it becomes feasible. As the feasibility of ambitious space ventures increases, it seems likely that decisions about how—and whether—to proceed into space will be subject to considerably more serious critical scrutiny than one finds among space advocates. In the face of arguments such as the ones raised here, it is doubtful that the governments—or government—of the Earth would embark upon ventures laden with such profoundly intrinsic major perils for human well-being and survival. To pursue the ambitious space expansionist project in the face of these many foreseeable downsides would be a colossally irrational move. As space habitat expansion becomes feasible, its undesirability might become sufficiently evident to preclude its realization.

The numerous ways in which ambitious space expansion can amplify and activate catastrophic and existential threats also has interesting implications for the emergence and survival—and visibility—of intelligent life elsewhere in the universe. The Fermi Paradox asks, "Where is everybody?" If intelligent life exists elsewhere in the universe, why do we not see evidence for it?[29] Preliminary searches for evidence of technological civilizations in this galaxy, while hardly exhaustive or conclusive, have produced the Great Silence: if such civilizations exist, we as yet see no evidence for them. This may be because they do not exist, at least in this galaxy; because we have not looked hard enough; or because they have advanced so far as to be effectively invisible to human observational techniques.

But as awareness has grown of the many ways, both natural and anthropogenic, that humanity might be rendered extinct on this planet, thinkers on the intelligent life question have suggested that there is a series of Great Filters operating to winnow out life forms between the emergence of life on a planet and the expansion of intelligent life forms across the galaxy. These lines of reasoning assume that other intelligent species confront a set of existential threats roughly comparable to the ones humanity faces, and then assert that the Great Silence is explained by the operation of these Great Filters. In sum, all other intelligent life forms eventually succumb to one or another peril and become extinct, thus answering the question of why we do not see evidence for them.

Once ambitious space expansion is itself accurately viewed as posing severe catastrophic and existential threats, another explanation for the Fermi Paradox suggests itself. The threats posed by ambitious space expansion are sufficiently general in their logic that they can reasonably be expected to apply to any intelligent species that emerges anywhere. If this is the case, and an intelligent species emerges and pursues ambitious space expansion, it would significantly *raise* its chances of becoming extinct. If, as many space expansionists believe, it is inevitable that life forms inevitably expand, and that intelligent life forms will inevitably expand into space, then space expansion leading to alien astrocide itself becomes a Great Filter. If, on the other hand, intelligent life forms elsewhere on the threshold of becoming significantly spacefaring are able, as we are, to anticipate the numerous perils stemming from this path, they might then decide, as we can and should, to relinquish large-scale space expansion. If they demonstrate their intelligence in the face of this cluster of perils, they stay at home, thus rendering themselves effectively invisible to us. In short, if we are intelligent enough—as we surely are, at least in principle—to relinquish large-scale space expansion, other intelligent species can be expected to do so as well. The reason we do not see evidence for other intelligent species in the cosmos is that they either succumbed to the perils of expansion or intelligently eschewed this path. They have not come here because they are smart enough to not leave there.

Conclusion

Space for Earth

> If we can't make it in this beautifully equipped [space] colony, we're not
> going to make it anywhere else, either.
> —Buckminster Fuller (1978)[1]

> What we don't know can kill us, but so can what we refuse to know.
> —Duncan Lunan (2014)[2]

> If we do not steer, we run the danger of ending up where we are going.
> —Eliezer Yudkowsky (2008)[3]

Dreams and Nightmares

Probably the most oft-quoted passage in space expansionist thought is from its
very beginnings, from Tsiolkovsky: "Earth is the cradle of humanity, but one
cannot live in a cradle forever."[4] Imagining Earth-bound humans in the bed
of species infancy creates a progressive trajectory of human development as a
movement into the cosmos. Children leave their cradles as they grow, and so
too humanity will—and must—leave its Earthly cradle. But this analogy also
suggests a message very different from the one its author surely intended and
which space enthusiasts routinely assume. If humans on Earth are indeed in
an infant state, then it also stands to reason that many—if not most—of their
visions of the future are essentially infantile as well, marked by the complete triumph of wishful and imaginary thinking over actual practical possibilities. Any
adolescent or adult who maintained all the aspirations and anticipations they
fancied as small children would be catastrophically maladjusted and prone to
disastrously life-threatening actions.

Coming of age means putting aside the fairy tales of childhood. Growing
up does not mean the realization of all childhood dreams, but rather their
winnowing and modification with the benefit of new knowledge and experience,
recognizing realities and making hard decisions involving painful trade-offs. The

maturation of humanity as a species should be marked by a sober—if wistful— setting aside of the limitless space fantasies of the species' infancy. The intellectual coming of age of humanity can thus be measured by its rejection of its childish dreams of escaping from what it must live with, of becoming something it cannot be, and of going places where it cannot thrive. It means disciplining actions in the light of their consequences. Childhood's end means learning to live well on Earth, not escaping from it.

With the globalization of machine civilization and the astounding empowerment produced by accelerating scientific and technological advance, humanity finds itself in a situation where its choices have massively amplified consequences. Humanity is no longer a teen playing with matches but a child playing with flamethrowers.[5] The avoidance of civilizational disaster and species extinction now depends on discerning what not to do, and then making sure it is not done. Previously harmless activities now have consequences of bewildering complexity, sobering magnitude, and awesome duration. Decisions with large and long-term consequences must increasingly be made, often with frighteningly inadequate information.

The overall human response to this sobering new world of very adult species choices looks largely adolescent in character. Impulses still outrun prudent calculation of risks. Impatience is great and attention spans are short; no one wants to make their bed or take out the garbage. Restraints chafe; no one wants to close off options or forgo possibilities. Interdependence seems threatening to freedom. Responsibility is dreary and must be evaded. Hopes and dreams seem more real than dangers and problems. We act as if we are immortal and playing in a sandbox. We proceed as if we will be rescued if things go awry by someone who knows better. We imagine escaping from problems rather than solving them. If we proceed into space mainly on the basis of childish dreams, we run the risk of realizing very adult nightmares.

Illusions and Evasions

Dream-walking into space is sleepwalking into space. Of the many domains of choice demanding prudent decisions and sober restraints, space thinking is particularly prone to dreamy assumptions, beguiling illusions, and stark disorientations. Space is radically unlike any place on the terrestrial Earth, and our thinking about its possibilities is marred by major misplacements and disorientations, sustained by mesmerizing but radically misleading technological imaginaries. The deeply rooted ascentionist assumption that going higher means getting better leads to the unwarranted conclusion that going into space will produce desirable consequences. The credibility of space expansionism is massively enhanced by the multiverses of science fictions and the intensely realistic images conjured by modern cinematic technologies. An arsenal of geophysical and geohistorical analogies, cherry-picked by advocates, makes space familiar and expansion desirable, if not inevitable. And to a remarkable extent, the ancient view of the heavens as a special place occupied by beings of great power has been transposed into a secular technological aspiration.

Space expansionist thinking is sustained by an imposing and seductive edifice of illusions and evasions. While advocates tout space as a frontier for expansion to escape and ameliorate planetary closure, almost all space activities have occurred in the space part of this planet and have intensified closure. With their eyes fixed on the distant and enormous, space advocates overlook the proximate and small realities of the astrosphere. The basic problem with expansionist views of space—past, present, and future—is the same: a massive discounting of the violence potentials inherent in the enterprise. Simple and convenient errors in classification and placement hide the fact that the dominant space activity—weaponization and militarization—has amplified the primary contemporary existential threat to humanity and has sustained the illusion that space activities have a positive relation to national and global security. Blind to the perils of long-standing space weaponization by their "not in my department" mentality, most space expansionists are much more eager to hitch a ride on renewed interstate rivalry than to use space to diminish the dangers to the planet arising from interstate conflicts.[6]

Interstate military rivalry propelled much of human space activity, but space expansionists ask us to believe conflicts will not be carried into solar space. Overcoming interstate rivalries on the highly interdependent Earth where large-scale violence is effectively suicidal is deemed utopian. But a Solar Archipelago populated by radically different polities, perhaps different species, and equipped with titanic violence potentials is, somehow, no problem. Space expansionists assure us that the arid, frigid, and lifeless wastelands of Mars can be turned into habitable space for humanity, but that sustaining the habitability of Terra teeming with life is too difficult. The religion of cosmism at the core of habitat space expansionism proposes steps deemed in the interest of life in general which eventually will almost assuredly terminate humanity. What advances itself as a cosmic life cult has at its core a human death destiny.

Humanity's problem is not that it is stuck on Earth but that it is stuck in an inherited, fragmented, stratified, and violence-prone international system. If humanity is unable to overcome anarchy to establish mutual restraints and pursue mutually beneficial problem-solving on Earth, where so many factors are supportive, it is more unlikely to be able to do so in geopolitically malefic solar space. Space-political problems are at least as challenging as the space environment but much less likely to be overcome. Humans and their institutions are not—and are not likely to become—capable enough to meet daunting solar space governance challenges.

The space expansionist expectation that a large-scale human movement into space will advance freedom is especially dubious. From Tsiolkovsky's giddy anticipation that weightlessness, a freedom from gravity, will somehow be a liberation rather than a biomedical hazard, to the current astrolibertarian craze, space expansionist thinking is consistently naive about the potentials for space activity to produce new comprehensive forms of confinement and domination. Space colonies, strongly disposed to be highly oppressive, are advanced as oases of freedom. Vast orbital infrastructures with the potential to dominate the Earth are advanced as a vital objective for "the free world." Anyone who values human political freedom must be an opponent of large-scale human expansion into space.

Space expansionism should be recognized as having not only a plethora of bad proposals but also a frightening potential for evil. The record of history amply demonstrates that salvation religions and strong modernist secular ideologies are sometimes prone to fanaticism with genocidal outcomes. Space expansionism, a secular religion infused with the highest modernist technological ambitions for a heavenly elevation of humanity, should be seen as a particularly dangerous potential fanaticism. For any religion or ideology promising heavenly ascent, the goal is so transcendently valuable that it becomes all too easy to justify *any* step leading forward and upward.

To help keep this ultimately evil potential of space fanaticism from slipping out of sight, a memorable warning of the underside of the space expansionist quest for Übermensch elevation should be emblazoned at the base of the stairway to the heavens and burned into our species' collective consciousness. The liquidation of the hapless denizens of Planet Dora by the ruthless "master race" builders of the first large rockets is commonly treated as an unfortunate historical accident having nothing to do with the space enterprise and everything to do with the contingent features of the Hitler regime. But when von Braun promotes nuclear-armed space stations for worldwide domination, the mentality of "the end justifies any means" is being taken to cosmic dimensions, further "aiming for the stars, but hitting London." The ease and frequency with which high-modernist technocratic and macro-engineering technological imaginaries are combined with horrifically genocidal projects warns that once very big things start getting moved around, multitudes of little people tend to get crushed. And when space expansionists embrace a narrative of human expansion into space that silently jumps from promoting the interests of *humanity* to those of *life*, they are clearly trafficking in an ideology that will all too easily be employed to justify ghastly crimes when circumstances make them seem vital to realizing their ascending path.

Oasis Earth, the Biosphere One Project, and Double NOPE

The most important practical discovery of Space Age astronomy, that the Earth is a minuscule oasis of flourishing life in an unfathomably vast and desolate wilderness, has not yet adequately transformed human behavior. The implication of this discovery is captured in the environmentalist slogan "There is no planet B." In the years around the beginning of the twentieth century, when the core ideas of space expansionism were coalescing, it was plausible to suppose that other bodies in the solar system harbored life, perhaps even intelligent life. While there may be microbes in watery nooks here or there, scientific investigations across the twentieth century clearly established that Terra is a very special place, an oasis teeming with a splendid diversity of life in a stupendously large and inhospitable cosmic wasteland stretching many trillions of miles in all directions. Every time a species on Earth becomes extinct, it is probably an event of galactic significance. The discovery of the specialness of Earth, reversing the Principle of Mediocrity erroneously inferred from the plurality of worlds of the Copernican Revolution, means that humanity's first cosmic duty is to protect life on Earth. Humans who purport to be guardians and evolutionary agents of life have a terrestrial, not a space expansionist, mission to accomplish.[7]

The major contemporary threats to Oasis Earth are of human making. Reforming human practices to sustain rather than jeopardize Earth life in all its wondrous diversity is the foremost task of humanity in this century and beyond. The imperatives of a Biosphere One Project must guide the overall priorities of humanity, and space activities must be measured by their contribution to this enterprise. Learning to live on Earth in ways consistent with the continued viability of the biosphere clearly requires an acceptance of limits. Unlimited extensive growth, the goal of Promethean modernity, is the ideology of a cancer cell and a planetary menace. Recognizing these realities, environmental thinkers speak of classes of activities, such as the detonation of large numbers of nuclear weapons or the significant alteration of the planet's atmosphere, that must be firmly and permanently prohibited and to which humanity must always say NOPE—Not On Planet Earth.

Inspired by Promethean visions of unlimited expansion, space advocates have responded to NOPE restraints by proposing perpetual growth off the planet in the unlimited reaches of space, turning terrestrial limits into a mandate for extraterrestrial expansion. OPEN!—Off Planet Earth Now!—they insist. But these proposals, realistically assessed, promise not solutions to Earth limits, problems, and troubles, but rather their amplification and the creation of a whole new set of catastrophic and existential threats. This assessment thus points to the need for an additional NOPE standard: Not Off Planet Earth. Filling the planet's astrosphere with large infrastructures, colonizing other celestial bodies, and routinely rerouting asteroids will produce major new threats to the Earth and humanity, and thus must be met with the second NOPE. Fundamental interests of the human species and the Earth now require the pursuit of this double NOPE program. Large-scale space expansion promises astrocide, not reduction of existential risks. With each enlargement in human technological power, the survival of civilization and humanity comes to hinge further on capacities of restraint, on our collective ability to say no. The good news is that species death by astrocide can be avoided much more easily than by cosmocidal, terracidal, or other technogenic threats, simply by saying no.

The basic facts of Earth and space need to be registered in the ledger sheet of life in a realistic manner, and in a way that will make a meaningful difference on Earth. Perhaps the simplest way to do this would be to adopt a "space replacement cost" yardstick for pricing natural assets on the Earth in all calculations and decisions that result in the degradation of the biosphere. All across the planet, wetlands are being drained, reefs destroyed, soils eroded, and forests felled by actors making some semblance of cost-benefit analysis. In a few far-sighted places, developers are forced to take into account at least some of the externalities of their activities. The appropriate standard should be to despoil only when the benefits imputed to development exceed the cost of replacement with a comparable ecological resource *in space*. The costs today of replacing a forest or wetland on Earth with something comparable in space are literally incalculable and surely astronomical.[8] By measuring the value of what we blithely ravage on Oasis Earth with the enormous costs of replacement in space, we acquire a cosmically calibrated metric of restraint.

Toward an Earth-Centered Space Program

The negative consequences of space activities have been far more significant than space expansionists acknowledge. Future space activities hold far less positive and vastly more negative potential than space expansionists believe. Many of the positive potentials of space, while more modest than their advocates think, are significantly underpursued. Overall, what should be *undone* and *not done* is far more important than what should be *done*. Once freed from pervasive space expansionist illusions and errors about space past, present, and future, it becomes possible to construct a space program for Oasis Earth that is better configured to avoid dangers and seize opportunities. An Earth Age space program pursues activities that contribute, to the limited extent possible, to solving Earth problems while avoiding the creation of further problems. An Earth-centered space program differs significantly from what has been occurring in space, and differs almost completely from the large and ambitious agenda of military and habitat space expansionists. Because so many current and prospective activities have been, or promise to be, extremely harmful, an Earth-oriented space program is heavily—but certainly not entirely—slanted to the negative, toward restraint through reversals, regulations, and relinquishments.

Guided by the medical dictum "First do no harm," reversals, regulations, and relinquishments are necessarily the most important parts of an Oasis Earth space program. With these restraints, the path is cleared for the pursuit of a more modest but less dangerous set of space activities. The elements of an Earth-oriented space program fall into three broad groupings (see Table C.1): activities that should either be reversed or relinquished; activities that should be

Table C.1 **Elements of an Earth-Oriented Space Program**

Activity	Policy	Rationale
Ballistic missiles and orbital weapons	Reverse and relinquish	Reduce likelihood of nuclear war
Large Earth orbital infrastructures	Relinquish	Reduce prospects for hierarchical world government
Colonization of Mars and asteroids	Relinquish	Eliminate danger of catastrophic interworld war and antagonistic species radiation
National or corporate asteroidal orbit alteration	Relinquish	Reduce probability of military use
International consortium of asteroidal orbit alteration	Expand	Provide planetary defense with minimum risk of military use
Outer Space Treaty	Strengthen	Provide framework for civil space activity, arms control, and debris mitigation
Earth system science	Expand	Increase knowledge to sustain planetary habitability
Astronomy from space	Expand	Increase knowledge of the cosmos

conducted only by broadly representative international consortia; and activities currently under way that should be expanded, strengthened, and redirected.

Reverse, Regulate, and Relinquish

First and most important, the weaponization and militarization of space should be restrained. What matters most about the events of the Space Age is how they have interacted with the possibilities of the Nuclear Age and their cata-strophic and existential threats to humanity and the Earth. By excluding ballistic missiles from the space story, space advocates have, ironically, underestimated the magnitude—and direction—of space impacts. Because the single most con-sequential impact of actual space activities has been to increase the risk of nu-clear war, the single most important goal for an Earth-oriented space program is to continue and complete the dismantlement of ballistic missiles for the de-livery of nuclear weapons. Next in importance is preventing the development and deployment of orbiting weapons designed to attack objects in orbital space. Because the most successful actual space program in terms of contributing to the reduction of catastrophic and existential risks is what has gone under the name of "nuclear arms control," an effort to complete this project builds on what has been learned during the Space Age rather than the fantasies that preceded it.

Second, the construction of large infrastructures in Earth orbital space should be relinquished. While such megastructures may be increasingly feasible as engineering projects, their ability to positively contribute to solving terres-trial energy and environmental problems is quite doubtful. It may be possible to build infrastructures to collect and beam energy from near space through the Earth's atmosphere or to partially shade the planet from sunlight. But whether such megatechnics will have their intended consequences, rather than severe unintended ones, is far beyond the current abilities of Earth system science to predict. Space-based geo-engineering should not be seen as Plan B but rather as a plan to avoid at all costs, Plan F. Furthermore, large Earth space infrastructures should be relinquished because any structure large and important enough to make a decisive contribution to solving important Earth problems is also likely to either require or produce a highly hierarchical world state that would itself be a catastrophic outcome of historically unprecedented magnitude.

Third, the alteration of the orbits of asteroidal bodies by any single gov-ernment or corporation should be explicitly relinquished. Once the orbits of these bodies have been fully mapped and techniques to alter their orbits have been demonstrated, humanity will have acquired a destructive capability vastly exceeding nuclear weapons. How, when, and by whom this technology is de-veloped has first-order implications for the human species and the fate of the

Earth. Acquiring this knowledge and developing these technologies is vital, and it is probably just a matter of time until there is a sudden urgency to do so. Mapping asteroidal orbits and developing the capabilities to alter their orbits in the context of militarized interstate rivalry would be the most undesirable path. Allowing private corporations to map and alter would also be extremely undesirable; rival governments probably would rush in once the destructive potential of these activities is recognized. Furthermore, allowing the potential mineral wealth of asteroids to be harvested by a tiny handful of the wealthiest of the wealthy would further exacerbate the already obscene levels of inequality marring the human world. Given the inherent mass destructive potential of asteroidal orbital alteration, allowing private companies answerable to only a handful of corporate owners to develop this technology would be like allowing private firms to develop the hydrogen bomb in the 1950s.

Fourth, the expansionist objective of colonizing Mars and other celestial bodies beyond the Earth should be explicitly relinquished. Reversing the employment of space capabilities for waging nuclear war and abandoning the construction of large orbital infrastructures do not fundamentally impair the most central of expansionist aspirations, but relinquishing the colonization of Mars cuts to its heart. Once a viable human colony on Mars has been established, a crucial threshold will have been passed and the path opened to the full range of catastrophic and existential threats likely to result from solar space expansion. It is no more inevitable that humans will settle Mars than that they will colonize Antarctica or the ocean floor.

But what, it might be objected, is the actual harm of a colony on Mars, which would be vastly distant from the Earth, have a tiny population, and initially be focused on surviving the harsh rigors of an inhospitable environment? How could a few hundred humans, out of a total population of billions, located tens of millions of miles from Earth, be in any way a threat? An initially small and precarious colony on Mars would itself not be any threat whatsoever, and thus would seem a questionable candidate for relinquishment. The problem is not what a Mars colony initially would be, but what it very likely would eventually become. A small and harmless colony might eventually become a large and threatening colony. The best way to think about a colony on Mars is the way we think about the first cancer cell that appears in a human body. It is extremely tiny and not itself the cause of any harm whatsoever. Its peril lies in what it will become once it has started its path of growth. Unlike the first cancer cell that emerges invisibly and cannot be readily stopped, a Mars colony will be highly visible and can be readily stopped. Along with fabricating nuclear arsenals capable of obliterating civilization and wrecking this planet's habitat, planting a settlement seed on Mars is a foreseeable and avoidable species-scope mistake that future generations will curse us for making.

In making these four big relinquishments, humanity takes the decisive steps to align space activities with the general interests of humanity and the Earth. Three of these relinquishments—weaponization, large infrastructures, and colonization—are straightforward: just say no. But choices about asteroids are filled with difficult dilemmas. Completely relinquishing the mapping and alteration of asteroidal orbits is very unwise because the collision of such bodies with the Earth is inevitable. If they are not deflected, they will eventually strike the Earth; if they are diverted, they eventually might be directed to strike the Earth even more frequently. While Sagan advised delaying such measures until some semblance of effective world government had emerged, he also embraced the colonization agenda whose eventual outcome would be off-world actors with both the capabilities to catastrophically bombard the Earth and plausible incentives to do so. The relinquishment of colonization means there will be no actors elsewhere to possibly act, leaving only Earth-based actors in play.

If the longer term and larger threat posed by spacekind wielding these gargantuan violence capabilities can be thwarted, then there may be a serviceable solution to the deflection dilemma: asteroidal mapping and diversion should be undertaken *only* by a consortium of leading states on Earth.[9] Such a deflection consortium should be assigned the task, given the sole legal authority, and equipped with the resources to develop the capacity to defend the planet from cosmic bombardment. Such an effort would fall far short of bringing a world government into existence, and the enduring mutual suspicion of states would impede the asteroid apparat from becoming the nucleus of a world state. It would be appropriately staffed and operated not by a distinct body of international civil servants but rather by members of the militaries of the contributing states.[10] After this consortium is operating, the path for possibly eventually mining asteroids for the benefit of the many would also open. Like any human venture, a strategy of military cooperation for planetary security would have its own risks and potential paths of breakdown. Once asteroidal orbits are mapped and techniques to divert them tested, a vast destructive potential is placed permanently into human hands. If the planetary protection consortium were to break down, this violence capacity would be possessed by several states. But as long as this agency remained solely focused on its narrow mission, and no private or off-world actors were permitted to engage in these activities, states would have a strong incentive to sustain the arrangement. Once this fearsome technology has been demonstrated, the relinquishment of colonization would also probably be reinforced, as the scope of Earth's vulnerability would be inescapably obvious.

Taken together, these relinquishments would terminate the core parts of both the von Braun and Tsiolkovsky programs, while realizing the arms control goals of the Clarke-Sagan program. While conceptually discrete, these regulations and relinquishments are also organically interconnected with one another and depend on one another, in much the same way that the parts of the militarization and habitation programs are and do. If one part succeeds, the success of other parts is more likely; if one part fails, other parts will be more prone to fail as well.

Strengthen, Expand, and Redirect

Three positive parts of an Oasis Earth space program have the potential to make valuable but probably ancillary contributions to solving significant Earth problems. First in importance is expanding the study of the Earth from space through the use of orbital platforms for observing and monitoring of this planet's bio-geophysical systems. Because anthropogenic climate change is a planetary problem of the first magnitude, the most important contribution space activity can make to the human situation in the Anthropocene is to provide scientists with more and better information. The resources allocated to this vital enterprise remain scandalously low, reflecting both the insufficient priority governments place on climate research and the limited focus space advocates place on Earth studies. More knowledge harvested from satellites will not in itself slow climate change, but it can play a critical contributing role and is arguably the single most important contribution space activities can make in sustaining the habitability of the Earth.

Second, the provisions of the Outer Space Treaty should be preserved and strengthened.[11] For governing the small and already crowded and degraded astrosphere, an environmentalist sensibility is needed. Far from being obsolete, the treaty provides an essential framework for building an Oasis Earth space program. The treaty is incomplete in not restraining ballistic missiles and orbital weapons, and it is under attack by space advocates and by the small but powerful special interests who want to appropriate asteroids for private economic gain. Strengthening this regime complements the reversals and relinquishments of the Earth Age space program. Phasing out ballistic missiles and banning their tests will eliminate any need for antiballistic missile systems. Expanding the treaty to outlaw weapons tests in orbit prevents an orbital weapons arms race. Preventing weapons tests also eliminates a large source of space debris. Relinquishing colonization will help sustain the treaty's provisions prohibiting the appropriation of celestial bodies. If mapping asteroidal orbits, assessing their mineral resources, and developing techniques to alter their orbits are done solely by an international consortium, competitive pressures to assert sovereignty or ownership will be minimized. If asteroids are mined, profits should be widely distributed.[12] Similarly, abandoning the construction of large orbital infrastructures will diminish pressures to abandon the free passage provisions of the treaty. And an expanded commitment to deploy much more extensive Earth-monitoring satellites will entail more international scientific cooperation. Military and colonization programs should not be relinquished in order to preserve and expand the Outer Space Treaty; rather they should be relinquished because their consequences are undesirable. The treaty regime can assist in achieving these relinquishments, which can in turn help strengthen the treaty regime.

Third, more resources should be devoted to space science, conducted cooperatively. More robotic missions of steadily increasing capabilities should be sent throughout the solar system. More and larger orbital observatories to study the cosmos should be built. More astrobiological searches for evidence of life elsewhere in the cosmos should be conducted. China and India should be invited to join and help expand the ISS, and possible future science bases should be cooperatively constructed. Crewed scientific exploratory missions to the moon, Mars, and the asteroids may become cost effective in conducting some kinds of important scientific research. But the desirability of sending humans and building bases should not be assessed solely on calculations of cost and efficiency for scientific yields. In building scientific bases, we would approach a very dangerous line to colonization. It is vital to conduct such scientific ventures in a way that prevents exploration from sliding into colonization. To the extent there is a danger of this happening, outposts on other celestial bodies should be proportionately avoided.

Pursuing this Earth-centered space program will bring human space activities into line with actual major human interests far better than the von Braun and Tsiolkovsky programs. And it builds on the successes of the arms control and information-centric Clarke-Sagan program. But nothing lasts forever and unexpected change is inevitable, posing the question: How long should this restraint-heavy agenda govern human space activities? New information will inevitably arise, and new situations will present themselves. Arguments and concerns that seem compelling now may fade and be replaced by others, potentially more favorable to large-scale space expansion.[13] At a minimum this Earth-centered program should prevail for at least a long century, and probably several centuries. Only after humanity has figured out how to order its political affairs by effectively regulating nuclear weapons, and not wrecking the planetary life support system, can space expansion be anything but a potentially dangerous diversion or amplification. And only after humanity has ridden through the daunting choices posed by the unfolding biotechnology and cybernetic revolutions should space colonization be seriously entertained.

Whatever emerges on Earth after these adjustments and revolutions have run their course will be better able than humanity today to weigh the consequences of large-scale space expansion. My hunch is that the basic profile of threats related to interplanetary war and the radiation of intelligent species in solar space will provide very long-lasting reasons to avoid the siren call of expansion into the ultimate frontier. Even if the neo-eugenic promise of human improvement through bio- and cyberengineering can be realized and the crooked timber of humanity be straightened and strengthened, large-scale expansion into space may still be judged something to avoid. The more fully rational creatures promised by transhumanism may find large-scale violence to be consistent with their rational self-interest in the structural setting of a solar space diaspora. Furthermore, a human or posthuman civilization with full mastery of genetic and cybernetic enhancement technologies will be much better equipped to foresee the full range of the superintelligent and superpowerful monstrosities and menaces that technologically enabled species radiation in off-worlds might be capable of birthing. And to the extent the survival of human successor species on Earth depends upon preventing the emergence of a self-directing artificial superintelligence, an enduring relinquishment of space expansion becomes necessary.

Slippery Slopes, Trivial Pursuits, and Dubious Dawns

Current thinking about space is overwhelmingly informed by the assumption that doing more in space is good, and anything contributing to this end is therefore also desirable. Once major space activities are accurately understood as posing catastrophic and astrocidal threats, measures now deemed valuable as stepping stones to something of supreme value are transformed into slippery slopes to dangerous abysses, and therefore are to be carefully avoided. Three interrelated efforts—lowering costs of accessing space, space tourism, and privatization—are currently viewed by space advocates as useful steps to the eventual realization of the larger space expansionist program. They are actually a mix of trouble and trivia leading to danger precisely because of their potential to open the larger door to extensive space activities.

Everything space expansionists want to do in space depends upon accessing space more cheaply. But substantially lowering access costs is very much a double-edged sword. If it is cheaper and easier to get to orbit, then all space activities become cheaper and easier to accomplish, whether or not their effects are desirable. The main reason so many space expansionist projects with ultimately undesirable outcomes have not yet been undertaken is simply because they cost too much. Given that colonization, infrastructure construction, and Earth Net weaponization are particularly sensitive to the costs of accessing orbit, lowering costs is probably more harmful than beneficial. If technological breakthroughs make possible cost reductions of several orders of magnitude, reversals and relinquishments will become vastly harder to achieve and maintain. Given all this, substantially lowering the costs of accessing space should be viewed as similar to advances in uranium enrichment technology, which enable more actors to acquire nuclear weapons. In a world with robust regulation of nuclear material, lower cost enrichment is probably tolerable, but if costs become extremely low, even the best regulatory arrangements become difficult to sustain.

Space tourism also looms on the near horizon. In any accurate ledger of planetary and species priorities, space tourism is a trivial pursuit. It does not help solve any major Earth problem, or indeed any problem, beyond the boredom of the excessively wealthy.[14] But it seems harmless enough in itself. Space tourism could also turn out to be more appealing in theory than in practice.[15] Barring some biomedical advance, an appreciable percentage of people experiencing weightlessness are likely to suffer from "space sickness," making for many very expensive "vomit comets." Such ventures are also likely to be fairly dangerous, a form of extreme adventure tourism, and the occurrence of a catastrophic accident could quickly send its economics plummeting. On the other hand, ringing the Earth with frivolous tourist hotels might create a modest break on further space weaponization and militarization activities. Barring massive reductions in the cost of reaching orbit, space tourism will remain very expensive, available to only a minuscule share of the world's population. Circling the planet with what will amount to sex hotels and meditation pads for the superwealthy will thus be a highly visible symbol of the highly stratified condition of humanity, a sort of cosmic advertisement for one of the planet's major maladies. But the emergence of a robust space tourism sector could also contribute to the lowering of costs to access Earth orbit, turning a trivial pursuit into a slippery slope to colonization, making its relinquishment more difficult.

The recent push to privatize as much space activity as possible, propelled by American space activists, antigovernment ideologues, and entrepreneurs, has placed much of its emphasis on lowering orbital access costs, launching space tourism and mining asteroids as steps to greater ambitions. Overall, privatization has very mixed implications for establishing an Earth Age space program. On the one hand, privatization is mildly subversive of the establishment and maintenance of restraints and relinquishments. Getting governments to agree to regulate private actors is a degree more difficult than getting governments to restrain their own activities. And the more actors there are, the more difficult it will be to establish and maintain the relinquishment of space colonization and large infrastructure deployment, as well as to keep asteroidal manipulation solely in the hands of an interstate consortium. Many astro-entrepreneurs are not just seeking profits but view themselves as providing a vital service to humanity by making space expansion more feasible. They envision plowing profits from space into further space ventures, making suitable restraints more difficult to establish and maintain.

Despite the fervent conviction of astrolibertarians that privatization will accelerate the development of space, it is more likely to retard the overall enterprise. Libertarianism, the political philosophy of the politically naive (or the cynical rich), is adept at privatizing the benefits of public expenditures but is unlikely to propel significant human expansion into space. Libertarian-inspired space expansionism may produce some spectacular vanity projects for the planetary Peter Pans, while diverting valuable attention and resources away from real planetary priorities. And relying on a handful of superrich visionaries means the enterprise is only a death, a change of whim, or a business setback from collapsing.[16] Allowing a handful of messianic internet billionaires to steer the space enterprise is an extremely dubious way to make decisions with species-existential consequences. Space choices are too important to be left to the space cadets.

In reality, only governments and groups of governments have the staying power and resources to surmount the large costs, high risks, doubtful profitability, and long lead-times needed for major space advances.[17] China, with its mega-engineering tradition and powerful central government, is now better situated to make large-scale space happen than the fiscally hollowed, politically gridlocked, and captured states in the West. But the fact that so many governments are too strapped and burdened to make large-scale commitments to space spares humanity from early realization of space menaces. And looking at the knuckleheads ruling many major states, the pathetic condition of global governance, and the rise of stridently backward-looking neonationalist antiglobalism, it would be folly to anticipate beneficial outcomes. The combination of deeply recalcitrant Epimethean governments and peoples and ever more potent Promethean technologies bodes ill for humanity.

The full realization of an Earth-oriented space program will not solve the problems of nuclear insecurity and environmental destruction and will not trigger the emergence of a limited confederal world government suitable to the densely interconnected and vulnerable contemporary Earth. Preventing a cosmic resource grab of asteroidal minerals by a small handful of the Earth's wealthiest inhabitants and countries will not in itself reduce the chasm of extreme inequality afflicting humanity. But realizing an Earth Age space program will make contributions toward important planetary security and habitability goals, will prevent problems from getting worse, and will foreclose the emergence of a whole new set of catastrophic and existential risks inherent in large-scale space expansion. While modest, they are the most positive contributions that space activities can make to the overall human situation for the foreseeable future.

Choices, Destinies, and Inevitabilities

Seasoned observers of space politics might well respond to this Oasis Earth space program by noting how difficult it will be to realize. After all, many of these measures have been proposed before, and many have been extensively discussed in negotiations by leading states. Their realization runs against the apparent interests and goals of a wide range of powerful and entrenched groups. What is going to convert desirable proposals into realized programs? This is a question space expansionists should be very concerned with answering, because if these modest measures to employ space technologies in desirable ways cannot be achieved now, how can one expect choices toward desirable outcomes will be made when the ventures—and stakes—are much larger?

Space expansionists also frequently proclaim that the movement of humanity, or at least some favored part of it, to other celestial bodies is not just desirable but also inevitable. But nothing so difficult and dangerous as space colonization can realistically be viewed as inevitable. Space expansionists point out that the Earth will inevitably become uninhabitable for life as the sun begins its expansive trajectory to explosive death. These arguments entail completely irrelevant time scales for current choices. The fact that the extended death throes of the sun will assuredly start making the Earth uninhabitable in a half-billion years or so has absolutely no relevance to any human choice about space for at least hundreds of millions of years to come. In an era when time horizons of so many actors are shrinking while the temporal consequences of so many human activities are growing, more extended time horizons for decision-making are imperative. But the long-term time horizons that now matter extend into centuries and millennia, not into hundreds of millions of years. Our choice, at least for millions of years, is not, as Wells breathlessly proclaimed, between "all the universe or nothing."

Measured against the aspirations of space expansionists, the Space Age has largely been a disappointment. Space activities, as diverse and spectacular as they have been, do not lay plausible claim to being the defining events of this period of human history. The pursuit of ambitious space expansion must now prudentially be judged to be deeply undesirable for humanity and the Earth for at least several centuries. As long as large-scale space ventures have been infeasible, it has been possible to view them as desirable without suffering any consequences from our illusions. But the time when we can escape doing the undesirable because it is largely infeasible will not last indefinitely. Eventually, and perhaps soon, we will no longer be protected from the consequences of our delusions by our incapacities, and we will suffer severely unless we learn to firmly say no. The only inevitabilities are that we must choose, that our foresight, steering, and restraint capacities are limited, and that we will live—or die—with the consequences of our choices.

NOTES

Prologue: Machine Civilization and the Transformation of the Earth

1. John von Neumann, "Can We Survive Technology?" *Fortune*, 51(6), June 1955, 106.
2. Robert Salkeld, *War and Space* (Englewood Cliffs, NJ: Prentice-Hall, 1970), xvi.
3. Accounts of these destructions now fill whole libraries. Landmark accounts are William L. Thomas, ed., *Man's Role in Changing the Face of the Earth*, 2 vols. (Chicago: University of Chicago Press, 1956); B. L. Turner, W. C. Clark, R. W. Kates, J. F. Richards, J. T. Mathews, and W. B. Meyer, *The Earth as Transformed by Human Action* (Cambridge, UK: Cambridge University Press, 1990).
4. Among theorists of international politics, the term "globalization" has long been used to characterize this multidimensional and multicentury process, but it came into much wider use in the 1990s in a much narrower sense, to refer only to the post–Cold War expansion of international trade. For an example of the broad use, see George Modelski, *Principles of World Politics* (New York: Free Press, 1972), 10, 46–49.
5. Among the numerous accounts of this expansion, Daniel R. Headrick, *Power over Peoples: Technology, Environments, and Western Imperialism, 1400 to the Present* (Princeton, NJ: Princeton University Press, 2010) links its pace and direction to advances in technology and the obstacles posed by different geographies and ecologies.
6. For Bacon as a founder of Western modernity, see Jerry Weinberger, *Science, Faith, and Politics: Francis Bacon and the Utopian Roots of the Modern Age* (Ithaca, NY: Cornell University Press, 1985).
7. Stephen Kern, *The Culture of Time and Space* (Cambridge, MA: Harvard University Press, 1983); David Landis, *The Unbound Prometheus: Technological Change and Industrial Development in Western Europe 1750 to the Present* (Cambridge, UK: Cambridge University Press, 1969).
8 Stephen Pinker, *Enlightenment Now: The Case for Reason, Science, Humanism and Progress* (New York: Penguin, 2018).
9. The now commonplace characterization of scientific discovery with the geographic construct of the frontier appears in the 1945 report by President Roosevelt's science adviser that led to the creation of the National Science Foundation. Vannevar Bush, *Science: The Endless Frontier* (Washington, DC: National Printing Office, 1945). Characterizing scientific and technological advance as the conquest of nature has been widespread over the last several centuries. John Nef, *The Conquest of the Material World* (Chicago: University of Chicago Press, 1964).
10. For the religious dimensions of Bacon's "great instauration," see Stephen A. McKnight, *The Religious Foundations of Francis Bacon's Thought* (Columbia: University of Missouri Press, 2006). And more generally Mary Midgley, *Science as Salvation: A Modern Myth and Its Meaning* (London: Routledge, 1992); David F. Noble, *The Religion of Technology: The Divinity of Man and the Spirit of Invention* (New York: Penguin, 1999).

11. For the range and sophistication of ancient thinking on this topic, see Adrienne Mayor, *Gods and Robots: Myths, Machines and Ancient Dreams of Technology* (Princeton, NJ: Princeton University Press, 2018).

12. For Butler's thought, see George Dyson, *Darwin among the Machines: The Evolution of Global Intelligence* (New York: Basic Books, 2001).

13. H. G. Wells, "The Discovery of the Future," *Nature* 65.1684 (1902): 326–31, at 331. For science in shaping Wells's views of the future, see Roslynn D. Haynes, *H. G. Wells: Discover of the Future* (New York: New York University Press, 1980).

14. A wide-ranging account of the effect of these disasters on Enlightenment optimism is provided by Ira Katznelson, *Desolation and Enlightenment: Political Knowledge after Total War, Totalitarianism, and the Holocaust* (New York: Columbia University Press, 2003).

15. For apocalyptic thinking past and present, see W. Warren Wager, *Terminal Visions: The Literature of Last Things* (Bloomington: Indiana University Press, 1982).

16. The best general account of a full-scale nuclear war and its implications for human survival remains Jonathan Schell, *The Fate of the Earth* (New York: Knopf, 1982). Further ecological consequences are described in Paul R. Ehrlich, Carl Sagan, Donald Kennedy, and Walter Orr Roberts, *The Cold and the Dark: The World after Nuclear War* (New York: Norton, 1984).

17. George Church and Ed Regis, *Regenesis: How Synthetic Biology Will Reinvent Nature and Ourselves* (New York: Basic Books, 2012).

18. The far-reaching implications of the miniaturization and diffusion of highly potent weapons are discussed in Fred Charles Ikle, *Annihilation from Within: The Ultimate Threat to Nations* (New York: Columbia University Press, 2006); Benjamin Witte and Gabriella Blum, *The Future of Violence: Robots and Germs, Hacker and Drones, Confronting a New Age of Threat* (New York: Basic Books, 2015).

19. For this emerging peril and potential difficulties in restraining it, see Nick Bostrom, *Superintelligence: Paths, Dangers, Strategies* (New York: Oxford University Press, 2014). For a tour d'horizon of the actors and arguments in the debate about artificial superintelligence, see James Barrat, *Our Final Invention: Artificial Intelligence and the End of the Human Era* (New York: St. Martin's Press, 2013).

20. Environmental history has become a large branch of historical studies. For synoptic accounts, see Jared Diamond, *Guns, Germs and Steel: The Fates of Human Societies* (New York: Norton, 1997); J. R. McNeill, *Something New under the Sun: An Environmental History of the Twentieth Century* (New York: Norton, 2001).

21. For synoptic accounts of trends, consequences, and implications, see Fred Pierce, *With Speed and Violence: Why Scientists Fear Tipping Points in Climate Change* (Boston: Beacon Press, 2007); Elizabeth Kolbert, *Field Notes from a Catastrophe: Man, Nature and Climate Change* (New York: Bloomsbury, 2005); Clive Hamilton, *Defiant Earth: Humans in the Anthropocene* (Cambridge, UK: Polity, 2017); David Wallace-Wells, *The Uninhabitable Earth: Life After Warming* (New York: Tim Duggan Books, 2019).

22. Elizabeth Kolbert, *The Sixth Extinction: An Unnatural History* (New York: Henry Holt, 2014); Donald Worster, *Shrinking Earth: The Rise and Decline of American Natural Abundance* (New York: Oxford University Press, 2016).

23. Drawing from the Russian geologist A. P. Pavlov, the visionary Russian geochemist Vladimir Vernadsky described the newly emerging "anthropogenic era" in which humanity had become "a mighty and ever-growing geological force." V. I. Vernadsky, "The Biosphere and the Noosphere," *American Scientist* 33.1 (January 1945): 8. With the rise of anthropogenic climate change, geologists now posit the present as the "Anthropocene." P. J. Crutzen, "Geology of Mankind," *Nature* 415.6867 (2002): 2–23; W. Steffen et al., "The Anthropocene: Are Humans Now Overwhelming the Great Forces of Nature?," *AMBIO: A Journal of the Human Environment* 36.8 (2007): 614–21. For plutonium fallout as the geological "golden spike" demarking the era, see Colin N. Water et al., "Can Nuclear Weapons Fallout Mark the Beginning of the Anthropocene Epoch?," *Bulletin of the Atomic Scientists* 7.3 (2015): 46–57.

24. Martin Rees, *Our Final Hour: A Scientist's Warning* (New York: Basic Books, 2003), 8. Nick Bostrom estimates that there is a 20 percent chance of human extinction over the twenty-first century. See his "The Future of Humanity," in Jan-Kyre Berg and Evan Selinger, eds., *New Waves in Philosophy of Technology* (New York: Palgrave Macmillan, 2007).

25. For forecasting and control efforts and the difficulties they confront, see Wendell Wallach, *A Dangerous Master: How to Keep Technology from Slipping Beyond Our Control* (New York: Basic Books, 2015). For dehumanizing implications and remedies, see Bill McKibben, *Enough: Staying Human in an Engineered Age* (New York: Henry Holt, 2003)

26. For numerous recent cases, see Richard A. Clarke and R. P. Eddy, *Warnings: Finding Cassandras to Stop Catastrophes* (New York: HarperCollins, 2017).

27. Barry Buzan and Richard Little observe, "But short of some very big surprises, at present the international system has reached geographical closure. It has only the option to grow more intense, and not the option to expand." *International Systems and World History* (New York: Oxford University Press, 2000), 350.

28. A good indicator of the status of human space expansion in the growing literature on catastrophic and existential threats is that space is discussed in the most comprehensive survey to date only in relation to a range of natural threats emanating from beyond the Earth, some of which (most notably asteroidal collision) might be averted. Nick Bostrom and Milan M. Cirkovic, eds., *Global Catastrophic Risks* (New York: Oxford University Press, 2008). No space threat of any sort is discussed in Vaclav Smil, *Global Catastrophes and Trends: The Next Fifty Years* (Cambridge, MA: MIT Press, 2008).

Chapter 1

1. Robert Zubrin, *Entering Space: Creating a Spacefaring Civilization* (New York: Tarcher, 1999), 275.

2. Stephen Hawking, "Our Only Chance," in James Benford and Gregory Benford, eds., *Starship Century* (Lucky Bat Books, 2013), 10. See also Rees, *Final Hour*, 170.

3. Frank White, *The Overview Effect: Space Exploration and Human Evolution* (Boston: Houghton, Mifflin, 2987), xvii.

4. For the many ways in which premodern peoples assigned importance to celestial phenomena, see Anthony Aveni, *People and the Sky: Our Ancestors and the Cosmos* (London: Thames & Hudson, 2008); Anthony Aveni, *In the Shadow of the Moon: The Science, Magic, and Mystery of Solar Eclipses* (New Haven, CT: Yale University Press, 2017).

5. Astronomical knowledge is so central to understanding the configurations and purposes of early megastructures that an entire branch of archeological studies, known as astro-archeology, has emerged. Peter Lancaster Brown, *Megaliths, Myths, and Men: An Introduction to Astro-Archaeology* (New York: Harper Colophon Books, 1978).

6. E. C. Krupp, *Skywatchers, Shamans and Kings: Astronomy and the Archaeology of Power* (New York: John Wiley & Sons, 1997).

7. For astrology's long history and wide influence, see Benson Bobrick, *The Fated Sky: Astrology in History* (New York: Simon & Schuster, 2005).

8. For a magisterial account of these interactions, see Neil deGrasse Tyson and Avis Lang, *Accessory to War: The Unspoken Alliance between Astrophysics and the Military* (New York: Norton, 2018).

9. Marjorie Hope Nicholson, *Voyages to the Moon* (New York: Macmillan, 1948); Scott L. Montgomery, *The Moon and the Western Imagination* (Tucson: University of Arizona Press, 1999).

10. For accounts of these early promotional efforts, see Frank H. Winter, *Prelude to the Space Age: The Rocket Societies: 1924–1940* (Washington, DC: Smithsonian Institution Press, 1983); William Bainbridge, *The Spaceflight Revolution* (New York: John Wiley & Sons, 1976). The pioneering work of the historian Asif A. Siddiqi has documented the extent of such organizations in late tsarist and early communist Russia: *The Red Rockets' Glare: Spaceflight and the Soviet Imagination, 1857–1957* (Cambridge, UK: Cambridge University Press, 2010).

11. The definitive historical account, emphasizing the importance of Hitler's enthusiasm, is Michael J. Neufeld, *The Rocket and the Reich: Peenemunde and the Coming of the Ballistic Missile Era* (New York: Free Press, 1995).

12. For the wide range of responses, see Matthew D. Tribbe, *No Requiem for the Space Age: The Apollo Moon Landings and American Culture* (New York: Oxford University Press, 2014); Ronald Weber, *Seeing Earth: Literary Responses to Space Exploration* (Athens: Ohio University Press, 1985).

13. "The Talk from Space on the Last Leg," *New York Times*, July 24, 1969, 20.

14. Norman Mailer, *Of a Fire on the Moon* (Boston: Little, Brown, 1971), 11.

15. Amitai Etzioni, *Moondoggle: Domestic and International Implications of the Space Race* (New York: Doubleday, 1964). Also comprehensively negative is Gerard J. DeGroot, *The Dark Side of the Moon: The Magnificent Madness of the American Lunar Quest* (New York: New York University Press, 2006).

16. Lewis Mumford, *The Myth of the Machine* (New York: Knopf, 1970), 303-11.

17. Discussed in "C. S. Lewis and His Space Trilogy, Then and Now," *Space Review*, January 10, 2011.

18. For example, Bill Kaysing and Randy Reid, *We Never Went to the Moon: America's Thirty Billion Dollar Swindle* (Pomeroy, OR: Health Research, 2002). Some 6 percent of Americans do not believe the Apollo landings happened. John Schwartz, "Vocal Minority Insists It Was All Smoke and Mirrors," *New York Times*, July 14, 2009, D7. Roger D. Launius describes the extensive scope of such "Apollo deniers" and explains their emergence in "American Spaceflight History: Master Narrative and the Meaning of Memory," in Steven J. Dick, ed., *Remembering the Space Age* (Washington, DC: NASA, 2008), 373-84. Another version of Apollo denialism holds that there was no US-Soviet race to the moon, refuted in John Logsdon and Alain Dupas, "Was the Race to the Moon Real?," *Scientific American*, June 1994, 36-43.

19. For conspiracies and religions, see Jodi Dean, *Aliens in America: Conspiracy Cultures from Outerspace to Cyberspace* (Ithaca, NY: Cornell University Press, 1998); James R. Lewis, ed., *The Gods Have Landed: New Religions from Other Worlds* (Albany: SUNY Press, 1995). Over the past half-century Erich von Däniken has produced a shelf of books, selling millions of copies, describing fantastic interventions of extraterrestrials across history, starting with *Chariots of the Gods: Unsolved Mysteries of the Past* (New York: G. P. Putnam's Sons, 1970).

20. Eugene Emme, ed., *Science Fiction and Space Futures: Past and Present* (Washington, DC: American Astronautical Association, 1982); F. I. Ordway III and R. Liebermann, *Blueprint for Space: Science Fiction to Science Fact* (Washington, DC: Smithsonian Institution Press, 1992).

21. Alexander C. T. Geppert, "European Astrofuturism, Cosmic Provincialism: Historicizing the Space Age," in Alexander C. T. Geppert, ed., *Imagining Outer Space: European Astroculture in the Twentieth Century* (London: Palgrave Macmillan, 2012).

22. W. Patrick McCray, *The Visioneers: How a Small Group of Elite Scientists Pursued Space Colonies, Nanotechnologies, and a Limitless Future* (Princeton, NJ: Princeton University Press, 2013), 17.

23. Particularly good on this interplay is Tom D. Crouch, *Aiming for the Stars: The Dreamers and Doers of the Space Age* (Washington, DC: Smithsonian Press, 1999).

24. Ben Bova, *Vision of the Future: The Art of Robert McCall* (New York: Harry N. Abrams, 1982).

25. Among recent full statements are Robert Zubrin, *The Case for Space: How the Revolution in Spaceflight Opens a Future of Limitless Possibility* (Amhert, NY: Prometheus Books, 2019); Michio Kaku, *The Future of Humanity: Terraforming Mars, Interstellar Travel, Immortality, and Our Destiny Beyond Earth* (New York: Doubleday, 2018); James Vedda, *Choice, Not Fate: Shaping a Sustainable Future in the Space Age* (Xlibris, 2009). For macro-natural-social narratives, see David Christian, *Maps of Time: An Introduction to Big History* (Berkeley: University of California Press, 2004).

26. For many statements of this perspective, see David Lavery, *Late for the Sky: The Mentality of the Space Age* (Carbondale: Southern Illinois University Press, 1992), 108-15.

27. Emerson was "obsessed with astronomy throughout his life" and wrote, "I hope the time will come when there will be a telescope in every street." Michael Crowe, *The Extraterrestrial Life Debate, 1750-1900: The Idea of a Plurality of Worlds from Kant to Lowell* (Cambridge, UK: Cambridge University Press, 1986), 235.

28. Sweeping criticisms, frequently voiced in the fevered 1960s, are richly chronicled in Tribbe, *No Requiem*, and Neil M. Maher, *Apollo in the Age of Aquarius* (Cambridge, MA: Harvard University Press, 2018).

29. For this long-running feud and its larger ramifications, see Roger D. Launius and Howard E. McCurdy, *Robots in Space: Technology, Evolution, and Interplanetary Travel* (Baltimore, MD: Johns Hopkins University Press, 2008).

30. A full and balanced account is provided in Robert Poole, *Earthrise: How Man First Saw the Earth* (New Haven, CT: Yale University Press, 2008).

31. Space law is now an established branch of international and domestic law, with its own law journals and institutes in many countries. A good overview, with key documents and influential articles, is provided in Glenn H. Reynolds and Robert P. Merges, *Outer Space: Problems of Law and Policy* (Boulder, CO: Westview, 1997).

32. A good example of this nearly universal pattern can be seen in the magisterial seven hundred–page history by William Burrows, *This New Ocean: The Story of the First Space Age* (New York: Random House, 1998), the most balanced and comprehensive account of space activities. Burrows begins by announcing his belief that he is telling the story of "one of the truly great and lasting human endeavors: the beginning of the human migration to space" (ix). He then observes in the opening pages of the first chapter, "Rockets were conceived, and reconceived time and again, expressly to wreak unparalleled destruction and kill large numbers of the very people whose enlightenment and salvation they promised" (4). He devotes a full chapter to the early development of rockets for war, centered on the German V-2 program, as well as a chapter on the American and Soviet crash programs to develop powerful rockets for intercontinental bombardment during the 1950s. But then, after the International Geophysical Year and the launch of Sputnik in 1957, his story focuses *solely* on space activities *other* than the ballistic missile programs, telling his readers nothing about expanded development and deployment of ICBMs in the 1960s and beyond, the pivotal role these weapons played in the nuclear competition and crises of the Cold War, or the central role their great reduction played in the ending of the Cold War and its arms control settlement.

33. A concise account of this shortfall is provided by Launius and McCurdy, *Robots in Space*, 220–36.

34. For a vivid political history of the early military space race in its Cold War setting, see Walter A. McDougall, *The Heavens and the Earth: A Political History of the Space Age* (New York: Basic Books, 1985).

35. Dandridge M. Cole, *Beyond Tomorrow: The Next Fifty Years in Space* (Amherst, WI: Amherst Press, 1965). See also Erik Berghaust, *The Next Fifty Years in Space* (New York: Macmillan, 1964).

36. For American space decision-making in this period, see John M. Logsdon, *After Apollo: Richard Nixon and the American Space Program* (New York: Palgrave, 2015).

37. Particularly in the 1990s, described in Brian Harvey, *Russia in Space: The Failed Frontier?* (Chichester, UK: Praxis, 2001).

38. For a bullish anticipation of the shuttle's potential, see Jerry Grey, *Enterprise* (New York: Morrow, 1979). Grey was a longtime congressional staff member and then head of the leading US aerospace trade organization, the American Institute for Aeronautics and Astronautics.

39. An account of the entire shuttle program is provided in Pat Duggins, *Final Countdown: NASA and the End of the Space Shuttle Program* (Gainesville: University Press of Florida, 2007). The two catastrophic malfunctions are treated in a large literature: Diane Vaughan, *The Challenger Launch Decision: Risky Technology, Culture, and Deviance at NASA* (New York: Columbia University Press, 1996); Richard Lewis, *Challenger: The Final Voyage* (New York: Columbia University Press, 1988).

40. Francis Fitzgerald, *Way Out There in the Blue: Reagan, Star Wars and the End of the Cold War* (New York: Simon & Schuster, 2000).

41. Donald A. Beattie, *ISScapades: The Crippling of America's Space Program* (Burlington, Ontario: Apogee Books, 2006).

42. Jeff Foust, "The Asteroid Mining Bubble Has Burst," *Space Review*, January 7, 2019.

43. Roger D. Launius, "Between a Rocket and a Hard Place: The Challenge of Space Access," in W. Henry Lambright, ed., *Space Policy in the Twenty-First Century* (Baltimore, MD: Johns Hopkins University Press, 2003), 15–54.

44. Roger D. Launius, "Perceptions of Apollo: Myth, Nostalgia, Memory, or All of the Above?," *Space Policy* 21.2 (2005): 129–39.

45. Walter A. McDougall, "A Melancholic Space Anniversary," in Dick, ed., *Remembering the Space Age*, 390; John Hickman, "Coping with the Closing," *Space Review*, August 24, 2009. A particularly evocative account of unrealized ambitions is Marina Benjamin, *Rocket Dreams: How the Space Age Shaped Our Vision of a World Beyond* (New York: Free Press, 2003).

46. No one would now imagine implementing the proposal of the philosopher Paul Kurtz, that 1969 mark the "transformation of the calendar of time from an era B.C. (Before Christ) to A.C. (After Christ) to an era of B.S. (before Space) to A.S. (after Space)." "The Year One (A.S.)," *The Humanist*, March–April 1969, 1.

47. For the ways in which space shaped design and architecture in the 1950s and 1960s, see Donna Goodman, *A History of the Future* (New York: Monacelli Press, 2008), chapter 5, "The Space Age."

48. John Schwartz, "NASA Is Facing a Climate Change Countdown," *New York Times*, April 5, 2016, D1.

49. For an encyclopedic treatment, see Brian Harvey, Henk H. F. Smid, and Theo Pirard, *Emerging Space Powers: The New Space Programs of Asia, the Middle East, and South America* (Chichester, UK: Springer, 2010). The space analyst James Clay Moltz explores the rapid rise of these new programs as a case of the "advantages of backwardness" in *Asia's Space Race: National Motivations, Regional Rivalries, and International Risks* (New York: Colubia University Press, 2012).

50. Tim Fernholtz, "Space is not a 'global commons' top Trump space official says," *Quartz*, December 19, 2017.

51. President Barack Obama, "State of the Union Address, 2016."

52. Leonard David, *Moon Rush: The New Space Race* (Washington, DC: National Geographic Press, 2019).

53 For description, see David H. Freedman, "Birth of a Rocket," *Scientific American*, 312(6), June 2015, pp. 56–65.

54. Multiple journalistic accounts, largely hagiographic, chart these efforts: Julian Gutherie, *How to Make a Spaceship: A Band of Renegades, an Epic Race, and the Birth of Private Spaceflight* (New York: Penguin, 2016); Christian Davenport, *The Space Barons: Elon Musk, Jeff Bezos, and the Quest to Colonize the Cosmos* (New York: Public Affairs, 2018); Greg Klerkx, *Lost in Space: The Fall of NASA and the Dream of a New Space Age* (New York: Random House, 2005); Tim Fernholz, *Rocket Billionaires: Elon Musk, Jeff Bezos, and the New Space Race* (Boston: Houghton Mifflin Harcourt, 2018). For sobering overviews of the difficulties such efforts face, see Lan Chan, "Hard Road to Commercial Space," *Spaceflight* 48.11 (November 2006): 427–31; Scott Pace, "The Future of Space Commerce," in Lambright, *Space Policy*, 55–86.

55. David Victor, "Introducing New Glenn, the Blue Origin Rocket That May Someday Take You to Space," *New York Times*, September 13, 2016, B2.

56. A similarly bullish account is provided in Kenny Kemp, *Destination Space: How Space Tourism Is Making Science Fiction a Reality* (London: Virgin Books, 2007). Virgin Books is owned by Richard Branson.

57. For the more general pattern of extremely wealthy individuals setting science policy, see William J. Broad, "Billionaires with Big Ideas Are Privatizing American Science," *New York Times*, March 16, 2014, A1. For early patron-driven astronomy, see Alexander MacDonald, *The Long Space Age: The Economic Origins of Space Exploration from Colonial America to the Cold War* (New Haven, CT: Yale University Press, 2017).

58. For a full and balanced picture of current space developments and trends, see James Clay Moltz, "The Changing Dynamics of Twenty-First Century Space Power," *Strategic Studies Quarterly* 13.1 (Spring 2019): 66–94.

59. A. P. J. Abdul Kalam, "Space Solar Power: Key to a Liveable Planet Earth," Address to 32nd International Space Development Conference, San Diego, California, May 24, 2013; Peter A. Garretson, *Sky's No Limit: Space-Based Solar Power, the Next Major Step in the Indo-US Strategic Partnership* (New Delhi: Institute for Defence Studies and Analysis, 2010); Molly K. Macauley and Jinh-Shyang Shih, "Satellite Solar Power: Renewed Interest in an Age of Climate Change?," *Space Policy* 23.10 (2007): 108–20.

60. For asteroidal collision as a triggering event, see Daniel H. Deudney, "High Impacts: Asteroidal Utilization, Collision Avoidance, and the Outer Space Regime, " in Lambright, *Space Policy*, 147-72.

61. William J. Broad, "Agencies, Hoping to Deflect Comets and Asteroids, Step Up Earth Defense," *New York Times*, June 19, 2015, A14; Valerie A. Olson, "Political Ecology in the Extreme: Asteroid Activism and the Making of an Environmental Solar System," *Anthropological Quarterly* 85.4 (2012): 1027-44.

Chapter 2

1. Bezos quoted in Kenneth Chang, "Jeff Bezos Lifts Veil on His Secretive Rocket Company," *New York Times*, March 9, 2016, B8.

2. Roger D. Launius, "Perfect Worlds, Perfect Societies: the Persistent Goal of Utopia in Human Spaceflight," *Journal of the British Interplanetary Society* 56.20 (September–October 2003): 338-49, at 345.

3. James A. Dator, *Social Foundations of Human Space Exploration* (New York: Springer, 2012), 53.

4. The closest to a net assessment is provided in a short essay by the noted environmental historian J. R. McNeill, who argues that the "space program changed the history of our times, but not (yet) in any fundamental ways." He concludes that barring some major new development, such as the discovery of alien intelligence, the space program amounts to "a small step for mankind that led to nowhere." But he does not include ballistic missiles on his ledger sheet of space activities. J. R. McNeill, "Gigantic Follies? Human Exploration and the Space Age in Long-Term Historical Perspective," in Steven J. Dick, ed., *Remembering the Space Age* (Washington, DC: NASA, 2008), 15-6.

5. In an important exception, McDougall argues that the consequence of American space activities in the 1950s and 1960s was to bring Soviet-model technocracy to the United States. McDougall, *The Heavens and the Earth*, 237-49.

6. Using here the expression "planetary security" for this approach, in contrast to "planetary protection" (efforts to prevent the contamination of the Earth, or other celestial bodies, with alien microbes), and "planetary defense" (measures to prevent asteroidal collisions with the Earth).

7. Cf. Kenneth Boulding's "fivefold fan of the future" in Joseph F. Coates, *What Futurists Believe* (Bethesda, MD: World Futures Society, 1989), 105.

8. R. Buckminster Fuller, *Utopia or Oblivion* (New York: Overlook, 1969).

9. For recent statements, see Ben Goertzel, *A Cosmist Manifesto* (Atlantic Highlands, NJ: Humanities Press, 2010); Max Tegmark, *Life 3.0: Being Human in the Age of Artificial Intelligence* (New York: Knopf, 2017).

10. Ray Kurzweil, *The Singularity Is Near* (New York: Viking, 2005); Murray Shanahan, *The Technological Singularity* (Cambridge, MA: MIT Press, 2015).

11. For example, the riskologist Seth D. Baum sees "relatively little risk" in space colonization: "The Great Downside Dilemma for Risky Emerging Technologies," *Physica Scripta*, November 2014, 1-10, at 8.

12. A telling example of this nonengagement can be seen in the recent book by the astronomer Donald Y. Yeomans, who is the manager of NASA's Near-Earth Object Program Office: *Near-Earth Objects: Finding Them before They Find Us* (Princeton, NJ: Princeton University Press, 2013). Yeomans begins his chapter 10 on asteroid deflection with a lengthy quote from Sagan on the necessity of deflection (140), drawn from the book in which Sagan makes his extended argument. Even though Yeomans labels a section of this chapter "the deflection dilemma" (149), which is Sagan's term for his argument, Yeomans ignores Sagan's argument entirely.

13. W. Warren Wager, *The City of Man: Prophecies of a World Civilization in Twentieth-Century Thought* (Boston: Houghton Mifflin, 1963); Joseph P. Baratta, *Strengthening the United Nations: A Bibliography on U.N. Reform and World Federalism* (Westport, CT: Greenwood, 1987).

14. John S. Partington, *Building Cosmopolis: The Political Thought of H. G. Wells* (Aldershot, UK: Ashgate, 2003).

15. For contemporary advocates, see Luis Cabrera, *Global Governance, Global Government: Institutional Visions for an Evolving World System* (Albany: SUNY Press, 2011); William E. Scheuerman, *The Realist Case for Global Reform* (Cambridge, UK: Polity, 2011).

16. Among classic statements are Harold and Margaret Sprout, *Toward a Politics of the Planet Earth* (New York: Van Nostrand Reinhold, 1971); William Ophuls, *Ecology and the Politics of Scarcity* (San Francisco: W. H. Freeman, 1977); Garrett Hardin, *Living within Limits* (New York: Oxford University Press, 1993); Bill McKibben, *The End of Nature* (New York: Random House, 1989); Al Gore, *Earth in the Balance* (London: Earthscan, 1996); Kolbert, *Sixth Extinction*.

17. For the most recent formulation, see Johan Rockstrom and Mattias Klum, *Big World, Small Planet: Abundance within Planetary Boundaries* (New Haven, CT: Yale University Press, 2015).

18. Particularly insightful treatments of the debate are Charles C. Mann, *The Wizard and the Prophet: Two Remarkable Scientists and Their Dueling Visions to Shape Tomorrow's World* (New York: Knopf, 2018); Hayward Alker and Peter Haas, "The Rise of Global Ecopolitics," in Nazli Choucri, ed., *Global Accord: Environmental Challenges and International Responses* (Cambridge, MA: MIT Press, 1993).

19. J. Peter Vajk, *Doomsday Has Been Cancelled* (Culver City, CA: Peace Press, 1978).

20. Particularly thorough on some of these images is Sabine Hohler, *Spaceship Earth in the Environmental Age, 1960–1990* (New York: Routledge, 2015).

21. Ronald J. Deibert, *Parchment, Printing, and Hypermedia: Communication in World Order Transformation* (New York: Columbia University Press, 1997).

22. H. G Wells, *The World Brain* (London: Macmillan, 1925); Vernadsky, "Biosphere and Noosphere"; ; Teilhard de Chardin, *The Phenomenon of Man* (Garden City, NY: Doubleday, 1965); Marshall McLuhan, *Gutenberg's Galaxy* (New York: Random House, 1968); Benjamin H. Bratton, *The Stack: On Software and Sovereignty* (Cambridge, MA: MIT Press, 2015).

23. Thomas Rid, *Rise of the Machines: A Cybernetic History* (New York: Norton, 2016).

24. Ronald Deibert, "The World Brain War," unpublished manuscript, 2019.

25. And just as the extremes of the left-right spectrum converge in totalitarianism, the far extremes of technopolitical thought converge in the elimination of humanity. Particularly notable among the Luddites is the voluntary extinction movement, described and insightfully discussed in James S. Ormrod, "Making Room for the Tigers and Polar Bears: Biography, Phantasy and Ideology in the Voluntary Human Extinction Movement," *Psychoanalysis, Culture and Society*, 16(2) June 2011:142–161.

26. In addition to Gertzweil and Tegmark, see Mark Lynas, *The God Species* (London: 4th Estate, 2011).

27. For a leading Promethean space expansionist on environmentalism, see Robert Zubrin, *Merchants of Death: Radical Environmentalists, Criminal Pseudo-Scientists and the Fatal Cult of Antihumanism* (New York: Encounter Books, 2013).

28. For example, Julian Simon, *The Ultimate Resource* (Princeton, NJ: Princeton University Press, 1981); Kevin Kelley, *Out of Control: The Rise of Neo-Biological Civilization* (Reading, MA: Addison-Wesley, 1994); Ronald Bailey, *The End of Doom: Environmental Renewal in the Twenty-First Century* (New York: Thomas Dunne, 2015).

29. For sophisticated briefs for hopeful optimism, see Stewart Brand, *Whole Earth Disciple: An Ecopragmatist Manifesto* (New York: Viking, 2009); David Grinspoon, *Earth in Human Hands: Shaping Our Planet's Future* (New York: Grand Central, 2016).

30. Usefully surveyed in Steven E. Jones, *Against Technology: From the Luddites to Neo-Luddism* (New York: Routledge, 2006). Particularly influential is Martin Heidegger, *The Question concerning Technology and Other Essays* (New York: Harper & Row, 1977).

31. The father of post- or late modern posthumanism is the German existential phenomenologist Martin Heidegger. Whether his ardent embrace of Hitler's Nazi regime says something about the politics of posthumanism remains vigorously disputed. For a good synthesis of recent progressive posthumanism, see Timothy Morton, *Humankind: Solidarity with Nonhuman People* (London: Verso, 2017). Posthumanism here refers to the rejection of the Humanist priviledging of humans over other species, not humans enhanced by genetic or cybernetic technology.

32. For an encyclopedic survey, see Vaclav Smil, *Growth: From Microorganisms to Megacities* (Cambridge, MA: MIT Press, 2019). For the de-growth movement, see Giorgas Kallis et al., "Research on Degrowth," *Annual Review of Environment and Resources*, 2018.43:291–316.

33. Clive Hamilton, *The Earthmasters: The Dawn of the Age of Planetary Engineering* (New Haven, CT: Yale University Press, 2013), 18.

34. Particularly good on this point is John McPhee, *The Control of Nature* (New York: Farrar, Straus and Giroux, 1989).

35 Despite its prominence and great practical successes, this strain of early modern theory and practice is now often overshadowed by libertarian and free market readings. For a recent corrective, see Dennis C. Rasmussen, *The Pragmatic Enlightenment: Recovering the Liberalism of Hume, Smith, Montesquieu and Voltaire* (Cambridge, UK: Cambridge University Press, 2014).

36 For varieties of practical knowledge, see Jurgen Habermas, *Knowledge and Human Interests* (Boston, MA: Beacon Press, 1968).

37. W. H. Parker, *Mackinder: Geography as an Aid to Statecraft* (New York: Oxford University Press, 1982), 114–118.

38. This story appears in Plato's *Theaetetus* (174a) and has been subject to considerable interest and several differing interpretations. For Martin Heidegger, it is "the laughter of the uncomprehending non philosopher," while for Hannah Arendt it embodies "the natural hostility of the many and their opinions towards the few and their truths." Hannah Arendt, *The Life of the Mind* (Orlando, FL: Harcourt, 1978), 81–82. For discussion, see Michael Gendie, ed., *The Thracian Maid and the Professional Thinker: Arendt and Heidegger* (Albany: SUNY Press, 1997).

39. Aristotle, *Politics*, 1.11, 1259a9–18. While it is unlikely that Thales was able to predict the weather, this folkloric story underscores the fact that early astronomy was valued in significant measure because celestial phenomena were thought to determine meteorological patterns, of crucial concern for agricultural societies dependent on reliable rainfall for food production.

Chapter 3

1. Allan O. Kelly and Frank Dachille, *Target Earth* (Pensacola, FL: Pensacola Publishing,1953), 256.

2. Cousins, quoted in Poole, *Earthrise*, 3.

3. Unless otherwise indicated, quantitative data in this chapter come from relevant NASA, Lunar and Planetary Institute, and Wikapedia web sites, and Stuart Lowe and Chris North, *Cosmos: The Infographic Book of Space* (London: Aurum Press, 2015).

4. Chris Impey and Holly Henry, *Dreams of Other Worlds: The Amazing Story of Unmanned Space Exploration* (Princeton, NJ: Princeton University Press, 2013); Patrick Moore, *Philip's Atlas of the Universe* (London: Octopus, 2000); Mark A. Garlick, *Atlas of the Universe* (Sydney: Weldon Owen Party, 2009); Martin Rees, ed., *Universe: The Definitive Visual Guide* (New York: DK Publishing, 2009).

5. Willy Ley, *Watchers of the Sky: An Informal History of Astronomy from Babylon to the Space Age* (New York: Viking, 1963); Jared Buss, *Willy Ley: Prophet of the Space Age* (Gainesville: University Press of Florida, 2017). For the role of instrumentation advances, see Steven J. Dick, *Discovery and Classification in Astronomy: Controversy and Consensus* (Cambridge, UK: Cambridge University Press, 2013), 279–312.

6. Stephen J. Pyne, "Space: A Third Great Age of Discovery," *Space Policy*, August 1988, 187–99. Particularly insightful on these interactions is Hubert Krivine, *The Earth: From Myth to Knowledge* (London: Verso, 2015).

7. Greek astronomy, cosmology, and philosophy were far more diverse than the Aristotelian ideas that became established and enforced truths during the medieval period. Other Greek astronomers hypothesized that the Earth rotated around the sun, and the school of Democritus and the Epicureans proposed a view of the universe's size, composition, and evolution that anticipated many of the key views of late modern cosmology.

8. The new astronomy also produced a new concept of space as infinite, unchanging, homogeneous, and inert, within which all objects existed. In terms of this broader sense of space, outer space is an immensely numerous set of places. For the history of spatiality, see Margaret

Wertheim, *The Pearly Gates of Cyberspace: A History of Space from Dante to the Internet* (New York: Norton, 1999).

9. Henry Fountain, "Two Trillion Galaxies, at the Very Least," *New York Times*, October 18, 2016, D3.

10. For Galileo's advances and travails, see John L. Heilbron, *Galileo* (New York: Oxford University Press, 2010); Thomas F. Mayer, *The Trial of Galileo, 1612–1633* (Toronto: University of Toronto Press, 2012).

11. For the origins and consequences of the scientific revolution, see Alfred North Whitehead, *Science and the Modern World* (Cambridge, UK: Cambridge University Press, 1926); Stephen Gaukroger, *The Emergence of a Scientific Culture: Science and the Shaping of Modernity, 1210–1685* (Oxford: Clarendon Press, 2008); Andrew Cunningham and Perry Williams, "De-centring the 'Big Picture': The Origins of Modern Science and the Modern Origins of Science," *British Journal for the History of Science* 26.4 (1993): 407–32; Steven Shapin, *The Scientific Revolution* (Chicago: University of Chicago Press, 1996); David Wootton, *Inventing Science: A New History of the Scientific Revolution* (New York: HarperCollins, 2015).

12. For Newton, see Rob Iliffe and George E. Smith, eds., *The Cambridge Companion to Newton*, 2nd edition (Cambridge, UK: Cambridge University Press, 2016). For far-ranging political consequences of the new cosmology, see Sigfried Giedion, *Mechanization Takes Command: A Contribution to Anonymous History* (London: Oxford University Press, 1948); Bentley Allan, *Scientific Cosmology and International Order* (Cambridge, UK: Cambridge University Press, 2015).

13. Stephen Toulmin, *Cosmopolis* (New York: Basic Books, 1998).

14. With the important exception of Carl Sagan, *Pale Blue Dot: A Vision of the Human Future in Space* (New York: Random House, 1994), 275.

15. Neil J. Comins, *The Hazards of Space Travel: A Tourist's Guide* (New York: Villard, 2007); Albert A. Harrison, *Spacefaring: The Human Dimension* (Berkeley: University of California Press, 2001).

16. Graham Swinerd, *How Spacecraft Fly: Spaceflight without Formulae* (New York: Copernicus Books, 2008).

17. Neil F. Comins, *What If the Moon Didn't Exist? Voyages to Earths That Might Have Been* (New York: HarperCollins, 1993).

18. Jeff Kanipe, *The Cosmic Connection: How Astronomical Events Impact Life on Earth* (Amherst, NY: Prometheus Books, 2009).

19. Emma Kiele Fry, "The Risks and Impacts of Space Weather: Policy Recommendations and Initiatives," *Space Policy* 28.10 (2012): 180–84; Nicole Homelar and Lisa Wei, *Solar System Risk to the North American Power Grid* (London: Lloyd's of London, 2013).

20. K. Maria Lane, *Geographies of Mars: Seeing and Knowing the Red Planet* (Chicago: University of Chicago Press, 2011).

21. Donald Goldsmith, *The Hunt for Life on Mars* (New York: Dutton, 1997); W. Henry Lambright, *Why Mars: NASA and the Politics of Space Exploration* (Baltimore, MD: Johns Hopkins University Press, 2014).

22. For the history of asteroid astronomy, see Curtis Peebles, *Asteroids: A History* (Washington, DC: Smithsonian Institution Press, 2001).

23. Kenneth Chang, "A Metal Ball the Size of Massachusetts That NASA Wants to Explore," *New York Times*, January 6, 2017, D2.

24. For a synthesis of the new perspective, see Derek Ager, *The New Catastrophism: The Importance of Rare Events in Geological History* (Cambridge, UK: Cambridge University Press, 1993).

25. W. G. Hoyt, *Coon Mountain Controversies: Meteor Crater and the Development of Impact Theory* (Tucson: University of Arizona Press, 1987).

26. John S. Lewis, *Rain of Iron and Ice: The Very Real Threat of Comet and Asteroid Bombardment* (Boston: Addison-Wesley, 1996); Victor Club and Paul Napier, *The Cosmic Winter* (Oxford: Blackwell, 1990).

27. Walter Alvarez, *T. Rex and the Crater of Doom* (Princeton, NJ: Princeton University Press, 1997); J. L. Powell, *Night Comes to the Cretaceous: Dinosaur Extinction and the Transformation of Modern Geology* (New York: W. H. Freeman, 1998).

28. Peter Brannen, *The Ends of the World: Volcanic Apocalypses, Lethal Oceans, and Our Quest to Understand Earth's Past Mass Extinctions* (New York: Ecco Books, 2017).

29 Emma Goldberg, "How to Cool a Planet With Extraterrestrial Dust," *New York Times,* September 18, 2019, p.C1.

30. Giuseppe Longo, "The Tunguska Event," in Peter T. Bobrowsky and Hans Richman, eds., *Comet/Asteroid Impacts and Human Society* (Heidelberg: Springer, 2007), 303–30.

31. Duncan Lunan, *Incoming Asteroid! What Could We Do about It?* (New York: Springer, n.d.), 91.

32. Zubrin claims, quite implausibly, that if the object had struck in European Russia it would have done no more than "possibly caused the cancellation of one of the social events at the Tsar's summer palace" (*Entering Space,* 129).

33. For how such events were interpreted in prescientific times, see William T. Hartwell, "The Sky on the Ground: Celestial Objects and Events in Archaeology and Popular Culture," in Bobrowsky and Richman, *Comet/Asteroid Impacts,* 71–87.

34. National Science and Technology Council, "National Near-Earth-Object Preparedness Strategy," December 2016.

35. Peebles, *Asteroids,* 209–13.

36. Kelly and Dachille, *Target Earth.* They also precociously hypothesize that asteroidal collision caused the demise of the dinosaurs, and propose an international effort to develop diversion technology. The implications of framing solar space events as part of the Earth's environment are also insightfully explored in Valerie Olson, *Into the Extreme: U.S. Environmental Systems and Politics beyond the Earth* (Minneapolis: University of Minnesota Press, 2018).

37. Immanuel Velikovsky, *Worlds in Collision* (New York: Dell, 1950); David Goldsmith, ed., *Scientists Confront Velikovsky* (Ithaca, NY: Cornell University Press, 1977); Michael D. Gordin, *The Pseudo-Science Wars: Immanuel Velikovsky and the Birth of the Modern Fringe* (Chicago: University of Chicago Press, 2012).

38. For a detailed status report, see Rob Landis and Lindley Johnson, "Advances in Planetary Defense in the United States," *Acta Astronautica,* 156.3 (March 2019): 394–408.

39. For detailed accounts, see William Burrows, *The Survival Imperative: Using Space to Protect Earth* (New York: Doherty, 2006); William Burrows, *The Asteroid Threat: Defending Our Planet from Deadly Near-Earth Objects* (Amherst, NY: Prometheus Books, 2014).

40. Short accounts of these three missions and other recent activities are found in Gordon L. Dillow, *Fire in the Sky: Cosmic Collisions, Killer Asteroids, and the Race to Defend Earth* (New York: Scribner, 2019).

41. William G. Hoyt, *Planet X and Pluto* (Tucson: University of Arizona Press, 1980).

42. For lively accounts, see Mike Brown, *How I Killed Pluto: And Why It Had It Coming* (New York: Spiegel and Grau, 2012); Neil deGrasse Tyson, *The Pluto Files: The Rise and Fall of America's Favorite Planet* (New York: Norton, 2009).

43. For classification debates, see Dick, *Discovery and Classification in Astronomy,* 173–312.

44. Donald H. Yeomans, *Comets: A Chronological History of Observation, Science, Myth, and Folklore* (New York: John Wiley & Sons, 1991).

45. For a vivid account of comet hysteria, see Nigel Calder, *The Comet Is Coming!* (New York: Viking Press, 1981).

46. B. G. Marsden and D. I. Steel, "Warning Times and Impact Probabilities for Long-Period Comets," in Tom Gehrels, ed., *Hazards Due to Comets and Asteroids* (Tucson: University of Arizona Press, 1994), 221–40.

47. David H. Levy, *Impact Jupiter: The Crash of Comet Shoemaker-Levy 9* (New York: Basic Books, 1995); J. R. Spencer and J. Mitton, eds., *The Great Comet Crash* (Cambridge, UK: Cambridge University Press, 1995).

48. For a trenchant formulation of this point, see Arthur C. Clarke, *Profiles of the Future: An Inquiry into the Limits of the Possible* (New York: Harper & Row, 1962), 113–22.

49. These and other potential threats are assessed in Arnon Dar, "Influence of Supernovae, Gamma Ray Bursts, Solar Flares, and Cosmic Rays on the Terrestrial Environment," in Bostrom and Cirkovic, *Global Catastrophic Risks.*

50. This fascinating topic has been treated in several magisterial scholarly works: Steven J. Dick, *Plurality of Worlds: The Origins of the Extraterrestrial Life Debate from Democritus to Kant* (Cambridge, UK: Cambridge University Press, 1982); Crowe, *The Extraterrestrial*

Life Debate; Karl S. Guthke, *The Last Frontier: Imagining Other Worlds from the Copernican Revolution to Modern Science Fiction* (Ithaca, NY: Cornell University Press, 1990); Steven J. Dick, *The Biological Universe: The Twentieth-Century Extraterrestrial Life Debate and the Limits of Science* (Cambridge, UK: Cambridge University Press, 1996).

51. Christiaan Huygens, *The Celestial Worlds Discovered* (London: Frank Cass, 1968 [1698]), 34.

52. Among those with general reputations who subscribed to this view and wrote about it during the eighteenth and nineteenth centuries are Alexander Pope, Lord Bolingbroke, William Blake, David Hume, Cotton Mather, Philip Freneau, David Rittenhouse, John Adams, Ezra Styles, Voltaire, Rousseau, Diderot, d'Alembert, Holbach, Buffon, Kant, Paine, Malebranche, William Wordsworth, Lord Byron, Samuel Taylor Coleridge, Timothy Dwight, DuPont de Nemours, Necker, Madame de Staël, Joseph de Maistre, Ralph Waldo Emerson, Henry David Thoreau, Charles Fourier, and Auguste Comte. See Crowe, *Extraterrestrial Life Debate*.

53. The Rev. Thomas Dick, a prolific writer on the topic, estimated that there were 2.4 billion inhabited worlds in the visible universe and, using the population density of England as his yardstick, estimated that the population of intelligent beings in this solar system at a bit under 21 trillion (Crowe, *Extraterrestrial Life Debate*, 198–99).

54. Speaking of the French writers on the topic, Crowe observes that "the great majority of authors, be they atheists, deists, or clergy, Protestant or Catholic, philosophers, physicists, poets, or biologists, favored the doctrine" (*Extraterrestrial Life Debate*, 139).

55. David Clark, "Kant's Aliens: The Anthropology and Its Others," *New Centennial Review* 1.2 (2001): 201–89.

56. I. S. Shklovskii and Carl Sagan, *Intelligent Life in the Universe* (New York: Dell, 1966). Isaac Asimov speculates on these civilizations in *Extraterrestrial Civilization* (New York: Crown, 1979).

57. For a survey of recent thinking, see Jim Al-Khalili, *Aliens: The World's Leading Scientists on the Search for Extraterrestrial Life* (New York: Picador, 2016).

58. Michael A. G. Michaud, *Contact with Alien Civilizations: Our Hopes and Fears about Encountering Extraterrestrials* (New York: Copernicus Books, 2007); Albert A. Harrison, *After Contact: The Human Response to Extraterrestrial Life* (New York: Plenum, 1997); Steven J. Dick, *Astrobiology: Science and Societal Impact* (Cambridge, UK: Cambridge University Press, 2003).

59. Peter D. Ward and Donald Brownlee, *Rare Earth: Why Complex Life Is Uncommon in the Universe* (New York: Springer-Verlag, 2000); David Waltham, *Lucky Planet: Why Earth Is Exceptional* (New York: Basic Books, 2014).

60. For debates about the character of life, see Lynn Margulis and Dorian Sagan, *What Is Life?* (Berkeley: University of California Press, 1995); Chris Impey, ed., *Talking about Life: Conversations on Astrobiology* (Cambridge, UK: Cambridge University Press, 2010).

61. What constitutes "intelligent life" is not sharply defined. Several species of marine mammals have brain sizes and forms of social interaction and communication that warrant their being considered intelligent, but they have little prospect for using tools and developing technological civilizations because they lack appendages comparable to the hands of humans and are forever precluded from using metals because fire cannot burn in water.

62. For the role of space perspectives in this revolution, see Poole, *Earthrise*, 140–89.

63. Ralph D. Lorenz, *Exploring Planetary Climate: A History of Scientific Discovery on Earth, Mars, Venus and Titan* (Cambridge, UK: Cambridge University Press, 2019).

64. Starting with James Lovelock, *Gaia: A New Look at Life on Earth* (New York: Oxford University Press, 1979) and Lynn Margulis, *Symbiotic Planet: A New Look at Evolution* (New York: Basic Books, 1998), to the full synthesis in Peter Ward and Joe Kirschvink, *A New History of Life on Earth* (New York: Bloomsbury Press, 2015).

65. Edward O. Wilson, *The Future of Life* (New York: Vintage, 2002).

66. Ed Yong, *I Contain Multitudes: The Microbes within Us and a Grander View of Life* (New York: HarperCollins, 2016).

67. S. A. Kaufman, *At Home in the Universe: The Search for the Laws of Self-Organization and Complexity* (New York: Oxford University Press, 1995); M. Mitchell Waldrop, *Complexity: The Emerging Science at the Edge of Order and Chaos* (New York: Simon and Schuster, 1992).

68. Daniel B. Botkin, *Discordant Harmonies: A New Ecology for the Twenty-First Century* (New York: Oxford University Press, 1990); Daniel B. Botkin, *The Moon in the Nautilus Shell: Discordant Harmonies Reconsidered* (New York: Oxford University Press, 2012).

Chapter 4

1. Quoted in Siddiqui, *Red Rockets' Glare*, 16.
2. Sagan, *Pale Blue Dot: A Vision of the Human Future in Space* (New York: Random House, 1994), 317.
3. Ray Kurzweil, "Promise and Peril," in Alan Lightman et al eds., *Living with the Genie: Essays on Technology and the Quest for Human Mastery* (Washington, DC: Island Press, 2003), 54.
4. Plato, *Protagoras*, 320c–322b, discussed in Mayor, *Gods and Robots*, 61–62.
5. For an early formulation, see Kenneth P. Oakley, *Man the Tool-Maker* (1949; Chicago: University of Chicago Press, 1961).
6. Gregory Cochran and Henry Harpending, *The 10,000 Year Explosion: How Civilization Accelerated Human Evolution* (New York: Basic Books, 2010).
7. As Cole observed, "Prediction of future events is one of the commonest and most important activities of the human brain" (*Beyond Tomorrow*, 17).
8. For social imaginaries generally, see Charles Taylor, *Modern Social Imaginaries* (Durham,NC: Duke University Press, 2004).
9. Jean Chesneaux, *The Political and Social Ideas of Jules Verne* (London: Thames and Hudson, 1972); Herbert Lottman, *Jules Verne: An Exploratory Biography* (New York: St. Martin's, 1997). For a magisterial account of early French SF, see Brian Stableford, *The Plurality of Imaginary Worlds: The Evolution of French Roman Scientifique* (Encino, CA: Black Coat Press, 2016). For Marxist SF, see Mark Bould and China Mieville, eds., *Red Planets: Marxism and Science Fiction* (Middletown, CT: Wesleyan University Press, 2009).
10. For analysis of his ideas and their legacies, see Leslie A. Fiedler, *Olaf Stapledon: A Man Divided* (New York: Oxford University Press, 1983); Robert Crossly, *Olaf Stapledon: Speaking for the Future* (Syracuse, NY: Syracuse University Press, 1994).
11. Mark R. Hillegas, *The Future as Nightmare: H. G. Wells and the Anti-Utopians* (New York: Oxford University Press, 1967).
12. Global closure in Verne's work is explored in Rosalind Williams, *The Triumph of Human Empire: Verne, Morris, and Stevenson at the End of the World* (Chicago: University of Chicago Press, 2013).
13. Paul Carter, *The Creation of Tomorrow: Fifty Years of Magazine Science Fiction* (New York: Columbia University Press 1977); Brian Aldiss with David Wingrove, *Trillion Year Spree: The History of Science Fiction* (London: Paladin, 1988).
14. Laurence Davis and Peter Stillman, eds., *The New Utopian Politics of Ursula K. Le Guin's* The Dispossessed (Lanham, MD: Lexington Books, 2005).
15. For example, Frederic Jameson, *Archaeologies of the Future: The Desire Called Utopia and Other Science Fictions* (London: Verso, 2005). Jutta Weldes, ed., *To Seek Out New Worlds* (New York: Palgrave Macmillan, 2002).
16. Spencer Weart and Gertrud Weiss Szilard, eds., *Leo Szilard: His Version of the Facts* (Cambridge, MA: MIT Press, 1978).
17. Nikolai Federovich Fedorov, *What Was Man Created For? The Philosophy of the Common Task* (Lausanne: Honeyglen, 1990); George M. Young, *The Russian Cosmists: The Esoteric Futurism of Nikolai Fedorov and His Followers* (New York: Oxford University Press, 2012);Albert A. Harrison, "Russian and American Cosmism: Religions, National Psyche, and Spaceflight," *Astropolitics* 11.1–2 (2013): 25–44.
18. These links are traced in Mark L. Brako and Neil Hook, *Different Engines: How Science Drives Fiction and Fiction Drives Science* (New York: Macmillan, 2008).
19. Marjorie Hope Nicholson, *Voyages to the Moon* (New York: Macmillan, 1948); Scott L. Montgomery, *The Moon and the Western Imagination* (Tucson: University of Arizona Press, 1999); Aaron Parrett, *The Translunar Lunar Narrative in the Western Tradition* (Aldershot, UK: Ashgate, 2004).

20. Robert Markley, *Dying Planet: Mars in Science and the Imagination* (Durham, NC: Duke University Press, 2005); Robert Crossley, *Imagining Mars: A Literary History* (Middletown, CT: Wesleyan University Press, 2011).

21. Norman Spinard, "Rubber Sciences," in Reginald Bretnor, ed., *The Craft of Science Fiction: A Symposium on Writing Science Fiction and Science Fantasy* (New York: Barnes and Noble, 1976), 54–72.

22. Stephen Webb, *All the Wonder That Would Be: Exploring Past Notions of the Future* (New York: Springer, 2017).

23. Raffaekka Baccolini and Tom Moylan, eds., *Dark Horizons: Science Fiction and the Dystopian Imagination* (New York: Routledge, 2003).

24. I. F. Clarke, *The Pattern of Expectation: 1644–2001* (New York: Basic Books, 1979).

25. The full title captures its ambition: H. G. Wells, *Anticipations of the Reaction of Mechanical and Scientific Progress upon Human Life and Thought* (New York and London: Harper & Brothers, 1902).

26. For the many techniques developed for forecasting, see Jib Fowles, ed., *Handbook of Futures Research* (Westport, CT: Greenwood Press, 1978). For the current state of the art, see Philip E. Tetlock and Dan Gardiner, *Superforecasting: The Art and Science of Forecasting* (New York: Crown, 2015).

27. Herman Kahn et al., *The Next 200 Years: A Scenario for America and the World* (New York: William Morrow, 1976). For the political agendas of futurists and the political uses of futurism, see Jenny Andersson, *The Future of the World: Futurology, Futurists and the Struggle for the Post Cold War Imagination* (Oxford: Oxford University Press, 2018).

28. Hugh Kenner, *Bucky: A Guided Tour of Buckminster Fuller* (New York: William Morrow, 1973); Robert W. Marks, *The Dymaxion World of Buckminster Fuller* (New York: Reinhold, 1960).

29. This line of thinking is explored in William Irwin Thompson, *Passages about Earth: An Exploration of the New Planetary Culture* (New York: Harper & Row, 1973).

30. Paul E. Ceruzzi, "Moore's Law and Technological Determinism: Reflections of the History of Technology," *Technology and Culture* 46.3 (July 2005):584–593 .

31. Numerous examples provided in Clarke, *Profiles of the Future.*

32. Sharply higher fuel prices, also not anticipated, also played a role in aborting the wide commercial use of the SST. Mel Horowitch, *Clipped Wings: The American SST Conflict* (Cambridge, MA: MIT Press, 1982).

33. For types of impossibility, see Michio Kaku, *The Physics of the Impossible* (New York: Doubleday, 2008); John D. Barrow, *Impossibility: the Limits of Science and the Science of Limits* (New York: Oxford University Press, 1998).

34. Scott Pace, "Merchant and Guardian Challenges in the Exercise of Spacepower," in Charles D. Lutes and Peter Hays, eds., *Toward a Theory of Spacepower: Selected Essays* (Washington, DC: National Defense University Press, 2011), 241–73, at 263–64.

35. Particularly insightful on these realities is John Hickman, "The Political Economy of Very Large Space Projects," *Journal of Evolution and Technology* 4 (November 1999) .

36. Todd Harrison et al., *The Implications of Ultra-Low-Cost Access to Space* (Washington, DC: CSIS Aerospace Security Project, 2017).

37. Howard E. McCurdy, "The Cost of Space Flight," *Space Policy* 10.4 (November 1994): 277–89.

38. Bradley C. Edwards and Philip Ragan, *Leaving the Planet by Space Elevator* (Seattle, WA: Lulu. com Press, 2006); Peter A. Swan, David I. Raitt, Cathy W. Swan, Robert E, Penny, and John M. Knapman, eds., *Space Elevators: An Assessment of the Technological Feasibility and the Way Forward* (Paris: International Academy of Astronautics, 2013).

39. Louis A. Kleiman, ed., *Project Icarus* (Cambridge, MA: MIT Press, 1968).

40. Yeomans, *Near-Earth Objects.*

41. John S. Lewis, *Asteroid Mining 101: Wealth for the New Space Economy* (Seattle, WA: Deep Space Industries, 2015).

42. John S. Lewis, *Mining the Sky: Untold Riches from the Asteroids, Comets and Planets* (Reading, MA: Helix Books, 1996).

43. The ambitious goals of the project are set forth by several of its leaders: A. Alling and M. Nelson, *Life under the Glass: The Inside Story of Biosphere 2* (Oracle, AZ: Biosphere Press,

1993); J. Allen and M. Nelson, *Space Biospheres* (Oracle, AZ: Synergetic Press, 1989). For its travails, see William Broad, "Paradise Lost: Biosphere Retooled as Atmospheric Nightmare," *New York Times*, November 19, 1996; Linnea Gentry and Karen Liptak, *The Glass Ark: The Story of Biosphere 2* (New York: Puffin Books, 2001). Research results are described in Howard T. Odum and Bruno D. Marino, eds., "Biosphere 2: Research Past and Present," *Ecological Engineering* 13.1–4 (1999) . For critical evaluations and space implications, see Dorion Sagan and Lynn Margulis, *Biospheres: From Earth to Space* (Hillsdale, NJ: Enslow, 1989); Tim W. Luke, *Ecocritique: Contesting the Politics of Nature, Ecology and Culture* (Minneapolis: University of Minnesota Press, 1997), 95–114; Hohler, *Spaceship Earth in the Environmental Age*, 108–27.

44. These and other difficulties are insightfully discussed in Kim Stanley Robinson, "Our Generation Ships Will Sink," *Boing, Boing*, November 16, 2015.

45. For the origins of this concern, see Audra J. Wolfe, "Germs in Space: Joshua Lederberg, Exobiology, and the Public Imagination, 1958–1964," *Isis* 93 (2002): 183–205. For ongoing disputes, see Robert Walker, "Debunked: The Planetary Protection Racket—Zubrin's Claim That There Is No Need to Protect Earth from Mars Microbes," *Science 2.0*, August 28, 2017.

46. Ken Roy and Robert G. Kennedy, "Mirrors & Smoke: Ameliorating Climate Change with Giant Solar Sails," *World Earth Review*, Summer 2001; Greg Matloff, C. Bangs, and Les Johnson, *Harvesting Space for a Greener Earth*, 2nd edition (New York: Springer, 2014), chapter 16, "Mitigating Global Warming Using Space-Based Approaches," 173–84.

47. James Oberg, *New Earths: Restructuring the Earth and Other Planets* (Harrisburg, PA: Stackpole Books, 1981); Marvin Beech, *Terraforming: The Creating of Habitable Worlds* (New York: Springer, 2009); James Lovelock and Michael Allaby, *The Greening of Mars* (New York: Warner Books, 1984).

48. Marjus Schmidt, ed., *Synthetic Biology: The Technoscience and Its Societal Consequences* (London: Springer, 2009).

49. Jon Turney, *Frankenstein's Footsteps: Science, Genetics, and Popular Culture* (New Haven, CT: Yale University Press, 1998).

50. James Hughes, "The Politics of Transhumanism and the Techno-Millennial Imagination, 1626–2030," *Zygon* 47.4 (December 2012): 757–76; James Hughes, *Citizen Cyborg: How Democratic Societies Must Respond to the Redesigned Human of the Future* (Boulder, CO: Westview, 2004).

51. K. Eric Drexler, *Engines of Creation: The Coming Era of Nanotechnology* (New York: Anchor Books, 1986); K. Eric Drexler, *Radical Abundance: How a Revolution in Nanotechnology Will Change Civilization* (New York: Public Affairs, 2013). For Drexler and his influence, see McCray, *Visioneers*, 146–257.

52. K. Eric Drexler, "Molecular Manufacturing for Space Systems: An Overview," *Journal of the British Interplanetary Society* 45.10 (1992): 401–5.

53. For an extended description, see George Dyson, *Turing's Cathedral: The Origins of the Digital Universe* (New York: Pantheon, 2012).

54. Joel N. Surkin, *Engines of the Mind: The Evolution of the Computer from the Mainframes to the Microprocessors* (New York: Norton, 1996).

55. Norman Macrae, *John von Neumann: The Scientific Genius Who Pioneered the Modern Computer, Game Theory, Nuclear Deterrence and Much More* (New York: Pantheon Books, 1992).

56. Steve Lohr, "The Promise of Artificial Intelligence Unfolds in Small Steps," *New York Times*, February 29, 2016, B1.

57. Steve Lohr, "Google Computer Beats World Go Champion," *New York Times*, June 6, 2018, B1.

58. John Markoff and Steve Lohr, "The Race Is On to Control Artificial Intelligence, and Tech's Future," *New York Times*, March 26, 2016, B1; John Markoff, "Pentagon Turns to Silicon Valley for Edge in Artificial Intelligence," *New York Times*, May 12, 2016, B1.

59. A lucid formulation of this point is made by Launius in "Perfect Worlds, Perfect Societies," 338–49.

60. The classic overview of the founding arguments remains Langdon Winner, *Autonomous Technology: Technics-out-of-Control as a Theme in Political Thought* (Cambridge, MA: MIT Press, 1977).

61. Ulrich Beck, *The Risk Society: Towards a New Modernity* (London: Sage, 1993); Ulrich Beck, *World Risk Society* (Malden, MA: Polity Press, 1999).

62. Raphael G. Kasper, ed., *Technology Assessment: Understanding the Social Consequences of Technology* (New York: Praeger, 1972).

63. Bruce Bimber, *The Politics of Expertise: The Rise and Fall of the Office of Technology Assessment* (Albany: SUNY Press, 1996).

64. Lydia Dotto and Harold Schiff, *The Ozone War* (Garden City, NY: Doubleday, 1978); Karen Litfin, *Ozone Discourse: Science and Politics in Global Environmental Cooperation* (New York: Columbia University Press, 1994); Edward A. Parson, *Protecting the Ozone Layer: Science and Strategy* (New York: Oxford University Press, 2013).

65. Samuel Arbesman, *Overcomplicated: Technology at the Limits of Comprehension* (New York: Penguin, 2016).

66. For their pervasiveness, see Edward Tenner, *Why Things Bite Back: Technology and the Revenge of Unintended Consequences* (New York: Knopf, 1996).

67. The classic statement, giving rise to "the Collingridge Dilemma," is David Collingridge, *The Social Control of Technology* (New York: St. Martin's Press, 1980).

68. Charles Perrow, *Normal Accidents: Living with High-Risk Technologies* (New York: Basic Books, 1984).

69. Alvin M. Weinberg, "Social Institutions and Nuclear Energy," *Science*, 177 (1972): 34.

70. For discussions of technocracy and machine-dependent polities, see Peter Medawar, *Pluto's Republic* (Oxford: Oxford University Press, 1982); Jean Meynaud, *Technocracy* (New York: Free Press, 1968).

71. In his fullest statement, a caste of virtuous technical experts modeled after Japanese warrior orders will rule. H. G. Wells, *A Modern Utopia* (New York: Scribner, 1905). For Wellsian technocracy as necessary to avoid the catastrophic breakdown of modern industrial polities, see W. Warren Wager, *H. G. Wells and the World State* (New Haven, CT: Yale University Press, 1961).

72. For the oppressions produced by authoritarian high modernism, see James C. Scott, *Seeing Like a State: How Certain Schemes to Improve the Human Condition Have Failed* (New Haven, CT: Yale University Press, 1998).

73. Wells, "Discovery of the Future," 331.

74. Dandridge Cole and Donald Cox, *Islands in Space: The Challenge of the Planetoids* (Radnor, PA: Chilton Books, 1962), 105-7.

75. Bill Joy, "Why the Future Doesn't Need Us," *Wired*, April 2000.

76. Ed Torres, *The End:What Science and Religion Tell Us about the Apocalypse* (Durham, NC: Pitchstone, 2016) 230. On the basis of his reading of an early version of this manuscript, Torres reverses his position in Phil Torres, *Morality, Foresight and Human Flourishing: An Introduction to Existential Risks* (Durham, NC: Pitchstone, 2017), 209. Taking a hundred thousand year perspective, Roger-Maurice Bonnet and Lodewijk Woltjer detail the case for the essential role of space rescue and escape. *Surviving 1,000 Centuries: Can We Do It?* (Berlin: Springer-Praxis, 2008), 281-365.

77. National Academy of Sciences, *Long-Term Worldwide Effects of Multiple Nuclear-Weapons Detonations* (Washington, DC: National Academy Press, 1975).

78 Schell, *Fate of the Earth*.

79 Nick Bostrom, "Existential Risk Prevention as Global Priority," *Global Policy* 4.1 (February 2013): 15-31. For a lucid overview, see Cass R. Sunstein, *Worst-Case Scenarios* (Cambridge, MA: Harvard University Press, 2007).

80. Global Challenges Foundation, "12 Risks That Threaten Human Civilization," February 2015.

81. Bill McGuire, *Apocalypse: A Natural History of Global Disaster* (London: Cassell, 1999).

82. Henry Stommel and Elizabeth Stommel, *Volcano Weather: The Story of 1816, the Year without a Summer* (Newport, RI: Seven Seas, 1983).

83. Michael R. Rampino, "Super-Vulcanism and Other Geophysical Processes of Catastrophic Impact," in Bostrom and Cirkovic, *Global Catastrophic Risks*, 205-21.

84. But see David Denkenberger and Robert W. Blair Jr., "Interventions That May Prevent or Mollify Supervolcanic Eruptions," *Futures*, Spring 2019.

85. Arnon Dar, "Influence," in Bostrom and Cirkovic, *Global Catastrophic Risks*, 238–59.

86. Nathan Wolfe, *The Viral Storm: The Dawn of a New Pandemic Age* (New York: Henry Holt, 2011).

87. The prospects and consequences of rapid and extreme change are analyzed in John Cox, *Climate Crash: Abrupt Climate Change and What It Means for Our Future* (Washington, DC: John Henry Press, 2005); Fred Pearce, *With Speed and Violence: Why Scientists Fear Tipping Points in Climate Change* (Boston: Beacon, 2007).

88. Thomas Homer-Dixon et al., "Synchronous Failure: The Emerging Causal Architecture of Global Crisis," *Ecology and Society* 20.3 (2015):1–13 ; Joseph Tainter, *The Collapse of Complex Societies* (Cambridge, UK: Cambridge University Press, 1988).

89. James Lovelock, *The Vanishing Face of Gaia* (New York: Basic Books, 2009).

90. Richard L. Garwin and Georges Charpak, *Megawatts and Megatons: The Future of Nuclear Power and Nuclear Weapons* (Chicago: University of Chicago Press, 2003).

91. For synoptic accounts, see Graham Allison, *Nuclear Terrorism: The Ultimate Preventable Catastrophe* (New York: Henry Holt, 2004); Charles D. Ferguson and William C. Potter, *The Four Faces of Nuclear Terrorism* (New York: Routledge, 2006). For diffusion, see Audrey Kurth Cronin, *Power to the People: How Open Technological Innovation Is Arming Tomorrow's Terrorists* (New York: Oxford University Press, 2020).

92. Harold A. Feiveson, Alexander Glaser, Zia Mian, and Frank von Hippel, *Unmaking the Bomb: A Fissile Material Approach to Nuclear Disarmament and Nonproliferation* (Cambridge, MA: MIT Press, 2014).

93. Jonathan Tucker, "Could Terrorists Exploit Synthetic Biology?," *New Atlantis*, Spring 2011.

94. Office of Technology Assessment, *Technologies Underlying Weapons of Mass Destruction* (Washington, DC: GPO, 1993); Joshua Lederberg, ed., *Biological Weapons: Limiting the Threat* (Cambridge, MA: MIT Press, 1999); Andreas Wenger and Reto Wollenmann, eds., *Bioterrorism: Confronting a Complex Threat* (Boulder, CO: Lynne Rienner, 2007).

95. Francis L. Flannery, "The Human Pox versus Green Fire: Eco-Terrorism and Activists," in *Understanding Apocalyptic Terrorism* (New York: Routledge, 2016). For religions, see Torres, *The End*, 160–220.

96. Discussed at length in Mayor, *Gods and Robots*.

97. Daniel J. Kevles, *In the Name of Eugenics: Genetics and the Uses of Human Heredity* (New York: Knopf, 1985).

98. Mark Walker, "Ship of Fools: Why Transhumanism Is the Best Bet to Present the Extinction of Civilization," in Gregory R. Hansell and William Grassie, eds., *Transhumanism and Its Critics* (Philadelphia: Metanexus Institute, 2011).

99. For bioconservatism, see Francis Fukuyama, *Our Posthuman Future: Consequences of the Biotechnology Revolution* (New York: Farrar, Straus and Giroux, 2002); Nicholas Agar, *Humanity's End: Why We Should Reject Radical Enhancement* (Cambridge, MA: MIT Press, 2010); and especially, for links with space thinking, Charles T. Rubin, *Eclipse of Man: Human Extinction and the Meaning of Progress* (New York: Encounter Books, 2014). For debates, see Hansell and Grassie, *Transhumanism and Its Critics*; Julian Savulescu and Nick Bostrom, eds., *Human Enhancement* (New York: Oxford University Press, 2009).

100. Maxwell J. Mehlman, *Transhumanist Dreams and Dystopian Nightmares: The Promise and Peril of Genetic Engineering* (Baltimore, MD: Johns Hopkins University Press, 2012).

101. Hugo de Garis, *The Artilect War: Cosmists vs Terrans. A Bitter Controversy concerning Whether Humanity Should Build Godlike Massively Intelligent Machines* (Etc. Publishers, 2005).

102. For existing regulations, see Heidi Ledford, "The Landscape for Human Genome Editing," *Nature* 526 (October 15, 2015): 310–11. For ambitious proposals, see George Annas, Lori Andrews, and Rosario Isasi, "Protecting the Endangered Human: Toward an International Treaty Prohibiting Cloning and Inheritable Alterations," *American Journal of Law and Medicine* 28 (2002): 151–78.

103. Center for Responsible Nanotechnology, "Dangers of Molecular Manufacturing," accessed January 15, 2019.

104. Chris Phoenix and Mike Treder, "Nanotechnology as Global Catastrophic Risk," in Bostrom and Cirkovic, *Global Catastrophic Risks*.

105. Eliezer Yudkowsky, "Artificial Intelligence as a Positive and Negative Factor in Global Risks," in Bostrom and Cirkovic, *Global Catastrophic Risks*, 315.

106. Patricia S. Warrick, *The Cybernetic Imagination in Science Fiction* (Cambridge, MA: MIT Press, 1980).

107. Bostrom, *Superintelligence*, 105–14.

108. Quite implausibly, James Lovelock argues that humans have little to fear from advanced AI, now initiating a new epoch of Earth history, which he calls the "novacene," because humans and advanced AI will need to work together to sustain the "Gaia system" keeping the planet from overheating. James Lovelock, *Novacene: The Coming Age of Hyperintelligence* (London: Penguin, 2019).

109. For "intelligence explosion," see Yudkowsky, "Artificial Intelligence," 323–28; Bostrom, *Superintelligence*, 62–77.

110. Yudkowsky, "Artificial Intelligence," 333–43; Bostrom, *Superintelligence*, 115–254. More optimistic about the prospects for human control is Stuart Russell, *Human Compatible: Artificial Intelligence and the Problem of Control* (New York: Viking, 2019).

111. For advocates, who amount to a Promethean voluntary extinction movement, and their employment of religious imaginaries, see Robert M. Geraci, *Apocalyptic AI: Visions of Heaven in Robotics, Artificial Intelligence, and Virtual Reality* (New York: Oxford University Press, 2010).

112. The 1857 words of the Russian liberal Alexander Herzon, cited in Bertram D. Wolf, *Revolution and Reality: Essays on the Origin and Fate of the Soviet System* (Chapel Hill: University of North Carolina Press, 1981), chapter 19, "The Totalitarian Potentials of the Modern Great State," 330.

113. Michael Halberstam, *Totalitarianism and the Modern Conception of Politics* (New Haven, CT: Yale University Press, 1999).

114. Olaf Stapledon, "Interplanetary Man," *Journal of the British Interplanetary Society* 7.6 (November 1948): 215.

115. Ronald J. Deibert, "Cyberspace Under Siege," *Journal of Democracy* 26.3 (July 2015): 64–78.

116. Bryan Caplan, "The Totalitarian Threat," in Bostrom and Cirkovic, *Global Catastrophic Risks*.

117. Olle Haggstrom, *Here Be Dragons: Science, Technology and the Future of Humanity* (New York: Oxford University Press, 2016), 61.

118. For scenarios of war with alien species, see John W. Macvey, *Space Weapons Space War* (New York: Stein and Day, 1979); Travis S. Taylor and Bob Roan, *An Introduction to Planetary Defense: A Study of Modern Warfare Applied to Extra-Terrestrial Invasion* (Boca Raton, FL: BrownWalker Press, 2006).

119. John Leslie, *The End of the World* (London: Routledge, 1996), 9; Torres, *The End*, 143.

120. For a reading of the development of Western thought about political order, violence capability, and restraint, see my *Bounding Power: Republican Security Theory from the Polis to the Global Village* (Princeton, NJ: Princeton University Press, 2007).

121. For the difficulties of repressing knowledge, see Roger Shattuck, *Forbidden Knowledge: From Prometheus to Pornography* (New York: St. Martin's, 1996).

122. Particularly good on these difficulties is Jonathan B. Tucker, *Innovation, Dual Use, and Security* (Cambridge, MA: MIT Press, 2012), especially 19–34.

Chapter 5

1. David Lasser, "The Rocket and the Next War," *AIS Bulletin*, no.13, November 1931, 7.

2. Quoted in DeGroot, *The Dark Side of the Moon*, 17.

3. Senator Lyndon B. Johnson, speech, January 7, 1958, cited in Salkeld, *War and Space*, 135.

4. For synoptic accounts, see Bernard Brodie and Fawn M. Brodie, *From Crossbow to H-Bomb*, revised edition (Bloomington: Indiana University Press, 1973); William McNeill, *The Pursuit of Power: Technology, Armed Force, and Society, AD 1000–1945* (Chicago: University of Chicago Press, 1982). Competitive armament innovation, moving at the much slower pace of biological evolution, also marks other life forms. Douglas J. Emlen, *Animal Weapons: The Evolution of Battle* (New York: Henry Holt, 2014).

5. Despite, or perhaps because of, their staggering cumulative costs, no official overall estimates exist. In a monumental public interest research project, analysts from the Natural Resources Defense Council put the total cost, in inflation-adjusted 1988 dollars, at $14 trillion for US nuclear forces. No estimate exists for overall Soviet outlays, which can be assumed to be roughly comparable. Stephen I. Schwartz, ed., *Atomic Audit: The Costs and Consequences of U.S. Nuclear Weapons since 1940* (Washington, DC: Brookings Institution, 1998). For the enlarged spatial scope of deployments, see William M. Arkin and Richard W. Fieldhouse, *Nuclear Battlefields: Global Links in the Arms Race* (Lexington, MA: Ballinger, 1985).

6. Estimated numbers from Feiveson et al., *Unmaking the Bomb*.

7. The best overall account of war futurism remains I. F. Clarke, *Voices Prophesying War, 1783–1984* (New York: Oxford University Press, 1966). For American fascination with military innovation, see H. Bruce Franklin, *War Stars: The Superweapon and the American Imagination* (New York: Oxford University Press, 1988).

8. Eliot A. Cohen and John Gooch, *Military Misfortunes: The Anatomy of Failure in War* (New York: Free Press, 1990).

9. For an overview of the central institution in the American scientific-technological-military-industrial-complex, see Sharon Weinberger, *The Imagineers of War: The Untold Story of DARPA, the Pentagon Agency That Changed the World* (New York: Random House, 2017).

10. Dwayne A. Day, "Paradigm Lost," *Space Policy* 11.10 (August 1995): 153–59; Michael J. Neufield, "The von Braun Paradigm and NASA's Long-Term Planning for Human Spaceflight," in Steven J. Dick, *NASA's First 50 Years: Historical Perspectives* (Washington, DC: NASA, 2009); and especially Launius and McCurdy, *Robots in Space*, 220–30. In another typology, Klerkx designates the von Braunian as an approach to space relying on government agencies and large corporations (*Lost in Space*, 63–65).

11. Michael J. Neufeld, "'Space Superiority': Wernher von Braun's Campaign for Nuclear Armed Space Station, 1946–1956." *Space Policy* 22.10 (February 2006): 52–62.

12. Dora was the name of the camp for the V-2 labor force, a satellite of the much larger Breslau concentration and extermination camp. Yves Béon, *Planet Dora: A Memoir of the Holocaust and the Birth of the Space Age,* ed. with an introduction by Michael J. Neufeld (Boulder, CO: Westview, 1997). See also Jean Michel with Louis Nucera, *Dora* (New York: Holt, Rinehart and Winston, 1979).

13. Michael J. Neufeld, *von Braun: Dreamer of Space, Engineer of War* (New York: Knopf, 2007).

14. Paraphrasing the quip widely attributed to the satirist Mort Sahl. The most recent indictment is particularly incisive: Wayne Biddle, *The Dark Side of the Moon: Wernher von Braun, the Third Reich, and the Space Race* (New York: Norton, 2009).

15. Paraphrasing lines in Tom Lehrer's song *Wernher von Braun*.

16. Alfred W. Crosby, *Throwing Fire: Projectile Technology through History* (Cambridge, UK: Cambridge University Press, 2002).

17. Milton Lehman, *This High Moon: The Life of Robert A. Goddard* (New York: Farrar, Strauss, 1963); David A. Clary, *Rocket Man: Robert H. Goddard and the Birth of the Space Age* (New York: Hyperion, 2003).

18. G. Harry Stine, *ICBM: The Making of the Weapon That Changed the World* (New York: Orion, 1991); M. P. Petersen, *Missiles for the Fatherland: Peenemunde, National Socialism and the V-2* (Cambridge, UK: Cambridge University Press, 2009).

19. Frederick I. Ordway III and Mitchell R. Sharpe, *The Rocket Team* (New York: Crowell, 1979).

20. Nicholas Michael Sambaluk, *The Other Space Race: Eisenhower and the Quest for Aerospace Security* (Annapolis, MD: Naval Institute Press, 2015).

21. For ballistic missile proliferation, see Aaron Karp, *Ballistic Missile Proliferation: The Politics and Technics* (Stockholm: SIPRI, 1996); Janne E. Nolan, *Trappings of Power: Ballistic Missiles in the Third World* (Washington, DC: Brookings, 1991). For the control regime, see Dinshaw Mistry, *Containing Missile Proliferation: Strategic Technology, Security Regimes and International Cooperation in Arms Control* (Seattle: University of Washington Press, 2003; Leonard S. Spector, "The Missile Technology Control Regime and Shifting Proliferation Challenges," *Arms Control Today*, April 2018.

22. Interceptor rockets with small nuclear warheads were deployed around many coastal American cities but dismantled after the deployment of ICBMs. Christopher Bright,

Continental Defense in the Eisenhower Era: Nuclear Antiaircraft Arms and the Cold War (London: Palgrave, 2010).

23. For discussion of speed and war, see Paul Virilio, *Politics and Speed: An Essay on Dromology* (New York: Foreign Agents, 1977); James der Derian, ed., *The Virilio Reader* (New York: Basil Blackwell, 1998).

24. William L. Borden, *There Will Be No Time* (New York: Macmillan, 1946).

25. For examples, see Tyson and Lang, *Accessory to War*, 257.

26. Described and discussed in Burrows, *New Ocean*, 127–29.

27. Among book-length accounts of this pivotal episode are Paul Dickson, *Sputnik: The Shock of the Century* (New York: Walker, 2001); Yanek Mieczkowski, *Eisenhower's Sputnik Moment: The Race for Space and World Prestige* (Ithaca, NY: Cornell University Press, 2013). Wide-ranging assessments are found in Roger D. Launius, John M. Logsdon, and Robert W. Smith, eds., *Reconsidering Sputnik: Forty Years Since the Soviet Satellite* (London: Routledge, 2000).

28. Matt Bille and Erika Lishock, *The First Space Race: Launching the World's First Satellites* (College Station: Texas A&M University Press, 2004).

29. Audra J. Wolfe, *Competing with the Soviets: Science, Technology, and the State in Cold War America* (Baltimore, MD: Johns Hopkins University Press, 2013).

30. For an early treatment of the transparency revolution and its relation to advances in the Earth sciences, see Daniel Deudney *Whole Earth Security: A Geopolitics of Peace* (Washington, DC: Worldwatch Institute, 1983), 20–32.

31. The high drama of this crisis is fully captured in Michael R. Beschloss, *May Day: Eisenhower, Khrushchev and the U-2 Affair* (New York: Harper and Row, 1986).

32. The saga of the early American military observation satellites, long obscured by secrecy, is recounted in Dwayne A. Day, John M. Logsdon, and Brian Latell, eds., *Eye in the Sky: The Story of the CORONA Spy Satellite* (Washington, DC: Smithsonian Press, 1998), 306.

33. Jeffrey T. Richelson, *America's Secret Eyes in Space: The Keyhole Satellite Program* (New York: Harper & Row, 1990).

34. Pat Norris, *Spies in the Sky: Surveillance Satellites in War and Peace* (New York: Springer-Praxis, 2008).

35. Moltz, "Changing Dynamics of Twenty-First Century Space Power," 78–83.

36. Allan Krass, *Verification: How Much Is Enough?* (Lexington, MA: Lexington Books, 1985).

37. Jeffrey T. Richelson, *America's Space Sentinels: DSP Satellites and National Security* (Lawrence: University Press of Kansas, 1999).

38. For detailed analysis of basing alternatives, see Office of Technology Assessment, *MX Missile Basing* (Washington, DC: OTA, 1981). For possible lunar basing, see Dwayne A. Day, "Nuking the site from orbit: when the Air Force wanted a base on the Moon," *The Space Review*, November 4, 2019. For the erosion of oceanic opacity and its implications, Elizabeth Mendenhall, "Fluid Foundations: Ocean Transparency, Submarine Opacity, and Strategic Nuclear Stability," *Journal of Military and Strategic Studies*, 19.1 (2018):119–58.

39. Simon Furchette and Peder Roberts, eds., *The Surveillance Imperative: Geosciences during the Cold War and Beyond* (London: Palgrave, 2014).

40. For these influences, see Harold A. Winters, ed., *Battling the Elements: Weather and Terrain in the Conduct of War* (Baltimore, MD: Johns Hopkins University Press, 1998).

41. Peter Anson and Dennis Cummings, "The First Space War: the Contribution of Satellites to the Gulf War," in Alan Cummings, ed., *The First Information War* (Fairfax, VA: AFCEA International Press, 1992).

42. A large literature, marked by extremely varied assessments and often outpaced by events, addresses the character and possibilities of cyber conflicts. Particularly interesting for analogies with other geophysical domains is George Perkovitch and Ariel E. Levite, eds., *Understanding Cyber Conflict: 14 Analogies* (Washington, DC: George Washington University Press, 2018). For nuclear linkages, see Erik Gatzke and Jon R. Lindsay, "Thermonuclear Cyberwar," *Journal of Cybersecurity*, February 2017, 1–12; Andrew Futter, *Hacking the Bomb: Cyber Threats and Nuclear Weapons* (Washington, DC: Georgetown University Press, 2018).

43. Hans M. Kristensen et al., "How US Nuclear Force Modernization Is Undermining Strategic Stability," *Bulletin of the Atomic Scientists*, March 2017.

44. Kier A. Lieber and Daryl G. Press, "The New Era of Counterforce: Technological Change and the Future of Deterrence," *International Security* 41.4 (Spring 2017): 9–49. A detailed description and critical evaluation is provided in James M. Acton, *Silver Bullet? Asking the Right Questions about Conventional Prompt Global Strike* (Washington, DC: Carnegie Endowment for International Peace, 2013).

45. P. W. Singer, *Wired for War: The Robotics Revolution and Conflict in the 21st Century* (New York: Penguin, 2009).

46. Benjamin S. Lambeth, *Mastering the Ultimate High Ground* (Washington, DC: RAND, 2003); Bleddyn E. Bowen, "From the Sea to Outer Space: The Command of Space as the Foundation of Spacepower Theory," *Journal of Strategic Studies* 10.10 (2017): 1–25. Barry Posen examines this topic but does not attribute any significance to the geographic aspects of the commons in "The Command of the Commons: The Military Foundations of American Hegemony," *International Security* 28.1 (Summer 2003): 5–46.

47. Mark Wolverton, *Burning the Sky: Operation Argus and the Untold Story of the Cold War Nuclear Tests in Outer Space* (New York: Overlook Press, 2018).

48. For historical development of ASAT technologies, see Thomas Karas, *The New High Ground: Systems and Weapons of Space Age War* (New York: Simon and Schuster, 1983), 147–200.

49. Namrata Goswani, "China in Space: Ambitions and Possible Conflict," *Strategic Studies Quarterly*, Spring 2018, 74–97; Michael Krepon and Julia Thompson, eds., *Anti-Satellite Weapons, Deterrence and Sino-American Space Relations* (Washington DC: Stimson Center, 2013).

50. For example, see Elbridge Colby, *From·Sanctuary to Battlefield: A Framework for a U.S. Defense and Deterrence Strategy for Space* (Washington, DC: Center for a New American Security, 2016).

51. For a detailed account of current efforts, see Brian Weeden and Victoria Samson, *Global Counterspace Capabilities: An Open Source Assessment* (Washington, DC: Secure World Foundation, 2018).

52. These interactions are described in Ashton Carter, "The Relationship of ASAT and BMD Systems," in Franklin Long, ed., *Weapons in Space* (New York: Norton, 1986).

53. For the earliest thinking, see Donald R. Baucom, *The Origins of SDI: 1944–1983* (Lawrence: University Press of Kansas, 1992). For the 1960s and 1970s, see James Cameron, *The Double Game: The Demise of America's First Missile Defense System and the Rise of Strategic Arms Limitation* (New York: Oxford University Press, 2018).

54. Deployment of ABM batteries around US cities was also politically difficult due to widespread popular opposition, described in Joel Primack and Frank von Hippel, "Invoking the Experts: The Antiballistic Missile Debate," in *Advice and Dissent* (New York: Basic Books, 1974).

55. Reagan's speech, related SDI documents, and multiple assessments are found in Steven Miller and Stephen Van Evera, eds., *The Star Wars Controversy* (Princeton, NJ: Princeton University Press, 1986). For all aspects of BMD, see Ashton Carter and David Schwartz, eds., *Ballistic Missile Defense* (Washington, DC: Brookings, 1983).

56. Daniel Graham, *The High Frontier: A New National Strategy* (Washington, DC: High Frontier, Inc., 1982); Daniel Graham, *The Non-Nuclear Defense of Cities* (Cambridge, MA: Abt Books, 1983); Jerry Pournelle and Dean Ing, *Mutual Assured Survival* (New York: Bean Enterprises, 1984); Ben Bova, *Assured Survival* (Boston: Houghton Mifflin, 1984); Fusion Energy Foundation, *Beam Defense: An Alternative to Nuclear Destruction* (Fallbrook, CA.: Aero, 1983). Analysts from the techno-optimist cult of Lyndon LaRouche envision these technologies catalyzing a wholesale civilizational renaissance.

57. For this view, see Peter Schweitzer, *Victory: The Reagan Administration's Secret Strategy That Hastened the Collapse of the Soviet Union* (New York: Atlantic Monthly Press, 1994).

58. This is the view of the distinguished Russian American diplomatic historian Vladislav M. Zubok, *A Failed Empire: The Soviet Union in the Cold War from Stalin to Gorbachev* (Chapel Hill: University Press of North Carolina, 2007), chapter 10, "Gorbachev and the End of Soviet Power," 303–35.

59. A detailed account of this scaled-back and refocused ABM effort is provided in Bradley Graham, *Hit to Kill: The New Battle over Shielding America from Missile Attack* (New York: Public Affairs, 2001). For the logic of this direction, see James M. Lindsay and Michael E. O'Hanlon, *Defending America: The Case for Limited National Missile Defense* (Washington, DC: Brookings, 2001). For programmatic and technical aspects, see K. Scott McMahon, *Pursuit of the Shield: The U.S. Quest for Limited Ballistic Missile Defense* (Lanham, MD: University Press of America, 1997).

60. Multiple perspectives on the abrogation of the ABM Treaty and the consequences of BMD deployment are provided in James J. Wirtz and Jeffrey A. Larsen, eds., *Rocket's Red Glare: Missile Defense and the Future of World Politics* (Boulder, CO: Westview, 2001).

61. Laura Grego, "US Ground-Based Midcourse Missile Defense: Expensive and Unreliable," *Bulletin of the Atomic Scientists* 74.4 (2018): 220–26.

62. George Lewis and Frank von Hippel, "Limitation on Ballistic Missile Defense—Past and Possibly Future," *Bulletin of the Atomic Scientists* 74.4 (2018): 199–209.

63. For a detailed analysis of the technical and strategic issues involved in extensive space weapons deployment, see Office of Technology Assessment, *Ballistic Missile Defense Technologies* (Washington, DC: GPO, 1985).

64. The technical features and limitations of these systems are concisely laid out in Richard Garwin and Hans Bethe, "Anti-Ballistic-Missile Systems," *Scientific American*, March 1968. For citizen action in hindering ABM deployment in the United States, see Primack and von Hippel, "Invoking the Experts."

65. Thomas G. Roberts, "Why a Space-Based Missile Interceptor System Is Not Viable," *Bulletin of the Atomic Scientists* 74.4 (2018): 238–42.

66. For an early account of how compressed time for decisions makes the dangerous strategy of DEAD (destruction entrusted automatic devices) appealing, see Deudney, *Whole Earth Security*, 32–39.

67. D. R. Baucom, "The Rise and Fall of Brilliant Pebbles," *Journal of Social and Political Economic Studies* 29.2 (2004): 143–90.

68. For a recent accessible overview, see R. Jeffrey Smith, "Hypersonic Missiles Are Unstoppable. And They're Starting a New Global Arms Race," *New York Times Magazine*, June 19, 2019. For first deployment, see Julian E. Barnes and David E. Sanger "Russia Deploys Hypersonic Weapon, Potentially Renewing Arms Race," *New York Times*, December 27, 2019, A8.

69. For these pervasive technological imaginaries and their employment by advocates, see Rebecca Slayton, "From Death Rays to Light Sabers," *Technology and Culture* 52.1 (2011): 45–74. For critical theory perspective, see Columba Peoples, *Justifying Ballistic Missile Defence: Technology, Security and Culture* (Cambridge, UK: Cambridge University Press, 2010).

70. For history and prospects, see Jeff Hecht, *Lasers, Death Rays, and the Long Strange Quest for the Ultimate Weapon* (Amherst, NY: Prometheus Books, 2019). For early ambitious speculations on military roles, see Keith B. Payne, ed., *Laser Weapons in Space: Policy and Doctrine* (Boulder, CO: Westview, 1983).

71. Cole and Cox, *Islands in Space*, 106.

72. Salkeld, *War and Space*, 42.

73. Salkeld, *War and Space*, 42.

74. Salkeld, *War and Space*, xvi–xvii.

75. Salkeld, *War and Space*, xviii.

76. Salkeld, *War and Space*, 51.

77. Salkeld, *War and Space*, 59.

78. Cole and Cox, *Islands in Space*, 157.

79. Cole and Cox, *Islands in Space*, 157.

80. Cole and Cox, *Islands in Space*, 158.

81. Cole and Cox, *Islands in Space*, 156.

82. Cole and Cox, *Islands in Space*, 158.

83. James Rogers Fleming, *Fixing the Sky: The Checkered History of Weather and Climate Control* (New York: Columbia University Press, 2010), 165–224; Jacob Darwin Hamblin, *Arming Mother Nature: The Birth of Catastrophic Environmentalism* (New York: Oxford University

Press, 2013); Nigel Calder, ed., *Unless Peace Comes: A Scientific Forecast of New Weapons* (London: Allan Lane, 1968).

84. "Give me a place to stand on and I will move the Earth." Archimedes, third century BCE, quoted in Pappus of Alexandria, in *Synagogue*, book 8, from Wikipedia, "Archimedes." Archimedes is also said to have designed large mirrors that ignited enemy warships by focusing intense sunlight on them, making him the first beam-weapon warrior.

85. Dandridge Cole, "Strategic Areas in Space: The Panama Theory" (working paper, Institute of Aerospace Studies, Los Angeles, 1962).

86. G. Harry Stine, "Defending the Third Industrial Revolution," in Reginald Bretnor, ed., *The Future of War, Vol. 1: Thor's Hammer* (New York: Baen, 1979), 22, 27.

87. Marc Vaucher, "Geopolitical Parameters for Military Doctrines in Space and the Defense of Space-Based Enterprise," in Uri Ra'annan and Robert Pfaltzgraff, eds., *International Dimensions of Space* (Hamden, CT: Archon Books, 1984), 43, 39.

88. Everett C. Dolman, *Astropolitik: Classical Geopolitics in the Space Age* (London: Frank Cass, 2002), 68. Dolman is a former graduate student of mine.

89. Dolman, *Astropolitik*, 8.

90. Dolman, *Astropolitik*, 157. The critical geographer Fraser MacDonald observes that Dolman is "writing in the service of his empire" and that his "veneer of transcendent humanism" masks "brazen self-interest." Fraser MacDonald, "Anti-*Astropolitik*: Outer Space and the Orbit of Geography," *Progress in Human Geography* 31.5 (2007): 592–615, at 607. For penetrating analysis of astropolitik, see Raymond Duvall and Jonathan Havercroft, "Taking Sovereignty out of this World: Space Weapons and the Empire of the Future," *Review of International Studies*, 34.4 (2008): 755–75.

91. Dolman, *Astropolitik*, 165, 159.

92. For the fullest critique, see Colin S. Gray, *House of Cards: Why Arms Control Must Fail* (Ithaca, NY: Cornell University Press, 1992).

93. For nuclear schools, see Daniel Deudney, "The Great Debate: The Nuclear-Political Question and World Order," in William Wohlforth and Alexandra Gheciu, eds., *The Oxford Handbook on International Security* (New York: Oxford University Press, 2018), 334–49.

94. Robert Jervis, *The Meaning of the Nuclear Revolution: Statecraft and the Prospect of Armageddon* (Ithaca, NY: Cornell University Press, 1989).

95. Colin Gray, "Nuclear Strategy: The Case for a Theory of Victory," *International Security* 4.1 (Summer 1979): 54–87.

Chapter 6

1. Kenneth E. Boulding, "The Economics of the Coming Spaceship Earth," in Henry Jarrett, ed., *Environmental Quality in a Growing Economy* (Baltimore: Johns Hopkins University Press, 1966), xx.

2. Marsha Freeman, *Krafft Ehricke's Extraterrestrial Imperative* (Burlington, Ontario: Apogee Books, 2008), 226.

3. Quoted in Robert Zubrin, *Entering Space*, 3.

4. Pascal, *Pensées*, no. 91/199. Guthke observes that this passage is "the classic expression of the insecurity brought about by the cosmology of the new science" (*The Last Frontier*, 188).

5. Hannah Arendt, "The Conquest of Space and the Stature of Man," in *Between Past and Future: Eight Exercises in Political Thought* (New York: Viking, 1968).

6. George Bernard Shaw, *Back to Methuselah: A Metabiological Pentateuch* (1921), revised edition (New York: Oxford University Press, 1947), 300.

7. Lavery, *Late for the Sky*, 3.

8. The main ideas are found in Konstantin Tsiolkovsky *Beyond the Planet Earth* (*Vne Zemli* [1920]), trans. K. Syers (New York: Pergamon Press, 1960). In Klerkx's tripartite typology, "O'Neillian" is proposed as the space approach responsive to terrestrial resource limits and viewing "space as a *personal* frontier" (*Lost in Space*, 69–72, at 72).

9. Konstantin Tsiolkovski, *The Aims of Astronautics* (Barcelona: Athena University Press, 2004), 38.

10. Zubrin, *Entering Space*, 5.
11. Freeman, *Ehricke's Extraterrestrial Imperative*, 25.
12. Zubrin, *Entering Space*, 146.
13. Zubrin, *Entering Space*, 9, 8.
14. Arthur C. Clarke, "The Challenge of the Space Ship: Astronautics and Its Impact upon Human Society," *Journal of the British Interplanetary Society*, 6.3, (December 1946), 72.
15. For a synthesis of the Earth-rescue agenda, see C.M. Hempsell, "A History of Space and Limits to Growth," *Journal of the British Interplanetary Society*, 51 1998: 323–36; C. M. Hempsell, "The Potential for Space Intervention in Natural Global Catastrophes," *Journal of the British Interplanetary Society*, 47 (2004): 14–21.
16. Zubrin, *Entering Space*, 7.
17. Zubrin, *Entering Space*, 7.
18. Zubrin, *Entering Space*, 275.
19. Zubrin, *Entering Space*, 226. For other examples and critique, see James S. J. Schwartz, Myth-Free Space Advocacy, Part I: The Myth of Innate Exploratory and Migratory Urges," *Acta Astronautica* 137 (2017): 450–60.
20. Zubrin, *Entering Space*, 226.
21. Zubrin, *Entering Space*, 225. Ehricke had made this point as his "third law of astronautics": "By expanding through the universe, man fulfills his destiny as an element of life." Krafft Ehricke "The Anthropology of Astronautics," *Astronautics* 2.4 (November 1957): 28.
22. Zubrin, *Entering Space*, 225, his emphasis.
23. See also Marshall Savage, *The Millennial Project: Colonizing the Galaxy in Eight Easy Steps* (Boston: Little, Brown, 1994).
24. For insightful analyses, see John Woodcock, "The Garden in the Machine: Variations on Spaceship Earth," *Michigan Quarterly Review* 18.2 (Spring 1979): 308–17; Hohler, *Spaceship Earth in the Environmental Age*.
25. An earlier version of some of the points in this section appeared in Daniel Deudney and Jairus Grove, "Geoengineering and World Order: The Emerging Debate," paper presented at the Annual Convention of the American Political Science Association, Toronto, September 2009.
26. Benton MacKaye, *From Geography to Geotechnics* (Urbana: University of Illinois Press, 1968).
27. For a manifesto of contemporary macro-engineering futurism, see Frank Davidson with John Stuart Cox, *Macro: A Clear Vision of How Science and Technology Will Shape Our Future* (New York: Morrow, 1983). Numerous historical projects and ambitious proposals are treated in Frank Davidson, L. J. Giacolletto, and Robert Salkeld, eds., *Macro-Engineering and the Infrastructure of Tomorrow* (Boulder, CO: Westview Press, 1978); Frank Davidson, C. Lawrence Meader, and Robert Salkeld, eds., *How Big and Still Beautiful? Macro-Engineering Revisited* (Boulder, CO: Westview Press, 1980).
28. Karl Wittfogel, *Asiatic Despotism* (New Haven, CT: Yale University Press, 1957); see also evaluations in Brendan O'Leary, *The Asiatic Mode of Production: Oriental Despotism, Historical Materialism and Indian History* (Oxford: Basil Blackwell, 1989).
29. For example, Henry A. Millon and Linda Nochlin, *Art and Architecture in the Service of Politics* (Cambridge, MA: MIT Press, 1978). Particularly insightful is Keller Easterling, *Extrastatecraft: The Power of Infrastructural Space* (London: Verso, 2014).
30. This "interior environmentalism" is analyzed at length in Joachim Radkau, *Nature and Power: A Global History of the Environment* (Cambridge, UK: Cambridge University Press, 2008).
31. Robert Fishman, *Urban Utopias in the Twentieth Century: Ebenezer Howard, Frank Lloyd Wright, and Le Corbusier* (New York: Basic Books, 1977).
32. For the range and diversity of population engineering and its politics, see Alison Bashford, *Global Population: History, Geopolitics, and Life on Earth* (New York: Columbia University Press, 2014).
33. William Delisle Hay, *Three Hundred Years Hence* (New York, 1881). For Hay's influence, see Clarke, *Pattern of Expectation*, 156–61.
34. Wells, *Anticipations*, 230. He later recanted this passage and was a stalwart defender of liberal democracy against communism and fascism.
35. Konstantin Tsiolkovsky, "The Future of the Earth and Mankind," in Boris Groys, ed., *Russian Cosmism* (Cambridge, MA: MIT Press, 2018), 122. A careful assessment of the ultimate carry

capacity of the Earth, done before the emergence of significant climate change, puts the maximum at between nine and eleven billion. Joel E. Cohen, *How Many People Can the Earth Support?* (New York: Norton, 1995).

36. Tsiolkovsky, "The Future of the Earth and Mankind," 130.

37. Milan Cirkovic, "Cosmological Forecast and Its Practical Significance," *Journal of Evolution and Technology* 12 (2002): 1-13; Nick Bostrom, "Astronomical Waste: The Opportunity Cost of Delayed Technological Development," *Utilitas* 15.3 (2003): 308-14.

38. For these early schemes, see Willy Ley, *Engineers' Dreams* (New York: Viking, 1954).

39. Scott Kirsh, *Proving Grounds: Project Plowshare and the Unrealized Dream of Nuclear Engineering* (New Brunswick, NJ: Rutgers University Press, 2005).

40. The basic logic of this extrapolation is concisely made by Robert Salkeld, "Space: Macro-Arena for Macro-Engineering," in Davidson, Giacolletto, and Salkeld, *Macro-Engineering and the Infrastructure of Tomorrow*. For a wildly imaginative tour of visionary planetary engineering, brimming with evocative neologisms, see Richard Brook Cathcart, *Medicative Macro-Engineering: Earth and Mars Megaprojects* (Burbank, CA: Geographos, 2014).

41. Plato, *The Republic*, 488a-489c.

42. This statist discourse is explored in Norma Thompson, *The Ship of State: Statecraft and Politics from Ancient Greece to Democratic America* (New Haven, CT: Yale University Press, 2001).

43. For further discussion and sources, see Deudney, *Bounding Power*, 115-35.

44. I concur with Robert Poole's assessment that Fuller was "one of the great original thinkers of the twentieth century" (*Earthrise*, 146).

45. For descriptive and hagiographic accounts, see Hugh Kenner, *Bucky: A Guided Tour of Buckminster Fuller* (New York: William Morrow, 1973); Robert W. Marks, *The Dymaxion World of Buckminster Fuller* (New York: Reinhold, 1960). Particularly good for the links between Fuller and the military, played down in other accounts, as well as a succinct overview of his main ideas, is Peder Anker, "Buckminster Fuller as Captain of Spaceship Earth," *Minerva* 45.4 (2007): 417-34.

46. Paolo Soleri, "Archology: The City in the Image of Man," in Alan Trachtenberg, Peter Neill, and Peter C. Bunnell, eds., *The City: The American Experience* (New York: Oxford University Press, 1971), 591, 594.

47. R. S. Deese points out that this notion was employed by the American socialist Henry George in *Progress and Poverty* (1879): "It is a well-provisioned ship on which we sail through space." R. S. Deese "The Artifact of Nature: 'Spaceship Earth' and the Dawn of Global Environmentalism," *Endeavor* 33.2(June 2009), 70.

48. R. Buckminster Fuller, *Operating Manual for Spaceship Earth* (Carbondale: Southern Illinois University Press, 1969), 42.

49. Fuller, *Utopia or Oblivion*.

50. Fuller, *Operating Manual*, 52.

51. R. Buckminster Fuller, *Critical Path* (New York: St. Martin's Press, 1981). Fuller characterizes his global megastructures as the next step up from American New Deal infrastructural programs for rural electrification and the Tennessee Valley Authority.

52. Buckminster Fuller, "Prolog: Universe Is Technology," in Larry Gels and Fabrice Florin, eds., *Worlds Beyond: The Everlasting Frontier* (Berkeley, CA: And/Or Press, 1978), 33.

53. Fuller, *Critical Path*, xxiv.

54. Hermann Oberth, *Rockets into Planetary Space (Die Rakete zu den Planetenramon)* (Washington, DC: NASA, 1965).

55. The Soviet engineer P. M. Borisov, in *Can Man Control the Climate?* (Moscow: Progress, 1973) proposes a combination of space-based and terrestrial interventions to melt the polar ice cap to bring a wide range of benefits.

56. For a critical overview, see Hamilton, *Earthmasters*. A more sympathetic account is David Keith, *A Case for Climate Engineering* (Cambridge, MA: MIT Press, 2013).

57. Jerome Pearson, Johns Oldson, and Eugene Levin, "Earth Rings for Planetary Environmental Control," *Acta Astronautica* 58 (2006); John Hickman, "The Political Economy of a Planetary Sunshade," *Astropolitics* 16.1 (2018): 49-58.

58. Athena Lord, *Pilot for Spaceship Earth* (New York: Macmillan, 1978).

59. Fuller, *Operating Manual*, 15-35.

60. In his book *Grunch of Giants* (New York: St. Martin's Press, 1983) Fuller vividly denounces the capitalist system as the "Gross Universal Cash Heist" (i.e., GRUNCH).

61. Fuller, *Critical Path*, xvii.

62. See Fuller's detailed account of how he came to see himself as having the potential to revolutionize the human condition, and the code of discipline, heavily influenced by his naval training, guiding his selfless pursuit of human betterment: "Self-Disciplines of Buckminster Fuller," chapter 4 of *Critical Path*, 123–60.

63. Freeman, *Ehricke's Extraterrestrial Imperative*, 202.

64. Peter E. Glaser, "Power from the Sun: Its Future," *Science*, November 22, 1968, 857–61; Peter E. Glaser, "Solar Power from Satellites," *Physics Today*, February 1977, 30–38.

65. National Security Space Office, *Space-Based Solar Power as an Opportunity for Strategic Security*, October 2007.

66. Department of Energy and NASA, *Satellite Power Systems: Concept Development Program* (Washington, DC: US Department of Energy, October 1978); Office of Technology Assessment, *Solar Power Satellites* (Washington, DC:OTA, August 1981); Committee on Satellite Power Systems, National Academy of Science, *Electric Power from Orbit: A Critique of a Satellite Power System* (Washington, DC: National Academy Press, 1981).

67. Claud N. Bain, *Solar Power System (SPS) Military Implications* (Washington, DC: US Department of Energy, 1978).

68. Danny Royce Jones and Ali Baghchehsara, *Electric Space: Solar-Based Solar Power Technologies and Applications* (North Charleston, SC: CreateSpace Independent Publishing, 2013); John Mankin, *The Case for Space Solar Power* (Houston, TX: Virginia Edition Publishing, 2014).

69. Molly K. Macauley and Jinh-Shyang Shih, "Satellite Solar Power: Renewed Interest in an Age of Climate Change?," *Space Policy* 23.10 (2007): 108–20.

70. Krafft A. Ehricke, "In-Depth Exploration of the Solar System and Its Utilization for the Benefit of Earth," *Annals of the New York Academy of Sciences*,187 (1972),427–456; Michael J. Gaffey and Thomas B. McCord, "Mining Outer Space," *Technology Review*, June 1977, 51–59; V. Badescu, ed., *Asteroids: Prospective Energy and Material Resources* (Berlin: Springer, 2013), 256.

71. G. Harry Stine, *The Third Industrial Revolution* (New York: G. P. Putnam's Sons, 1975).

72. Lewis, *Mining the Sky*, 234–35.

73. Lewis, *Mining the Sky*, 255.

74. Aaron Bastini, *Fully Automated Luxury Communism: A Manifesto* (London: Verso, 2019), 117–37.

75. E. E. Hale, "The Brick Moon," *Atlantic Monthly* 24 (October–December 1869). Intended as a navigational beacon, the satellite becomes an accidental long-term habitat through a series of highly implausible mishaps. For discussion, see Burrows, *This New Ocean*, 33.

76. For an illustrated tour of stations, imagined and actual, see Roger Launius, *Space Stations: Base Camps to the Stars* (Old Saybrook, CT: Konecky & Konecky, 2003); Jay Chaladek, *Outposts on the Frontier: A Fifty-Year History of Space Stations* (Lincoln: University of Nebraska Press, 2017).

77. An excellent overview of the International Space Station is provided in Charles Fishman, "5,200 Days in Space," *Atlantic Monthly*, January–February 2015. Book-length treatments include Peter Bond, *The Continuing Story of the International Space Station* (Chichester, UK: Springer Praxis, 2002); David M. Harland and John E. Catchpole, *Creating the International Space Station* (Guilford, CT: Springer-Verlag, 2002).

78. The first iteration is in G. K. O'Neill, "The Colonization of Space," *Physics Today* 27.9 (September 1974): 32–42, and the full version in Gerard O'Neill, *The High Frontier* (New York: William Morrow, 1977). For another popular account, see T. A. Heppenheimer, *Colonies in Space* (Harrisburg, PA: Stackpole Books, 1977).

79. A detailed account of O'Neill's efforts is provided in McCray, *Visioneers*, 40–145. For the L5 Society, see Michaud Michaud, *Reaching for the High Frontier: The American Pro-Space Movement, 1972–1984* (New York: Praeger, 1986).

80. O'Neill anticipates that in establishing ecosystems within space colonies it would be possible "to take along those species we want and which form parts of a complete ecosystem chain, but leave behind some parasitic types" (*High Frontier*, 49).

81. O'Neill, *High Frontier*, 265–66.

82. O'Neill, *High Frontier*, 64, 23.

83. O'Neill, *High Frontier*, 111.

84. O'Neill, *High Frontier*, 148.

85. O'Neill, *High Frontier*, 111.

86. O'Neill, *High Frontier*, 111.

87. O'Neill, *High Frontier*, 180.

88. O'Neill, *High Frontier*, 234.

89. O'Neill, *High Frontier*, 17, 235.

90. O'Neill, *High Frontier*, 236.

91. This suburban space vision is even accompanied by a racially tinged "white flight." In his *2081: A Hopeful View of the Human Future* (New York: Simon and Schuster, 1981), 205–6 O'Neill intersperses his technological futurist account with fictional reportage in which visitors to space colonies, and from space colonies to Earth, describe what they observe, including an Africa where nuclear proliferation has become complete and where capitols are routinely obliterated by nuclear detonations by terrorists or coups. Kilgore observes that O'Neill "reinvents the segregationist ethic." De Witt Douglas Kilgore, *Astrofuturism: Science, Race and Visions of Utopia in Space* (Philadelphia: University of Pennsylvania Press, 2003), chapter 5, "The Domestication of Space: Gerard K. O'Neill's Suburban Diaspora," 176.

92. J. D. Bernal, *The World, the Flesh, and the Devil: An Inquiry into the Future of the Three Enemies of the Rational Soul* (1929; Bloomington: Indiana University Press, 1969).

93. Bernal, *World, Flesh and Devil*, 33, 38–41.

94. Bernal, *World, Flesh and Devil*, 64, 44.

95. Bernal, *World, Flesh and Devil*, 18–19.

96. Bernal, *World, Flesh and Devil*, 18–19.

97. Bernal, *World, Flesh and Devil*, 25.

98. Bernal, *World, Flesh and Devil*, 78.

99. Bernal, *World, Flesh and Devil*, 79–80.

100. White, *Overview Effect*, 150, 143.

101. White, *Overview Effect*, 148.

102. White, *Overview Effect*, 166–67.

103. For possible Lunar activities, see Neil P. Ruzic, *Where the Winds Sleep: Man's Future on the Moon. A Projected History* (Garden City, NY: Doubleday, 1970); Rick N. Tumlinson and Erin R. Medlicott, eds., *Return to the Moon* (Burlington, Ontario: Apogee Books, 2005); Erik Seedhouse, *Luna Outpost: The Challenge of a Human Settlement on the Moon* (Berlin: Springer, 2009); Paul D. Spudis, *The Value of the Moon: How to Explore, Live, and Prosper in Space Using the Moon's Resources* (Washington, DC: Smithsonian Books, 2016).

104. Wernher von Braun, *The Mars Project* (1953; Urbana: University of Illinois Press, 1991).

105. David Portree, *Humans to Mars: Fifty Years of Mission Planning* (Washington, DC: NASA, 2001); Andrew Chaikin, *A Passion for Mars: Intrepid Explorers of the Red Planet* (New York: Abrams, 2008); W. Henry Lambright, *Why Mars: NASA and the Politics of Space Exploration* (Baltimore, MD: Johns Hopkins University Press, 2014).

106. Buzz Aldrin and Leonard David, *Mission to Mars: My Vision for Space Exploration* (Washington, DC: National Geographic Press, 2013).

107. Robert Zubrin with Richard Wagner, *The Case for Mars: The Plan to Settle the Red Planet and Why We Must* (New York: Free Press, 1997); Robert Zubrin, *How to Live on Mars: A Trusty Guidebook to Surviving and Thriving on the Red Planet* (New York: Three Rivers, 2008).

108. Zubrin and Wagner, *Case for Mars*, 218, 223.

109. Zubrin and Wagner, *Case for Mars*, 230.

110. Zubrin and Wagner, *Case for Mars*, 230.

111. Zubrin, *Entering Space*, 123.

112. Bould and Mieville, *Red Planets*; Loren R. Graham and Richard Stites, eds., *Red Star: The First Bolshevik Utopia by Alexander Bogdanov* (Bloomington: Indiana University Press, 1984).

113. Cameron Smith and Evan Davies, *Emigrating beyond Earth: Human Adaptation and Space Colonization* (New York: Springer, 2013), xix.

114. Zubrin and Wagner, *Case for Mars*, 218.

115. Oberg, *New Earths*, 258.
116. Oberg, *New Earths*, 255.
117. Oberg, *New Earths*, 254–55.
118. Oberg, *New Earths*, 255.
119. Oberg, *New Earths*, 259.
120. Zubrin, *Entering Space*, 150.
121. Further developed in Donald W. Cox and James H. Chester, "Colonizing the Minor Planets," in *Doomsday Asteroid: Can We Survive?* (Amherst, NY: Prometheus Books, 1996), 167–230.
122. Cole and Cox, *Islands in Space*, 108.
123. Cole and Cox, *Islands in Space*, 110.
124. Cole and Cox, *Islands in Space*, 104–5.
125. Cole and Cox, *Islands in Space*, 110.
126. Cole and Cox, *Islands in Space*, 103.
127. Cole and Cox, *Islands in Space*, 149.
128. Cole and Cox, *Islands in Space*, 149.
129. Cole and Cox, *Islands in Space*, 149.
130. Cole and Cox, *Islands in Space*, 149.
131. Cole and Cox, *Islands in Space*, 149.
132. Cole and Cox, *Islands in Space*, 150.
133. Charles S. Cockell, *Extra-Terrestrial Liberty: An Enquiry into the Nature and Causes of Tyrannical Government beyond the Earth* (Edinburgh: Shoving Leopard, 2013); Charles S. Cockell, ed., *The Meaning of Liberty beyond Earth* (New York: Springer, 2015). Cockell's understanding of freedom and its foundations is drawn primarily from early modern liberal thought, with a selective admixture of Berlin and Hayek, and curiously does not draw from those theorists within this tradition who examine the role of environmental and material-contextual factors in shaping "free states," most notably Montesquieu, Rousseau, and the American founders. Nor does he value or consider direct or representative democracy. The outcome he opposes is referred to as tyranny, but is more accurately labeled despotism, as tyranny is highly individualized and capricious while despotism systemic and bureaucratic.
134. Cockell, *Extra-Terrestrial Liberty*, 172, 29.
135. Cockell, *Extra-Terrestrial Liberty*, 205.
136. Cockell, *Extra-Terrestrial Liberty*, 27–39, 171, 203.
137. Cockell, *Extra-Terrestrial Liberty*, 24, 171.
138. Cockell, *Extra-Terrestrial Liberty*, 172.
139. Cockell, *Extra-Terrestrial Liberty*, 173.
140. Cockell, *Extra-Terrestrial Liberty*, 30.
141. Cockell, *Extra-Terrestrial Liberty*, 23, 164, 200–201.
142. Cockell, *Extra-Terrestrial Liberty*, 172–3, 179–80, 195.
143. Cockell, *Extra-Terrestrial Liberty*, 47–50, 196–98.
144. Cockell, *Extra-Terrestrial Liberty*, 196.
145. Cockell, *Extra-Terrestrial Liberty*, 181–82.
146. Cockell, *Extra-Terrestrial Liberty*, 183–85.
147. Cockell, *Extra-Terrestrial Liberty*, 151–59, 158.
148. Charles S. Cockell, "Freedom Engineering – Using Engineering to Mitigate Tyranny in Space," *Space Policy*, 49 (August 2019). For insights on alternative colony designs and their implications for colony activities, see Fred Scharmen, *Space Settlements* (New York: Columbia Books on Architecture and the City, 2019).
149. Ian A. Crawford and Stephen Baxter, "The Lethality of Interplanetary Warfare: A Fundamental Constraint on Extraterrestrial Liberty," in Cockell, *The Meaning of Liberty beyond Earth*, 187.
150. Crawford and Baxter, "Lethality," 188.
151. Crawford and Baxter, "Lethality," 197.
152. Crawford and Baxter, "Lethality," 188.
153. Olaf Stapledon, "Interplanetary Man?," *Journal of the British Interplanetary Society* 7 (1948): 213–33; I. A. Crawford, "Stapledon's Interplanetary Man: A Commonwealth of Worlds and the Ultimate Purpose of Space Colonization," *Journal of the British Interplanetary Society* 65 (2012): 13–19.

154. Ian A. Crawford, "Interplanetary Federalism: Maximizing the Chances of Extraterrestrial Peace, Diversity and Liberty," in Cockell, *The Meaning of Liberty beyond Earth*, 199–218.

155. Crawford, "Interplanetary Federalism," 209.

156. I. W. Crawford, "Space Development: Social and Political Implications," *Space Policy* 11.4 (November 1995): 219–25.

157. Crawford, "Interplanetary Federalism," 212.

158. Thomas Gangale, *Outer Space Territories and Sovereignties: Politics beyond the Earth into the 22nd Century* (Santa Barbara, CA: Praeger, 2014).

159. Dyson's essays and lectures have been assembled in a series of books whose titles vividly convey his worldview: *Disturbing the Universe* (New York: Harper & Row, 1979); *Infinite in All Directions* (New York: Harper & Row, 1988); *Imagined Worlds* (Cambridge, MA: Harvard University Press, 1997); *The Scientist as Rebel* (New York: New York Review of Books, 2006); *Dreams of Earth and Sky* (New York: New York Review of Books, 2015).

160. Freeman J. Dyson, "The Future Development of Nuclear Weapons," *Foreign Affairs* 38.3 (1960): 457–64.

161. A history of this project is provided by his son: George Dyson, *Project Orion: The Atomic Spaceship, 1957–1965* (New York: Allen Lane Science, 2002).

162. Dyson, "Peacemaking," chapter 12 in *Disturbing the Universe*, 129–30.

163. A splendid collection of documents and interviews on this topic is provided by Chris Hables Gray, ed., *The Cyborg Handbook* (New York: Routledge, 1995).

164. Manfred Clynes and Nathan Kline, "Cyborgs and Space," *Astronautics* September 1960, 26–27 and 74–76.

165. Cole, *Beyond Tomorrow*, 116–19.

166. Cole, *Beyond Tomorrow*, 118.

167. Cole, *Beyond Tomorrow*, 106.

168. White, *Overview Effect*, 173.

169. Jones and Finney, in *Overview Effect*, 173.

170. Dyson, "The Greening of the Galaxy," chapter 21 in *Disturbing the Universe*.

171. Dyson, "Greening," 233.

172. Dyson, "Greening," 233.

173. Dyson, "Greening," 233.

174. Dyson, "Greening," 233.

175. Martin Rees, *On the Future* (Princeton, NJ: Princeton University Press, 2018).

176. Dyson, "Greening," 234.

177. Dyson, "Greening," 235. This point is also discussed by the eminent environmental historian Alfred W. Crosby, "Life (With All Its Problems) in Space," in Ben R. Finney and Eric M. Jones, eds., *Interstellar Migration and the Human Experience* (Berkeley: University of California Press, 1985).

178. Dyson, "Greening," 234.

179. Dyson, "Greening," 235.

180. Clarke, *Profiles*, 223.

181. Clarke, *Profiles*, 224.

182. Bostrom, *Superintelligence*, 100.

183. Simon Young, *Designer Evolution: A Transhumanist Manifesto* (Amherst, NY: Prometheus Books, 2006), 44. This vision was probably formulated and then widely given currency by Winwood Reade, *The Martyrdom of Man* (1872; London: Jonathan Cape, 1930), 423.

184. For the variety of such schemes and their evolution, see Adam Crowl, "Starship Pioneers," in James Benford and Gregory Benford, eds., *Starship Century: Toward the Grandest Horizon* (Lucky Bat Books, 2013); Paul Gilster, *Centauri Dreams: Imaging and Planning Interstellar Exploration* (New York: Copernicus Books, 2004); Yoni Kondo, Frederick Bruhweiler, John Moore, and Charles Sheffield eds., *Interstellar Travel and Multi-Generational Ships* (Burlington, Ontario: Apogee Books, 2003).

185. Peter Garretson, "What Our Civilization Needs Is a Billion-Year Plan," *Kurzweil Accelerating Intelligence Blog*, September 23, 2012.

186. It is telling that Zubrin's fervent presentation of the main steps in the Tsiolkovsky program says nothing about possible warfare among very diverse space polities with posthuman

species-radiated populations in solar space, only briefly raising this possibility when considering eventual possible interaction with intelligent alien life originating elsewhere in the galaxy (*Entering Space*, 271–73).

Chapter 7

1. Franklin D. Roosevelt, "Radio Address on United Flag Day," June 14, 1942, quoted in Gerhard Peters and John T. Woolley, *The American Presidency Project*, University of California Santa Barbara.
2. Schell, *The Fate of the Earth*, 12.
3. Sagan, *Pale Blue Dot*, 260.
4. Klerkx identifies Sagan as articulating one of three fundamental approaches to space, centered on avoiding nuclear war and protecting planetary habitability, but neglects his support for ambitious cooperative space ventures as steps to terrestrial pacification (*Lost in Space*, 65–67).
5. For a classic statement on the disjuncture, see Richard A. Falk, *This Endangered Planet* (New York: Random House, 1971).
6. World Commission on Environment and Development, *Our Common Future* (New York: Oxford University Press, 1987), 27. As a consultant to the Commission, this author assisted in drafting parts of the report on space.
7. For the full range of analogues, see Paul Crook, *Darwinism, War and History: The Debate over the Biology of War from the Origins of Species to the First World War* (Cambridge, UK: Cambridge University Press, 1994).
8 John Dewey, *The Public and Its Problems* (New York: Swallow, 1957[1927]). Discussed in Deudney, *Bounding Power*, 178-9.
9. For how this approach leads to a planetary republican constitution, see Daniel Deudney, "Earth Orders: Intergenerational Public Sovereignty, Republican Earth Constitutions, and Planetary Identities," in Karen Litfin, ed., *The Greening of Sovereignty* (Cambridge, MA: MIT Press, 1998), 299–325.
10. Joann Pemberton, *Global Metaphors: Modernity and the Quest for One World* (London: Pluto Press, 1991); Mark Mazower, *Governing the World: The History of an Idea* (New York: Penguin, 2012); Or Rosenboim, *The Emergence of Globalism* (Princeton, NJ: Princeton University Press, 2017).
11. Among early statements, see Harrison Brown, *Must Destruction Be Our Destiny?* (New York: Simon and Schuster, 1946); discussions in Campbell Craig, *Glimmer of a New Leviathan: Total War in the Realism of Niebuhr, Morgenthau, and Waltz* (New York: Columbia University Press, 2004); Deudney, "Anticipations of World Nuclear Government," in *Bounding Power*; Rens van Munster and Casper Sylvest, *Nuclear Realism: Global Political Thought during the Thermonuclear Revolution* (New York: Routledge, 2016).
12. For the classic statement, see John Herz, *International Politics in the Atomic Age* (New York: Columbia University Press, 1960).
13. For the impasse, see Daniel Deudney, "Going Critical: Toward a Modified Nuclear One Worldism," *Journal of International Political Theory* 15.1 (October 2019), 367–85.
14. Hedley Bull, *The Control of the Arms Race* (London: Weidenfeld & Nicolson, 1961); Thomas Schelling and Morton Halperin, *Strategy and Arms Control* (New York: Twentieth Century Fund, 1961).
15. For an overview and assessment, see Joseph Cirincione, *Bomb Scare: The History and Future of Nuclear Weapons* (New York: Columbia University Press, 2007).
16. Joseph Nye, "Nuclear Learning and U.S.-Soviet Security Regimes," *International Organization* 41.3 (1987): 371–402.
17. Alton Frye, "Zero Ballistic Missiles," *Foreign Policy*, no. 88 (Fall 1992): 3–20; Andrew Lichterman, Zia Mian, M. V. Ramana, and Jurgen Scheffran, "Beyond Missile Defense," International Network of Engineers and Scientists Against Proliferation, October 2002.

18. For American, Chinese, and Indian views, see three articles by Mark Gubrud, Tong Zhao, and Rajaram Nagappa, each entitled "Going Too Fast: Time to Ban Hypersonic Missile Tests?," *Bulletin of the Atomic Scientists* 7.5 (2015).

19. This accomplishment was partially dimmed because the Soviets, shortly after signing the treaty, tested a partial version of this technology, called the Fractional Orbital Bombardment System, by putting nuclear weapons into orbit, but then de-orbiting them before they had completed a single full orbit, thus, the Soviets claimed, staying within the letter of the treaty. This apparent Soviet attempt to evade the purpose of the newly signed treaty caused a political uproar in the United States, and no further additional tests of this system were ever conducted. Raymond Gartoff, "Banning the Bomb in Outer Space," *International Security* 5.3 (Winter 1980–81):25–40.

20. John Lewis Gaddis, "The Evolution of a Satellite Reconnaissance Regime," in Alexander George, Philip Farley, and Alexander Dallin, eds., *US-Soviet Security Cooperation* (New York: Oxford University Press, 1988), 353–72; Gerald Steinberg, *Satellite Reconnaissance: The Role of Informal Bargaining* (New York: Praeger, 1983).

21. Thomas Graham Jr. and Keith A. Hansen, *Spy Satellites and Other Intelligence Technologies That Changed History* (Seattle: University of Washington Press, 2007).

22. Walter H. Dorn, *Peacekeeping Satellites: The Case for International Surveillance and Verification* (Dundas, Canada: Peace Research Institute, 1978).

23. Particularly good on the logic of ASAT restraint are Paul Stares, *The Militarization of Space, U.S. Policy, 1945–1984* (Ithaca, NY: Cornell University Press, 1985); Karl P. Mueller, "Totem and Taboo: Depolarizing the Space Weapons Debate," *Astropolitics* 1.1 (Spring 2003): 4–28; James Clay Moltz, *The Politics of Space Security; Strategic Restraint and the Pursuit of National Interests* (Palo Alto, CA: Stanford University Press, 2011).

24. John Pike, personal communication, July 15, 2017.

25. James M. Acton, "Escalation through Entanglement: How the Vulnerability of Command-and-Control Systems Raises the Risks of Inadvertent Nuclear War," *International Security* 43.1 (Summer 2018): 56–99.

26. Anthony Milne, *Sky Static: The Space Debris Crisis* (New York: Praeger, 2002).

27. For space debris in comparison with other high-technology governance problems, see Dave Baiocchi and William Welser IV, *Confronting Space Debris: Strategies and Warnings from Comparable Examples* (Washington, DC: RAND, 2010).

28. Space debris data from Jessica West et al., *Space Security Index 2018* (Waterloo, Ontario: Project Ploughshares, 2018), 19.

29. Donald Kesseler and Burton G. Cour-Palais, "Collision Frequency of Artifical Satellites: The Creation of a Debris Belt," *Journal of Geophysical Research*, 83 (1978): 2637-46.

30. James Clay Moltz, *Crowded Orbits: Conflict and Cooperation in Space* (New York: Columbia University Press, 2014).

31. Daniel Deudney, "Unlocking Space," *Foreign Policy*, no. 53 (Winter 1983–84): 101.

32. Theresa Hitchens, *The Future in Space: Charting a Cooperative Course* (Washington, DC: Center for Defense Information, 2004); Michael Krepon, "Setting Norms for Activities in Space," in Scott Jasper, ed., *Conflict and Cooperation in the Global Commons* (Washington, DC: Georgetown University Press, 2012), 201–14.

33. Ross Liemer and Christopher F. Chyba, "A Verifiable Ban for Anti-Satellite Weapons," *Washington Quarterly* 33.3 (Summer 2010): 149–63. For incisive critique of space control ambitions, see Joan Johnson-Freese, *Heavenly Ambitions: America's Quest to Dominate Space* (Philadelphia: University of Pennsylvania Press, 2009).

34. Rees, *On the Future*, 150.

35. William Hartman, "Space Exploration and Environmental Issues," *Environmental Ethics* 6.2 (1984): 227–39.

36. Lavery, *Late for the Sky*, 48. And Space Age thinking is "placeless, ageographical, ahistorical, postmodern, Protean, senseless, narcissistic, unaccommodated, weightless, puerile and Gnostic" ,(3).

37. For classic collections of arguments, see Eugene Hargrove, ed., *Beyond Spaceship Earth: Environmental Ethics and the Solar System* (San Francisco: Sierra Club Books, 1986); Stewart Brand, ed., *Space Colonies* (New York: Penguin, 1977). For unsuccessful efforts to

link space and environmental movements, see Kim McQuaid, "Earthly Environmentalism and the Space Exploration Movement, 1960–1990: A Study in Irresolution," *Space Policy*, 26, 2010: 163–73. For atmospheric pollution, Martin N. Ross and Darin W. Toohey, "The Coming Surge of Rocket Emissions," *Eos*, September 24, 2019. For parks, Charles S. Cockell and Gerda Horneck, "Planetary Parks: Formulating a Wilderness Policy for Planetary Bodies," *Space Policy*, 22.4 (November 2006: 256–61.

38. Barbara War, *Spaceship Earth* (New York: Columbia University Press, 1965); Barbara Ward and Rene Dubos, *Only One Earth* (Harmondsworth, UK: Penguin, 1972).

39. Garrett Hardin, *The Voyage of the Spaceship Beagle* (New York: Viking, 1972).

40. Charles S. Cockell, *Space on Earth: Saving Our World by Seeking Others* (New York: Macmillan, 2006).

41. Quoted in Bastini, *Fully Automated Luxury Communism*, 129.

42. William K. Hartman, Ron Miller, and Pamela Lee, "Epilogue: The Golden Rule," in *Out of the Cradle: Exploring the Frontiers beyond Earth* (New York: Workman, 1984), 182. Another carefully considered process standard is advanced in Wolfgang Bender, "Ethical Criteria for the Assessment of Space Projects," in Wolfgang Bender et al., eds., *Space Use and Ethics* (Munster: Agend-Verlag, 2001), 35–92. For socialist left critiques, see Peter Dickens, "The Humanization of the Cosmos – To What Ends?" *The Monthly Review*, 62.6 (November 2010); Nick Levine, "Democratize the Universe," *Jacobin*, March 21, 2015.

43. Leading works are Philip C. Jessup and Howard J. Taubenfeld, *Controls for Outer Space and the Antarctic Analogy* (New York: Columbia University Press, 1959); Myres S. McDougal, Harold D. Lasswell, and Ivan A. Vlasic, *Law and Public Order in Outer Space* (New Haven, CT: Yale University Press, 1963); Jerome Morenoff, *World Peace through Space Law* (Charlottesville, VA: Law Publishers, 1967).

44. Peter John Brobst, "'Icarian Geography': Air Power, Closed Space, and British Internationalism," *Geopolitics* 9 (Summer 2004): 426–39.

45. Philip W. Quigg, *A Pole Apart* (New York: Twentieth Century Fund, 1983).

46. For how analogies from the Law of the Sea influenced the provisions of the Outer Space Treaty, see M. J. Peterson, *International Regimes for the Final Frontier* (Albany: SUNY Press, 2005).

47. Jessup and Taubenfeld, *Controls for Outer Space*.

48. Moltz, *Politics of Space Security*, 149.

49. Andrew Brearley, "Mining the Moon: Owning the Night Sky?," *Astropolitics* 4.1 (Spring 2006): 43–67.

50. Dolman, *Astropolitik*, 140–41.

51. Zubrin, *Entering Space*, 14.

52. Fabio Tronchetti, "Private Property Rights on Asteroid Resources: Assessing the Legality of the ASTEROIDS Act," *Space Policy* 30 (2014): 193–96.

53. The idea of establishing a space control regime modeled on the aerial one was proposed in the 1960s and beyond by a retired airline executive, Howard Kurtz, as a key element of what he termed a "war control system." For discussion of recent proposals, see Michael Krepon, "Setting Norms for Activities in Space," in Scott Jasper, ed., *Conflict and Cooperation in the Global Commons* (Washington, DC: Georgetown University Press, 2012), 201–14.

54. David Lasser, *The Conquest of Space* (1931), introduction by Arthur C. Clarke (Burlington, Ontario: Apogee Books, 2002). Lasser's thought has been largely overlooked, with this important exception, on which this paragraph is based: Kilgore, *Astrofuturism*, chapter 1, "Knocking on Heaven's Door: David Lasser and the First Conquest of Space."

55. Lasser, cited in Kilgore, *Astrofuturism*, 3.

56. Lasser, cited in Kilgore, *Astrofuturism*, 47, 40.

57. Daniel Deudney, "Forging Missiles into Spaceships," *World Policy Journal*, Spring 1985, 271–303.

58. William James, "The Moral Equivalent of War," *Popular Science Monthly* 77 (1910): 400–410.

59. David Mitrany, "A Working Peace System" (1943) and "The Functional Approach and Federalism," in *A Working Peace System* (Chicago: Quadrangle, 1966), 25–103, 149–215.

60. Deudney, "Forging Missiles into Spaceships."

61. Edward Ezell and Linda Ezell, *The Partnership: A History of the Apollo-Soyuz Test Project* (Washington, DC: NASA, 1978).

62. Carl Sagan, "A Proposal for a Joint U.S./Soviet Expedition," *Parade Magazine*, February 2, 1986.

63. Roald Sagdeyev, "To Mars Together—A Soviet Proposal," *Washington Post*, December 13, 1987; Burton I. Edelson and John L. McLucas, "US and Soviet Planetary Exploration: The Next Step Is Mars, Together," *Space Policy*, November 1988, 337–49; Spark Matsunaga, "U.S.-Soviet Space Cooperation and Arms Control," *Bulletin of the Atomic Scientists* 41.3 (March 1985). Edelson was a former associate administrator of NASA; McLucas was a former assistant secretary of the US Air Force; and Matsunaga was a US senator from Hawaii.

64. For detailed accounts, see Susan Eisenhower, *Partners in Space: US-Russian Cooperation after the Cold War* (Gettysburg, PA: Eisenhower Institute, 2004); James Oberg, *Star-Crossed Orbits: Inside the U.S.-Russian Space Alliance* (New York: McGraw-Hill, 2002).

65. John M. Logsdon, *John F. Kennedy and the Race to the Moon* (New York: Palgrave, 2011).

66. When Kennedy came into office in early 1961, the US military was pursuing several ambitious space programs: manned military orbital flights (Blue Gemini), a military space shuttle (Dyna-soar), and a military space station (Manned Orbital Laboratory, MOL), all of which were canceled before deployment. McDougall, *The Heavens and the Earth*, 321.

67. The first formulations of the argument appear in Carl Sagan and Steven Ostro, "Dangers of Asteroid Deflection," *Nature* 369 (1994): 501; Carl Sagan and Steven J. Ostro, "Long-Range Consequences of Interplanetary Collision Hazards," *Issues in Science and Technology*, Summer 1994, 67–72. They are developed at length in chapter 18, "The Marshes of Camarina," in Sagan, *Pale Blue Dot*.

68. Keay Davidson, *Carl Sagan: A Life* (New York: Crown, 1999); William Poundstone, *Carl Sagan: A Life in the Cosmos* (New York: Henry Holt, 1999); Ray Spangenburg and Kit Moser, *Carl Sagan: A Biography* (Amherst, NY: Prometheus, 2009).

69. For Sagan's leading role in researching and publicizing the nuclear winter and in opposing space weapons, see Lawrence Badash, *A Nuclear Winter's Tale: Science and Politics in the 1980s* (Cambridge, MA: MIT Press, 2009); Matthias Dorries, "The Politics of Atmospheric Sciences: 'Nuclear Winter' and Global Climate Change," *Osiris* 26.1 (2011): 198–223.

70. Carl Sagan, *Cosmos* (New York: Random House, 1980).

71. Sagan, *Pale Blue Dot*, 250, 254.

72. Author calculations, based on NASA NEOWISE data and Wikipedia pages on "Nuclear Weapons," "Asteroids," and "Impact Events." Impact energies of specific objects can vary widely on the basis of their composition and velocity. Main Belt asteroids, not included here, contain some 99 percent of solar system asteroid mass. Kuiper Belt and Oort Cloud objects, not included here, may number into the hundreds of billions or trillions.

73. Sagan, *Pale Blue Dot*, 258.

74. Sagan, *Pale Blue Dot*, 259.

75. Sagan, *Pale Blue Dot*, 261, 263.

76. Sagan, *Pale Blue Dot*, 261.

77. Sagan, *Pale Blue Dot*, 262–63.

78. Sagan, *Pale Blue Dot*, 263.

79. Lunan, *Incoming!*, 165–76.

80. Preston et al., *Space Weapons, Earth Wars*, "Natural Meteoroids as Weapons," Appendix C, 173–83, at 183.

81. Sagan, *Pale Blue Dot*, 329.

82. Sagan, *Pale Blue Dot*, 317.

83. Akira Iriye, *Cultural Internationalism and World Order* (Baltimore, MD: Johns Hopkins University Press, 1997).

84. For Clarke's fascinating life, see Neil McAleer, *Odyssey* (London: Gallanez, 1992).

85. Michael Benson, *Space Odyssey: Stanley Kubrick, Arthur C. Clarke, and the Making of a Masterpiece* (New York: Simon & Schuster, 2018).

86. Arthur C. Clarke, "The Challenge of the Space Ship" 72. Robert Poole, "The Challenge of the Spaceship: Arthur C. Clarke and the History of the Future, 1930–1970," *History and Technology* 28.3 (September 2012): 255–80, at 255. See also Thore Bjornvig, "Transcendence of Gravity: Arthur C. Clarke and the Apocalypse of Weightlessness," in Geppert, *Imagining Outer Space*; Kilgore, *Astrofuturism*, chapter 4, "Will There Always Be an England? Arthur C. Clarke's New Eden.".

87. Marshall McLuhan, *War and Peace in the Global Village* (New York: Bantam, 1968).

88. Marshall McLuhan, *The Medium Is the Message* (New York: Random House, 1967), 3.

89. Arthur C. Clarke, *Greetings, Carbon Based Bipeds! Collected Essays, 1934–1998* (London: Voyager, 1999), 520.

90. Clarke, *Greetings*, 40.

91. Clarke, *Greetings*, 39.

92. Clarke, *Greetings*, 248.

93. The scope of such thinking is superbly chronicled in Poole, *Earthrise*; Ursula K. Heise, *Sense of Place, and Sense of Planet: The Environmental Imagination of the Global* (New York: Oxford University Press, 2008). An alternative argument, that viewing the Earth from "above" is linked to imperial projects and mentalities, is developed at length in Denis Cosgrove, *Apollo's Eye: A Cartographic Genealogy of the Earth in the Western Imagination* (Baltimore, MD: Johns Hopkins University Press, 2001). For Whole Earth–inspired planetary reenchantment, see Daniel Noel, *Approaching Earth: A Search for the Mythic Significance of the Space Age* (Amity, NY: Amity House, 1986).

94. Holly Henry, *Virginia Woolf and the Discourse of Science: The Aesthetics of Science* (Cambridge, UK: Cambridge University Press, 2003), 134.

95. Nancy Ellen Abrams and Joel R. Primack, *The New Universe and the Human Future: How a Shared Cosmology Could Transform the World* (New Haven, CT: Yale University Press, 2011), xii–xii; Joel R. Primack and Nancy Ellen Abrams, *The View from the Center of the Universe: Discovering Our Extraordinary Place in the Cosmos* (New York: Riverhead, 2006).

96. Lisa H. Sideris, *Consecrating Science: Wonder, Knowledge, and the Natural World* (Oakland: University of California Press, 2017).

97. Henry, *Woolf and Science*, 109.

98. Fred Hoyle, *The Nature of the Universe* (Oxford: Oxford University Press, 1950), iii.

99. Quoted in White, *Overview Effect*, 12–13. Further developed in Frank White, *The Cosma Hypothesis: Implications of the Overview Effect* (New York: Morgan Brook Media, 2019). Similar ideas are developed by former NASA astronaut Ron Garan, *The Orbital Perspective* (Oakland, CA: Berrett-Koehler, 2015).

100. Building from Yi-Fu Tuan, *Topophilia: A Study of Environmental Perception, Attitudes, and Values* (Englewood Cliffs, NJ: Prentice-Hall, 1974). For doubts, see Ursula Heise, *Sense of Place, Sense of Planet*, 37. For Earth nationalism, see Daniel Deudney, "Ground Identity: Nature, Place and Space in Nationalism," in Yosef Lapid and Friedrich Kratochwil, ed., *The Return of Culture and Identity in IR Theory* (Boulder, CO: Lynne Reinner, 1996),129–45.

101. White, *Overview Effect*, 3.

102. White, *Overview Effect*, 4.

103. White, *Overview Effect*, 27, 84, 92.

104. White, *Overview Effect*, 84, 61.

105. White, *Overview Effect*, 150–51.

106. White, *Overview Effect*, 73.

107. White, *Overview Effect*, 61, 188.

108. White, *Overview Effect*, 166.

109. Daniel H. Deudney, "All Together Now: Geography, the Three Cosmopolitanisms, and Planetary Earth," in Luis Cabrera, ed., *Institutional Cosmopolitanism* (New York: Oxford University Press, 2018), 253–76.

Chapter 8

1. Colin S. Gray, "The Continued Primacy of Geography," *Orbis*, 40:2 (Spring 1996), 256.

2. Karl Marx, *The Eighteenth Brumaire of Louis Napoleon Bonaparte* (New York: International Publishers, 1963[1852]), 15.

3. Richard Langworth, ed., *Churchill By Himself: The Definitive Collection of Quotations* (New York: Public Affairs, 2006), 18.

4. John Noble Wilford, *The Mapmakers* (New York: Knopf, 1981).

5. Particularly insightful on these links are Wootton, *Inventing Science*; Hubert Krivine, *The Earth: From Myths to Knowledge* (London: Verso, 2015); Joyce Appleby, *Shores of Knowledge: New World Discoveries and the Scientific Imagination* (New York: Norton, 2013)

6. For example, the British exploration of the Pacific Ocean led by Captain Cook also aimed to take observations of the transit of Venus across the sun, which could provide information to determine the absolute distance between the planets. Eli Maor, *Venus in Transit* (Princeton, NJ: Princeton University Press, 2000).

7. The title of chapter 13 of David Livingstone, *The Geographical Tradition: Episodes in the History of a Contested Enterprise* (Oxford: Blackwell, 1993). See also Anne Godlewska and Neil Smith, eds., *Geography and Empire* (Oxford: Blackwell, 1994); D. R. Stoddart, *On Geography and Its History* (Oxford: Blackwell, 1986); Martin W. Lewis and Karen E. Wigen, *The Myth of the Continents: A Critique of Metageography* (Berkeley: University of California Press, 1997).

8. Particularly good on the overall approach, as well as map propaganda, are Gearoid O Tuathail, *Critical Geopolitics* (Minneapolis: University of Minnesota Press, 1996); Mark Monmonier, *How to Lie with Maps* (Chicago: University of Chicago Press, 1996).

9. For thinking by geographers on different kinds of misperceptions and their often significant consequences, see Steve Pickney, *Understanding Geography and War: Misperceptions, Foundations and Prospects* (London: Palgrave, 2017).

10. This being the basis for Nicolas Spykman's influential critique of pre–World War II American hemispheric isolationism, discussed in Michael Vhalos, *America: Images of Empire* (Washington, DC: School of Advanced International Study, 1982), 51 For ways in which classification systems distort perceptions and behavior, see Geoffrey C. Bowker and Susan Leigh Star, *Sorting Things Out: Classification and Its Consequences* (Cambridge, MA: MIT Press, 1999).

11. Maurice Merleau-Ponty, "The Body," part one (1945), in *The Phenomenology of Perception* (London: Routledge, 2014), 64–208. For the philosophical annihilation of place by abstract space, see Edward S. Casey, *The Fate of Place: A Philosophical History* (Berkeley: University of California Press, 1997).

12. Husserl quoted and discussed in Benjamin Lazier, "Earthrise: Or the Globalization of the World Picture," *American Historical Review* 116.3 (2011): 602–30. The German philosopher Hans Blumenberg discusses the Copernican Revolution at great length in *The Genesis of the Copernican World* (Cambridge, MA: MIT Press, 1987).

13. Emphasizing the lower location of sexual organs, Sigmund Freud makes a somewhat similar argument in *Civilization and Its Discontents* (1930; New York: Norton, 1962), ch. 4, notes 1, 7.

14. R. Buckminster Fuller, "Vertical is to Live – Horizontal Is to Die," *The American Scholar*, 39.1 (winter 1969–70), 27.

15. Francis Bacon, *The New Organon* (1620; Indianapolis, IN: Bobbs-Merrill, 1960), aphorism 41, p. 48. See also Timothy Morton, *Hyperobjects* (Minneapolis: University of Minnesota Press, 2013).

16. In a classic of space studies, the civil—but not military—applications of the railroad are explored as a guide to the consequences of the development of rockets. Bruce Mazlish, ed., *The Railroad and the Space Program: An Exploration in Historical Analogy* (Cambridge, MA: MIT Press, 1965). Roger D. Launius, "The Railroads and the Space Program Revisited: Historical Analogies and the Stimulation of Commercial Space Operations," *Astropolitics* 12.10 (2014): 167–79.

17. For the role of analogies in thinking, see Dedre Gentner, Keith J. Holyoak, and Boicho N. Kokinov, eds., *The Analogical Mind: Perspectives from Cognitive Science* (Cambridge, MA: MIT Press, 2011); Douglas Hofstader and Emmanuel Sander, *Surfaces and Essences: Analogy as the Fuel and Fire of Thinking* (New York: Basic Books, 2013). For analogies as aids to innovation, see Mary B. Hesse, *Models and Analogies in Science* (Notre Dame, IN.: University of Notre Dame Press, 1966); Keith J. Holyoak and Paul Thagard, *Mental Images: Analogy in Creative Thought* (Cambridge, MA: MIT Press, 1995).

18. Patricia Limerick, "Imagined Frontiers: Westward Expansion and the Future of the Space Program," in Radford Byerly, ed., *Space Policy Alternatives* (Boulder, CO: Westview Press, 1992), 250.

19. Howard E. McCurdy, *Space and the American Imagination*, 2nd edition (Baltimore, MD: Johns Hopkins University Press, 2011). But frontier mythology is widespread in many modern national narratives, documented in Frank H. Tucker, *The Frontier Spirit and Progress* (Chicago: Nelson-Hall, 1980).

20. M. J. Peterson, "The Use of Analogies in Developing Outer Space Law," *International Organization* 51.2 (Spring 1997): 245–74; M. J. Peterson, *International Regimes for the Final Frontier* (Albany: SUNY Press, 2005).

21. Steven J. Dick, "Analogy and the Societal Implications of Astrobiology," *Astropolitics* 12.10 (2014): 210–30.

22. Paul Bartha, *By Parallel Reasoning: The Construction and Evaluation of Analogical Arguments* (New York: Oxford University Press, 2010).

23. Yuen Foong Khong, *Analogies at War: Korea, Munich, Dien Bien Phu, and the Vietnam Decisions of 1965* (Princeton, NJ: Princeton University Press, 1992).

24. Clarence Glacken, *Traces on the Rhodian Shore: Nature and Culture in Western Thought from Ancient Times to the End of the Eighteenth Century* (Berkeley: University of California Press, 1967).

25. "Historical materialism" is commonly used to describe the ideas of Karl Marx about the ways in which "forces of production" shape the viability and occurrence of different "modes of production" (such as capitalism and socialism) and their accompanying institutions and ideas. In reality, Marxism is but one of several families of "historical production materialism" in debate with liberal capitalist and authoritarian statist versions. Many thinkers commonly called "early Realists," as well as the global geopoliticians of the industrial era, make "historical security materialist" arguments about how different material contexts composed of geography and technologies of violence shape the viability and occurrence of different sets of security practices and their accompanying institutions and ideas.

26. In the large secondary literature, concise summaries and evaluations are provided in Ladis K. D. Kristof, "The Origin and Evolution of Geopolitics," *Journal of Conflict Resolution* 4.2 (March 1960): 15–51; Geoffrey Parker, *Western Geopolitical Thought in the Twentieth Century* (New York: St. Martin's Press, 1985); Klaus Dodds and David Atkinson, ed., *Geopolitical Traditions: Critical Histories of a Century of Geopolitical Thought* (London: Routledge, 2002).

27. To take a leading example, the constructivist IR theorist Alexander Wendt at great length attempts to dispel the importance of material factors, leaving them only a residual "rump" influence, but then, in attempting to theorize the motors of change in contemporary world politics, assigns a key role to the material factors of nuclear weapons and climate change. Alexander Wendt, *Social Theory of International Politics* (Cambridge, UK: Cambridge University Press, 1999).

28. Leo Marx and Merritt Roe Smith, eds., *Does Technology Drive History? The Dilemma of Technological Determinism* (Cambridge, MA: MIT Press, 1994); Allan Dafoe, "On Technology Determinism: A Typology of, Scope Conditions, and a Mechanism," *Science, Technology, and Human Values*, 40.6 (2015):1047–76. For doubts, see Kier A. Lieber, *War and the Engineers: The Primacy of Politics over Technology* (Ithaca, NY: Cornell University Press, 2005).

29. Geoffrey L. Herrera, *Technology and International Transformation: The Railroad, the Atom Bomb and the Politics of Technological Change* (Albany: SUNY Press, 2006); Leonard Dudley, *The Word and the Sword: How Techniques of Information and Violence Have Shaped Our World* (Oxford: Blackwell, 1991); Daniel R. McCarthy, ed., *Technology and World Politics: An Introduction* (New York: Routledge, 2018); and Maximillian Mayer and Michele Acuto, "The Global Governance of Large Technical Systems," *Millennium*, 43.2 (21–25): 660–83.

30. For an overview of diverse contemporary approaches, see Benjamin K. Sovacool and David J. Hess, "Ordering Theories: Typologies and Conceptual Frameworks for Sociotechnical Change," *Social Studies of Science* 47.5 (2017): 703–50.

31. W. Brian Arthur, *The Nature of Technology: What It Is, How It Evolves* (New York: Free Press, 2009); Sheila Jasanoff, "Is Science Socially Constructed – And Can It Still Influence Public Policy?" *Science and Engineering Ethics*, 2.4 (1996):263–76.

32. For the shaping role of social forces, see Andrew Feenberg, *Questioning Technology* (London: Routledge, 1999). For how geographic location shapes scientific activities, see Harold D. Dorn, *The Geography of Science* (Baltimore, MD: Johns Hopkins University Press, 1991).

33. This section is derived from Deudney, *Bounding Power*, chapter 1, "Republican Security Theory." Another variant of this way of thinking, centered on "interaction capacity," is used

to conceptualize anarchy and system scope by Barry Buzan, Charles Jones, and Richard Little, *The Logic of Anarchy: Neorealism to Structural Realism* (New York: Columbia University Press, 1993).

34. Frederick Jackson Turner, *The Frontier in American History* (New York: Henry Holt, 1920).

35. Stuart Eldon, "Secure the Volume: Vertical Geopolitics and the Depth of Power," *Political Geography*, 34 (May 2013):35–51.

36. Derived from Deudney, "Republican Security Theory." For difficulties in creating unions, see Joseph M. Parent, *Uniting States: Voluntary Union in World Politics* (New York: Oxford University Press, 2011).

37. Harold Innis, *Empire and Communications* (1950; Toronto: University of Toronto Press, 1972).

38. Daniel Deudney, "Geopolitics as Theory: Historical Security Materialism," *European Journal of International Relations* 6.1 (Spring 2000): 77–108. For other recent revivalist approaches, see Tomasz Klin, *Conducting the Study of Geopolitics: Three Approaches* (London: SAGE, 2018); Terrence Haverluk, et al., "The Three Critical Flaws of Critical Geopolitics: Toward a Neo-Classical Geopolitics," *Geopolitics*, 19.2 (2014): 19–39.

39. Initially formulated by Hobbes and Rousseau, these ideas have been elaborately developed by Kenneth Waltz and others as "neorealism" or "structural realism." Kenneth N. Waltz, *Theory of International Politics* (New York: Random House, 1979). Among the vast literature, influential evaluations include Robert O. Keohane, ed., *Neorealism and Its Critics* (New York: Columbia University Press, 1986).

40. For sources of failure, see Randall Schweller, *Unanswered Threats: Political Constraints on the Balance of Power* (Princeton, NJ: Princeton University Press, 2006).

41. Theodor W. Adorno, *Negative Dialectics* (New York: Continuum, 1973), 320.

42. William McNeill, "Human Migration: Historical Overview," in William McNeill and Ruth Adams, eds., *Human Migrations: Patterns and Policies* (Bloomington: Indiana University Press, 1978).

43. Like pretty much everything else in the field of human paleontology, the evidence is thin and the disputes are vigorous on the question how these extinctions occurred. Among recent synoptic accounts of the evidence and arguments are Clive Finlayson, *The Humans Who Went Extinct* (New York: Oxford University Press, 2009); Pat Shipman, *The Invaders: How Humans and Their Dogs Drove Neanderthals to Extinction* (Cambridge, MA: Harvard University Press, 2015).

44. Robert Carneiro, "Political Expansion as an Expression of the Principle of Competitive Exclusion," in Ronald Cohen and Elman Service, eds., *The Origins of the State* (Philadelphia: Institute for the Study of Human Issues, 1978).

45. For extensive evidence of prehistoric warfare, see Lawrence H. Keeley, *War before Civilization: The Myth of the Peaceful Savage* (New York: Oxford University Press, 1996); Steven LeBlanc, *Constant Battles* (New York: St. Martin's Press, 2003).

46. Chris Smaje, *Natural Hierarchies: The Historical Sociology of Race and Caste* (Oxford: Basil Blackwell, 2000).

47. Dominic Sachsenmaier, *Global Perspectives on Global History: Theories and Approaches in a Connected World* (Cambridge, UK: Cambridge University Press, 2011); David C. Krakauer, John Lewis Gaddis and Kenneth Pomeranz, eds., *History, Big History & Metahistory* (Santa Fe, MN: Santa Fe Institute Press, 2017).

48. Walter Prescott Webb, *The Great Frontier* (Austin: University of Texas Press, 1952).

49. Charles Mann, *1493: Uncovering the New World Columbus Created* (New York: Knopf, 2011).

50. Alfred Crosby, *Ecological Imperialism: The Biological Expansion of Europe 900–1900* (Cambridge, UK: Cambridge University Press, 1988).

51. Paul Kennedy, *The Rise and Fall of British Naval Mastery* (London: Lane Allan, 1976).

52. Halford J. Mackinder, *Democratic Ideals and Realities* (New York: Henry Holt, 1919), 40; Barney Warf, *Time-Space Compression: Historical Geographies* (New York: Routledge, 2008)

53. John McHale, *World Facts and Trends*, 2nd edition (New York: Macmillan, 1972).

54. The basic point is made by the publisher of *Scientific American*, Gerald Piel, *The Acceleration of History* (New York: Knopf, 1968). The pervasive effects of acceleration are analyzed in Hartmut Rosa, *Social Acceleration: A New Theory of Modernity* (New York: Columbia

University Press, 2015); Simon Glezos, *Speed: Capitalism, the State and War in an Accelerating World* (London: Routledge, 2012).

55. For doubts about contemporary intense violence interdependence, see Patrick Porter, *The Global Village Myth: Distance, War, and the Limits of Power* (Washington, DC: Georgetown University Press, 2015).

56. The IR theorist James N. Rosenau analyzes this situation as "fragmagration" in *Distant Proximities: Dynamics beyond Globalization* (Princeton, NJ: Princeton University Press, 2003). For accounts of the growing gap between the demand and supply of global problem-solving, see Ian Golden, *Divided Nations: Why Global Governance Is Failing, and What We Can Do about It* (New York: Oxford University Press, 2013); Thomas Hale, David Held, and Kevin Young, *Gridlock: Why Global Cooperation Is Failing When We Need It Most* (Oxford: Polity, 2013).

Chapter 9

1. Teilhard de Chardin, *Building the Earth and The Psychological Conditions of Human Unification* (New York: Avon, 1973), 11.

2. Marshall McLuhan, *From Cliche to Archetype* (New York: Viking, 1970), 9.

3. Nigel Calder, *Spaceships of the Mind* (New York: Penguin, 1979), 113.

4. Salkeld, *War and Space*, 46–47.

5. At length in John J. Klein, *Space Warfare: Strategy, Principles and Policy* (London: Routledge, 2006).

6. Shannon Hall, "As SpaceX Launches 60 Starlink Satellites, Scientists See Threat to 'Astronomy Itself'," *New York Times*, November 11, 2019, 1.

7. Salkeld, *War and Space*, 59.

8. Dimitry Adamsky, *Russian Nuclear Orthodoxy: Religion, Politics, and Strategy* (Palo Alto, CA: Stanford University Press, 2019).

9. Arthur Schlesinger Jr., "Foreword," in Robert F. Kennedy, *Thirteen Days: A Memoir of the Cuban Missile Crisis* (New York: Norton, 1999), 7.

10. Sherwin quoted in Sheldon M. Stern, *The Cuban Missile Crisis in American Memory: Myth versus Reality* (Palo Alto, CA: Stanford University Press, 2012), 159.

11. In the wake of the Cold War several conferences of participants in the crisis revealed that, unbeknownst to US intelligence, the Soviet Union had also deployed short-range nuclear cruise missiles, the Luna, which would have been fired at US naval vessels in the event of an invasion, that the Soviet military commander on the island had predelegated authorization to fire the missiles under his command through much of the crisis, and that the Soviets had forty-two thousand rather than eight thousand troops in Cuba. James Blight and David A. Welch, *On the Brink: Americans and Soviets Reexamine the Cuban Missile Crisis* (New York: Noonday, 1990); Michael Dobbs, *One Minute to Midnight: Kennedy, Khrushchev, and Castro on the Brink of Nuclear War* (New York: Knopf, 2008).

12. Within the vast literature on this crisis, a balanced overview of the political and military aspects is provided in Don Munton and David A. Welch, *The Cuban Missile Crisis: A Concise History* (New York: Oxford University Press, 2007). For a detailed account of the military dimensions, see Norman Polmar and John D. Gresham, *DEFCON-2: Standing on the Brink of Nuclear War during the Cuban Missile Crisis* (New York: Wiley, 2006).

13. For the fear of losing control in motivating both sides to draw back, see James G. Blight, *The Shattered Crystal Ball: Fear and Learning in the Cuban Missile Crisis* (Lanham, MD: Rowman & Littlefield, 1992). For accidents and warning system errors stemming from the high alert levels, see Bruce G. Blair, *The Logic of Accidental Nuclear War* (Washington, DC: Brookings, 1993); Scott D. Sagan, *The Limits of Safety: Organizations, Accidents and Nuclear Weapons* (Princeton, NJ: Princeton University Press, 1993), 53–155.

14. The American concession on the removal of the European missiles was secretly agreed to, thus contributing to the widespread view in the United States that the crisis ended with the Soviets backing down in the face of American resolve and superior military capability.

15. For the origins and consequences of Reagan's views, see Paul Lettow, *Ronald Reagan and His Quest to Abolish Nuclear Weapons* (New York: Random House, 2005); James Mann, *The Rebellion of Ronald Reagan: A History of the End of the Cold War* (New York: Viking, 2009). On

Gorbachev as a liberal internationalist and the role of nuclear vulnerability in late Soviet "New Thinking," see Zubok, *A Failed Empire*, 303–35.

16. For why nuclear weapons make claims of post–Cold War American unipolarity illusory, see Daniel Deudney, "Unipolarity and Nuclear Weapons," in G. John Ikenberry, Michael Mastanduno, and William C. Wohlforth, eds., *International Relations Theory and the Consequences of Unipolarity* (Cambridge, UK: Cambridge University Press, 2011), 282–316.

17. Henry R. Hertzfeld and Ray A. Williamson, "The Social and Economic Impact of Earth Observing Satellites," in Steven J. Dick and Roger D. Launius, eds., *Societal Impact of Spaceflight* (Washington, DC: NASA, 2007);Jennifer Gabrys, *Program Earth: Environmental Sensing Technology and the Making of a Computational Planet* (Minneapolis: University of Minnesota Press, 2016).

18. Yaakov Jerome Garb, "The Use and Misuse of the Whole Earth Image," *Whole Earth Review*, 44 (March 1995),18-25; Wolfgang Sachs, ed., *Global Ecology: A New Arena for Global Conflict* (London, Zed, 1993) .

19. Thore Bjornvig, "Outer Space Religions and the Overview Effect: A Critical Inquiry into a Classic of the Pro-Space Movement," *Astropolitics* 11.1–2 (January–August 2013): 4–24; Paul Levinson and Michael Waltemathe, eds., *Touching the Face of the Cosmos: On the Intersection of Space Travel and Religion* (New York: Connected Editions, 2016). Perhaps efforts by researchers using virtual reality and flotation tanks to stimulate a cognitively transformative Overview Effect will make orbital flights unnecessary. Ian Sample, "Scientists attempt to recreate 'Overview Effect' from Earth, *Guardian*, December 26, 2019. But scaling up this technology for mass access will be difficult. States, religious groups and others might also employ such conversion technology to propagate their worldviews.

20. John C. Baker, Kevin M. O'Connell, and Ray A. Williamson, eds., *Commercial Observation Satellites: At the Leading Edge of Global Transparency* (Washington, DC: RAND, 2001).

21. For GPS development and diverse uses, see Greg Milner, *Pinpoint: How GPS Is Changing Technology, Culture, and Our Minds* (New York: Norton, 2016); Rick W. Sturdevant, "The Global Positioning System: A Sampling of Its Military, Civil, and Commercial Impacts," in Dick and Launius, *Societal Impact of Spaceflight*; Paul E. Ceruzzi, *GPS* (Cambridge, MA: MIT Press, 2018).

22. Described in Shoshana Zuboff, *Surveillance Capitalism* (New York: Public Affairs, 2019).

23. For spatial mapping as a product of science, and a tour of micro and macro advances, see Stephen S. Hall, *Mapping the Next Millennium: The Discovery of New Geographies* (New York: Random House, 1992); Caleb Scharf, *The Zoomable Universe* (New York: Scientific American, 2017).

24. Richard P. Feynman, "Plenty of Room at the Bottom," *Engineering and Science* 23.5 (February 1960): 22–36.

25. Particularly insightful is James Clay Moltz, "Toward Cooperation of Conflict on the Moon? Considering Lunar Governance in Historical Perspective," *Strategic Studies Quarterly*, Fall 2009, 82–103.

26. For scenarios, see David Langford, *War in 2080: The Future of Military Technology* (New York: Morrow, 1979), 150–56.

27. This point is made by Kieran Coleman in "Space-Based Solar Power: Avoiding Potential Negative Consequences for Human Security," unpublished paper, Johns Hopkins University, January 2012.

28. A brief discussion of this point is found in Calder, *Spaceships*, 111–14.

29. Calder, *Spaceships*, 113.

30. An earlier version of some of the points in this paragraph appears in Daniel Deudney and Elizabeth Mendenhall, "New Earths: Assessing Planetary Geographic Constructs," in Rens van Munster and Casper Sylvest, eds., *The Politics of Globality since 1945* (London: Routledge, 2016), 20–43.

31. Daniel Deudney, "Turbo Change: Accelerating Technological Disruption, Planetary Geopolitics, and Architectonic Metaphors," *International Studies Review* 20 (2018): 223–31.

Chapter 10

1. Johannes Kepler, quoted in Dick, *Biological Universe*, 515.

2. Raymond Aron, *Peace and War: A Theory of International Relations* (Garden City, NY: Doubleday and Company, 1966), 664.

3. Dyson, "Greening the Galaxy," 231.

4. Burrows, *This New Ocean*, 317-18.

5. Writing in 1977, Michael A. G. Michaud forecast a Mars colony by 2015-20 and self-propelled asteroids and Saturn moon colonization by 2040-50: "Spaceflight, Colonization and Independence: A Synthesis, Part One: Expanding the Human Biosphere," *Journal of the British Interplanetary Society* 30 (1977), 83-95, at 87.

6. Jared Diamond, *Collapse: How Societies Choose to Fail or Succeed* (New York: Penguin, 2005).

7. Martin Elvis, "How Many Ore-Bearing Asteroids," *Planetary & Space Science* 91 (2014): 20-26.

8. Chris Stringer, *Lone Survivors: How We Came to Be the Only Humans on Earth* (New York: St. Martin's, 2012).

9. Olaf Stapledon, "Interplanetary Man?," *Journal of the British Interplanetary Society* 7 (1948): 213-33. I. A. Crawford, "Stapledon's Interplanetary Man: A Commonwealth of Worlds and the Ultimate Purpose of Space Colonization," *Journal of the British Interplanetary Society* 65 (2012): 13-19.

10. Dolman suggests that energy-efficient orbital transfer paths could be "chokepoints" (*Astropolitik*, 72-76).

11. An early attempt to model these shifts, leading to a bipolar solar system with Earth in rivalry with an empire based on Jupiter's moon Callisto, is discussed in Calder, *Spaceships*, 103-8.

12. For many examples and a critique, see James S. J. Schwartz, "Myth-Free Space Advocacy Part II: The Myth of the Space Frontier," *Astropolitics* 16.1 (2017): 167-84.

13. Finney and Jones, *Interstellar Migration and the Human Experience*.

14. For many examples and a critique, see Limerick, "Imagined Frontiers."

15. The long puzzle of a biological mechanism to explain how variations in solar insolation cause variations in skin pigmentation has now been convincingly solved. N. G. Jablonski and G. Chaplin, "The Evolution of Human Skin Coloration," *Journal of Human Evolution* 39.10 (2000): 57-106.

16. In the preface to his *War of the Worlds*, Wells references the Kepler passage I quote in the first epigraph to this chapter.

17. For example, George S. Robinson and Harold M. White Jr., *Envoys of Mankind: A Declaration of First Principles for the Governance of Space Societies* (Washington, DC: Smithsonian Institution Press, 1986).

18. The neglected topic is explored in Louis Hartz, *The Founding of New Societies* (New York: Harcourt, Brace & World, 1964).

19. See Deudney, "Maritime Whiggery" in *Bounding Power*; Scott Gordon, "The Republic of Venice," in *Controlling the State* (Cambridge, MA: Harvard University Press, 1999); William J. Bouwsma, *Venice and the Defense of Republican Liberty* (Berkeley: University of California Press, 1966).

20. J. R. Seeley, *The Expansion of England* (1884; Chicago: University of Chicago Press, 1971).

21. For these barriers, see Daniel Deudney, "Greater Britain or Greater Synthesis? Seeley, Mackinder and Wells on Britain in the Global Industrial Era," *Review of International Studies* 27.2 (2001): 187-208. For variations and influences, see Duncan Bell, *The Idea of Greater Britain: Empire and the Future of World Order, 1860-1900* (Princeton, NJ: Princeton University Press, 2007).

22. Among the many places this historical event is deployed are Ben Bova, *The High Road* (Boston: Houghton Mifflin, 1981) 258; Lewis, *Mining the Sky*, 2-3; Zubrin, *Entering Space*, x-xi, Smith and Davies, *Emigrating beyond Earth*, 138.

23. Edward L. Dreyer, *Zheng He: China and the Oceans in the Early Ming Dynasty 1405-1433* (New York: Pierson-Longman, 2007); Louise Levanthes, *When China Ruled the Seas: The Treasure Fleet of the Dragon Throne, 1405-1433* (New York: Oxford University Press, 1994).

24. Arthur Waldron, *The Great Wall of China: From History to Myth* (Cambridge, UK: Cambridge University Press, 1990).

25. Hawking, "Our Only Chance," 10.

26. The notion that an ASI driven by self-preservation and resource-acquisition goals would rapidly expand in space is vividly advanced in Bostrom's account, where he anticipates an ASI that would "develop the technology to build and launch von Neumann probes, machines capable of interstellar travel that can use resources such as asteroids, planets, and stars to make copies of themselves," thus embarking on an "open-ended process of space colonization" that would result in the "colonizing of a substantial portion of the Hubble volume, that part of the universe that is theoretically accessible from where we are now" (*Superintelligence*, 100). But perhaps the logic of relinquishing human colonization might also apply to an ASI. Doubtful of its ability to sustain control over, or the benevolent disposition of, its offspring across the vast reaches of interstellar space, an ASI might rationally choose not to expand beyond its natal solar system, fearing its offshoots would outstrip its technological abilities and resource base, and then expand back at its expense.

27. Hans Moravec, *Robot: Mere Machine to Transcendent Mind* (New York: Oxford University Press, 1999), 133.

28. Dyson, "Greening the Galaxy," 236.

29. For a comprehensive survey of explanations, see Stephen Webb, *If the Universe Is Teeming with Aliens. .. Where Is Everybody? Seventy-Five Solutions to the Fermi Paradox and the Problem of Extraterrestrial Life*, 2nd edition (New York: Copernicus Books, 2015); Particularly insightful on the possible role of catastrophes is Milan M. Cirkovic, *The Great Silence: The Science and Philosophy of the Fermi Paradox* (New York: Oxford University Press, 2018).

Conclusion

1. Fuller, "Prolog: The Universe Is Technology," in Larry Gels and Fabrice Florin, eds., *Worlds Beyond: The Everlasting Frontier* (Berkeley, CA: And/Or Press, 1978), 33.

2. Lunan, *Incoming Asteroid!*, 81.

3. Yudkowsky, "Artificial Intelligence," in Bostrom and Cirkovic, eds., *Global Catastrophic Risks*, 316.

4. For other limitations of this imagery, see Deudney and Mendenhall, "New Earths," 37. Similarly, Ehricke's characterization of terrestrial humanity as being in a womb, waiting birth into the cosmos, suggest that our notions are pre-infantile and embryonic. See Freeman, *Extraterrestrial Imperative*, 245.

5. Torres, *The End*, 33.

6. For example, Peter Garretson, "Why the Next Space Policy Directive Needs to Be to the Secretary of Energy," *Space Review*, July 1, 2019.

7. In the words of the philosopher Clive Hamilton, "The struggle to learn how to live collectively on the earth and within its limits is *the way*, the opportunity for humankind to find its place in the cosmos" (*Defiant Earth*, 125).

8. For the case for keeping half the planet undeveloped, see Edward O. Wilson, *Half-Earth: Our Planet's Fight for Life* (New York: Everlight, 2016).

9. For governance possibilities, see Nikola Schmidt, *Planetary Defense: Global Collaboration for Defending Earth from Asteroids and Comets* (New York: Springer, 2019).

10. Mark Bucknam and Robert Gold, "Asteroid Threat? The Problem of Planetary Defence," *Survival* 50.5 (October–November 2008): 141–56.

11. For measures to refurbish the Outer Space Treaty, see Ram Jaku and Joseph N. Pelton, *Global Governance in Outer Space* (New York: Springer, 2017).

12. For models of equitable distribution, see Morgan Sterling Saletta and Kevin Orrman-Rossiter, "Can Space Mining Benefit All of Humanity?," *Space Policy* 43.10 (2018): 1–6.

13. For how many established verities of every era are eventually overthrown, see Chuck Klosterman, *But What If We're Wrong? Thinking about the Present As If It Were the Past* (New York: Blue Rider Press, 2016).

14. Sheila Marikar, "The Rich Are Planning to Leave This Wretched Planet," *New York Times*, June 9, 2018.

15. Sober assessments are provided in Roger D. Launius and Dennis R. Jenkins, "Is It Finally Time for Space Tourism?," *Astropolitics* 4.10 (2006): 253–80; Jacqueline Feldscher, "A 'Wild Environment': Uncertain Safety Rules Await Space Tourists," *Politico*, December 25, 2019.

16. Roger Handberg, "Seeking the Future: The Fragility of the Patron," *Space Review*, February 18, 2019; Dwayne A. Day, "The End of the Egolauncher," *Space Review*, June 3, 2019. For private sector dependence on public research efforts, see Marianna Mazzucato, *The Entrepreneurial State: Debunking Public vs Private Sector Myths* (New York: Public Affairs, 2015).

17. Zubrin, *Entering Space*, 75–76.

INDEX

Figures are indicated by *f* and tables by *t*, respectively, following the page number.

For the benefit of digital users, indexed terms that span two pages (e.g., 52–53) may, on occasion, appear on only one of those pages.